THE
INFOURGE

COMPENDIUM
of MODELS and
THEORIES

for COACHES
FACILITATORS
and CONSULTANTS

Former Executive Coach To The FBI

Max Palomeque

Edited by Frank Steele
Design by Stefan Merour
Branding and design by Joshua Kwassman
Production managed by Bethany Kelly and Publishing Partner

Printed and bound in the United States of America

ISBN:
Hardback: 979-8-9905803-0-5
Paperback: 979-8-9905803-1-2

INTRODUCTION

The Infourge Compendium of Models and Theories for Coaches, Facilitators, and Consultants (ICMT) is a repository of knowledge relevant to industry professionals. The resources contained in this compendium cover a wide array of subject matter that professionals may encounter with their clients, be they individuals, groups, teams, or organizations.

The ICMT is a guide, a means for professionals to quickly familiarize themselves with some of the most significant concepts and resources available. Presenting profuse information in a usable way requires categorizing and sorting these disparate concepts in some fashion. The Infourge Compendium of Models and Theories for Coaches, Facilitators, and Consultants divides the material into three volumes.

- **The Infourge Compendium of Models and Theories** This tome includes over 300 different frameworks covering topics like behavioral change, coaching models, leadership models, and personality typing. Many of the concepts presented in the first volume serve as a foundation for the assessments, tools, and techniques contained in the second volume.

- **The Infourge Compendium of Assessments:** This volume currently under development contains over 220 instruments designed to <u>evaluate or measure</u> the client's position on one or more dimensions.

- **The Infourge Compendium of Tools & Techniques** Currently under development

  Section 1: Tools: This section contains over 70 exercises in which the <u>use of physical materials</u> (e.g., worksheets, charts, pictures, technology) is essential to helping the client achieve a desired outcome.

  Section 2: Techniques: This section contains over 80 exercises in which <u>prescriptive or structured coaching actions</u> are essential to helping client achieve a desired outcome.

Facilitating the utility of this compendium, the ICMT classifies each entry into at least one of 26 categories. The categorizations depicted in the ICMT are subjective. Users may perceive their applicability differently than presented here, and that is okay.

• Bias • Change (individual) • Change (organizational) • Coaching Models • Communication • Confidence/Resilience • Conflict • Crisis Management • Culture • Decision-Making • Emotional Intelligence/Social Intelligence • Employee Engagement • Feedback • Goal Setting • Influence • Leadership (styles/theories) • Learning/Development • Motivation • Personality-Behavioral Styles • Polarities • Problem-Solving • Reflection • Self-Awareness/Actualization • Stress Management • Teaming • Values

Disclaimers:

- **The ICMT is not a substitute for formal training**, nor does reading the ICMT qualify readers to apply the concepts contained herein. The purpose of this compendium is to provide a high-level awareness of these resources and relevant literature, nothing more.

- The inclusion or exclusion of entries into the ICMT is not an endorsement or rejection of any resource. **The ICMT does not advocate for or against any product, resource, or service listed herein.**

- There is no scientific standard or threshold required for an entry's inclusion in the ICMT. In other words, the concepts presented here vary regarding the quality of academic and scientific rigor supporting them. While most of the entries contained herein are based on some measure of research, there are countervailing arguments for almost every entry. It is important that readers understand that many of the theories presented here come with criticism or alternative viewpoints, and **it is incumbent upon the reader to thoroughly explore a resource prior to adopting it.**

- Some theories contained in this desk reference have enjoyed decades of acceptance; however, several have recently come under scrutiny based on emerging research. The ICMT includes these theories because it is important that professionals understand how knowledge of these domains has evolved over time. Additionally, it is critical that professionals possess awareness of the many concepts they may encounter when collaborating with clients and colleagues. **It is the reader's responsibility to explore and examine the validity of any concept prior to incorporating it into practice**.

- Regarding the use of certain language and labels in the ICMT, some readers may disagree with words like "weakness" and "vulnerability." These words may carry negative connotations and suggest judgment or criticism; therefore, some may find such language archaic. The ICMT adopts language directly from the supporting source material to avoid confusing, obfuscating, or compromising the accuracy of the information.

- Regarding the inclusion of theories associated with therapy, it is important to note three key points.

  1. Many theories born of clinical therapy and psychology are appropriate for coaching. One example of this is *Cognitive Behavioral Coaching (CBC)*, which derives from Cognitive Behavioral Therapy (CBT). While CBT is not appropriate for coaching, CBC is an accepted form of coaching for those with proper training.

  2. The ICMT does include several theories that are the domain of clinical therapy. This is because some coaches also serve as licensed clinical therapists or counselors. Therefore, it is possible some of these theories and concepts may come up as therapist coaches and non-therapist coaches collaborate. The ICMT includes a note to make the reader aware when a certain concept is the domain of therapy. In these cases, the inclusion of such an entry is solely for the readers' awareness and it's not intended for use by individuals who are not professionally trained clinical practitioners.

  3. When it comes to the boundary between coaching and therapy, professionals should follow the guidelines defined by their parent organization, certifying/regulatory body, or personally defined precincts. What constitutes "appropriate" for coaching is sometimes a matter of opinion. As such, there may be entries in this compendium which some may find inappropriate for coaching and better suited for therapy. The following distinction reflects how the ICMT views the boundary between therapy and coaching. Readers may possess different distinctions, and that is okay.

     - Therapy seeks to **diagnose and treat** psychopathologies (which may include maladaptive cognitions, feelings, trauma, and behaviors that may involve a variety of conditions and disorders). Though coaches do not diagnose or treat these conditions, they may present in a client, and by having sufficient awareness to recognize the presence of indicators, coaches may encourage their clients to seek professional help. Awareness of these factors may also protect the coach and the client from delving into inappropriate topics, causing unintentional harm.

     - Coaching, on the other hand, focuses on developing a client's awareness and understanding of self, others, the environment, and the ensuing relationships between these variables, typically within the context of a professional setting. Coaching seeks to help clients achieve the personal and professional changes and goals they desire.

- The list of resources contained in *The Infourge Compendium of Models and Theories for Coaches, Facilitators, and Consultants* is not all-inclusive. To submit a framework for a future edition of the ICMT, please email your recommendations to compendium@infourge.co

WHY THIS BOOK

The *Infourge Compendium of Models and Theories for Coaches, Facilitators, and Consultants* serves four functions. First, it provides easy access to a foundation for shared knowledge. There are many different training programs available to coaches, facilitators, and consultants. These programs vary in their focus and approach to the work. Consequently, these professionals possess different foundations of knowledge. The ICMT seeks to provide a repository of information to allow collaborating professionals to work together with greater understanding and awareness. For example, an internal leadership coach working for a company may find herself working with an external organizational development consultant during a time of organizational change. The internal leadership coach can use the ICMT to learn about the many organizational change frameworks the consultant uses, allowing her to better support the organization's leadership through their journey.

Second, the number of theories, assessments, and tools relevant to coaches, facilitators, and consultants makes it difficult for professionals to know the extent of the resources available, let alone determine which ones would be most appropriate for them and their client. The ICMT strives to include a broad range of models, theories, and frameworks to give professionals insight into the wide and diverse array of resources that relate to their profession. This will allow the professional to choose the framework or assessment most appropriate for both them and their client.

Third, the ICMT strives to help professionals who may become stuck when working with their client. Because clients often face a dizzying array of challenges and topics, the coach, facilitator, or consultant may encounter a topic that exceeds their knowledge and ability. The ICMT allows professionals to explore frameworks and theories across a range of topics, helping them find a way forward. This may be as simple as incorporating a newly discovered framework to influence your technique, or introducing the client to a new framework in an explicit fashion so they may better understand the situation.

Fourth, most professionals dedicate themselves to continuous improvement. Deciding what training and certification to seek can be a daunting task, especially given the vast number of options available. To help coaches, facilitators, and consultants make more informed decisions, the ICMT offers a high-level overview of these options that can inform their professional growth and development.

At the heart of this text is a core fundamental belief: that "right" looks a lot of different ways and that there is usually more than one way to move forward. The ICMT strives to expand the professional's toolbox so that each coach, facilitator, and consultant has the added flexibility and adaptability needed to meet clients where they are.

DEFINITIONS

It is important to define certain terms and make a few distinctions. The entries included in *The Infourge Compendium of Models and Theories for Coaches, Facilitators, and Consultants* are based on the work of countless academics, researchers, and scientists. The vast array of professionals exploring human behavior, testing hypotheses, and developing theories provides significant insights into the human condition and the complexities involved. The breadth and depth of knowledge is substantial and often includes a dizzying assortment of labels, many of them used interchangeably despite meaning different things to different people.

To that end, the ICMT opens with a dictionary to define some of these labels, so each reader possesses the same understanding of how key terms apply in this reference guide. Some of these are "informal," meaning there is no formal rule where one distinction applies and the other does not. The definitions provided here serve to create a common frame of reference for all readers, not to officially define terms. Some readers will disagree with the definitions provided here, and that is okay.

Approaches and Techniques (*herein used interchangeably*):[1] exercises in which <u>prescriptive or structured coaching actions</u> are the essential component to helping the client achieve a specific outcome. These exercises serve as conduits to aid the client in making discoveries, exploring topics, and facilitating new ways of examining an issue.

For example, a coach seeking to help the client adopt an objective perspective of a specific experience (the specific outcome) might use a technique (or approach) called "View from the Balcony" in which the coach asks the client to envision the experience playing out on a stage. Once the client adopts this image, the coach may ask a series of specific questions (structured coaching action) designed to reinforce the third-person perspective (e.g., "What is happening for the main character in this moment?").

Clinical Professionals: individuals trained, certified, and licensed in the fields of therapy, psychology, counseling, or other behavioral health professions. While some coaches are licensed therapists, psychologists, or psychiatrists, most are not. The ICMT occasionally makes reference to clinical professionals; in these cases, the text means a licensed therapist, psychologist, psychiatrist, or counselor.

Depth of Knowledge: an individual's level of knowledge about a topic. Possessing significant depth of knowledge implies the user can dissect a concept or tool into its base components and recognize when and how to adapt the concept when necessary. Conversely, a shallow depth of knowledge suggests a rudimentary awareness of the concept. Readers interested in learning more about depth of knowledge should consider the *Dreyfus Model* or *Bloom's Taxonomy (Revised)*.

For example: Reading the ICMT provides an awareness (nothing more) of the concepts contained herein. Therefore, readers are unable to provide detailed explanations about the science or mechanics of these concepts solely by reading this book.

Instruments and Assessments: material tools (e.g., worksheets, tests, forms) that <u>evaluate</u> the client and/or <u>measure</u> their position on one or more dimensions.

Examples of assessments include The Personal DISCernment Inventory (PDI), the Myers-Briggs Type Indicator (MBTI), the Emotional Quotient Inventory (EQ-i), and the Revised NEO Personality Inventory (NEO-PI-R). Many of the instruments listed in this compendium derive from a model, theory, or framework, and include techniques and approaches to aid the client and facilitate their understanding.

---

1   The distinction between tools and approaches is vague and a matter of opinion. Typically, tools and approaches go hand in hand. For the purposes of this text, if an exercise requires the client to fill out a worksheet or chart or use some form of technology, then we categorized it as a tool. If the exercise does not require the client to complete a worksheet or chart, we classified it as an approach or technique.

Models, Theories, and Frameworks (*used interchangeably*): The ICMT defines Models, Frameworks and Theories as a systematic presentation of information that fosters a deeper understanding of complex or complicated subjects by demonstrating flow, process, sequence, and/or component relationships. Academia makes a distinction between these; however, these distinctions are not generally relevant to the practicing coach. Therefore, the ICMT uses the terms interchangeably.

Examples of models (theories/frameworks) include the *Transtheoretical Model, Intentional Change Theory, DiSC,* and *Myers-Briggs.*

Tools[1] are exercises in which material resources (e.g., worksheets, charts, or technology) are essential components in helping clients make discoveries, explore topics, and facilitate new ways of examining an issue. Tools are distinct from instruments and assessments in that tools are not diagnostic and do not provide measurements. All assessments are tools, but not all tools are assessments.

Examples of tools include the State of Mind Chart, the Polarity Map, and the Immunity to Change Map.

Coach, Facilitator, and Consultant (*used interchangeably*): The ICMT recognizes the distinctions between these three professions. However, the content contained in this compendium is as useful to one as to all. Therefore, in this text, the ICMT uses the three terms interchangeably. At times the text uses "the professional" instead.

USING INFOURGE'S COMPENDIUM OF MODELS AND THEORIES

To simplify ease of use, each entry in the ICMT is a single page in length. At the start of each entry is a quick-glance table which offers an overview of key information pertaining to the entry. For example:

Model, theory, or framework name

Certification Available: yes
Certification Required: no
Assessments: yes
Proprietary: no
Client: individuals
Cost: $1,000
Category: communication, personality

- **Certification Available**: This denotes if certification or formal training is available in the model or theory. It is important that readers understand the following points:

  1. Some vendors offer options for training in a theory without certification or training in a theory with certification.

  2. In some cases, training or certification in a theory is only available through formal training in the associated assessment.

     For example, there is no certification in the *Emotional Intelligence Competencies Model (EICM)*; those seeking formal training in EICM must seek certification in the EICM-derived assessment, the Emotional Quotient Inventory (EQ-i).

- **Certification Required**: This denotes if formal use of the model or theory (not the assessment) requires certification, credentialing, or licensing. It is important for readers to understand the following points:

  1. In cases where using the model does not require certification or training, we urge readers to con-

sider certification as a means of increasing depth of knowledge. See the "Proprietary" section for additional legal considerations.

  2. Some theories may not require certification, though they may require certification to administer the associated assessment.

     For example, professionals do not require certification to incorporate the *Five-Factor Model* into their coaching sessions; however, use of one of its associated assessments like the Hogan Assessment requires certification.

- **Assessments**: This denotes if there are assessments designed to <u>evaluate</u> the client and/or <u>measure</u> their position on one or more dimensions or spectra within this framework.

     For example, the Emotional and Social Competency Inventory (ESCI) is an assessment that measures a client's emotional quotient based on the *Emotional Intelligence Performance Model*. Assessments identified in this volume will feature in The Infourge Compendium of Assessments.

- **Proprietary**: This indicates if the content is proprietary, and if so, to whom. Often, proprietary tools and frameworks require certification or authorization prior to formal use. In some cases, professionals seeking to use an assessment or tool may need to hire a representative from the parent company to administer the instrument. When using proprietary tools, instruments, or models, coordinate with the owner in advance to avoid legal issues. To be safe, readers should verify the proprietary nature of any resources listed in the ICMT regardless of its classification in the quick-glance table.

- **Client**: This denotes if the model applies to individuals, groups, teams, organizations, or all.

- **Cost**: This pertains to the cost of training, certification, credentialing, or licensing in the model or theory, not the cost of using the assessment. In some cases, multiple vendors may offer training in a framework at different price points and in different currencies. When this is the case, the ICMT denotes this with "pricing varies." Prices quoted are current as of May 2022 and are subject to change. Professionals should verify all costs before deciding.

- **Category**: This denotes which of the twenty-six subject categories apply to the entry. A single entry may cover multiple categories.

    For example, the *Appreciative Inquiry Model* is a useful framework when discussing organizational change or problem-solving.

Following the quick-glance table, the ICMT provides a high-level overview of the resource that includes a brief explanation of the theory's origin, a general description of the framework, an identification of potential providers who offer training in the framework, and a citation of the most relevant publications associated with the theory. At the end of each entry is an endnote sourcing the information. It is important to note that the sources cited in the bibliography were current as of the time of writing. Since then, links may have changed or become invalid. In some cases, links which do not seem to work when clicked may work when copied and pasted (or typed) into a browser.

Often, when describing a framework, the ICMT may reference similar frameworks (also contained in the ICMT). In this case, the ICMT italicizes the term to let the reader know the model in italics has its own entry in the text.

For ease of use, the ICMT provides a table of contents listing all entries alphabetically and a table of contents listing entries by category.

ABOUT THE AUTHOR

Max Palomeque is the founder of Infourge Leadership LLC, a private firm specializing in the application of behavioral science to foster leadership development. Max has worked with over 450 clients, including individuals, groups, and teams; from new frontline supervisors to experienced C-Suite executives in government and private-sector organizations across multiple countries. In addition to leadership coaching, Max develops tailor-made workshops and curricula to meet the unique experiential learning needs of his clients. Max is an accomplished public speaker, having addressed groups at Georgetown University, the Federal Bureau of Investigation, the Department of Justice, the Department of State, and the US Air Force.

Max's experience as a coach, facilitator, and consultant crosses multiple domains, including organizational change, emotional intelligence, behavioral intelligence, leadership development, and business development. In addition to his work at Infourge Leadership LLC, Max serves as a leadership coach for Georgetown University's McDonough School of Business and an advisor to KAVEO Leadership LLC, an international leadership development and coaching company.

Max holds a BA in Political Science from Louisiana State University, an Executive MBA from Georgetown University, and he is a certified leadership coach from Georgetown University's Institute for Transformational Leadership. Max lives outside of Washington D.C. with his wife, three Bengal cats, a Maine Coon cat, and one English Lab.

Want to contact Max? He is available through LinkedIn and www.infourge.co

ABOUT THE REVIEWERS

The *Infourge Compendium of Models and Theories for Coaches, Consultants, and Facilitators* (Volume I) utilized several industry professionals to serve as peer reviewers. These professionals come from diverse backgrounds and experiences and help ensure the material is accurate and relevant to a wide range of users.

I would like to personally thank each one of these amazing individuals for their support in helping me build a product useful to the many professionals in our industry.

Anthony Cerella, EdD, is a retired US Army Lt. Col. and the current Director of Operations for KAVEO Leadership LLC, where he coaches and facilitates. Tony is an Associate Certified Coach by the International Coach Federation (ICF) and certified leadership coach from Georgetown University.

Theresa Garcia, MS, is the founder of Trust Leadership and Growth LLC, a private executive and team coaching practice with an emphasis on brain-based coaching. Theresa holds master's degrees in Human Resources from the University of Arizona and in Organizational Development from Pepperdine University. She is a Professional Certified Coach by the ICF, and holds certification in Applied Neuroleadership from Pepperdine University and in leadership coaching from Georgetown University. Theresa maintains certifications in multiple behavioral assessments.

Libby Graves, MBA, is the founder of Core Citizen LLC, a leadership coaching practice. Libby holds a master's in Business Administration from the Wharton School of Business. She is a Master Certified Coach by the ICF and serves as adjunct faculty for Georgetown University's Institute for Transformational Leadership.

Judy King, MBA, is the founder of Crown Consulting and Coaching, her executive coaching practice. Judy holds a master's in Business Administration from the NYU Stern School of Business. She is an Associate Certified Coach by the ICF and certified leadership coach from Georgetown University.

Louiza Kiritopoulos-Adams, MS, PCC, is a seasoned Organizational Psychologist focusing on leadership development and performance psychology. She presently serves as an executive and leadership development coach on a number of global benches and consults on human capital initiatives. She earned her master's in Organizational Psychology from Columbia University and is currently a Professional Certified Coach from the ICF and certified leadership coach from Georgetown University. Louiza sits on the board of directors as Programs Chair for Georgetown University's Institute for Transformational Leadership Network.

Pam Krulitz is the founder and CEO of Optify, a leadership coaching and development company. Pam is a Professional Certified Coach by the ICF and a certified leadership coach from Georgetown University. Pam also serves as an advisor for the International Coach Federation.

Alejandro Rodriguez, MA, is a retired US Air Force Lt. Col. and the founder and CEO of KAVEO Leadership, an international leadership development firm. Alejandro holds both a master's in Leadership and a certificate in leadership coaching from Georgetown University. Alejandro is an Associate Certified Coach by the ICF. He serves as an adjunct faculty member for Georgetown University's School of Continuing Studies.

Maureen Rudell, MBA, is the Director of Coaching for KAVEO Leadership. She holds a master's in Business Administration from Mount St. Mary's University and a master's in Military Operational Art and Science from Air University. Maureen is an Associate Certified Coach by the ICF and a certified leadership and performance coach from Brown University.

Peter Siu, JD/MBA, is an organizational development advisor/coach with a track record of helping leaders and their teams become more impactful, inspired, and inclusive. He is a certified leadership coach from Georgetown University.

MODELS & THEORIES

Some of the models, theories, and frameworks presented in the ICMT are quite complex. To keep entries to a maximum of one page, this text may omit certain aspects of a model. In these cases, the ICMT informs the reader of this and encourages further study before incorporating the framework into practice.

The content contained in the ICMT serves only to provide an awareness of the theory or framework. In most cases, professionals seeking to incorporate the theory or model will need to further study the content or seek out formal training and certification prior to use.

TABLE OF CONTENTS (ALPHABETICAL)

TABLE OF CONTENTS (BY CATEGORY)

COACHING MODELS

COMMUNICATION

CONFIDENCE AND RESILIENCE

CONFLICT

CRISIS MANAGEMENT

CULTURE

DECISION-MAKING

EMOTIONAL AND SOCIAL INTELLIGENCE

EMPLOYEE ENGAGEMENT

FEEDBACK

GOAL SETTING

INFLUENCE

LEADERSHIP

LEARNING AND DEVELOPMENT

MOTIVATION

PERSONALITY AND BEHAVIORAL STYLES

POLARITIES

PROBLEM-SOLVING

REFLECTION

SELF-ACTUALIZATION/SELF-AWARENESS

STRESS MANAGEMENT

TEAMING

VALUES

4A MODEL FOR STRESS MANAGEMENT

Certification Available: no
Certification Required: no
Assessments: no
Proprietary: no
Client: individuals
Cost: not applicable
Category: stress mgt., confidence/resilience

The 4A Model for Stress Management is a discourse-driven process designed to help clients identify and examine the stress-inducing variables in their life. Commonly used in *Cognitive Behavioral Coaching (CBC)*, the model provides four lenses which facilitate the client's ability to mitigate these stress-inducing variables.

The process begins with an exploration of the client's pattern of life to identify all obligations, commitments, and activities that require the client's time and attention. These can include people, situations, and environments. The client should not discriminate between positive and negative activities because both are potential sources of stress.

As the client identifies their obligations, they make distinctions about which commitments are essential to life and work, which ones are strictly for pleasure and enjoyment, and which ones are essentially unnecessary. The client may create a list to track these obligations.

Once a picture comes into focus, indicated by a robust list of commitments, the client examines each commitment through the following four lenses.

Avoid: Assess each commitment to determine which obligations are avoidable. Clients may prioritize these avoidable obligations into three groups (e.g., groups A, B, and C). On days when stress is high, the client may decide to reject commitments that fall into group C. The client should consider how behavioral changes can help them avoid committing to similar stress-inducing obligations in the future.

Alter: Examine each obligation to determine how the client may mitigate stress by changing the way they engage in the activity. This might include establishing parameters or limits on how much time they spend on the activity.

In this phase, it is important for the client to determine what is and is not within their span of control. Clients who fixate on variables outside their span of control will incur additional stress and anxiety.

Altering some behaviors or habits may require the client to communicate with peers and managers for their support. For example, a client may determine the two-hour commute to work is a significant source of stress. Upon further discussion, the client may decide that shifting their work hours will not only allow them to avoid rush hour going into work, but also going home. To shift their hours, the client will need their supervisor's permission.

Adapt: Explore the role of a client's thoughts and feelings about an obligation in amplifying their stress. Bringing awareness to these thoughts and feelings enables the client to adapt and decrease the stress associated with the activity.

Accept: Explore and embrace the stress-inducing variables outside the client's span of control. A challenging step in the process, achieving acceptance requires the client's patience and may test their resilience.

A common obstacle to acceptance occurs when a client's obligations diametrically oppose their value or belief system, an experience called dissonance. When this happens, acceptance may make the client feel like they are compromising their values. Frameworks useful when helping clients deal with dissonance include *Cognitive Dissonance Theory*, *Consistency Theories*, *Congruity Theory*, and the *Polarity Management Model* among many others.

Finding equilibrium through acceptance often requires frequent conversation and reinforcement from the coach, and positive self-talk for the client.

Sources[1]

4C MODEL FOR MENTAL TOUGHNESS

Certification Available: yes
Certification Required: no (yes for assessments)
Assessments: yes (MTQ48, MTQPlus)
Proprietary: no
Client: individuals
Cost: $1,480
Category: confidence/resilience

Developed by psychologist Peter Clough in 2002, the 4C Model for Mental Toughness provides a framework to help clients develop their resilience. Clough's model suggests that mental toughness is a personality trait which can improve an individual's performance.

The 4C Model consists of four elements grouped into two categories: resilience and confidence. Thus, the 4C Model suggests that mental toughness requires both resilience and confidence.

RESILIENCE

• **Control**: This is the degree to which the client believes they have control over their life; that they can make a difference and effect change. This element reflects a client's sense of self-worth (i.e., self-esteem).

Individuals high on control feel comfortable in their own skin, they believe they can regulate their emotions, and they are less susceptible to the emotions of other people.

Individuals low on control may feel most events are out of their control and that they lack the ability to make any meaningful changes in their life.

• **Commitment**: This is the client's ability to set clear goals and dedicate themselves to achieving them, especially when they encounter obstacles.

Individuals high on commitment often set clear goals, define the tasks necessary to achieve the goal, then persevere in pursuit of each objective despite setbacks and distractions.

Individuals low on commitment find it difficult to set goals and follow through.

CONFIDENCE

• **Challenge**: This is the extent to which clients will intentionally push their personal boundaries, confront change, and take risks.

Individuals high on challenge may view change and adversity as opportunities to learn and grow.

Conversely, individuals low on challenge will see change as a threat to be avoided at all costs.

• **Confidence**: This is the client's belief in their ability to deal with adversity, change, and conflict as well as their ability to influence others.

Individuals high on confidence may weather setbacks well, quickly overcoming them. They remain grounded when processing a setback and maintain their resolve.

Individuals low on confidence are more likely to give up when they encounter a setback.

The 4C Model is common in professional sports and includes an assessment called the Mental Toughness Questionnaire (MTQ), which comes in multiple versions, including the MTQ48 and MTQPlus.

Using the framework does not require certification; however, use of the MTQ48 requires licensing or certification. Training in the 4 C Model is available through multiple vendors, including Mental Toughness Partner's MTQ accreditation program and AQR International licensed user training.

Professionals seeking additional information may consider Clough's 2015 book, *Developing Mental Toughness: Coaching Strategies to Improve Performance, Resilience, and Well-Being*, co-written by Doug Strycharczyk.

Sources[2]

4MAT LEARNING STYLES

Certification Available: yes
Certification Required: no (yes for assessment)
Assessments: yes (LTM)
Proprietary: yes
Client: individuals, groups, teams
Cost: $349–$1,950
Category: learning/development

Developed in 1979 by educational theorist Bernice McCarthy, the 4MAT Learning Styles provides a framework for identifying and understanding an individual's learning preference.

The 4MAT model, also known as the 4MAT Cycle, suggests every person forms a pattern for how they integrate ideas and knowledge to create meaning. These patterns represent the individual's learning preference, which falls into one of four types.

TYPE 1—These learners are natural observers, preferring to watch and listen closely. They favor feelings, often preferring to talk about experiences and **reflect** on how they made them **feel**. Type 1 learners tend to make decisions based on feelings and are more prone to subjective observations than objective facts.

Type 1 learners need instruction that connects the learning content to their personal lives. Establishing the "so what" or relevance of the content is critical for the learner to advance. Type 1 learners work well with groups, learning from the experience of others.

TYPE 2—These learners are analytical and fascinated by structure and process. Adept at conceptualizing, they seek out details and data to form understanding and meaning.

Like Type 1 learners, Type 2s also favor **reflection**, but their focus is on **thinking** about the experience through a more objective examination, not how it made them feel.

These learners prefer solitary work and favor learning through traditional lectures. They are vulnerable to noise and distraction. They struggle with nonlinear/nonsequential instruction, role-playing, and presentations.

TYPE 3—These learners are problem-solvers that seek opportunities to get their hands dirty. Like Type 2 learners, Type 3s favor **thinking** about and understanding how things work, though they prefer to learn through **active experience** (working the problem) rather than by reflecting on past experiences.

Type 3 learners gravitate to experiments, building, tinkering, and demonstrations. These learners need to work things out for themselves and often create unique solutions in the process. They are vulnerable to ambiguity of purpose, subtlety in relationships, and expressing feelings.

TYPE 4—These learners are creative risk-takers. Like Type 3s, Type 4 learners prefer learning through **active experience**, though they are more comfortable with ambiguity and include subjective **feelings** in their learning. A characteristic of Type 4s is that they seek to challenge the boundaries of their world and enjoy out-of-the-box thinking.

Though Type 4s can work alone or with others., they are vulnerable to highly structured learning settings, overly methodical tasks, and learning environments which prevent them from challenging or questioning the content.

The 4MAT Cycle is useful in understanding a client's learning preferences, thus enabling the coach to adapt their coaching style to meet the client's learning preferences.

4MAT is more complex than presented here and incorporates multiple theories based on the works of Carl Jung, Roger W. Sperry, John Dewey, Isabel Myers, and many others.

Use of the model's assessment, Learning Type Measure (LTM), requires certification. Professionals seeking additional information may consider McCarthy's 2006 book, *Teaching Around the 4MAT Cycle: Designing Instruction for Diverse Learners with Diverse Learning Styles*.

Sources[3]

4S COACHING MODEL

Certification Available: no
Certification Required: no
Assessments: no
Proprietary: no
Client: individuals
Cost: not applicable
Category: coaching model

Developed by coaches Sue Coleman and Susan Sussman, the 4S Coaching Model is a framework designed specifically for coaching individuals with attention deficit hyperactivity disorder (ADHD). The model provides coaches with a flexible process capable of meeting the unique needs of clients with ADHD, helping them benefit from the coaching experience.

The 4S Coaching Model consists of four distinct frameworks that combine to provide the client with a complete coaching experience.

Structure is essential to providing the client with the means to be proactive in the face of change and anxiety. This framework includes six components.

- Clear goals and purpose: Work with the client to determine their sense of self and what they want to achieve.
- Systems: Create routines or repetitive patterns of behavior to help the client manage daily life.
- Time management: Help the client develop and commit to a schedule.
- Regularly scheduled appointments: Reoccurring events help establish consistency for the client.
- Single Day Action (SDA): This is a specific action the client accomplishes every single day no matter what.

This creates a sense of accomplishment and increases self-esteem.
- Daily habits: Small incremental actions done every day create the foundation for greater change.

Support pertains to how the coach helps the client. This framework includes some of the following actions.

- Witness and Empathize with the client and their story.
- Validate and Provide feedback encouraging the client to consider their options.
- Acknowledge their wins early and often to help them build momentum.
- Hold the client's vision for them, as they may forget along the way.

Skills involve working with the client to build skills and coping mechanisms to maintain consistency in the world. Topical areas for consideration include:

- Time management
- Goal setting
- Setting boundaries
- Dealing with transitions
- Managing the inner critic

Strategies involve the use of tools and techniques designed to help the client manage daily life. These may include the following approaches.

- Pattern learning (i.e., piggybacking one task on top of another)
- Managing energy
- Establishing rewards

Professionals seeking additional information on the 4S Coaching Model will find limited information beyond Coleman and Sussman's article, "The Four S's: A Comprehensive Program for Coaching People with ADD." Alternatively, an array of literature exists on the topic of coaching clients with ADHD, including Sarah D. Wright's 2014 book, *ADHD Coaching Matters: The Definitive Guide.*

Professionals interested in ADHD-focused coaching may consider certification through MentorCoach LLC or the Professional Association for ADHD Coaches (PAAC).

Sources[4]

4 TERRITORIES COACHING MODEL

Certification Available: no
Certification Required: no
Assessments: no
Proprietary: no
Client: individuals
Cost: not applicable
Category: coaching model

Developed in 2008 by coaches Mike Munro Turner and Diane Newell, the 4 Territories Model is a coaching process emphasizing individual change. Like many coaching models, the 4 Territories Model focuses on where a client is, where they want to be, and how to bridge the gap between. The model provides a process for coaching individuals through the changes needed to achieve their desired goals.

The 4 Territories Model, also known as the Jericho Model and the Renewal Model, consists of four key phases.

Readiness: During the first phase, the client works to define themselves (i.e., who they are and where they are at the moment). They seek to develop responsibility and autonomy for their choices so that they are unconstrained by personal history.

Coaches working with clients in this phase should adopt a nurturing and judgment-free approach to help the client develop a strong positive self-image.

Authentic vision: In the second phase, the client works to determine where they want to be. This typically involves discourse regarding the client's values and belief systems as well as their vision for the future. The resulting dissonance between values and vision may result in tension for the client.

Coaches should help the client "create and hold this tension between their current reality and their vision." This will prevent the vision (future state) and reality (present state) from merging, which may result in the vision becoming nothing more than a reinforcement of the status quo.

Skillful action: During the third phase, the client works to identify the goals, objectives, and tasks that will help them achieve their vision. This work involves the client strategizing, brainstorming, identifying, and prioritizing the specific steps they need to take.

Once they have an action plan, they must establish a timeframe with deadlines to help them with accountability. This includes defining indicators of success.

Insight: During the final phase, the client seeks out and receives feedback on how well they are moving toward achieving their vision. This examination considers the efficacy of their actions (as identified in the previous phase).

Along the way, it is important for the client to accept responsibility for both the successes and failures of their actions. In this, the coach is instrumental in helping the client learn from their experiences.

There are multiple variations of the 4 Territories Model, each based on the application of the model in different arenas. With each variation there are different labels; however, they are fundamentally the same in that they consist of segmenting the issue into four quadrants or components (i.e., phases). The various versions include emphasis on leadership, communication, creative process, shifts (i.e., personal growth), and many more.

There is no formal certification in the 4 Territories Model, and despite the model's similarities to other coaching theories, there is limited information available on the framework. Professionals seeking additional information may consider Turner and Newell's 2008 article, "A Model of Coaching for Renewal."

Sources[5]

5 ELEMENTS OF COOPERATIVE LEARNING

Certification Available: no
Certification Required: no
Assessments: no
Proprietary: no
Client: groups, teams
Cost: not applicable
Category: learning/development, teaming

Developed in the 1940s by social psychologist Morton Deutsch, Cooperative Learning is an approach to education that utilizes teams or groups to facilitate the learning experience. According to Deutsch, Cooperative Learning requires five elements to succeed. These elements foster the collective learning process and are essential for effective teaming.

Positive interdependence: This occurs when each member commits to both their own personal success and the success of their teammates. A state of positive interdependence exists when the group realizes that they sink or swim together.

Achieving a state of positive interdependence requires the team members share responsibility for a clearly defined goal (or task), have an equal share in the rewards, and are assigned specific roles/functions.

Individual and group accountability: This occurs when each member of the group can demonstrate an acceptable understanding of the lesson content and there is an equal balance of contribution between members. In other words, everyone contributes to the group's effort.

Achieving individual and group accountability requires that the group assess and share individual performance outcomes. This requires transparency in how each person performs their assigned function. This will dissuade members from social loafing (i.e., letting others do the work for them).

Interpersonal and small group skills: This element pertains to the quality and efficacy of individual social skills. These skills can include conflict management, trust building, communication, decision-making, and consensus building.

Face-to-face promotive interactions: This element consists of two behaviors. The first involves individuals supporting the learning process through peer-to-peer engagement. In other words, members of the team actively work to help each other understand the content.

The second behavior involves individual members proactively acknowledging or promoting each other's successes. This form of encouragement and support increases the collective mood and positivity of the group.

Group processing: The final element pertains to the group's ability to evaluate its progress toward achieving the goal and the performance of its individual members. Often, this may require structure or a framework to guide the team's processing.

There are many exercises that support cooperative learning and a variety of techniques that facilitate each of the five elements. Professionals considering use of this method should explore the options available to increase depth of knowledge.

Despite the longevity of this method, educators advise caution before committing to cooperative learning. This method is not appropriate for all environments, and if there are too many teams or groups, the facilitator may become overwhelmed and be unable to facilitate effectively.

Additionally, some caution that the model does not account for individual learning preferences or personality characteristics like introversion, shyness, or other patterns of behavior that challenge effective teaming.

Cooperative Learning is useful when coaching or facilitating teams and groups. Professionals seeking additional information will find ample literature available on the subject, including Spencer and Miguel Kagan's 1994 book, *Cooperative Learning*.

Sources[6]

5 VOICES

Certification Available: yes (GiANT University)
Certification Required: yes
Assessments: yes
Proprietary: yes
Client: individuals, groups, teams
Cost: pricing not available
Category: leadership, communication

Developed by leadership development professionals Jeremie Kubicek and Steve Cockram, the 5 Voices framework provides an easy-to-use system for characterizing and understanding individual leadership styles.

The foundation of 5 Voices suggests everyone has an ability to lead. They call this ability "voice." A person's voice can guide others, influence them, or dominate them. The 5 Voices framework seeks to help clients, groups, and teams better understand their respective voices, manage overbearing voices, and provide an environment where every voice matters.

The framework consists of five distinct leadership styles. A person with a preference for one voice (style) may also possess traits from the other voices.

Nurturers: For these leaders, people come first. Known for strong empathy and intuition, Nurturers often function as the social glue that keeps a team together. They have a strong ability to understand individual and organizational sentiments. Nurturers appreciate harmony and genuinely celebrate the accomplishments of others.

Accounting for almost half of the population, Nurturers tend to avoid conflict, often choosing silence over vocalizing their point if doing so risks confrontation. This can lead them to be passive-aggressive and undervalue their own contributions.

Creatives: These leaders can think outside the box with an eye to what lies over the horizon. Designers and architects, these leaders strive for continuous improvement and new opportunities. Never satisfied with the status quo, they believe there are always better ways. Creatives value integrity and innovation.

Creative leaders can struggle to communicate their vision, leading them to become frustrated with themselves and others. When this occurs, or if the group rejects too many of their ideas, Creatives can shut down.

Guardians: These leaders value logic and reason, often grounding the group to ensure the team's vision remains realistic and achievable. Known for their stewardship, Guardians strive to follow protocols and processes, adhere to timelines, and come in at or under budget. Able to set aside personal feelings during decision-making, they ensure that facts drive decisions, not emotion.

Guardians are risk averse, and their tendency for asking tough questions can appear hypercritical, leading others to remain silent.

Connectors: Highly charismatic and influential, these leaders are consummate team builders. They possess the ability to establish new social connections in support of the team's effort. A significant source of energy, they drive the collaborative process and ensure the right stakeholders come to the table.

These leaders strive to please others to maintain their relationships, which can lead them to take any challenge to their ideas personally.

Pioneers: Ardent believers that anything is possible, these leaders serve as a source of inspiration. Their ability to see the bigger (strategic) picture allows them to align people, resources, and systems to support goal attainment. Driven to win, they relish problem-solving, challenges, and obstacles, and they will not give up.

The passion and persistence of Pioneers can make them appear insensitive and arrogant. The drive to be in control and find solutions can lead them to ignore others.

Professionals seeking additional information may consider Kubicek and Cockram's 2016 book, *5 Voices: How to Communicate Effectively with Everyone You Lead.*

Sources[7]

6M FOUNDATIONS OF FLOURISHING

Certification Available: yes
Certification Required: yes
Assessments: no
Proprietary: yes (The Positivity Institute)
Client: individuals, groups, teams
Cost: $330
Category: confidence/resilience

Developed by psychologist Suzy Green, 6M Foundations of Flourishing (6M) is a framework of interconnected psychological skills that foster an individual's resilience to challenges and setbacks. Dr. Green suggests that clients who develop these skills will position themselves to weather unexpected situations and bounce back more quickly. The 6M framework falls under the banner of *Positive Psychology Coaching (PPC)*.

The 6M Foundations of Flourishing consists of six categories or domains of well-being. Within each domain are multiple skill sets and techniques a person can develop to enhance their well-being and resilience.

Mood: Skills within this category encompass the client's ability to process a full range of emotions and moods. 6M, true to positive psychology, does not ignore the client's negative emotions but includes them while simultaneously harnessing the power of positive emotions. This means helping the client recognize and process these negative emotions to limit the emotion's ability to control or dominate them.

Motivation: Skills within this domain involve exploring the client's intrinsic motivations and goals which support the client's well-being. These can include traditional goals focused on achievement or performance. Research indicates people often set and strive for goals to the detriment of their well-being. Therefore, these skill sets seek to help the client identify goals that foster their well-being and achieve their desired end state.

It is important to note that some clients may find it challenging to identify and commit to goals with the sole justification of making them feel better about themselves, their situation, or simply to recharge their energy.

Might: These skills help the client better understand their character and increase their self-awareness. Skills under the domain of Might include those necessary to help the client explore their values and develop an understanding of the role those values play in shaping their character. This step also endeavors to help the client recognize their strengths and vulnerabilities and help them develop a better sense of their capabilities.

Meaning: Skills under this domain help the client identify their authentic desires and translate them into meaningful life goals. Sometimes clients can struggle to accurately determine what they want, often striving for goals that are not truly desired or that are counterproductive to their well-being.

Mindfulness: Skills within this domain foster the client's ability to meditate, find their center, and focus on the here and now. Mindfulness avoids fixation on the future (what-ifs) as well as the past (what could have been) and brings their awareness to the moment.

Mindset: This domain seeks to leverage the client's basic cognitive skills to provide them with insight on their relationship with negative thoughts and allow them to hold these thoughts and examine them without them consuming the client.

6M does not include a formal assessment; however, practitioners may use an array of external assessments in conjunction with the model. Certification in 6M Foundations of Flourishing is available via a six-week course from Dr. Green's The Positivity Institute.

Professionals seeking to learn more about the 6M Foundations of Flourishing might consider Suzy Green's 2019 book, *The Positivity Prescription*, and her 2020 6-part podcast series on the 6M framework, *The Positivity Prescription with Dr. Suzy Green*.

Sources[8]

7 Cs OF EFFECTIVE COMMUNICATION

Certification Available: no
Certification Required: no
Assessments: no
Proprietary: no
Client: individuals, groups, teams
Cost: not applicable
Category: communication

Developed in 1952 by Professor of Public Relations Scott M. Cutlip, the 7 Cs of Effective Communication is a simple framework consisting of seven criteria to facilitate the development of impactful messages. These criteria apply to both written and verbal messaging.

Clarity: Avoid language that is pedantic, ambiguous, overly full of jargon, or excessively implicit. Limit the number of goals or ideas you wish to share through your message. Focus on precision and specificity.

Correctness: This criterion applies on two levels. First, ensure your use of grammar and language is accurate. Be mindful of homophones and spelling errors by proofreading your message (or speech) before disseminating it.

Second, review the accuracy of the information you provide in your message. Identify which elements within your message are fact and which are assumptions, then consider how the assumptions could become fact in the mind of the reader if misunderstood.

Conciseness: Brevity is key; avoid using unnecessary words when conveying your message. Consider how to deliver your message with the fewest words possible, without compromising clarity or intent.

Courtesy: Ensure your message is respectful to your audience. Beyond basic politeness, this includes emotional acknowledgment when appropriate, and careful thought to avoid passive-aggressive tones and condescending language.

A word of caution: Some recipients will expect a professional tone while others may prefer a more personal touch. Be mindful of these preferences when crafting your message.

Concreteness: While this appears like a combination of clarity and correctness, concreteness means that the message contains sufficiently explicit information so that the recipient fully understands the intent of the message. To achieve this, avoid the use of ambiguous language and ensure that any requests or instructions are clear and not open to interpretation. Concreteness ensures that a large and diverse audience possesses the same understanding of the message.

Consideration: This involves perspective-taking, putting yourself in the shoes of your recipients. What do they want/need to know? How will they interpret the message and how will they receive it coming from you? This element seeks to incorporate a measure of emotional and social awareness into the messaging. By considering the point of view of your audience, you can craft a message that better resonates with them.

Completeness: Though you want your message to be concise, you do not want to leave out critical information. Make sure that your audience has all the information they need to embrace your message and act.

The 7 Cs framework often serves as a useful checklist for those developing high-stakes messaging. In these cases, clients may elect to incorporate the 7 Cs as an additional framework for proofing their work.

It is important to note, sources differ on how they label the elements of this framework. Alternatives include the use of labels such as Creative and Credible.

Also known as the 7 Cs for Effective Business Communication, many have written about Cutlip's framework. Professionals seeking additional information may consider the book *Effective Public Relations*, written by Cutlip and his colleagues Allen H. Center and Glen M. Broom.

For a more current resource, consider the article "The 7 Cs of Communication," authored by the Mind Tools Content Team, free on their website.

Sources[9]

7-EYED SUPERVISION MODEL

Certification Available: no
Certification Required: no
Assessments: no
Proprietary: no
Client: individuals
Cost: not applicable
Category: coaching model

Developed in 1985 by professor of leadership Peter Hawkins and leadership consultant Robin Shohet, the 7-Eyed Supervision Model is a framework designed to facilitate the supervision of therapists, counselors, and coaches. The model presents seven domains supervisors can use to foster the professional development of their coaches.

The Client: This domain pertains to the coach's observations of their client, including the client's challenges and goals for coaching. To avoid subjective opinion, the supervisor should encourage the coach to focus on objective observations (i.e., what they saw and what the client said) instead of their interpretations. This technique helps the supervisor determine if the coach sees the client as a person or as a problem to solve.

The Intervention: This domain involves an exploration of all deliberate coaching actions originating from the coach, and includes the coach's use of models, tools, techniques, humor, silence, etc. This discussion seeks to understand the rationale behind the coach's decisions and involves brainstorming and role-playing different options.

Another purpose of this step is to identify opportunities to introduce new tools and skills to the coach, enabling their growth and development.

The Client-Coach Relationship: This domain involves the exploration of the coaching relationship from an outside perspective to assess the impact of the coach-client relationship on the client. One purpose of this approach is to help the coach and supervisor notice any dynamics which may influence the coach's objectivity.

The Coach: This domain analyzes the impact of the coach-client relationship on the coach. In other words, how does the client's experience make the coach feel? One purpose for this is to determine if and how the client affects the coach, which in turn could influence their ability to provide meaningful coaching.

The Coach-Supervisor Relationship: This domain involves the exploration of how the supervisor's relationship with the coach is similar to or different from that of the coach and client. A reason for this is to determine if the coach is transferring the client's emotions to the supervisor. This can indicate if the client's impact on the coach extends beyond the coaching relationship into other aspects of the coach's life.

The Supervisor Process: This domain examines the supervisor's internal processes. By examining what is happening for them during the coach-supervisor relationship, they can better recognize potential bias, transference, and loss of objectivity.

The Wider Context: This domain involves an exploration of how the client's social environment, professional environment, organization, and culture may impact their mindset, emotions, and behaviors.

The model adopts both a relational and systemic approach to supervising coaches. Put another way, it examines the relationship between the client, coach, and supervisor; and it considers the impact of these interactions on the wider system.

The 7-Eyed Supervision Model is a useful framework for those who supervise or mentor coaches. The seven domains can also facilitate performance reviews for coaches.

The model is slightly more complex than presented here. Professionals seeking additional information may consider Joan and Robin Shohet's 2020 book, *In Love with Supervision: Creating Transformative Conversations.*

Sources[10]

8 Cs OF SELF-LEADERSHIP

Certification Available: no (yes for IFS)
Certification Required: no (yes for IFS)
Assessments: no
Proprietary: yes (IFS Institute)
Client: individuals, groups, teams
Cost: not applicable
Category: self-awareness, confidence/resilience

Created by family therapist Richard Schwartz, the 8 Cs of Self-Leadership provides a framework consisting of eight domains to facilitate a client's development of self-awareness. The 8 Cs is a component of Schwartz's *Internal Family Systems Model (IFS)*.

Calmness: This is the client's ability to respond vs. react to their environment, which means being less vulnerable to the traditional fight, flight, or freeze triggers.

Clients with high levels of calmness tend to present a "go with the flow" or "ride the wave" mentality, suggesting a lower susceptibility to becoming overwhelmed.

Clarity: This is the client's ability to maintain an objective perspective despite the potential for personal or emotional compromise. This requires minimizing distortions that come from beliefs and emotions. Clarity mitigates biases by reflecting on how the client's perspective can obfuscate truth.

Curiosity: This is the client's genuine sense of wonder, and their desire to understand the world around them. Prejudgment is the antithesis of curiosity; therefore, it is important to emphasize that a genuine yearning to learn means that the client should avoid forming preconceptions before having enough facts. When a client prejudges something, it implies they know enough of that thing that further exploration is unwarranted.

A key function of curiosity is witnessing. Both the coach and client can foster curiosity by striving to be a witness to experience, not a judge of it.

Compassion: This pertains to having an open heart, receptive mind, and sincere empathy for others and self. Sometimes, when people protect themselves, they engage in behavior that is defensive or caustic. Compassion allows the coach and client to minimize the impact of this defensive behavior by fostering an understanding of the behavior.

Confidence: This refers to a person's trust in their ability to handle what life throws at them. This may come from past experiences which serve as a source of knowledge and wisdom. Other theories call this self-efficacy.

Courage: This refers to the client's willingness to take chances, venture into uncomfortable discourse, and explore for the sake of personal learning, growth, and development. Courage is not the absence of fear but doing what is right in the presence of it.

Creativity: This pertains to the client's ability to think in more abstract ways, to consider multiple possibilities, and to apply imagination. Creativity is a key component to expanding the client's horizon and enhancing the depth of their perspective.

Connectedness: Refers to the state of the client's connections with the individuals, groups, and culture around them. These sources influence the client and are important to reinforcing the client's growth and development.

Within IFS is a concept called **self-energy**, a quality that allows a client to feel as if they know themselves, their strengths, their patterns, and their blind spots. Developing and nurturing self-energy requires attention and insight in the 8 domains.

The 8 Cs of Self-Leadership are far more complex than presented here. Though primarily used in therapy, IFS's presence in coaching continues to grow. The framework has broad utility, especially when discussing self-care and self-compassion with clients.

Professionals seeking additional information will find both IFS and the 8 Cs of Self-Leadership featured in Schwartz's books, *Introduction to the Internal Family Systems Model* (2001), and *Internal Family Systems Therapy* (1995).

Sources[11]

8 DISCIPLINES OF PROBLEM-SOLVING

Certification Available: yes (multiple vendors)
Certification Required: no
Assessments: no
Proprietary: no
Client: groups, teams
Cost: $800–$2,000
Category: problem-solving

Developed by the US Department of Defense during World War II, the 8 Disciplines of Problem-Solving (8D) contain a methodical eight-step approach to solving high-stakes complex problems.

D0—Plan: The first step involves developing an approach plan which includes a basic description of the problem and takes into consideration any time constraints, resources needed to solve the problem, and the relevant stakeholders who should join the solutions team.

Because the 8D model is a cascading process, many argue the first step is the most important, cautioning that a failure to properly plan will lead to future failures and missteps.

D1—Team: The second step involves organizing a team of stakeholders to address the problem. In this stage, clients can use a variety of theories to help them build the ideal team construct. Though situationally dependent, considerations for effective team constructs typically include cross-functional perspectives, diversity of experience, and broad subject matter expertise.

D1 also includes the establishment of parameters regarding how the team will function, who will lead, and what deliverables the team will produce.

D2—Define the problem: The team examines the construct of the problem to identify its base elements or components. The team may use one or more models to facilitate this examination, including a Fishbone Diagram, Process Variables Map, Is-Is Not Matrix, and SWOT Analysis.

D3—Containment: During this step, the team acts to temporarily contain the problem to prevent further harm or inconvenience to the client or customer. In some cases, this may include removing the product from shelves or halting production until the team can develop a permanent solution.

D4—Identify root cause: During this step the team uses all available data to develop theories which might explain the cause of the problem. Through a process of examination and elimination, the team seeks to test these theories until the root cause is determined.

D5—Identify corrective actions: In this stage, the team develops actions to permanently correct the problem.

D6—Implement and validate actions: Once the team identifies the corrective actions, they (or the company) must implement them. As the implementation process unfolds, it is important to measure progress against key performance indicators to validate the efficacy of the plan.

D7—Prevention: During this step, the team takes proactive steps to prevent the same problem or one like it from reoccurring.

D8—Acknowledgment: The final step involves management publicly recognizing the team's efforts.

Professionals exploring the 8D model will discover that the original model consisted of eight steps. The ninth step, D0, came about sometime later.

In the 1980s, the Ford Motor Company adopted the methodology as a best practice. Since then, the process has enjoyed wide use across multiple industries and has gone by many names, including the Global 8D Standard, G8D, 8D, or Team-Oriented Problem-Solving (TOPS).

The 8D process is more involved than presented here. Professionals seeking additional information may consider the 2017 book, *Introduction to 8D Problem-Solving* by D. Benbow and A. Zarghami.

Multiple vendors offer training in 8D; however, much of the available training incorporates 8D as an element of a larger course.

Sources[12]

8 FACTORS OF ENGAGEMENT

Certification Available: yes (Sicora Consulting)
Certification Required: yes
Assessments: yes
Proprietary: yes (Sicora Consulting)
Client: individuals, teams, organizations
Cost: pricing not available
Category: culture, employee engagement

Developed in the early 2000s by organizational development professional Dr. Robert T. Sicora, the 8 Factors of Engagement provides an actionable science-based model to help organizations improve employee engagement.

The framework consists of eight factors allowing an organization to create and sustain a culture of positive employee engagement.

Purpose: Considered the most important factor, this element requires that an employee's work align closely with their passion and values. The individual's purpose, consequently, should align with the team's purpose. Establishing and defining a clear purpose that aligns with the team can foster resilience during times of change and difficulties.

Agility: Employees encouraged to seek new ways of thinking and find more efficient ways of accomplishing tasks develop an enhanced ability to adapt to their environment. This agility gives them confidence to rise to meet challenges instead of running from them.

Recognition: Acknowledging an individual's contributions is essential to engagement. The challenge rests in knowing the most appropriate and effective way to recognize each person. People differ in their preference for recognition. Some may prefer public praise while others may respond better to private acknowledgment. One employee might prefer a cash bonus while another might prefer a time-off award.

Care: Employees need to feel that the company cares for them; that they are not an easily replaceable cog in the wheel. Care is essential to an employee's sense of belonging. If they feel the organization does not care for them, they will probably feel as if they do not belong.

Trust: Employee engagement depends greatly on how deeply and broadly the employee trusts the organization, its leaders, and its workforce. Trust threads through all other factors in symbiotic fashion. A lack of trust may undermine an employee's sense of purpose in the mission; also, an employee who feels uncared for will have less trust in the organization.

Development: Employees want opportunities to grow by acquiring new skills and knowledge. Some want to leverage this toward gaining higher positions and responsibilities within the organization. Simply making opportunities available is not enough; they must be meaningful opportunities that align with employee desires for professional growth and development.

Resources: Employees not provided adequate tools and resources to accomplish the job may become less engaged. Ensuring employees have access to knowledge, skills, tools, and other resources is essential to their engagement.

Accountability: This factor requires consideration on multiple levels. First, employees must possess a clear understanding of what the organization expects of them. To accomplish this, set clear and measurable goals. Second, acknowledge and take responsibility for shortfalls and mistakes. Ensure feedback is clear and includes a clearly articulated path for improvement.

Many scholars influenced Sicora's work, including Carl Jung, William Marston, and Five-Factor Model scholars Ernest Tupes, Raymond Christal, and John M. Digman. Because of this, readers may notice an emphasis on introverted/extraverted thinking perspectives.

The 8 Factors of Engagement is proprietary to Sicora Consulting and includes the assessment 8 Factors of Engagement Individual Profile. Professionals seeking additional information on the 8 Factors of Engagement may consider Sicora's 2020 book, *Grab the Helm: Navigating with Purpose*, or his *Chart Your Course: A Student's Guide to Navigating Life and Finding Purpose*.

Sources[13]

ABC MODEL OF BEHAVIOR (BIJOU)

Certification Available: no
Certification Required: no
Assessments: no
Proprietary: no
Client: individuals
Cost: not applicable
Category: change, reflection, self-awareness

Developed by psychologist Sidney Bijou in the 1960s, and further refined in the 1970s by psychologist Edward Carr, the ABC Model of Behavior provides a framework to facilitate a client's exploration of the relationship between their behavior, the triggers which cause the behavior, and the subsequent impact of the behavior on others.

The ABC Model of Behavior applies to both positive and negative behaviors. Therefore, the model can help the client change undesirable behavior in favor of more desirable behavior. The ABC Model consists of three components.

Antecedent: This refers to the trigger or catalyst of the client's behavior. These triggers may come from the environment, individuals in the client's life, or from the client's own perceptions. During the coaching process, patterns will likely emerge that reveal the client's potential triggers.

The client's awareness of these triggers is the essential first step to understanding how it affects them and how they might adapt. Therefore it is important to spend time with the client as they explore these triggers and develop a better understanding of where they come from and how they might develop heightened awareness in the future. It is important for the client to recognize they are having a moment as the moment is taking place.

Behavior: This refers to the client's actions in response to the trigger. We can categorize these behaviors as Positive, Problematic, or Pivotal.

- Positive: refers to behavior the client wishes to see more of, also known as desirable behavior.

- Problematic: refers to behavior the client wants to change, also known as undesirable behavior.

- Pivotal: refers to behavior that is not in and of itself problematic, but leads to problematic behavior.

Consequences: This refers to the outcome of a behavior. Consequences can be negative or positive. Working with the client to explore consequences means examining the impact of their behavior on themselves (i.e., how their behavior may perpetuate the problem they encounter), as well as its impact on others.

These consequences can play a pivotal role in whether the client continues to engage in the same behavior or seek out change.

The ABC Model of Behavior, also known as the Antecedent-Behavior-Consequence Model, is frequently used in conjunction with the ABC Chart, a tool which allows the coach and client to track behaviors and identify patterns.

Often associated with *Cognitive Behavioral Coaching (CBC)*, and frequently combined with B.F. Skinner's *Reinforcement Theory*, the ABC Model enjoys wide use in therapy, counseling, and coaching because it is a simple framework based on observable patterns. Because Bijou and Carr focused their research on individuals with autism, many professionals find the ABC Model useful when working with autistic clients.

The ABC Model of Behavior should not be confused with the ABC Model (later *ABCDE Model*) developed by Albert Ellis. Though very similar, the two models are distinct in that Bijou's model is simpler and looks at the relationship between triggers, behaviors, and consequences. Ellis' model looks at how triggers may influence a client's belief system, which in turn influences behaviors.

Professionals seeking additional information on the ABC Model will find much written on the topic freely available online.

Sources[14]

ABCDE MODEL (ELLIS)

> **Certification Available:** no
> **Certification Required:** no
> **Assessments:** no
> **Proprietary:** no
> **Client:** individuals
> **Cost:** not applicable
> **Category:** self-awareness, reflection, confidence

Developed by psychologist Albert Ellis in the 1950s, the ABCDE Model (originally called the ABC Model) is part of his Rational Emotive Behavior Therapy (REBT) and falls under the field of Cognitive Behavioral Therapy (CBT). The model provides a framework for helping clients understand the relationship between their thoughts, feelings, and behaviors.

The ABCDE Model consists of five steps designed to facilitate the client's exploration of recent experiences to better understand what happened and why, and better position themselves to respond in a more desirable way in the future.

Step 1—Activating event (A): This step explores the event which triggered an emotional response for the client. This can include changes in the environment, interactions with other people, or performance issues. It is important for clients to describe the catalyst for their emotion in objective terms (i.e., what happened, minus attributions).

Step 2—Belief system (B): This step involves the client exploring the meaning behind the activating event. During this stage, the client makes attributions and interpretations of how or why the event transpired. These beliefs often include a combination of the rational and the irrational. The client's responses in this stage may reveal patterns which indicate possible counterproductive thinking.

This stage focuses on the types of faulty or detrimental beliefs the client may hold. Often called irrational beliefs, they include the use of absolutes (e.g., always, and never) and unrealistic demands (i.e., perfectionism, or winning is the only option).

Other examples of irrational beliefs include catastrophizing, intolerance, and Global Rating in which the client criticizes their entire being (e.g., "I did not receive the promotion, I am worthless"). This stage often reveals insight into the client's self-esteem, self-confidence, and level of anxiety.

Step 3—Consequences (C): This step involves the client discovering how the triggering event (A) and their existing belief system (B) result in external and internal outcomes (C). These outcomes include observable behaviors (e.g., avoiding certain people) and less obvious emotional states (e.g., feelings of insignificance around a specific person). Consequences can often serve to reinforce negative behaviors or feelings (e.g., believing they will not do well in their presentation leads them to underperform, which in turn solidifies their belief they are not a good presenter).

Step 4—Disputing (D): This step involves challenging the harmful or negative belief (B) that perpetuates the undesirable outcomes (C). In this, the coach must tread carefully, as challenging a client's beliefs (negative or otherwise) is risky. Doing so often requires the use of specific questions designed to engage the client in creative thinking. Disputing a client's beliefs is both a logical/cognitive effort and an emotional one.

Step 5—Effect (E): The final step takes place after the client has recognized the presence of faulty beliefs and has considered what healthy beliefs might look like (D). During this stage, the client begins the process of adopting the new belief into their life, leading to improved outcomes.

Widely used in *Cognitive Behavioral Coaching (CBC)*, the ABCDE Model applies to a wide range of client experiences, from fear of public speaking to relationship management, and is highly useful in helping clients challenge irrational thoughts.

Professionals seeking additional information will find substantial literature available on the ABCDE Model. An excellent source of information on the model and Ellis' other works is available online at The Albert Ellis Institute.

Sources[15]

ABCDE MODEL (SELIGMAN)

Certification Available: no
Certification Required: no
Assessments: no
Proprietary: no
Client: individuals
Cost: not applicable
Category: self-awareness, reflection

Developed in the 1960s by psychologist Martin Seligman, the ABCDE Model provides a framework to help clients understand how a pessimistic mindset can influence the way they perceive and process their daily experiences. The model allows clients to challenge negative thoughts and facilitate the integration of positive thoughts.

Seligman's Model, frequently used in a variety of coaching fields, consists of five steps.

Step 1—Adversity: The first step involves the client selecting an event or experience that resulted in negative feelings. Typically, this involves some form of adversity or problem. The client explores the event in an objective manner, recounting the facts of the event absent attribution and interpretation. Clients may experience the sense of reliving the event during this step; therefore the coach may consider techniques to help the client adopt a third-person or objective perspective of the event.

Step 2—Belief: During the second step, the client identifies the thoughts present in them at the time of the event. Honesty is critical as these thoughts indicate the beliefs which influence their perception of the experience. Sometimes these thoughts may manifest implicitly, so it is important to make them explicit.

Step 3—Consequence: The third step involves the client's consideration of how their thoughts affected their feelings and behavior. Often, intensely negative beliefs lead to an equally intense feeling and consequent reaction. This step is not about the justification for those feelings, but acknowledgment of them and the role they played.

Step 4—Disputation: During the fourth step, the client challenges their own belief system by searching for evidence to dispute their beliefs. This can prove difficult for inflexible clients or those with a tendency to catastrophize. By questioning the validity of their own beliefs and examining their usefulness, clients may begin to consider alternative ways to look at the issue. In the process, clients may now open themselves to more optimistic beliefs.

Step 5—Energization: Once the client has fully challenged their beliefs and considered more optimistic perspectives, they may begin to experience a shift in mood and emotion. Identifying and labeling these new feelings will help establish a connection between these positive thoughts and feelings which will lead to new behaviors.

In this final step, clients should develop a strategy for how they intend to adopt changes in both their mindset and behavior to maintain these positive feelings.

Readers will notice strong similarities between Seligman's ABCDE Model, Ellis' *ABCDE Model*, and Bijou's *ABC Model*. Ellis' model predates the others and serves as the original framework from which the others drew inspiration. Distinctions between these models are subtle but important (e.g., Ellis' model focuses on "irrational thoughts" while Seligman's model focuses on "pessimistic thoughts").

As a theory, Seligman's ABCDE Model falls under the umbrella of *Positive Psychology Coaching (PPC)*, a school of psychology also developed by Martin Seligman. Professionals seeking formal training in Seligman's model will find a variety of positive psychology programs available through multiple vendors.

For related theories, see the *PERMA Coaching Model, Learned Helplessness Theory*, and *Learned Optimism Theory*, all developed by Seligman.

Additionally, readers may consider Seligman's 1990 book, *Learned Optimism: How to Change Your Mind and Your Life*, which explores the ABCDE Model in further detail.

Sources[16]

ACCEPTANCE AND COMMITMENT THERAPY

<table>
<tr><td>Certification Available: yes (clinicians only)</td></tr>
<tr><td>Certification Required: yes (clinicians only)</td></tr>
<tr><td>Assessments: no</td></tr>
<tr><td>Proprietary: no</td></tr>
<tr><td>Client: individuals</td></tr>
<tr><td>Cost: not applicable</td></tr>
<tr><td>Category: change (ind.), confidence/resilience, self-awareness</td></tr>
</table>

Developed in 1986 by psychologist Steven C. Hayes, Acceptance and Commitment Therapy (ACT) provides a framework to help clients process painful experiences by accepting what is beyond their control and committing to actions that enrich their lives. These processes may also help clients who feel stuck to become unstuck.

The ACT framework consists of six core processes, with each process designed to facilitate the client's psychological flexibility. In other words, these processes help clients reframe the experience and their perceptions so that they may benefit and grow from the experience.

Acceptance: The first process involves the client accepting the presence of a painful or negative experience. Achieving acceptance means the client must cease avoiding, rejecting, denying, or repressing the negative event. Instead, the client works to find a space so they may acknowledge and recognize the experience; only then can they begin to explore and examine the experience.

Cognitive diffusion: The second process consists of a variety of techniques designed to help the client adjust their thoughts and feelings about the experience. This can include the adoption of a more objective perspective, thereby allowing the client to face the experience with some measure of psychological safety.

Being present: This process helps the client focus on the moment through the practice of mindfulness. Creating awareness for the client about how they think and feel in the moment can provide them with insight into how the experience affects them.

Self as context: This is a critical process that helps the client recognize they are more than the sum of their experiences. In other words, they are not what happens to them. Some variations of ACT identify this step as the Observing Self or Transcendent Self. This process pulls from Gestalt Theory, which states that the whole of anything is greater than the sum of its parts.

Values: The fifth process seeks to help clients identify their core values and leverage them to further process the experience. The client's application of their values can help them chart a new course and create consistency and congruity between their actions and beliefs.

Committed actions: This process helps the client create a path of tangible actions to help them accept the experience, learn from it, and grow.

Hayes created ACT because he fundamentally disagreed with the popular belief that people should avoid pain and suffering whenever possible. He not only believed pain is unavoidable, but understood it to be a necessary part of the human experience.

ACT, as a form of therapy, is only for clinical professionals. However, aspects of this framework have utility for coaches working with clients who struggle to accept things they cannot change or who feel stuck (assuming the issue is appropriate for coaching).

An awareness of ACT can help coaches make informed distinctions between coaching and therapy when working with clients. This may help the coach avoid crossing boundaries on issues better suited for therapy.

ACT is more complex than presented here and includes many different techniques and tools to facilitate the client's journey through these processes. Certification in ACT is available to clinical professionals.

Coaches seeking additional information may consider Hayes' 2011 book, *Acceptance and Commitment Therapy: The Process and Practice of Mindful Change* (2nd Edition), co-authored with Kirk D. Strosahl and Kelly G. Wilson.

Sources[17]

ACHIEVE COACHING MODEL

Certification Available: no
Certification Required: no
Assessments: no
Proprietary: yes
Client: individuals
Cost: not applicable
Category: coaching model

Developed in the early 2000s by executive coaches Sabine Dembkowski and Fiona Eldridge, the ACHIEVE Coaching Model provides a framework for coaching that focuses on the use of transparency to foster trust within the coaching relationship.

The ACHIEVE Model depends on five essential skill sets which form the foundation of the coaching style: rapport building, deep listening, creative and open-ended questioning, open and honest feedback, and intuition.

The ACHIEVE Model process consists of seven steps to facilitate the coaching relationship.

Step 1—Assess the current situation: During this first step in the process, the coach works with the client to explore their current state. This includes an examination of how the status quo came about, what role the client played in getting there, and reflections of past experiences. At the core of this step is the belief that the client needs to know exactly where they are and how they got there so they can decide where they want to go and how they will get there.

Step 2—Creative brainstorming: In the second step, the client explores possible options and diversifies their perspective to create a foundation for change. The model suggests it is in this stage where clients may become "stuck," or encounter tunnel vision, and the coach may need to work with them to overcome this challenge through creativity and perspective-taking.

Step 3—Hone goals: During this step, the client takes the options they identified in the previous stage and articulates them as explicitly defined goals. The model warns coaches to be aware of clients who fixate on "what they don't want" and to encourage clients to focus on "what they want." Above all, the goals must be meaningful and clearly defined for the client. For this step, Dembkowski and Eldridge recommend using the *SMART Model for Goal Setting*.

Step 4—Initiate options: During the fourth step, the client considers multiple ways they might achieve their desired goals. The idea is for the client to develop a list of possible actions, ranging from the more immediate steps they might take to longer-term actions.

Step 5—Evaluate options: In this stage, the client examines their list of actions to assess the potential efficacy of each action to move them toward their desired goal. The result of this step is a prioritized list of behaviors the client believes is necessary to achieving their goals.

Step 6—Valid action program design: During this stage, the client uses their prioritized list of actions/behaviors to develop a plan of execution. It is in this stage where the client may discover a need to break actions into smaller subgoals to ensure success. It is also in this stage where the client carries out their plan.

Step 7—Encourage momentum: During this stage, the coach uses coaching behaviors which encourage the client and celebrates their successes, no matter how small.

The ACHIEVE Coaching Model is useful for coaches searching for a more comprehensive coaching framework. The broad utility of the model allows it to easily integrate with other theories and frameworks to support the coaching process. It is important to note that the ACHIEVE Model, like so many coaching frameworks, derives from Whitmore's *GROW Model*.

Though there is no training or certification readily available in the ACHIEVE Coaching Model, professionals seeking additional information may consider Dembkowski and Eldridge's 2006 book, *The Seven Steps of Effective Executive Coaching*, co-written by Ian Hunter.

Sources[18]

ACTION-CENTERED LEADERSHIP MODEL

Certification Available: no
Certification Required: no
Assessments: no
Proprietary: no
Client: individuals
Cost: not applicable
Category: leadership

Developed in 1973 by leadership theorist John Eric Adair, the Action-Centered Leadership Model (ACL) provides a blueprint for fostering effective leadership.

ACL consists of the three management elements and six functional abilities Adair believes are critical to effective leadership.

Managerial elements: These are aspects of management which a leader is responsible for.

• **Task**: This element pertains to the specific objectives the group must accomplish. Aspects of this functional element include defining the goal, setting clear objectives, establishing the group's purpose, identifying the processes necessary for success, setting standards and expectations, establishing time frames, and more.

• **Team**: This element pertains to the group's behaviors and needs. These include establishing group expectations, norms, culture, discipline, and integrity. This element also considers group construct. Put another way, are the right people part of the team or do others need to join the effort? Leaders seeking to satisfy this element must put the needs of the group before their own.

Within this managerial element, leaders will often play a critical role, ensuring group cohesion and fostering morale. They facilitate group communication, manage conflict, and maintain balance between accountability and group freedom.

• **Individual**: This element pertains to the individual needs of group members. Leaders must take into consideration the personalities, desires, fears, and concerns of team members.

Within this element, leaders must apply a proper balance of intrinsic and extrinsic motivations based on the individual's preferences. This includes providing the appropriate amount of freedom, empowerment, and structure sought by each member of the group.

Functional abilities: These are the leadership abilities a leader must possess.

• **Planning**: the ability to seek out information and clearly define goals and objectives.

• **Initiating**: the ability to set expectations of behavior and performance, as well as allocate and assign tasks.

• **Controlling**: the ability to maintain standards, ensure group progress, and make decisions as needed.

• **Supporting**: the ability to resolve group conflict, motivate members of the team, and satisfy the needs of the group and its members.

• **Informing**: the ability to clarify assignments, mitigate ambiguity, and receive and interpret feedback.

• **Evaluating**: the ability to assess performance (self and others), measure progress, and consider the efficacy of group/individual ideas.

John Adair was among the first academics to demonstrate that leadership is both learnable and transferable, countering long-held theories that suggested leadership was an inborn trait. See *Trait Theory (Carlyle/Galton)*.

ACL, also known as the Three Circles Model, is one of two theories included in the ICMT which fall under the umbrella of *Functional Leadership Models*.

Variations of ACL exist which may use different labels to describe the elements/abilities; some versions include additional functions. ACL is more complex than presented here. Professionals seeking additional information may consider Adair's 1979 book, *The Action-Centered Leader*, or his 2010 book, *Effective Leadership: How to Be a Successful Leader*.

Sources[19]

ACTION LEARNING

Certification Available: yes (multiple vendors)
Certification Required: no
Assessments: no
Proprietary: no
Client: groups, teams
Cost: pricing varies
Category: problem-solving, teaming

Developed in 1983 by industrial management professor Reginald "Reg" Revans, Action Learning provides a conceptual framework to facilitate team-based problem-solving. The model consists of six elements, each representing an aspect of the team-based problem-solving process.

Team construct: The first element pertains to the identification and selection of team members. The ideal team size is between five and eight people of diverse experiences and expertise. The diversity of the team's composition should include varying ages, cultural backgrounds, skill sets, and other dimensions. Once formed, one person should assume responsibility for the team (leader).

Facilitator: The second element involves selecting the right person to guide the team. This is a person skilled at asking powerful questions, capable of guiding but not leading the team, and who can maintain a neutral stance on the issue (i.e., can remain objective).

Some variations of Action Learning suggest the facilitator can be a member of the team while others suggest the facilitator should not be part of the team.

Problem: The third element requires stakeholders to select a single relevant problem for the team to address. The organization's leadership must demonstrate continued support for the team and the team must have confidence that the problem presented to them is important to the organization.

Discourse: At the heart of Action Learning is productive team-based discourse. Using powerful questions, the facilitator guides the team in their examination and exploration of the problem, where they develop a greater understanding of the problem and its impact on the organization. Through discourse, the team brainstorms and generates ideas. This discourse fosters peer-to-peer learning and growth.

Possibilities: The fifth element involves the team identifying possible actions which may solve the problem. These possibilities will spur further discourse as the team explores the efficacy of each option.

Decisions: Throughout the Action Learning process, the team will make multiple decisions requiring them to listen to and consider the diverse perspectives represented on the team.

A valuable aspect of this model is its dependence on the diversity of the team. Action Learning champions the belief that diverse teams possess the greatest potential for solving problems by leveraging the unique perspectives of their members.

The purpose of Action Learning is to create a learning experience that results in real-world outcomes. For example, a large organization struggling with discord between its different job roles brought together teams of mixed roles to address real problems facing the company. By focusing on a shared problem, these teams not only created solutions, they also learned to appreciate what each role brings to the mission.

Action Learning is a time-intensive process influenced by the complexity of the problem and team cohesion. Depending on circumstances, this may require days to months for a successful outcome.

Action Learning inspired several alternative processes with different levels of complexity and structure. Due to these differences, professionals should explore all options to determine which is appropriate.

Multiple vendors offer certification in Action Learning. Pricing for certification varies greatly by vendor and level of mastery.

Professionals seeking additional information on Action Learning may consider Revans' 1983 book, *ABC of Action Learning*.

Sources[20]

ADAPTIVE LEADERSHIP

Certification Available: no
Certification Required: no
Assessments: no
Proprietary: no
Client: individuals
Cost: not applicable
Category: leadership, problem-solving, change (org.)

Developed in the 1990s by professors Marty Linsky and Ronald Heifetz, Adaptive Leadership combines theories of change management, leadership, problem-solving, and decision-making to provide a framework for leading organizations and people in times of change. According to Linsky and Heifetz, Adaptive Leadership is the practice of mobilizing people to adopt the changes that enable their capacity to thrive.

The framework begins with an important distinction between two types of problems.

Technical problems are problems with known solutions that utilize existing knowledge and capabilities. Though technical problems may vary in complexity, their solutions depend on current know-how.

Adaptive problems are problems whose solutions require changes in priorities, beliefs, habits, and loyalties.

According to Linsky and Heifetz, the most common source of leadership failure lies in mistaking adaptive problems for technical ones. The four principles of Adaptive Leadership speak to a leader's ability to leverage the organization in making accurate distinctions while leading the organization as they adapt to the problem and thrive as a consequence.

Emotional intelligence: Organizations facing change and adaptation may find their employees experiencing challenges to their beliefs, resulting in intense emotions. Adaptive leaders require a heightened awareness of how others think and feel about change. Central to this is empathy, the ability to feel with others as they navigate the challenges ahead.

Organizational justice: Organizations are complex, with as many perspectives as there are employees. For successful adaptation to take place, leaders must create an open and honest environment to ensure employees have a voice in the change. Giving voice to others allows them to feel heard and fosters greater acceptance of the changes ahead.

Development: When existing knowledge and skills cannot solve a challenge, it becomes an adaptive challenge, meaning the organization and its employees must acquire new skills, new knowledge, and new ways of doing business. Leaders must, for themselves and their employees, encourage and pursue continuous growth, learning, and development.

Character: Leading organizations and people through significant change requires leaders to possess the trust of their employees. Earning trust necessitates leaders be transparent in their thoughts and decisions, adhere to a code of ethics, and accept responsibility for mistakes.

Influenced by Charles Darwin, Adaptive Leadership suggests organizations capable of adapting to the changing environment stand the best chance of thriving. Drawing from the theory of evolution, Linsky and Heifetz liken organizational change to the subtle changes in DNA over time which enable a species to thrive. They argue organizational change should build on the past, not jettison it. This means the relevant change is both conservative and progressive, just like changes in DNA. To prevent the shock of abrupt change, adaptive leaders should possess an anticipatory eye to the future and lead accordingly.

Like its biological comparison, one of the most important requirements for successful organizational change is diversity. This means creating an environment that values diverse experiences, opinions, views, and beliefs.

Adaptive Leadership is more complex than presented here. Professionals seeking additional information may consider Linsky and Heifetz's 2009 book, *The Practice of Adaptive Leadership: Tools and Tactics for Changing Your Organization and the World*, co-authored by A. Grashow.

Sources[21]

ADKAR MODEL

Certification Available: yes
Certification Required: yes
Assessments: no
Proprietary: yes (Prosci)
Client: individuals, organizations
Cost: $4,500–$4,800
Category: change (ind., org.)

Developed in the 1990s by change management professional Jeff Hiatt, the ADKAR Model provides a multidimensional framework to facilitate meaningful organizational change efforts. The model examines organizational and individual change and how these two dimensions interrelate for meaningful change.

The foundation of ADKAR is the belief that successful organizational change requires that individuals within the organization accept and commit to change. Where many organizational change models focus primarily on the organization, ADKAR begins with the individual. The individual dimension of this framework consists of five elements focusing on the individual's path to change adoption.

Awareness: Each employee should possess sufficient awareness of the forces driving the need for change. Identifying the catalyst for change in a way that people understand and can accept will limit misunderstandings and false assumptions about the change. Failure to foster this awareness may lead some people to resist or challenge the organization's change efforts.

Desire: Once they possess awareness, allow employees the freedom to choose change. Forcing them to change can lead employees to resist or reject the change. Ensure employees understand the consequences of maintaining the status quo and allow them an opportunity to see the potential benefits of successful change. In time, many will realize the current situation is undesirable and they may seek out change.

Knowledge: Educate employees on how to change. Provide clear and specific steps for the new behaviors or processes. This includes demonstrating how to adapt their behaviors to meet the new norm.

Ability: Develop each employee's ability/capability to perform the new functions, tasks, or behaviors associated with the change. Give employees the opportunity to practice the new changes so they may develop confidence in the change and self-confidence in their ability to successfully change.

Reinforcement: Generate momentum and encourage employees to continue supporting change by using reinforcement mechanisms like feedback, rewards, and recognition to motivate employees. Consider the intrinsic and extrinsic motivations of employees when selecting the appropriate reinforcement technique.

The organizational dimension of the ADKAR Model focuses on the technical or program management aspects of change, like the business need for change, adjustments to policies, development of new processes and systems, and other considerations for implementing change.

One variation of the ADKAR Model amalgamates the process into three phases: the current state, the transition state, and the future state. Readers will notice similarities between the ADKAR Model and other theories on organizational change management like *Kotter's Change Management Theory* and *Bridges' Transition Model*.

This framework includes multiple tools, exercises, and resources designed to facilitate the client's application of the change management process. The ADKAR Model is significantly more complex and involved than presented here.

Professionals interested in formally using the ADKAR Model must obtain certification from Hiatt's company, Prosci. Certification, offered in both proximate and virtual learning formats, typically lasting several days.

Professionals seeking additional information on the ADKAR Model may consider Hiatt's 2006 book, *ADKAR: A Model for Change in Business, Government, and Our Community,* and his 2003 book, *Change Management: The People Side of Change,* co-authored by T.J. Creasey.

Sources[22]

AFFECTIVE-COGNITIVE CONSISTENCY MODEL

Certification Available: no
Certification Required: no
Assessments: no
Proprietary: no
Client: individuals
Cost: not applicable
Category: conflict, polarities, values

Developed in 1956 by psychologists Milton J. Rosenberg and Robert P. Abelson, the Affective-Cognitive Consistency Model (ACCM) is a theory which strives to explain the relationship between a person's feelings, thoughts, and values.

Like most frameworks under the banner of Consistency Theory, we can use *Heider's Triad* as a foundation to explain the theory.

• Prime Person (A): This is the individual experiencing the balance or imbalance within the relationship.

• Other Person (B): This is the person with whom the Prime Person has a relationship. Typically, this relationship classifies as either positive, negative, or neutral.

• Issue, Idea, Object (X): This is the source or catalyst of the disconnect. This could be a controversial topic, a political position on an issue, a polarizing object, or other target of disagreement or strong opinion.

• Prime Person's Values (Y1, Y2, etc): These are the core values of Person A. This is not an original component of Heider's Triad and is unique to ACCM.

The following scenario best represents the ACCM. Suppose Adam (A) and Ben (B) are good friends. Further suppose that Adam takes a favorable position on an issue (X), but Ben strongly opposes the issue. Adam values loyalty (Y1) to Ben, but the issue pertains to a topic relevant to another of Adam's values (Y2). At this moment, Adam's values (Y1 and Y2) conflict. This can create an imbalance for Adam, potentially leading to tension, anxiety, discomfort, and conflict.

In response, ACCM suggests that Adam might increase his feelings for Ben until they outweigh any negative feelings he has about Ben's position on the issue. Put another way, Adam devalues (Y2) the importance of the issue, by increasing his emotional connection to Ben. Alternatively, Adam might devalue (Y1) his sense of loyalty to Ben in favor of his commitment (Y2) to the issue.

ACCM is one of several subtheories which fall under the umbrella of *Consistency Theories*.

Other Consistency Theories offer alternative pathways to achieve balance. For example, some models suggest Adam might adjust how he thinks about the issue, or he might change how he feels about Ben, or he might try to influence Ben's attitude toward the issue so that it conforms to his own beliefs (see *Newcomb's Symmetry Theory*).

A unique aspect of ACCM is that it suggests the possibility that other people may experience greater tension than the person with the inconsistency. Therefore, ACCM suggests that a person may seek consistency for the comfort of others more than for themselves.

Consistency Theories, like the Affective-Cognitive Consistency Model, are useful when working with clients experiencing internal tension resulting from conflicting values. Professionals may also find Consistency Theories useful with clients facing issues of polarities.

ACCM is significantly more complex than presented here. Professionals seeking depth of knowledge will find most information on ACCM relegated to academic sources; however, there remains significant literature available on the broader topic of Consistency Theories, *Congruity Theories*, and *Cognitive Dissonance Theory*. Readers may consider the 1983 book, *Consistency and Cognition: A Theory of Causal Attribution*, written by psychologists S. Duval, V.H. Duval, and F.S. Mayer.

Sources[23]

AFTER-ACTION REVIEW

Certification Available: no
Certification Required: no
Assessments: no
Proprietary: no
Client: individuals, groups, teams
Cost: not applicable
Category: reflection

Developed in the 1970s by the US military, the After-Action Review (AAR) provides a framework to facilitate immediate learning from an experience, event, or performance. Designed to support soldiers in the field and enhance their ability to adapt to setbacks, the AAR became a best practice for many companies in the 1990s.

The After-Action Review is a simple process often used immediately following the implementation of a project or action to determine the efficacy of said action. For example, a company may use an AAR following delivery of a new training program or service.

Though simple by design, it is easy to underutilize the AAR, thereby mitigating its positive impact. To maximize the efficacy of the process, it is important that users meet five criteria when applying the AAR.

Timely: The AAR must quickly follow the event, project, or action. Allowing days to pass before conducting a review will risk losing sight of key details and increase the presence of inaccurate recollections.

Team focus: The AAR focuses on the collective performance of the team. This does not mean it excludes individual performance; it means that individual performance only arises inasmuch as it impacts the team's overall mission.

Open discourse: To ensure relevance, each member of the team must be able to give voice to their observations and opinions during the After-Action Review.

Objectivity: The AAR examines the components of what worked and what did not work without assigning blame or delving into personal attacks.

Facilitator: Utilizing a third-party facilitator is useful given the tendency for participants to fall into subjective or biased self-evaluations, especially when emotions run high.

The AAR process consists of three phases, with each phase incorporating a variety of powerful questions designed to facilitate a thorough examination of events.

Phase 1—What worked (and why): This phase focuses on the aspects of the project/mission that worked. Doing this often requires a comparison of the project's goals, objectives, and projected outcomes with the actual results. It is important to note that a project can fail and still have many elements in the "what worked" category.

Phase 2—What didn't work (and why): This phase seeks to identify all the elements that hindered the project's success. This can include individual performance failures, process failures, or external factors. It is important to note that a successful project may have multiple elements that don't work. It is a common oversight among AAR users to skip this step when a project is successful.

Phase 3—What can we do differently: This phase involves the team identifying concrete steps or actions that can fix the problems identified in phase 2 and expand on the effective actions identified in phase 1.

Making the most of an AAR requires taking detailed notes of the meeting, generating a full report of the findings, and establishing commitments for follow-ups.

Professionals may use the AAR during project or mission implementation, not just after the fact. Often, teams working on long-term projects will use the AAR at key points or milestones along the project timeline.

Professionals seeking additional information will find much written on the AAR freely available online.

Sources[24]

AGILE METHODOLOGY

Certification Available: yes
Certification Required: recommended
Assessments: no
Proprietary: no
Client: groups, teams, organizations
Cost: pricing varies
Category: decision-making, problem-solving, teaming

Originally introduced in 2001 as a process for effective software development, the Agile Methodology evolved into one of the most popular project management frameworks.

The Agile framework consists of four pillars, twelve principles, a variety of subprocesses or approaches, and several terms specific to the methodology. The four pillars create a foundation that emphasizes teamwork, flexibility, and relevance in project management.

Pillar 1: Individuals over process and tools

Pillar 2: Working software over comprehensive documentation

Pillar 3: Customer collaboration over contract negotiation

Pillar 4: Responding to change over following a plan

The twelve principles serve to foster the Agile mindset and guide practitioners.

Principle 1: customer satisfaction

Principle 2: embrace change

Principle 3: deliver value frequently

Principle 4: collaborate across boundaries

Principle 5: motivated team construct

Principle 6: personal communication

Principle 7: functional products

Principle 8: sustainable work pace

Principle 9: excellence

Principle 10: simplicity

Principle 11: self-organized teams

Principle 12: reflective learning

The Agile Methodology includes over a dozen approaches or subprocesses, each providing an important function in project management. Agile users may select from these approaches based on what is most appropriate for the situation.

Three of the most popular approaches are **Scrum**, which emphasizes creative and adaptive teamwork for problem-solving; **Kanban**, which helps to reduce the amount of work in the process and save time; and **Lean Development**, which helps identify and eliminate waste within the project.

Sources vary in the number of steps in the Agile lifecycle, their complexity, and how they label them. One version presents the following five steps:

Step 1: Requirements, definition, and analysis of concepts.

Step 2: Planning and sprints

Step 3: Collaboration, design, and development

Step 4: Create and implement

Step 5: Review and monitor

Another representation of the Agile process identifies seven steps labeled as Plan, Design, Develop, Test, Deploy, Review, and Launch.

The Agile Methodology is significantly more complex than presented here. The different perspectives and representations of the methodology only further complicate how professionals may perceive the methodology.

Professionals seeking additional information will find much written on the topic, including the original *Agile Manifesto*. Additionally, multiple vendors offer training and certification in Agile.

Sources[25]

AGS CHANGE MANAGEMENT FRAMEWORK

Certification Available: yes
Certification Required: yes
Assessments: no
Proprietary: yes (OCM Solutions)
Client: individuals, groups, teams
Cost: not applicable
Category: change (org.)

Developed by senior change management consultant Ogbe Airiodion, the AGS Change Management Framework provides a comprehensive framework to facilitate large-scale organizational change.

The AGS Change Management Framework, also known as the OCM Solution Organizational Change Management Framework, consists of five phases, each including multiple steps, techniques, and objectives for effecting meaningful organizational change.

Phase 1—Assess: The initial phase of AGS involves a methodical analysis of all relevant variables affecting the change process. This multifaceted assessment requires insight into the principal stakeholders, the employees and customers impacted by change, an assessment of the organization's culture and readiness for change, and the identification of potential obstacles and resistance to the change effort. Phase 1 results in a deeper understanding of the client, their organization, and the change.

Phase 2—Develop: During this phase, change agents create a comprehensive change management strategy which includes a detailed plan for change implementation. Elements critical to the change management plan include identifying tools and technology necessary for change to take place, assigning responsibilities for deliverables, developing a project plan, and formulating a communication strategy to ensure everyone possesses the same understanding of the change and to garner support for the effort.

In perhaps the most complex and involved stage of the AGS Change Management Framework, change agents strategize ways to mitigate resistance while simultaneously identifying champions for change and ensuring change endures.

Phase 3—Deploy: During this stage, change agents implement the change plan developed in phase 2. This may include the use of new training programs, coaching, and mentorship. Phase 3 requires consistent interaction with relevant parties to observe and measure indicators of progress or threats to the change effort. Phase 3 may involve continuous adjustments to the plan based on the information and results gathered.

Phase 4—Normalize: During this stage, the organizational transition begins as people adopt the changes as their new status quo. This may involve using a system of rewards to encourage participants to continue to perform the new behaviors, and the use of positive public acknowledgments to ensure the change becomes part of the organization's culture.

Phase 5—Exit: As the new status quo becomes a normal part of the organization, the fifth phase involves developing and executing a plan to transfer the remaining responsibilities for change to long-term permanent parties. This also includes a post-change implementation review to determine the overall efficacy of the change project and ascertain areas for improvement.

The AGS Change Management Framework is significantly more complex than presented here. Literature on the model does not provide insight into how much time the process requires or the duration of each phase.

OCM Solutions makes multiple resources available (for a fee) to facilitate the process, including templates for meetings, communication plans, project plans, and timelines. Additionally, OCM offers an extensive library of tools for each phase and every step of the process. These include tools for coaching, metrics, key performance indicators, managing resistance, managing leaders, and more.

Professionals seeking additional information about the AGS Change Management Framework may consider OCM Solutions' free multimodule training program for change management professionals.

Sources[26]

AID FEEDBACK MODEL

> **Certification Available:** no
> **Certification Required:** no
> **Assessments:** no
> **Proprietary:** no
> **Client:** individuals
> **Cost:** not applicable
> **Category:** feedback

Developed in the 1990s by leadership coach Max Landsberg, the AID Feedback Model provides a simple framework for delivering meaningful feedback, especially when the feedback is critical or constructive in nature. The model consists of three steps.

Step 1—Action: As a first step, review the catalyst for the feedback. Ensure you focus on the specific behavior you observed, or the actions as brought to your attention, not your interpretation of the action. This can present a challenge for some, especially when the behavior elicits a strong emotional response.

When delivering the feedback, you should avoid language that questions the recipient's intent or indicates judgment of their character or personality. Put another way, keep it about the behavior, not the person.

When using the AID Model, Landsberg recommends limiting feedback to one or two issues or topics. Combining too many different issues risks overwhelming the recipient, which may cause them to shut down.

Step 2—Impact: In step 2, provide details on how the recipient's behaviors or actions impacted you, the team, or the company. These details can help demonstrate the potential long-term consequences should the behavior persist. It is important that these consequences are quantifiable and tangible. In other words, recipients must be able to observe for themselves the consequences of their actions.

When providing positive feedback, explain how the recipient's actions benefited the team or company. The AID Model suggests that simply saying "that was really good," without demonstrating the impact, lessens the meaningfulness of the feedback.

Step 3—Desired outcome: In the final step, suggest to the recipient how they might change or adapt their behavior to avoid repeating the same outcomes. The AID Model recommends presenting this in positive terms. Another way to think of this is by focusing on what is missing, not what is wrong.

The AID Model encourages users to consider incorporating the *SMART Model for Goal Setting* as part of the third step to help the recipient develop a plan. Doing so will ensure the recipient understands clearly what they need to do and how, as well as any other expectations that may arise.

The AID Model is a useful framework when working with clients who struggle to give constructive or critical feedback. This is due, in part, to its simplicity and the provider eliminating their emotional and subjective considerations from the experience.

The AID Model is one of many feedback models included in the ICMT and is among a small group of virtually identical processes such as *BIFF*, *BEEF*, *BOOST*, and *SBI*. Due to these similarities, we encourage professionals to familiarize themselves with these variations, as both clients and colleagues may have established preferences.

Professionals seeking additional information on the AID Model may consider Landsberg's 1996 book, *The Tao of Coaching*.

Sources[27]

AIM CHANGE MANAGEMENT METHODOLOGY

Certification Available: yes
Certification Required: yes
Assessments: no
Proprietary: yes (IMA)
Client: organizations
Cost: $1,800–$3,100
Category: change (org.)

Developed by change management expert Don Harrison, the AIM Change Management Methodology provides a comprehensive roadmap for effective organizational change. The framework, also known as the Accelerating Implementation Methodology (AIM), offers professionals a meticulous and detailed process to facilitate enterprise-wide change efforts.

AIM consists of a 10-step, dynamic and nonlinear (cyclical) process.

Step 1—Define the change: Stakeholders must possess a common understanding of the current state and share the same vision for the future state. The first step seeks to establish a common picture of the present and future.

Step 2—Build agent capacity: Successful change requires the right number of people with the right skills, experiences, and characteristics. These individuals serve as change agents who will drive the change effort.

Step 3—Assess the climate: A thorough understanding of the environment is essential to effective planning. This entails the exploration of an organization's culture, strengths, and vulnerabilities. Knowing the organization's resource constraints as well as its obligations and politics will enable change agents to adapt their change strategy accordingly.

Step 4—Generate sponsorship: Change agents need a network of influential members within the organization to serve as sponsors. These sponsors should represent all levels within the organization.

Step 5—Determine change approach: Successful change often requires a multifaceted approach to meet the needs and expectations of organizational members where they are. This includes a combination of indirect and direct methods for influencing others to adopt change.

Step 6—Develop target readiness: Change agents must prepare the organization for change. Those resistant or hostile to the change may reject forced or coerced change; therefore, change agents may need to prepare them slowly but persistently over time.

Step 7—Build communication plan: Explaining the change in a way that others may receive and understand the effort is essential. Change agents must use a communication process that includes feedback, which in turn may reveal early adopters and resisters.

Step 8—Develop reinforcement strategy: It is important to consider how the organization's metrics and culture support or undermine the desired change.

Step 9—Create culture fit: In a conflict between change and culture, often culture wins out. Therefore, it is important to ensure reinforcements align with the change.

Step 10—Prioritize action: This involves the blending of the technical and human aspects of project management.

The AIM Methodology pulls from older change management theories like *Kotter's Change Management Theory*. Though many of the steps presented in the AIM framework manifest in other models, the explicit articulation of these steps makes AIM one of the more detailed change management structures available.

Using the AIM Change Management Methodology requires training, certification, and licensing, only available through Don Harrison's company, Implementation Management Associates (IMA). IMA offers both certification and accreditation in the AIM Methodology.

Professionals authorized to use AIM have access to multiple tools and resources designed to facilitate the AIM process.

Sources[28]

APPRECIATIVE COACHING MODEL

Certification Available: no
Certification Required: no
Assessments: no
Proprietary: no
Client: individuals, groups, organizations
Cost: not applicable
Category: coaching model

The Appreciative Coaching Model (ACM) is a style of coaching that facilitates a client's growth by developing their existing strengths. Influenced by the *Appreciative Inquiry Model*, ACM consists of five core principles.

Constructionist principle: What we believe to be true often determines or influences our behavior (i.e., what we do and how we do it). These beliefs then reflect in the language we use to shape our social reality. The constructionist principle suggests there are many ways to look at our social realities or truths, and accordingly, the use of absolute claims is impossible (e.g., "always," and "never").

Coaching by this principle means the coach should avoid telling the client what to do or how to think. These coaching sessions involve an exploration from multiple perspectives and an open dialogue that considers various possibilities and raises awareness for the client.

Poetic principle: People tend to filter and alter what they see by emphasizing some details and deemphasizing others. This principle includes several forms of bias, including confirmation bias (i.e., the tendency to ignore evidence which conflicts or contradicts an existing thought or belief).

Adopting this principle in coaching involves working with clients to examine all the evidence available so they may more accurately see their reality and confront the potential presence of bias.

Anticipatory principle: Our expectations of the future can influence our present behavior. Consequently, it is during this stage that motivations become critical drivers of behavior.

Adopting this principle in coaching involves the client's exploration of the future they want. Facilitating this exploration may include the use of visioning exercises to help the client create a positive vision of their future.

Simultaneity principle: The types of questions we ask, the emphasis (i.e., focus) of our questions, and act of asking them can serve as the catalyst for change. They may even influence the nature of change (i.e., how change takes place).

Adopting this principle in coaching involves using powerful and carefully worded questions to ensure the client is exploring the issues in a way that is both methodical and holistic.

Positive principle: The more positive the inquiry for change, the more effective and lasting the change.

Adopting this principle in coaching involves helping the client create a positive emotional connection with the change.

While ACM acknowledges a client's problems, it does not focus on them. Instead, the model's approach to problem-solving centers on enhancing the client's strengths, thereby expanding their capacity to perform and ultimately address the problem. By taking the client "from good to great," it fosters transformation through the client's innate talent and inherent strengths.

ACM is a collaborative process designed to help the client build a vision for the future, develop strategies for success, and create a plan of action. The model does this through client empowerment and enhancing self-awareness. In addition to the Appreciative Inquiry Model, ACM shares many similarities with *Positive Psychology Coaching*. While certification in ACM is not available, several vendors offer training and certification in Appreciative Inquiry.

Professionals seeking additional information may consider the 2007 book, *Appreciative Coaching: A Positive Process for Change*, authored by Ann L. Clancy, Jacqueline Binkert, and Sara Orem.

Sources[29]

APPRECIATIVE INQUIRY MODEL

Certification Available: yes (multiple vendors)
Certification Required: no
Assessments: no
Proprietary: no
Client: individuals, organizations
Cost: pricing varies
Category: change (org.), problem-solving

Developed in 1986 by organizational behaviorist David Cooperrider, the Appreciative Inquiry Model (AI) provides an alternative method to traditional problem-solving approaches. The AI Model consists of a four-step process, often referred to as the 4D Model.

Step 1—Discovery: This step involves an exploration of the organization's (or client's) past successes to identify the factors which enabled those successes. This step, often characterized as one of inquiry, serves to shift the client's mindset away from deficit thinking (fixating on the problem) to positive thinking (exploring what has worked).

Step 2—Dream: The second step involves the client imagining the constructive and optimistic possibilities regarding their future. This requires creativity, brainstorming, positive questioning, and visioning.

Step 3—Design: The third step involves the client's examination of the multiple possibilities identified from the previous step to determine the appropriate goal or end state. When groups or teams are involved, this step should result in a shared vision.

Step 4—Destiny: The fourth step involves the client designing a strategy or action plan to help them achieve or realize their desired vision. Older versions of Appreciative Inquiry label this step **Delivery**.

In addition to the four-step process, AI includes five principles which help facilitate application of the model.

- Constructionist Principle: This element suggests that our subjective beliefs about what is true determine our thoughts, actions, and behaviors. This affects our use of language, which in turn influences our social environment.

- Poetic Principle: This principle suggests that people within a human system like a group, team, or organization share their life through stories. These stories are subjective and often adjusted to justify certain actions or influence the narrative in favor of the protagonist. Appreciative Inquiry looks to create positive, but realistic, stories about the future.

- Simultaneity Principle: This concept suggests that inquiries into systems can, in and of themselves, cause changes to that system. The questions used during an inquiry can influence how people think about things, which in turn affects how they learn, discover, and grow.

- Anticipatory Principle: This principle suggests that our expectations and anticipations of the future shape our current actions and behaviors.

- Positive Principle: This suggests that asking positive questions about positive aspects of the organization leads to lasting positive change.

In contrast to traditional models that seek to fix "what is broken," AI focuses on "what is working." In other words, AI explores the positive core strengths of the organization. AI can also apply to individuals, as seen in the *Appreciative Coaching Model*.

Appreciative Inquiry continues to grow in popularity, and with this growth come variations of the framework. Professionals may encounter versions of AI which incorporate additional principles like awareness, free choice, synchronicity, and more.

Professionals may obtain certification in the Appreciative Inquiry Model from multiple vendors, including The Center for Appreciative Inquiry. The Center offers five different levels of certification in virtual and proximate formats.

For additional information on Appreciative Inquiry, consider Cooperrider's 1999 book, *Appreciative Inquiry: A Positive Revolution in Change*, co-authored with Diana Whitney.

Sources[30]

ARROW COACHING MODEL

Certification Available: yes (Matt Somers)
Certification Required: no
Assessments: no
Proprietary: no
Client: individuals, groups, organizations
Cost: $450
Category: coaching model

Developed in the early 2000s by leadership coach Matt Somers, the ARROW Model provides the framework for a five-step, inquiry-based coaching process.

Step 1—Aim: The first step involves the client looking over the horizon to determine what they want to achieve. This means developing a list of potential goals and exploring the relevance of each goal. A component of this exploration involves the client differentiating between dreams and performance goals.

As with many coaching models, the ARROW Coaching Model recommends the *SMART Model for Goal Setting* to help the client set goals that are clear, measurable, achievable, and timely.

Step 2—Reality: In the second step, the client explores their current reality. This involves the client looking at their world from multiple perspectives which, in turn, enables them to more accurately assess where they are and how they got there. Helping the client visualize their present state allows them the ability to compare it with their desired future state (Aim) and better define the gap in-between.

An exploration of their current reality also allows the client to identify obstacles that may prevent them from bridging the gap between their current state and their future state. This exploration includes examining what is working for the client and what is not.

Step 3—Reflection: The third step involves the client exploring the gap between their current state and their goal. While the act of reflection is present in each step of the ARROW Model, as a separate step in the process, it serves to integrate all the client's learning thus far to better prepare them to bridge the gap.

A variation of the ARROW Model labels this step **Resources**. This alternative model suggests the client consider the resources (tangible and intangible) which may support them in achieving their goals.

Step 4—Options: In the fourth step, the client explores all the possible scenarios which can help them bridge the gap between their present state and their goal. This includes creating a strategy to overcome challenges, thinking outside the box, and creative brainstorming.

Step 5—Way-Forward: In the final step, the client begins the process of narrowing down their options through a critical examination of the pros and cons of each option. The ensuing prioritization allows the client to identify the course of action most likely to help them achieve their goals.

Once the client selects the best option, it is time for them to put it into action. In this step, Somers encourages coaches to use language which emphasizes what the client "will do" and avoid language which suggests what the client "could do." In this regard, the coach is helping the client by holding them accountable to their plan of action.

Like so many coaching models, the ARROW Model is an expanded variation of Sir John Whitmore's *GROW Coaching Model*.

It is important to note that there are other coaching models which use the ARROW acronym. These variations include Arise, Recognize, Reinvent, Own-it, and Win. Alternatively, another version of the model is Ambition, Reflection, Reality, Options, and Will-do.

Professionals seeking additional information may consider Somers' 2006 book, *Coaching at Work*. Matt Somers offers training in the ARROW Model.

Sources[31]

ATKINS MURPHY MODEL OF REFLECTION

Certification Available: no
Certification Required: no
Assessments: no
Proprietary: no
Client: individuals
Cost: not applicable
Category: reflection

Developed in 1994 by Registered Nurses Sue Atkins and Kathy Murphy, the Atkins Murphy Model of Reflection (AMMR) provides a structured approach to help clients reflect on significant recent experiences and enable learning that is both immediate and meaningful. The AMMR cycle consists of five steps.

Step 1—Awareness: This first step involves developing the client's awareness of and desire to reflect on the experience. This includes an exploration of how they felt during the experience as well as their current feelings.

During this stage of the process, the client should acknowledge that the experience is worthy of reflection. Sometimes, a client may reject the idea of reflecting on an experience because the event creates anxiety, or they dismiss it as inconsequential when, in fact, it is not. This acknowledgment is especially important if the client feels discomfort which might otherwise dissuade them from reflecting on the experience.

Step 2—Describe the situation/experience: The second step involves the client recounting the experience by highlighting the details of what happened and the sequence of how the event unfolded. The client's ability to describe the event should include their thoughts and feelings throughout the experience. In other words, what were they feeling and thinking as the experience took place?

Step 3—Analyze feelings and knowledge: This step involves the client's ability to apply critical thinking and logic while reflecting on the experience. The client's examination of their assumptions and biases is crucial as a means of identifying their role in the experience, how they behaved, and how things could have been different.

This step depends on the client's creative ability to imagine and consider how alternative scenarios might have occurred in the presence of different assumptions or actions (on the client's part). This technique, called counterfactual thinking, is a useful means of exploring the road not taken and ensuring the client does not respond in the same way in the future.

Step 4—Evaluate the relevance of knowledge: During this step, the client evaluates the role knowledge played in their experience. Being able to identify gaps in their knowledge and understand how those gaps influenced their behavior and perceptions of the experience is crucial to the client's learning process.

Step 5—Identify any learning: The final step brings everything together and involves the client explicitly acknowledging what they learned from the experience and their ensuing reflection of the event.

Though originally designed to examine a recent and significant experience in nursing, the utility of AMMR applies across all professions and experiences. AMMR is useful for clients struggling to acknowledge the consequences of their actions, those experiencing intense emotions, or those who find it difficult to break patterns of detrimental behaviors. Another useful application of the AMMR is its utility in helping clients who want to reflect on an experience but find it difficult because of the discomfort that arises when reliving the experience.

AMMR, though simple in appearance, is complex in practice. The model may not be ideal for those seeking a quick reflection process or for those who resist the idea of examining past experiences on a deep level.

Professionals seeking additional information may consider Atkins and Murphy's 1995 article, "Reflective Practice," found in the *Nursing Standard Journal*.

Sources[32]

ATTRIBUTION THEORY

Certification Available: no
Certification Required: no
Assessments: no
Proprietary: no
Client: individuals
Cost: not applicable
Category: bias

Introduced in 1958 by psychologist Fritz Heider, Attribution Theory examines how people make sense of their world through the causal attribution of observed behavior. In other words, Attribution Theory seeks to explain the process we use to understand why people do what they do.

This process involves using information to determine the cause (attribution) of the behavior. Heider's original theory identifies two forms of attribution.

Dispositional (internal): This occurs when the observer attributes the cause of observed behavior to an internal characteristic of the person. For example, we might say a person driving aggressively does so because they are a bad driver.

Situational (external): This occurs when the observer attributes the cause of observed behavior to the person's environment. For example, we might say a person driving aggressively (and we see smoke coming from their car) does so because they are trying to pull off the road before their car catches fire.

Attribution Theory identifies several sources of inaccuracies that can negatively affect the attribution process.

Fundamental attribution error: This happens when we make an inaccurate attribution based on an assumption about the person's personality or character. For example, we might say a person driving aggressively does so because they are a jerk.

Actor-observer bias: This form of inaccuracy typically occurs when we try to explain our own actions by attributing our behavior to situational or external factors. For example, I drive the way I do because no one else knows how to.

Self-serving bias: This is the act of making attributions based on a positive (or negative) self-interpretation of our behavior. Typically, when we perceive our behavior as positive, we tend to make an internal attribution. When our behavior is negative, we tend to make an external attribution.

For example, a person driving too fast in the rain who loses control of their car and then regains control might say they are a good driver, because they avoided a crash. Conversely, if they lose control and crash, they might blame the wet road conditions.

Studies in Attribution Theory suggest when a person's behavior occurs in a socially desirable way, we tend to assign no meaning to the behavior or the person. If the behavior runs counter to what is socially acceptable, we will likely make an inference (possibly negative) about the person. For more information on how we create and maintain balance when this occurs, see *Heider's Balance Theory*.

Because the theory deals with understanding why people do what they do, professionals often combine this with other germane theories like *Consistency Theories*.

Attribution Theory has since become an umbrella term for a collection of subtheories that further explore this question. Psychologists contributing to these theories include Edward E. Jones, Keith E. Davis, Harold Kelly, Bernard Weiner, and others. Theories under the Attribution Theory umbrella include:

- *Covariation Model of Attribution* (embedded within the entry for Correspondent Inference Theory)

- *Three-Dimensional Model of Attribution*

- *Correspondent Inference Theory*

Attribution Theory is more complex than presented here. Professionals should thoroughly research the theory before incorporating it into practice. Readers seeking additional information on Attribution Theory may consider Heider's 1958 book, *The Psychology of Interpersonal Relations*.

Sources[33]

BARRETT MODEL

Certification Available: yes
Certification Required: yes
Assessments: yes (PVA, LDR, IVA, LVA)
Proprietary: yes (Barrett Values Center)
Client: individuals, groups, organizations
Cost: $1,600–$1,800
Category: values, self-actualization, motivation, culture, leadership

Created in 1997 by leadership development consultant Richard Barrett, the Barrett Model provides a framework to foster insight into a client's values and motivations. Influenced by *Maslow's Hierarchy of Needs*, the Barrett Model consists of seven domains that comprise human motivation. We list the seven domains sequentially starting from the base level.

Level 1—Viability: This speaks to the fundamental need for stability. This includes financial stability and surety of safety and health.

Level 2—Relationships: This is the need to build relationships, form communities, develop a sense of belonging, communicate with others, and establish connections.

Level 3—Performance: This motivation speaks to a person's drive to achieve. This includes a desire for quality, efficiency, and results. These needs can motivate people to build their competencies and enhance their self-esteem.

Level 4—Evolution: This is the drive for personal transformation, which includes a person's desire for autonomy and empowerment. This level of motivation inspires a person to learn and seek out new and novel experiences.

Level 5—Alignment: This is the need to express oneself in an honest and open way. This includes a person's desire for creativity, need for transparency, and development of their passions.

Level 6—Collaboration: This is the need to cultivate one's community. This involves a person's need to derive internal fulfillment from their work, engage in mentorship and coaching, and contribute to their community.

Level 7—Contribution: This is the pinnacle of motivations and speaks to a person's desire for purpose. Within this level, a person feels social responsibility, a need to be of service, and a desire to strive for a greater vision.

Using his original model, Barrett developed a variation for use with leaders, called the **Barrett Leadership Model**. This model lists the seven levels as follows.

Level 1—Crisis Manager
Level 2—Relationship Manager
Level 3—Performance Manager
Level 4—Facilitator/Innovator
Level 5—Authentic Leader
Level 6—Mentor/Partner Leader
Level 7—Visionary Leader

The Barrett Model, also known as Barrett 7 Levels of Consciousness, has evolved over the years, resulting in multiple variations of the framework. Despite an official version, older versions of the model persist, meaning the reader may encounter them during their coaching career.

The Barrett Model is useful with a variety of clients, groups, and organizations, and supports the client's journey toward self-actualization by helping them identify strengths and weakness across multiple competency areas. The model also facilitates a client's understanding of their values and how those values influence them.

The Barrett Model is significantly more complex than presented here and includes a litany of assessments and tools to facilitate a client's exploration of their values and motivations. These include resources designed for individuals, groups, and organizations. Using the Barrett Model and its affiliated assessments requires certification provided solely by the Barrett Values Center.

Professionals seeking additional information on the Barrett Model may consider Barrett's 2018 book, *Everything I Have Learned About Values*.

Sources[34]

BASADUR PROFILE

> **Certification Available:** yes (Basadur)
> **Certification Required:** yes
> **Assessments:** yes (CPSP)
> **Proprietary:** yes (Basadur)
> **Client:** individuals, groups
> **Cost:** not applicable
> **Category:** problem-solving, teaming

Developed in the 1980s by organizational psychologist Marino "Min" Basadur, the Basadur Profile provides a generalized framework that identifies the following "four stages of creativity" used to spur innovation: generation, conceptualization, optimization, and implementation.

According to Basadur, every person possesses a preference for how they like to solve problems. Some prefer action, others contemplation, but all bring a unique and necessary skill to the table. To characterize these preferences, Basadur uses the corresponding stages of creativity.

Generators (generation stage): These individuals excel during the generation stage of innovation. They love to find new problems and opportunities to work on. They are often the spark that lights the fire of inno-vation. Generators prefer the early stages of the inno-vation process, thriving in the ambiguity and explora-tion of problem sets.

Conceptualizers (conceptualization stage): These individuals relish a deep and methodical exploration of the problem, but first they must understand the problem in relation to the bigger picture. Driven to understand the problem, conceptualizers take their time for thorough examination. Once they define the problem to their satisfaction, they enjoy brainstorming ideas and possible solutions.

Optimizers (optimization stage): These individuals excel at evaluating ideas and potential solutions. They take abstract solutions and refine them into more practical ideas. Optimizers strive to eliminate any ambiguity sur-rounding the problem and its potential solutions. Keen on metrics and measurements, they establish scorecards and milestones to measure the efficacy of solutions.

Implementors (implementation stage): These individ-uals are all about action. Highly adaptable, they are almost single-minded in their pursuit of getting the job done. Sometimes seen as impatient or pushy, these individuals are essential to the successful implementation of solutions.

The Basadur Profile is useful to help ensure problem-solving teams include an effective balance of skills and prefer-ences. A team made up entirely of generators and conceptualizers will likely struggle to design pragmatic solutions and implement them successfully.

To facilitate this framework, Basadur developed the Creative Problem-Solving Profile Inventory (CPSP), which allows a client to characterize individual team members based on their preferences for four stages. The CPSP results in the Team Scatter Report that identifies any potential imbalance in the team construct, allowing leaders to adjust accordingly.

Professionals seeking a more methodical process than the generalized overview offered by the Basadur Profile might consider the *Simplexity* model, also developed by Basadur. This model provides a detailed process for prob-lem-solving and innovation that complements the Basadur Profile.

Professionals seeking additional information on the Basadur Profile may consider Basadur's 1995 book, *The Power of Innovation: How to Make Innovation a Way of Life and Put Creative Solutions to Work.*

Sources[35]

BASIC ID MODEL

Certification Available: no
Certification Required: no
Assessments: yes (SPI)
Proprietary: no
Client: individuals
Cost: not applicable
Category: coaching model, problem-solving

Developed in the 1980s by psychologist Arnold Lazarus, Multimodal Therapy (MMT) is a form of psychotherapy based on the belief that most psychological problems are multifaceted, requiring an equally multifaceted approach for treatment. Lazarus called these multiple facets modalities, and he identified seven of them, represented by the acronym BASIC ID. The ICMT presents these seven modalities through a coaching optic.

Behavior: This modality explores the client's actions, past, present, and future. To discern actual behavior from isolated actions, the client should look for repetitive patterns which may have created, perpetuated, or exacerbated the problems they are experiencing.

In a coaching context, a common question that reflects this modality is "What behavior do you want to do more of (or less of)?"

Affect: This modality explores the emotional impact of the experience on the client. This includes the client's consideration of both positive and negative feelings, and their self-assessment of how these emotions influenced their behavior.

In a coaching context, this modality involves developing the client's self-awareness so they may recognize and understand when they are having a moment as it is happening.

Sensation: This modality explores the physiological results of the behavior. When a client encounters an intense emotion, the result often manifests in the body.

In a coaching context, this modality pertains to the work we do in somatics. For example, a client who experiences fear at public speaking may shake uncontrollably before giving a speech, which in turn influences the tone, pitch, and rate of their speech.

Imagery: This modality explores the client's ability to visualize or think in pictures. Often, the mental pictures a client forms can play a vital role in their success or failure. In a coaching context, performance coaches use this modality when they ask an athlete to imagine themselves winning or performing their personal best.

Cognition: This modality explores the client's attitudes, beliefs, values, and language-based thought. Because many clients are not explicitly aware of their own core values, developing their awareness of this domain is essential.

Interpersonal relationships: This modality explores the client's ability to form social and professional relationships that are meaningful and capable of fostering the changes the client desires.

Drugs and biological functions: Despite its name, this modality explores the client's habits which may create or exacerbate their problems. In clinical settings, these lifestyle choices often involve drug use; hence the label. In a coaching context, coaches often work with clients on less dangerous habits like working excessive hours or procrastination.

It is important to note that MMT is the domain of clinical therapy. However, because MMT focuses on the relationship between how a person thinks, feels, and behaves, it is commonly associated with *Cognitive Behavioral Therapy (CBT)* and thus, to an extent, *Cognitive Behavioral Coaching (CBC)*. Therefore, aspects of MMT have utility in coaching.

For example, a client may want to run more inclusive meetings (Behavior), they may want to change how they feel about a project (Affect), they may want to stop biting their nails (Sensation), or they may want to become more efficient in the morning as they get ready for work (Biological: habits). Professionals seeking additional information may consider Lazarus' 1981 book, *The Practice of Multimodal Therapy*.

Sources[36]

BEEF FEEDBACK MODEL

Certification Available: no
Certification Required: no
Assessments: no
Proprietary: no
Client: individuals
Cost: not applicable
Category: feedback

Developed by leadership coach Russell Stratton, the BEEF Feedback Model is a simple framework to help managers have difficult conversations in which constructive or critical feedback is necessary. The model presents four elements to consider when preparing to provide someone with critical feedback.

Behavior: Identify the problematic behavior for the employee in clear and unambiguous terms. Specify what the employee is or is not doing that is causing friction. Explain why the behavior is problematic.

Examples: Provide multiple examples to demonstrate how the employee's actions are part of a repetitive pattern of behavior. In other words, demonstrate how the person's actions represent a trend.

Effect: Show the employee how their behavior is affecting others, the group, and the organization. Use impact statements from those affected to reinforce the point.

Future: Explain what you want to see from the employee going forward. Provide clear and unambiguous behaviors to help the person understand how to correct the problem.

The BEEF Model helps managers address problematic behavior with employees with the intention of inducing a change to correct the problem. Conceptually, the BEEF Model presents less as a conversation and more as a one-way corrective process. In other words, the framework adopts only the perspective of the manager delivering the feedback and does not explicitly include how the provider and recipient should converse about the issue.

It is important to note, Stratton presents this model as one part of a larger process for productive discourse. The model simply helps the provider prepare for their conversation.

An important aspect of the model is that it removes the emotional impact the problematic behavior may cause the manager. Some practitioners see this as preferable since emotions can complicate the situation, while others believe demonstrating emotional impact is critical to conveying the consequences of problematic behavior.

The BEEF Model is one of many feedback models included in the ICMT and is among a small group of virtually identical processes like *BIFF, BOOST,* or *SBI.*

Because many of these feedback models are similar in design and intent, professionals should familiarize themselves with these variations as both clients and peers may possess awareness of these frameworks.

Professionals seeking additional information on the BEEF Model and its accompanying conversational strategies may consider Stratton's 2020 book, *I Need to F***ing Talk to You: The Art of Navigating Difficult Workplace Conversations,* co-authored by Ken Cameron.

Sources[37]

BEHAVIORAL EQ MODEL

Certification Available: yes (multiple vendors)
Certification Required: no
Assessments: yes (multiple vendors)
Proprietary: some versions (multiple vendors)
Client: individuals, groups, organizations
Cost: pricing not available
Category: emotional intelligence

The exact origin of the Behavioral Intelligence Model (BEQ) is ambiguous. A few sources suggest the concept emerged from military strategy (i.e., out of a desire to know one's adversary), while others suggest BEQ arose from the early emotional intelligence work of Goleman, Boyatzis, and others. However, most agree that regardless of its origin, BEQ is an evolution of emotional intelligence (EI), with some sources calling it the third generation of EI.

Several variations of BEQ exist. This entry presents the Tracom version of BEQ, which consists of four domains: emotional intelligence—self, emotional intelligence—others, behavioral intelligence—self, and behavioral intelligence—others. Each domain, in turn, includes several components.

Emotional Intelligence—Self

• Emotional awareness: the cognizance of and relationship between one's emotions and behaviors.

• Self-insight: an accurate self-assessment of one's strengths and limitations.

• Self-confidence: one's feelings of worth and competence.

Behavioral Intelligence—Self

• Self-control: the ability to manage impulses and emotions.

• Self-management: the ability to regulate reactions to stress.

• Conscientiousness: the level of responsibility for one's personal behavior.

• Optimism: one's ability for positivity in the face of adversity.

Emotional Intelligence—Others

• Emotion perception: the ability to identify and understand the emotions of others.

• Empathy-openness: the ability to consider another's perspective and be receptive to feedback.

• Listening: the ability to actively listen.

Behavioral Intelligence—Others

• Building relationships: the ability to establish and maintain positive relationships.

• Influencing others: the ability to persuade others.

• Motivating others: the ability to inspire others.

• Flexibility: the ability to adapt to new circumstances.

• Innovativeness: the ability to generate new ideas.

A common question of BEQ involves how it is different from other EI models. On this, Tracom offers the following distinction, "EI focuses on developing emotional awareness, recognition, and understanding, while BEQ focuses on the practical skills necessary for influencing others, thus affecting individual and team performance."

Multiple variations of BEQ exist, with each using different labels and different frameworks. These differences are not subtle; professionals should fully research each variation to determine which is appropriate for them and their client. For more information, see the *Emotional Intelligence (general)* entry in this text.

Each version of BEQ includes its own suite of assessments requiring certification from the parent company.

Sources[38]

BEHAVIORAL LEARNING THEORY

Certification Available: no
Certification Required: no
Assessments: no
Proprietary: no
Client: individuals
Cost: not applicable
Category: learning/development, behavioral styles

ntroduced in 1913 by psychologist John B. Watson, Behavioral Learning Theory (BLT) suggests a person's behavior is a result of their experiences with their environment. Put another way, BLT suggests our experiences are a key determinant in who we become.

In the 1930s, famed psychologist B.F. Skinner further refined Watson's theory by focusing on observable and measurable behaviors. He suggested individuals learn from their environment through a process called conditioning. Skinner identified two types of conditioning.

Classical conditioning: This form of conditioning occurs by pairing a neutral stimulus (e.g., sound of a bell) with a naturally occurring stimulus (e.g., food). Over time, the neutral stimulus influences the individual in the same way as the naturally occurring stimulus. A well-known example of this is Ivan Pavlov's experiment using a bell to induce the same response (salivation) from a dog that normally occurs when the dog receives food.

Operant conditioning: This form of conditioning occurs by pairing a positive or negative stimulus (e.g., a dog treat) with a specific behavior (e.g., raising the left paw). This type of conditioning seeks to establish an association between a specific behavior and the consequences of that behavior. An example of this is an experiment in which the subject receives a reward for pressing a green button and a shock for pressing the red button. In time, the subject learns to press the green button and avoid the red one. This type of conditioning is the focus of B.F. Skinner's *Reinforcement Theory*.

Watson felt so strongly about BLT that he claimed if given a dozen healthy infants, he could train them to be anything from doctors and lawyers to thieves and beggars, regardless of their predispositions or talents, simply by controlling their environment.

A commonly held belief among proponents of BLT is that personality is not a predetermined construct; rather it is a product of culture, societal conditions, and upbringing. This implies that innate or inherited factors such as genetics or temperament have little to no influence on a person's personality.

Another principal characteristic of BLT, also called Behavioral Psychology or Behaviorism, is its focus on observable/measurable behaviors. Behaviorists typically do not consider internal factors (i.e., unobservable, or unmeasurable variables) such as thoughts, feelings, emotions, or intrinsic motivations when exploring human behavior.

It is important to note that both practitioners and opponents of BLT question the efficacy of the theory, believing it's too rigid because it ignores biological factors that influence both an individual's behavior and personality.

Nevertheless, BLT is a useful theory for practicing coaches, facilitators, and consultants because of its focus on observable behaviors. Professionals may use BLT to further develop their observational skills and enable them to notice patterns in the client's behavior which can help inform the coaching process.

Behaviorism is also useful when working with clients considering change. The use of conditioning as a lens to examine the origin of current behaviors and explore strategies to create new and more desirable behaviors can provide value for the client.

Practitioners seeking to enhance their depth of knowledge on Behaviorism will find significant literature available on the subject. The foundational work from Watson features in his 1913 paper, "Psychology as the Behaviorist Views It." Professionals may also consider the 1984 book, *Learning Theory and Behavior Modification,* from Stephen Walker.

Sources[39]

BELBIN'S TEAM ROLE THEORY

> **Certification Available:** yes
> **Certification Required:** yes
> **Assessments:** yes (BSPI)
> **Proprietary:** yes (Belbin Associates)
> **Client:** groups, teams
> **Cost:** $1,700
> **Category:** teaming, behavioral styles

Developed in 1981 by management consultant Meredith Belbin, Team Role Theory explores the different styles of team-member behaviors and how these behaviors contribute to the team's performance. Belbin's research led to the identification of nine roles, organized in three categories.

Action-Oriented Roles

• Shaper: This style pertains to highly motivated individuals who help the team achieve and maintain momentum. They challenge the team to overcome obstacles but can provoke intense feelings in others.

• Implementor: Practical and reliable, these individuals help convert ideas into a concrete plan. They lean toward inflexibility, though they can make the team more efficient.

• Completer-finisher: Meticulous and detail oriented, these individuals tend to make their contributions at the end of team projects. They help teams with quality control, though they lean toward perfectionism.

People-Oriented Roles

• Coordinator: Highly focused and goal oriented, these individuals help the team stay on track. Capable of effective delegation, they sometimes overdelegate, to the point of passing on their responsibilities to others.

• Team worker: Diplomatic and perceptive, these individuals help the team coalesce and cooperate. They can help manage personalities and conflict, though they may struggle to make decisions and tend to avoid confrontation.

• Resource investigator: Outgoing and enthusiastic, these individuals seek out resources to meet the team's needs. They can help the team think through their requirements, though they can sometimes lose interest in the team's purpose.

Thought-Oriented Roles

• Plant: Highly creative and imaginative, these individuals are critical to the team's problem-solving ability. They can generate ideas through unconventional thinking but sometimes lack the ability to inspire others.

• Monitor-evaluator: Strategic and logical, these individuals help track the team's progress. They contribute to the team's decision-making process by providing impartial and dispassionate input, though they may struggle to connect with others.

• Specialist: Single-minded and highly determined, they bring subject matter expertise to the team. Though sometimes overly technical and myopic, their insight can reveal important details for the team.

Belbin's research focused on what he called useful behaviors, or behaviors that positively contribute to the team's mission. He believed that understanding these behaviors allows individuals to develop their strengths, manage weaknesses, and allow leaders to create better balanced teams.

Belbin's Team Roles is significantly more complex than presented here and includes an array of assessments and tools to facilitate the application of the theory. Formal use of these resources requires training, certification, and accreditation from Belbin Associates.

Because Belbin's assessment categorizes individual behavioral tendencies, we also classify it as a personality-typing instrument.

Professionals seeking additional information may consider Belbin's 1981 book, *Management Teams: Why They Succeed or Fail*, and his 1993 book, *Team Roles at Work*.

Sources[40]

BENZIGER THINKING STYLES

Certification Available: yes
Certification Required: yes
Assessments: yes (BTSA)
Proprietary: yes (MyBenziger)
Client: individuals
Cost: pricing not available
Category: learning/development, personality

Developed in the 1980s by psychologist Katherine Benziger, the Benziger Thinking Styles offers a framework for personality typing based on the four regions of the brain. Unique among personality theories, Benziger's work examines personality based on brain function. The model looks at the four regions (called modes) of the brain through the optic of psychologist Carl Jung's four psychological types.

Benziger identified four styles of personality corresponding to the modes (regions) of the brain. She noted that while each person possesses a natural preference for one mode, we can develop skills in multiple modes. The four personality modes are:

Mode 1—Basal left: This region of the brain favors process and routine. Mode 1 individuals tend to be practical, sensible, and ordered. They prefer clearly defined rules and tend to stick with what they know. They are not naturally creative or comfortable with improvisation.

Mode 2—Basal right: This region of the brain favors spiritual experience and feelings. Mode 2 individuals tend to be highly intuitive and deeply empathetic. Known to be personable and humane, these individuals prefer building and maintaining relationships to following a highly structured process. They are creative and thrive in dynamic social settings.

Mode 3—Frontal right: This region of the brain favors creativity and imagination. Mode 3 individuals tend to be visionary and speculative. They prefer following intuition to a strict adherence to facts. They crave meaning in their work and resist mundane and repetitive tasks.

Mode 4—Frontal left: This region of the brain favors logic and analytical structure. Mode 4 individuals prefer a structured approach to task performance. They respond well to methodical tasks and possess a meticulous attention to detail. Mode 4 individuals want expectations laid out for them and are not well suited for tasks that require creativity or spontaneity.

In her work, Benziger expresses concern about a vulnerability in most personality assessments she calls "falsification of type," which happens when a person answers an assessment question in a less than honest way. For example, a candidate for an open position might answer questions based on what he thinks the organization is looking for.

Benziger further determined that falsification of type occurs when people create an alternate personality type so they can better fit a desired role. This may lead to *Prolonged Adaptation Stress Syndrome (PASS)*. Benziger's framework and associated assessments help clients identify their true preferences and avoid the adoption of false typing, thus mitigating the risk of PASS.

Benziger provides a general list of professions commonly associated with each of the four modes, so her model has utility in career coaching. The model is also known as Benziger's Personality Assessment Model, Benziger's Personality and Brain Type Theory, and Benziger's Working Model of Brain Function.

Benziger's model is more complex than presented here. Use of Benziger Thinking Styles and its affiliated assessments requires training, certification, and licensing from Benziger International.

Professionals seeking depth of knowledge may consider Benziger's 1989 book, *The Art of Using Your Whole Brain*, or her 1994 book, *The BTSA User Manual*.

Sources[41]

BIF/BIFFOF/BIFF FEEDBACK MODELS

Certification Available: no
Certification Required: no
Assessments: no
Proprietary: no
Client: individuals
Cost: not applicable
Category: feedback

The exact origin of the BIFF Feedback Model is ambiguous. An exploration into this model revealed multiple variations with subtle differences. One variation, created by leadership development professional John Tomlinson, is the BIF Feedback Model. This version provides a simple three-step framework for delivering feedback.

BIF Model

Step 1—Behavior: Describe the behavior at issue with as much specificity as possible. Avoid commenting on the recipient's personality and do not share your opinions on the recipient's attitudes, beliefs, or feelings.

Variations of this model recommend including information not directly observed by the provider (i.e., what others have said or observed).

Step 2—Impact: Explain how the problematic behavior affected others by using concrete examples. Include tangible examples like metrics or quantifiable outcomes, when possible (e.g., loss of a client, loss of revenue, project failure).

Step 3—Future: Explain, in detail, the desired change you wish to see in the recipient. Provide a clear picture of behaviors you want the recipient to adopt or cease.

BIFFOF Model

Should the recipient fail to follow through on the original feedback, Tomlinson recommends using the BIFFOF process, which adds a fourth step to the BIF Model: Behavior, Impact, Future, and Feedback on Feedback.

Step 4—Feedback on Feedback: The provider focuses their commentary on the recipient's ability, or lack thereof, to follow through or effect meaningful change based on the initial feedback.

BIFF Model

Another similar feedback model, called BIFF (unknown attribution), includes the addition of feelings (third step) into the feedback process. Behavior, Impact, Feelings, and Future.

Step 3—Feelings: After discussing the impact of the recipient's behavior, but before discussing the changes you want to see, explain how the recipient's behavior makes you and others feel. This may add additional context for the recipient and help them better understand the consequences of their behavior. Avoid criticizing the individual and personal attacks (i.e., do not be judgmental); instead focus on the behavior.

Another variation of the BIFF Model switches the sequence of steps to Behavior, Impact, Future, and Feelings. In this version, Feelings refers to how the recipient feels following the feedback. This distinction highlights the importance of inquiring about how the feedback landed for the recipient.

Each of these feedback models has strengths and limitations. Before selecting the most appropriate framework, the provider should consider the nature of the feedback and the recipient (e.g., their needs).

It is important to note that a second model exists which uses the acronym BIFF. Called the BIFF Conflict Model, this is a separate and unrelated framework used in responding to conflict.

The BIF/BIFFOF/BIFF Models are among many feedback models included in *The Infourge Compendium of Models and Theories* and among a small group of similar processes, including the *AID, BEEF, BOOST,* and *SBI Models*.

Because many of these feedback models are similar in design and intent, professionals should familiarize themselves with these variations as both clients and peers may already possess awareness of these frameworks.

Sources[42]

BIRKMAN METHOD

Certification Available: yes
Certification Required: yes
Assessments: yes (several)
Proprietary: yes
Client: individuals, groups
Cost: $3,995
Category: personality, motivation, engagement

Developed in 1951 by organizational psychologist Roger W. Birkman, the Birkman Method provides a framework for exploring the way a person's perspective influences their personality. The model consists of four perspectives that Birkman believed play a significant role in influencing a person's personality and consequently their behavior.

Perspective 1—Motivation: This component of the model explores a person's level of interest in the different roles and tasks found within their work environment. This allows the person to distinguish tasks that motivate and inspire them from those that drain their energy. When exploring this perspective, a person seeks to identify their passions and any opportunities to pursue those passions within their professional setting. From this, a person can better determine which tasks and roles align with their interests and passions.

Perspective 2—Self-perception: This component pertains to how people see themselves. In a professional context, this includes how they perform their assigned tasks, how they manage their relationships, and how they present to others in their environment, also called Usual Behavior. Additionally, this involves a person's perception of their strengths and weaknesses. One of the underlying principles of the Birkman Method is the belief that a person's experience will heavily influence their perceptions.

Perspective 3—Social perception: This component pertains to the view a person has of the world around them. This includes the context they draw upon to determine if a situation or environment is comfortable. Highly influential of behavior, a person's social perceptions often remain hidden from much of the external world, meaning that others may not understand why this person behaves the way they do because they cannot see the underlying context. Also referred to as Needs, insight into this element allows a person to anticipate their reaction to the ever-changing environment.

Perspective 4—Mindset: This component pertains to a person's fundamental belief system, specifically as it affects interpersonal and intrapersonal relationships. The mindset perspective explores the "why" behind a person's behavior by bringing together the various perspectives to understand their belief system. This includes consideration of the impact on behavior of the subconscious (e.g., bias) and of heuristics.

Birkman developed his model to explain why pilots in World War II behaved and reacted differently to similar situations. He determined that the primary cause of this phenomenon was a person's underlying perceptions and motivations.

Fundamentally, Birkman's Method draws upon other psychological frameworks like *Lewin's Behavior Equation*. In application, the method employs Positive Psychology to help the client learn, grow, and flourish.

One aspect differentiating the Birkman Method from many other personality frameworks is its incorporation of occupational data in the survey. This provides insight into a person's motivation and passion for specific roles within the organization. For this reason, professionals will use the method to support hiring practices and help connect employees with positions that better fit.

The Birkman Method instrument, originally known as the Test of Social Comprehension, is very complex and encompasses an array of assessments for individuals and groups, as well as extensive reports and graphs. Formal use of the framework and the assessments requires certification. Professionals seeking additional information may consider Birkman's 1995 book, *True Colors: Get to Know Yourself and Others Better with the Highly Acclaimed Birkman Method*, and the 2013 book, *The Birkman Method: Your Personality at Work*, by Sharon Birkman Fink and Stephanie Capparell.

Sources[43]

BLOOM'S TAXONOMY (REVISED)

Certification Available: no
Certification Required: no
Assessments: no
Proprietary: no
Client: individuals, groups
Cost: not applicable
Category: learning/development

Developed in 1956 by educational psychologists Benjamin Bloom, Max Englehart, Edward Furst, Walter Hill, and David Krathwohl, Bloom's Taxonomy provides a framework to help educators set learning objectives at a level appropriate for students.

The original Bloom's Taxonomy consisted of the following six levels of learning: Knowledge, Comprehension, Application, Analysis, Synthesis, and Evaluation. In 2001, educational professors Lorin Anderson and David Krathwohl revised the model, changing the labels for each level and transitioning from nouns to verbs to describe the learning-level behaviors. This subtle but significant change allowed curriculum developers to design more meaningful learning objectives.

Level 1—Remember: This is the ability to recognize, recall, and retrieve relevant information from memory. Verbs describing these learning behaviors include define, describe, identify, and recite. Example learning objective: Identify the management structure of a company.

Level 2—Understand: This is the ability to construct meaning from oral, written, and graphic messages, also known as comprehension. Verbs describing these learning behaviors include explain, compare, contrast, and summarize. Example learning objective: Explain the firm's 5-year financial projections.

Level 3—Apply: This is the ability to functionally use the concept, also known as implementation or execution. Verbs describing these learning behaviors include demonstrate, examine, solve. Example learning objective: Use the Generally Accepted Accounting Principles (GAAP) to solve errors in the company's income statement.

Level 4—Analyze: This is the ability to dissect the concept into its base components and determine their relationship to one another. Verbs describing these learning behaviors include differentiate, distinguish, and deconstruct. Example learning objective: Analyze the elements of a company's supply chain.

Level 5—Evaluate: This is the ability to make logical judgments based on criteria and standards. Verbs describing these learning behaviors include assess, conclude, critique, and validate. Example learning objective: Assess a new product/service based on the company's core values, mission, and ethics.

Level 6—Create: This involves putting the components of the concept into a new pattern or new coherent whole. Verbs describing these learning behaviors include design, construct, develop. Example learning objective: Use the *Systematic Inventive Thinking* process to find new uses for existing products or services.

The model is sequential, meaning a person cannot achieve one level of competence without reaching the previous levels. For example, a person cannot apply a concept without first knowing and comprehending the concept.

Bloom's Taxonomy is useful for professionals who design training curricula. The model also provides a common frame of reference to define a person's depth of knowledge.

The Revised Bloom's Taxonomy is significantly more complex than presented here. This comprehensive framework also includes a taxonomy of the types of knowledge used in cognition: Factual, Conceptual, Procedural, and Metacognitive.

Professionals seeking additional information may consider Bloom's 1956 book, *Taxonomy of Educational Objectives*, or Anderson and Krathwohl's 2013 book, *A Taxonomy for Learning, Teaching, and Assessing: A Revision of Bloom's Taxonomy of Educational Objectives*. Readers may also consider Niall McNulty's book, *Bloom's Digital Taxonomy: A Reference Guide for Teachers*.

Sources[44]

BOOST FEEDBACK MODEL

Certification Available: no
Certification Required: no
Assessments: no
Proprietary: no
Client: individuals
Cost: not applicable
Category: feedback

The BOOST Feedback Model is a simple framework useful for delivering informal feedback. Though widely written about, the origins of BOOST remain ambiguous.

The BOOST Model consists of five criteria.

Balanced: The first criterion involves feedback which consists of both positive and constructive elements. The provider should avoid feedback that relies solely on critical commentary. By focusing only on the recipient's vulnerabilities, weak points, problems, or behavioral issues, the provider risks the recipient becoming defensive and potentially shutting down.

Conversely, focusing solely on the positive aspects of the recipient's performance risks the recipient becoming stagnant. By including a balance of positive and negative elements, the provider demonstrates to the recipient that they recognize the recipient's strengths and their contributions but also see opportunities for them to grow.

Observed: The second criterion requires the provider to focus their feedback on behavior directly observed by the provider. This means avoiding using hearsay or unverifiable information in the feedback process. Focusing on observed behavior means the provider owns the feedback. Providing feedback based solely on what others observe means the provider is just passing along the information.

Objective: The third criterion requires that the provider focus on the recipient's tangible and explicit actions. This means the feedback should address the recipient's specific behaviors and avoid any criticism of the recipient's personality. Put another way, describe the behavior; do not attribute the behavior to some aspect of the recipient's character.

Specific: The fourth criterion requires that the feedback include as much detail about the recipient's behavior or actions as possible. This includes providing real details like when the behavior took place, where, and who was present or involved.

Timely: The final criterion of effective feedback requires that the provider deliver feedback as soon as possible following the action in question. The sooner the feedback follows the action, the less likely the recipient will remember events differently.

Many laud the BOOST Model as a framework to facilitate the delivery of informal feedback; in other words, feedback that is spontaneous or as needed. As such, the BOOST Model may not be ideal as a mechanism for formal feedback sessions like annual performance appraisals.

It is important to note that some sources switch the sequence of Observed and Objective criteria. Despite this, the model remains the same.

Critics of the model cite the absence of criteria which address the impact or consequences from the recipient's behavior and the absence of criteria to facilitate a two-way conversation between recipient and provider. Proponents argue that these elements are inherent in the process.

The BOOST Model is one among many feedback models included in this compendium and among a small group of virtually identical processes. See *AID, BIFF, BEEF, SBI*.

Because many of these feedback models are similar in design and intent, professionals should familiarize themselves with these variations, as both clients and peers may possess awareness of these frameworks.

Sources[45]

BORTON'S MODEL OF REFLECTION

Certification Available: no
Certification Required: no
Assessments: no
Proprietary: no
Client: individuals
Cost: not applicable
Category: reflection

Developed in 1970 by educator Terry Borton, Borton's Model of Reflection provides a framework to foster a client's experiential learning through reflecting on their past experiences. Put another way, Borton's Model allows clients to process, learn, and grow from past experiences. Valued for its simplicity, Borton's Model of Reflection consists of three steps, each represented by a simple question to facilitate the reflective examination process.

Step 1—What? In the first step of the reflection process, the client focuses solely on the facts surrounding the event or experience they want to explore. The client should strive to be as specific as possible by explaining what happened, when and where the event occurred, and who was involved. The client should provide a narrative of what each person said and did during the event in question.

Encourage the client to remain objective and avoid interpretations of what happened and why. It is also important that the client avoid ascribing meaning to their own behavior as well as that of others. Ask them to focus only on the observable facts.

Step 2—So what? With the facts on the table, the client can begin to seek meaning in what happened, to understand why the event happened the way it did, and gain insight into why those involved behaved the way they did. This includes the client's own behavior.

Making sense of the experience requires the client to consider their own feelings at different times. First, what were the client's feelings at the time of the event? Second, what are the client's feelings as they reflect on the experience?

Now the client may begin to examine the consequences of their actions (or inaction), how the behavior of others may have influenced their own actions, and what lessons the client might learn from the experience.

Step 3—Now what? During the final step in the reflective process, the client uses everything they learned from the previous steps to imagine how they might like to respond (or act) in the future. A popular technique in this stage of the process is counterfactual thinking, where the client considers the past that did not happen. This includes "if only…" or "had I known…" statements.

During this stage, the client acknowledges the consequences of their actions and compares them to the potential consequences had they responded or behaved in a more desirable way.

Borton's Model of Reflection is one of the most influential frameworks on the topic of reflection, having inspired subsequent frameworks like *Driscoll's Reflection Cycle* and *Rolfe's Reflective Learning*.

Though originally designed for students in a classroom setting, the utility of Borton's Model makes it a useful framework for coaching, particularly with clients looking for a quick, easy, and effective reflective experience.

It is important to note, some practitioners caution against using this model to reflect on deeply personal or intense experiences. For these more complex experiences, professionals recommend more methodical frameworks like *Johns' Model for Structured Reflection* or the *ABCDE Model (Ellis)*.

Though formal certification in Borton's Model of Reflection does not exist, professionals seeking additional information will find much written on the topic, including Borton's 1970 book, *Reach, Touch, and Teach*.

Sources[46]

BRIDGES' TRANSITION MODEL

Certification Available: yes
Certification Required: yes
Assessments: no
Proprietary: yes (William Bridges Associates)
Client: groups, teams, organizations
Cost: pricing not available
Category: change (org.), change (ind.)

Developed in 1991 by business consultant William Bridges, Bridges' Transition Model provides a comprehensive framework to facilitate organizational change by focusing on the individual employee's personal transition in response to the change. The model consists of three stages which describe the process of individual transition.

Stage 1—Endings: The first stage of any transition begins with the ending of something (e.g., the end of the status quo). According to Bridges, before people accept change, they must accept that something is ending. Therefore, clients in this stage will need to consider what they are losing, what they are keeping, and how they will manage the impact of change.

When presented with change, clients may experience intense feelings like anxiety, grief, and stress, which may drive them to resist the change or become hostile to its agents. For this reason, the first stage involves the client getting to a place where they feel they can let go of what they will lose during the transition.

Stage 2—Neutral Zone: The second stage marks the heart of any transition and can only occur once the client lets go of the past and becomes receptive or open to the idea of change. In this stage, the client does not accept the change; rather they commit to exploring the change.

The Neutral Zone stage occurs after the old way is gone, but before the new way becomes an established norm. This stage can present the client with a sense of confusion, anxiety, resentment, and skepticism as they begin to develop and learn new processes. This stage also involves the client developing an awareness of their new role, which can lead to role identity confusion.

Stage 3—New Beginnings: The final stage occurs when individuals embrace their new role identity and adopt the change as the new norm. The New Beginnings stage may also involve the integration of new values and beliefs with old ones. This stage often leads to increased energy and optimism for the client.

Though classified in this text as a framework for organizational and individual change, Bridges describes it as a model for transition, not change. Bridges offers the following distinction.

• Change is an external event or situation that happens to someone (e.g., new product launch, change in leadership, new business strategy).

• Transition is the internal psychological process a person goes through in response to the external change. A unique feature of this model is that it recognizes the potential for change to put people into crisis.

The model's emphasis on the individual psychology of change is like two other change management frameworks featured in *The Infourge Compendium of Models and Theories*, the *ADKAR Model* and the *Transtheoretical Model*. These models also focus on individual change within a larger organizational change effort.

Bridges' Transition Model is useful for clients struggling to adopt or accept organizational change. The framework may also support leadership-level clients preparing for an enterprise-wide change initiative. Many coaches use this model as a process to help clients explore their feelings about change, be it personal or organizational.

Formal use of Bridges' Transition Model requires training and certification from William Bridges Associates. Professionals seeking additional information may consider William and Susan Bridges' 2017 book, *Managing Transitions: Making the Most of Change*, and their 2019 book, *Transitions: Making Sense of Life's Changes*.

Sources[47]

BROOKFIELD MODEL OF REFLECTION

Certification Available: no
Certification Required: no
Assessments: no
Proprietary: no
Client: individuals
Cost: not applicable
Category: reflection

Developed in 2005 by professor of adult learning Stephen Brookfield, the Brookfield Model of Reflection provides a framework to help teachers foster reflective learning and improve the quality of their teaching. The model consists of four lenses, each representing a specific point of view. We present the four lenses from the coaching perspective.

Autobiographical Lens: This involves the client exploring the relationship between their past experiences and their current reality. In other words, how do the client's previous experiences influence their present situation? This exploration is vital to determining the presence of inaccurate assumptions and detrimental heuristics.

For example, a client may explore their experiences with good and bad leaders over the years to determine how those experiences influence their current approach to leading others. Exploring why the client considered particular leaders good or bad may help the client discover how those perceptions, born of past experiences, now influence their leadership style.

Student's Lens: In leadership coaching we call this the Follower's Lens. This involves the client exploring experiences from the perspective of their employees. This step tests the client's ability to think from someone else's point of view without judgment and bias.

The client's initial findings are speculative; however, clients should engage their employees to test their assumptions and form a more accurate understanding of each employee's point of view. The client can do this through direct interactions with each employee or by using anonymous surveys.

Colleague's Lens: Also called the Peer Lens, this involves the client exploring an experience from the point of view of their peers. For example, a client might consider how a peer may have handled a specific situation differently.

The client may explore this conceptually or they can explicitly engage their peers, either individually or in a group setting.

Theoretical Lens: Also called the Literature Lens, this involves the client reading books and articles to expand their knowledge of concepts and constructs. This will foster the client's ability to engage in experiential learning.

For example, a client may read a book about emotional intelligence and, in so doing, learn a new framework that changes how they interpret or perceive a recent experience. This newly acquired knowledge may influence how they view their own behavior or the behavior of others.

A distinct feature of the Brookfield Model is its emphasis on "critical reflection," the act of exploring an experience through multiple lenses to challenge the client's own perceptions and assumptions. One way the framework achieves this is through the combined use of subjective contemplation and objective examination. As the client develops their speculative perceptions of how others may perceive an experience, they will need to test their assumptions by engaging others. This is critical to the reflection process as it reveals to the client how their assumptions and perceptions may differ from reality.

Curriculum development professionals may use this model to ensure the content and its delivery is relevant and effective for the learner. Though created for use in teaching, the model has broad utility across professions. The Brookfield Model of Reflection, also known as Brookfield's Lenses Model, can help clients struggling to process difficult feedback or challenging experiences.

Professionals seeking additional information on the Brookfield Model of Reflection may consider Brookfield's 1995 book, *Becoming a Critically Reflective Teacher*.

Sources[48]

BURKE-LITWIN CHANGE MODEL

<table>
<tr><td>

Certification Available: no
Certification Required: no
Assessments: no
Proprietary: no
Client: organizations
Cost: not applicable
Category: change (org.)

</td></tr>
</table>

Developed in the 1960s by organizational psychologists W. Warner Burke and George H. Litwin, their model provides a multifaceted framework to facilitate organizational change.

The Burke-Litwin Change Model consists of two levels (Transformational and Transactional) and 12 elements which explore the variables that influence organizational change.

Transformational Level

• External factors: These pertain to variables outside of the organization which impact the organization. These include regulations, economic forces, supply chain, social forces, culture, and more. Because these variables have consequences for the organization, they often become the catalyst for change.

• Mission and strategy: Mission pertains to the organization's purpose, what the organization does. Strategy describes how the organization carries out the mission. This involves goals and objectives.

• Leadership: This pertains to the responsibilities of organizational leaders. These include their ability to establish a forward-leaning vision, the efficacy and quality of their decision-making, and their capacity for change and adaptation.

• Culture: This is the internal context of the organization and includes the accepted ways of performing and behaving.

Transactional Level

• Structure: the organization of corporate functions and relationships.

• Management practices: the day-to-day behaviors of managers.

• Systems and policy: the complex constellation of processes, policies, and procedures the organization adopts and follows. This also includes budgeting and resource allocation.

• Work climate: the collective perceptions employees have about how they are managed. This includes clarity of purpose, standards, psychological safety, and accountability.

• Motivation: the degree to which the organization satisfies the individual's needs.

• Skills and tasks: Are people matched to the appropriate task based on their skill?

• Needs and values: the degree of congruence between the individual's values and the organization's values.

• Performance: The cumulative effect of the 11 previous elements will manifest in this final element. Performance pertains to both individual and organizational outcomes.

The model presents the 12 elements in a linear fashion, though the relationship between elements is nonlinear and interconnected. In other words, each element has a relationship with all other elements.

The broad utility of the model includes its use as a resource for assessing, diagnosing, planning, and managing large-scale organizational change efforts. The Burke-Litwin Model is a useful resource for clients facing organizational change.

Sources on the model offer a wide range of material and information, though it is important to note that sources differ on their use of labels and depiction of the model. Some sources segment the elements on as many as five levels. The entry we present derives directly from Burke's material.

The Burke-Litwin Change Model is significantly more complex than presented here. Professionals seeking additional information may consider Burke's 2002 book, *Organization Change: Theory and Practice*.

Sources[49]

BURNETT MODEL OF CRISIS MANAGEMENT

Certification Available: no
Certification Required: no
Assessments: no
Proprietary: no
Client: organizations
Cost: not applicable
Category: crisis management

Developed in 1998 by marketing professor John Burnett, his Model of Crisis Management provides a multilayered framework for understanding how organizations prepare for and respond to crisis situations.

Burnett's Model consists of four factors, three stages, and six steps to crisis management.

Four Factors Impeding Crisis Response

• **Time pressure**: Typical strategic planning occurs over a period of months and involves potential actions that may not take place for years; crises often require immediate action. The limited time available to make decisions, real or perceived, creates a psychological stress on both leaders and the organization.

• **Control issues**: The presence of a crisis often pushes the limits of organizational processes and operational procedures designed for a status quo environment. An organization's inability to adapt and a loss of organizational control undermines its ability to respond to the crisis.

• **Threat-level concern**: This is a complex assessment of the potential risks to the organization stemming from the crisis. The higher the risk level, the more difficult it is to respond.

• **Response option constraints**: A crisis inevitably limits an organization's ability to operate. The typical problem-solving approaches a leader may use to guide the organization may lose efficacy during a crisis.

Only once the organization considers these four factors can it begin the process for crisis management, which Burnett divides into three stages: Identification, Confrontation, and Reconfiguration.

Identification Stage

Step 1—Goal formation: Determine what matters most to the organization, considering the array of possible crises it could face.

Step 2—Environmental analysis: Conduct an internal and external analysis of data pertaining to opportunities, vulnerabilities, risks, patterns, and trends. Understand the crisis (cause and consequences) and how it could impact the organization.

Confrontation Stage

Step 3—Strategy formulation: Use the assessment derived from the environmental analysis to develop a strategy plan for how the organization can best adapt in response to the crisis.

Step 4—Strategy evaluation: Assess the efficacy of the response strategy to identify potential risks and vulnerabilities of the plan.

Reconfiguration Stage

Step 5—Strategy implementation: Execute the response strategy.

Step 6—Strategic control: Observe and influence how leaders manage the organization and its response during the crisis.

To facilitate the application of his framework, Burnett developed a classification matrix to measure the severity of potential crises by assessing an organization based on the four factors which impede the organization's ability to respond to a crisis.

Burnett's model is more complex than presented here. Professionals seeking additional information may consider Burnett's 2008 book, *Managing Business Crises,* or his 2013 paper, "Proactive Crisis Management."

Sources[50]

BUSINESS CHEMISTRY

Certification Available: yes
Certification Required: yes
Assessments: yes (BC Self-Assessment)
Proprietary: yes (Deloitte)
Client: groups, teams
Cost: pricing not available
Category: personality, teaming

Developed in 2018 by Deloitte consultants Kim Christfort and Suzanne Vickberg, Business Chemistry provides a framework to identify a person's working style and understand how their style connects with a team. The model consists of four styles, each representing a distinct set of characteristics.

Pioneers: This working style includes big-picture thinkers drawn to bold ideas and creative approaches. On teams, they tend to provide a creative spark to drive innovation. Described as outgoing and risk-seeking, they can also overlook details and disregard the feelings of others.

Drivers: This working style consists of results-oriented individuals typically driven to win. On teams, they serve as a source of momentum and keep the team focused on the goal. Described as logical and competitive, they can resist rules and may lack empathy.

Within the category of Drivers are two subtypes: Commanders and Scientists.

- Commanders: These are hyperfocused and competitive individuals; often seen as those who "get it done."

- Scientists: These are deeply curious individuals, often seen as explorers keen on experimentation and deduction.

Guardians: This working style includes pragmatic and methodically minded individuals. On teams, they can provide stability and help the team focus on facts and pay attention to detail. Described as structured, they are sometimes averse to risk and can struggle to communicate with others.

Integrators: This working style consists of diplomatic and relationship-oriented individuals. On teams, they help maintain group cohesion. Described as empathetic consensus builders, they can fall to indecision and may ignore or fail to embrace facts.

Within the category of Integrators are two subtypes: Teamers and Dreamers.

- Teamers: These are very outgoing individuals known for bringing people together to form teams.

- Dreamers: These are highly introspective individuals. Despite a strong aversion to conflict, their ability to understand others makes them essential to maintaining team stability.

The Business Chemistry framework suggests we are a composite of all four styles, though our thought process and behavior tend to align with one or two of the styles. Like William Marston's *DISC*, this model provides users with a framework based on observable traits and characteristics, making it useful to help clients improve their interpersonal connection with others.

Though presented as a framework describing work styles, the model contains striking similarities to personality frameworks like *DISC*, *Myers-Briggs*, and *Keirsey's Four Temperaments*. For this reason, we classify Business Chemistry as a personality framework. The model's utility in team construct development also warrants its inclusion in the teaming category.

Business Chemistry is more complex than presented here. The framework includes a litany of resources to help clients develop an awareness of styles and facilitate their efforts to adapt their style to meet the style of others.

Professionals seeking additional information may consider Christfort and Vickberg's 2018 book, *Business Chemistry: Practical Magic for Crafting Powerful Work Relationships*.

Business Chemistry is proprietary to Deloitte. Use of this framework and its associated assessment requires training available only from Deloitte.

Sources[51]

CARPER'S FUNDAMENTAL WAYS OF KNOWING

> **Certification Available:** no
> **Certification Required:** no
> **Assessments:** no
> **Proprietary:** no
> **Client:** individuals
> **Cost:** not applicable
> **Category:** learning/development, reflection

Developed in 1978 by nursing school professor Barbara A. Carper, Carper's Fundamental Ways of Knowing provides a framework to explain how people acquire, organize, test, and apply information. Carper's research revealed four patterns or sources of knowledge, presented here through a coaching optic.

Empirics: This pertains to knowledge acquired through science and includes a combination of objective and abstract information that is quantifiable, verifiable, and testable. This source of knowledge consists of theories and laws which describe and explain observable phenomena.

For example, a coach may observe a pattern of behavior in which the client presents a persistent defeatist attitude to challenges they encounter. Theories which may provide insight into this observed pattern include the *4C Model for Mental Toughness* and *Learned Helplessness Theory*. A coach's comprehension of these theories constitutes empirical knowing.

Ethics: This pertains to knowledge which derives from a person's experience with internal conflict, often involving a determination of right and wrong. Of the four ways of knowing, ethics is the most frequent catalyst for reflection, hence why Carper's model often appears in conjunction with other models of reflection.

For example, a coach may wrestle with actions that are in line with organizationally established ethical guidelines but that violate their personal values. This dissonance will lead the coach to reflect on their choices and associated consequences. This reflection can result in new knowledge for the coach.

Aesthetics: This pertains to knowledge derived from nature and an appreciation of beauty. In this context, beauty is that which moves, inspires, or evokes us. Some sources describe this as knowledge derived from art (as opposed to science). Some professions value aesthetic knowledge less than empirical knowing. This is based on the false belief that the only reliable knowledge is that which is factual and testable. In other professions, however, aesthetic knowing has greater acceptance.

For example, the skills of active listening are based in the empirical, but the application of active listening is as much art as science. Coaches listen to what a client says and does not say. The coach's effort to "read between the lines" requires the coach to make meaning from the client. Though meaning-making has foundations in science, how the coach and client discover this meaning is very much art.

Personal: This source of knowledge is the most problematic because it is difficult to teach. Personal knowledge derives from an individual's awareness of self as a human being, which includes awareness of one's strengths, vulnerabilities, tendencies, triggers, and predispositions. Personal knowledge also includes an awareness of self in relation to others. This involves the ability to acquire knowledge through the adoption of alternative perspectives.

For example, this is the ability of a coach to use their past experiences, consider the client's perspective, and leverage the coaching relationship to the benefit of the client.

In Carper's framework, the concept of "ways of knowing" refers to how people know what they know within their field or profession. Though Carper's original work focused on the field of nursing, her work has broad utility and applies to any profession.

Carper's work went on to influence other theories on learning and reflection like *Johns' Model of Reflection*.

Professionals seeking additional information on Carper's Fundamental Ways of Knowing may consider her 1978 paper, "Fundamental Patterns of Knowing in Nursing."

Sources[52]

CEDAR FEEDBACK MODEL

Certification Available: no
Certification Required: no
Assessments: no
Proprietary: no
Client: individuals
Cost: not applicable
Category: feedback

Developed in 2003 by facilitator and management consultant Anna Wildman, the CEDAR Model provides a conversational approach to delivering feedback. The model consists of five steps represented by the acronym CEDAR.

Step 1—Context: The first step involves the provider establishing how the feedback process will work for the recipient. This includes how feedback connects with the recipient's overall performance plan. During this step, a two-way conversation ensues in which both parties explore the topical area. The provider explicates (i.e., analyzes to ascertain meaning) how the recipient's behavior affected the environment, mission, and others and impacts the recipient's ability to achieve goals.

Step 2—Examples: In the second step, the provider cites clear examples of the observed behavior (good or problematic). Relevant details include when, where, and who else might have been involved. Be judicious in the number of examples you provide. Any more than three or four examples risks the recipient becoming overwhelmed, shutting down, or becoming defensive.

Step 3—Diagnosis: This step involves an exploration of the behavior. Ask the recipient to examine the issue and share insight into what may have contributed to the behavior. This allows the recipient to engage in self-exploration and identify potential patterns for themselves. This stage is critical to the process because it involves insight, awareness, and understanding, all crucial to development.

According to Wildman, when providing constructive feedback, it is important to allow the recipient to lead the conversation as much as practical. This will foster self-discovery for the recipient, resulting in a greater impact on their relationship to change. When providing positive feedback, however, it is more important the provider lead the conversation since this is about recognizing achievement or good performance.

Step 4—Actions: During the fourth step, the recipient uses insight gleaned from the previous step to identify relevant actions which will address the issue. By continuing to allow the recipient to engage in productive discourse, it increases their ownership in the process, which in turn increases their likelihood of committing to change.

Step 5—Review: In the final step, the provider works with the recipient to determine the best way to check in with them. Touching base too often risks sending the wrong message to the recipient; too infrequent, and the recipient may lose momentum. Discuss with the recipient what they believe is best.

A unique aspect of the CEDAR Model is that it integrates both the provider's and the recipient's feedback into a larger conversation. This method encourages the recipient of the feedback to drive the conversation as much as possible, allowing for a greater sense of ownership in the process.

The model's collaborative approach to delivering feedback makes it highly useful for leadership-level clients, particularly those seeking to add coaching to their leadership style.

The CEDAR Model's integration of individual change theories like the *Transtheoretical Model* and *Intentional Change Theory*, with the principles of meaningful discourse, make it one of the more effective feedback processes included in *The Infourge Compendium of Models and Theories*.

Though no formal training exists in the CEDAR Model, professionals seeking additional information may consider Wildman's 2021 book, *Now You're Talking: The Manager's Complete Handbook to Leading Great Conversations at Work—Even the Tough Ones*.

Sources[53]

CHARISMATIC LEADERSHIP THEORY

Certification Available: no
Certification Required: no
Assessments: no
Proprietary: no
Client: individuals
Cost: not applicable
Category: leadership

Developed in the early 1920s by sociologist Max Weber, Charismatic Leadership Theory (CLT) describes a style of leadership where the source of a leader's authority derives from their personality. He identified three dimensions that influence the development of a charismatic leader.

Psychological dimension: This is arguably the most critical dimension in Charismatic Leadership Theory. This facet pertains to the psychological characteristics and qualities of the leader and includes factors like personality type, psychopathology, and other variables associated with a person's psychological construct.

Social dimension: This domain pertains to the socio-environmental factors that shape and influence the leader. Facets of this dimension include the leader's cultural and socio-political environment.

Relational dimension: This facet pertains to the relationship between leaders and those who follow them. Weber argues that the stronger the relationship, the more devoted and intense the follower's commitment.

Since Weber's introduction of Charismatic Leadership Theory, many scholars have advanced upon his origi-nal work. One of these scholars was leadership professor Robert J. House, who discovered that charismatic leaders possessed certain psychological characteristics that encouraged people to follow them. These qualities include the creative mindset necessary to develop a vision and the ability to communicate that vision in a way that resonates with people.

Like most theories of leadership, scholars debate the benefits and limitations of the theory. Some caution that charismatic leaders can instill such a deep sense of loyalty that it crosses into an unhealthy level of devotion.

Additionally, opponents of CLT warn that while charismatic leaders can develop stability by virtue of who they are, once they die, they tend to leave a power vacuum that often proves difficult to fill.

Even Weber worried that charismatic leadership was unsustainable because the charismatic leader changed the leadership status quo to something implicit and not easily maintained beyond the life of the leader.

Despite the risks, charismatic leadership has served a valuable role in society. During times of crisis and despair, charismatic leaders possess the ability to inspire hope in others. For organizations looking to engage in significant change, charismatic leaders are more readily able to build the support needed for change.

When considering a list of characteristics representative of charismatic leaders, most sources cite positive attributes like active listening, maturity, and humility. Certainly, these qualities apply; however, not all charismatic leaders possess these qualities. History is full of charismatic leaders who were despots and dictators with questionable levels of maturity and humility. Weber described this style of leadership as one influenced more by appearances than by actions.

Charismatic Leadership Theory is one of three theories born of *Weber's Theory of Authority*, which examines the sources of a leader's power. The other two, *Transformational Leadership Theory* and *Transactional Leadership Theory*, also feature in the ICMT.

Professionals seeking additional depth of knowledge on Charismatic Leadership Theory will find much written on the topic. The available literature varies in scope and viewpoint, but presents a wide-ranging perspective of the theory.

The two seminal works on Charismatic Leadership Theory are Weber's 1958 article, "The Three Types of Legitimate Rule," and House's 1976 paper, "A 1976 Theory of Charismatic Leadership."

Sources[54]

CIGAR COACHING MODEL

Certification Available: no
Certification Required: no
Assessments: no
Proprietary: no
Client: individuals, groups, teams
Cost: not applicable
Category: coaching model

Developed by psychologists Suzy Green and Anthony Grant in 2003, the CIGAR Coaching Model provides a five-step coaching process designed to use a "gap analysis" approach to coaching. This means the process works by having the client consider their current state, their desired future state, and then explore the gap between the two.

Step 1—Current reality: During the first step in the process, the client explores their current state or status quo. This may involve comparing the client's perceptions of reality with those of others to help them form a more accurate picture. An important aspect of this step involves the client's use of perspective-taking as part of the exploration process.

Using an analogy of going on a long journey, the purpose of the first step is for the client to figure out their current position on the map.

Step 2—Ideal outcome: During the second step, the client considers their desired goal or end state. A critical part of this step involves the client exploring what makes the goal or desired end state meaningful and relevant for them.

In this step of the journey, clients are considering all of the possible destinations they want to reach. Ultimately, the client will evaluate these options and select a primary destination.

Step 3—Gap analysis: In the third stage of the process, the client explores the gap between their current reality and their desired end state or goal. During this examination, clients will identify obstacles, challenges, and other considerations which may influence how they achieve their goal.

Using the journey analogy, the client has determined where they are on a map and where they want to go. Now they examine the map and study the terrain, roads, and obstacles between their starting point and their destination. The knowledge resulting from this stage will facilitate the next step in the process.

Step 4—Action plan: In the fourth stage, the client develops a list of actions they believe will help them achieve their goals. These actions should include a combination of simple and complex tasks.

In this phase of their journey preparation, clients sketch out the route they want to take to reach their destination. They factor in detours and side excursions as appropriate. They should strive to create a plan that is detailed enough to prepare them for the journey but flexible enough to allow them to adapt when needed.

Step 5—Review: In the final stage, the client evaluates their progress by examining the results of each of their tasks. The client accomplishes this by measuring each outcome in relation to how much closer it got them to their goal.

In this stage, the client has begun their journey. As is often the case, the route intended is rarely the route followed. As the client follows their route plan, they may encounter unexpected setbacks, road closures, flat tires, or other unforeseen events that require them to adjust their plan.

Some sources classify this as a feedback model. Though it has utility in this domain, the most common characterization of this model is as a performance coaching framework. Readers will notice similarities between the CIGAR Model and other coaching models like *GROW* and *ACHIEVE*. The CIGAR Model is one of many coaching frameworks inspired by Whitmore's *GROW Model*.

There is no certification in the model itself; however, available literature provides sufficient depth of knowledge for coaches to incorporate the model into practice.

Sources[55]

CLEAR COACHING MODEL

Certification Available: no
Certification Required: no
Assessments: no
Proprietary: no
Client: individuals, groups, teams
Cost: not applicable
Category: coaching model

Created in the 1980s by professor of leadership Peter Hawkins, the CLEAR Coaching Model provides a five-step framework designed to facilitate the coaching process.

Step 1—Contract: During the first stage, the coach reviews the coaching contract with the client. This allows the coach to set the rules for coaching and manage the client's expectations. This includes logistical concerns, meeting times, communication methods, payment details, and other relevant information as appropriate.

During this step, the client explores and identifies a desired goal or outcome for coaching. Once the coach and client agree to the coaching agreement and the client's desired goals, the coaching relationship may begin.

Step 2—Listen: In the second stage, the coach uses narrative-inducing questions to encourage the client to talk about their current situation. This includes what is happening for the client, why, and any perceptions they have of their situation. The coach uses active listening skills to learn from the client and develop an understanding of how the client perceives the situation and how they make sense of the world around them.

Step 3—Explore: In the third stage, the coach transitions from general narrative-inducing questions (or catalytic questions) to more focused questions that probe the issue to foster a deeper exploration of the client's situation.

Meaningful exploration requires the client to consider how the situation affects them, and how their behaviors, actions, and choices affected the situation. Then the client may begin to consider possible options to improve or correct the situation.

Step 4—Action: During the fourth stage, the client begins to identify steps or actions they can take to move them toward their goals. A key objective of this stage is to secure the client's commitment to change or follow through on the action plan they come up with.

Step 5—Review: In the final stage, the client summarizes key points from the session and reviews their overall progress to date. The coach revisits the coaching agreement (contract) to ensure the session supported the client's goal as defined in the agreement.

A distinct feature of the CLEAR Model is that it factors procedural coaching requirements into the process. For example, where most models solely focus on the client, CLEAR goes further and takes into consideration what a coach needs to effectively coach the client. For example, the first step of the CLEAR process involves reviewing the coaching agreement at the start and end of each session to ensure that the coach and client focus on what is most important to the client.

CLEAR is one of the oldest and most widely used coaching models. Many of the coaching models presented in this compendium derive from CLEAR, either by building on the framework or incorporating it into a larger methodology.

It is worth noting that Peter Hawkins also developed the *7-Eyed Supervision Model,* useful for supervising other coaches.

Professionals seeking additional information will find much written on the CLEAR Model. Additionally, Hawkins has authored multiple books on coaching and leadership. Some include the CLEAR Model, like his 2011 book, *Leadership Team Coaching: Developing Collective Transformational Leadership.*

Sources[56]

CO-ACTIVE COACHING MODEL

> **Certification Available:** yes
> **Certification Required:** yes
> **Assessments:** no
> **Proprietary:** yes (Co-Active Training Inst.)
> **Client:** individuals, groups, teams
> **Cost:** $14,497
> **Category:** coaching model

Developed in the 1980s by coaches Laura Whitworth, Henry Kimsey-House, and Phil Sandahl, the Co-Active Coaching Model provides a complex and methodical approach to coaching. The framework consists of four Cornerstones, three Principles, five Contexts, and the concept of Designed Alliance.

Cornerstones

• **People are naturally creative, resourceful, and whole**: This is the belief that clients inherently possess the capacity to find the answers they need with the support of a Co-Active Coach. A fundamental aspect of this belief is acknowledging that the client is not broken and does not require fixing. The model implies that clients possess an innate wisdom about how they live their lives which can prove valuable during the coaching process.

• **Dance in the moment**: This is a metaphor for being able to adapt during the coaching process. As the client adjusts, so too must the coach.

• **Focus on the whole person**: Though a client may have a specific issue they want to focus on, that issue likely impacts other aspects of the client's life. Therefore, it is important to consider the whole person and not just the issue.

• **Evoke transformation**: This is not about small incremental change but calling forth radical change for the client.

Principles

• **Fulfillment**: This is what fills the client's heart and soul and makes them whole.

• **Balance**: This principle seeks to add choices and expand the scope of the client's perspective; "saying yes to some things and no to others."

• **Process**: This is focusing on the client's journey, not their destination.

Contexts

• **Listening**: The coach listens and observes body language, breathing, hesitation, excitement, and tone. The coach looks for key themes like the client's vision, values, and purpose.

• **Intuition**: As the coach listens, they subconsciously synthesize information and impressions. This can lead to a gut feeling, or intuition about the client.

• **Curiosity**: To help the client discover their solution (see the first cornerstone), both coach and client should be curious and explore the issues.

• **Forward and deepen learning**: Learning generates new resourcefulness, expanded possibilities, and stronger muscles for change.

• **Self-management**: This is the ability of the coach to set aside personal options, preferences, pride, defensiveness, and ego to foster the coaching process.

Designed alliance: This is the relationship between coach and client, which varies from relationship to relationship. This involves an intentional conversation about the process and clarifies the desired outcomes.

The Co-Active Coaching Model is one of the most popular coaching methodologies in the world. Though several coaching programs may discuss the model, official certification is only available from the Co-Active Training Institute.

Co-Active Coaching is significantly more complex than presented here. Professionals seeking additional information may consider Whitworth, Kimsey-House, and Sandahl's 2018 book, *Co-Active Coaching* (4th Edition).

Sources[57]

COACH MODEL

Certification Available: yes
Certification Required: yes
Assessments: no
Proprietary: yes (Creative Results Management)
Client: individuals, groups, teams
Cost: $2,997–$3,247
Category: coaching model

Developed by leadership coach Keith E. Webb, the COACH Model is a five-step, faith-based coaching framework that emphasizes Christian principles and beliefs through the coaching process.

Step 1—Connect: Stage 1 consists of two objectives. The first involves the coach establishing trust and building rapport with the client. The second involves revisiting outcomes and progress from previous sessions.

Webb recommends several approaches for building rapport, including questions centered on what the client learned since their last coaching session, their feelings about God's role in their life, what behaviors they did well, which behaviors they could improve upon, and how they might behave differently in the future.

Step 2—Outcome: The second stage in the process, also called agenda setting, involves the client identifying their goals for the coaching session. This allows the coach to guide the conversation and ensure the focus remains on the topics and issues important to the client.

In addition to articulating their goals, it is important that the client understand why the goal is important to them. This means the client must consider what matters to them.

Step 3—Awareness: The third stage in this process involves a robust exploration of the client's perceptions to foster personal discovery, develop new insight, and increase the scope of the client's perspectives. This may require an examination of the client's challenges and obstacles.

During this stage, the client will benefit from the use of creativity and brainstorming to expand their point of view and consider alternative perspectives.

Step 4—Course: The fourth stage capitalizes on the insight and awareness gained from the previous stage by allowing the client to develop actions which will help them achieve their goals.

When developing their action plan, it is important that the client identifies their own solutions. This increases their sense of ownership in the process and their commitment to change.

Step 5—Highlights: The final stage in this process involves the client reflecting on the coaching relationship. Asking the client to identify important lessons from their coaching sessions, recognize their accomplishments, and codify key takeaways will reinforce the coaching experience for them.

Functionally, the COACH Model is like other coaching models presented in the ICMT. However, a key differentiator is that this model emphasizes coaching within Christian ministries. Many consider this framework useful when coaching members of the clergy or ministry.

Certification in the COACH Model is available through Creative Results Management and Active Results LLC, both owned by Keith E. Webb. Professionals seeking additional information may consider Webb's 2019 book: *The Coach Model for Christian Leaders: Powerful Leadership Skills for Solving Problems, Reaching Goals, and Developing Others*.

Sources[58]

COACHING MODELS (GENERAL ENTRY)

Category: coaching model

This entry provides a general overview of coaching models as presented in *The Infourge Compendium of Models and Theories*. As of publication, there are scores of coaching models available to professionals. The volume of available frameworks exceeds the capacity of this compendium. To narrow the list of models, we focused on those with longevity and those with sufficient literature available to enable learning.

Due to similarities between some of these models, the author considered selecting certain models and omitting others to avoid redundancy. However, the process proved highly subjective. We decided to present these models and allow readers to determine for themselves which is most appropriate.

While exploring coaching models, the author noticed a pattern that led to a distinction between **coaching styles** and **coaching models**.

- **Coaching style**: This refers to the underlying beliefs or philosophical foundations that influence a coach's approach to coaching clients.

For example, *Cognitive Behavioral Coaching (CBC)* is a style of coaching based on scientific theories pertaining to the relationship between thoughts, feelings, and actions. In other words, what a client thinks about something influences how they feel about that thing, and how they feel about that thing influences how they respond or react to that thing.

Coaching styles included in *The Infourge Compendium of Models and Theories* include:

- *Cognitive Behavioral Coaching (CBC)*
- *Neuroscience-Based Coaching (NBC)*
- *Positive Psychology Coaching (PPC)*

- **Coaching model**: This term refers to the structured process a coach uses to conduct their coaching session. Some, though not all, coaching models fall under a coaching style.

For example, coaching models under the CBC style of coaching include:

- *ABCDE Model (Ellis)*
- *PRACTICE Model*
- *SPACE Model*

Coaching models under the Positive Psychology Coaching style include:

- *PERMA Model*
- *6M Foundations*
- *RAW Model*
- *ABCDE Model (Seligman)*
- *Positive Intelligence*

Some coaching models are universal and do not fall under a specific coaching style. These models typically have broad utility and transcend multiple different styles. Examples of coaching models that do not fall under a single coaching style include:

- *GROW Model*
- *CLEAR Model*
- *CIGAR Model*

The author recognizes that not all share in this distinction; therefore, the ICMT groups both coaching styles and coaching models under the category of coaching models.

Sources[59]

COGNITIVE BEHAVIORAL COACHING

Certification Available: yes
Certification Required: yes
Assessments: not applicable
Proprietary: no
Client: individuals
Cost: prices vary based on vendor
Category: coaching model

Derived from Cognitive Behavioral Therapy (CBT), Cognitive Behavioral Coaching (CBC) is a coaching style that shares the same fundamental principles as CBT, but CBC adapts the skills and techniques of CBT in a way that is appropriate for coaching.

The fundamental focus of CBC is on the relationship between a client's thoughts, feelings, and behavior. Put another way, what the client thinks about a stimulus affects how they feel about that stimulus, and how they feel about that stimulus affects how they behave in response to that stimulus.

The aim of CBC is to explore a client's experiences, develop the client's perceptions of the events that trigger them, and finally help the client cultivate new ways of looking at their experiences to foster the kinds of behavioral change which can help them achieve their goals.

Exploration using CBC allows the coach to challenge the client's beliefs in a positive and meaningful way, often through exercises designed to reveal alternative perspectives. Therefore, a prominent characteristic of CBC is working with the client to identify the emotional and cognitive root of an issue which may prevent the client from achieving their potential.

CBC consists of many different coaching models, among the first and most popular is psychologist Albert Ellis' *ABCDE Model,* which consists of five steps.

Step 1—Activating event: This is an event or events (stimuli) which trigger an intense emotional response in the client. These can be significant events or trivial events. In this stage the coach and client work to identify and understand the triggering event.

Step 2—Beliefs: These are the beliefs which facilitate the client's actions in response to the activating event. This involves awareness of the client's personal core values, beliefs, and culture.

Step 3—Consequences: This is the outcome of the client's belief system on their actions. This stage seeks to establish the relationship between the client's beliefs and their actions.

Step 4—Disputes: In this step, the coach and client challenge the client's beliefs. Clients should consider if their existing beliefs have an empirical basis. During this stage they also explore the functional purpose of the belief (i.e., what goal does the belief support) and consider the logic of the belief (i.e., does this belief make sense and how do they know this).

Step 5—Effects: In the final stage, the coach and client explore what happens if the client removes or alters the belief. This often involves visioning exercises.

Other models under the umbrella of CBC include *PRACTICE, SPACE* and *ABCDE.*

CBC is one of few coaching styles to include the client's emotional and psychological barriers in the coaching process. CBC is useful when working with clients across a variety of issues including stage fright, emotional and behavioral self-regulation, performance anxiety, relationship management, self-confidence, and much more.

Due to the similarities between CBC and CBT, professionals should be mindful to avoid crossing into therapy. Therefore, training in CBC is highly recommended before incorporating the model into practice. It is important to stress that CBT is the domain of therapy, though CBC is appropriate for trained coaches.

There are multiple options for certification in CBC. Professionals seeking additional information may consider Michael Neenan and Stephen Palmer's 2012 book, *Cognitive Behavioral Coaching in Practice,* and Helen Whitten's 2009 book, *Cognitive Behavioral Coaching Techniques for Dummies.*

Sources[60]

COGNITIVE DISSONANCE THEORY

Certification Available: no
Certification Required: no
Assessments: no
Proprietary: no
Client: individuals
Cost: not applicable
Category: conflict, confidence/resilience, polarities

Developed in the 1950s by psychologist Leon Festinger, Cognitive Dissonance Theory (CDT) falls under the umbrella of *Consistency Theories*, a collection of theories that suggest humans strive for a balance between cognition (what we think) and behavior (how we act).

The theory defines cognitive dissonance as a feeling of mental discomfort resulting from conflict between a person's beliefs, values, attitudes, and behaviors. This imbalance can lead to real emotional and physical (somatic) discomfort. When this occurs, a person's natural response is to resolve the dissonance in the simplest way possible.

Some of the more common sources of cognitive dissonance include:

Forced compliance: This form of dissonance occurs when an external source compels a person to do something that violates their values or beliefs. Dissonance may manifest immediately or long after the action is complete. An example of forced compliance is peer pressure.

Decision-making: This happens when a person faces a decision in which all available choices are undesirable. The expression "damned if you do, damned if you don't" exemplifies this scenario. A client compelled to choose from undesirable choices (i.e., the lesser of two evils) may experience dissonance as a result.

Effort: This occurs when a person dedicates a lot of time to accomplishing something and the results fail to meet expectations. A person who invests a lot of time and effort in a task may resist or resent a negative outcome resulting in dissonance. An expression which can precipitate this is "practice makes perfect."

New information: This happens when a person learns new information that suggests their behavior, long assumed correct, is wrong. For example, a senior employee may experience dissonance when presented with a newer and more effective way of performing tasks at work.

When confronted with dissonance, CDT suggests an individual will inherently try to reestablish balance. The most common approaches people use to achieve balance include:

Justification: Seek out any information that justifies the original behavior, no matter how illogical or unsound.

Confirmation bias: Avoid or reject any information that does not align with the original behavior.

Value reduction: Reduce the importance of the conflicting value.

Reconciliation: This involves the person changing their behaviors to align with their beliefs. This is the ideal solution, but also the most difficult.

When exploring cognitive dissonance, it is important to understand the source of the dissonance to determine how the client intends to resolve the conflict. Because it is natural to seek the easiest path to resolution, the client's ensuing actions may lead to undesirable consequences.

Modern researchers are now calling into question the validity of CDT, after nearly fifty years as a prominent theory in social psychology. For now, CDT remains a widely accepted theory used across professions including coaching.

CDT is useful when working with clients experiencing internal conflict and issues involving polarities. Professionals seeking additional information may consider Festinger's 1957 book, *A Theory of Cognitive Dissonance*.

Sources[61]

COILED FEEDBACK MODEL

Certification Available: no
Certification Required: no
Assessments: no
Proprietary: no
Client: individuals
Cost: not applicable
Category: feedback

The COILED Model is a six-stage process for conducting discourse-based feedback. Derived from Anna Carroll's *COIN Feedback Model*, the COILED Model adopts a conversational approach to feedback.

Step 1—Conversation: During the first step, the provider establishes a personal and positive connection with the recipient before discussing the issue. Put another way, the provider builds rapport with the recipient to create a level of comfort between provider and recipient.

Step 2—Observation: In the second step, the provider transitions the conversation to the feedback. To do this, the provider cites specific examples of the observed behavior, including details like the day the behavior occurred, the names of those involved, and other information as appropriate.

It is important that the provider avoid hearsay by focusing only on behavior they observed and avoid mixing issues or unrelated behaviors.

The provider must remain neutral and objective, both in tone and language.

Step 3—Impact: During the third stage, the provider gives an impact statement that explains how the behavior (positive or negative) impacted the team, clients, customers, and the company. It is important to deliver the impact statement in a neutral tone with the provider citing clear examples of the consequences.

Step 4—Listen: The fourth stage involves the provider facilitating additional trust by asking the recipient to reflect on the situation (i.e., their thoughts and feelings about what happened). As they share their perspective, the provider listens intently to foster an understanding of the recipient's point of view.

Step 5—Establish solution: During the fifth stage, the provider and recipient discuss potential solutions which take into consideration both perspectives (i.e., the provider's and the recipient's). This stage involves a collaborative approach to problem-solving in which both parties seek resolution.

Step 6—Definite agreement: The final stage involves the recipient revisiting the details of the feedback session and demonstrating a clear and explicit understanding of the resulting expectations. In other words, the recipient summarizes what the issue is and what they need to do to correct the situation.

Among the many feedback models included in *The Infourge Compendium of Models and Theories*, COILED presents as one of the more robust and methodically structured frameworks. Its conversational style may not be appropriate for all situations; however, its inclusive approach is likely to lead to more desirable outcomes and greater buy-in by the recipient.

Professionals seeking additional information on the COILED Model will find very little written on the subject. However, the process remains simple and easy to use.

Because many of the models are similar in their design and intent, professionals should familiarize themselves with these variations as leadership-level clients will probably possess awareness of one or more of these frameworks.

Sources[62]

COIN FEEDBACK MODEL

Certification Available: no
Certification Required: no
Assessments: no
Proprietary: no
Client: individuals
Cost: not applicable
Category: feedback

Created by executive coach Anna Carroll, the COIN Feedback Model offers a four-stage process for delivering feedback.

Stage 1—Context: The first step of the process involves the provider establishing a personal and positive connection with the recipient. This sets the tone for the feedback session and makes the recipient more comfortable.

During this stage, the provider sets the context for the feedback and begins to focus on the behavior requiring the recipient's attention. In this, it is imperative that the provider stay on topic and avoid injecting other issues or behaviors into the session.

Stage 2—Observation: During the second step, the provider describes what they observed. It is important that the provider specifies events in detail, including when the behavior occurred, the names of other people involved, and any additional information as appropriate.

It is important that the provider avoid adding hearsay (i.e., unvalidated or unverified details) not directly witnessed. The provider must remain neutral and objective, both in tone and language.

Stage 3—Impact: During the third stage, the provider explains how the recipient's behavior (problematic or beneficial) impacted the team, clients, customers, and the company. The provider should present the impact statement in a neutral tone and cite clear examples.

Stage 4—Next steps: The final stage of the COIN Feedback Model involves developing solutions to correct the behavior. Though the provider may have ideas, it is important that the recipient contribute to the solution development discussion. This provides the recipient an opportunity to participate in the feedback process, have a say in the outcome, and develop a sense of ownership in what comes next.

It is important to note that variations exist of the COIN Model which use different labels to describe the steps of the process. Despite this, these variations are essentially the same process.

The COIN Model is one of many feedback models included in this compendium and among a small group of virtually identical processes like *AID*, *BIFF*, *BEEF*, *BOOST*, and *SBI Models*.

Because many of the models are similar in their design and intent, professionals should familiarize themselves with these variations as clients and peers may possess awareness of one or more of these acronyms.

Professionals seeking additional information on the COIN Feedback Model may consider Carroll's 2003 book, *The Feedback Imperative: How to Give Everyday Feedback to Speed Up Your Team's Success.*

Sources[63]

COMMUNICATION THEORY OF IDENTITY

Certification Available: no
Certification Required: no
Assessments: no
Proprietary: no
Client: individuals
Cost: not applicable
Category: culture

Developed in the 1980s by communications professor Michael L. Hecht, the Communication Theory of Identity (CTI) suggests that communication is a component of identity, not a product of identity.

CTI consists of four distinct perspectives, each representing a continuous process in the relationship between communication and identity. These interconnected perspectives do not exist independent of one another but engage in a reciprocal relationship.

Personal (person): This perspective focuses on the individual as a source of identity and includes concepts like self-image and self-esteem. This also includes the individual's perception of self and the labels they use to define who they are and how they see themselves. For example, "I am smart and funny."

Enactment (communication): This perspective focuses on the individual's style of communication as a source of identity. Put another way, when a person communicates, they are, in essence, putting on a show which may originate from their identity. Within this domain, one may examine a variety of indicators, from style of speech to the labels a person uses when communicating.

Relational (relationships): This perspective explores an individual's personal relationships as a source of identity. This focus includes how a person's relationships influence their identity. Within the relational component are three aspects of relationships which can foster a greater understanding of the complex association between communication and identity.

The first of these aspects involves the perceptions (made explicit) others have of the person. For example, when a close friend describes the client as "a good person," this may influence the client's identity of self.

The second involves the aspect of identity which derives from the type of relationship. For example, a client who identifies as a husband or wife does so because of their relationship with their spouse.

The third involves the aspect of identity which derives from the relationship with a specific person. In other words, it is not simply that the client is a spouse, but they are the spouse of someone specific. For example, "I am Ashley's husband."

Communal (community): The final perspective considers the group as a source of identity. Generally, a group possesses social rules, customs, and norms which constitute the group's identity. Consequently, the group identity may further influence an individual's identity. This collective identity often manifests in communication, on both the part of the group and the individual members. Another theory which explores this perspective is *Social Identity Theory*.

CTI suggests that communication and identity are involved in a reciprocal relationship with neither solely responsible for defining the other. CTI also suggests that an individual may possess multiple identities which assert themselves at different times and in different situations.

CTI is a useful framework to help clients seeking to better understand their own identity and that of others. Using this model may foster improved self- and social awareness.

Communication Theory of Identity is more complex than presented here. Professionals seeking additional information will find much written on the theory, as CTI continues to be the focus of research among communication and cultural scientists.

Sources[64]

COMPETING VALUES FRAMEWORK

> **Certification Available:** yes
> **Certification Required:** yes (OCAI Online)
> **Assessments:** yes (OCAI, CVA)
> **Proprietary:** yes
> **Client:** organizations
> **Cost:** $127 (OCAI Online)
> **Category:** culture, leadership

Developed in the late 1980s by management professors Kim Cameron and Robert Quinn, their Competing Values Framework provides a complex and multifaceted tool designed to evaluate and understand an organization's culture, behavioral patterns, effectiveness, leadership competencies, information processes, roles, structure, and more.

Based on decades of research in organizational effectiveness, CVF looks at two key dimensions often depicted as a grid. The first dimension is **Organizational Structure**, characterized on a scale ranging between **Flexible** and **Control** (visually depicted as the vertical axis). This dimension seeks to assess the degree of empowerment, delegation, and decision-making within the organization.

The second dimension is **Organizational Focus**, characterized on a scale ranging from **Internal** to **External** (depicted as the horizontal axis). This dimension seeks to assess how much attention an organization pays to the external variables vs. internal variables which affect them.

These two dimensions form four quadrants, with each quadrant representing a multitude of characteristics describing everything from the organization's leadership to its strategy, and more.

Collaborate (upper/left): This quadrant describes organizations with a **Clan** style of culture where people work together in teams and value relationships. These organizations thrive on a shared vision, and employees operate in an autonomous fashion. Leadership styles in this quadrant include facilitators, mentors, and teambuilders.

Create (upper/right): This quadrant describes organizations with an **Adhocracy** style of culture, a highly dynamic environment where employees take risks and strive for creativity and innovation. These organizations are quick and agile, able to react to their environment. Leadership styles in this quadrant include the innovator, entrepreneur, and visionary.

Control (lower/left): This quadrant describes organizations with a **Hierarchy** style of culture. This is a highly structured work environment with clearly defined protocols and an emphasis on efficiency. These organizations value position power and favor bureaucratic authority. Leadership styles in this quadrant include the coordinator, monitor, and organizer.

Compete (lower/right): This quadrant describes organizations with a **Market** style of culture. These organizations are results-driven with a focus on deadlines and goals. They pay close attention to rivals and the competitive environment. Leadership styles in this quadrant include the hard-driver, competitor, and producer.

CVF's broad utility makes it an ideal framework to integrate with other theories and frameworks, like *Weber's Theory of Authority*. The framework's name derives from the idea that the values within each dimension (and quadrant) represent competing opposites.

Because CVF originates from decades of validated research, the model enjoys broad use in organizational development circles. CVF is an ideal model for organizational change initiatives, leadership development planning, and myriad other applications. CVF includes several tools and assessments, including the Organizational Culture Assessment Instrument (OCAI) and the Competing Values Assessment (CVA).

The Competing Values Framework is significantly more complex than presented here. Formal video-based training is available from OCAI Online. Professionals seeking additional information may consider Cameron and Quinn's 2011 book, *Diagnosing and Changing Organizational Culture: Based on the Competing Values Framework* (3rd edition).

Sources[65]

CONGRUITY THEORY

Certification Available: no
Certification Required: no
Assessments: no
Proprietary: no
Client: individuals
Cost: not applicable
Category: influence, polarities, communication

Introduced in 1955 by psychologists Charles Osgood and Percy Tannenbaum, Congruity Theory seeks to explain the role of persuasive communications in influencing attitude change.

Congruity Theory falls under the umbrella of *Consistency Theories*, a collection of theories that suggest humans inherently strive for a balance between cognition (what we think) and behavior (how we act). According to these theories, when an imbalance occurs, people will act to reestablish equilibrium or seek resolution to such conflict. Often, this may result in the recipient changing their feelings about the issue or the sender, depending on which one they value more.

Congruity Theory suggests that people tend to adopt the path of least resistance when looking for a solution to imbalance. This means a person may bypass critical thought to save time, energy, and the effort needed for meaningful self-reflection.

Even when a person does engage in critical thought, Congruity Theory suggests they are likely to choose the simplest approach (i.e., path of least resistance) when making discriminations. Rather than refined or detailed discriminations, a person may oversimplify with generalizations and stereotypes. The failure to make meticulous distinctions may lead to extreme perspectives and even polarities.

Like most Consistency Theories, Congruity Theory uses *Heider's Triad* to demonstrate a simple framework for exploring the complex relationship between three specific variables.

- Source (O): This is the person sending a message. The conduit of messaging includes verbal and written forms of communication, and the message may deliver either a positive or negative sentiment.

- Object (X): This pertains to the subject of the message. This is often a thing, a person, or an issue.

- Receiver (P): This is the person receiving the message. Often, the recipient is the target of intentional influence by the message sender.

Congruity Theory suggests that a recipient's (P) thoughts and feelings about the sender (O) may influence the way they perceive the sender's message (X). If the recipient holds the message sender in high regard, then the message may have greater influence. Internal conflict may arise if there is a discrepancy between the receiver's feelings about the message and their feelings about the sender.

For example, Anne opposes Proposition 41 but is a staunch supporter of Councilwoman Knope.

Councilwoman Knope sends a message to her constituents that she intends to vote in favor of Proposition 41 because she believes it is the right thing to do. The fact that Anne supports Knope, but opposes the proposition Knope favors, may create internal conflict or dissonance for Anne.

It is important that professionals considering Congruity Theory also review other frameworks under the umbrella of Consistency Theories. All of these theories focus on a distinct aspect or perspective of Heider's Triad and include *Balance Theory*, *Newcomb's Symmetry Theory*, and *Cognitive Dissonance Theory*. Several theories focus on communication and influence, like the *Elaboration Likelihood Model* and the *Six Principles of Influence*.

Much of the available literature on Congruity Theory, as with other models under Consistency Theory, comes primarily from academic sources. However, there is sufficient information available for professionals seeking to enhance their depth of knowledge on the topic.

Sources[66]

CONSISTENCY THEORIES (GENERAL ENTRY)

Certification Available: no
Certification Required: no
Assessments: no
Proprietary: no
Client: individuals
Cost: not applicable
Category: conflict, polarities

Consistency Theories is an umbrella term encompassing multiple theories which suggest people possess a natural motivation to seek balance between their attitudes, thoughts, beliefs, values, behaviors, and feelings.

The origin of Consistency Theories dates to the 1920s, emerging from the Gestalt field of psychology. After nearly a century, research on cognitive consistency led to a variety of subtheories and produced volumes of literature on the subject.

Though many concepts fall under the umbrella of Consistency Theories, these are the four major theories.

Heider's Balance Theory: focuses on the triadic relationship between two people and an issue, object, or third person. The theory explores the thoughts and feelings both people have about the issue or object and each other, and how those thoughts and feelings influence them to change their attitude, either toward the issue or each other.

Heider's Balance Theory introduced the concept of Heider's Triad, which uses a formula to suggest eight possible relationships, four balanced and four imbalanced. See *Heider's Balance Theory.*

Congruity Theory: focuses on the effect of persuasive messaging within Heider's Triad. This theory explores how the client's thoughts and feelings about a messenger might influence how they think and feel about the message.

Affective-Cognitive Consistency Model (ACCM): focuses on the relational and social implications of Heider's Triad. This model explores the relationship between feelings and cognition in a social-relational context.

For example, suppose the client has positive feelings for Joe but feels negatively about the newly proposed organizational changes. Now suppose Joe favors these changes. How does the resulting inconsistency impact the relationship between the client and Joe?

Cognitive Dissonance Theory (CDT): Perhaps the most well-known of Consistency Theories, CDT focuses on the consistency between an individual's thoughts and feelings, and their actions. Dissonance is common when clients experience conflict between their actions and their values.

At the heart of these theories is the belief that people inherently strive for a state of balance between affective, cognitive, and behavioral domains. In other words, on a subconscious level people desire consistency between their thoughts, feelings, and behavior.

These theories further suggest that a misalignment between cognition, emotion, and behavior creates a state of imbalance which leads to tension as well as internal and external conflict. The consequences of this internal conflict can result in very real physical (somatic) and emotional discomfort. The ensuing dissonance may also lead to interpersonal conflict, often manifesting in hostile communication between parties.

Consistency Theories are relevant to coaching because they provide useful frameworks for working with clients experiencing internal conflict resulting from polarities or conflicting values. These theories also provide insight for clients who struggle when someone they like takes a position counter to their own.

Professionals seeking additional information will find much written on the topic. Due to the variety and complexity of these theories, professionals should explore these frameworks prior to application.

Sources[67]

CONTINGENCY THEORIES (GENERAL ENTRY)

Certification Available: no
Certification Required: no
Assessments: no
Proprietary: no
Client: individuals
Cost: not applicable
Category: leadership

Contingency Theories (CT) is an umbrella term that applies to multiple leadership theories which suggest that no single style or set of traits constitutes an effective leader; rather it is the situation that determines which style is appropriate. This means that different situations call for different styles of leadership or require different leadership traits. Thus, while some leaders may excel in certain situations, they may struggle in others. Consequently, CT argues against the idea that there is a best leadership style.

Generally, most Contingency Theories present factors which can help assess a situation and identify the leader or leadership style best for the given situation. These factors can include consideration of the leader's personality style, the nature of the task at hand, the skills required for the task, the abilities of the leader, and the composition of the team. Some CT subtheories emphasize the importance of considering the team's psychological composition and needs when selecting the right person to lead them.

Though CT includes many subtheories, six have emerged as the most widely known. Despite their apparent similarities, each offers a slightly different view on leadership.

Fiedler's Contingency Theory: focuses on the relationship between an individual's leadership style and the situation.

Path-Goal Theory: focuses on the relationship between an individual's leadership style and the employees who follow them.

Vroom-Yetton Decision Model: focuses on the relationship between an individual's leadership style and their decision-making process.

Lewin's Leadership Styles: discusses three generalized styles of leadership and offers examples of situations to highlight the benefits and risks associated with each style.

Tannenbaum-Schmidt Leadership Continuum Model (LCM): describes seven different leadership styles leaders may consider when responding to a specific situation.

Goleman's Six Styles of Leadership: describes six styles of leadership and recommends their appropriateness for certain situations.

Though other leadership theories exist, some more popular, Contingency Theories provide a valuable lens through which to explore a client's approach to leadership.

These theories can help professionals working with executive-level clients dealing with daunting challenges that stress their leadership capacity.

Contingency Theories are useful when working with clients contemplating the selection of leaders for specific roles or succession planning. These frameworks offer structure when considering external and situational factors which may require certain skills, abilities, and leadership styles.

The Infourge Compendium of Models and Theories for Coaches includes several Contingency Theories to help professionals explore the topic and enhance their understanding.

Sources[68]

CORE MODEL FOR CRITICAL REFLECTION

Certification Available: no
Certification Required: no
Assessments: no
Proprietary: no
Client: individuals
Cost: not applicable
Category: reflection

Developed in 2010 by the former Director of Lifelong Learning at the University of Leeds, Stella Cottrell, the Core Model for Critical Reflection (CMCR) is a process that facilitates a thorough and methodical approach to reflection. CMCR consists of five steps, each intended to foster critical thinking during the reflection process.

Step 1—Evaluate significance: Reflection using the CMCR model requires significant time and energy. Therefore, the first stage in the process involves the client making an honest determination of whether the experience is worth the investment. Not all experiences warrant such deep and intensive reflection.

To help clients determine the appropriateness of an experience for inclusion in the CMCR process, the model encourages clients to consider several factors.

- Uniqueness of the experience.
- Potential learning value.
- Comparative analysis to other experiences.
- Potential impact on self and others.

Step 2—Reconstruct the experience: The second stage involves the client recounting the experience. It is important the client understand that recalling any experience is a reconstruction at best, not an exact record. Factors like time and emotion can distort a client's memory of an event, thus influencing the reflection process. For more details on this phenomenon, see *Neuroscience-Based Coaching*.

Facilitating the client's meaningful reconstruction of the experience includes an examination of the events moment by moment, point by point, including the intent and feelings of all persons involved, and the outcome of the event.

Step 3—Analyze: The third stage in the process involves a critical examination of the event to help the client extrapolate or find meaning from the experience. A highly subjective moment in the process, it is important that the client consider multiple perspectives when seeking to understand why the event occurred.

A consequential analysis of the experience includes contemplation of alternative points of view, a review of available literature and theories which may explain the event or behavior of those involved, and an exploration of external factors which may have influenced the experience. These actions will help the client challenge their own assumptions and perceptions of the experience.

Step 4—Distill: The fourth stage involves the synthesis of information gleaned from the previous steps to identify valuable lessons learned from the experience.

Maximizing the learning potential from an experience requires that the client consider the specific behaviors and factors that triggered them, techniques to foster deliberate responses to a situation versus succumbing to instinctive reactions, and opportunities for self-awareness and training.

Step 5—Apply: The final stage involves the client creating a plan to prepare for the future. This includes brainstorming future scenarios which may challenge the client, role-playing these scenarios to help the client visualize desirable responses to the situation, and examining the potential consequences.

The Core Model for Critical Reflection is one of the more methodical reflective processes contained in this compendium. While some models are better suited for quick surface-level reflection, the Core Model is ideal for experiences requiring a deeper level of reflection with a component of critical thinking.

Professionals seeking additional information may consider Cottrell's book: *Skills for Success* (3rd edition, 2015), and her 2007 book: *Critical Thinking Skills*.

Sources[69]

CORRESPONDENT INFERENCE THEORY

Certification Available: no
Certification Required: no
Assessments: no
Proprietary: no
Client: individuals
Cost: not applicable
Category: bias

Introduced in 1965 by psychologists Edward E. Jones and Keith E. Davis, their Correspondent Inference Theory (CIT) explains how and why people make inferences and attributions about people from their behavior. CIT consists of two factors that determine if it is appropriate to attribute a person's behavior to an aspect of their personality.

- First, if a person's behavior is generally representative of how others would react in the same situation, it is not appropriate to attribute behavior to personality. For example, if a person wins a hundred million dollars and jumps up and down in excitement, one cannot say their behavior is a result of having a positive or happy personality, as most would react this way.

- Second, if it is not clear what trait or characteristic the behavior suggests, it is not appropriate to attribute the behavior to personality. For example, a person wins a giant yacht but abruptly declines the boat. Without clear context we cannot assume the reason for the behavior. Perhaps the winner has aquaphobia, or lives in Kansas with no access to the ocean.

Several factors can influence the inferences we draw when attributing behavior to an aspect of personality.

Choice: Does the person have the freedom to choose the behavior or was the choice forced upon them by the situation? For example, the inference changes when a teacher tasks a student to debate in favor of capitalism versus when a student chooses to debate for capitalism.

Social desirability: A person behaving in a socially acceptable way provides little insight into their personality. However, a person acting outside normal social protocol might provide some indication of true personality. For example, an audience member clapping for an award recipient (along with everyone else) tells us little about the person. An audience member not clapping for an award recipient, while others do, may tell us something.

Expectancies: Does the person meet our expectations of them? This comes in two forms.

- Categorical: Does the behavior conform with our expectations of the group we associate the person with? For example, we see a priest sitting alone at a bar drinking a beer. Does this say something about the priest or about our assumptions about priests?

- Targeted: Does the behavior conform with our expectations of the person. For example, if a friend admires Mother Teresa, we might expect certain behaviors from them. Deviations from those expected behaviors might lead us to make inferences.

Non-common effects: This involves a comparison between the consequences of the available choices. When the consequences are similar, making an inference is difficult. When the consequences are dissimilar, making an inference is easier. For example, inference is difficult if a person is deciding between a trip to Cancun or Cozumel. Making an inference is easy when the decision is between Cancun in the winter or Siberia in the winter.

Incorporated within CIT, Harold Kelley's Covariation Model explores the tendency to assign attributions based on situational explanations (i.e., the environment explains the behavior) or dispositional explanations (i.e., the individual's personality explains the behavior).

Correspondent Inference Theory is more complex than presented here and includes additional variables and theories of attribution. Professionals seeking additional information may consider the book, *The Selected Works of Edward E. Jones*, edited by Daniel T. Gilbert, or *Attribution and Social Interaction: The Legacy of Edward E. Jones*, authored by John M. Darley and Joel Cooper.

Sources[70]

CRISIS MANAGEMENT MODEL (G-HERRERO/PRATT)

Certification Available: no
Certification Required: no
Assessments: no
Proprietary: no
Client: individuals, organizations
Cost: not applicable
Category: crisis management

Developed in the 1990s by Alfonso González-Herrero and Cornelius Pratt, their Crisis Management Model segments crisis management into three stages and examines each stage through the optic of communication strategy and planning.

Stage 1—Diagnosing crisis: The first stage focuses on an organization's ability to recognize the early warning signs of an imminent crisis. Because the potential sources of a crisis vary, it is important that leaders maintain open, honest, and consistent communication with employees at all levels of the organization to identify indicators in advance. This occurs on two levels.

• Internal: This level focuses on the indicators of a crisis born from within the organization. These internal warning signs include declining morale, decreasing employee engagement, poor performance, and more.

To better spot these indicators, leaders must first know the organization's baseline (i.e., they must regularly monitor the company and employees to maintain an awareness of the patterns and trends typical to the organization). One framework useful in identifying the organization's baseline is the *McKinsey 7S Model*.

• External: This level focuses on the indicators of a crisis born outside the company. To accomplish this, the organization should dedicate individuals to the collection and analysis of information which may indicate a crisis looming on the horizon. This information includes identifying patterns and trends in the economy, industry, market forces, competitors, regulatory decisions and more.

Additionally, leaders (and organizations) should establish and maintain open conduits of communication to multiple sources external to the organization. This includes various forms of relationships like liaison contacts and partnerships.

Stage 2—Planning: The second stage involves creating a team, or leveraging an existing team, to manage and respond to the crisis. As the crisis unfolds, fear and anxiety begin to take effect; therefore it is important that the crisis management team communicate with everyone in a clear and calm fashion. The planning stage consists of many objectives, including:

• Develop strategies to help the organization transition and adapt as needed to survive the crisis.

• Develop subteams as needed to address specific elements of the crisis.

• Maintain morale, focus, and direction for the organization.

• Spearhead analysis of the crisis to identify cause and effect.

• Review predeveloped contingency plans if available or develop a deliberate and methodical plan if a preexisting contingency plan is not available.

• Communicate to the organization the facts, the plan, the expectations, and progress.

Stage 3—Implementation: The third, and final, stage involves executing the plan developed in the previous stage. Two-way communication is essential because leaders depend on information from multiple perspectives to determine the efficacy of the plan. It is important that data influence adjustments to the plan as necessary.

The G-Herrero/Pratt model for crisis management allows integration with other theories like *Diffusion of Innovation Theory* to facilitate the process. Professionals seeking additional information may consider González-Herrero's 1995 book, *An Integrated Symmetrical Model for Crisis-Communications Management*.

Sources[71]

CRISIS MANAGEMENT MODELS (GENERAL ENTRY)

Category: crisis management

Crisis Management Models are theories and frameworks that seek to understand how individuals and organizations prepare for, deal with, overcome, and recover from crisis situations.

What constitutes a crisis differs across organizations, industries, and individuals. A new or small company may consider a harsh review of a product as a crisis, while a larger, more established firm may not. The sources and causes of crises are many and include natural disasters, workplace violence, social and political unrest, leadership failures, widespread ethics violations, and regulatory or legal judgments.

While definitions for crisis vary, thematically, three characteristics appear universal.

- The event presents a risk of negative consequences (i.e., the event is a threat). In other words, the event results in undesirable outcomes. In the case of an organization, the negative consequences may include loss of profits, legal or regulatory actions, loss of intellectual property or proprietary information, or the loss of physical property and life.

- Secondly, the event is unexpected, or it surprises the organization. This distinction is important because the organization may not see the event coming, or they may know the event is coming but fail to anticipate the severity of the impact.

- The third characteristic is that there is limited time to react or make decisions in response to the event. The pressure of making decisions under time constraints only adds to the severity of the crisis. Acting too quickly may risk moving before all the facts are known, while moving too slowly risks the possibility of negative public perceptions.

Available crisis management models differ on several levels. Some models adopt a more proactive approach by focusing on the preemptive identification of potential crises before they impact the organization. Other models focus on crisis response using scenarios to simulate real-world conditions and prepare decision-makers for the experience of leading during crisis. These models frequently use role-playing as a means of testing individuals, organizations, and protocols against a crisis with set parameters. Other models focus on the client's capacity to respond to a crisis.

Some crisis management models focus on specific functions and roles within an organization. These include frameworks for leading during a crisis, making decisions during a crisis, and communicating during a crisis.

The Infourge Compendium of Models and Theories for Coaches includes multiple models under the umbrella of crisis management for two reasons. First, to support coaches who work with executives responsible for leading their organizations through a crisis.

Second, there is utility in crisis management theories as a framework to foster an understanding of personal crisis. Put another way, a crisis may threaten an individual's sense of self and negatively influence their perceptions of the world (i.e., how they make sense of and relate to the world).

While many models exist, the frameworks included herein are those with a management/executive-level perspective. These models include:

- *Fink's Crisis Management Model*
- *Mitroff's Crisis Management Model*
- *González-Herrero and Pratt Crisis Management Model*
- *Burnett Model of Crisis Management*
- *Crisis Management Relational Model*

Sources[72]

CRISIS MANAGEMENT RELATIONAL MODEL

Certification Available: no
Certification Required: no
Assessments: no
Proprietary: no
Client: individuals, organizations
Cost: not applicable
Category: crisis management

Developed in 2007 by crisis management expert Tony Jaques, the Crisis Management Relational Model (CMRM) provides a framework based on the belief that effective crisis management is a discipline, not a process.

CMRM consists of two phases, the Pre-Crisis Management phase and the Crisis Management phase. Within each phase are two elements, each consisting of a cluster of activities that are key to effective crisis management. The components of CMRM are overlapping and can occur simultaneously in a nonlinear fashion.

Pre-Crisis Management Phase:

• **Crisis preparedness element**: This element focuses on the organization's current level of readiness to face a crisis. The activities associated with this element include an examination of the organization's planning processes to determine their capability to prepare contingency plans proactively and effectively.

Expanding upon this element requires an exploration of the organization's policies and protocols to identify procedures which support crisis management or hinder it. Another critical component of crisis preparation is the use of training simulations and practical exercises to allow stakeholders at all levels to practice their response to a crisis.

• **Crisis prevention element**: This element focuses on the organization's ability to proactively monitor for signs of a pending crisis. Activities associated with this element include evaluating the organization's capability for early warning detection (i.e., do they have a system in place to detect indicators of a crisis). This includes their capability for analyzing data to identify trends and patterns. Critical to crisis prevention is the organization's ability to use these assessments to respond preemptively to mitigate the crisis.

Crisis Management Phase:

• **Crisis event management element**: This element focuses on the organization's ability to effectively manage the crisis event as it unfolds. Activities associated with this element include the ability to acknowledge a crisis is underway, the speed and efficiency of the organization to activate crisis protocols (developed in the Pre-Crisis Management phase), and the capacity to function effectively as an organization while simultaneously managing the crisis.

• **Post-crisis management element**: This element focuses on the period following a crisis event, which can be as dangerous and consequential as the crisis itself. Activities associated with this element include the development and execution of post-crisis recovery plans, the analysis of issues and problems stemming from the after-effects of the crisis, and the adaptation of best practices to foster recovery.

A unique aspect of CMRM is its fundamental belief that crisis management is a continuous discipline, not a formulaic process. Adding to the distinctiveness of CMRM is that it considers the possibility that the consequences of a crisis may persist beyond the event and potentially lead to future crises.

CMRM asserts that understanding the relationship between the two phases and four elements and their associated activities can help mitigate crisis-induced losses. Focusing on the strengths and vulnerabilities of the organization across multiple levels allows crisis management professionals to position their organizations to anticipate crisis, respond during crisis, and recover post-crisis.

Professionals seeking additional information on the Crisis Management Relational Model may consider Tony Jaques' 2014 book, *Issue and Crisis Management: Exploring Issues, Crises, Risk, and Reputation.*

Sources[73]

CULTURAL IDENTITY THEORY

Certification Available: no
Certification Required: no
Assessments: no
Proprietary: no
Client: not applicable
Cost: not applicable
Category: culture, communication, bias, self-awareness

Cultural Identity Theory (CIT) is a broad term used to encompass a variety of concepts which offer insight into the complex relationship between an individual's identity and the people, groups, and culture they associate with. The origin of CIT remains ambiguous; however, contributions from notable academics like Stuart Hall, Jane Collier, and Milt Thomas date to the 1980s.

The array of literature available on CIT offers a diversity of perspectives, with some focusing on culture as expressed through communication, and others studying group influence on identity. Exploring CIT with a client can involve multiple topics for consideration. Three common areas to focus on include:

• The client's perceptions and sense of belonging to a specific group or groups. In other words, what groups does the client identify with or believe they belong to?

• The extent to which the client integrates aspects of their group's culture into their life. How many of the group's norms, beliefs, social rules, etc., does the client accept and follow? Which rules do they choose not to follow?

• The relationship between the multiple cultures that exist within the client. A person may identify with more than one culture, which may give rise to conflict between competing cultures, resulting in internal dissonance. For example, how does an individual maintain equilibrium between two distinct cultures they value?

CIT borrows from *Maslow's Hierarchy of Needs* by suggesting that a person's need to belong often leads them to adopt the norms and rules of the group to which they belong, which in turn influences their perception of self and others.

A common focus for studies in cultural identity is the communicative processes used to navigate personal and cultural relationships. (See *Communication Theory of Identity*.) Such research suggests that cultural identities are frequently expressed in verbal communication. To facilitate this understanding, researchers Jane Collier and Milt Thomas offer several concepts for examining cultural identity through communication. We include three of these concepts.

• Avowal: This pertains to how the client articulates their view about group identity. In other words, how does a person outwardly (explicitly) identify the culture to which they belong?

• Ascription: This pertains to how others view or perceive the client and their culture, as well as how the client perceives other cultures.

• Modes of expression: This pertains to the symbols, gestures, emblems, labels, language, etc., considered acceptable by a group. While there are generally accepted norms within a group, there also exist differences within groups. In other words, groups within a single culture may hold opposing beliefs about what is appropriate behavior.

Research on cultural identity is prolific, resulting in knowledge on a variety of areas of interest to coaches and consultants. These include the role of proxemics in forming cultural identity, as well as the role of organizational culture on an individual's cultural identity.

CIT is useful for clients seeking to better understand the potential impact of organizational culture on individuals, or to develop additional insight into factors which may contribute to social groupings and prejudice.

CIT is significantly more complex than presented here. Professionals seeking additional information may consider Hall's 1996 book, *Questions of Cultural Identity*.

Sources[74]

CULTURAL INTELLIGENCE

Certification Available: yes
Certification Required: no
Assessments: yes (CQS, E-CQS, others)
Proprietary: no
Client: not applicable
Cost: $3,000 (prices vary based on provider)
Category: culture

Developed in 2003 by professors Christopher Earley and Soon Ang, Cultural Intelligence (CQ) provides a framework to determine "a person's capability to adapt effectively to new cultural contexts." The CQ framework identifies three sources of cultural intelligence.

Head: the ability to observe, gather information, research, and develop learning strategies to foster their cultural understanding and awareness.

Body: the physical manifestations of cultural norms, including the capability to recognize, understand, and mirror the gestures, emblems, proxemics, linguistics, and body language of other cultures.

Heart: the presence of confidence and self-efficacy when encountering new and unfamiliar cultures. The courage to explore, learn, and make mistakes is essential to cultural intelligence.

Since its introduction, many scholars have contributed to the development and advancement of Cultural Intelligence. In 2011, sociologist David Livermore extended the CQ framework when he identified four areas critical to develop individual Cultural Intelligence.

CQ-Drive: pertains to a person's motivation to learn about new cultures. This includes a combination of intrinsic and extrinsic interests and a person's confidence to successfully encounter new cultures. In other words, does the person genuinely enjoy exposure to new cultures and are they confident engaging with new cultures.

CQ-Knowledge: pertains to a general understanding of how a person's culture can shape their beliefs, values, and behaviors. This includes an awareness of rules and norms across multiple domains like business, legal, social, linguistic, and religious.

CQ-Strategy: pertains to a person's ability to incorporate cultural knowledge into their considerations, planning, and judgments in an accurate, meaningful, and relevant way. This includes consideration for the potential of cultural misunderstandings resulting from an overreliance on assumptions, generalizations, and stereotypes.

CQ-Action: pertains to a person's ability to apply the previous steps in a way that fosters culturally aware behaviors. This includes using cultural awareness to shape nonverbal, verbal, and other behaviors as appropriate.

CQ is frequently described as an evolution of *Emotional Intelligence (EI)*. While EI focuses on our ability to understand ourselves and others on an individual basis, CQ applies the same ability on a larger level. Like EI, variations of CQ exist, which include the use of different labels and frameworks.

CQ includes several assessments which require certification prior to use. These instruments are proprietary and include the Cultural Intelligence Scale (CQS), the Extended Cultural Intelligence Scale (E-CQS), and the Eight Poles Assessment, among others. These assessments represent variations of the CQ framework presented here. We encourage professionals to explore available resources before selecting one.

CQ is useful when working with clients facing geographic relocation, organizations expanding office locations, and leaders struggling with organizational culture. Many find the inclusion of both EI and CQ essential to leadership development.

Training on CQ is available from multiple providers at different price points. Professionals seeking additional information on Cultural Intelligence may consider Earley and Ang's 2003 book, *Cultural Intelligence: Individual Interactions Across Cultures*, and Livermore's 2011 book, *The Cultural Intelligence Difference*.

Sources[75]

CULTURAL WEB

Certification Available: no
Certification Required: no
Assessments: no
Proprietary: no
Client: organizations
Cost: not applicable
Category: culture, change (org.)

Developed in 1992 by management professors Gerry Johnson and Kevan Scholes, the Cultural Web provides a multifaceted framework for exploring organizational culture. The model consists of six interrelated elements or aspects that form an organization's culture.

Stories: These are the people and events employees talk about long after they have passed. These narratives immortalize aspects of the organization's history. Stories persisting over time will influence employees to behave in certain ways. What stories persist and why provide insight into what the organization values most (i.e., values and beliefs). Stories also help to establish what will constitute traditions, and they create role models to inspire others.

Rituals and routines: These are the daily behaviors of employees. Behaviors repeated often and regularly suggest the organization considers them appropriate. In this way, rituals and routines form the basis of the organization's social norms. Though behavior itself is observable, rituals and routines often manifest from the implicit expectations of an organization. In other words, it is possible for an organization to explicitly claim one thing, but for its collective behavior to say something else.

Symbols: These pertain to a collection of inward- and outward-directed visual manifestations of the organization's culture. They include logos, dress codes, office décor, and more.

Organizational structure: This component explores the relationship between departments or units within the organization, specifically how they influence one another. Often associated with the organizational chart, this aspect of culture examines the flow of reporting, where decision-making takes place, and the delegation of roles, responsibilities, and authority.

Control systems: This pertains to how an organization exerts control over employees and their work. This includes mechanisms used to incentivize, track, measure, and evaluate performance like bonuses, punishment protocols, quality control, and more.

Power structures: The final element pertains to the distribution of influential power within the organization. Dictatorial-style power structures often result when power rests with only a few leaders. Conversely, a wider distribution of influential power often results in a more empowered workforce.

According to Johnson and Scholes, the six elements overlap in what they call the Paradigm. The Paradigm represents the organization's actual values, beliefs, and behaviors which define the organization's culture.

Though not one of the six elements, the model does take into consideration national or regional context. This involves exploring how a country or region's culture influences the organization's culture. Sometimes, the organization's culture may conflict with the host nation culture, creating friction within the organization.

Cultural Web is popular within organizational development because of its utility in helping professionals analyze an organization's culture as it is now, explore the culture an organization aspires to create, and develop a strategy to bridge the gap.

Though not a stand-alone change management framework, the Cultural Web model complements any organizational change management approach.

Professionals seeking additional information will find much written about the Cultural Web, including Gerry Johnson's 1992 article from *Long Range Planning*, "Managing Strategic Change—Strategy, Culture, and Action." Readers may also find insight in Johnson and Scholes' 1998 book, *Exploring Corporate Strategy*, co-authored by Richard Whittington.

Sources[76]

DECIDE MODEL

Certification Available: no
Certification Required: no
Assessments: no
Proprietary: no
Client: not applicable
Cost: not applicable
Category: decision-making, problem-solving

Developed in 2008 by professor of public administration Kristina L. Guo, the DECIDE Model provides a simple decision-making framework consisting of six steps.

Step 1—Define the problem: The first step in the process is both time consuming and cognitively intensive as the client works to articulate the problem. This requires the client to conduct a thorough examination of the issue to distinguish cause and effect (catalyst and symptom).

Exploring these distinctions along with other contributing variables can help the client develop an enhanced understanding of the problem, enabling them to define the issue in detail. Well-defined problems often hint at causes and consequences paving the way to solution development.

Step 2—Establish criteria: The second step of the process involves the client identifying and setting parameters concerning the decision or problem. This includes articulating their desired goals, what they want to change, what they want to preserve, and what they want to avoid.

Communicating these factors allows both the client and coach to discover potential preemptive roadblocks as well as identify core motivations and values that may influence the decision-making process.

Step 3—Consider the alternatives: During the third step of the process, the client explores multiple potential solutions to the problem. Often, this stage begins with robust brainstorming where the client formulates multiple options.

The client's creativity and open-mindedness are essential to this stage of the process. For clients who struggle with this, the coach can help the client by broadening their horizon, encouraging them to consider possibilities without preemptively dismissing them, and ensuring the client allows facts, not assumptions, to influence the process.

Step 4—Identify best alternative: The fourth step involves the client evaluating the potential solutions identified in the previous stage. The ensuing analysis requires a combination of logic, intuition, and experience. In this stage, the coach is vital to ensuring the client applies these three elements consistently across each option.

Step 5—Develop and implement plan: The fifth step consists of two distinct components. First, the client must develop a detailed plan including all of the tasks necessary to address the problem, performance parameters for each task, the people who are key to accomplishing each task, a strategy for communicating the plan to others, and the metrics that will inform progress.

The second component involves executing the plan, collecting metrics, and adhering to the original strategy while maintaining the flexibility to adjust as necessary.

Step 6—Evaluate: The final step is a thorough review to determine the efficacy of the plan. This involves identifying elements of the plan that worked or did not work, and developing improvements to strengthen the plan.

Guo developed the DECIDE Model to provide health-care workers with a methodical decision-making process. Citing several gaps in existing decision-making models, Guo wanted to create a framework to facilitate the kinds of high-stakes decisions health-care workers face on a regular basis.

It is important to note that other decision-making models exist which use the acronym DECIDE, including a model designed specifically for use in aviation.

Professionals seeking additional information may consider Guo's 2008 article, "DECIDE: A Decision-Making Model for More Effective Decision-Making by Health Care Managers."

Sources[77]

DEMING CYCLE

Certification Available: no
Certification Required: no
Assessments: no
Proprietary: no
Client: not applicable
Cost: not applicable
Category: problem-solving, change (ind., org.)

Introduced in the 1950s by statistician William Deming, the Deming Cycle (PDCA/PDSA) is a four-step iterative process designed to help businesses continually improve their processes, products, and services. Though only a four-step framework, the PDCA is complex and multifaceted.

Step 1—Plan: The first step involves multiple substeps which begin with the client analyzing the problem or obstacle to identify potential root causes. Once identified, the client should develop multiple hypotheses to potentially explain these causes. Next, the client begins testing each hypothesis.

Once a valid hypothesis emerges, the client develops a plan to make the changes needed to correct the problem. This plan should take into consideration the company's mission, vision, and core values to ensure alignment with the organization's strategies.

When coaching clients in the first stage, it is useful to incorporate tools to facilitate the client's examination of cause and effect, problem-solving, and creative thinking.

Step 2—Do: During the second stage, the client tests the efficacy of the plan by implementation. PDCA encourages users to enact the plan in small increments (not enterprise-wide) and, if possible, in a controlled environment to avoid interrupting actual operations.

To facilitate the testing process, clients should identify and define the metrics and measurements which will indicate progress, and eventually, success.

When coaching clients in the second stage, it is useful to incorporate tools which facilitate the establishment of goals and performance measures.

Step 3—Check/Study: During the third step, the client analyzes the data from step 2 to determine the efficacy of the plan. This analysis can include a before-and-after comparison.

When coaching clients in the third stage, it is useful to incorporate tools which facilitate the processing and analysis of data, like matrixes, charts, and graphs.

Subsequent to unveiling the PDCA framework, Deming felt the "check" step in the process underemphasized the importance of the analysis required in this step. Therefore, he renamed the process to PDSA, the "S" representing Study.

Step 4—Act: If the initial implementation proves effective, then the client is ready for the final step, where they consider applying the changes on a larger scale. If the data suggests flaws in the efficacy of the plan, the client may make modifications based on the resulting analysis.

Though one of the earliest frameworks to emerge from the field of quality control, the use of PDSA persists in lean management programs across the world. Deming presents the PDSA as a loop, not an end-to-end process, to emphasize its functionality as a mechanism to drive continuous improvement.

Also known as the Shewhart Cycle, the PDCA Cycle, and the PDSA Cycle, the model derives from the work of Deming's mentor, physicist Walter Shewhart. It is important to note, some sources question Deming's role as the originator of this cycle, though most continue to attribute the work to him.

PDCA is a useful resource when starting a new project, exploring potential problems and challenges, or implementing change.

Professionals seeking additional information will find much written on the Deming Cycle, including Deming's 1993 book, *The New Economics for Industry, Government, Education.*

Sources[78]

DENISON MODEL

Certification Available: yes
Certification Required: yes
Assessments: yes (DOCS)
Proprietary: yes (Denison Consulting)
Client: organizations
Cost: $1,950
Category: culture, change (org.)

Developed in 1990 by organizational psychologist Dan Denison, The Denison Model provides a framework for analyzing organizational culture to determine its impact on organizational performance (e.g., return on investment, equity, innovation, employee satisfaction, etc.).

The Denison Model consists of four cultural traits, each containing three management practices or indexes which provide a structured approach for analyzing and assessing performance from the optic of organizational culture.

Mission: This cultural trait pertains to the organization's goals, direction, purpose, and strategy. An examination of this trait seeks to answer questions like, "Does the organization know where it's going? Does it have clear goals and a plan to achieve them?"

The three indexes measured under this trait are:
- Strategic Direction and Intent
- Goals and Objectives
- Vision

Adaptability: This cultural trait pertains to the organization's ability to make accurate and meaningful observations of patterns, trends, and market direction. An examination of this trait seeks to answer questions like, "Does the organization listen to the market? How well does it listen to customers? Is it responsive to consumer needs and feedback?"

The three indexes measured under this trait are:
- Creating Change
- Customer Focus
- Organizational Learning

Involvement: This cultural trait relates to the organization's level of commitment to the mission, sense of ownership in the work, and responsibility to employees. An examination of this trait seeks to answer questions like, "Are the organization's people aligned and engaged? How well does the organization empower its employees and build teams?"

The three indexes measured under this trait are:
- Empowerment
- Team Orientation
- Capability Development

Consistency: This cultural trait applies to the organization's systems, processes, and structures. An examination of this trait seeks to answer questions like, "Do the organization's interconnected policies, practices, procedures, and protocols support or hinder mission achievement?"

The three indexes measured under this trait are:
- Core Values
- Agreement
- Coordination and Integration

Visually, the Denison Model presents as a color-coded circumplex which includes two hemispheres of culture characterizing the four cultural traits.
- External or Internal Focus
- Flexibility or Stability

The Denison Model has broad utility, including as a tool to diagnose and treat organizational "cultural malaise," improve strategic alignment, prepare organizations for mergers and acquisitions, and facilitate organizational transformation planning.

The Denison Model is significantly more complex than presented here and includes an assessment called the *Denison Organizational Culture Survey (DOCS)*. Both the model and the instrument are proprietary to Denison Consulting and require training and certification from Denison Consulting LLC prior to formal use.

Professionals seeking additional information may consider Denison's 2012 book, *Leading Culture Change in Global Organizations*, co-authored with Robert Hooijberg, Nancy Lane, and Colleen Lief.

Sources[79]

DESC MODEL

Developed in the 1970s by Sharon Anthony Bower and Gordon Bower, the DESC Model provides a simple framework to solve interpersonal conflict and facilitate feedback.

DESC consists of four steps to enable users to express themselves effectively when engaged in intense or highly emotional conversations.

Step 1—Describe: In a formal feedback setting (e.g., a performance evaluation), the first step involves providing a detailed description of the recipient's behaviors. It is important that the provider focus only on the behavior they observed directly. The provider should avoid making interpretations or assumptions relating to the observed behaviors.

When using DESC to address interpersonal conflict, the first step involves the provider describing the situation as they perceive it, acknowledging to the recipient that this is their point of view.

Step 2—Express: In a formal feedback session, this step involves an explanation of how the recipient's behavior impacts other employees, the team, and the organization. It is important for the provider to offer clear and unambiguous examples of the negative or positive effects on others. This provides context for the consequences to the recipient.

When resolving interpersonal conflict, this step involves the provider explaining how the recipient's behavior makes them feel and how those feelings affect them.

Variations of this model identify this step differently, using labels like Effect or Emotion.

Step 3—Specify: In a formal feedback session, this step involves the provider presenting a clear and specific description of the behavior they wish to see from the recipient.

When resolving interpersonal conflict, the provider describes possible solutions that could resolve the conflict. Though not part of the DESC Model, most conflict resolution models suggest a collaborative approach whereby the provider and recipient of feedback work together to identify a solution.

Variations of this model identify this step differently, using labels like Solution.

Step 4—Consequences: In both formal feedback and interpersonal conflict resolution settings, the final step involves providing the recipient with a positive explanation of how the desired behavior will benefit all involved.

Variations of this model identify this step differently, using labels like Conclusion.

In one version of the DESC Model, the fourth step is Contract of Commitment. This requires verbal acknowledgment from the recipient to ensure they understand the provider's expectations of them.

An important aspect of the DESC Model is the provider's use of the pronoun "I" and limited use of "you." This helps the provider avoid making the recipient feel judged or attacked, which risks the recipient shutting down.

In addition to facilitating conflict resolution and formal feedback, the DESC Model also provides a framework for having difficult conversations in which there is little room for negotiations. To help clients prepare for these difficult conversations, the Bowers developed the DESC Script. This worksheet allows the client to script out key points within each step of the DESC process.

DESC is one of the oldest feedback models used by coaches in a variety of settings and contexts. Professionals seeking additional information on the DESC Model may consider the Bowers' 1976 book, *Asserting Yourself: A Practical Guide for Positive Change.*

Sources[80]

DESIGN THINKING

Certification Available: yes (multiple vendors)
Certification Required: no
Assessments: no
Proprietary: no
Client: individuals, groups, teams
Cost: prices vary by vendor
Category: problem-solving

Design Thinking is a methodology for creative problem-solving that adopts a human-centric approach to solution creation. The Design Thinking mindset encompasses multiple frameworks, each providing a unique approach to problem-solving, like *IBM's Design Thinking*.

Design Thinking frameworks vary in the number of process steps and labels used to describe each step. Some models consist of only three steps while others provide a more structured six-step process. Conceptually, however, these frameworks are fundamentally the same and they all incorporate the user's perspective in the process.

One common Design Thinking framework emerged from The Hasso Plattner Institute of Design at Stanford University.

Step 1—Empathize: Also known as user-centricity, this step involves researching the user's needs, then developing an understanding of how those needs affect the user. Adopting the user's perspective allows designers to shed their assumptions about the problem or challenge before them, giving them a different and potentially less biased view of the problem.

Step 2 –Define: In this step, the designer considers all the data collected from the first step to articulate the user's needs in a problem statement that clearly synthesizes and defines the elements of the problem. The Design Thinking mindset requires the problem statement come from the perspective of the user to ensure the process remains relevant to the end user. This stage, also called collaboration, encourages diverse groups of designers to work together toward identifying a solution.

Step 3—Ideate: During this stage, designers develop multiple potential solutions to each problem statement by thinking outside the box.

Step 4—Prototype: Considered the experimental phase; during this stage, designers create scaled-down versions of potential solutions.

Step 5—Test: In the final phase, designers test the solutions, measure efficacy, and adjust as needed.

Another popular framework comes from global design company IDEO.

Step 1—Frame question: Frame the problem in the form of a question that inspires others to seek a solution.

Step 2—Gather inspiration: Build inspiration by learning what needs other people have.

Step 3—Generate ideas: Push idea generation beyond the obvious to find creative options.

Step 4—Make ideas tangible: Build prototypes to make ideas concrete.

Step 5—Test to learn: Experiment with the prototypes, learn, adjust.

Step 6—Share the story: Develop a humanistic story to inspire others to adopt the solution.

Design Thinking processes are iterative and nonlinear. Designers may jump back and forth across stages or implement multiple stages simultaneously, as appropriate.

Though used heavily in engineering and software development, the Design Thinking mindset is an effective methodology for innovation and solving highly complex problems, sometimes called "wicked problems."

Professionals will find many books and articles available on Design Thinking, including *Harvard Business Review's 10 Must Reads on Design Thinking*.

Sources[81]

DESTINY MODEL

Certification Available: no
Certification Required: no
Assessments: no
Proprietary: no
Client: individuals
Cost: not applicable
Category: goal setting

The DESTINY Model is a seven-step framework which facilitates individual goal setting.

Step 1—Detailed: The first step involves two parts. First, the client conducts a focused examination of the facts and data relevant to the issue or problem at hand. This includes identifying stakeholders who have a vested interest in the client's position. It is important that the client consider all external factors influencing the situation, like organizational politics and culture, resource limitations, and other variables.

Second, the client applies what they learned from the above examination to identify a goal which satisfies their interest or desire. This includes identifying a list of actions, tasks, and behaviors that will move the client toward goal attainment.

Step 2—Exciting: The second step involves exploring the client's commitment to achieving their goal. It is essential the client consider the reasons why the goal is important to them. This contemplative effort may lead the client to adjust their initial goal to one that resonates on a deeper level or presents the potential for a more significant reward.

Step 3—Specific: During the third step of the process, the client defines success and describes what it looks like.

This will help them recognize goal attainment when it happens. Achieving this often requires the use of visioning exercises to help the client imagine a desired future state.

Additionally, this step helps the client explore their perceptions of success and may reveal self-biased assumptions like overconfidence or competency bias. The client's effort in this stage may also indicate if the client's goal conflicts with their best interest or well-being, a consideration which manifests again in the seventh step.

Step 4—Timeline: The fourth stage involves the client developing a timeline which allows them to sequence the actions, tasks, and behaviors they need to adopt to achieve their goal.

Step 5—Identifiable: In the fifth step, the client identifies clear and measurable indicators of progress. These milestones serve as a barometer to help the client track their progress.

Step 6—Noticeable: The sixth step introduces a perspective unique among goal-setting models. During this stage of the process, the client considers what indicators others might observe which tell them the client has achieved their goal. Adopting this outside perspective allows the client to explore their goals from different points of view and opens them up to new ideas and ways of measuring success.

Step 7—Your future: In the final step, the client explores how their goals might impact their future life and career. Like the third step (Specific), this involves the client envisioning how success could improve their situation. This exercise can reveal assumptions or perceptions that may risk the client's success. These can include tasks, actions, and behaviors that may advance a client's career but prove detrimental to their well-being, like working 14-hour days, seven days a week.

The DESTINY Model is useful with clients struggling to set goals which are beneficial to both their professional careers and their well-being. While presented as a linear process, the model is nonlinear. This allows the client to move across stages as needed.

Professionals seeking additional information will find limited material available on the DESTINY Model. Though the origins of this model remain unclear, the framework features in Helen Whitten's 2011 book, *Cognitive Behavioral Coaching Techniques for Dummies*.

Practicing coaches may consider integrating elements of DESTINY with other goal-setting models like the *SMART Model*.

Sources[82]

DIFFUSION OF INNOVATION THEORY

Certification Available: no
Certification Required: no
Assessments: no
Proprietary: no
Client: groups, teams, organizations
Cost: not applicable
Category: change (org. and ind.), influence

Developed in 1962 by sociologist E.M. Rogers, Diffusion of Innovation Theory (DOI) is a complex framework that explains how an idea gains momentum and spreads (diffuses) throughout a population. The theory consists of the following three interrelated frameworks: Adopter Categories, Stages of Adoption, and Factors of Adoption.

Adopter categories: Researchers discovered that the adoption of new ideas (or change) within a group setting does not happen simultaneously or in the same way; rather people adopt change at five different rates.

- **Innovators:** These individuals want to be the first to try new ideas; they are risk-takers, adventurous, and interested in new ideas.

- **Early adopters:** Typically, these are leaders who understand the importance of change, are comfortable adopting new ideas, and require little convincing.

- **Early majority:** Typically, individuals in this group are not leaders, though they tend to adopt ideas before the average person. They require proof that change works or some evidence of viability (i.e., success stories).

- **Late majority:** Typically, these individuals are skeptical of change and will only consider change once most others

have successfully adopted change. They require more information about how others have adopted change successfully.

- **Laggards:** Typically, these people are bound to tradition and the status quo. They require all available information about the change and need pressure from individuals in different adopter groups before they will consider adoption.

Stages of Adoption: Researchers identified four stages a person goes through on the way to adoption.

- **Awareness:** The person recognizes a need for change or adoption.

- **Decision to adopt:** The person accepts the change.

- **Initial use:** The person tests the change to determine viability.

- **Continued use:** The person fully adopts the change.

Factors: Researchers identified five variables that influence a person's adoption of change. These factors play a different role depending on the individual's Adopter Category.

- **Relative advantage:** the degree to which a person perceives the change as preferable to the status quo.

- **Compatibility:** how closely aligned the change is with the individual's values.

- **Complexity:** how difficult the change is to understand.

- **Triability:** extent to which a person can test the change.

- **Observability:** extent to which the change produces tangible, measurable results.

DOI is a useful framework, especially when working with clients undergoing organizational change as well as large groups considering the adoption of new innovations.

DOI has proven useful in many fields, including marketing, social work, public health, and criminal justice. DOI is more complex than presented here. Professionals seeking additional information may consider Rogers' 1962 book, *Diffusion of Innovations*.

Sources[83]

DISC

Certification Available: yes (multiple vendors)
Certification Required: no (yes, certain versions)
Assessments: yes (several)
Proprietary: no (yes, certain versions)
Client: individuals, groups
Cost: pricing varies
Category: communication, personality type

Created in the 1920s by psychologist William Marston, the DISC Model provides a simple framework for classifying individual personality, preferences, and behavior. Influenced by classical theories of personality (Empedocles and Hippocrates), DISC consists of four categories or styles.

Dominant: Individuals in this category are direct, sometimes forceful, result-oriented, and persistent.

Influence: Individuals in this category are outgoing, enthusiastic, and high-spirited.

Steadiness: Individuals in this category are humble, patient, and empathetic.

Conscientiousness: Individuals in this category are logical, methodical, and highly analytical.

Though individuals may possess characteristics across each of the four domains, typically one style emerges as the preferential mode of behavior. For this reason, most DISC assessments will identify both a primary and secondary style.

Variations of the DISC framework adopt different lenses when exploring the four styles. For example, some versions of DISC examine individual preferences for communication while others use DISC to explore leadership styles. Regardless of the focus, each version includes a number of descriptors to help clients better understand themselves, others, and their relationships.

Marston created the model using observable traits and characteristics, which means one does not need an assessment to use the DISC framework. In fact, Marston never created an assessment for his theory. The existing slate of assessments emerged long after Marston's passing.

Marston developed DISC as a theory to explain how normal human emotions lead to behavioral differences among groups of people, and how a person's behavior might change over time. Therefore, a person taking the DISC assessment multiple times over several years may produce different results.

Though very popular in business and leadership circles, many clinicians and academics question the scientific efficacy of DISC. Though largely discredited as a diagnostic instrument in clinical circles, DISC's utility in coaching remains undeniable given its widespread use.

As a framework, DISC is useful in many different areas, including interpersonal communication, relationship development, self-awareness enhancement, perspective-taking, leadership development, and conflict resolution.

Use of the original DISC framework does not require certification, and several assessments are available for purchase without certification. However, we highly encourage professionals to seek certification prior to use. Interpreting the results for clients and applying the framework in complex environments requires significant depth of knowledge.

Though the original DISC framework is not proprietary, some variations and expanded versions of DISC are and require certification or permission before use. Multiple vendors offer training in DISC at different price points.

DISC is significantly more complex than presented here. Professionals seeking additional information may consider Marston's 1931 book, *Integrative Psychology: A Study of Unit Response*, which provides insight into the proto version of his framework. Readers will find ample literature available on the many variations of DISC. Due to the differences between these versions, professionals should thoroughly explore their options before selecting the version of DISC appropriate for their practice.

Sources[84]

DISTRIBUTED WORK'S FIVE LEVELS OF AUTONOMY

Certification Available: no
Certification Required: no
Assessments: no
Proprietary: no
Client: organizations
Cost: not applicable
Category: employee engagement

Developed in 2020 by software developer and entrepreneur Matt Mullenweg, Distributed Work's Five Levels of Autonomy provides a framework for assessing and characterizing an organization's ability to function effectively while supporting telework or remote work, which Mullenweg calls "distributed work."

Level 0: These are professions that cannot support remote work. For this reason, Level 0 is not one of the five levels. Level 0 professions include doctors, firefighters, first responders, cooks, massage therapists, and more.

Level 1: These are companies that do not foster a "remote-friendly" environment. Typically, these organizations do not have the culture, policies, or resources available to facilitate employees working outside of the office. Those who work in Level 1 companies relegate their efforts to company space and company time.

While Level 1 firms may survive a day or two of remote-based work, their effectiveness drops quickly as they lack the infrastructure (technologically and psychologically) to function in a remote fashion. Mullenweg suggests approximately 98% of companies were in Level 1 when COVID-19 hit.

Level 2: These are companies that attempt to re-create the office experience within the home environment, often leading to detrimental consequences. When fabricating a 9-to-5 workday, companies may inundate employees with virtual meetings, conference calls, and emails, all while failing to take into consideration home-based distractions.

Level 2 organizations assume because an employee is at home, they can respond to requests immediately. This assumption proved false during COVID-19 when parents found themselves struggling to meet their employee obligations while simultaneously functioning as a teacher to their quarantined children. Mullenweg compares Level 2 to fitting a synchronous peg in an asynchronous hole.

Level 3: These are companies that invest in remote work by dedicating resources to facilitate the employee's ability to work outside the office. This includes adjusting corporate protocols, policies, and practices to reinforce the demands of remote work. Employees working off-site for Level 3 organizations begin to adopt an asynchronous schedule. In other words, work does not happen all at once or on a predetermined schedule. Level 3 employees complete their work with a measure of autonomy.

Organizations operating on Level 3 hold meetings infrequently but ensure each session is effective and efficient. This includes the effective use of digital resources and virtual conduits of communication. Mullenweg says Level 3 is the start of a company's move to becoming "distributed."

Level 4: These are companies transitioning to asynchronous work. Leaders in Level 4 organizations evaluate employees based on the quality of the work produced, not when or how they produce it. Employees become more efficient communicators and can delegate and share responsibilities seamlessly.

Level 5: Mullenweg calls Level 5 Nirvana. At Level 5, a company performs better with a fully distributed (remote) workforce than a co-located one. Level 5 means a company's culture, policies, and resources align to foster a distributed workforce.

The Five Levels of Autonomy emerged in response to the COVID-19 pandemic, which forced companies around the world to transition to telework. The model is more complex than presented here. Professionals seeking additional information may consider Matt Mullenweg's podcast interview on "Making Sense with Sam Harris."

Sources[85]

DOBLIN'S TEN TYPES OF INNOVATION

> **Certification Available:** no
> **Certification Required:** no
> **Assessments:** no
> **Proprietary:** yes (Deloitte LLP)
> **Client:** organizations
> **Cost:** not applicable
> **Category:** problem-solving

Developed by innovation strategists Larry Keeley and Jay Doblin, the Ten Types of Innovation provides a framework for exploring innovation opportunities across ten domains.

Profit model: This domain focuses on how the organization makes money and examines opportunities for innovation in pricing strategies, revenue collection, bundling, and more.

Network: These pertain to innovation opportunities within an organization's relationships and seek to leverage these relationships to the benefit of both parties.

Structure: This domain explores opportunities to innovate the structure and alignment of an organization's assets and talent.

Process: This domain explores innovation of an organization's way of doing business, building products, and delivering services.

Product performance: This domain explores product innovation and is the focus of traditional innovation efforts.

Product system: This domain explores innovation through the integration and interconnectivity of products.

Service: This pertains to innovation focusing on the services offered by an organization.

Channel: This domain explores innovation in how the organization's products and services get to customers.

Brand: This domain explores innovation in client capture and reputation development.

Customer engagement: This domain explores innovation focused on the organization's understanding of customer needs and desires.

The ten domains amalgamate into three distinct categories.

Category 1—Configuration: These innovations focus on the organization's innermost workings and systems and consist of profit model, network, structure, and process.

Category 2—Offering: These innovations focus on the organization's core products and consist of product performance and product system.

Category 3—Experience: These innovations focus on the customer-facing aspect of the organization and include service, channel, brand, and customer engagement.

Doblin's model pushes back on two common misconceptions about innovation: first, that innovation applies only to product development, and second, that funding R&D is the primary way to foster innovation.

The Ten Types of Innovation has broad utility, including as a diagnostic tool to help companies identify opportunities for improving operations, as a means of combining internal and external innovation, and as a strategy to adapt to market forces.

Doblin's model includes over 100 tactics or actions designed to foster innovation within key areas of each domain. These tactics spur creative thinking and facilitate innovation.

Doblin's framework is more complex than presented here. Professionals seeking additional information may consider Keeley's 2013 book, *Ten Types of Innovation: The Discipline of Building Breakthroughs.* Doblin's Ten Types of Innovation is proprietary to Doblin, a subsidiary of Deloitte LLP.

Sources[86]

DREXLER-SIBBET TEAM PERFORMANCE MODEL

> **Certification Available:** yes
> **Certification Required:** no (yes, for assessment)
> **Assessments:** yes (TPS)
> **Proprietary:** yes (The Grove)
> **Client:** teams, groups, organizations
> **Cost:** pricing not available
> **Category:** teaming

Developed in the 1980s by organizational consultants Allan Drexler and David Sibbet, their Team Performance Model (TPM) provides a framework to facilitate the creation and sustainment of teams. The TPM framework consists of seven stages: four devoted to creating the team and three to sustaining the team's performance.

Creating the Team Phase

Stage 1—Orientation: In this stage, there is no team, only a group of individuals curious about their selection. Therefore, it is important to explain the rationale for each person's selection. Equally critical, the collective must understand the purpose behind the team's creation. This includes defining the team's mission and setting expectations for team performance.

Indicators of a team struggling in this stage include a collective sense of disorientation, uncertainty, and fear among selected members.

Stage 2—Trust building: This stage involves developing the willingness of individual members to work together and depend on each other to perform the tasks necessary for team success. This typically requires team members to possess an understanding of each person's skills, competencies, and vulnerabilities.

Indicators of a team struggling in this stage include hesitancy allowing others to perform tasks, false displays of trust, a façade of confidence in the team, and a general mistrust in others.

Stage 3—Goal clarification: Building on the "why" behind the team's formation, this stage involves providing the team with details regarding their collective goals. In cases where the team receives a general mandate (vision) without a specific goal, the team uses this stage to define their goals in clear, measurable, and objective ways.

Indicators of a team struggling in stage 3 include skepticism over the team's efficacy or purpose, a lack of enthusiasm for the team's effort, or active resistance to the tasks required for team success.

Stage 4—Commitment: During this stage, the team assigns roles and delegates responsibilities among members, creating momentum as they pursue their goals.

Indicators of a team struggling in stage 4 include a refusal to perform required tasks and the abdication of individual or collective responsibility for mission achievement.

Sustaining the Team Phase

Stage 5—Implementation: This stage involves the development and execution of an action plan consisting of tasks necessary for goal attainment. Indicators of stage 5 challenges include missed deadlines, conflict, and ineffectual results.

Stage 6—High performance: In this stage, the team performs in a synergistic fashion. The seamless interactions of members allow for efficient goal attainment and a rapid response to obstacles. Indicators of challenges in stage 6 include discord and disharmony.

Stage 7—Renewal: Over time, even high-performance teams burn out or need renewal. This stage involves teams revisiting previous stages to reaffirm their purpose and regain momentum.

Though presented as a linear process, a team's movement through the process is nonlinear. A team may move across stages randomly.

Training in the TPM framework is available from The Grove Consultants International. Professionals seeking additional information may consider Drexler and Sibbet's 1993 book, *Team Performance: Creating and Sustaining Results*.

Sources[87]

DREYFUS MODEL

Certification Available: no
Certification Required: no
Assessments: no
Proprietary: no
Client: individuals
Cost: not applicable
Category: learning/development

Developed in 1980 by professors Stuart Dreyfus and Hubert Dreyfus, the Dreyfus Model provides a framework consisting of five levels of learning adults may experience as they acquire new skills.

Level 1—Novice: The first level of skill acquisition. Individuals in this stage have little to no experience with the desired skill. Their incomplete understanding means they approach learning in a mechanical way, often needing direct supervision or instruction. Providing a formal learning structure and dissecting complex issues into basic components can help learners in the novice stage.

Level 2—Advanced beginner: In this stage, the individual has learned the basic rules and concepts associated with the skill and experiments by applying them to new situations. Each application (right or wrong) represents new experiences that foster the individual's learning. While this step marks progress toward greater autonomy, the individual still depends on rules and examples, and to a lesser extent oversight. One useful teaching approach in this stage is to demonstrate the relationship between elements and concepts, which increases the learner's depth of knowledge.

Level 3—Competent: In this stage, the individual learns additional rules and concepts associated with the skill. This can encourage individuals to move into new situations where the rules they know may not apply. When this happens, the individual may not be able to determine which rules do apply. This can lead to feelings of confusion and anxiety. The number of rules may overwhelm the learner; as a result, the learner may develop an internal process to determine when to apply certain rules or ignore them. If they are unable to learn and adapt, they may never transition to the next stage of development. Individuals in this stage have a greater capacity to problem-solve and can work independently, though mentorship is highly recommended. In this stage, including additional frameworks can expand the scope of the individual's frame of reference.

Level 4—Proficient: Individuals in this stage see the bigger picture, understand the rules, and can select the correct application of skills with little conscious thought. Individuals at the proficient level can examine their own mistakes and those of others to foster further learning, and they routinely perform to higher standards.

Level 5—Expert: In appearance, individuals in this stage look like those at the proficient level with a key exception: They can make subtle discriminations because their depth of knowledge reaches a granular level. Individuals at the expert level become a source of knowledge able to interpret the application of rules and theory for others. To the novice, the expert's grasp of the content appears almost magical.

The Dreyfus Model suggests that learners depend less on abstract principles and more on experience the more skilled they become. By the time an individual reaches the Expert level, they trust intuition more than heuristics or formulaic rules.

The Dreyfus Model has broad utility, especially for those developing curricula. Leaders creating teams may use the model to evaluate individual levels of expertise to ensure their teams include a diverse range of experience levels.

Some sources use different labels to describe the five levels. The original version of the model labeled the fifth stage **Mastery**. In 2004, they renamed this stage **Expert**. As a result, practitioners may encounter older versions of the model which still use the term mastery. The Dreyfus Model is also known as the Dreyfus and Dreyfus Model.

Professionals seeking additional information on the Dreyfus Model may consider Stuart Dreyfus' 2004 article, "The Five-Stage Model of Adult Skill Acquisition," or the 2021 book, *Teaching and Learning for Adult Skill Acquisition: Applying the Dreyfus and Dreyfus Model in Different Fields*, edited by E.S. Mangiante, K. Peno, and J. Northup.

Sources[88]

DRISCOLL'S REFLECTION CYCLE

Certification Available: no
Certification Required: no
Assessments: no
Proprietary: no
Client: individuals
Cost: not applicable
Category: reflection

Developed between 1994 and 2007 by registered nurse John Driscoll, Driscoll's Reflection Cycle provides a framework to facilitate reflection that fosters experiential growth and understanding. Driscoll's Reflection Cycle consists of three stages.

Stage 1—Reflection (description): In the first stage of Driscoll's process, the client examines a selected experience, beginning with a description of the event. This is not a summary, but a methodical recounting of the experience.

Characterized by the question "What," the client explains what happened, what they did, what they saw, and more. Details relevant to this examination include who was involved, the behaviors or actions of those involved, and any pertinent observations. Complete objectivity is difficult to achieve; however, clients should be as dispassionate as possible in their recollection.

Stage 2—Discover (analysis): In the second stage, the client analyzes the experience presented in the prior stage (Reflection).

Characterized by the question "So what," the client examines their feelings at the time of the event, noticing any changes in their emotional state as the experience unfolded. The client should also consider how their reactions impacted those around them. Another optic the client should explore is how the experience compares with other experiences. Stage 2 is more subjective than the previous stage as the client's perceptions will influence their interpretations.

The analysis performed in stage 2 should help the client find meaning in the experience. This can include a better understanding of why others behaved the way they did or appreciating how the event came to pass.

Stage 3—Actioning: The third stage involves the client reconsidering their behavior during the experience and engaging in an imaginative exploration of alternative behaviors they could adopt in the future. Though the incident has passed, the act of envisioning alternative ways they could have handled the situation creates the potential for a more effective response, in the event a similar experience takes place. This technique, sometimes called counterfactual thinking, is an essential part of social functioning.

Characterized by the question "Now what," the client considers what happens if they change nothing about their behavior as well as what might happen if they adopt one or more possible changes. The client explores what kind of information might be useful to them in deciding on the most appropriate course of action.

Driscoll's Reflection Cycle, also known as Driscoll's Model of Reflection and the What Model, applies across a variety of professional settings and situations. Driscoll's framework is ideal for clients new to reflection, or those who struggle with deeper or more intensive reflection frameworks.

Driscoll's Reflection Cycle, like other models of reflection, is based on the work of educator Terry Borton and his *Borton's Model of Reflection*. Borton's framework focused on reflection within academic settings; however, Driscoll adapted the framework to foster reflection in nursing and medical settings.

The similarity of Driscoll's Reflection Model to *Rolfe's Reflective Model* and *Borton's Model of Reflection* makes it difficult to distinguish between them. Much of the available literature appears to present these models in near identical fashion, often presenting them as interchangeable. Professionals considering one of these models should research all three models.

For additional information on these similar frameworks, consider Borton's 1970 book, *Reach, Touch and Teach*.

Sources[89]

DRiV MODEL

Certification Available: yes
Certification Required: yes
Assessments: yes (several)
Proprietary: yes (Leadership Worth Following)
Client: individuals, organizations
Cost: $2,000
Category: motivation, values, decision-making

Developed by organizational psychologists Chris W. Coultas and Myranda Grahek, the DRiV Model provides a framework to help clients identify and distinguish between the drivers that motivate them and the ones that drain them. The model allows clients to better understand the relationship between their values and behaviors, and as a result, help them make better decisions.

The DRiV Model (pronounced "drive") consists of 28 motivational drivers categorized by six factors.

Insight: This factor speaks to a person's motivation for knowledge, their desire to seek understanding and to learn about the world around them. Insight explores how much the individual values creativity in comparison to their need for explicit rules. Drivers associated with this factor include Creativity, Growth, Wisdom, and Compliance.

Connection: This factor pertains to a person's motivation to build and maintain meaningful relationships. Connection explores how much the individual values relationship building in comparison to their need for independence. Drivers associated with this factor include Collaboration, Inclusion, Rapport, and Autonomy.

Harmony: This factor pertains to a person's motivation to treat others well and support them. This includes an individual's ability to put others before self. Harmony speaks to the quality and stability of the relationships a person maintains. Drivers associated with this factor include Honesty, Forgiveness, Service, Authority, Competition, Personal Wealth, and Status.

Productivity: This factor pertains to a person's motivation to accomplish tasks and produce results. Productivity explores how much the individual values a commitment to reliability in comparison to their need for personal enjoyment. Drivers associated with this factor include Alignment, Excellence, Persistence, and Enjoyment.

Meaning: This factor pertains to a person's motivation to make meaning from one's own life. This includes defining one's purpose and the desire to make lasting contributions to the world. Drivers associated with this factor include Authenticity, Legacy, Purpose, and Recognition.

Impact: This factor speaks to a person's desire to influence the world around them. Impact explores how much an individual values the ability to influence change in comparison to their need for certainty. Drivers associated with this factor include Charisma, Commercial Focus, Courage, Caution, and Deliberation.

The DRiV Model is useful with clients struggling to align their behaviors and values. The framework can also help clients considering significant personal or professional changes. Based on the *Theory of Planned Behavior*, DRiV allows clients to determine what matters most to them, help them recognize their expectations of self, and consequently, lead them to make better-informed decisions.

The DRiV Model has broad utility, reflected in the array of assessments and tools based on the framework. These include a leadership report, a 360 tool, an assessment workbook, and a team version of the assessment. Use of these resources requires certification.

Professionals seeking formal training in DRiV will find multiple vendors offering certification. DRiV is a trademark of Leadership Worth Following, and their primary training provider is Otto Kroeger Associates (OKA).

Professionals seeking additional information on DRiV may consider Coultas' 2021 book, *Driven, Not Drained: Discover Your Path to Career Happiness, Effectiveness, and Influence.*

Sources[90]

DUAL PROCESS THEORY (KAHNEMAN)

Certification Available: no
Certification Required: no
Assessments: no
Proprietary: no
Client: individuals
Cost: not applicable
Category: decision-making, problem-solving

The origins of Dual Process Theory date to the late 19th century. Since then, many have contributed to the evolution of the theory. This entry presents Dual Process Theory as described by noted psychologist and Nobel Laureate economist Daniel Kahneman.

Kahneman's Dual Process Theory suggests that the human mind possesses two different decision-making systems. Each system presents different strengths and risks depending on the situation.

System 1: This is the fast process, also called the lower-level process. System 1 decision-making is automatic, often taking place on an unconscious level and is based on a combination of past experiences, pattern recognition, and intuition, a process commonly referred to as heuristics.

The System 1 process is useful in situations requiring immediate decisions or when there is insufficient time to consider all options. Some suggest System 1 is a product of evolution, influenced by the fight, flight, or freeze experience in which human beings often needed to make quick decisions about threats to survive. Therefore, System 1 is beneficial in certain situations.

Because System 1 relies on past experiences to create mental shortcuts, it is highly susceptible to multiple forms of bias. These biases negatively influence decision-making, leading some to oversimplify complicated solutions. Applying System 1 in the wrong circumstances can result in snap decisions and subconscious reactions which undermine effective decision-making.

System 2: This is the slow process, also called the higher-level process. System 2 decision-making is deliberate, methodical, conscious, and structured. Individuals using System 2 for decision-making rely on preexisting or well-established frameworks to facilitate problem-solving.

System 2 is useful in complex, high-stakes situations that require analytical techniques, like "cause and effect" or "compare and contrast." Individuals can use System 2 to reflect and evaluate outcomes from System 1 thinking to determine relevance and accuracy. While System 2 processes make for more thorough decision-making, there are limitations.

System 2 processing requires time. In situations where there is insufficient time to thoroughly examine an issue, a System 2 approach may fall short. When distractions are present, those using System 2 may find themselves subconsciously moving back to System 1.

It is important to note that some sources will use the term "dual systems theory" interchangeably with Dual Process Theory. We caution against this because the term "dual systems model" also applies to an unrelated field of cognitive study focusing on adolescent development.

"Dual process theory" also applies as an umbrella term referring to a collection of models and frameworks dealing with competing cognitive processes. Models under this umbrella term span a variety of topics, including communication, persuasion, learning, decision-making, and many more. Kahneman's Dual Process Theory is one such model and falls under the category of decision-making.

There is no formal certification or training in Dual Process Theory. However, significant literature is available (under both Dual Process Theory and Dual Systems Theory) to enhance depth of knowledge for practitioners wishing to incorporate Kahneman's model into practice.

Professionals seeking additional information may consider Kahneman's popular 2011 book, *Thinking, Fast and Slow*.

Sources[91]

DUNBAR'S NUMBER

Certification Available: no
Certification Required: no
Assessments: no
Proprietary: no
Client: individuals
Cost: not applicable
Category: communication

Developed in the 1990s by anthropologist and evolutionary psychologist Robin Dunbar, Dunbar's Number suggests there is a limit to the number of social connections an individual can maintain at any given time. Though often misconstrued as a single number (150 the most frequently cited), the theory consists of several numbers based on the level of social intimacy.

The following depicts Dunbar's Number for each level of relationship, from the most intimate to the most superficial.

- Loved ones: 5 connections
- Good friends: 15 connections
- Friends: 50 connections
- Meaningful contacts: 150 connections
- Acquaintances: 500 connections
- People you can recognize: 1,500 connections

Dunbar suggests these numbers are generalizations and may vary from person to person. He also recognizes the existence of variables that may increase or decrease these numbers, like introversion and extroversion.

Dunbar's research stems from a combination of observational studies of both humans and nonhuman primates, neuroimaging, and brain size measurements. The results of his research indicate a correlation between brain size, specifically the frontal lobe of the neocortex, and a person's ability to maintain meaningful social connections.

A common way to visualize Dunbar's Number is by using a set of six concentric circles (e.g., a bull's-eye target). Each circle represents a level of social intimacy, with the center (bull's-eye) representing the closest and most meaningful relationships. The labels used to describe each level vary from source to source; we present one such variation.

Though research continues into Dunbar's Number, many remain skeptical of his theory. Some claim the number of meaningful connections (150) is more like 290, while others suggest attempting to assign a number is impractical. Other skeptics question the veracity of the theory on methodological grounds, citing other factors that may influence limitations on a person's social connections like diet and culture.

Further fueling the debate around Dunbar's Number is the existence of social media (e.g., LinkedIn and Facebook) which facilitate quick and easy connections. To date, research into the effect of social media on Dunbar's Number has resulted in conflicted findings.

Proponents of the theory argue that although social media simplifies a person's ability to make connections, its impact on a person's actual capacity for maintaining relationships is minimal. Researchers suggest many of the hundreds of connections a person has on social media fall under the category of people you can recognize (1,500 connections), not meaningful contacts (150 connections).

Dunbar's Number is a useful lens through which a client may explore their existing social and professional networks. Bringing awareness to their bandwidth for expanding and maintaining relationships may allow the client to better manage their current network.

The science behind Dunbar's Number is robust and multifaceted, yielding significant literature on the matter, both in favor of and opposed to the theory. We encourage coaches to research both perspectives prior to adopting the framework.

Professionals seeking additional information will find much written about Dunbar's Number, including Dunbar's 2010 book, *How Many Friends Does One Person Need: Dunbar's Number and Other Evolutionary Quirks.*

Sources[92]

DUNN AND DUNN LEARNING STYLES

Certification Available: no
Certification Required: no
Assessments: yes (LSI)
Proprietary: no
Client: individuals
Cost: not applicable
Category: learning/development

Developed in the 1970s by Dr. Rita Dunn and Dr. Kenneth Dunn, the Dunn and Dunn Learning Styles model provides a framework for examining student learning preferences across five domains. The model encourages teachers to identify a learner's preferences in each domain, thereby allowing the teacher to tailor their instructional approach to better resonate with the student.

Environmental: This domain pertains to the physical learning environment. This includes traditional classrooms, auditoriums, and breakout rooms, or in the case of real-world practical exercises, the setting where students will apply their learning. Factors to consider within this domain include noise level, lighting, temperature, safety, privacy, space, and seating.

Emotional: This domain focuses on the student's motivation to learn, their tendency for task persistence (i.e., ability to see things through), and their willingness to conform to the learning task (i.e., receptivity to authority/taking direction).

Another component involves the student's learning structure preferences (i.e., do they want to receive detailed instructions or would they prefer to do the work with minimal direction). In other words, does the student prefer a lot of oversight, or will they assume personal responsibility for learning?

Sociological: This domain refers to the student's preference for learning by themselves or with others. Possible constructs within this domain include self-guided learning, pair-based learning, learning with peers or a team, learning from an authority figure, or a combination of these options.

Physiological: This domain applies to the student's sensory preference for information intake. This includes auditory, visual, tactile, or kinesthetic learning (e.g., hearing, seeing, touching, or doing). Other components of this domain include the learner's preferences for learning during a specific time of day and their predilection for static or kinetic learning (i.e., learning while still or moving).

Psychological: This domain focuses on the student's preference for receiving and processing information. Does the student prefer an analytical approach where the instructor provides focused details first, followed by the concept, or do they prefer to see the global concept first, followed by the details? Does the student prefer to take time to process and reflect on the information or are they impulsive and want to move on quickly?

Dunn and Dunn developed their model based on a review of 80 years of research data. Their effort led them to better understand student learning styles, which they define as "the way students begin to concentrate on, process, internalize, and remember new and difficult information."

Though Dunn and Dunn Learning Styles focuses on adolescent learning, the fundamental concepts have broad application in coaching. Understanding a client's preferences for learning and processing new information can help the coach develop meaningful approaches that resonate with the client.

In addition to their original work, Rita Dunn also studied learning styles across five subcultures within the United States. Her work on this topic features in the 1995 book, *Multiculturalism and Learning Style: Teaching and Counseling Adolescents*, co-authored by Shirley A. Griggs.

Dunn and Dunn Learning Styles is more complex than presented here. The framework includes an assessment called the Learning Styles Inventory (LSI).

Professionals seeking additional information will find many books written on the subject, including Rita Dunn and Shirley A. Griggs' 2000 book, *Practical Approaches to Using Learning Styles in Higher Education*.

Sources[93]

EDMONDSON'S THEORY OF TEAMING

> **Certification Available:** no
> **Certification Required:** no
> **Assessments:** no
> **Proprietary:** no
> **Client:** groups, teams
> **Cost:** not applicable
> **Category:** teaming

Developed by organizational psychologist and Harvard Business School professor Amy C. Edmondson, her Theory of Teaming identifies three pillars (or characteristics) necessary for individuals to effectively engage in teaming.

Curiosity: This pillar involves an individual's genuine curiosity about the skills and competencies of other members assigned to the project. This characteristic also includes an individual's desire to learn more about other members of the collective and understand what strengths they bring to the project.

Passion: The second pillar involves the individual's level of interest in the project. A deep passion for the project will drive quality and enthusiasm for the effort.

Empathy: The third pillar pertains to an individual's ability to understand other people's perspectives. Within this context, empathy is critical to fostering collaboration during periods of intense pressure.

Fundamental to Edmondson's Theory of Teaming is the belief that team and teaming are not one and the same. Edmondson reasons that teaming is a dynamic activity (action), not a bounded static entity (team).

Furthermore, the theory advocates a mindset shift from the noun (team) to the verb (teaming). Thus, teaming includes the characteristics an individual develops which enable them to work collaboratively with others across multiple proj-ects and groups at the spur of the moment. Edmondson describes it this way: "Teaming is teamwork on the fly."

The Theory of Teaming further suggests that the traditional idea of static teams is not universally applicable in today's dynamic and global business environment. Citing the need for employees to be able to work on different projects, with different groups of individuals, with disparate functions, in dynamic circumstances, she advocates teaming as a more appropriate solution.

Edmondson's work suggests that traditional static teams are ill-suited for environments with high staffing turnover, or in circumstances where team membership is part-time, the project is temporary, or members work in geographically separate areas.

In traditional static teams, individuals have time and opportunity to learn how to work together, to learn each other's strengths and skills. In teaming, individuals do not have such opportunities and must be able to function quickly and efficiently.

This theory may help clients who find themselves part of multiple teams and struggle to integrate meaningfully in each one. Coaches may use the theory with leadership-level clients who want to better understand how their leadership style may impact their employees' ability to engage in meaningful teaming activities.

To facilitate the use of her theory with leaders, Edmondson incorporates leadership perspectives into her theory. For example, the Theory of Teaming encourages leaders to be aware of how they model behavior by asking questions, actively listening, and showing enthusiasm for the team's efforts.

When applied effectively, professionals using Edmondson's Theory of Teaming observed some of the following results:

- Increased employee engagement
- Increased sense of accomplishment
- Increased sense of growth
- Enhanced peer relationships

Though formal training in Edmondson's Theory of Teaming does not currently exist, professionals seeking additional information will find much written on the topic, including Edmondson's 2012 book, *Teaming: How Organizations Learn, Innovate, and Compete in the Knowledge Economy.*

Sources[94]

EFFORT-REWARD IMBALANCE MODEL

Certification Available: no
Certification Required: no
Assessments: yes (ERI Questionnaire)
Proprietary: no
Client: individuals
Cost: not applicable
Category: emp. engagement, stress management

Developed in 1986 by professor of medical sociology Johannes Siegrist, the Effort-Reward Imbalance Model explores the relationship between an employee's level of effort performing their job and the rewards they receive from the job. To better understand the effort vs. reward dichotomy, we offer the following distinctions.

Effort: This pertains to all the costs and requirements associated with performing the job. Two distinct perspectives exist within this domain: external (job) and internal (employee).

• External: These are the costs of the job itself. They include the demands of the position, the level of responsibility placed on the employee doing the job, the pressure to work a certain number of hours, and environmental factors like working conditions and cultural atmosphere.

• Internal: These are the personal sacrifices made when doing the job. They include the employee's motivational level, which may lead to an overcommitment, and the individual's capacity to cope with obstacles in performing the job and their ability to adapt to their environment. Other internal factors within this domain include the individual's self-efficacy and self-esteem.

Reward: This pertains to the benefits that result from doing the job. Two forms of rewards exist within this domain: extrinsic (tangible rewards) and intrinsic (intangible rewards).

• Extrinsic: These are tangible and explicit rewards that include pay, bonuses, time off, health benefits, and other forms of compensation.

• Intrinsic: These are intangible and subjective rewards that include job satisfaction, job security, stability, safe work environment, personal satisfaction and fulfillment, and developmental opportunities.

The ERI Model suggests that work-related stress occurs when there is an imbalance between effort and reward. The lack of reciprocity between the effort an employee provides and the rewards they receive in response to that effort can lead to lower employee engagement.

ERI further suggests that when an employee's effort is greater than the reward they receive, the resulting stress can also lead to health and performance issues for the employee.

Effort-Reward Imbalance Model (ERI) is among the most influential job stress models in the field of occupational health psychology. ERI is a popular framework used in the analysis of job stress and employee engagement.

Several ERI-based studies (2013) revealed that an imbalance between effort and reward may also lead to workplace bullying. This suggests that individuals experiencing an effort/reward imbalance are at risk of increasing their vulnerability to bullying by engaging in socially harmful behavior, thereby eliciting negative responses from others.

ERI, along with the *Job Demands-Control Model (JD-C)* and the *Job Demands-Resources Model (JD-R)* make up three of the most popular frameworks for exploring occupational stress, with each model adopting a slightly different perspective on the causes of workplace stress.

The Effort-Reward Imbalance Model includes a self-report style assessment called the ERI Questionnaire, which measures the effort-reward balance from the individual employee's perspective.

Professionals seeking additional information on the Effort-Reward Imbalance Model will find much written on the topic, including Siegrist's 2016 book, *Work Stress and Health in a Globalized Economy.*

Sources[95]

EGO DEVELOPMENT THEORY

> **Certification Available:** no
> **Certification Required:** no (yes, for assessments)
> **Assessments:** yes (multiple)
> **Proprietary:** no
> **Client:** individuals
> **Cost:** not applicable
> **Category:** learning/development, self-actualization

The origins of Ego Development Theory (EDT) date to the early 1900s; however, the theory did not gain popularity until the work of noted psychologist Jane Loevinger in the 1960s. EDT consists of nine stages which describe the developmental process of an individual's interaction with and attempt to make meaning of the world around them. Though often presented in terms of the human life cycle (i.e., infancy, childhood, adolescence, etc.), we present the theory as it might apply to adults.

Stage 1—Pre-social (E1): This stage represents infancy, during which time the child has little ego. Because infants cannot perform the sentence completion assessment associated with Ego Development Theory, many articles will omit this stage.

Stage 2—Impulsive (E2): In this stage, people tend to see the world in binary terms, often judging the world by how it affects them. Driven by a need to satisfy urges (emotions), they often judge the world as good or bad based on whether the world satisfies their needs.

Stage 3—Self-protective (E3): In this stage, individuals possess a basic level of self-control but still strive to satisfy needs, often taking risks so long as they can avoid detection. Adults in E3 often engage in hedonistic and opportunistic behavior.

Stage 4—Conformist (E4): In this stage, individuals begin associating with groups based on a preferential bias. In other words, they join groups that look like them, believe like them, or behave like them. It is during this phase of development when concepts like social identity and norms apply.

Stage 5—Self-aware (E5): In this stage, individuals engage in self-critique. Those in E5 begin to distinguish between their real self and the self that society or the group expects.

Stage 6—Conscientiousness (E6): In this stage, individuals consider the consequences of their behavior on others. They do not just feel bad for violating rules, but for causing another person pain. They will acknowledge rules but also recognize special circumstances which may justify deviations from the rules.

Stage 7—Individualistic (E7): In this stage, individuals develop respect for individuality and the differences between individuals.

Stage 8—Autonomous (E8): In this stage, individuals strive for self-fulfillment over external achievements. Those in E8 possess the ability to embrace the polarities of life and respect the autonomy of others.

Stage 9—Integrated (E9): This is the self-actualization stage. Those in E9 possess deep wisdom, empathy, and an acceptance of others.

Loevinger's model is linear, suggesting people cannot jump stages. However, some variations of EDT argue that people can skip stages.

To facilitate her research, Loevinger developed a sentence-completion-style assessment to gather data. To this day, many assessments based on Ego Development Theory use a similar sentence-completion-style format, like the Leadership Maturity Profile (MAP).

Professionals may notice similarities between EDT and psychologist Susanne Cook-Greuter's *Leadership Maturity Framework (LMF)*. The LMF provides a robust expansion of EDT, one that focuses more on the adult perspective of ego development.

Professionals seeking additional information on Ego Development Theory may consider Loevinger's 1976 book, *Ego Development*. Readers may also consider Cook-Greuter's published dissertation from 1999, *Postautonomous Ego Development: A Study of Its Nature and Measurement*.

Sources[96]

EI ABILITY MODEL (MAYER, SALOVEY, CARUSO)

Certification Available: yes (multiple vendors)
Certification Required: no (yes, for assessment)
Assessments: yes (MSCEIT)
Proprietary: no
Client: individuals
Cost: $1,100–$2,500 (multiple vendors)
Category: emotional intelligence

Developed in the 1990s by John D. Mayer, Peter Salovey, and David R. Caruso, the Emotional Intelligence Ability Model defines emotional intelligence as "the ability to monitor and regulate one's own and others' feelings, and to use feelings to guide thought and action."

The EI Ability Model consists of four branches which present emotional intelligence as a mental ability.

Perceiving emotion: This branch involves an individual's ability to perceive and identify emotions, internally and externally. From an internal perspective, this pertains to a person's ability to recognize their own feelings, especially as they experience them.

Externally, this relates to an individual's ability to perceive and identify the emotions of other people by observing nonverbal indicators like facial expressions and body language. This also includes observation of verbal indicators like the voice, tone, and inflection.

Using emotion: This branch focuses on the individual's ability to use emotion or their awareness of emotion to influence and inform decision-making. This includes recognizing the relationship between emotions and moods and developing an understanding of the relationship between feelings and actions.

Understanding emotions: This branch pertains to an individual's ability to understand a broad range of emotions, analyze the presence of emotions in self and others to determine patterns and trends, and the ability to discriminate between different types of emotions, moods, and their causes.

Managing emotions: This branch involves a person's ability to regulate the effect emotions have on them. This includes possessing an appreciation for the value of emotions, both positive and negative, in our life. Developing enhanced abilities within this branch includes being able to influence the emotions and feelings of others.

The EI Ability Model suggests that information originating from our perceived understanding of emotion, coupled with our ability to manage emotion, can facilitate our thinking and guide our decision-making. This intimates that we have some capacity to reason about emotions and can use those emotions to affect decision-making.

The EI Ability Model has evolved since its introduction in the 1990s, which means coaches may encounter older versions which use different labels and list different components. The earliest version consisted of 16 components; the newest version developed in 2016 reflects 26 components.

Measuring EQ within the EI Ability Model construct requires the Mayer-Salovey-Caruso Emotional Intelligence Test (MSCEIT). Many classify the MSCEIT as a performance-based assessment; this means the instrument presents scenarios and the client must answer how they, or the person in the scenario, would feel or react.

Like all EI frameworks, some call into question the validity and efficacy of both the EI Ability Model and the MSCEIT. Despite these concerns, both remain widely used.

Formal training in the model only comes from certification in the MSCEIT assessment. Multiple vendors offer MSCEIT certification at different price points.

Professionals seeking depth of knowledge in the Mayer-Salovey-Caruso Emotional Intelligence Test and the EI Ability Model may consider Salovey and Mayer's 2004 book, *Emotional Intelligence: Key Readings on the Mayer and Salovey Model*, co-authored with Marc A. Brackett.

Sources[97]

EI COMPETENCIES MODEL (BAR-ON)

Certification Available: yes (multiple vendors)
Certification Required: yes
Assessments: yes (EQ-i and EQ-i 360)
Proprietary: no
Client: individuals
Cost: $1,600–$2,300 (multiple vendors)
Category: emotional intelligence

Developed in the mid-1980s by psychologist Reuven Bar-On, the EI Competencies Model, also known as the Bar-On Model, describes emotional intelligence as a behavior. The framework consists of five scales which explore the individual's ability to adapt and use emotional intelligence. Each domain contains three competencies or subscales.

Self-perception: This scale pertains to how well individuals know themselves.

- Self-regard: respecting oneself while recognizing one's strengths and weaknesses.

- Self-actualization: willingness to persistently improve oneself.

- Emotional self-awareness: recognizing and understanding one's own emotions.

Self-expression: This scale focuses on an individual's ability to present in an effective manner.

- Emotional expression: openly expressing feelings, verbally and nonverbally.

- Assertiveness: defending one's thoughts, feelings, and beliefs in a nonoffensive and respectful manner.

- Independence: the ability for self-direction and freedom from dependencies.

Interpersonal: This scale involves an individual's ability to form and manage meaningful relationships.

- Interpersonal relationships: the ability to develop and maintain healthy relationships.

- Empathy: the ability to recognize, understand, and appreciate how others feel.

- Social responsibility: the willingness to contribute to the greater community and act responsibly.

Decision-making: this scale pertains to an individual's ability to apply emotional intelligence in decision-making.

- Problem-solving: the ability to solve problems involving emotions.

- Reality testing: the ability to maintain perspective in the presence of intense emotions.

- Impulse control: the ability to resist impulses.

Stress management: The fifth scale involves an individual's resiliency.

- Flexibility: the ability to adapt to dynamic and unpredictable circumstances.

- Stress tolerance: the ability to cope with difficult situations.

- Optimism: the ability to maintain a positive outlook in the face of adversity.

The EI Competencies Model defines emotional intelligence as a system of interconnected behaviors that arise from emotional and social competencies. The model derives much of its influence from Charles Darwin, who studied the role of emotional expression in survival and adaptation. Therefore, this model views emotionally and socially intelligent behaviors in Darwinian terms of effective adaptation.

Measuring EQ within the EI Competencies Model construct requires the Emotional Quotient Inventory (EQ-i). Professionals seeking depth of knowledge in the model may consider Bar-On's 2000 book, *The Handbook of Emotional Intelligence*, co-edited by J. D. A. Parker. Additionally, multiple vendors offer certification in the EQ-i assessment.

Sources[98]

EI PERFORMANCE MODEL (GOLEMAN)

Certification Available: yes
Certification Required: yes
Assessments: yes (ESCI, PSI, MDBP)
Proprietary: no
Client: individuals
Cost: $1,800
Category: emotional intelligence

Developed in 1995 by psychologist Daniel Goleman, the EI Performance Model defines emotional intelligence as "the capacity for recognizing our own feelings and those of others, for motivating ourselves, and for managing emotions well in ourselves and in our relationships."

The EI Performance Model provides a framework consisting of four domains and twelve subscales or competencies. The model describes emotional intelligence as a set of learned skills or competencies.

Self-awareness: how well individuals know themselves.

- Emotional self-awareness: the ability to know one's own emotions and tendencies.

Self-management: how well individuals can control themselves.

- Emotional self-control: the ability to regulate and manage one's own emotions.

- Adaptability: the ability to emotionally adapt to dynamic circumstances.

- Achievement orientation: the ability to strive for self-improvement.

- Positive outlook: the ability to maintain an optimistic perspective in the face of adversity.

Social awareness: how well an individual knows other people and the social world.

- Empathy: the ability to understand the emotional makeup of other people.

- Organizational awareness: the ability to recognize the emotional and political realities of groups.

Relationship management: how well an individual maintains healthy relationships.

- Influence: the ability to manage emotions in other people.

- Coach and mentor: the ability to guide and help others.

- Conflict management: the ability to identify and resolve conflict.

- Teamwork: the ability to collaborate in diverse groups.

- Inspirational leadership: the ability to inspire others to work together toward a common goal.

Though the EI Performance Model is among the most widely used emotional intelligence frameworks in the world, coaches may encounter alternative or hybrid variations of Goleman's model, like the Mixed Model of Emotional Intelligence or Travis Bradberry's EI 2.0. These variations may use different labels or present a different structure; however, fundamentally they are the same.

Measuring EQ within the EI Performance Model construct requires the Emotional and Social Competency Inventory (ESCI). Additional assessments associated with Goleman's model include the Personal Sustainability Index (PSI) and the Motivational Drivers and Behavioral Preferences (MDBP) assessment. Certification in the EI Performance Model, ESCI, PSI, and MDBP is available only from Korn Ferry.

Professionals seeking additional information on the EI Performance Model may consider Daniel Goleman's 1995 book, *Emotional Intelligence: Why It Can Matter More Than IQ*, and his 2006 book, *Social Intelligence: The New Science of Human Relationships*.

Sources[99]

EI TRAIT MODEL (PETRIDES)

> **Certification Available:** no (yes, for assessment)
> **Certification Required:** yes
> **Assessments:** yes (TEIQue)
> **Proprietary:** no
> **Client:** individuals
> **Cost:** pricing not available
> **Category:** emotional intelligence

Developed in 2009 by psychologist Konstantinos V. Petrides, the EI Trait Model defines emotional intelligence as "a theoretical framework that integrates emotions, personality traits, and intelligence, broadly defined."

The EI Trait Model consists of four domains and 15 facets which describe emotional intelligence as a personality trait that influences an individual's perception of their emotional abilities.

Well-being: how an individual feels about their self and their life. A person's well-being is associated with their level of job satisfaction, mood, and somatic feeling.

- Happiness: how a person feels about the present.

- Optimism: how a person feels about the future.

- Self-esteem: how a person feels about their self.

Self-control: how well an individual can regulate their desires and urges.

- Emotional regulation: the ability to control one's feelings and emotional state.

- Impulse control: the ability to think before acting.

- Stress management: the ability to manage stress using emotional control and coping mechanisms.

Emotionality: how in touch a person is with their own emotions and those of others.

- Emotional management: the ability to manage other people's emotional states.

- Assertiveness: the ability to engage others in a forthright and frank way.

- Social awareness: the ability to "read" the social environment and adapt social skills accordingly.

Sociability: how an individual forms and maintains social relationships and influence.

- Empathy: the ability to see the world from someone else's point of view.

- Emotional perception: the ability to recognize one's own emotional state and that of others.

- Emotional expression: the ability to express one's feelings accurately and effectively.

- Relationships: the ability to form and maintain relationships.

There are two facets that apply across all four domains.

- Adaptability: the ability to adapt to new and changing environments.

- Motivation: the ability to strive and achieve.

Recent studies compared the EI Trait Model to the *Five-Factor Model of Personality* and identified several correlations between the two frameworks. For example, high scores in the relationships facet (EI Trait Model) correlate positively with the facets of Agreeableness and Openness (Five-Factor Model of Personality).

Measuring EQ within the EI Trait Model construct requires the Trait Emotional Intelligence Questionnaire (TEIQue). Formal use of Petrides' model and assessment requires training and certification from Petrides' company, TraitEI.

Professionals seeking additional information will find much written on the EI Trait Model, including Petrides' 2010 *Industrial and Organizational Psychology* article, "Trait Emotional Intelligence Theory."

Sources[100]

ELABORATION LIKELIHOOD MODEL

Certification Available: no
Certification Required: no
Assessments: no
Proprietary: no
Client: individuals
Cost: not applicable
Category: influence, comm., decision-making

Developed in the 1980s by psychologists Richard E. Petty and John T. Cacioppo, the Elaboration Likelihood Model (ELM) provides a framework for exploring the effect of persuasion on individual attitudes and beliefs, specifically on how much effort a person uses to process an external stimulus like messaging.

ELM suggests that when an individual receives an external stimulus like a message, they process the message through one of two channels. Each channel requires a different level of effort to fully process the message.

Central route: This channel requires the greatest effort because the individual gives careful thought and consideration to the message. Called the high-level process of elaboration, individuals using the central route apply a methodical approach to their examination of the message.

There are two prerequisites necessary for central route processing to take place. The first is motivation; the recipient of the message must care about the issue enough to seek elaboration. In other words, if the recipient does not care about the issue, they may lack the motivation to elaborate on the message and thereby move to the peripheral route.

Second, they must possess the ability to process the message. This depends on the individual's cognitive ability. However, external factors may impede a person's cognitive ability to process the message. For example, a person distracted by significant life events may lack the ability to process the message and thereby move to the peripheral route.

Peripheral route: This channel requires the least amount of effort because the individual defaults to heuristics, emotions, or the path of least resistance. Called the low-level process of elaboration, the individual abdicates responsibility for critical thought in favor of what is easiest and requires the least time and energy.

The peripheral route often sees the strength of the message giving way to more subjective or superficial factors. For example, instead of comparing products and researching customer reviews (central route), a person buys a product simply because their favorite celebrity endorses it (peripheral route).

ELM suggests a person may use the central route on some issues and the peripheral for others. Factors that influence which path an individual chooses can include the importance of the product, the cost, and their level of interest. For example, a passionate car enthusiast buying an expensive car may use the central route when processing the salesperson's statements. They will examine every detail to make an informed decision. But the same consumer may use the peripheral route when buying a new computer. A lack of time or motivation to research memory, speed, storage capacity, and processing power may lead the consumer to buy the first computer the salesperson recommends.

Research into ELM revealed that attitude changes resulting from central route processing will have a different effect on the individual than those resulting from the peripheral route. Additionally, research shows that change resulting from the central route will have greater temporal persistence (i.e., will last longer) than those from the peripheral route.

ELM is useful in understanding how messaging can influence individuals to change their attitude about something (e.g., service, product, issue). Other models that provide insight into this relationship include the *Heuristic-Systematic Model of Information Processing* and *Dual Process Theory*.

ELM is more complex than presented here. Professionals seeking additional information will find much written on ELM, including Petty's 1981 book, *Attitudes and Persuasion: Classic and Contemporary Approaches*.

Sources[101]

EMOTIONAL INTELLIGENCE (GENERAL ENTRY)

> **Category:** emotional intelligence

Modern emotional intelligence (EI) emerged in the latter part of the 20th century, and its evolution is based on contributions from scholars like Peter Salovey, John Mayer, Daniel Goleman, Travis Bradberry, Reuven Bar-On, Konstantinos V. Petrides, and many others.

Prior to the formal establishment of emotional intelligence as a structured concept, many sources credit a variety of early scholars for laying the foundation of emotional intelligence, including Charles Darwin, E. L. Thorndike, and Howard Gardner.

While so many academics advanced our understanding of emotional intelligence, this also led to the development of multiple models which provide different frameworks and use different definitions and labels. As a result, there is no universally accepted definition of EI.

Though debate continues to surround the impact of EI on individual success, emotional intelligence remains a popular and widely used concept. Advocates claim EI is highly important to leadership development as it fosters an individual's understanding of self and others.

The components and how they are labeled vary from one EI framework to another; however, every major model of EI includes the concept of self-awareness, a component universally attributed to effective leadership.

Every year, new studies and articles add to our understanding of EI. Despite the abundant research, there remains a great deal we do not know about EI and its potential correlations. For example, debate continues (as do the studies) regarding the relationship between emotional intelligence and cognitive intelligence as predictors of success.

Other frequently asked questions: Do emotional and cognitive intelligence complement or compensate each other? What role does emotional intelligence play for people facing tasks that exceed their cognitive capabilities? To date, studies offer mixed findings, leaving few definitive answers. However, each study nudges the needle of understanding just enough to help us consider and apply EI in ever more meaningful ways.

There are a variety of emotional intelligence models available, each adopting a different perspective on the concept. The four most popular EI models and their perspectives are:

- EI Ability Model: EI is a mental ability.

- EI Competencies Model: EI is a behavior.

- EI Performance Model: EI is a learned skill.

- EI Trait Model: EI is a personality trait.

What constitutes the better model is subjective, as each model has its own strengths and limitations. All four models enjoy widespread use in coaching, facilitation, and consulting. Until research indicates otherwise, professionals will have to make their own judgments on which model and assessment is best for them and their client.

Many use the abbreviation EI interchangeably with the abbreviation EQ (emotional quotient). For the purposes of this desk reference, we do not. We offer the following distinction between EI and EQ. EI refers to the model (theory) of emotional intelligence. EQ refers to the measurement of an individual's emotional intelligence, much like a person's cognitive intelligence measurement is their IQ. We consider EQ the outcome of an EI assessment instrument.

For example, Daniel Goleman's Performance Model is EI. A person's outcome using Goleman's ESCI assessment is their EQ.

Professionals looking to incorporate emotional intelligence into their practice should thoroughly research the models and assessments available to determine the best fit.

Sources[102]

ENNEAGRAM OF PERSONALITY

Certification Available: yes (multiple vendors)
Certification Required: yes
Assessments: yes (RHETI, IVQ)
Proprietary: no
Client: individuals
Cost: $1,700–$2,900
Category: personality, learning/development

Developed in the 1960s by philosopher Oscar Ichazo, the Enneagram of Personality provides a framework for characterizing an individual's personality into one of nine types.

Type 1 (The Reformer): This person is principled, purposeful, self-controlled.

Type 2 (The Helper): This person is demonstrative, generous, people-pleasing.

Type 3 (The Achiever): This person is adaptive, excelling, driven.

Type 4 (The Individualist): This person is expressive, dramatic, self-absorbed.

Type 5 (The Investigator): This person is perceptive, innovative, secretive.

Type 6 (The Loyalist): This person is engaging, responsible, anxious.

Type 7 (The Enthusiast). This person is spontaneous, versatile, distractible.

Type 8 (The Challenger): This person is self-confident, decisive, willful.

Type 9 (The Peacemaker): This person is receptive, reassuring, agreeable.

The nine personality types organize into three groupings called **Centers**. The three Centers are **Instinctive**, **Thinking**, and **Feeling** (sometimes referred to as the heart, the head, and the body). Each Center contains a dominant emotion which further characterizes the individual.

Visually, the Enneagram uses a nine-point star to represent the personality types, with the Centers reflected in the middle of the star. According to the theory, the personality types adjacent to a person's position on the star may influence the characteristics of their personality. The model calls these adjacent positions the **Wings**.

In addition to providing a model for typing individual personality, the Enneagram also characterizes the strategies by which the human psyche develops and establishes a worldview. This includes how individuals cope with their environment, how they adapt to challenges, and what motivations drive their behaviors.

Though widely used, the Enneagram is not without controversy. Many scientists claim there is insufficient testing to validate the diagnostic efficacy of the model. As a result, numerous clinical and evidence-based psychologists reject the model and its assessment.

Despite this controversy, Enneagram's popularity continues to grow within coaching and organizational psychology because of its ability to function as a conduit for self-awareness and self-exploration.

The exact origin of the Enneagram is difficult to ascertain, though some sources claim the theory originated in Asia and was subsequently brought to South America by Ichazo.

The Enneagram of Personality is significantly more complex than presented here and includes several assessments, like the Riso-Hudson Enneagram Type Indicator (RHETI).

Incorporating the Enneagram into practice and use of the RHETI requires certification offered by multiple vendors at different price points.

Professionals seeking additional information will find much written on the Enneagram, including Adelaida Harrison's 2020 book, *The Neuroscience Behind the Enneagram: How Changing Yourself … Changes Everything.* Another popular reference is Riso and Hudson's 1999 book, *The Wisdom of the Enneagram: The Complete Guide to Psychological and Spiritual Growth for the Nine Personality Types.*

Sources[103]

EQUITY THEORY OF MOTIVATION

Certification Available: no
Certification Required: no
Assessments: no
Proprietary: no
Client: individuals
Cost: not applicable
Category: motivation, employee engagement

Developed in 1963 by workplace and behavioral psychologist John Stacey Adams, Equity Theory of Motivation provides a framework for exploring individual motivation based on the idea that fairness is at the core of employee motivation.

Adams' framework consists of three components (inputs, outputs, and referent groups) which help professionals explore the motivations and engagement levels of employees. The first two components (inputs and outputs) explore the employee's perceived balance between effort and reward, while the third component (referent groups) examines the multiple ways a person compares and evaluates their input/output for fairness.

Inputs: This component focuses on the actions and behaviors the employee (or client) performs so they may receive a desired output.

Examples of inputs include the number of hours worked, the number of products developed, the number of personal sacrifices made, the sense of loyalty to the firm, doing more than asked, and much more.

Outputs: This component applies to the results which stem from the employee's inputs. Sometimes called outcomes, these pertain to the rewards employees receive for their effort.

Examples of outputs include a person's salary, bonuses, perks, time off, promotions, and much more.

Referent groups: This component involves the various lenses a person may use to make comparisons of their experiences (i.e., inputs/outputs) to determine fairness and equity.

Categorically, Adams identified four types of referent groups.

- Self-inside: This lens involves the client comparing their recent experiences to other experiences they had within their current organization.

- Self-outside: This lens involves the client comparing their recent experiences to the experiences they had in other organizations.

- Others-inside: This lens involves the client comparing their recent experiences to people within their current organization.

- Others-outside: This lens involves the client comparing their recent experiences to people outside their current organization.

Adams' Theory of Motivation, also known as Adams' Equity Theory, suggests if an individual perceives their situation as fair, their motivation increases. Conversely, if the individual perceives their situation as unfair, they become less motivated and may even seek to adjust their performance to achieve the balance (or fairness) they desire.

Research into Adams' theory indicates that individuals who perceive a lack of equity will react in different ways. Some will decrease the quality and volume of work (i.e., a decrease in employee engagement), some will feel distressed, and others will experience significant anger or grief. The bottom line: Inequity leads to lower employee engagement, lower morale, and lower motivation.

Adams' Theory of Motivation is a useful framework with leadership-level clients struggling with employee engagement or employee motivation.

Adams' Equity Theory of Motivation does not require certification or specialized training. Professionals seeking additional information will find much written on Adams' Theory of Motivation.

Sources[104]

EXISTENCE, RELATEDNESS, AND GROWTH THEORY

Certification Available: no
Certification Required: no
Assessments: no
Proprietary: no
Client: individuals
Cost: not applicable
Category: motivation, employee engagement

Developed in 1969 by psychologist Clayton Alderfer, the Existence, Relatedness, and Growth Theory (ERG) provides a framework for understanding individual needs and motivations. Based on *Maslow's Hierarchy of Needs*, ERG reorganizes the five levels Maslow identified into three groups.

Group 1—Existence needs: This grouping refers to an individual's physical needs. These include shelter, food, and water. From the professional perspective, they include secure employment, health insurance, and more.

Group 2—Relatedness needs: This group pertains to an individual's sense of belonging, which includes their relationships to coworkers, the maintenance of meaningful friendships, and the quality of their family connections. Relatedness applies beyond the social realm and includes the relationship people have with themselves.

Group 3—Growth needs: This grouping refers to an individual's intrinsic motivation for personal development, which includes opportunities for training, experiential learning, and professional skills development. Needs within this category foster self-actualization and self-esteem.

In addition to restructuring Maslow's work, Alderfer presents a distinctly different take on motivation from Maslow. Where Maslow presents hierarchy as a strictly linear or static framework (i.e., the order of needs does not change), ERG Theory suggests that once satisfied, the order of the hierarchy shifts accordingly.

Maslow's theory states that before satisfying a higher-level need, a person must first satisfy their base needs. ERG says this is not the case; individuals may elect to pursue higher-level needs over more fundamental needs. Alderfer observed many instances of individuals who sacrificed a base need (e.g., an actor in need of buying food or paying rent) in favor of a higher-level need (e.g., spending the money to attend an acting school).

These can provide rich grounds for exploration with the client and include discourse on the client's distinctions between needs and wants, as well as the role of pragmatics in their decision-making process.

During his research, Alderfer observed that a person's life view and personal preferences can impact the prioritization of their needs. As one's view of life changes, or as their preferences evolve, so will their priority of needs.

ERG Theory research focusing on the workplace revealed that employees typically have multiple needs at all levels. If managers neglect one or two levels by focusing on a single level, they risk failing to effectively motivate an employee. Leaders seeking to improve employee engagement and motivation should develop an awareness of each employee's "blend of needs" to best support them.

Accompanying ERG is a concept called the **Frustration-Regression Principle**. This phenomenon occurs when an employee's higher-level needs are not satisfied. For example, an employee not afforded personal development opportunities may become frustrated (consciously or subconsciously) and turn their focus and energy to their relatedness needs, thereby socializing more at work.

Professionals seeking additional information on ERG may consider Alderfer's 1969 article, "An Empirical Test of a New Theory of Human Needs."

Sources[105]

EXPECTANCY THEORY OF MOTIVATION

```
Certification Available: no
Certification Required: no
Assessments: no
Proprietary: no
Client: individuals
Cost: not applicable
Category: motivation
```

Developed in 1964 by Yale Business School professor Victor H. Vroom, Expectancy Theory is a theory of motivation that states an individual's choice of behaviors is based on what will result in the most desirable outcome. In 1968, professors Edward Lawler and Lyman Porter joined Vroom to further develop the theory.

Expectancy Theory identifies three variables that help explain individual motivation. The order of variables differs from source to source, suggesting there is no formal sequence.

Valence (V): This variable represents the significance an individual assigns to the reward. This valuation is based on the individual's needs, desires, values, and goals.

The valence variable includes both extrinsic and intrinsic rewards. This means a person may hold an emotional connection to the reward. Leaders seeking to include this variable in their leadership style should know the motivations of each employee.

Expectancy (E): This variable represents the individual's beliefs regarding the relationship between their effort and their resulting performance. Put another way, does the individual believe that putting forth increased effort will result in increased performance?

A principle fundamental to the expectancy variable is self-efficacy (i.e., the client's belief that they possess the necessary skills to succeed). Factors that influence an individual's sense of self-efficacy include past experiences, current confidence level, and the availability of relevant resources to support them. Clients considering the issue of self-efficacy often ask the question, "Can I do this?"

Instrumentality (I): This variable represents the individual's belief that meeting their performance goals will result in the expected outcome or reward. Clients exploring the issue of instrumentality often ask the question, "If I accomplish these tasks or perform these behaviors, will I receive this (specific) outcome?"

Facilitating instrumentality requires several considerations, such as the client developing clear goals in advance of the effort. When exploring incentives, it is important that the proposed reward be consistent with the individual's motivational preferences (i.e., intrinsic or extrinsic). For leaders seeking to guide employees within this domain, trust is essential to instrumentality. If the employee does not trust that the leader or organization will make good on their promise of reward, they are not likely to put forth the effort.

Expectancy Theory, therefore, offers a formula which suggests that motivation is a function of valence, expectancy, and instrumentality.

$$M = V * E * I$$

Note that the formula uses multiplication and not addition. This is because the theory suggests that if any variable is zero, then motivation is zero, no matter how large the other variables.

Expectancy Theory of Motivation, unlike other theories of motivation, focuses on the outcome of behavior instead of the individual's needs like *Maslow's Hierarchy of Needs*, *Two-Factor Theory*, and *ERG Theory*. In other words, the theory suggests that a person's motivation derives from how much they desire a specific reward and their belief that they can achieve the reward.

Some sources refer to Vroom's theory as Expectancy Value Theory (EVT), though the term also applies to the work of other researchers like psychologists John Atkinson (1950s), Martin Fishbein (1970s), and Jacquelynne Eccles (1980s).

Professionals seeking additional information on the Expectancy Theory of Motivation will find much written on the topic, including Vroom's 1964 book, *Work and Motivation*.

Sources[106]

EYSENCK'S PEN MODEL

Certification Available: no
Certification Required: no
Assessments: yes (EPI)
Proprietary: yes (EPI)
Client: individuals
Cost: not applicable
Category: personality

Developed in the 1940s by psychologist Hans Eysenck, the PEN Model provides a framework for exploring personality. His work marks one of the first theories to examine the relationship between a person's biology (e.g., brain activity and hormones), environment, and personality. Though Eysenck believed personality is part genetic and part learned, his research focused primarily on the biological aspect, leaving the learned component for others to explore.

The original framework consisted of two dimensions (also called super factors), with a third dimension added in 1976. According to Eysenck, these three broad dimensions collectively form the foundations of an individual's personality.

Psychoticism: The last dimension added to Eysenck's model, this is a person's tendency to engage in irresponsible behavior. The spectrum of psychoticism ranges from harmlessly rejecting social norms on one extreme to criminal behavior on the other.

Though individuals scoring high on psychoticism tend to engage in antisocial behavior, Eysenick discovered that some individuals with high psychoticism scores also possessed more creative abilities.

Extraversion/Introversion: Individuals high on extraversion tend to be more conversational, gregarious, and open. They seek out communal activities, prefer social gatherings, and enjoy being the center of attention.

On the opposite side of the spectrum are those labeled introverts. Individuals high on introversion tend to prefer more solitary activities and experiences that require introspection or contemplation. They tend to avoid social gatherings, though they enjoy the company of close friends.

Neuroticism: This dimension examines a person's emotional stability. Individuals high on neuroticism tend to experience higher levels and greater frequency of stress and anxiety. Constantly worrying, they often see only the negative in a situation or experience.

Individuals low on neuroticism tend to handle stress better, able to cope accordingly. Able to handle crisis and remain calm, they tend to be more tolerant of others and of variables beyond their control.

Eysenck's model is among the first to adopt a biological view of personality, suggesting that much of it derives from genetic inheritance. In fact, the model's associated assessment, the Eysenck Personality Inventory (EPI), provides insight into a person's temperament, an aspect of personality believed by some to be 50% genetic. The EPI is available online.

Eysenck developed his PEN Model as an alternative to the *Five-Factor Model of Personality*, which he perceived as a compilation of muddled theorizing. Both frameworks share the same dimensions of extraversion and neuroticism, and like the Five-Factor Model of Personality, PEN also includes a variety of subtraits. For example, the dimension of extraversion includes the subtraits of sociability and positive affect.

As with most theories, the PEN Model is not without controversy. Some sources question the inclusion of psychoticism as a super factor, claiming that elements of psychoticism measured by the EPI more closely align with neuroticism than psychoticism. Additionally, sources claim that neither the model nor the EPI accurately measures the predisposition to psychotic-like experiences.

Despite these concerns, Eysenck's contributions to exploring personality remain undeniable. Professionals seeking additional information on Eysenck's work may consider his 1947 book, *Dimensions of Personality*, or his 1987 book, *Personality Dimensions and Arousal*, co-authored by Jan Strelau.

Sources[107]

FACTS COACHING MODEL

Certification Available: yes
Certification Required: no
Assessments: no
Proprietary: yes
Client: individuals, groups
Cost: not available
Category: coaching model

Developed in 2012 by executive coaches Ian Day and John Blakey, the FACTS Coaching Model provides a framework designed to engage clients using direct observations, accountability, and tension to effectively challenge clients.

The FACTS Coaching Model is a nonlinear framework consisting of five core elements which enable the coach to push the client in a positive and meaningful way.

Feedback: The first element involves providing the client with direct feedback that is meaningful and useful for the client, even if it involves the coach sharing their own feelings and perceptions. Day and Blakey caution that feedback must come from an intention to help the client develop their self-awareness, and not the coach's ego.

Accountability: The second element focuses on methods the coach may use to hold the client accountable for their actions and encourage them to follow through on their commitment to the coaching process. A potential obstacle when holding clients accountable is doing so without using guilt or shame, or without compromising the coach's neutrality.

Courageous goals: The third component builds upon more traditional goal-setting models like the *SMART Model* by introducing the three elements of **Dream** (what could be), **Share** (who can help), and **Start** (what is the first step). This process helps the client strive for higher and more ambitious goals, ones that require courage.

Tension: The fourth component involves creating a healthy or optimal level of tension for the client, which in turn will foster increased performance. Building tension for the client is challenging, as too much can lead the client to experience anxiety and shut down. Many traditional coaching philosophies eschew the idea of coaches creating tension; instead they advocate creating a safe and comfortable environment for the client. The FACTS approach claims that creating healthy tension and a safe space are not mutually exclusive.

Systems thinking: The final element involves guiding the client to see a bigger picture. This includes expanding their perceptions and exploring how their behavior affects their environment. A systems thinking approach involves adopting new and different perspectives like considering another person's point of view.

To facilitate the positive and productive use of tension, the model also includes the concept of **Zone of Uncomfortable Debate (ZOUD)**. This concept involves building tension and challenging the client even though it may risk rapport and the coaching relationship. In this, Day and Blakey encourage coaches to have the courage to push the client to address the "elephant in the room" when it is appropriate to do so. They recommend entering ZOUD only when the situation demands.

The FACTS Model differs from many coaching theories by encouraging coaches to adopt a more assertive role in the coaching relationship. Day and Blakey argue that clients can benefit from coaches who adopt a more direct and emphatic approach with them. They do stress, however, the importance of balance and timing when confronting a client.

The FACTS Model does not wholly dismiss early coaching philosophies; it simply provides an alternative style to help coaches adopt a more proactive and assertive role with their clients.

Professionals seeking additional information on the FACTS Coaching Model should consider Day and Blakey's 2012 book, *Challenging Coaching: Going Beyond Traditional Coaching to Face the FACTS*. Day and Blakey offer training through their company The Trusted Executive Ltd, accessible through their website, Challenging Coaching.

Sources[108]

FEEDBACK MODELS (GENERAL ENTRY)

Category: feedback

Feedback models are frameworks that facilitate delivery of praise or criticism. This may include sharing one's experiences, observations, perceptions, thoughts, or feelings. The feedback process can provide a pathway for reviewing the results of an individual's assessment or discussing their performance. Delivered effectively, feedback can lead to growth and development.

The Infourge Compendium of Models and Theories reviewed over 30 different feedback models. Many of these frameworks are fundamentally similar, with several adopting synonymous labels to enable the use of creative acronyms. After careful consideration, we determined that due to the similarities between many of these models and to manage the size of this text, we would limit entries in this category to the following 18 feedback models based on the volume of supporting literature and their distinctiveness compared to other models.

- *AID*
- *BEEF*
- *BIF/BIFFOF/BIFF*
- *BOOST*
- *CEDAR*
- *COILED*
- *COIN*
- *DESC*
- *Heron's Six Categories of Intervention*
- *IDEA*
- *OASIS Conversation*
- *Pendleton*
- *Radical Candor*
- *SBI*
- *STAR*
- *Start, Stop, Continue Model*

These models provide a broad range of frameworks to suit a client's specific needs. For example, a leadership-level client lacking awareness of how their feedback lands for others may benefit from *Heron's Six Categories of Intervention*, which examines feedback delivery through a combination of leadership styles and communication styles.

Other examples include the *AID Model* for those seeking a simple framework. Professionals who desire a more methodical approach may prefer the *COILED Model*. For engagements with a high risk of conflict, the *OASIS Model* may prove more appropriate. Clients who struggle to provide honest and direct feedback may benefit from the *Radical Candor Model*.

While exploring the many feedback models, six characteristics appeared repeatedly among these frameworks. The frequency with which these characteristics manifest suggests they are fundamental to delivering effective feedback.

1. Conduct an objective and methodical examination of the event or behavior.

2. Determine the behavior of everyone involved.

3. Make meaning of the event or behaviors.

4. Determine the consequences of the behavior.

5. Apply counterfactual thinking to explore alternative behaviors and consider how these alternative behaviors could have impacted the event.

6. Imagine the consequences of those potential behaviors.

For the sake of transparency with the reader, we list the following feedback models omitted from this edition of the ICMT.

- BROFF
- DESICA
- EEC
- McKinsey's Feedback Model
- PEAR
- Praise Burger (feedback sandwich)
- SIPP
- SKS Model
- SLC
- Stanford Model ("I like, I wish, what if…")
- W3

We encourage professionals to thoroughly explore all available options before selecting the appropriate model for themselves, their clients, and the situation.

FELDER-SILVERMAN LEARNING STYLES

Certification Available: no
Certification Required: no
Assessments: yes (ILS)
Proprietary: no
Client: individuals
Cost: not applicable
Category: learning/development

Developed in 1988 by professor of chemical engineering Richard Felder and educational psychologist Linda Silverman, the Felder-Silverman Learning Styles provides a framework for understanding the learning preferences of students.

The framework consists of four domains which pertain to how we use information. The theory suggests we have a preference within each domain. The combination of these preferences results in a person's learning style.

Domain 1—Accepting Information

• **Sensing**: A learner with this preference favors concrete thinking that focuses on verifiable facts and figures. These learners do not tolerate ambiguous or abstract thinking.

• **Intuitive**: A learner with this preference favors conceptual thinking that gravitates toward theories and meaning-making. These learners are comfortable with abstract ideas.

Domain 2—Presentation of Information

• **Visual**: A learner with this preference favors information presented via charts, graphs, and images. These learners enjoy seeing the information. For this reason, many processes, though codified meticulously, often include a flow chart or visual.

• **Verbal**: A learner with this preference favors information presented via language and oral explanation. These learners relish information obtained through meaningful discourse.

Domain 3—Processing Information

• **Active**: A learner with this preference favors working through problems by doing (i.e., getting their hands dirty). These learners tend to appreciate working in groups or with random partners.

• **Reflective**: A learner with this preference favors thinking through problems before application. These learners tend to prefer working alone or with a trusted (known) partner.

Domain 4—Organizing Information

• **Sequential**: A learner with this preference favors linear thinking. These people approach problems using a methodical and orderly process, often in small incremental steps.

• **Global**: A learner with this preference favors a more holistic approach to learning. They focus on entire systems and consider the larger picture. These learners often move in leaps and bounds.

According to the model, a person possesses preferences in each of the four dimensions. Though individuals may fluctuate between preferences on occasion, over time they will demonstrate a predominant preference.

Though originally focused on identifying the learning preferences of students in science and engineering fields, the model has since found wide-reaching utility across multiple fields of study. Professionals developing curricula may find this model useful to the learning experience.

The Felder-Silverman Learning Styles framework shares similarities to other learning styles included in the ICMT, like *Honey Mumford Learning Styles*. A key differentiator from these other models is that the Felder-Silverman model goes further in helping teachers adapt their instructional methodologies to better resonate with students.

In addition to its broad utility, the Felder-Silverman Learning Styles includes an instrument designed to help identify the user's learning preferences across the four dimensions called the Index of Learning Styles Questionnaire (ILS). The ILS Questionnaire is freely available online from North Carolina State University.

Sources[109]

FIEDLER'S CONTINGENCY THEORY

Certification Available: no
Certification Required: no
Assessments: yes (LPC Scale)
Proprietary: no
Client: individuals
Cost: not applicable
Category: leadership, crisis management

Developed in 1963 by psychologist Fred Fiedler, Fiedler's Contingency Theory explores the relationship between a person's leadership style and the situation. Fiedler's framework consists of two dimensions which help characterize this relationship.

Leadership orientation: This dimension pertains to a person's way of leading and includes their approach to communicating, their temperament, and other characteristics. According to Fiedler, a person's disposition is the main trait that defines their ability to lead.

An examination of this dimension seeks to identify and understand a leader's style along with the strengths and weaknesses associated with that style. Fiedler suggests leadership styles fall into one of two camps.

• Task oriented: This style pertains to leaders who focus on organizing and managing complex projects. They tend to favor a methodical approach to projects and are frequently mindful of metrics, timelines, agendas, and process.

• Relationship oriented: This style pertains to leaders who focus on building and maintaining relationships at work. These leaders tend to be effective at conflict management and are inclusive in their decision-making.

Situational favorableness: This dimension provides a framework for examining the situation, which may include the environment or a crisis. Fiedler suggests that by understanding the situation, senior leaders may select more appropriate leaders for a given situation. To facilitate an assessment of the situation, Fiedler provides three factors to consider.

• Leader-member relations: This pertains to the level of trust and respect people have for their leader. Leaders with high leader-member relations tend to have greater influence within their environment.

• Task structure: This refers to the level of clarity and precision of the tasks, objectives, and goals associated with the situation. The clearer and more well defined the goals and tasks, the better. More ambiguous objectives may require leaders better suited to vague and abstract situations.

• Leader's position power: This pertains to the leader's ability to effectively issue rewards and punishments. Fiedler's theory contends that leaders with minimal position power are at a disadvantage, especially with less experienced or more dependent followers.

Fiedler believed there was a direct correlation between the traits of a leader and their effectiveness as a leader. He asserted that the environment would dictate the traits necessary for success. Consequently, leaders who did not possess those traits were not ideal to lead in that circumstance. Fiedler argued that leadership styles do not change, advocating for the replacement of leaders who proved unfit for a given situation.

Originally called Contingency Trait Theory, then Contingency Management Theory, Fiedler's model is frequently cited as one of the first theories to fall under the umbrella of *Contingency Theories*.

To facilitate the use of Fiedler's Contingency Theory, the model includes an assessment called the Least Preferred Coworker Scale (LPC). This assessment allows users to ascertain a person's leadership orientation and situational favorableness. The LPC is available from multiple vendors, including several free versions.

Fiedler's theory is useful in crisis planning, helping planners identify prospective leaders suitable for crisis management.

Professionals seeking additional information on Fiedler's Contingency Theory may consider Fiedler's 1964 article, "A Contingency Model of Leadership Effectiveness," or his 1967 book, *A Theory of Leadership Effectiveness*.

Sources[110]

FINK'S CRISIS MANAGEMENT MODEL

Certification Available: no
Certification Required: no
Assessments: yes (CIV)
Proprietary: no
Client: organizations
Cost: not applicable
Category: crisis management

Developed in the mid-1980s by communication expert Steven Fink, his Crisis Management Model provides a four-stage framework representing the lifecycle of crisis management.

Stage 1—Prodromal: The first stage in Fink's model, also called the "pre-crisis" stage, takes place between the emergence of crisis indicators and the onset of the crisis. Put another way, this is the time between the first signs of a crisis and the crisis event itself.

During the Prodromal stage, organizational leaders should proactively monitor the environment for signs of a crisis looming on the horizon. For large-scale companies, where it is impractical for leaders to serve this function, it is important to empower a collective within the organization to monitor for these indicators.

Characterized as the proactive stage of Fink's model, individuals tasked with monitoring for early warning signs must act on the earliest indications of a potential crisis. The use of exploratory techniques designed to facilitate creative thinking can help observers recognize ambiguous indicators. These approaches include gaming techniques and red teaming. Crisis managers can use these techniques across an array of potential crisis types (e.g., brand crisis, financial crisis, natural disaster crisis, among many others).

The results of these exploratory and creative techniques will influence the organization's crisis planning and better prepare people for multiple scenarios.

Fink argues that a thorough and thoughtful Prodromal stage can minimize the impact and damage caused by a crisis. This can also lead an organization to adopt a more deliberate decision-making process. Conversely, a superficial Prodromal stage can lead an organization to reactionary decision-making.

Stage 2—Acute: The second stage in Fink's model begins with the onset of the crisis. Also called the "crisis" stage, this is where the organization executes the crisis plan developed during the prodromal stage. During the acute stage, the organization attempts to adapt to the changing environment to mitigate the risks and damage to the organization.

Stage 3—Chronic: The third stage, also called the "cleanup" stage, takes place in the aftermath of the crisis event. Though the crisis event has passed, the consequences may endure for months or years post-event. How the organization handles these long-term (chronic) consequences is essential to successful crisis resolution. Fink argues that a thoughtful crisis management plan should include the consideration of long-term implications stemming from the crisis event.

Stage 4—Resolution: The final stage, also called "post-crisis," takes place following the end of the crisis event. Unlike the chronic stage, which focuses on long-term consequences, the resolution stage seeks to evaluate the organization's performance during the crisis. This involves a thorough after-action review to help the organization improve future crisis planning and preparation.

Fink's Crisis Management Model includes a Prodromal-stage assessment called the Crisis Impact Value (CIV). The CIV assessment facilitates crisis forecasting, allowing professionals to characterize a potential crisis by its impact and probability using a four-quadrant matrix.

Professionals seeking additional information may consider Fink's seminal 1986 book, *Crisis Management: Planning for the Inevitable*. Additionally, Fink's work includes an emphasis on crisis management through communications. For further details, see Fink's 2013 book, *Crisis Communications: The Definitive Guide to Managing the Message*.

Sources[111]

FISHER'S THEORY OF DECISION EMERGENCE

Certification Available: no
Certification Required: no
Assessments: no
Proprietary: no
Client: individuals
Cost: not applicable
Category: teaming, decision-making

Developed in 1970 by professor B. Aubrey Fisher, Decision Emergence Theory is a developmental model describing four phases of group evolution from the perspective of communication and decision-making. Put another way, Fisher's theory focuses on the interaction of team members with an emphasis on how they communicate with one another and make decisions.

Phase 1—Orientation: The first phase of group development involves individuals coming together to form the team. Fisher characterizes phase one communication as minimal and overly polite, though there is some tension as members get to know one another. The initial communication between members is sparse but will increase as members use communication to reduce uncertainty and social tension.

Fisher observed that individuals in the orientation phase will communicate with more ambiguity to avoid conflict and maintain a measure of amity with other members of the team.

Phase 2—Conflict: The second phase takes place once team members acclimate to each other and are ready to discuss the relevant issues and advocate their positions. According to Fisher, it is normal for tensions to rise during this stage and for healthy conflict to occur as debate ensues between individuals of different positions and experiences. He says healthy conflict is important as it can deter "groupthink."

Fisher characterizes phase two communication as persuasive, with individuals shifting from ambiguous positions to explicit ones to influence others. It is in this phase where coalitions form and leaders emerge.

Phase 3—Emergence: During the third phase, a direction begins to form, allowing the team to begin working toward their goals and objectives. This phase is both the longest and most gradual, marked by extensive discourse and decision-making. Not all members will agree with the team's direction, and those in opposition may adopt a more ambiguous position to save face.

During his research, Fisher noted a difference between the ambiguity observed in the orientation phase and that of the emergence phase. The ambiguity observed during orientation served as a tentative agreement between members to maintain amity. During the emergence phase, it serves as muted disapproval.

Phase 4—Reinforcement: During the final phase, the team comes to a consensus and unites in support of the collective's decisions. The shortest phase, teams in reinforcement address internal and external conflicts quickly and efficiently.

Fisher noted that not every group will go through all four phases. Some may get stuck in a phase and never progress. Teams which struggle often do so while making decisions about the team's direction, purpose, or tasks.

Fisher defines teams as a complex "open" system of set units bound by defined parameters whose components interact to produce an outcome. An open system means that individual members of the team are susceptible to outside influence or external factors, which can contribute to a team getting stuck.

Fisher also noted that teams are more than just the combined personalities of their individual members and they possess the capacity to learn and adapt. He suggests teams are greater than the sum of their parts.

Like other models on teaming, Decision Emergence Theory pulls from a variety of frameworks, including *Uncertainty Reduction Theory*, *Cognitive Dissonance Theory* and *Elaboration Likelihood Model*.

Professionals seeking additional information on Decision Emergence Theory may consider Fisher's 1974 book, *Small Group Decision-Making: Communication and the Group Process*.

Sources[112]

FIVE DYNAMICS OF TEAMWORK & COLLABORATION

Certification Available: no
Certification Required: no
Assessments: no
Proprietary: no
Client: teams, groups
Cost: not applicable
Category: teaming

Developed in 2001 by management expert Frank LaFasto and professor of communication Carl Larson, the Five Dynamics of Teamwork and Collaboration is a multifaceted framework for team effectiveness. Based on a study of more than 600 teams and 6,000 team members, the model consists of five variables deemed essential for team effectiveness.

Team members: This variable focuses on the individuals who make up the team. According to LaFasto and Larson, six characteristics are essential for an effective team member.

- **Experience**: This is an individual's practical knowledge relevant to the team's objective. An effective team member should possess the capacity to apply their knowledge in meaningful ways to help the team achieve objectives.

- **Problem-solving ability**: This is the individual's capacity to work through problems and arrive at solutions.

- **Openness**: This is the individual's ability and willingness to participate with other team members using direct communication.

- **Supportiveness**: This is the individual's willingness to help other members of the team in task completion and goal attainment.

- **Action oriented**: This is the degree to which an individual actively works on behalf of the team's objective and purpose.

- **Personal style**: This pertains to the individual's general demeanor and temperament.

Team relationships: This variable focuses on how individual team members interrelate with one another. A key component of relationship building is the ability to provide and receive honest and meaningful feedback.

Team problem-solving: This variable pertains to the team's ability to collectively solve problems. Though members may possess the individual ability to solve problems, it is the collective's ability that is critical.

Three factors crucial to a team's problem-solving ability include the degree to which the team focuses on the problem, the collaborative climate of the team's environment, and the level of openness in their communication.

Team leader: This variable pertains to the individual tasked with leading the team. LaFasto and Larson identified the following six behaviors with effective leadership: focusing on the team's goals, ensuring a collaborative environment, building confidence among members, possessing sufficient knowledge about the relevant matter (i.e., technical, or subject matter expertise), setting clear priorities, and managing team performance.

Organizational environment: The final variable involves the environment in which the team operates. A positive working environment requires three elements.

- **Management support**: External leaders and stakeholders are key to reinforcing the team's mission and morale.

- **Structure and process**: The team must operate in an environment where the organization's policies and practices are conducive to the team's mission.

- **Systems**: This pertains to how well the organization treats members of the team. This includes the use of personal, financial, and psychological rewards.

The Five Dynamics model is slightly more complex than presented here. Professionals seeking to learn more about the framework may consider LaFasto and Larson's 2001 book, *When Teams Work Best: 6,000 Team Members and Leaders Tell What It Takes to Succeed.*

Sources[113]

FIVE DYSFUNCTIONS OF A TEAM

Certification Available: no
Certification Required: no
Assessments: yes
Proprietary: yes (The Table Group Inc.)
Client: groups, teams
Cost: not applicable
Category: teaming

Developed in 2002 by business management expert Patrick Lencioni, the Five Dysfunctions of a Team identifies five common obstacles, presented as a cascading framework, which can prevent effective teaming.

Absence of trust: Arguably the greatest threat to teaming, a lack of trust often results in team members unwilling to be honest with one another. The reluctance to be honest can lead to various forms of deception, including fabrication, omission, or evasion among team members. Without trust, individuals feel they cannot be their genuine self. They lack the comfort necessary to be vulnerable, admit mistakes, and share weaknesses.

Fear of conflict: A lack of trust within the team often leads to a lack of courage and general unwillingness to engage in conflict. Consequently, a conflict-avoidant team cannot engage in the type of open and meaningful discourse needed for problem-solving and decision-making. In fact, a conflict-avoidant team is one that fails to understand the role of healthy conflict as a critical component in problem-solving.

Lack of commitment: The absence of healthy conflict means the collective will be unable to establish a sense of ownership and commitment to the project. The ability for individuals to voice their point of view and feel heard is critical to their sense of commitment to the team and the team's effort. For individuals to believe in the team, they must have the opportunity to question one another, to explore, and to seek understanding. A commitment to the team and the team's mission (or purpose) requires that everyone engage in passionate discourse.

Avoidance of accountability: The absence of an individual's commitment to the team and the team's mission makes it difficult to hold them accountable. If individual members feel they have no voice, they are unheard, or have little trust in the team, they will resist any attempt at accountability. Without a clear, well-established, and agreed-on plan of action, accountability is nearly impossible.

Inattention to results: The presence of any one of the previous obstacles presents a threat to the team's ability to perform. Without accountability, clear goals, and agreed-on strategies, individuals may lose sight of the team's results, positive and negative. Inattention to results means the team becomes blind to indicators of performance, limiting their ability to adapt and adjust. In some cases, the needs of the team give way to the needs and ego of the individual members.

Lencioni argues that the five obstacles are natural (normal) and are often mistaken as independent factors, though they are interdependent. In other words, one factor influences the others in a cascading effect.

To facilitate application of the framework, Lencioni offers a survey (using a Likert scale) to help individuals determine their team's susceptibility to the five dysfunctions. In addition to his model, Lencioni also offers a series of exercises to help teams overcome these obstacles.

Professionals considering the Dysfunctions of a Team framework may incorporate other models and theories to address individual obstacles. For example, when addressing the absence of trust, practitioners may consider incorporating *The Platinum Rule* or *Uncertainty Reduction Theory* to foster trust and rapport among team members. *Equity Theory of Motivation* and the *Existence, Relatedness, and Growth Theory* may prove valuable when dealing with a lack of commitment among individual members.

Professionals seeking additional information may consider Lencioni's 2002 book, *The Five Dysfunctions of a Team*, and his 2016 book, *The Ideal Team Player: How to Recognize and Cultivate the Three Essential Virtues*.

Sources[114]

FIVE-FACTOR MODEL OF PERSONALITY

Certification Available: yes
Certification Required: no
Assessments: yes (NEO-PI-R, Big Five Workplace Profile, Birkman Method, Hogan Assessment)
Proprietary: no
Client: individuals
Cost: prices vary by vendor
Category: personality types

Though the foundations of the Five-Factor Model of Personality date to the 1930s and 1940s, the framework we see today emerged in the 1980s based on the work of psychologists Paul Costa and Robert McCrae. The model provides a framework for exploring the construct of an individual's personality. The framework consists of five factors, each composed of six facets.

Openness: This factor pertains to an individual's receptivity to new experiences. Facets contributing to a person's openness are fantasy, aesthetics, feelings, actions, ideas, values.

Conscientiousness: This factor pertains to an individual's tendency to strive and act responsibly. Facets contributing to a person's conscientiousness are competence, order, dutifulness, achievement, self-discipline, deliberation.

Extraversion: This factor pertains to how an individual derives energy from the world. Facets contributing to a person's level of extraversion are warmth, gregariousness, assertiveness, activity, excitement seeking, positive emotions.

Agreeableness: This factor pertains to an individual's concern for others and the world. Facets contributing to a person's agreeableness are trust, straightforwardness, altruism, compliance, modesty, tender-mindedness.

Neuroticism: This factor pertains to an individual's emotional stability. Facets contributing to a person's neuroticism include anxiety, hostility, depression, self-consciousness, impulsiveness, vulnerability.

When exploring the Five-Factor Model, it is important to consider each factor and its associated facets as a set of continuums that apply to everyone; the question is to what degree. The combination of where a person falls on each continuum paints a picture of that person's personality.

The Five-Factor Model, also known as the Big Five, OCEAN, or CANOE, is one of the most widely used personality frameworks. The Five-Factor Model has proved effective in multiple languages, including English, German, and Chinese. This suggests that the model has potential utility across cultures. The model is useful with clients seeking an enhanced awareness of self and it provides a framework to better understand others.

It is important to note that opponents of the Five-Factor Model consider it an overly simple framework limited to organizing personality traits and not an actual theory to explain personality. Still, the model remains widely used in executive coaching and has broad utility in leadership and followership development.

The formal assessment for the Five-Factor Model is the NEO-PI-R; however, professionals will find many other assessments influenced by the Five-Factor Model, including the Big Five Workplace Profile, the Birkman Method, and the Hogan Assessment. Use of these assessments requires certification.

Though many credit Costa and McCrae with the modern Five-Factor Model, many others added to its development over the years. Sources also acknowledge Ernest Tupes, Raymond Christal, J.M. Digman, and Lewis Goldberg as contributors.

Professionals seeking additional information on the Five-Factor Model will find much written on the framework from both academic and non-scholarly sources. Those who wish to learn more about the modern version of OCEAN from Costa and McCrae may consider their 1990 book, *Personality in Adulthood: A Five-Factor Theory Perspective*. Those looking for alternative perspectives may consider the 1996 book, *The Five-Factor Model of Personality: Theoretical Perspectives*, edited by Jerry S. Wiggins.

Sources[115]

FIVE LEADERSHIP PRACTICES

Certification Available: yes
Certification Required: yes (formal use)
Assessments: yes (LPI)
Proprietary: yes (a Wiley brand)
Client: individuals
Cost: $1,500
Category: leadership

In 1983, professors James Kouzes and Barry Z. Posner initiated a research project based on *Trait Theory (Carlyle/Galton)* to understand "what people did when they were at their personal best leading others." Their study questioned the efficacy of measuring leadership traits which, in turn, led them to develop a more sophisticated model for examining leadership. Through their research, they identified a pattern of five functions common among the most effective leaders.

In 1987, Kouzes and Posner codified these five functions into their theory of leadership, called the Five Leadership Practices. Also known as the Leadership Challenge Model, this framework consists of five practices effective leaders engage in which foster meaningful leadership.

Model the way: This practice involves setting an example for followers. It requires the leader to possess a deep understanding of their own values and actively demonstrate a commitment to those values. This will allow the leader to embody these values for those who follow in both voice and deed.

Modeling the way requires that the leader establish what they stand for, how they (and others) are to behave, and demonstrate a commitment to these principles as a beacon for others. It also requires leaders to help their people achieve small wins to build momentum.

Inspire a shared vision: Effective leaders create exciting, meaningful, and thought-provoking visions for the future. In the process, these leaders enlist their people to contribute to the vision, giving them a foundational sense of understanding and ownership in the long-term goal.

Sharing a vision requires the leader to employ language that inspires commitment and encourages input from everyone. Giving voice to the thoughts and feelings of followers is an essential component to obtaining their commitment.

Challenge the process: Considered the "crucible for greatness," this practice involves the courage to question the status quo, to experiment, to seek out opportunities for growth, and to embrace risk. Effective leaders not only possess this courage but also inspire it in others.

Enabling others to act: Good leaders understand that success does not happen in a vacuum. Therefore, the best leaders create an environment that fosters collaboration and teamwork. They also recognize the importance of delegating and empowering their people to act in support of the vision and the goal.

Encourage the heart: This practice involves a celebration of the people, a recognition of their accomplishments, their contributions, and their victories. Effective leaders validate and acknowledge the work of those who support the vision.

It is worth noting that the Five Leadership Practices falls under the umbrellas of *Functional Leadership Theory, Transformational Leadership Theory,* and *Trait Theory.*

Though among the newer frameworks of leadership, some argue the model ignores the concept of shared leadership, a notion found in theories like the *Team Effectiveness Model* and *Postindustrial Leadership Theory.*

To learn more about the traits which underlie the Five Leadership Practices, see *Trait Theory (Kouzes and Posner).* Professionals interested in formal training in the Five Leadership Practices may obtain certification in the model's primary assessment instrument, the Leadership Practices Inventory (LPI). Because the model is proprietary to the Wiley brand, they are the sole source of training. For additional information, see Kouzes and Posner's 2012 book, *The Leadership Challenge: How to Make Extraordinary Things Happen in Organizations.*

Sources[116]

FIVE LEVELS OF FOCUS MODEL

Certification Available: no
Certification Required: no
Assessments: no
Proprietary: no
Client: individuals, groups, teams
Cost: not applicable
Category: problem-solving, communication

Developed in the mid-2000s by neuroscientist Dr. David Rock, the Five Levels of Focus Model provides a framework demonstrating how a person's focus (or perspective) may impact their ability to deal with a problem, crisis, or obstacle.

The framework consists of five levels. Dr. Rock further categorizes these into two groups: counterproductive and productive. The counterproductive group, levels 5–3, consists of perspectives that undermine the client's ability to process and address problems. The productive group, levels 3–1, consists of perspectives that support the client's ability to address the problem.

Level 5—Drama: The most counterproductive perspective, Level 5 involves highly emotional and often hearsay-type information pertaining to the problem or challenge. Conversations at level 5 can feel like gossip with a sense of "he said/she said." On this level, facts give way to biased thought and base sentiments. Level 5 discourse rarely provides any useful information or results.

Level 4—Problems: A client on this level fixates on the problem or on what went wrong. Often, clients on level 4 will get stuck in the past, unable to progress or learn from an experience. This fixation typically results in a negative attitude, which subsequently influences the client's perceptions and decision-making ability. Clients exploring a problem while in level 4 tend to cause more harm than good.

Level 3—Details: This level pertains to how much focus a client gives to the details of the issues. Level 3 borders the productive and counterproductive portions of the model. Consequently, this level may fall into either productive or counterproductive realms based on its application.

A productive application of level 3 involves the client's exploration of a problem with the intention of advancing their understanding of the issue.

A counterproductive application may occur if a client only considers the negative aspects of the problem, leading them to regress to level 4 or level 5. Leaders experiencing a counterproductive level 3 tend to engage in micromanagement as a means of exerting a sense of control over the problem.

Level 2—Planning: During this productive phase, the client explores "how" they intend to achieve a goal or realize a vision. Their focus centers on identifying explicit steps or actions they believe essential to goal attainment.

Level 1—Vision: A client on this productive level is one who looks at the big picture and seeks to understand "why" an issue is important to them and "what" they want to achieve. Put another way, the client looks to the future and considers what goals matter most to them.

The model suggests that our focus, when facing an issue, greatly influences how we perceive the issue, how we communicate the issue to others, and how we address the issue. For this reason, the ICMT includes the Five Levels of Focus in the communication category. Clients on levels 4 and 5 are more likely to present biased and negative information, while clients on levels 1–3 are more likely to deliver optimistic, positive messaging.

The Five Levels of Focus is useful with leaders considering organizational change or striving to solve or address a problem. The utility of this framework comes by helping clients lead organizational change from a position of level 1.

Professionals seeking additional information on the Five Levels of Focus Model will find little information available beyond Dr. David Rock's 2006 book, *Quiet Leadership*.

Sources[117]

FORMULA FOR CHANGE

Certification Available: no
Certification Required: no
Assessments: no
Proprietary: no
Client: individuals, organizations
Cost: not applicable
Category: change (org. and ind.)

Developed in the 1960s by management consultant David Gleicher, the Change Formula provides a simple framework for determining an organization's ability to achieve change by examining the relationship between four key variables. Gleicher applies these variables in a formula to demonstrate the concept.

The variables:

A: the level of dissatisfaction with the status quo

B: the clear presence of a desire for an alternative state

D: the presence of practical steps to achieve the desired state

X: the cost of change

C: the change or desired state

The formula:

$$C = (A \times B \times D) > X$$

The Change Formula suggests that an organization's ability to achieve meaningful and lasting change is only likely when their level of dissatisfaction with the status quo (A), the presence of a more desirable alternative (B), and a clear path to reaching the goal (D) are collectively greater than the cost of change (X).

Since Gleicher's introduction of the formula in the late 1960s, many have expanded upon the concept. In 1977, Richard Beckhard and Reuben T. Harris popularized the formula, leading some to call this the Beckhard-Harris Formula, though neither created the framework.

In the 1980s, business consultant Kathleen Dannemiller revised Gleicher's original formula to the version most often seen today. Though functionally identical to the original formula, Dannemiller's version labels the variables differently and expands on the concept.

$$C = (D \times V \times F) > R$$

D: the level of dissatisfaction with the status quo. Also known as the "motivation" factor, this variable must reach a high level to motivate a person or organization to consider the idea of change.

V: the presence of a vision for a better state. Called the "what" factor, this requires a clear and broadly messaged vision. An unambiguous vision may offset the fear and anxiety often associated with change efforts.

F: the presence of concrete actions that move a person or organization toward the vision. Called the "how" factor, this provides a roadmap for those expected to effect the change. Clearly defined steps and expectations also serve to minimize fear and anxiety.

R: the presence of obstacles that undermine change, which can include individuals, culture, systems, and processes. Often, the value of this variable is high, contributing to the difficulty of change efforts.

C: change

The construct of the formula (i.e., the use of multiplication) implies that if any one of the first three variables (D, V, F) are low or zero, the combined value of the three variables will be low or zero. This suggests that change will not occur because the value of resistance (cost of change) will be greater than the motivation, desire, and plan to change combined.

Professionals seeking additional information may consider Beckhard and Harris's 1977 book, *Organizational Transitions: Managing Complex Change*, or Dannemiller's 1999 book, *Whole-Scale Change*, co-authored with S.L. James and P.D. Tolchinsky.

Sources[118]

FOUR-DIMENSIONAL MODEL OF VIRTUAL TEAMS

Certification Available: no
Certification Required: no
Assessments: yes (Virtual Team Assessment)
Proprietary: yes (NetAge)
Client: groups, organizations
Cost: pricing not available
Category: teaming

Developed in 2000 by virtual team researchers Jessica Lipnack and Jeff Stamps, the Four-Dimensional Model of Virtual Teams provides a comprehensive framework for understanding how virtual teams operate. Created prior to the COVID-19 pandemic, theirs is among the earliest frameworks on virtual teaming.

Purpose (why): Successful virtual teams require a clearly defined objective. Considered a major predictor of success, a well-defined goal can unite a virtual team. The model recommends making the purpose explicit through group discussion so that all may share a common understanding of the goal. This will mitigate the risk of misunderstandings and conflicting interpretations.

People (who): When assigning members to the virtual team, it is important to select individuals who serve as complements, not opposites, to one another. Each person must possess a balance of independence and interdependence and they must have clear roles within the team. This dimension also involves the number of members assigned to the team, taking into consideration the advantages and disadvantages of team size.

Links (how): This dimension explores the many conduits a virtual team may use to communicate. Each method has strengths and weaknesses. Careful consideration for how each mode of communication can influence the relationship between members of the team is essential to protecting team cohesion and efficacy. It is important to include the benefits and risks associated with each mode on how the team communicates with entities external to the team.

Time (when): Virtual teams are social organisms that have a life cycle; they require time to form and gain momentum. This dimension explores the frequency and duration of team meetings as well as the phases or stages of the team's project.

Each dimension consists of three systems (inputs, processes, and outputs) to provide additional structure to support virtual teaming. The combination of four dimensions and 12 systems forms a matrix called the "Periodic Table" of virtual teaming, allowing leaders to methodically prepare a virtual team for success.

Periodic Table

Purpose-Inputs: Goals
Purpose-Processes: Tasks
Purpose-Outputs: Results

People-Inputs: Members
People-Processes: Leadership
People-Outputs: Levels

Links-Inputs: Media
Links-Processes: Interactions
Links-Outputs: Relationships

Time-Inputs: Calendar
Time-Processes: Interactions
Time-Outputs: Life Cycles

The Four-Dimensional Model has utility with leadership-level clients adapting to remote work environments where managing high-performance virtual teams is imperative. This model can facilitate the creation of new virtual teams or help teams transitioning to virtual teaming.

The Four-Dimensional Model of Virtual Teams is significantly more complex than presented here. Professionals seeking additional information may consider Lipnack and Stamps' 2000 book, *Virtual Teams: People Working Across Boundaries with Technology*. Additionally, Lipnack and Stamps make chapters relevant to the four dimensions freely available on their company website, NetAge.

The Four-Dimensional Model of Virtual Teaming is proprietary to NetAge. Formal use of the model and its associated assessment require training and licensing from NetAge.

Sources[119]

FOUR-FACTOR THEORY OF LEADERSHIP

Certification Available: no
Certification Required: no
Assessments: no
Proprietary: no
Client: individuals
Cost: not applicable
Category: leadership, employee engagement

Developed in 1966 by organizational psychologists David Bowers and Stanley Seashore, the Four-Factor Theory of Leadership provides a framework which explores the relationship between leadership and organizational effectiveness. The model identifies four key leadership behaviors that influence the efficacy of an organization.

Support: These behaviors involve leaders acting to increase the feeling of value and self-worth in the people around them. The Four-Factor Theory emphasizes the importance of leaders engaging in positive interaction (e.g., motivating, inspiring) with both direct reports and peers to improve organizational morale.

Research into the Four-Factor Theory of Leadership revealed that among organizations without engaging leaders, there is a greater tendency for lower morale and decreased compliance. Consequently, lower employee engagement and a reluctance to follow directions significantly decreased the organization's effectiveness.

Goal emphasis: These leadership behaviors inspire others, create a sense of excitement, and secure a commitment to achieve shared goals. The ability to leverage an individual's intrinsic motivation as opposed to their extrinsic (e.g., pay), results in higher-quality work and increased employee engagement.

Leaders proficient in goal-emphasizing behaviors inspire others to develop enthusiasm for the work at hand. Research into the Four-Factor Theory of Leadership revealed that the presence of goal-emphasizing behaviors among leaders is a predictive indicator of enhanced organizational output and improved profit margin.

Work facilitation: These behaviors involve leaders taking a proactive role to support the team's work. This means ensuring team members have all the resources they need to succeed. One aspect of this involves the leader facilitating effective planning and operations management to help the team avoid bureaucratic obstacles.

Organizations with leaders weak in this domain often have a growing divide between management and employees. Research into the Four-Factor Theory revealed that organizations deficient in this behavior experience higher employee turnover and decreased productivity. Conversely, organizations with leaders engaged in work facilitation experience higher morale and productivity.

Interaction facilitation: These behaviors involve leaders encouraging employees to develop relationships and improve communications with one another. This style of facilitation centers on a leader's ability to actively engage in and foster team building.

Research into the Four-Factor Theory revealed that organizations with leaders supporting interaction facilitation tended toward greater efficiency and productivity.

Variations of the Four-Factor Theory of Leadership adopt different labels to describe the four factors. These include focusing on goals, encouraging teamwork, providing personal support, and encouraging efficiency.

The Four-Factor Theory of Leadership remains in use today, often in leadership development circles and with organizational development practitioners.

Professionals seeking additional information on the Four-Factor Theory of Leadership may consider Bowers and Seashore's 1966 paper, "Predicting Organizational Effectiveness with a Four-Factor Theory of Leadership," and their follow-on 1967 paper, "Peer Leadership within Work Groups."

Sources[120]

FOUR STAGES OF COMPETENCE MODEL

Certification Available: no
Certification Required: no
Assessments: no
Proprietary: no
Client: individuals
Cost: not applicable
Category: learning/development

The origin of the Four Stages of Competence is a matter of some debate. The model, or some variation, appears in literature as far back as the 1960s. Though difficult to attribute, and often adopting different names and labels, these frameworks remain fundamentally the same. We present one version of a competency model.

The Four Stages of Competence provides a framework describing the sequential process a person goes through when learning a new skill.

Stage 1—Unconscious incompetence: In this stage, a person is unaware a knowledge gap exists. In some cases, they may recognize the gap but fail to see the value of learning to bridge the gap. In other cases, a person may simply be unaware of that which they do not know. Some versions of the model refer to this stage as "ignorance."

A common mistake instructors make with stage 1 learners derives from the false assumption that students understand the importance of the content. For this reason, curriculum developers should explain the rationale behind the content. Helping students understand why a concept or skill is relevant facilitates their learning.

Stage 2—Conscious incompetence: In this stage, a person acknowledges the existence of a knowledge gap. More than that, a person in this stage appreciates the importance of learning to acquire the knowledge or skill. This stage marks the commencement of learning. Some versions of the model call this stage "awareness."

Stage 3—Conscious competence: In this stage, a person has acquired the knowledge or skill sought. Though they know how to use the knowledge or skill, doing so requires significant effort. In other words, they can perform the task but may lack the depth of knowledge or experience to perform effortlessly. Some versions of the model call this stage "learning."

Stage 4—Unconscious competence: In this stage, an individual has so much experience with the knowledge or skill that it becomes second nature. Executing the skill occurs on a subconscious level, allowing a person to perform the task simultaneously with other skills. Some versions of the model call this stage "mastery."

Though presented in a linear fashion, the Four Stages of Competence Model is also cyclical. Individuals reaching stage 4 may develop a deep sense of confidence that blinds them to future gaps in knowledge, consequently bringing them back to stage 1.

A recent variation of the model presents a fifth stage that suggests that a person who becomes so skilled as to no longer remember the theory behind the skill loses the ability to teach the skill to others. Sources call this stage Conscious Competence of Unconscious Incompetence.

The Four Stages of Competence Model is useful with clients learning new skills or those pursuing additional academic training (e.g., bachelor's, master's degrees). Additionally, the model may serve as a lens to help clients understand what to expect in their journey to acquire knowledge.

Though the origins of the Four Stages of Competence Model remain ambiguous, some of the most cited contributors include Martin M. Broadwell, Noel Burch, Paul R. Curtiss, Phillip W. Warren, and many others.

Readers may encounter variations of this mode called the Conscious Competence Matrix, Learning Matrix, Four Stages of Learning, Conscious Competence Learning Model, Conscious Competence Learning Theory, and the Conscious Competence Ladder.

Professionals seeking additional information on the Four Stages of Competence Model will find articles freely available online.

Sources[121]

FUEL COACHING MODEL

Certification Available: yes
Certification Required: yes
Assessments: no
Proprietary: yes (Zenger/Folkman)
Client: individuals
Cost: pricing not available
Category: coaching model

Developed in 2010 by leadership coaches John H. Zenger and Kathleen Stinnett, the FUEL Coaching Model provides a four-step process for coaching that applies to both the coaching session and the coaching relationship.

Step 1—Frame the conversation: In the first step, the coach and client work to frame the conversation by exploring the client's expectations for coaching, the topics they want to focus on, and the purpose for the coaching session. This requires both coach and client to agree to tentative objectives for each session and an overall goal for the coaching relationship. Clients will revisit and modify their goals in stage 3, after a thorough examination of their current state.

Step 2—Understand the current state: The second step involves the coach helping the client develop an enhanced understanding of their current situation. This requires a deep exploration of the client's perceptions and perspectives which contribute to how the client perceives their experiences. This enables them to examine the issue holistically so they may better understand where they are and how they got there.

In this stage, the coach and client explore the presence of existing patterns of behavior which may impede the client's ability to achieve desired outcomes, or which negatively influence their perception of the issue.

Step 3—Explore the desired state: The client applies what they learned in stage 2 to their initial goal. Through this process, the coach helps the client define a revised goal based on where they are and where they want to be. This involves the client bridging the gap and generating multiple options through a combination of creativity and brainstorming.

Exploring the client's desired end state includes a consideration of potential obstacles that could prevent them from achieving their goal. To prepare for these potential challenges, the client may consider alternative pathways to success consistent with their vision.

Step 4—Lay out a success plan: In the final step, the coach works with the client to develop a success plan consisting of specific actions the client considers essential to achieving their goal. The success plan consists of multiple components, including an established timeframe with deadlines to help the client achieve and maintain momentum, and milestones and metrics to track progress. A thorough success plan fosters the client's accountability to the effort.

Another critical component of the success plan involves the client identifying key stakeholders to help support them along the way. These stakeholders can play a pivotal role in preventing the client from abandoning their effort and help them reengage should they experience setbacks or feel discouraged.

Discourse using the FUEL Model focuses heavily on the client's behavioral coaching needs and encourages them to take ownership of the process. This leads the client to a greater commitment to follow through as they execute the success plan.

It is important to note that several sources justify the FUEL Model over other coaching frameworks by highlighting shortcomings in other coaching models. The primary justification suggests the FUEL Coaching Model gets the client's buy-in while other models encourage coaches to use leading questions to guide the client, thereby undermining their sense of ownership in the process. These sources do not provide any evidence to back up their claims. Therefore, we encourage professionals to further explore all frameworks before selecting one.

Professionals seeking additional information on the FUEL Coaching Model may consider Zenger and Stinnett's 2010 book, *The Extraordinary Coach: How the Best Leaders Help Others Grow.*

Sources[122]

FULL RANGE LEADERSHIP MODEL

> **Certification Available:** no
> **Certification Required:** no
> **Assessments:** no
> **Proprietary:** no
> **Client:** individuals
> **Cost:** not applicable
> **Category:** leadership

Developed in the 1980s by leadership and organizational behavior researchers Bernard Bass and Bruce Avolio, the Full Range Leadership Model (FRLM) provides a framework for exploring different styles of leadership. FRLM consists of seven styles of leadership behavior ordered from least effective (or passive) to most effective (or active).

Laissez-faire (LF): Considered the most passive form of leadership, Bass and Avolio describe this style as hands-off or absent leadership, marked by an avoidance of conflict and the abdication of decision-making. The least effective style of leadership, studies strongly indicate laissez-faire is detrimental to organizational effectiveness.

Management by exception (MBE): Characterized as only leading before or after something goes wrong, this style of leader intervenes only when people fail to meet standards, often doling out punishment and criticism. MBE exists in two forms, active and passive MBE. Active MBE involves leaders who constantly monitor employees and intervene at the very first sign of a problem. Conversely, passive MBE involves leaders who wait until after the problem occurs to intervene.

Contingent reward (CR): These leaders use reward systems to entice and motivate employee actions. CR, though considered a positive leadership style, presents risks. These leaders may become dependent on rewards or overuse extrinsic rewards, which can demotivate followers (see *Self-Determination Theory* for details on this phenomenon).

Individualized consideration (IC): These leaders see every person as unique and strive to build relationships with each person based on their strengths, preferences, and needs.

Intellectual stimulation (IS): These leaders emphasize the intellect of employees and encourage them to challenge old ways of doing things to foster creativity and innovation.

Inspirational motivation (IM): These leaders emotionally stimulate followers by appealing to their intrinsic motivations, cultivating their confidence, and evoking optimism within them.

Idealized influence (II): Considered the highest form of leadership, these leaders set the example; they model the behaviors they expect of others.

The Full Range Leadership Model is one of the most popular frameworks used in leadership development because it combines aspects of other well-known models. These include the *Transformational Leadership Theory*, originally created by James Downton and popularized by James MacGregor Burns. Transformational Leadership Theory contributed idealized influence, inspirational motivation, intellectual stimulation, and individualized consideration to FRLM. *Transactional Leadership Theory*, created by Max Weber, contributed contingent reward and management by exception. The final contribution comes from Kurt Lewin's *Laissez-faire Leadership Theory*. Bass and Avolio combined these theories along with several enhancements to highlight the full range of leadership behaviors which characterize an individual's style of leadership.

FRLM is useful as a framework to help characterize patterns of leadership behavior. Understanding where a client's leadership style falls within this framework can help the client develop their self-awareness and set new developmental goals.

Professionals seeking additional information will find significant literature available on the Full Range Leadership Model, including Avolio's 2010 book, *Full Range Leadership Development* and Bass's 2009 book, *The Bass Handbook of Leadership: Theory, Research, and Managerial Applications*, co-authored by Ruth Bass.

Sources[123]

FUNCTIONAL LEADERSHIP MODELS

Certification Available: no
Certification Required: no
Assessments: no
Proprietary: no
Client: individuals, groups, teams
Cost: not applicable
Category: leadership, influence

Functional Leadership Models (FLM) refers to a category of theories that focus on the function of leadership, not the individual. In other words, FLM examines the mechanics of how effective leadership works, in contrast to other theories which focus on the environment and the situation (*Contingency Theories*), or the personalities, traits, and characteristics of the individual leaders (*Trait Theories*).

FLM defines leadership not as a mantle or designated authority, but as a function anyone can perform. This implies that the leader is not necessarily the one with the title, but the one who performs the functions required of leadership. These functions include maintaining group cohesion, resolving group conflict, facilitating decision-making, and more.

FLM's focus on the "how" of leadership and not the "who" suggests leadership is not the responsibility of one person; rather it is a function that any member of the team may perform to different degrees and at different times. Therefore, models under the FLM umbrella propose that the role of leader is fluid and may pass from one member of the team to another based on the needs of the team and the situation.

Functional Leadership Models point out that a designated leader and a functional leader may not be the same person. This distinction is useful in understanding the relationship between figureheads and those who drive the team to success. The relationship between designated leaders and functional leaders is worth exploring with leadership-level clients. The interaction between these two can range from symbiotic to contentious, either advancing the organization or undermining it.

Functional Leadership Models provide broad utility in leadership development. Clients tasked with leadership-level functions or responsibilities, but who do not possess the authority to lead, may find value in FLM frameworks that explore how to lead through influence (e.g., inspiration, motivation) rather than authority (i.e., fear of punishment).

Conversely, a client designated as a leader may struggle when individuals without formal leadership title serve as functional leaders. FLM frameworks may prove useful in helping the client navigate the dichotomy between designated and functional leadership.

It is important to note that some sources present the Functional Leadership Model as a singular framework and not an umbrella term. In most of these cases, what they describe is John Adair's *Action-Centered Leadership Model*. To provide a level of distinction, we present FLM as an umbrella term consisting of many frameworks. Within *The Infourge Compendium of Models and Theories for Coaches*, we present two frameworks that fall under the Functional Leadership Models umbrella.

- Action-Centered Leadership
- Five Leadership Practices

Sources[124]

FUNDAMENTAL INTERPERSONAL RELATIONS ORIENTATION

Certification Available: yes
Certification Required: yes
Assessments: yes (FIRO-B, Elements of Awareness)
Proprietary: yes
Client: individuals, groups, organizations
Cost: $1,000–$10,000 (based on vendor)
Category: communication, personality

Developed in 1958 by psychologist William C. Schutz, Fundamental Interpersonal Relations Orientation Theory (FIRO) provides a comprehensive framework for exploring the complex connection between human behavior and interpersonal relationships.

The FIRO framework consists of three specific needs that influence the way people interact.

- Inclusion: This pertains to a person's need to belong to a group, receive recognition from others, and relate to those around them.

- Control: This pertains to a person's need to influence their world, effect decisions, and assume responsibility for personal actions.

- Affection: This pertains to a person's need for closeness to others, their level of sensitivity, and degree of openness.

FIRO explores each need from two perspectives: how the person expresses the need (their behavior toward others) and how they wish others to treat them.

For example, when exploring Inclusion with a client, we might consider the extent to which a client includes others in their activities. How do they invite others or encourage them to participate or join in on activities? Conversely, we may consider the extent to which the client wants to be included in the activities of other people. How does the client want others to include them? Does the client want an explicit invitation or a more subtle invitation?

When exploring Control with a client, we might consider the extent to which a client seeks to control or influence other people. Does the client feel an overwhelming need to control their environment? Conversely, we may explore the extent to which a client needs their environment to have structure. How much influence does the client require from their environment?

It is important to note that some sources present FIRO Theory with fewer aspects, omitting some of the elements. This can lead to some confusion. Additionally, professionals may encounter older versions of FIRO. For this reason, we encourage professionals to thoroughly research the theory before incorporating it into practice.

FIRO is a useful framework to facilitate individual leadership development, improve interpersonal communication, and foster effective teaming. Fundamental Interpersonal Relations Orientation Theory includes an array of FIRO-based assessments like the FIRO-B (from the Myers-Briggs Company) and the Elements of Awareness (from the Human Element). The cost of certification varies by vendor.

Fundamental Interpersonal Relations Orientation Theory is significantly more complex than presented here. Professionals seeking additional information may consider Schutz's 1958 book, *FIRO: A Three-Dimensional Theory of Interpersonal Behavior*, and his 1992 article from *Psychological Reports*, "Beyond FIRO-B: Three New Theory-Derived Measures—Element B: Behavior, Element F: Feelings, Element S: Self."

For information on the FIRO-B, consider the book *Introduction to the FIRO-B Instrument in Organizations*, authored by E.R. Schnell and A.L. Hammer.

Sources[125]

GARDNER'S THEORY OF MULTIPLE INTELLIGENCES

Certification Available: no
Certification Required: no
Assessments: no
Proprietary: no
Client: individuals
Cost: not applicable
Category: learning/development

Developed in 1983 by psychologist Howard Gardner, his Theory of Multiple Intelligences challenges the traditional belief that we are born with a single type of intelligence that does not easily change, represented by the Intelligence Quotient (IQ). Instead, Gardner argues for the existence of multiple types of intelligence, the combination of which portrays a person's unique aptitude and set of capabilities.

Since Gardner's introduction of the theory, the number of intelligence types identified has grown over the years to the current count of nine.

Linguistic Intelligence (word smart): This refers to a capacity for learning, understanding, and using written and spoken language. Individuals high on this spectrum can analyze and produce works like books and speeches.

Mathematical Intelligence (number smart): This refers to a capacity for analysis, problem-solving, and examination using logic, math, and science. Individuals high on this spectrum tend to see patterns and think conceptually about numbers. They can also recognize and make meaning from the relationships between variables.

Spatial Intelligence (picture smart): This refers to the capacity for recognizing and manipulating patterns in both open and confined spaces. Individuals high on spatial intelligence possess excellent visual and spatial judgment, are good with directions and maps, and they excel at visualizing concepts.

Kinesthetic Intelligence (body smart): This refers to a person's ability to use their body to solve problems and achieve goals. Individuals high on this spectrum tend to have excellent hand-eye coordination, agility, and dexterity.

Musical Intelligence (music smart): This refers to the capacity for recognizing, composing, and performing musical patterns. These individuals excel at thinking and remembering melodies and rhythm.

Interpersonal Intelligence (people smart): This refers to the capacity for understanding the thoughts, feelings, and motivations of other people. These individuals excel at communicating and interacting with others.

Intrapersonal Intelligence (self-smart): Refers to the capacity for understanding one's own thoughts, feelings, and motivations. Individuals high on this spectrum tend to excel at introspection.

Naturalist Intelligence (nature smart): This refers to a person's capacity for recognizing and classifying the flora and fauna of their environment. These individuals are highly aware of changes to their environment.

Existentialist Intelligence (spiritual smart): This refers to the capacity for exploring questions about human existence.

Gardner claims each type of intelligence applies to everyone, though in different ways and to different degrees. While his theory touches on an individual's preference for learning, it is important to note that Gardner is clear on the fact that his Theory of Multiple Intelligences is not the same thing as learning styles.

Though widely used in curriculum design circles, Gardner's Theory of Multiple Intelligences is not without controversy. Arguments suggest there is insufficient research to validate the theory and point to an absence of instruments designed to measure a client's presence in each of the intelligences.

Gardner's Theory of Multiple Intelligences is more complex than presented here. Professionals seeking additional information may consider Gardner's 1983 book, *Frames of Mind: The Theory of Multiple Intelligences*.

Sources[126]

GENERAL ADAPTATION SYNDROME

Certification Available: no
Certification Required: no
Assessments: no
Proprietary: no
Client: individuals
Cost: not applicable
Category: stress management

Developed in 1936 by noted endocrinologist Hans Selye, General Adaptation Syndrome (GAS) provides a framework for exploring and understanding a person's physiological response to stress-inducing stimuli. In the 1950s, Selye codified the three stages of GAS we see today.

Alarm reaction stage: The first stage involves the body's initial reaction to stress-inducing stimuli. Also called the fight-or-flight (or freeze) stage, during this period, a person experiences sudden changes in hormone levels, allowing them to react to the situation.

The process begins with the hypothalamus secreting specific hormones that trigger the release of adrenaline and cortisol. These hormones facilitate the fight, flight, or freeze response by altering a person's heart rate, breathing, and muscle tension. Depending on the intensity and duration of this hormone release, the experience can "shock" the body.

Resistance stage: During the second stage, if the stress-inducing stimuli cease, the body begins recovering from the physiological shock by lowering adrenaline and cortisol levels. Eventually, the body will return to normal.

If stress-inducing stimuli persist, the body may remain in a prolonged state of alertness. Though the body may not produce the same spike in hormones as seen in the alarm reaction stage, these chemicals remain at elevated levels. Consequently, the resistance stage may involve the body adapting to the protracted presence of stress-inducing stimuli.

A person in the resistance stage who encounters new stress-inducing stimuli may return to the alarm reaction stage.

Exhaustion stage: In the event a stressor persists, and the body continues to produce elevated stress hormones, a person may enter the exhaustion stage. This occurs when the body, drained of physical, emotional, and mental resources, can no longer cope with stress. This stage can manifest as fatigue, burnout, depression, and hopelessness.

Extended time in the exhaustion stage risks serious long-term physical and mental consequences. For example, prolonged exposure to cortisol and adrenaline can compromise the immune system, leading to illness.

General Adaptation Syndrome identifies several types of stressors. These include traumatic events, daily exposure to environmental stresses, and sudden life changes. GAS also recognizes positive stress. These are positive but significant events that can induce stress, like winning the lottery or receiving a promotion at work.

Though called General Adaptation Syndrome, GAS is not a diagnosable medical condition. Rather it is simply the process the body goes through in response to a stress-inducing stimulus. Prolonged exposure to this process may result in diagnosable psychological conditions like post-traumatic stress, depression, anxiety, and obsessive-compulsive disorder. This process may also lead to diagnosable physical conditions like hypertension, stomach ulcers, and heart disease.

As a framework, GAS can help clients recognize their experience with stress and where they are in the process. Coaches can work with clients on techniques to address stressors or manage the impact of these hormones on the body. This includes breathing techniques, exercises, and cathartic discourse.

Professionals seeking additional information about General Adaptation Syndrome will find much written on the topic, including Selye's 1974 book, *Stress Without Distress: How to achieve a rewarding lifestyle, in harmony with the laws of Nature, by using stress as a positive force for personal achievement and happiness.*

Sources[127]

GIBBS' REFLECTIVE CYCLE

Certification Available: no
Certification Required: no
Assessments: no
Proprietary: no
Client: individuals
Cost: not applicable
Category: reflection

Developed in 1988 by Graham Gibbs, Gibbs' Reflective Cycle provides a comprehensive six-step framework to facilitate learning from experience. Each step in the process includes an assortment of questions designed to facilitate the client's reflective journey through meaningful discourse.

Step 1—Description: The first step in the process requires the client to describe the experience in as much detail as possible. While explaining what happened, it is important that the client avoid making attributions or meaning of the experience. Put another way, the client should focus on the facts of what happened without injecting an opinion (no matter how accurate) of why the event happened.

The client's description should also include who was present during the event, when and where the event took place, and what actions the client and others took before, during, and after the event.

Step 2—Feelings: This second step pertains to the client's thoughts and feelings before, during, and after the event in question. Asking the client to share this aspect of the experience may lead them to experience a sense of "reliving" the event. Thus coaches should remain mindful of the client during this stage.

For the client to feel safe to express their sentiments honestly and openly, it is important for the coach to avoid commenting on the client's perceptions and feelings during this stage of the process. In this, it is important that the coach serve as a witness to experience, not a judge of it.

Step 3—Evaluation: The third step involves an objective examination of the experience. In other words, the client evaluates the actions by all parties involved to better understand which behaviors served a positive role and which ones played a negative role in the event. To facilitate this evaluation, the client may consider classifying or grouping the observed actions.

Step 4—Analysis: The fourth step involves a subjective examination of the experience to make sense of the event. In other words, this step is about the client's attempt to understand the "why" behind the actions of those involved, including their own.

Typically, clients will try to apply meaning-making in the beginning as they explain the event. By keeping the client focused on the objective elements first, they can form a clearer picture of what happened, from which they may better determine why the event took place.

Step 5—Conclusion: In the fifth step, the client uses all the knowledge gained from the previous four steps to draw conclusions about the experience. These conclusions then serve to inform the client of what they could do differently, what they have learned from the experience, and what skills they could use for personal and professional improvement.

Step 6—Action plan: In the final step, the client identifies, considers, and commits to new behaviors that capitalize on the lessons learned from the experience. It is one thing to creatively identify multiple courses of action; it is an entirely different matter to position oneself to make that happen. Fostering the client's commitment to the action plan means the client must understand the value of the new behaviors and should develop a realistic and meaningful strategy based on their strengths.

Gibbs' Reflective Cycle offers a more methodical framework when compared to other models of reflection. A key difference in this model lies in its distinction between Evaluation and Analysis. By separating the objective examination from the subjective examination, it allows the client to explore the experience with greater focus and clarity. Professionals seeking additional information may consider Gibbs' 1988 book, *Learning by Doing*.

Sources[128]

GOLEMAN'S SIX STYLES OF LEADERSHIP

> **Certification Available:** no
> **Certification Required:** no
> **Assessments:** no
> **Proprietary:** no
> **Client:** individuals
> **Cost:** not applicable
> **Category:** leadership

Developed in the early 2000s by noted psychologist Daniel Goleman, the Six Styles of Leadership provides a framework useful for exploring leadership behaviors.

Commanding: Also known as the **Coercive** or **Directive** style, these types of leaders prefer to make all the decisions. They tend to give orders with minimal or no explanations and seek to exercise tight control over both the team and the project.

The commanding style is one of two styles (the other is Pacesetting) Goleman recommends using only in the rarest of occasions as it can kill creativity and flexibility. The phrase that best represents this style: "Do as I say."

Visionary: Also known as the **Authoritative** style, these types of leaders tend to establish a vision of where the team will go but avoid telling them how to get there. Visionary leaders possess the capability to inspire followers and relay their vision to others, so it becomes a shared vision between all members of the team. The phrase that best represents this style: "Come with me."

Affiliative: This type of leader is one who focuses on relationships, people, and the emotional well-being of the team. Affiliative leaders demonstrate great empathy to care for their people and build trust. This style is ideal for teams that have gone through a difficult experience or need healing. The phrase that best represents this style: "People come first."

Democratic: This style of leadership derives from other theories of the same name (see *Lewin's Leadership Styles*). Democratic leaders build consensus through participative and inclusive engagement. They openly ask team members to share their thoughts and ideas. The phrase that best represents this style: "What do you think?"

Pacesetting: This type of leader is one who focuses on performance and results. Pacesetting leaders tend to lead by example and expect others to follow suit without question. This is the second style for which Goleman urges caution before adopting. Like the commanding style, this form of leadership works in only a few situations. The phrase that best represents this style: "Do as I do, when I do it."

Coaching: This type of leader focuses on the development of followers. Coaching leaders strive to obtain the commitment and loyalty of their followers by providing them opportunities to grow and nurturing their development. The phrase that best represents this style: "Try this."

Goleman's Six Styles of Leadership partially derives from his *EI Performance Model* and his study of over 3,000 managers. Accordingly, users may benefit from understanding Goleman's emotional intelligence model prior to using this leadership framework.

Each of the six styles represented in this framework possesses its own unique strengths and weaknesses; one style does not fit all situations. What may work well in one situation with one team may fail in another situation or with a different team. Goleman suggests that the most effective leaders are ones with both the flexibility to adopt any of the six leadership styles as needed and the ability to determine (accurately) which style is appropriate for the given environment or situation.

Goleman's model is rooted in the belief that leadership is a tool, and like any tool, it is important to know which tool is appropriate for a given situation. For this reason, the Six Styles of Leadership falls under the umbrella of *Contingency Theories*.

The Six Styles of Leadership is more complex than presented here. Professionals seeking additional information may consider Goleman's 2002 book, *Primal Leadership: Unleashing the Power of Emotional Intelligence*, co-authored by Richard Boyatzis and Annie McKee.

Sources[129]

GROUPTHINK

Certification Available: no
Certification Required: no
Assessments: no
Proprietary: no
Client: groups, teams
Cost: not applicable
Category: teaming, decision-making

Popularized in the 1970s by psychologist Irving Janis, the term Groupthink describes a phenomenon in which a group makes irrational or illogical decisions influenced by social pressures like conformity, identity, or a negative perception of or against individual dissent.

The framework suggests there are four primary sources of Groupthink. Furthermore, the model provides eight observable signs which may indicate the presence of Groupthink.

Sources of Groupthink

• **Identity**: This pertains to both individual and group identity. If individual members of the group share an identity, there are fewer opportunities for alternative perspectives. If the group identity is insular, then the group becomes less receptive to outside opinions.

• **Leadership influence**: This element pertains to the group's leader. A leader possessing a domineering personality can restrict a group's willingness to openly share ideas and thoughts. Overbearing personalities in a leadership position can negatively influence the team's dynamics, style of communication, and undermine rational thought.

• **Lack of knowledge**: This pertains to the depth of knowledge of individual team members. When a person lacks sufficient knowledge to actively contribute to discourse and they strive to hide this fact, they may "go with the flow" and accept the opinion of others without challenge or question.

• **Stress**: The presence of stress and anxiety may lead individuals to avoid questioning the group's choices. Yet another variable that undermines critical thinking.

Indicators of Groupthink

• **Rationalization**: Occurs when the team convinces themselves that a decision is the best one despite evidence to the contrary. The act of rejecting facts to justify a decision is confirmation bias.

• **Peer pressure**: Occurs when the collective engages in affective conflict (i.e., attacks the person and not the idea). Castigating an individual for having a different opinion or taking a position counter to the majority is a clear indicator of Groupthink.

• **Complacency**: Occurs when the group develops a sense of superiority or invulnerability based on prior successes. The phrase "Our record speaks for itself" best captures this.

• **Moral high ground**: Occurs when individuals believe that because they are moral, they cannot make an immoral decision.

• **Stereotypes**: Occurs when the group applies generalizations and stereotypes to those whose position is counter to the majority, furthering the "us vs. them" divide.

• **Self-censorship**: Occurs when individuals censor themselves to conform with the group.

• **Illusion of unanimity**: This happens when the group perceives an absence of explicit debate as confirmation of unanimous agreement.

• **Mind guards**: Occurs when individuals withhold perspectives or evidence that counters the group's position with the intent of protecting the group.

During his research, Janis observed that teams suffering from Groupthink were more likely to make poor or immoral choices.

Professionals seeking additional information on Groupthink will find much written on the topic, including Janis' 1982 book, *Groupthink*.

Sources[130]

GROW COACHING MODEL

Certification Available: yes
Certification Required: yes
Assessments: no
Proprietary: yes (PCI)
Client: individuals
Cost: $8,400–$13,000
Category: coaching model

Developed in the 1980s by the late executive coach Sir John Whitmore in conjunction with Graham Alexander and Max Landsberg, the GROW Coaching Model is among the earliest frameworks designed to facilitate the coaching process.

The GROW process consists of four steps critical to an effective coaching session.

Step 1—Goal: The first step in the process involves the client articulating their desired objectives for coaching. These can include goals for individual sessions or a larger goal for the coaching relationship.

Professionals who use the GROW Model often incorporate the *SMART Model for Goal Setting* into the process to ensure clients develop goals that are specific, measurable, achievable, relevant, and time-bound. The GROW process also encourages clients to consider goals that are inspiring and challenging for both the long term and short term.

Step 2—Reality: The second step involves the client's exploration of where they are in the moment and how they got there. Such examination requires the client to consider what is happening for them, what challenges they are facing, and what actions they have tried.

Unlike other change models, GROW emphasizes the client's perspectives, not external sources of information.

Step 3—Options: The third step involves the client exploring all available options that can help them achieve their goal. This step utilizes the client's creativity combined with discourse designed to generate ideas.

In this phase, the client considers all the possibilities for how they might overcome challenges, adopt change, or achieve their goals.

Step 4—Will: The final step in the process sees the client developing a plan of action and new behaviors they believe will help them achieve their goal. During this step, the client agrees to commit to these new behaviors.

The GROW Model is among the most widely recognized coaching processes and is arguably one of the two most influential models in coaching (see the *CLEAR Coaching Model*). Many of the coaching models presented in this compendium derive from GROW, either by building on the framework or incorporating it into a larger methodology.

Several variations of the GROW Model exist. Given the proliferation of these variations, it is possible that collaborating professionals may adopt differing frameworks. It is important to recognize these informal variations, as they present slightly different processes. For example, in one variation, they label the third step Options and Obstacles. In the original GROW Model, addressing obstacles takes place in the second step of the process, whereas this variation addresses the topic in the third step.

The utility of GROW applies across all forms and styles of coaching, adding to its ubiquity in the industry. Professionals seeking formal training and certification will find programs available through Sir John Whitmore's company Performance Consultants International (PCI).

Professionals seeking additional information on the GROW Model will find a significant amount of information available, including Whitmore's 1992 book, *Coaching for Performance: The Principles and Practice of Coaching and Leadership*.

Sources[131]

GROWTH COACHING MODEL

Certification Available: yes
Certification Required: no
Assessments: no
Proprietary: no
Client: individuals, groups
Cost: $3,200
Category: coaching model, goal setting

Developed by educator John Campbell and coach Mandy O'Bree, the GROWTH Coaching Model is an extension of Sir John Whitmore's *GROW Coaching Model* and emphasizes a deeper exploration of how clients intend to achieve their goals. The GROWTH process consists of six steps designed to facilitate both the coaching relationship and the individual coaching sessions. The first four steps mirror Whitmore's GROW Model.

Step 1—Goal: The first step involves the client identifying what goals they want to achieve through coaching.

Step 2—Reality: During the second step, the client explores their current situation, including what actions led them to the present moment.

Step 3—Options: In the third step, the client considers all the possible ways they could achieve their goal.

Step 4—Will: The fourth step involves the client developing a plan of action and committing to these actions and new behaviors.

Step 5—Tactics: During the fifth step, the client considers how and when they will act to achieve their goal. Where "Will" identifies the actions, "Tactics" organizes the actions into a strategy for maximum efficacy.

Step 6—Habits: The final step involves the client considering how they will sustain their success. This involves making behavior changes "stick" and adopting effective reinforcements to encourage continued commitment to the client's plan.

In 1997, psychologist Peter Gollwitzer conducted research which contributed to the GROWTH Model. His work focused on the disparity between a client's desire (intention) to achieve a goal and their actual success achieving the goal. His research showed that intentions alone were insufficient predictors of success. Instead, a more reliable strategy involves the development of an "If-Then Plan," also known as Implementation Intention.

Comparisons between traditional goal-setting methods and Implementation Intention suggest typical goal-setting methods tend to result in vague and ambiguous goals. In contrast, Implementation Intentions are specific, concrete actions that the client decides to undertake under predefined conditions.

For example, a typical goal might be "I want to handle uncomfortable social situations at work better." An Implementation Intention would be "The next time my coworker asks me how my weekend went, I will answer 'good' and turn the question back on them to take the focus off me."

The key characteristic differentiating GROWTH from the original GROW Model is its meticulous focus on how the client realizes and actualizes their goals. For this reason, the GROWTH Model is useful with clients struggling to reach their goals. Though the GROWTH Model focuses on coaching within academic settings, its utility applies to many styles of coaching.

An inquiry into the GROWTH Model revealed a different version of the model created by Kenneth Acha, MD. Acha's model also derives from Whitmore's GROW Model, but the final two steps consist of Team Capabilities and Helper Systems. An inquiry into Acha's model revealed no additional sources of information or explanation of his model.

Professionals seeking additional information may consider Gollwitzer's chapter, "Goal Implementation: The Benefits and Costs of If-Then Planning," featured in the 2009 book, *The Psychology of Goals*, edited by G.B Moskowitz and H. Grant. Additionally, Campbell's chapter, "Coaching in Schools," featured in the 2015 book, *Coaching in Professional Contexts*, edited by C.V. Nieuwerburgh, may prove useful.

Sources[132]

GRPI MODEL

Certification Available: no
Certification Required: no
Assessments: no
Proprietary: no
Client: groups, teams
Cost: not applicable
Category: teaming

Developed in 1972 by organizational development theorist Dick Beckhard, the GRPI Model serves as both a project planning tool and a framework for team organization. Pronounced "grip-ee," the model also provides a method for diagnosing team dysfunction.

Popular among consultants, particularly in organizational development and project management circles, GRPI consists of four elements. When properly used, these elements may facilitate team development and enhance project efficacy.

Goals: This element pertains to the team's explicit goals (i.e., the team's purpose). When goals are vague or ambiguous, individuals will interpret the goals in a way that makes sense to them. This results in contrasting beliefs between team members that can vary greatly from one person to another, leading to misunderstandings and conflict among the team.

GRPI suggests that a shared goal is the foundation for team cohesion. This is based partly on studies which demonstrate that individuals with disparate motivations and desires are more likely to coalesce when striving toward a common goal.

To facilitate effective goal setting, GRPI encourages use of the *SMART Model for Goal Setting*.

Roles: The second element relates to the responsibilities and functions assigned to each member of the team. Problems can arise if roles overlap too much or if a gap exists between roles (e.g., important tasks go undone because no one thinks it is their responsibility). To avoid this, it is important that each individual team member has a clearly defined role with explicit responsibilities and functions.

Ensuring each member of the team understands their role and the role of others is essential to both the efficacy of the team and team cohesion. This requires transparency between team members and the ability to hold one another accountable.

Processes: The third element focuses on how the team members perform their work and how they make decisions. While the "Roles" element focuses on the responsibilities of individual members, "Processes" focuses on how the individual roles interconnect and function in furtherance of the team's goals.

This element requires team members to establish clear parameters regarding how they interact, how they communicate internally and externally, how they will address conflict and challenges along the way, and what authorities empower the team.

Interpersonal relationships: The final element emphasizes how people relate to each other. Often misattributed as the source of most team dysfunction, "interpersonal relationships" deals with the trust and respect between team members.

Creating strong interpersonal relationships requires individuals to develop a deeper understanding of each other, their thoughts, feelings, motivations, and desires. This requires an open dialogue and a willingness to learn.

The GRPI Model has broad utility. Its most common use is as a framework for examining the sources of team dysfunction. However, it also serves as a framework to proactively enhance team efficacy during project execution.

There is no formal certification in the GRPI Model; however, ample literature is available for practitioners looking to expand their depth of knowledge.

Professionals interested in additional information on Beckhard's work in organizational change and teaming may consider his 1977 book, *Organizational Transitions: Managing Complex Change*.

Sources[133]

HACKMAN'S MODEL OF TEAM EFFECTIVENESS

Certification Available: no
Certification Required: no
Assessments: no
Proprietary: no
Client: groups
Cost: not applicable
Category: teaming

Developed in the 1970s by organizational psychologist J. Richard Hackman, his Model of Team Effectiveness provides a framework consisting of five specific conditions necessary for teams to function effectively and successfully.

Real team: The first condition involves the presence of clarity in every aspect of teaming. Hackman defines this as providing clear boundaries for how the team operates (i.e., rules and procedures), specifying unambiguous tasks (i.e., defined responsibilities and roles for each member), plainly identifying team members, and ensuring membership stability (i.e., explicit expectations for each member).

Compelling direction: The second condition involves providing the team with a clear and well-defined goal that everyone may work toward. It is critical that the goal be challenging, though not impossible.

The stakes and consequences associated with the goal should motivate team members to strive for success. Satisfying this condition may require providing smaller objectives to help the team build momentum and confidence early in their effort.

Enabling structure: This condition focuses on the team's workflow, process, and other obligations. For a team to succeed, members require a structure that fosters effective teaming and facilitates flexibility and adaptability.

This condition covers both the team's structure and the supporting management's structure. A complicated or complex set of obligations to management can hamper team effectiveness (e.g., a team required to report to multiple supervisors across multiple branches or divisions is not likely to perform effectively).

Supportive context: The fourth condition involves team-member motivations and consists of three key elements. First, the group must receive rewards that satisfy the intrinsic and extrinsic needs of the group but also connect to performance. Second, individuals involved with the team must have access to developmental opportunities that foster professional growth.

Third, all members of the team must have access to all relevant information. This includes timely information needed to support group decision-making.

Expert coaching: The final condition involves the use of coaching, mentoring, or facilitation to help the group maintain momentum and positive progress. This involves a person, external to the group, guiding the team and providing encouragement.

The coach, mentor, or facilitator may share their past experiences for the benefit of the group, help the team process new information and experiences, foster perspective-taking, or facilitate the application of a new process.

The expert coaching condition is unique among theories of teaming and advocates the value of group and team coaching in fostering success.

Hackman's Model of Team Effectiveness is based on nearly 40 years of research. Unlike other models on teaming which focus on the characteristics of teams or team construct, Hackman's model focuses on the conditions of effective teaming. This makes Hackman's model ideal for integrating with other frameworks like *Tuckman's Stages of Group Development* or *Edmondson's Theory of Teaming*.

Hackman called his framework the Five-Factor Model, but it should not be confused with the *Five-Factor Model* of personality.

Professionals seeking additional information on the Model of Team Effectiveness may consider Hackman's 2002 book, *Leading Teams: Setting the Stage for Great Performance*.

Sources[134]

HANDY'S FOUR TYPES OF CULTURE

Certification Available: no
Certification Required: no
Assessments: no
Proprietary: no
Client: organizations
Cost: not applicable
Category: culture

Developed in the 1970s by management consultant Charles Handy, the Four Types of Culture provides a framework to characterize and explain organizational culture based on the style of management that contributed to its development.

Handy's model consists of four distinct styles of management and the cultures that result, each personified by an ancient Greek god to help people understand and remember the unique characteristics of each style.

Role: Personified by Apollo, the god of order and rules, this type of culture describes an organization that values protocol, process, and procedure. Often characterized as heavily bureaucratic, this type of organization typically adopts a functional structure. Put another way, these organizations assign each employee clearly defined roles and responsibilities, aligning groups of employees based on role function.

Organizations with this cultural style function well in stable environments, typically providing long-term continuity to ensure consistent and persistent operations. Unfortunately, these types of organizations often struggle in dynamic environments or when facing crisis. They often find it difficult to adapt to sudden or unforeseen changes.

Power (also called Club Culture): Personified by Zeus, the chief deity among ancient Greek gods and the leader of the rebellion that overthrew his father Chronos, this type of culture describes organizations with centralized power structures. Within this culture, decision-making authority rests with a select few, who in turn decide how much power to delegate to others.

Organizations with a power culture typically respond quickly to problems, able to make decisions on short notice. This can prove useful for organizations in crisis or for smaller companies and start-ups. Contrarily, employees within this type of organization tend to feel little empowerment and no sense of ownership in the mission. The lack of inclusivity in decision-making leaves these organizations vulnerable to a single point of failure, the leader.

Task: Personified by Athena, goddess of knowledge, this type of culture describes organizations not structured by function but by purpose. Commonly found in matrixed organizations, this style of culture typically involves disparate functions working collectively toward a shared goal.

Organizations of this cultural style are highly flexible and collaborative, able to adapt to dynamic, rapidly changing environments. A potential risk in a task culture is that employees can become myopic, fixating on the problem, leaving the organization blind to the bigger picture.

Person (also called Existential Culture): Personified by Dionysus, the god of wine and song, this type of culture describes organizations with employees who feel they are more important than the organization. Sometimes this involves the belief that the person does not serve the organization, but the organization serves the person. This can apply to some professions like doctors (hospitals) and lawyers (law firms), who provide services to benefit the welfare of others.

Organizations with a person culture tend to offer the greatest freedom to employees, providing services only as needed. Unfortunately, this style of culture risks the organization's needs and priorities taking a back seat to the needs and desires of the employee or the customer.

Handy's Four Types of Culture is more complex than presented here. Professionals seeking additional information may consider Handy's 1976 book, *Understanding Organizations*, and his 1978 book, *Gods of Management*.

Sources[135]

HAWTHORNE EFFECT

Certification Available: no
Certification Required: no
Assessments: no
Proprietary: no
Client: individuals, groups
Cost: not applicable
Category: employee engagement

The Hawthorne Effect, officially coined by sociologist Henry Landsberger in the 1950s, is based on a series of experiments conducted in the 1920s and 1930s by Elton Mayo, Fritz Roethlisberger, and William Dickerson at Western Electric's Hawthorne Works plant. This phenomenon, also known as the Hawthorne Studies, suggests that people will modify their behavior when they know others are observing them.

In the study, researchers observed employees working in a variety of different conditions to identify which factors negatively or positively affected productivity. To facilitate the experiment, researchers altered environmental variables like the lighting conditions, break rules, and working hours.

Researchers expected that lowering lighting levels and adjusting work hours to inconvenient times would result in a noticeable decrease in productivity. However, their observations revealed something completely unexpected. All changes, regardless of the anticipated negative or positive consequences, resulted in increased productivity.

To explain this, researchers suggested that the employees of Hawthorne increased their productivity simply because they knew the researchers were observing them. In other words, an awareness that others are observing you may lead you to behave in a way that deviates from your typical behavioral patterns.

Many years later, researchers called into question the veracity of the experiment, classifying the Hawthorne Effect and its results as "fictional." Despite this, social researchers continue to take into consideration the potential implications of observation on the results of an experiment.

We include the Hawthorne Effect in *The Infourge Compendium of Models and Theories for Coaches* because it is not uncommon for coaches to observe their clients as they go about their day. This typically includes attending meetings and observing interactions with subordinates, peers, and supervisors. Coaches do this to develop an understanding of the client's environment, how they interact with others, and their typical patterns of behavior.

Because of this, coaches should be aware of how their presence as an observer may affect their client's behavior. Clients may consciously or unconsciously alter their behavior because the coach is observing them. Other theories and concepts which may support or contribute to this phenomenon include impression management and socially desirable responding.

There is limited information on how to mitigate the Hawthorne Effect. A coach's awareness that a client's behavior, while under observation, may not reflect a wholly accurate picture can help the coach contextualize their observations.

It is worth noting that lessons learned from the experiment at the Hawthorne Works plant influenced the development of *Participative Leadership Theory*. Landsberger's examination of Mayo's work found that workers who felt supported through observation and participation experienced a greater sense of satisfaction which, in turn, increased their productivity. For this reason, we characterize the Hawthorne Effect under the category of employee engagement.

Professionals seeking additional information on the Hawthorne Effect will find much written about the topic. Those looking specifically for the Hawthorne Effect and its relationship to employee engagement may consider Richard Gillespie's 1991 book, *Manufacturing Knowledge: A History of the Hawthorne Experiments*.

Sources[136]

HEALTH BELIEF MODEL

Certification Available: no
Certification Required: no
Assessments: no
Proprietary: no
Client: individuals
Cost: not applicable
Category: change (ind.)

Developed in the 1950s by social psychologists at the US Department of Health, the Health Belief Model (HBM) provided a framework to explain why so few people sought screening for tuberculosis despite easy access. Since then, HBM has evolved to become one of the most widely used frameworks for understanding individual health behaviors.

HBM consists of six constructs, identified through research, which explain why an individual may resist medical treatment or testing. Many of these manifested in individuals refusing COVID-19 testing and vaccinations.

Perceived susceptibility: This construct pertains to the client's subjective assessment of the risks posed by the disease or virus. For example, a client may possess an irrational belief that their youth and fitness make them less susceptible to catching the illness.

Perceived severity: This involves the client's subjective assessment of how bad the risk is to them. For example, a client may believe the virus is no worse than the flu.

Perceived benefits: This construct pertains to the client's subjective assessment of the efficacy of the changes considered. For example, the client may doubt the effectiveness of a screening test or a vaccine.

Perceived barriers: These are the client's feelings about the obstacles and impediments to the changes considered. For example, the client may believe getting the vaccine could risk their exposure to others with the virus.

Cues to action: These pertain to indications supporting the need for change. These indicators can be internal and external in nature and are susceptible to confirmation bias.

Self-efficacy: This is the client's confidence in their capability to adopt the changes considered.

The fundamentals of HBM, born of cognitive psychology, suggest that a person's perceptions of the threat of illness, coupled with their belief in the efficacy of the recommended treatment, predict the likelihood a person will adopt the desired behavior. In other words, individuals who either do not believe the threat is real (or will happen to them), or who do not believe the prescribed courses of action are effective, will not likely adopt the desired behavior change.

The persistent presence of these constructs among individuals across decades of health epidemics and pandemics demonstrates the efficacy of the framework in explaining certain health behaviors.

The HBM framework is fundamental and has broad utility in the domain of individual change. For this reason, we include it in *The Infourge Compendium of Models and Theories*.

The elements of HBM can help clients adopt a more objective and systematic approach when considering the various aspects of personal and professional change. These may include their belief in their ability to adopt new behaviors, or their belief in the necessity for change. In coaching, we sometimes call these beliefs the client's perceptions.

Like other models on individual change, HBM is most effective when coupled with other theories, tools, and assessments that complement the process. For example, when discussing "perceived severity" with a client, it may be helpful to use resources designed to facilitate an objective risk analysis.

Professionals seeking additional information on the Health Belief Model will find much written on the topic, including Charles Abraham and Paschal Sheeran's chapter, "The Health Belief Model," featured in the *Cambridge Handbook of Psychology, Health, and Medicine* (2007).

Sources[137]

HEIDER'S BALANCE THEORY

Certification Available: no
Certification Required: no
Assessments: no
Proprietary: no
Client: individuals
Cost: not applicable
Category: conflict, polarities

Introduced in the early 1940s by social psychologist Fritz Heider, Balance Theory suggests that individuals inherently strive to maintain psychological equity and stability in social relationships. His theory is among the most influential models in the category of *Consistency Theories*.

Heider noted in his research that individuals tended to seek out interpersonal connections which foster a sense of balance while avoiding connections that create an imbalance. Heider also determined that when an imbalance exists, it can create uncomfortable tension for the individual experiencing the imbalance.

To demonstrate his theory, Heider created a formulaic representation. Sometimes called the POX Triangle, POX Model, POX Formula, or simply Heider's Triad, the concept introduces three variables involved in a person's quest to seek balance, maintain balance, and avoid imbalance. These three variables are:

• Prime Person (P): This is the individual who experiences the balance or imbalance in the relationship.

• Other Person (O): This is the other person in the relationship, the one who often serves as the catalyst for change.

• Object or Third Person (X): This is either an object (e.g., a car, money, etc.), an issue (e.g., controversial topic), or a third person. This often serves as the source of the conflict.

In addition to the above variables, the POX Formula includes two functions:

Likes (+): This denotes a positive opinion or relationship between two variables.

Dislikes (-): This denotes a negative opinion or relationship between two variables.

Given three variables, and the possibility for positive or negative sentiments, the results yield four possible combinations of balanced relationships and four possible combinations of imbalanced relationships.

Balanced relationships:
• P+O, P+X, O+X: prime person likes second person, prime person likes the object/issue, second person also likes the object/issue.
• P-O, P-X, O+X: prime person dislikes second person and issue, second person likes the issue.
• P-O, P+X, O-X: prime person dislikes second person but likes the issue, second person dislikes the issue.
• P+O, P-X, O-X: prime person likes the second person but dislikes the issue, second person dislikes the issue.

Imbalanced relationships:
• P+O, P-X, O+X: prime person likes second person but dislikes the issue, second person likes the issue.
• P+O, P+X, O-X: prime person likes second person and the issue, but second person dislikes the issue.
• P-O, P+X, O+X: prime person dislikes second person but likes the issue, second person likes the issue.
• P-O, P-X, O-X: prime person dislikes second person and issue, second person dislikes the issue.

Another manifestation of Heider's Balance Theory is the often-used expression:
My friend's friend is my friend,
My friend's enemy is my enemy,
My enemy's friend is my enemy,
My enemy's enemy is my friend.

Heider's theory is useful with clients struggling to build and maintain meaningful relationships at work or those experiencing discomfort between conflicting social polarities.

Professionals seeking additional information on Heider's Balance Theory will find much written on the topic, including Heider's seminal book from 1958, *The Psychology of Interpersonal Relations*.

Sources[138]

HELICAL MODEL OF COMMUNICATION

Certification Available: no
Certification Required: no
Assessments: no
Proprietary: no
Client: individuals
Cost: not applicable
Category: communication

Developed in 1967 by communications professor Frank E. X. Dance, the Helical Model of Communication is a visual framework depicting the natural evolution of human communication. The model uses a three-dimensional inverted, conical-shaped spiral to represent how an individual's ability to communicate progresses over time.

At the base of the model, the spiral is narrow and compressed. This represents the newborn, able to communicate solely through crying and limited noise making. As we move further up the spiral, the cone widens and the spring becomes less compressed, representing the individual's ability to form sentences, articulate concepts, and master more complex forms of communication (e.g., writing, drawing, language, storytelling, etc.).

With time, the infant becomes a child, an adolescent, and eventually an adult. With this maturation comes a natural increase in the individual's ability to communicate.

The Helical Model, though simple, includes several assumptions fundamental to the framework.

• Communication is cyclical, often drawing from previous outcomes to inform present approaches to communication. In this way, communication never truly repeats itself. When we receive information (feedback) about something we have said, we use that feedback to adjust our future messaging to better resonate with the recipient.

• Communication is cumulative; as we grow and learn, we acquire a greater capacity to make distinctions and label the world around us. This, in turn, allows us to form more complex methods of communication, facilitating a more efficient and precise level of messaging.

• Time is an essential variable in the evolution of communication. In typical circumstances, a person's ability to communicate is not static, but consistently evolving. This evolutionary change may appear so subtle and slow that it is imperceptible, but it evolves nonetheless.

• The widening of the spiral (over time) signifies our ability to utilize more complex forms of communication as we get older. The conical shape implies that regardless of how complex our present ability to communicate, the origins for all communication are simple.

For example, the first time we communicate with someone, we may rely on more verbose, detail-oriented language. Once we get to know the other person, we can rely on more complex conduits for communication, like nonverbal conduits (e.g., gestures and emblems), and the enhanced use of spoken language (e.g., words or phrases with alternative or ambiguous meaning).

• Our past experiences influence how we communicate in different environments. Over time we may learn some forms of communication are more acceptable in some settings and less so in others. As we learn these norms, we adjust how we communicate to better fit our specific circumstances.

Unlike most frameworks in the ICMT, the Helical Model of Communication does not provide a concrete structure or defined stages of progression. It simply presents the belief that our ability to communicate evolves with time and experience.

The Helical Model of Communication is useful for clients looking to explore, understand, and develop their style of communication.

The model is also known as Dance's Communication Model, and the Helix Model of Communication. Professionals seeking additional information will find significant literature available, including Dance's 1976 book, *Functions of Human Communication: A Theoretical Approach.*

Sources[139]

HERON'S SIX CATEGORIES OF INTERVENTION

Certification Available: no
Certification Required: no
Assessments: yes (Six Styles Questionnaire)
Proprietary: no
Client: individuals
Cost: not applicable
Category: communication, feedback

Developed by psychologist John Heron in 1975, the Six Categories of Intervention provides a framework for exploring the various ways leaders communicate with their followers. Heron uses the term "intervention" to include any form of communication intended to influence or create change (e.g., verbal, text, etc.). The framework identifies six types of communication Heron further categorizes into two leadership styles.

Authoritative styles: The first style describes an autocratic leader, one who prefers a hands-on approach to leadership and management.

- **Prescriptive**: Considered the most direct type of communication. This occurs when a leader provides meticulous directions to subordinates on what task to perform with instructions on how to perform the task.

  This style of intervention has utility when working with inexperienced teams or in time-sensitive situations requiring a rapid response. However, the prescriptive nature of this style may indicate a lack of trust between leaders and their subordinates.

- **Informative**: This style of communication involves the leader imparting knowledge and wisdom derived from their personal experiences. Their intention is to help guide the subordinate by using the leader's own experiences to influence the employee's work.

This form of intervention may work with skilled subordinates who lack experience. However, this style of communication can make employees feel micromanaged.

- **Confronting**: Considered the most aggressive type of communication, this style involves the leader questioning an employee's approach to task completion. The leader's intention is to challenge the employee to consider alternative ways to complete the task. This style of intervention is useful when trying to help subordinates think independently and creatively.

Facilitative styles: The second style of leadership communication describes a democratic leader, one who understands the subordinate's strengths and weaknesses and trusts in their ability to complete the tasks assigned.

- **Cathartic**: This type of communication occurs when a leader works with the employee to explore their feelings and frustrations with a task. The leader's intention is to help the employee better understand the issues.

  This style of intervention is useful with skilled employees experiencing a slowdown in performance or productivity.

- **Catalytic**: Believed to be the most common type of communication, this involves the leader fostering and supporting the employee's self-discovery.

  This style of intervention is useful with self-aware employees with an ability for introspection.

- **Supportive**: This type of communication occurs when a leader helps the employee build self-esteem and confidence by reinforcing their strengths and highlighting their achievements and contributions to the organization.

  This style of intervention may help employees experiencing self-doubt and a loss of confidence.

Heron's Six Categories of Intervention is a lens through which clients may explore their approach to leadership communication. The framework also allows clients to examine the way they provide feedback to their employees.

Professionals seeking additional knowledge will find literature online and in Heron's 1975 book, *Helping the Client: A Creative Practical Guide* (fifth edition, 2001). An assessment is available to help clients discover their preferred style of intervention.

Sources[140]

HERRMANN'S WHOLE BRAIN MODEL

Certification Available: yes
Certification Required: yes
Assessments: yes (HBDI)
Proprietary: yes (Herrmann Global LLC)
Client: individuals, groups, teams, orgs
Cost: pricing not available
Category: learning/development

Developed in 1976 by creative-thinking researcher Ned Herrmann, the Whole Brain Model provides a framework for identifying and understanding individual preferences for learning and thinking. The model uses the following four regions of the brain to characterize the four learning preferences.

Left side: This is the analytical, rational, and objective side of the brain.

Right side: This is the emotional, intuitive, and subjective side of the brain.

Upper side: This is the intellectual and theoretical portion of the brain.

Lower side: This is the instinctive and realistic portion of the brain.

Four Preferences

- **Analytical** (upper/left side): Individuals with this learning preference want to learn how things work by examining the issue and reviewing all available data and variables. Characteristically, these learners are logic driven and fact based. They prefer assessments based on quantitative analysis. They favor learning in a structured environment with a curriculum that is both methodical and process focused.

- **Experimental** (upper/right side): Individuals with this learning preference are imaginative explorers. They enjoy taking risks and trying new things, though they can be impulsive. These learners are dreamers capable of significant creativity and innovation. They respond well to subjective thinking and often use visual means to guide their learning (e.g., mind maps and brainstorming boards). Experimental learners possess a capacity to synthesize vague and ambiguous information and make meaning from chaotic facts and figures.

- **Relational** (lower/right side): Individuals with this learning preference are more emotional and expressive. They tend to have strong interpersonal skills and are caring of others. These learners are adept communicators and possess the ability to consider more subjective variables like the feelings of other people. Emotionally intelligent and empathetic, these learners tend to work well in group environments.

- **Practical** (lower/left side): Individuals with this learning preference are structured, organized, and methodical in their learning. They prefer timelines and logical sequencing in their curriculum. These learners are detail-oriented planners.

Further characterizing Herrmann's Whole Brain Model, the framework suggests that the upper brain styles, Analytical and Experimental, are more receptive to theoretical learning, while the lower brain styles, Relational and Practical, prefer realistic learning. Alternatively, left-brain styles, Analytical and Practical, tend to rely more on rational thought, while the right-brain styles, Relational and Experimental, prefer intuitive thinking.

Herrmann suggests that individuals may possess an ability to learn across these styles; however, we tend to develop a preference for at least two styles and as many as three. These findings are based on results from the primary assessment developed for this model, the Herrmann Brain Dominance Instrument (HBDI).

The Herrmann Whole Brain Model is proprietary to Herrmann Global LLC. Formal use of the model and its associated assessments requires prior training and certification provided by Herrmann Global LLC.

Professionals seeking additional information may consider Herrmann's 1988 book, *The Creative Brain*, or his 1996 book, *The Whole Brain Business Book: Unlocking the Power of Whole Brain Thinking in Organizations and Individuals*, co-authored by Ann Herrmann-Nehdi.

Sources[141]

HEURISTIC-SYSTEMATIC MODEL OF INFORMATION PROCESSING

Certification Available: no
Certification Required: no
Assessments: no
Proprietary: no
Client: individuals
Cost: not applicable
Category: influence, decision-making

Developed in the 1980s by social psychologist Shelly Chaiken, the Heuristic-Systematic Model of Information Processing (HSM) is a framework that explains how people process information intended to persuade them. Unlike other models that look at the content of a persuasive message, HSM explores influence from the perspective of how individuals consider and internalize the message.

HSM suggests that an individual receiving a message intended to persuade them will assess the message using either the heuristic process or the systematic process.

Heuristic process: This process involves the use of preexisting knowledge (i.e., experience) or a form of rule structure (i.e., if this, then that) to facilitate how we judge the information we receive. We then make decisions based on those judgments.

Considered a nonanalytical approach, the heuristic process's dependency on past experiences and rule structures makes it a quick and easy process to use. People using heuristics in decision-making will look for cues that indicate which rules or experiences may apply for a given situation.

For example, a person participating in a large group discussion may look to see if there is a simple majority. If so, they may apply the rule of "consensus implies correctness," which suggests that if most people believe one way, then they must be correct.

Other examples of heuristics include the sentiments "experts are usually right" and "if other people believe it, it must be true."

Systematic process: This process involves a careful and methodical examination of information using a logic-driven process based in critical thinking. Individuals using the systematic process often question the veracity and validity of the information they receive regardless of who is delivering the message.

For example, just because the CEO says something does not make that statement true. Individuals using the systematic process will seek out facts to inform their decision-making process.

Both heuristic and systematic processing have merits and risks. Systematic processing is more methodical and results in more thoughtful decisions. However, it requires more time and energy than heuristic processing. For individuals with limited cognitive bandwidth, the heuristic process offers a convenient alternative, though at a potential cost of decision-making efficacy. Between the two, people tend to use heuristic processing more often.

A person's selection of which process to use can occur on either a conscious or subconscious level. Other theories, like *Heider's Balance Theory*, suggest our sentiments about the person sending the message can lead us to automatically accept or reject the message.

HSM is a useful concept to consider when working with clients easily influenced by others within their environment or those who struggle to commit the time and energy to critical thinking.

HSM has broad utility, particularly in the fields of marketing and advertising, and can help clients design messaging to better resonate with consumers. HSM may also help leaders convey sensitive messages more effectively to the workforce.

Professionals seeking additional information on the Heuristic-Systematic Model of Information Processing may consider Chaiken's 1980 article in the *Journal of Personality and Social Psychology*, "Heuristic Versus Systematic Information Processing and the Use of Source Versus Message Cues in Persuasion."

Sources[142]

HONEY AND MUMFORD LEARNING STYLES

Certification Available: no
Certification Required: no
Assessments: yes (LSQ)
Proprietary: no
Client: individuals
Cost: not applicable
Category: learning, personality

Developed in 1986 by psychologists Peter Honey and Alan Mumford, the Honey and Mumford Learning Styles (HMM) provides a framework for identifying, understanding, and exploring an individual's learning preferences. The model consists of four styles.

Activists: These are individuals who prefer to learn by doing like experimentation, trial and error, and by getting their hands dirty. For these learners, the most effective source of learning involves hands-on activities like brainstorming, puzzle solving, group discussions, and competition. The least effective learning approaches to use with this group include long lectures and lengthy reading assignments.

Theorists: These learners prefer to understand the theory behind the subject or skill they will learn. For theorist learners, analysis and synthesis is critical to their learning process. Understanding how and why something works is essential for them before they can apply a concept. The most effective approach to teaching theorists is to provide them with data, metrics, visuals, quotes, stories, and statistics. The least effective learning approach to use with this group is any activity involving significant emotion or that is unstructured or disorganized. Asking these learners to act without explaining the principles or theories behind the action can frustrate them.

Pragmatists: These learners require justification or proof of efficacy before they commit to learning. In other words, they need to see that the skill or method successfully works before they will consider learning the skill. The most effective approach to teaching these learners is by providing them with case studies, real-world examples, success stories, and enough time to envision what practical application might look like. The least effective learning approaches to use with this group include the use of exercises that offer no immediate practical benefit, providing them with limited instructions, or the use of activities that focus too heavily on theory.

Reflectors: These are individuals whose learning preferences center on watching others apply the concepts, observing the outcomes, and then collecting data. The most effective approach to teaching reflectors is to provide them a structured way of examining and exploring their observations. This may include small group (or pair) discussions, worksheets designed to foster an exploration of the skill, and questionnaires. The least effective learning approaches to use with this group include forcing them to take the lead in group settings, tasking them to do things without sufficient time to prepare, and rushing them to complete activities.

HMM, also called the Honey Mumford Model, is based on *Kolb's Learning Styles*, and suggests that by becoming more aware of how they learn, clients can take steps to improve their learning.

A distinct trait of HMM is its integration of personality characteristics into the four styles. For this reason, we also include this model under the category of personality styles. For example, HMM describes an activist learner as one who is excitement seeking, impatient, and self-focused.

HMM is a useful framework for clients seeking to better understand their learning preferences. For coaches, recognizing which learning style applies to your clients can enable you to better adapt to meet them where they are and help you select more effective approaches.

To help determine which learning style applies to your client, Honey and Mumford developed an assessment called the Learning Styles Questionnaire (LSQ), available for free online.

Professionals seeking additional information on the Honey and Mumford Learning Styles may consider their 1982 book, *The Manual of Learning Styles*.

Sources[143]

HOY-TARTER DECISION-MAKING MODEL

Certification Available: no
Certification Required: no
Assessments: no
Proprietary: no
Client: individuals, groups, teams, orgs
Cost: not applicable
Category: decision-making, leadership, teaming

Developed in the late 1990s by professors Wayne K. Hoy and C. John Tarter, the Hoy-Tarter Decision-Making Model (HTDM), provides a multifaceted framework to prepare a client for effective decision-making. The model explores the decision-making process across multiple domains, beginning with the decision-makers.

The HTDM consists of a four-quadrant matrix used to determine if a person should participate in the decision-making process. The matrix considers two dimensions for each potential decision-maker.

Dimension 1—Relevance: This domain asks if the decision is relevant to the person. Does it matter to them? Will the decisions affect them in significant ways?

Dimension 2—Expertise: This domain considers if the person possesses a specific set of skills or experiences that allows them to contribute to the decision-making process. Are they the only ones with this skill or are there others?

- Expertise (Yes) and Relevance (Yes): This person should participate in the decision-making process. They possess both valuable knowledge and have a vested interest in the decision outcome.

- Expertise (No) and Relevance (Yes): This person should have a marginal role in the process. They may not bring expertise to the table, but they may bring dedication since the decision is relevant to them.

- Expertise (Yes) and Relevance (No): This person should participate only when their expertise provides value to the decision-making process.

- Expertise (No) and Relevance (No): This person should not participate in the decision-making process. They bring neither expertise nor relevance to the process.

HTDM incorporates several leadership styles to help facilitate the process. Depending on the participants selected to participate in the process, a leader may need to adopt one of five leadership styles, each with a distinct role. Some variations of HTDM only list four styles. The labels differ slightly among these variations; however, the concept is generally the same.

Democratic: The leader has maximum involvement in the process.
Conflictual: The leader limits their involvement, stepping in only to address conflict.
Stakeholder: The leader occasionally engages to educate decision-makers.
Expert: The leader occasionally engages to foster better decisions and provide subject matter expertise.
Noncollaborative: The leader is not involved in the process.

Within a decision-making group, individuals may serve in one of five distinct roles.

Integrator: This person seeks out or creates consensus among the group.
Parliamentarian: This person facilitates safe and open discourse among the team.
Educator: This person explains matters to the group to foster understanding.
Solicitor: This person fosters group participation by seeking input from participants.
Director: This person makes unilateral decisions.

HTDM is distinct among decision-making models in that it emphasizes the preparatory process for decision-making.

The Hoy-Tarter Decision-Making Model is significantly more complex than presented here. Professionals seeking additional information may consider Hoy and Tarter's 1995 book, *Administrators Solving the Problems of Practice: Decision-Making Concepts, Cases, and Consequences.*

Sources[144]

HUMAN SYNERGISTICS INTERNATIONAL CIRCUMPLEX

Certification Available: yes
Certification Required: yes
Assessments: yes (LSI, LWS, others)
Proprietary: yes (Human Synergistics Int'l.)
Client: individuals, groups, teams, organizations
Cost: $1,800–$2,100
Category: personality, leadership, culture

Introduced in 1971 by psychologist J. Clayton Lafferty and further developed by organizational behaviorist Robert A. Cooke, the Human Synergistics International Circumplex (HSI) is a complex, multifaceted framework designed to identify the behavioral styles of individuals, groups, teams, organizations, and organizational culture.

The HSI Circumplex consists of 12 behavioral styles, each presented through the optic of the individual, leader, group, organization, and customer. We present the 12 styles from the individual perspective.

Humanistic-Encouraging: These individuals are highly sensitive to the needs of others; they possess a high level of interest in the development of people, and often coach and mentor others.

Affiliative: These individuals focus on maintaining pleasant relationships, share their feelings, and strive to make others feel accepted.

Approval: These individuals need to feel accepted, often determining their self-worth based on how others feel about them. They are highly agreeable and strive to please others.

Conventional: These individuals strive to blend in with their environment and abhor attention of any kind. They prefer routine and value a safe and predictable work environment.

Dependent: These individuals believe they have little control over their life, often deferring to others when important decisions arise. They desire self-protection so much they depend on others to perform tasks.

Avoidance: Even more self-protective than dependents, these individuals go to great lengths to play it safe and avoid risks. They avoid group activities, and when faced with a choice, they offer noncommittal responses.

Oppositional: These individuals desire a sense of security, often protecting themselves using critical, invasive, and even cynical questioning. Though their questions may lead to innovations, they can fixate on the smallest of issues and blame others for their own mistakes.

Power: These individuals desire prestige through recognition, often associating their self-worth with how well they can manipulate and control others. They tend to adopt a dictatorial style coupled with an aggressive approach to micromanagement.

Competitive: These individuals determine their self-worth by comparing themselves to others. They desire recognition and adoration from others, often turning noncompetitive situations into competitive ones to prove themselves.

Perfectionistic: These individuals determine self-worth by how well they perform. They strive for flawless results, often putting extreme pressure on themselves and others. They tend to ignore the needs and feelings of others.

Achievement: These individuals strive for quality results, believing they are a by-product of effort, not luck. They plan, explore their options, and learn from their mistakes.

Self-Actualizing: These individuals strive for personal growth and fulfillment by seeking out new experiences.

The HSI Circumplex has broad utility, including organizational change, leadership development, culture, and more. It includes a variety of assessments, including the Life Styles Inventory (LSI) and the Acumen Leadership Workstyles (LWS).

The HSI Circumplex is significantly more complex than presented here. Professionals seeking additional information will find limited resources on the model; however, training is available from Human Synergistics International.

Sources[145]

IBM DESIGN THINKING MODEL

Certification Available: yes
Certification Required: yes
Assessments: no
Proprietary: yes
Client: groups, teams, organizations
Cost: pricing not available
Category: change (org.), problem-solving

Developed in 2013 by IBM designers Adam Cutler and Miroslav Azis, the IBM Design Thinking Model (DTM) provides a framework to foster consumer-driven organizational cultures. The comprehensive DTM framework combines concepts from teaming, decision-making, problem-solving, communications, and innovation.

The DTM consists of three key principles that guide the process, a three-step process called the Loop, and three tactics that align the process. To facilitate a better understanding of the framework, we adjusted some of the original technology-heavy language to reflect a broader business application.

Principle 1—User outcomes: It is essential to understand who the client is and what their needs are.

Principle 2—Reinvention: When is the last time the client rethought what they are making or the service they are providing?

Principle 3—Diverse empowered teams: Who are the right people from the client's organization and are they at the table?

The Loop Process

Step 1—Observe: Immerse yourself in the client's world; observe their needs, their environment, and their challenges. Develop an enhanced understanding and awareness of the client.

Step 2—Reflect: Synthesize and analyze the data you collect from your observations of the client. This is especially important when working in diverse teams, as a diversity of membership leads to different interpretations of the situation. These differing perspectives are important to the process, allowing for a more holistic assessment.

Step 3—Make: Use the resulting knowledge to influence the generation of new ideas. Test the efficacy of these ideas, analyze the results, and further innovate.

Tactics

• **Hills**: Develop concise statements and clear goals to share regularly with members and ensure everyone is working around a shared outcome.

• **Playbacks**: Check in regularly with the team to determine their status, share stories of lessons learned, exchange feedback, measure their progress, and correct misalignments.

• **Sponsor users**: Incorporate the client and the client's stakeholders into the process. They provide expertise and insight into both the client's challenges and the challenges faced by the client's customers. This helps the team stay aligned with the client's reality and ensure relevance.

The IBM Design Thinking Model is a useful framework for helping organizations apply large-scale teaming and innovation strategies in support of their end user or customer. The model inherently leads to change, so we include it in the category of organizational change.

The IBM Design Thinking Model is more complex than presented here. Professionals seeking additional information may consider Srikant M. Datar, Amram Migdal, and Paul Hamilton's 2021 *Harvard Business Review* case study, "IBM: Design Thinking."

A multiphase certification in the IBM Design Thinking Model is available through IBM. As of publication, the program is free, though IBM qualifies this as temporary. Those who complete the program gain access to a library of resources and tools designed to facilitate the IBM Design Thinking Model.

Sources[146]

IDEA FEEDBACK MODEL

Certification Available: no
Certification Required: no
Assessments: no
Proprietary: no
Client: individuals
Cost: not applicable
Category: feedback

The origin of the IDEA Feedback Model is difficult to ascertain. This model, like many other feedback models contained in this compendium, adopts a simple four-step process represented by an acronym.

Variations of this model exist and use slightly different labels to describe each step. We present two of these variations.

Step 1—Identify: The first step of the model requires the feedback provider to highlight the recipient's behavior, being as specific as reasonable. Where possible, provide examples citing the day, time, and location to reinforce the point.

Step 2—Describe: In the second step, the provider offers the recipient examples of how their behavior impacted the other members of the team, the customer, and the business. In this step, it is important to cite the specific, observable, or measurable consequences of the recipient's behavior on others.

Step 3—Encourage: In the third step, the provider encourages the recipient and boosts their motivation to seek out and commit to change.

The provider must demonstrate their support of the recipient's behavioral change (in the case of negative feedback). It is imperative that the provider avoid signaling judgment, as this may lead the recipient to reject any further feedback.

Step 4—Action: In the final step, both the provider and recipient identify and agree to a clear and measurable set of actions intended to correct the issue. This is critical to accountability and future feedback sessions.

An alternative version of the model presents a similar process using slightly different labels.

Step 1—Intent: This requires that the provider explain why they are sharing feedback with the recipient using positive framing. In this variation of the model, providing details on the problematic behavior does not occur until the second step.

Step 2—Describe: This step is the same as in the previous version, except the provider combines the problematic behavior with the impact of said behavior in one step.

Step 3—Exchange: In this variation of the model, the third step promotes a two-way conversation between the provider and the recipient which fosters deeper rapport and trust between both parties. The provider listens to the recipient's perspective and seeks common ground and understanding. Like the previous version, this increases the recipient's level of commitment to change.

Step 4—Action: This step is the same as the previous version.

The IDEA Feedback Model is one of many feedback models included in *The Infourge Compendium of Models and Theories* and among a small group of virtually identical processes like *BIFF, BEEF, BOOST, SBI,* and others.

Because many of the models are similar in their design and intent, professionals should familiarize themselves with these variations since clients and other coaches will likely use one or more of these frameworks.

Sources[147]

IDENTITY MANAGEMENT THEORY

> **Certification Available:** no
> **Certification Required:** no
> **Assessments:** no
> **Proprietary:** no
> **Client:** individuals, groups, teams, organizations
> **Cost:** not applicable
> **Category:** culture, communication, bias

Developed in the 1990s by communications professors William R. Cupach and Tadasu Todd Imahori, Identity Management Theory (IMT) provides a framework for examining the relationship between cultural identity, personal identity, and interpersonal communication.

Incorporating Identity Management Theory into practice requires understanding five core elements at the intersection of culture, identity, and communication.

Intercultural communication: This refers to any communication between two or more individuals from two or more different cultures.

Intracultural communication: This refers to communication between two or more individuals from the same culture.

Cultural identity: This pertains to the aspects of a culture that a person integrates into their self-image or identity. This distinction is important as individuals often adopt some but not all aspects of a culture and mix them with aspects of other cultures and subcultures. A person's cultural identity typically evolves and changes over time.

Face: These are external behaviors an individual chooses to present to the world. Face incorporates elements of an individual's culture and is a manifestation or reflection of cultural identity. Other models refer to this as the public persona or external identity.

Face work: This is the effort an individual puts into developing their face, which includes a collection of skills and strategies. A person's preference for autonomy (positive or negative) influences their face work.

- Positive autonomy is a desire for acceptance and approval from others.

- Negative autonomy is a desire for independence and freedom from imposition.

IMT suggests that effective intercultural relationships require that all parties successfully traverse a three-step process. Failure at any point risks the relationship.

Step 1—Trial and error: Also called the **Trial phase**, this occurs early in the relationship and involves both individuals seeking out similarities or commonalities between their respective cultural identities. Individuals who focus on the differences between their cultural identities will encounter greater difficulty finding common ground during this phase of the process.

It is important to note that this phase pertains to similarities between the cultural identity of interacting individuals, not their actual cultures. Therefore, two people from opposing cultures can form meaningful friendships.

Step 2—Mixing-up: Also called **Enmeshment**, this occurs when individuals can build upon the commonalities discovered in the first phase and form a new "relational identity." This is a distinct identity that belongs only to the interacting parties and represents the nature and manner of their relationship.

Step 3—Renegotiation: Over time, as the relationship strengthens, the relational identity developed in step two begins to influence each person's cultural identity. This might entail each person adopting some aspect of their partner's cultural identity into their own.

IMT is more complex than presented here and includes discussions of stereotypes, generalizations, bias, ignorance, and more. Professionals seeking additional information may consider psychologist Erving Goffman's 1967 book, *Interaction Ritual: Essays on Face-to-Face Behavior.*

Sources[148]

IMMUNITY TO CHANGE

Certification Available: yes (Minds at Work)
Certification Required: no
Assessments: no
Proprietary: yes (Minds at Work)
Client: individuals, groups, teams, organizations
Cost: not applicable
Category: change (ind.), change (org.), polarities

Created by developmental psychologist Robert Kegan and management professor Lisa Lahey, the Immunity to Change model provides a framework for identifying and understanding the sources of change resistance.

At the core of Immunity to Change is the concept of "competing commitments." These are often unconscious beliefs made up of assumptions that can undermine a person's attempt to change. Though a person may consciously want change, the presence of competing commitments may hinder or prevent them from the change they desire.

To facilitate the use of Immunity to Change in fostering meaningful and lasting change, Kegan and Lahey offer this three-stage method to help identify what is getting in the way of change.

Stage 1—Uncover competing commitments: During this stage, the client strives to identify some of the commitments undermining their ability to change. Often, these commitments manifest in the form of complaints.

For example, asking the client, "What changes would you like to see at work to help you be more effective" might result in them complaining that change is not necessary, that they have successfully performed their job for years and "you don't fix what isn't broken."

Stage 2—Examine big assumptions: At the core of each commitment or complaint lies one or more assumptions. These assumptions often evolve from a person's perceptions.

For example: The client in the previous example may perceive that forced changes to how they do the job implies that for years they were not performing the job correctly. The assumption that change only happens when something is wrong underpins his competing commitment.

Stage 3—Questioning the assumption and moving forward: Once the client identifies the competing commitment and understands the underlying assumption, they may begin to challenge their assumption. To facilitate this, Kegan and Lahey offer a five-step process.

Step 1—Notice and record: Ask the client to make observations of how these assumptions influence their behavior. Encourage them to consider the consequences of these behaviors on themselves and others.

Step 2—Contrary evidence: Ask the client to be on the lookout for facts or information that may cast doubt on their original assumptions. Often, people ignore evidence that contradicts their assumptions, preferring to see only the information that validates their beliefs.

Step 3—Explore history: Once the client begins to see contrary evidence, ask them to consider when and how their assumptions first took hold. Encourage them to explore these experiences and how, in light of new evidence, they might reflect differently on these experiences.

Step 4—Test assumptions: Ask the client to try subtle changes in behaviors that contrast with their original assumption. These should consist of incremental changes that give the client time and safety to experiment.

Step 5—Evaluate the results: Ask the client to reflect on these subtle changes and their results. Explore, with the client, how the results affect their underlying assumptions and how they may lead to different assumptions and commitments.

Immunity to Change is a widely used concept and includes a popular tool called the Immunity to Change Map. Sources offer differing perspectives and applications of the model. Professionals seeking additional information may consider Kegan and Lahey's 2009 book, *Immunity to Change.*

Sources[149]

INNOVATION FUNNEL

Certification Available: no
Certification Required: no
Assessments: no
Proprietary: no
Client: individuals, groups, teams, organizations
Cost: not applicable
Category: decision-making, problem-solving

An Innovation Funnel is an umbrella term referring to a variety of processes designed to facilitate the use of creative decision-making to sort, prioritize, and select from multiple options. These types of frameworks often involve creating a list of options or ideas, narrowing the list over a series of steps, and identifying a single desirable course of action.

Innovation Funnels include formal processes like the *Stage Gate Process*, and a variety of informal frameworks. We present a very generalized conceptual overview of an Innovation Funnel.

Most Innovation Funnels begin with a period of exploration and intensive research to collect as much relevant data as possible. Applied in a different context, this stage may include creative brainstorming to identify an extensive list of ideas or possibilities. The broad opening of the funnel visually depicts this first stage in the process and represents the collection of as much information as possible, which feeds the funnel.

The second step in the process, visually depicted by the narrowing of the funnel, represents an analysis of the available options. This analysis may include a comparison of each option to the client's goals, mission, vision, or relevant external factors. The client may also consider their limitations and their strengths when analyzing the options. The resulting assessment allows the client to eliminate unrealistic options in favor of ones more likely to produce the desired outcomes.

The third step of the process, often depicted as the narrow stem of the funnel, represents the prioritization and selection of the most logical options. In this step, the remaining options undergo comparison analysis to determine the cost/benefit of each option. This analysis may include an estimation of the possibility and probability of each option to help the client achieve their desired goals.

The bottom of the funnel represents the outcome of this process. The client selects the option they believe most appropriate for their needs. It is important to note, if the final option fails to satisfy the objective, the client may return to the prioritized list and select another course of action.

Between each stage in the Innovation Funnel, "screens" or "gates" facilitate the objective decision-making process. These gates allow stakeholders to review the process and provide feedback. It is critical that stakeholders use measurable metrics and key performance indicators when reviewing progress.

Variations of the Innovation Funnel range from simple three-step processes to more complex and methodical processes. More complex frameworks may expand on the option generation, option analysis, and option selection aspects of the process. Others may include additional steps to help the client actualize their selected option.

Because Innovation Funnels provide a methodical approach to the sorting, prioritization, and selection of options (or course of action), many professionals working in product development and process improvement find Innovation Funnels useful.

Despite their popularity, Innovation Funnels are not without criticism. Some express concern that funnel processes may perpetuate a mindset of "picking" vs. "creating" winners, thereby contributing to the fear that teams will pick from "what is given" to them versus creating a better solution. Though a valid concern, some funnel-style processes take this concern into consideration and build in safeguards to avoid this risk, like the use of a neutral process facilitator and added steps to facilitate brainstorming.

Professionals seeking additional information will find much written on the topic, including David O'Sullivan and Lawrence Dooley's 2015 book, *The Innovation Funnel: Planning Change in Any Organization.*

Sources[150]

INNOVATION MANAGEMENT

Certification Available: no
Certification Required: no
Assessments: no
Proprietary: no
Client: groups, teams
Cost: not applicable
Category: change, problem-solving, management

Innovation Management is a commonly used term in business and organizational development, though there is no universally accepted definition. This means innovation management can hold different meaning for different people, and the intent behind its use may vary from one person to another.

The term innovation, according to Webster's Dictionary, means the introduction of something new. Therefore, we present innovation management as an umbrella term encompassing a variety of processes and models used to create and facilitate the introduction of something new (i.e., change).

Though sources vary on what constitutes innovation and how to achieve innovation within an organization, a belief common to many sources is that innovation applies to more than an organization's products and services and includes some of the following:

• Culture: This involves helping an organization achieve meaningful cultural change.

• Structure: This type of innovation focuses on the hierarchy and reporting flow of an organization.

• Business processes: This type of innovation applies to how an organization conducts business and produces its products and services.

• Strategy: This type of innovation examines an organization's ability to identify trends, anticipate future needs, and plan accordingly.

• Networking: This type of innovation explores innovative opportunities through collaboration, partnerships, alliances, and mergers.

• Capabilities: This type of innovation considers opportunities for growth and development.

• Employee engagement: This type of innovation explores opportunities to innovate and improve employee engagement.

Readers exploring the topic of innovation management will find an array of methodologies, processes, and frameworks covering a range of innovation issues. These processes are often unique to the type of innovation. In other words, a framework used for innovating a new product is different from a framework used for innovating organizational culture.

Innovation management theories which focus on the creation and development of new products and services include the *Theory of Inventive Problem-Solving (TRIZ)*, *Systematic Inventive Thinking (SIT)*, and the Innovator's Dilemma.

Innovation management theories that facilitate the development and implementation of new processes include the *Stage Gate Process, Kaizen, Doblin's 10 Types of Innovation*, and the *Innovation Funnel*.

Innovation management theories that facilitate the innovation of organizational structure, culture, or employee engagement include *Bridges' Transition Model, Kotter's Change Management Model*, and the *Job Demands-Resources Model*.

The management aspect of innovation examines how leaders (formal and informal) manage initiatives designed to foster innovation. This inherently requires leaders to possess the ability to manage complex and multifaceted projects. For this reason, many innovation management frameworks incorporate project management skills like Project Management Institute's Project Management Body of Knowledge (PMBOK), which facilitate a methodical approach to managing and implementing innovation.

Professionals seeking additional information on innovation management will find significant literature on the issue.

Sources[151]

INTEGRAL THEORY

Certification Available: yes
Certification Required: no
Assessments: yes (several)
Proprietary: unknown
Client: individuals, groups, teams
Cost: pricing varies by vendor
Category: learning/development

Developed by philosopher Ken Wilber in the early 1970s, Integral Theory is a complex metatheory some sources describe as "a theory of everything," while others describe it as a map for the psychological and spiritual evolution of human beings.

Integral Theory incorporates a wide range of theories, Western and Eastern-based, from the fields of psychology, sociology, biology, religion, spirituality, and others. The ICMT categorizes Wilber's theory as adult development because it draws heavily from the works of Loevinger, Piaget, Freud, and Erikson.

Integral Theory consists of five essential elements or aspects, each based on multiple theories and philosophies.

Quadrants: Among the most widely used aspects of Integral Theory are the four quadrants, known by the acronym AQAL, which stands for All Quadrants, All Levels, All Lines, All States, All Types. The four quadrants describe four perspectives based on a combination of the interior subjective world, the exterior objective world, the collective reality, and the individual reality. Sources suggest the four quadrants serve to bring together all five elements and allow users to identify patterns and see connections between the various elements.

Wilber also uses the four quadrants to characterize and classify the many topics, theories, and academics/philosophers used to contribute to Integral Theory.

Levels of development: Also called Stages, these represent the vertical aspect of adult development. They consist of eight color-coded and labeled levels. In order, they are Archaic (infrared), Magic (magenta), Magic-Mythic (red), Mythic (amber), Rational (orange), Postmodern (green), Integral (teal), and Mature Integral (turquoise).

Lines of development: These represent the horizontal aspect of adult development. Influenced by *Gardner's Theory of Multiple Intelligences*, they consist of multiple aspects like cognitive intelligence, morals, spirituality, emotions, kinesthetics, creativity, self-identity, and many more.

States of consciousness: This describes a space of awareness that is fluid and ever changing. It includes several states, like the meditative state (achieved through practices like yoga and meditation), the altered state (achieved through the use of drugs), the dreaming state, the deep sleep state, and the waking state. According to Integral Theory, it is through these states that an individual may discover a spectrum of spiritual enlightenment.

Types: This aspect pertains to how different typologies manifest in each of the stages. Integral Theory accepts a wide array of typologies, including *Myers-Briggs*, *Keirsey's Four Temperaments*, the *Enneagram*, and others. One form of typology widely used in this theory is that of male/female and how men and women may process, perceive, and respond differently to experience.

Integral Theory has broad utility across topics like leadership, communication, learning, polarities, culture, and more. Several assessments, like Terri O'Fallon's STAGES Assessment, derive from Integral Theory. A variety of different tools, like Integral Mapping, exist to support application of the theory.

Integral Theory is significantly more complex than presented here. Multiple vendors offer training or certification in Integral Theory and its associated assessments and tools. Professionals seeking additional information may consider one of Wilber's many works, like his seminal 1995 book, *Sex, Ecology, Spirituality: The Spirit of Evolution*; or 2006's *Integral Life Practice*; or *A Brief History of Everything* (1996).

Sources[152]

INTEGRATED MODEL OF GROUP DEVELOPMENT

Certification Available: no
Certification Required: no
Assessments: yes (GDOS, GDQ)
Proprietary: no
Client: groups
Cost: not applicable
Category: teaming

Developed in the 1990s by psychologist Susan Wheelan, her Integrated Model of Group Development (IMGD) provides a framework for understanding the evolution of team development. Building on *Tuckman's Stages of Group Development*, IMGD identifies four stages that are similar to the stages of life development.

Stage 1—Infancy (dependency and inclusion): During this stage, individuals (like infants) experience a measure of uncertainty, leading them to depend heavily on leaders and other more experienced members of the group. Throughout stage 1, individuals avoid conflict and confrontation, seeking to establish rapport and a sense of belonging. During this period, the group's attention primarily focuses on relationship building, reducing uncertainty among members, and learning. This means the group makes little progress on its assigned project.

Indicators of stage 1 include overly compliant team members, limited conflict, heightened politeness between members, and a fear of rejection. Groups in stage 1 work to form a collective identity and provide a sense of safety for their members.

Stage 2—Adolescence (counter-dependency and fight): In stage 2, individuals begin to feel more comfortable with each other. Consequently, they express their thoughts and feelings more openly, often challenging each other in the process. The group actively debates how it will operate, which may lead to some early-stage conflict. Assuming healthy conflict occurs, group discourse surrounding shared goals and procedures will progress in a productive and positive direction. In stage 2, the team's attention adjusts, focusing a bit more on the tasks at hand, though members remain inefficient.

Stage 3—Adulthood (trust and structure): As groups reach stage 3, discourse yields to consensus. In this, the team agrees to a shared purpose, vision, and direction. Members establish relevant norms for how the team will interact and operate. The relationship between team members strengthens as they transition to focus on the work. Stage 3 sees the group's attention focus more on the mission as members work to complete tasks while addressing any conflicts quickly and efficiently.

Stage 4—Maturity (work and productivity): In the fourth stage, the team's focus and attention lies primarily on completing tasks and achieving its mission. Characterized as high-functioning, highly efficient, and intensely productive, teams do their best work in stage 4.

Termination: The team has accomplished its mission and disbands. Though not a formal developmental stage, how a team disbands is important to future groups and team effort.

Though influenced by Tuckman's framework, IMGD is not a linear model. Teams may move back and forth across stages randomly. Wheelan's work suggests there is a significant relationship between time and a group's progression through the stages. Her research indicates it takes groups an average of six months to reach stage 4.

In addition, Wheelan discovered that small teams tend to function more effectively than large teams, often reaching higher levels of development in a shorter time. According to Wheelan, smaller teams consist of between three and eight members.

The Integrated Model of Group Development is more complex than presented here and includes additional insights into team size, construct, and time, as well as two assessments/questionnaires.

Professionals seeking additional information may consider Wheelan's 1994 book, *Group Processes: A Developmental Perspective*, and her 2020 book, *Creating Effective Teams: A Guide for Members and Leaders*, co-authored by M. Åkerlund and C. Jacobsson.

Sources[153]

INTENTIONAL CHANGE THEORY

Certification Available: no
Certification Required: no
Assessments: no
Proprietary: no
Client: individuals
Cost: not applicable
Category: change (ind.), coaching model

Developed in 1967 by social psychologist Richard Boyatzis, Intentional Change Theory (ICT) provides a multilevel framework to facilitate individual change. The ICT framework consists of five stages called the Five Discoveries.

Stage 1—Ideal self: During the first stage, the client focuses on the vision of who they want to be and what they want. This requires an exploration of the client's identity and values as well as their thoughts, feelings, and perceptions.

Stage 2—Real self: In the second stage, the client explores how other people perceive them with the intention of discovering what kind of person others believe them to be. This may require the client to seek feedback from others to provide the insight needed.

The difference between who they want to be (stage 1) and who they are (stage 2) is "the gap" or the "personal balance sheet."

Stage 3—Learning agenda: In stage 3, the client develops a plan that outlines how they intend to bridge the gap and achieve their desired change. This requires the client to take into consideration what they learned from the first two stages.

Stage 4—Experiment and practice: This stage involves the client actualizing their learning agenda. The client's execution of their plan is inherently experimental as they test their assumptions of self. A critical aspect of stage 4 is the client's willingness to learn and grow from these experiments.

Stage 5—Relationships and trust: The final stage involves the client using their existing relationships to facilitate their learning experience.

The ICT framework can help predict an individual's readiness for "desired and sustained change." Boyatzis provides the following definitions to clarify these distinctions.

- Desired change: the specific changes that a person wants to occur.

- Sustained change: change that lasts a relatively long time.

Intentional Change Theory shares striking similarities with other coaching models like *GROW*, *GROWTH*, *Cognitive Behavioral Coaching*, and *OSKAR*. For this reason, we include ICT in the category of coaching models. ICT also shares commonalities with other change models like the *Transtheoretical Model*.

Like most coaching frameworks, ICT allows for integration with other theories, tools, and assessments. For example, clients in the first stage of discovery (ideal self) may benefit from a tool like CCL's Visual Explorer Cards, which can foster a client's creative visioning using pictures as analogs for desired outcomes.

The longevity of Intentional Change Theory has allowed others to thoroughly research the model. The resulting literature explains why ICT remains one of the most widely used frameworks by coaches and organizational development specialists.

Intentional Change Theory is more complex than presented here and includes a deeper exploration of the behavioral and psychological factors that influence individual change. Professionals seeking additional information will find much written about Intentional Change Theory, including Richard Boyatzis' 2006 article featured in the *Journal of Management Development*, "An Overview of Intentional Change from a Complexity Perspective."

Professionals may also consider Boyatzis' 2019 *Harvard Business Review* article, "Coaching for Change," co-authored by Melvin Smith and Ellen Van Oosten.

Sources[154]

INTERNAL FAMILY SYSTEMS MODEL

Certification Available: yes (IFS Institute)
Certification Required: yes
Assessments: no
Proprietary: yes
Client: individuals
Cost: pricing not available
Category: coaching model, resilience

Developed in the 1980s by family therapist Richard C. Schwartz, the Internal Family Systems Model (IFS) provides a framework for understanding how the relationship between different aspects of an individual's personality affects a client's well-being and state of mind.

Since its development, variations of the model have introduced the use of different labels and different constructs. We present the original IFS Model, which consists of the following three subpersonalities or aspects.

Exiles: These are the aspects of our personality that experience pain, trauma, fear, or shame. These are unwanted experiences, and a person may inherently work to exile them, hence the name.

For example, the client may experience judgment from their peers at work, leading them to feel strong negative emotions. The client may either attempt to avoid this experience (Manager behaviors) or attempt to mitigate the experience (Firefighter behaviors).

Managers: These are the self-protective aspects of our personality. They influence the way a person interacts with the world, striving to protect them from harm and painful experiences.

For example, to avoid the pain of judgment and ridicule from peers, clients may preemptively micromanage their employees or insist on perfection.

Firefighters: These are the response aspects of our personality that come out when an Exile breaks free and threatens us. These behaviors seek to distract or minimize the impact of Exiles and may include counterproductive or detrimental reactions.

For example, a client judged by their peers experiences a sense of embarrassment. To protect themselves from this feeling, the client may come down hard on employees, passing the blame on to them.

The relationship between these aspects, healthy or unhealthy, influences what Schwartz called the **Self**. This is the foundation of who a person truly is and represents the whole person. IFS strives to help the client disentangle the three subpersonalities from their true Self. This requires a client to develop a deeper understanding of Self, which involves the client managing the relationship between the three aspects and Self.

Schwartz identified eight qualities that allow a client to manage these relationships. He called these the *8 Cs of Self-Leadership*: Curiosity, Calmness, Confidence, Compassion, Clarity, Creativity, Courage, Connectedness.

IFS is primarily the domain of therapy; however, elements of the framework are informative and useful for coaching. Practitioners of *Cognitive Behavioral Coaching* will often incorporate elements of IFS into practice by focusing on the present state or recent past (with a concentration in the workspace). Delving too far into the past with IFS risks crossing into the realm of therapy.

IFS is an evidence-based framework of psychotherapy, popular with family therapists and professionals working with individuals processing trauma. When using the IFS Model, it is important to distinguish when the client's needs fall within the scope of coaching and when a referral to a clinical professional is appropriate.

IFS is significantly more complex than presented here; formal use of this model requires training and certification. Though multiple vendors offer certification, the primary provider is the IFS Institute, which offers three levels of certification.

Professionals seeking additional information will find much written on IFS, including Schwartz's 2001 book, *Introduction to the Family Systems Model.*

Sources[155]

JOB DEMANDS-CONTROL MODEL

> **Certification Available:** no
> **Certification Required:** no
> **Assessments:** no
> **Proprietary:** no
> **Client:** individuals
> **Cost:** not applicable
> **Category:** emp. engagement, stress management

Developed in 1979 by sociologist Robert Karasek, the Job Demands-Control Model (JD-C) provides a framework for understanding the relationship between characteristics of a job and an employee's psychological well-being.

The Job Demands-Control Model examines two dimensions that influence an employee's stress level.

Job demands: This dimension pertains to factors that consume an employee's time, attention, and energy. These include deadlines, resource limitations, competing priorities, conflict, interruptions, level of effort, task difficulty, and more.

Decision latitude: This dimension refers to an employee's autonomy, specifically their ability to influence or control their work. This can include the employee's ability to decline projects or tasks, to request and receive additional support, and to adjust project execution.

The combination of these two dimensions describes four job types which further explain Karasek's Job Demands-Control theory.

- Low-strain job: results when job demands are low and an employee's sense of autonomy is high. This can sometimes leave employees feeling unchallenged.

- Passive job: results when job demands and autonomy are low, sometimes leaving employees feeling demotivated.

- High-strain job: results when job demands are high, and autonomy is low. This can leave employees feeling overly tasked and undersupported, leading to burnout.

- Active job: occurs when both job demands and autonomy are high, often leaving employees feeling equally challenged by the tasks assigned them and supported by management.

Karasek's research suggests that the high demands of a job alone are not sufficient to lead to employee burnout or stress. However, when coupled with a lack of control over one's work, an employee may experience significant stress. Karasek observed that employees in positions with high demands and minimal autonomy regularly felt exhausted at the end of a day, struggled to wake up in the mornings, and experienced greater feelings of depression and anxiety.

Conversely, Karasek noticed that employees in positions with high demands but who also had high levels of autonomy often felt the highest level of job satisfaction.

Repeated studies into the JD-C Model suggest that an employee's perceived level of control is critical to their level of job satisfaction, engagement, and stress. Interestingly, other studies suggest that among younger workers, job demands factored more importantly than sense of autonomy.

Widely used in organizational psychology and organizational development, the Job Demands-Control Model provides a useful framework for exploring the workload of individual employees and how it impacts their stress level.

Karasek's JD-C Model would go on to influence many other theories, like the related *Job Demands-Resources Model*. This model, developed in the 2000s, explores the relationship between job demands and resource availability and their collective impact on an employee's level of engagement and stress.

Professionals seeking additional information will find much written on the Job Demands-Control Model, including Karasek's 1992 book, *Healthy Work: Stress, Productivity, and the Reconstruction of Working Life*, co-authored with Tores Theorell.

Sources[156]

JOB DEMANDS-RESOURCES MODEL

Certification Available: no
Certification Required: no
Assessments: no
Proprietary: no
Client: individuals
Cost: not applicable
Category: emp. engagement, stress management

Developed in 2006 by organizational psychologists Arnold Bakker and Evangelia Demerouti, the Job Demands-Resources Model (JD-R) provides a framework to help analyze and predict employee engagement and burnout by examining two key factors: job demands and job resources.

Job demands: This pertains to the physical and emotional stressors associated with the employee's role or position. Performance expectations associated with the job often require sustained effort and as a result involve some form of physiological and psychological cost. Variables affecting the demands of the job include workload, time pressures, interpersonal conflicts, job security, sense of safety, complexity of tasks, ambiguity of purpose, and more.

Job resources: These are physical, social, and organizational variables which reduce job stress. They include work-based relationships, genuine support from management, opportunities for advancement, coaching, mentoring, the employee's sense of control over their environment, self-efficacy, and more.

The JD-R model suggests that when job demands are high, stress-inducing pressures go up. The availability of job resources serves to counter this pressure. However, when demands are high and there are few resources, employee engagement decreases, absenteeism increases, and burnout becomes a risk.

Using a combination of job demands and job resources, the JD-R Model identifies four possible states.

• Demand (Low) and Resources (Low): Minimal job demands means minimal stress or strain on the employee. However, low resources may also lead to diminished motivation. Additionally, low demands may offer employees limited challenges, which may also decrease employee motivation.

• Demand (High) and Resources (Low): Elevated job demands may increase the stress and strain on the employee. When coupled with minimal resources, the employee experiences a decrease in motivation and the potential for burnout increases. Employees in this category are susceptible to higher absenteeism and lower engagement.

• Demand (High) and Resources (High): The presence of sufficient resources may offset some of the stress and strain associated with the job. Employees facing high-demand work with all the resources needed to accomplish the work often feel challenged but accomplished.

• Demand (Low) and Resources (High): Employees working in low-demand jobs with an overabundance of resources experience increased motivation with minimal stress or strain from the job.

JD-R is one of several models contained in the ICMT which explore the issue of employee engagement. As with many of these frameworks, the JD-R Model provides considerations for improving job resources (e.g., creating more favorable working conditions) while optimizing job demands (e.g., providing greater clarity and job security).

The JD-R Model is a useful framework to use with leadership-level clients facing employee engagement challenges. Studies by Bakker and others sought to explore the relationship between leadership and the variables of the JD-R Model. This research indicates multiple ways leaders can influence the demands of the job and the resources available to employees.

The Job Demands-Resources Model is more complex than presented here. Professionals seeking additional information will find much written about the Job Demands-Resource Model, including Bakker's 2010 book, *Work Engagement: A Handbook of Essential Theory and Research*, co-authored by Michael P. Leiter.

Sources[157]

JOHN DEWEY'S REFLECTIVE THINKING

Certification Available: no
Certification Required: no
Assessments: no
Proprietary: no
Client: individuals
Cost: not applicable
Category: reflection

Developed in the early 1900s by noted educator John Dewey, Reflective Thinking provides a philosophical exploration of reflection and its function in facilitating the individual learning experience. Though sources classify Reflective Thinking as a process, Dewey provided no formal or sequential procedure to support his idea. Thus, we suggest Dewey's work on reflection is more a philosophy than a formal process.

Dewey defined Reflective Thinking as a persistent and active consideration or contemplation of a belief or form of knowledge by identifying what we know, how we know it, what we do not know about it, and how this knowledge affects the way we act.

Dewey was among the first and most prominent philosophers of the 20th century to advocate questioning how we come to know what we know. This is because Dewey recognized that stereotypes and bias negatively influence how people acquire knowledge, and he declared these biases the antithesis of true knowledge. In fact, Dewey believed Reflective Thought was essential to combating the erroneous beliefs born of bias.

According to Dewey, "reflection is not a sequence of ideas (or a medley of ideas), but a consequence." In other words, reflection is more than one's thoughts about an experience; it is a part of the experience itself. In meaningful reflection, each thought emerges from the preceding thought, creating a logical chain of ideas where each link or idea supports the other.

Though some characterize Reflective Thinking as a method for problem-solving, it is more accurate to say its utility extends well beyond problem-solving. A staunch advocate of experiential learning, Dewey advocated the use of Reflective Thinking as an ideal process for learning from one's experiences.

Recently, some have used the terms critical thinking and Reflective Thinking interchangeably, though many argue the two terms are distinctly different.

One source offers the following distinction: Critical thinking involves a series of cognitive processes designed to make decisions and achieve desired outcomes. Reflective Thinking consists of a contemplative process designed to make judgments about what has already happened to develop a greater understanding of the experience. With these distinctions, it is easy to see that while similar, the two concepts are different.

The concept of Reflective Thinking is useful for professionals seeking to develop a greater understanding of the fundamentals behind experiential learning. Such knowledge will help professional coaches and consultants to select and implement the most appropriate reflective process for clients based on their needs.

Dewey's philosophy of Reflective Thinking would go on to influence many of the models on reflection contained within this compendium, like *Johns' Model for Structured Reflection* and *Kolb's Experiential Learning Cycle*.

Professionals interested in learning more about Dewey's Reflective Thinking will find much written on the topic, including Dewey's 1910 book, *How We Think*.

In 1933, Dewey revised his book, expanding upon the concept of Reflective Thinking. The updated version of the book is *How We Think: A Restatement of the Relation of Reflective Thinking to the Educative Process*.

Sources[158]

JOHN DEWEY'S THEORY OF EDUCATION

Certification Available: no
Certification Required: no
Assessments: no
Proprietary: no
Client: individuals
Cost: not applicable
Category: learning/development

Developed circa 1938 by noted psychologist and philosopher of education John Dewey, his Theory of Education provides a framework for understanding and exploring seven variables that influence an individual's learning experience. Awareness of these variables can lead to the development of more relevant curricula and a more effective instructional strategy.

Ownership: Learning is most effective when students can take an active role in their learning experience. This requires consideration of the students' preferences for learning. Without a sense of ownership, students may not take the material seriously.

Relevance: Optimal learning occurs when the content and style of instruction links directly to the students' past experiences and their future needs. In this way, students can see the value of the content. Dewey held that the content must present a clear value to the students to be meaningful. Without relevance, students may dismiss the content.

Environmental: Dewey argued that students should have the opportunity to learn from their environment and experiences. This allows students to draw from reality and establish context for the content. The ability for a student to draw from past experiences or learn from a peer's experiences enables them to make a connection between the content and the real world.

Instructor role: Dewey believed the teacher's role was a fluid one, influenced primarily by the needs of the student. This means the teacher may adopt the role of a facilitator, guide, mentor, or presenter based on the preferences of the students.

Structure: Dewey believed in the value of structured learning. He promoted the use of logical sequencing in curriculum development, especially when ordering learning objectives and instructional delivery.

Planning: Dewey advocated the planning of curriculum development, taking into consideration the content for inclusion, connecting content with the needs of the students (relevance), and developing a strategy for delivery.

Curriculum: Dewey argued that a curriculum should allow for individual learning differences among students based on their experiences. In this, Dewey rejected the idea of the universal, static, single-approach curriculum.

John Dewey's Theory of Education is among the first theories to advocate experiential learning over the more traditional educational methods of the time, which favored rote learning (i.e., presenting information for memorization).

A pioneer in the field of experiential learning, Dewey believed the social aspect of learning was key to a student's development. In other words, he recognized the value of learning in a collaborative environment. His Theory of Education would go on to influence theories across multiple fields of study, including pragmatism and instrumentalism, progressive education, and functional psychology.

John Dewey's Theory of Education is a useful framework for curriculum developers, especially those focused on leadership development. Any knowledge best acquired through experiential learning, like emotional intelligence, will benefit from curriculum that takes into consideration Dewey's theory.

Dewey's Theory of Education is significantly more complex than presented here. Professionals seeking additional information will find much written on the topic, including Dewey's 1938 book, *Experience and Education*.

Sources[159]

JOHNS' MODEL FOR STRUCTURED REFLECTION

Certification Available: no
Certification Required: no
Assessments: no
Proprietary: no
Client: individuals
Cost: not applicable
Category: reflection

Developed in the 1990s by nursing professor Christopher Johns, the Model for Structured Reflection (MSR) provides a five-step framework for reflection that includes the examination of a client's internal and external perspectives.

Step 1—Describe the experience: During the first step in the process, the client recalls the details of the event or experience they wish to reflect on. The client should limit details to firsthand observations and objective notes of what transpired. The client should avoid interpreting events or making attributions about the behaviors of other people involved in the experience.

Step 2—Reflection: In the second step, the client seeks insight from their experience by revisiting their own intentions and behaviors during the event. This involves the client exploring the rationale and motivation behind their actions. Additionally, the client explores the consequences of their behavior, both on self and others.

During this step, the client considers both internal and external perspectives. For example, the client should consider how the experience made them feel, as well as how it made others feel. Taking into consideration the impact of an experience on others expands the client's awareness of others.

Step 3—Influencing factors: The third step in the process involves the client exploring the internal and external factors that may have precipitated or influenced the experience. These may include heuristics, bias, politics, identity, culture, and more. The client should work to identify the many variables that influenced their decision-making processes and their behavior. This may require adopting different perspectives.

During the third step, the client should take into consideration the information available to them at the time of the event and how the presence or absence of certain information influenced their behavior. The client may also consider what information might have been useful to know prior to the experience.

Step 4—Could I have dealt with it better: During the fourth step, the client explores possible alternative behaviors they could have adopted. This act, sometimes called counterfactual thinking, depends on the client's creativity. For every alternative path they may have taken, the client should consider the potential consequences, positive and negative. This exercise will lead the client to determine if there might have been a better way to handle the situation.

Step 5—Learning: During the final step, the client identifies and articulates what they learned about the experience from the reflection process. The client then draws conclusions about these lessons and considers how these lessons may facilitate their personal and professional development.

Through the MSR process, the client will possess greater insight into what caused the experience, why it happened, and how their role impacted the situation and those around them. Using this awareness, clients can determine for themselves what aspects of their behavior they might change in the future.

Though originally designed for use in nursing, the efficacy of the MSR model applies equally in any field or profession. This is because the fundamental philosophy underlying the MSR framework is based on Barbara *Carper's Fundamental Ways of Knowing*, which examines how people gather, process, and apply knowledge.

Though one of many models on reflection, the MSR offers a more methodical approach with sufficient structure to facilitate the reflection process. The MSR is ideal for clients with the time, energy, and inclination to conduct a deep exploration of an experience or event.

Professionals seeking additional information on Johns' Model for Structured Reflection may consider his 2017 book, *Becoming a Reflective Practitioner*.

Sources[160]

KAIZEN

Certification Available: yes
Certification Required: no
Assessments: no
Proprietary: no
Client: organizations, teams
Cost: varies by provider
Category: problem-solving, change (org.)

Originating in post–World War II Japan, Kaizen is both a philosophy and a framework for continuous improvement, problem-solving, and innovation. Though the originator of Kaizen remains unknown, many credit organizational theorist Masaaki Imai with introducing modern Kaizen to the world in the late 1980s.

Central to the Kaizen philosophy is the **Kaizen Cycle**, a seven-step process designed to facilitate the continuous improvement of processes, products, and performance.

Step 1—Involve employees: Organizations, especially large ones, are complex constructs. Each employee, from senior leader to frontline worker, possesses a unique perspective of the organization. The Kaizen philosophy emphasizes the value of these distinct points of view and encourages participation from all levels of the organization to ensure a holistic and more accurate view of the company.

Kaizen holds that the diversity of perspectives is essential to identifying and diagnosing problems, creating innovation, and increasing engagement across the board.

Step 2—Identify problems/challenges: The second step in the Kaizen Cycle involves a thorough examination of the observed problem to discover the root cause of the issue. Practitioners of Kaizen often incorporate external problem-solving frameworks to facilitate this step, like the *8 Disciplines of Problem-Solving*.

When using the Kaizen Cycle for process improvement, this step seeks to identify waste or inefficiencies in existing processes.

Step 3—Create solutions: During the third step, the organization begins to develop potential solutions using the knowledge acquired about the root cause of the problem. Professionals will often incorporate tools and techniques designed to foster creative thinking and idea generation.

Kaizen stresses the importance of participation from employees at all levels during the solution development stage. The combination of distinct perspectives increases the efficacy of each possible solution.

Step 4—Test solutions: In the fourth step, the organization tests one or more of the solutions to gather important data which will facilitate the next step.

Step 5—Analyze results: In the fifth step, the organization applies methodologies, formulas, scorecards, and/or other tools to measure the efficacy of each solution. This data may reveal an ideal solution but also indicate areas for potential improvement.

Step 6—Standardize and adopt: In the sixth step, the organization selects the best solution and prepares for enterprise-wide implementation. This includes implementation of process and policy changes to support the new solution.

Step 7—Repeat cycle: The Kaizen Cycle applies to both large organizational change and the smaller incremental changes that support it. Organizations may need to repeat the process several times to achieve lasting organizational change.

Kazien's popularity grew in the late 1980s to early 1990s when Toyota cited the philosophy as a best practice. There are many variations of Kaizen; some present the cycle with as few as five steps while others offer an eight-step process. These variations also include the use of different labels to describe the steps. Professionals should study Kaizen before putting it into practice.

Professionals seeking additional information will find multiple opportunities for formal training and certification in Kaizen. Professionals may also consider Masaaki Imai's 1986 book, *Kaizen: The Key to Japan's Competitive Success*.

Sources[161]

KATZENBACH & SMITH TEAM EFFECTIVENESS MODEL

Certification Available: no
Certification Required: no
Assessments: no
Proprietary: no
Client: groups, teams
Cost: not applicable
Category: teaming

Developed in the 1990s by organizational consultant Jon Katzenbach and management advisor Douglas K. Smith, the Team Effectiveness Model provides a framework for exploring the various elements which contribute to successful teaming. The model groups these elements into two categories—behaviors and deliverables.

Team behaviors: This category pertains to the behaviors necessary for the team to achieve its goals or deliverables.

- **Commitment**: The team must share a mutual commitment to a common cause or goal. Three criteria are necessary to facilitate a team's commitment. These include a specific and well-defined goal to ensure the team possesses the same vision and may work toward the same outcome. The second element is a clear plan of action to ensure the team's effort is both efficient and effective. Finally, the project itself must satisfy the intrinsic motivation of team members.

This means individuals on the team must have the same understanding of their goal, they must agree on how they are going to achieve the goal, and the goal must resonate with them on a deeper level.

- **Skills**: The team must include a diverse range of skills. Three criteria essential to a successful team construct include the presence of individuals with problem-solving skills, those with technical or functional expertise, and those with strong interpersonal skills. This means the team must include a combination of members who possess subject matter expertise, are creative or gifted problem-solvers, and those with strong relationship-building skills.

- **Accountability**: The final behavior necessary for effective teaming is a sense of accountability. This requires the team's commitment to the task and to one another. Criteria for accountability include first, the ability to hold individual team members responsible for their performance without fear of judgment. Second, the team must possess the capacity for mutual accountability. This is the belief that the team, not the individual, succeeds or fails. Finally, the size of the team should be appropriate to foster the openness and honesty necessary for accountability to take place.

Team deliverables: This category focuses on elements related to expectations of team performance and their desired outcomes.

- **Collective work product**: This is the tangible outcome the team will produce. For example, a team may come together to innovate a more efficient product development process.

- **Performance results**: These are performance goals that a team may establish as a part of their effort. For example, the team wants to develop a new process that can get new products to market 50% quicker than past performance.

- **Personal growth**: This is the positive personal consequence of individuals working together. Typically, high-functioning teams facilitate both the personal and professional growth of their individual members. For example, when serving as part of a team, professionals only familiar with their own roles and functions will develop increased awareness and appreciation for professionals from other roles.

The Team Effectiveness Model is based on research into over 50 teams across 30 different companies. The outcome of this research highlights the importance of the relationship between the team's behavior and the expected deliverables.

Professionals seeking additional information may consider Katzenbach and Smith's 1992 book, *The Wisdom of Teams: Creating the High-Performance Organization.*

Sources[162]

KEGAN'S THEORY OF ADULT DEVELOPMENT

Certification Available: no
Certification Required: no
Assessments: no
Proprietary: no
Client: individuals
Cost: not applicable
Category: learning/development

Developed by Harvard psychologist Robert Kegan in the early 1980s, his Theory of Adult Development provides a framework for understanding and exploring the process of adult development. Kegan's model consists of four elements that contribute to a client's presence within the identified five stages of development.

Element 1—Subject: These are the subjective concepts, beliefs, and perceptions a client possesses, because they cannot fully engage in objective reflection. They may include the client's perceptions of the world, the behaviors they observe, the emotions they feel, and their sense of self.

Element 2—Object: These are the objective concepts, beliefs, and perceptions a client possesses about something because of their ability to reflect objectively. The balance between the client's ability to adopt objective vs. subjective concepts, beliefs, and perceptions will factor into their development.

Element 3—Information: This refers to any new knowledge the client acquires. It is an expansion of what the client knows.

Element 4—Transformation: Refers to the evolution in how a client knows what they know, which, in turn, supports the acquisition of more complex and multifaceted information.

The combination of these elements influences where a client is within Kegan's five stages of development, which he called the **Orders of Mind**. It is important to note this is not a linear process; clients may move back and forth.

Stage 1—Impulsive mind: Typically associated with children and not discussed here.

Stage 2—Imperial mind: Though primarily relevant to children, this stage does apply to some adults. This typically involves individuals heavily focused on self, who prioritize their own needs, interests, and agendas ahead of others. Their relationships tend to be transactional as they think of others as either helpers or barriers on the road to achieving their desires.

Stage 3—Socialized mind: Most adults are in this stage. Here, the most important things are the ideas, beliefs, and norms of the systems around us. We consider how others see us, and we judge our self-worth by how society judges us.

Stage 4—Self-authoring mind: In this stage we form our own seat of judgment, becoming independent of the thoughts and beliefs of society. We define who we are and do not allow society, our relationships, or our environment to do so. In this stage, we take accountability and responsibility for our choices and actions.

Stage 5—Self-transforming mind: In this stage, we are free to be who and what we want to be, and we are constantly exploring and adopting identities based on our experiences. We are less susceptible to the effects of polarities and more able to adapt as needed. Few ever reach this stage.

Kegan's framework falls under the umbrella of constructive-developmental psychology, a school of thought which believes that the systems or processes people use to make meaning grow and change over time.

Kegan's Theory of Adult Development is also known as the Theory of Evolutionary Consciousness, the Levels of Consciousness, and Subject-Object Theory. Different publications offer variations of the theory with alternative labels to describe the stages.

Kegan's theory is significantly more complex than presented here. Professionals seeking additional information may consider Kegan's 1982 book, *The Evolving Self: Problem and Process in Human Development,* and his 1994 book, *In Over Our Heads: The Mental Demands of Modern Life.*

Sources[163]

KEIRSEY'S FOUR TEMPERAMENTS

Certification Available: yes
Certification Required: yes
Assessments: yes (KTS)
Proprietary: yes (Keirsey Group)
Client: individuals
Cost: $3,400–$5,000
Category: personality

Introduced in the 1970s by psychologist David W. Keirsey, the Four Temperaments provides a framework for categorizing and exploring human personality types. Keirsey's model consists of 16 personality types grouped by four temperaments. Each personality is a unique combination of four domains:

- Introversion (I)—Extroversion (E)
- Thinking (T)—Feeling (F)
- Judging (J)—Perceiving (P)
- Sensation (S)—Intuition (I)

Guardian: This temperament characterizes personalities that are cooperative in action and concrete in communication. These individuals are factual and detail oriented. They are highly organized and considered planners. Personalities associated with the Guardian temperament include:

- Inspector (ISTJ)
- Protector (ISFJ)
- Provider (ESFJ)
- Supervisor (ESTJ)

Idealist: This temperament characterizes personalities that are cooperative in action and abstract in communication. These individuals think conceptually and value feelings.

They are creative and seek novelty. Personalities associated with the Idealist temperament include:

- Champion (ENFP)
- Counselor (INFJ)
- Healer (INFP)
- Teacher (ENFJ)

Artisan: This temperament characterizes personalities that are utilitarian in action and concrete in communication. These individuals prefer facts and details but are spontaneous, fun-loving, and risk-takers. Personalities associated with the Artisan temperament include:

- Composer (ISFP)
- Crafter (ISTP)
- Performer (ESFP)
- Promoter (ESTP)

Rational: This temperament characterizes personalities that are utilitarian in action and abstract in communication style. These individuals think conceptually but value logic and reason. They are natural problem-solvers and seek knowledge.

- Architect (INTP)
- Field Marshal (ENTJ)
- Inventor (ENTP)
- Mastermind (INTJ)

Professionals will notice similarities between Keirsey's Four Temperaments and *Myers-Briggs*. This is because both are based on Jungian psychology. Consequently, there is a correlation between these two theories of personality, and they utilize the same four-letter coding system.

To facilitate the application of the Four Temperaments, Keirsey developed an assessment called the Keirsey Temperament Sorter (KTS) which is available online for a fee. Because KTS derives from Jungian psychology, it shares similarities with the Myers-Briggs Type Indicator (MBTI). One distinction between the two assessments is that MBTI focuses on the client's thoughts and feelings, while KTS focuses on the client's behavior.

Professionals should familiarize themselves with both assessments prior to adopting one. Administering the KTS requires certification provided solely by the Keirsey Group.

The Keirsey Four Temperament model is significantly more complex than presented here. Professionals seeking additional information may consider Keirsey's 1978 book, *Please Understand Me*, and his 1998 book, *Please Understand Me II*.

Sources[164]

KELLEY'S COVARIATION MODEL

> **Certification Available:** no
> **Certification Required:** no
> **Assessments:** no
> **Proprietary:** no
> **Client:** individuals
> **Cost:** not applicable
> **Category:** bias

Introduced in the 1960s by social psychologist Harold Kelley, the Covariation Model provides a framework to explain how people determine the causes of another person's behavior. Because Kelley's model explores the attribution of behavior, it falls under the umbrella of *Attribution Theory*.

Kelley's Covariation Model consists of two types of attribution to explain behavior.

Dispositional attribution: This category of explanation suggests that the behavior we observe in another person results from that person's character or personality.

Situational attribution: This category of explanation suggests that the behavior we observe in another person results from that person's environment or situation.

Kelley's model suggests three variables influence our determination of behavior as dispositional or situational.

Consensus: This variable pertains to how the person's behavior compares to the behavior of others in similar circumstances. The more people who do the same behavior in similar situations, the higher the consensus of that behavior. If the person's behavior is unique or done by few others, then the behavior has low consensus. One question which captures consensus: Are others behaving the same way in this situation?

When consensus is high, we tend to make situational attributions. When consensus is low, we tend to make dispositional attributions.

Distinctiveness: This variable considers if a person's behavior is the same or different in similar (but not the same) situations. If a person behaves this way in many different circumstances, then the behavior has low distinctiveness. If the behavior is unique to certain situations, then the behavior is highly distinct. One question which captures distinctiveness: Is this behavior unique to the situation?

When distinctiveness is high, we tend to make situational attributions. When distinctiveness is low, we tend to make dispositional attributions.

Consistency: This variable pertains to how often the person replicates the behavior in the same situation. If a person behaves the same way every time they are in the same situation, then consistency is high. If the behavior does not manifest in the same situation often, consistency is low. One question which captures consistency: Is this behavior typical for this person in this situation?

When consistency is low, we tend to make situational attribution. Conversely, when consistency is high, we tend to make dispositional attributions.

Our interpretation of these variables is susceptible to many forms of bias, including fundamental attribution error, idiosyncratic error, confirmation bias, racial and cultural biases, and more. Kelley's Covariation Model is a useful lens to help clients explore their perceptions and assumptions of other people's behaviors.

Another vulnerability in this process lies in the absence of data. Much of our ability to assess consensus, distinctiveness, and consistency requires us to possess a measure of knowledge about the other person and their environment. Research suggests that when faced with the absence of data, we tend to replace knowledge with assumptions, often pulling from our most relevant experiences. The accuracy of these assumptions can lead us to make false attributions of behavior.

Professionals seeking additional information on Kelley's Covariation Model will find many articles available on the topic. For those interested in a broader perspective of Attribution Theory and the workplace, consider M.J. Martinko's 1995 book, *Attribution Theory: An Organizational Perspective*.

Sources[165]

KOLB'S EXPERIENTIAL LEARNING CYCLE

Certification Available: no
Certification Required: no
Assessments: yes (LSI)
Proprietary: no
Client: individuals
Cost: not applicable
Category: learning/development, reflection

Developed in 1984 by educational theorist David A. Kolb, his Experiential Learning Cycle provides a framework to understand individual preferences for experiential learning. The model consists of two interrelated subframeworks: the four stages of learning and the four learning styles.

The Four Stages of Learning involves the sequence a person goes through when processing an experience.

Stage 1—Concrete Experience (CE): The first stage is the specific experience affecting the client.

Stage 2—Reflective Observation (RO): The second stage involves the client taking the time to reflect on the experience. In this stage, the client examines what happened.

Stage 3—Abstract Conceptualization (AC): The third stage involves the client making sense of the experience to understand why it happened. This includes identifying the relationship between those variables precipitating the experience. In this stage, the client may also consider what they could have done differently.

Stage 4—Active Experimentation (AE): The final stage involves the client considering how to apply what they have learned.

Kolb's Four Learning Styles suggest a client's learning preferences may make them suited for some stages more than others. The four styles are based on an individual's learning preferences within two domains: thinking vs. feeling and doing vs. observing.

• Thinking vs. feeling: Does the person prefer to think about an experience, or do they focus on how the experience made them feel?

• Doing vs. observing: Does the person prefer to do the task themselves or observe another performing the task first?

Diverging (CE/RO): These learners prefer to watch others perform the task before performing the task themselves. They are sensitive and gravitate to creative tasks like brainstorming. Open-minded and emotional, they thrive in small groups and respond favorably to feedback.

Assimilating (AC/RO): These learners are logic driven, valuing facts and practical ideas. They prefer thinking through problems and observing others perform the task. They require clear guidelines and parameters. They prefer to work individually rather than on a team.

Converging (AC/AE): These learners prefer to perform the task rather than watch others. They strive to find practical solutions to problems. They gravitate to technical problems and are more focused on tasks than people.

Accommodating (CE/AE): These learners also prefer to perform the task over watching others. They rely on intuition more than logic when overcoming challenges. Because they rely on the analysis of others rather than conduct their own, they work well in teams and are known for using experimentation to find solutions.

Though not without controversy, Kolb's work remains widely used. His framework draws influence from Kurt *Lewin's Behavior Equation* and *John Dewey's Reflective Thinking* and *Theory of Education*, among others. Kolb's theory also includes an assessment called the Learning Styles Inventory (LSI). Variations of the LSI are freely available online.

The Experiential Learning Cycle, also known as Kolb's Reflective Cycle and Kolb's Learning Styles, is more complex than presented here. Professionals seeking additional information may consider Kolb's 1984 book, *Experiential Learning: Experience as the Source of Learning and Development.*

Sources[166]

KOTTER'S CHANGE MANAGEMENT THEORY

> **Certification Available:** no
> **Certification Required:** no
> **Assessments:** no
> **Proprietary:** no
> **Client:** organizations
> **Cost:** not applicable
> **Category:** change (org.)

Developed in 1996 by Harvard Business School professor John Kotter, Change Management Theory provides a framework for engineering successful organizational change. Kotter's model consists of eight criteria or steps essential to any enterprise-wide change effort.

Increase urgency: This involves creating a sense of urgency among change agents and key stakeholders. Establishing urgency requires that everyone understand the importance and need for change. To achieve this, change agents must facilitate discussions to raise awareness about the threats and issues facing the organization that require the company to adapt or change.

Form coalitions: This involves identifying key stakeholders at all levels of the organization who are essential to the change effort. These individuals understand the risks facing the organization and the need for change. Sharing a commitment to change, they become a collective of change agents who will inspire and drive change. It is important the coalition include a diverse combination of employees.

Develop vision and strategy: This involves creating a vision for change, establishing clear and measurable goals, aligning change with the organization's core values, and developing a strategy to achieve the desired goals and vision.

Communicate the vision: This involves disseminating the vision to all levels of the organization so people understand what is coming and why. In this step, it is important that all employees share a common understanding of the intent behind the change effort.

Remove obstacles: This step involves checking for barriers to change, which includes identifying individual resisters or pockets of resistance. To mitigate the impact of resisters on the organization, Kotter recommends rewarding key contributors to the change effort.

Create short-term wins: This is essential because it establishes momentum and enthusiasm for change. Short-term wins allow participants to see their progress toward change in more obvious ways than having goals that are long-term. Win early, win often.

Sustain and build on change: This involves capitalizing on the positive momentum (short-term wins) by taking on more challenging aspects of the change. This momentum may inspire others to join the change effort.

Anchor change in corporate culture: This involves integrating success stories into the status quo and ensuring new leaders are active supporters of the change. Change agents should continue to recognize key contributors and reinforce the relationship between change and the company's core values. This step serves to help the change endure.

Kotter's model is based on a study of hundreds of organizations undergoing change efforts. The result of Kotter's research indicates these eight criteria are essential to successful organizational change.

Kotter's Change Management Theory is one of the most popular frameworks used by consultants, coaches, and facilitators who work in organizational behavior. Professionals using Kotter's model often integrate it with other theories and tools to facilitate the individual steps of the process. For example, clients in stage 4 (communicate vision) may consider the *7 Cs of Effective Communication* or *Diffusion of Innovation Theory* when designing a communication strategy.

Kotter's Change Management Theory is more complex than presented here. Professionals seeking additional information may consider Kotter's seminal 1996 book, *Leading Change,* or his 2008 *Harvard Business Review* article, "Choosing Strategies for Change," co-authored by L.A. Schlesinger.

Sources[167]

KÜBLER-ROSS CHANGE CURVE

Certification Available: no
Certification Required: no
Assessments: no
Proprietary: yes (Kübler-Ross Foundation)
Client: individuals
Cost: not applicable
Category: change (ind.)

Developed by psychiatrist Elisabeth Kübler-Ross, the Kübler-Ross Change Curve expands upon Ross' earlier model on the five stages of grief, called the *Kübler-Ross Model* (1969). The Change Curve provides a useful framework for exploring a client's experience processing difficult or traumatic change. The model consists of seven stages.

Stage 1—Shock: This is the client's initial reaction at an unexpected event such as job loss, job transfer, or a project setback. The client may experience numbness and present an "I don't care" attitude.

Stage 2—Denial: In this stage, the client looks for evidence to prove that what happened is not real or true. They try to invalidate the event and its underlying cause. A client in this stage may say, "The reason I was fired was because my boss has it out for me." Bias and emotional wildfires run rampant in this stage.

Stage 3—Frustration: In this stage, the client begins to recognize the situation is real and expresses annoyance and possibly even anger. The client may even blame others for their situation.

Stage 4—Depression: In this stage, the client's lack of enjoyment may spread to other aspects of their life.

Experiences which should be cause for celebration and joy instead have little effect. This can lead to counterproductive behaviors which may exacerbate the situation.

Stage 5—Experiment: In this stage, the client begins to consider a new state of being or a new norm. The client may ask the question, "What might a new job look like for me?"

Stage 6—Decision: In this stage, the client accepts that changes are necessary, and a feeling of positivity starts to emerge. For example, the client may decide to apply for a new job that excites them.

Stage 7—Integration: The client adopts the changes as their new normal. They no longer dwell on what they lost but focus on what they have now.

Though typically presented through the lens of death or devastating circumstances, the Change Curve has broad utility. Clients facing job loss, job transition, mission failure, lawsuits, hostile work environments, etc., may find themselves in the grieving process.

The framework suggests that a client is likely to experience a roller coaster effect throughout the course of the grieving process, meaning there is an ebb and flow over time. This is because clients in the early portion of the process focus on preserving the status quo (they have high energy, put forth great effort, and experience intense feelings). Then, as realization sets in, the curve drops (they experience low energy, a decrease in effort, and depressed feelings). Finally, as a new possibility emerges, the curve moves upwards as revitalized energy increases effort with renewed positive feelings.

The Change Curve differs from the original Kübler-Ross Model in that it provides a more granular look at the grieving process by expanding from five to seven stages.

The Kübler-Ross Change Curve is useful in helping coaches understand where the client is so that they may meet them on their level. The Change Curve is more complex than presented here. While most of the literature on the Change Curve focuses on death and grief, articles are available online which present a more coaching-appropriate perspective.

It is important to note that despite decades of acceptance, some question the efficacy of the model. Professionals should thoroughly study the model prior to application to avoid crossing into therapy with a client.

Sources[168]

KÜBLER-ROSS MODEL

Certification Available: no
Certification Required: no
Assessments: no
Proprietary: no
Client: individuals
Cost: not applicable
Category: change (ind.)

Developed in 1969 by psychiatrist Elisabeth Kübler-Ross, the Kübler-Ross Model, also known as the Five Stages of Grief Model, provides a framework for understanding the stages clients go through when processing grief. The model consists of five stages.

Stage 1—Denial: Often the first observable stage, clients typically experience shock or numbness, and they may respond by avoiding the truth. A client may feel fear when thinking about how life will be different going forward. Individuals in this stage may reject reality, saying things like, "This isn't happening." Some sources explain this stage as the human mind's defense mechanisms kicking into high gear.

Stage 2—Anger: In this stage, reality begins to set in, and the client may experience anger over what happened, often looking for something or someone to blame. Because of this hostility, those closest to the client may be on the receiving end of that anger. This can lead a client's support network to limit their exposure to the client. When this happens, the client may experience an increased sense of solitude and loss.

Stage 3—Bargaining: The third stage typically involves the client acknowledging their reality; however, they may try to negotiate for a reprieve, if only temporary. Sometimes this comes in the form of making deals with God or postulating an endless series of "what if" scenarios.

Stage 4—Depression: The fourth stage, characterized by a sense of deep hopelessness, often sees the client asking, "What's the point?" This stage happens when the client begins to realize that bargaining is not really an option, and they begin to accept reality.

Stage 5—Acceptance: The final stage of the grieving process occurs when the client accepts their situation for what it is. Individuals in this stage may continue to experience sadness, frustration, and anger, though these experiences will be less severe than prior stages.

Though presented in a linear fashion, the Kübler-Ross Model is not linear. Individuals may move back and forth across the stages at different times for varying durations of time during the grieving process. It is important that professionals practice patience and active listening when working with a client processing grief.

It is important to stress that grief counseling is not the domain of coaches, facilitators, or consultants; however, it is reasonable that professionals may encounter clients who are going through the grieving process. A client's grief does not respect the boundary between therapy and coaching. Topics appropriate for coaching can come under the significant influence of a client's grief. Therefore, understanding the Kübler-Ross Model can prepare coaches for what they may encounter when working with these clients and allow them to adjust their coaching as appropriate.

Kübler-Ross created her model after working with terminally ill patients. She sought to better understand their experiences and those of their loved ones. Despite its original intent, the Kübler-Ross Model has broad utility in professional coaching. Clients facing job loss, a toxic work environment, or conflict at work may find themselves in the grieving process. Any significant life change or professional change may induce grief in a client. For these reasons we include the Kübler-Ross Model in this compendium.

Because significant organizational change can induce a state of grief in employees, the Kübler-Ross Model, or its more recent incarnation *Kübler-Ross Change Curve*, is frequently included in change management literature.

Professionals seeking additional information on the Kübler-Ross Model will find much written about the topic, including Kübler-Ross's seminal 1969 book, *On Death and Dying*. For those seeking a more workplace-focused application of the model, multiple sources online provide valuable insight for practicing coaches and consultants.

Sources[169]

LADDER OF INFERENCE

Certification Available: no
Certification Required: no
Assessments: no
Proprietary: no
Client: individuals
Cost: not applicable
Category: problem-solving, decision-making, bias

Developed in the 1970s by organizational psychologist Chris Argyris, the Ladder of Inference provides a framework to explain how individuals process information to facilitate decision-making. In 1994, MIT management professor Peter Senge revised the Ladder of Inference to reflect the popular model we see today, which consists of a seven-step cascading process.

Step 1—Observe facts: The first step applies to all available data we observe and have access to. This includes objective data like statistics and metrics, and subjective data like body language and tone of voice. The data we collect informs the process.

Step 2—Select facts: Typically, the amount of data available to us is overwhelming; this means we must select which facts to consider and which ones to discard. This selection process occurs on dual levels (conscious and subconscious). It is during this stage that confirmation bias can negatively influence the process. Ideally, the selection of data is based on logic and reason; however, a bias for or against specific types of data may lead a client to ignore certain facts.

Step 3—Interpret facts: Once we select the facts to consider, we begin to make and ascribe meaning to the selected data. Because this step involves our interpretation of the facts, it is highly susceptible to multiple forms of bias and heuristics.

Step 4—Form assumptions: When evaluating data, we frequently encounter gaps in our knowledge. A common response is to fill in the gaps with assumptions. These assumptions may derive from pattern recognition, heuristics, or other default beliefs. The greatest risk from these assumptions occurs when we forget which data point is an assumption and which is a fact. Treating an assumption as fact can derail the efficacy of our decision-making process.

Step 5—Draw conclusions: During this stage of the process, the combination of facts and assumptions leads us to draw a conclusion regarding what happened, why it happened, and what it means. A risk when drawing conclusions is the tendency to treat the conclusion as fact. To mitigate this risk, one should remain open to revisiting or challenging their conclusions.

Step 6—Adopt beliefs: Once we draw a conclusion, the next step involves adjusting our beliefs based on the conclusion. There is a natural tendency to draw our conclusions so they align with our existing belief systems; accordingly, much of the time our conclusions serve to reaffirm our beliefs.

Step 7—Act: The final step in the process involves acting on these beliefs.

The Ladder of Inference is a cascading process, meaning that each step affects all subsequent steps in the process. For example, the presence of bias when interpreting the facts will negatively influence the assumptions we make, the conclusions we draw, what we believe, and how we act.

The Ladder of Inference is a useful framework for helping clients understand how they make sense of the world around them and how that knowledge influences their decisions and actions. The model may also help clients better understand how others make sense of the world around them.

Variations of the Ladder of Inference exist which use alternative labels to describe the steps. Using the Ladder of Inference does not require certification, though a careful study of the framework will facilitate a more accurate application.

Professionals seeking additional information will find much written about the Ladder of Inference, including Peter Senge's 1994 book, *The Fifth Discipline: The Art and Practice of the Learning Organization.*

Sources[170]

LAISSEZ-FAIRE LEADERSHIP

Certification Available: no
Certification Required: no
Assessments: no
Proprietary: no
Client: individuals
Cost: not applicable
Category: leadership

In the 1930s, psychologist Kurt Lewin developed *Lewin's Leadership Styles* framework, which consists of three primary styles of leadership: Laissez-Faire Leadership, Autocratic Leadership, and Democratic Leadership. We present Laissez-Faire Leadership as its own entry because the concept, as Lewin described it, shows up in multiple theories of leadership.

Lewin describes Laissez-Faire Leadership as a hands-off approach to management, with the leader delegating most of the tasks, responsibilities, and decision-making authority to followers. Executed in an ineffective way, Laissez-Faire Leadership often appears like an abdication of leadership. Because of this, most leadership theories like the *Full Range Leadership Model* present Laissez-Faire Leadership as a negative or undesirable form of leadership. Even Lewin suggested laissez-faire was the least effective leadership style.

However, despite its negative reputation, subsequent research reveals that in certain situations and environments, the characteristics associated with Laissez-Faire Leadership can prove highly effective. This suggests that Laissez-Faire Leadership, as an undesirable style of leadership, represents the inappropriate application of positive leadership characteristics.

These positive characteristics include:

Effective delegation: Successful laissez-faire leaders understand how to delegate tasks to the most appropriate and qualified employee. They take into consideration which individuals desire additional responsibilities and possess the capabilities to complete the task.

Training and support: Because laissez-faire leaders depend on the competency and capability of their people, they tend to provide ample opportunities for training to ensure their people can continue to do the job and meet the needs of the organization.

Trust: Because laissez-faire leaders delegate so much responsibility to their people, they tend to show a great deal of trust in them which, in turn, fosters an increase in employee engagement.

Empowerment: Leaders using a laissez-faire style empower their people to make decisions, often giving them significant latitude to drive projects and goals. This can increase the employee's sense of ownership in the mission.

Safe to make mistakes: Laissez-faire leaders typically create an environment where it is safe for subordinates to experiment and fail. This can foster an employee's growth and development and encourage innovation.

The research which suggests Laissez-Faire Leadership consists of positive characteristics also suggests this style is not well suited for use with new employees or those who require structure and direction. Additionally, Laissez-Faire Leadership is not ideal for teams experiencing internal conflict. Laissez-Faire Leadership is more appropriate for use with seasoned, well-trained, and responsible employees who take initiative.

Though most sources and theories treat Laissez-Faire Leadership as an undesirable leadership style, we encourage professionals to study this style of leadership for both its strengths and limitations. History provides many examples of effective laissez-faire leaders and the achievements which resulted from Laissez-Faire Leadership. Several sources identify Warren Buffett, Steve Jobs, and Queen Victoria as effective laissez-faire leaders.

Professionals seeking additional information on Laissez-Faire Leadership will find volumes of literature available on the subject. We encourage readers to consider texts which present differing views of Laissez-Faire Leadership to ensure a more accurate understanding of the characteristics associated with this style.

Sources[171]

LASER COACHING MODEL

Certification Available: no
Certification Required: no
Assessments: no
Proprietary: no
Client: individuals, groups, teams
Cost: not applicable
Category: coaching model

Laser Coaching is a broad and somewhat ambiguous term with a variety of different meanings. This is important since the various meanings of Laser Coaching are far from similar and can confuse professionals who may hold distinct definitions in mind when using the term. We include this entry in the ICMT to make professionals aware of the ambiguity associated with the term Laser Coaching or LASER Coaching.

One version of LASER Coaching refers to a framework that falls under the umbrella of *Cognitive Behavioral Coaching (CBC)*. Developed by executive coach and psychotherapist Graham Lee, LASER consists of a five-step coaching process designed to help clients process and learn from their experiences. This version of LASER involves narrative-style coaching sessions consisting of the following five stages.

Stage 1—Learning
Stage 2—Assessing
Stage 3—Story-making
Stage 4—Enabling
Stage 5—Reframing

A different Laser Coaching model refers to coaching sessions designed for busy professionals. This framework provides for more direct and condensed coaching sessions. A form of speed coaching, each session lasts 20 minutes or less and allows busy clients to quickly focus on what is important. Though similar to Graham Lee's LASER, this version does not incorporate storytelling into the coaching process.

A third variation of the term, attributed to Jack Canfield, describes an eight-step coaching process.

Step 1—Permission to coach
Step 2—Clearly define the outcome
Step 3—Identify importance
Step 4—Identify consequences of inaction
Step 5—Identify obstacles and blocks
Step 6—Determine step-by-step actions
Step 7—Create accountability
Step 8—Acknowledge and reward

Like the second variation, a fourth version of Laser Coaching, also of unknown origin, provides a framework for short but direct coaching sessions consisting of four steps.

Step 1—What happened to the client?
Step 2—What is the client's ideal outcome?
Step 3—What are the barriers to the client?
Step 4—What ideas can the client come up with?

Other variations of Laser Coaching exist, but the point remains the same. Laser Coaching is an ambiguous and informal term that can have different meaning to different professionals.

Further adding to the confusion, some applications of Laser Coaching follow traditional models like Sir John Whitmore's *GROW Model*, while others deviate from these more traditional models.

Professionals should seek clarification when confronted with the term Laser Coaching to ensure all parties possess a common frame of reference.

Professionals seeking additional information on Laser Coaching as a focused approach to coaching sessions may consider the 2019 book by Marion Franklin, *The HeART of Laser-Focused Coaching: A Revolutionary Approach to Coaching.*

Sources[172]

LATERAL THINKING MODEL

Certification Available: yes
Certification Required: yes
Assessments: no
Proprietary: yes (The de Bono Group)
Client: individuals, groups, teams
Cost: $5,200
Category: problem-solving

Developed in 1967 by noted psychologist Dr. Edward de Bono, the Lateral Thinking Model provides a process to facilitate creative and out-of-the-box problem-solving. The framework includes a variety of techniques, including these seven popular approaches designed to foster creativity.

Alternatives: These techniques involve the client seeking alternative points of view to affect the way they see or perceive the problem. This may include the use of perspective-shifting techniques. Freeing the client from existing patterns of thinking which may stymie creativity will enable them to create new potential solutions.

Focus: These techniques involve the client's ability to shift their focus from one aspect of an issue to another. Often, clients fixate on a single aspect of the problem, which limits or stifles creativity. By helping clients shift their focus to aspects previously unconsidered, they open themselves to new possibilities.

Challenge: These techniques ask the question, "Is there a better way of doing this?" In other words, this approach challenges the status quo specific to how and why organizations and people do things. Like the previous technique, challenge techniques seek to break a set pattern of thinking and open the client to new possibilities.

Random entry: These techniques use seemingly disconnected or unrelated stimuli to inspire creative thought. Often, this involves using random terms, pictures, analogies, or sounds to stimulate creativity.

Provocation: These techniques use provocative statements as conduits to kindle creativity. By empowering the client to consider outlandish possibilities, the client becomes free of the anchors that may preemptively stymie the creative process.

Harvesting: These techniques help the client select the most sensible ideas and shape them for practical applications. In other words, this function takes a promising idea and advances it into a practical concept or course of action.

Treatment of ideas: These techniques help the client reshape previously selected ideas so they can thrive within a specific environment or organization.

De Bono developed Lateral Thinking as an alternative to the traditional logic-based *Vertical Thinking Model*. Though presented in the ICMT as two separate entries, the Lateral Thinking Model and Vertical Thinking Model are two halves of Dr. de Bono's problem-solving framework.

It is important to note that neither approach is wrong. In fact, both Vertical and Lateral Thinking present distinct advantages and warrant consideration when problem-solving or when developing a team to address a real-world problem. Having team members who represent a combination of these two approaches can improve the problem-solving process.

To facilitate the integration of Lateral and Vertical Thinking Models within group settings, Dr. de Bono created the Six Thinking Hats technique. This is a process which allows a group to simultaneously apply a creative and methodical approach to problem-solving.

The Lateral Thinking Model is more complex than presented here. Professionals seeking additional information may consider Dr. de Bono's 1967 book, *The Use of Lateral Thinking*, and his 1970 book, *Lateral Thinking: Creativity Step by Step*.

Formal training is available in Vertical and Lateral Thinking Models as well as the Six Thinking Hats from one of de Bono's authorized providers.

Sources[173]

LEADER-MEMBER EXCHANGE THEORY

Certification Available: no
Certification Required: no
Assessments: yes (LMX 7 Scale)
Proprietary: no
Client: individuals, groups, teams
Cost: not applicable
Category: leadership, employee engagement

Leader-Member Exchange Theory (LMX) emerged in the 1970s, though the exact origin of the theory remains ambiguous. Between 1980 and 1990, several scholars contributed to the theory, including organizational psychologists George Graen, Fred Dansereau, Mary Uhl-Bien, and William Haga among others.

Unlike leadership theories which focus on the characteristics, traits, or behaviors of leaders, LMX focuses on the relationship between leaders and their followers. This theory suggests that the effectiveness of leaders is contingent on the quality of the relationships they have with each individual follower. For this reason, LMX falls under the category of *Relational Leadership Theories*.

Research into the leader-member relationship revealed that these relationships tend to follow a three-phase developmental sequence.

Phase 1—Role-taking: The first phase occurs when a new member joins the leader's group. During this period, the leader begins evaluating the new member on both a conscious and subconscious level to determine what skills and abilities the person brings to the team.

Phase 2—Role-making: In this phase, the new member begins integrating into the group dynamic. During this period, an informal negotiation takes place between the leader and the new member as the member begins to establish a place or role for herself within the group. The new member's ability to establish and cultivate trust with the leader is essential to a strong relationship.

A consequence of the leader's evaluation (from phase 1) is the informal and often subconscious creation of two groups within the leader's team.

• In-group: This is a collective of the leader's most trusted members. Because of this, members of the in-group receive the best opportunities, increased responsibilities, and the most resources.

• Out-group: This is a collective of those who fail to earn the leader's confidence or trust. Because of this, they receive the easiest tasks, often mundane ones; they rarely receive opportunities for development or growth.

A commonly observed example of in-group/out-group is when leaders have their "go-to" people for important tasks while others feel they never get an opportunity to prove themselves.

LMX suggests that members who find themselves in the out-group may develop a strong dislike and distrust of the leader and those in the in-group. This can fracture team cohesion, damage morale, and decrease employee engagement.

Phase 3—Routinization: In this phase, the relationship between leader and member normalizes and becomes the new status quo. Habits and patterns form in the relationship that make deviation or change difficult.

LMX, also known as Vertical Dyad Linkage Theory, is useful in helping leadership-level clients examine their relationships. Much of the LMX process occurs on a subconscious level, therefore many leaders may lack awareness of their role in creating in-groups and out-groups. Some leaders may fail to recognize the need to rebuild trust and improve relationships with those in the out-group.

To facilitate the use of LMX, Graen and Uhl-Bien created the LMX 7 Scale. This seven-item Likert-style questionnaire is freely available online and helps users gain insight into their leadership style under the LMX framework.

Professionals seeking additional information will find much written about the theory, including the 2015 book, *The Oxford Handbook of Leader-Member Exchange*, authored by Talya N. Bauer and Berrin Erdogan.

Sources[174]

LEADERSHIP MATURITY FRAMEWORK

<table>
<tr><td>

Certification Available: yes
Certification Required: yes
Assessments: yes (MAP)
Proprietary: no
Client: individuals
Cost: pricing not available
Category: learning/development, leadership

</td></tr>
</table>

Developed by psychologist Susanne R. Cook-Greuter, the Leadership Maturity Framework (LMF) provides a model for understanding the evolution of individual adult development. The framework consists of nine levels, though most sources only depict eight levels. This is because it is not typical to see functional individuals at the first level. Each level represents a distinct and increasingly complex view of self and reality. LMF groups the nine levels into four stages: Preconventional, Conventional, Post-conventional, and Transcendent.

Self-centric (Preconventional): Individuals on this level focus primarily on their own needs, which in turn motivates their behavior. They often adopt a short-term view and seek out opportunities for personal advantage. Their opportunistic and self-protective nature influences their perspective of the world.

Group-centric (Conventional): Individuals on this level seek belonging and desire approval from their group. They strive to conform, meet social expectations, and satisfy group norms. They do not concern themselves with anyone outside their group and often develop an "us vs. them" attitude.

Skill-centric (Conventional): Individuals on this level strive to improve their skills and abilities, often comparing themselves to others. They may find themselves lost in the weeds, unable to see the bigger picture. They may believe their way is the right way and only way of doing things.

Self-determining (Conventional): Individuals on this level enjoy analyzing, are goal oriented, and are driven to achieve results. They seek rational ways around problems and strive for consensus.

Self-questioning (Post-conventional): Individuals on this level focus on "self" within relationships. They contextualize their experiences to facilitate meaning-making. They question their assumptions and views, going beyond facts to make interpretations.

Self-actualization (Post-conventional): Individuals on this level strive to integrate and transform "self" and systems. They seek out problems to solve. Those on this level develop a deep appreciation for others.

Construct-aware (Post-conventional): Individuals on this level are highly aware of "self" and the effect they have on others. Capable of complex meaning-making, they seek personal transformation of "self," and strive to help others along their journey.

Unitive (Transcendent): Cook-Greuter describes this as the catch-all level for the ego, the transcendent stage of human development. She acknowledges the possible existence of additional stages but explains that available data does not allow for further distinctions.

Cook-Greuter's LMF is based on Jane Loevinger's *Ego Development Theory* and is one of several frameworks that fall under the umbrella of Vertical Leadership Development.

The data supporting LMF derives from decades of research, including thousands of test results. This enables certified LMF facilitators to show clients how they compare to the larger population.

The Leadership Maturity Framework is more complex than presented here and contains multiple applications, advanced concepts, and assessments, including the Maturity Assessment Profile (MAP). Use of LMF and the MAP Assessment requires extensive training and certification.

Professionals seeking additional information on the Leadership Maturity Framework will find significant literature available, some drawing comparisons to the *Seven Transformations of Leadership*, like Susanne R. Cook-Greuter's paper, "Ego Development: Nine Levels of Increasing Embrace."

Sources[175]

LEADERSHIP THEORIES (GENERAL ENTRY)

Category: leadership

For centuries, scholars, philosophers, and researchers have studied leadership to better understand the factors, conditions, characteristics, and qualities that make for a good leader. The result of these disparate examinations is a collection of frameworks, each offering valuable insight into the construct of leadership. Though no single theory of leadership can claim universal acceptance, understanding these diverse perspectives can provide great insight into the world of leadership.

To understand the vast array of models, it helps to categorize them in some fashion. The ICMT adopts a widely used approach to classifying leadership theories which groups them into seven potential categories based on their underlying assumptions or beliefs. It is important to note that some leadership frameworks fall under more than one umbrella. For example, the *Full Range Leadership Model* applies to both Transactional and Transformational Theories.

Trait Theories: These leadership theories focus on the individual personality traits that contribute to effective leadership. The earliest versions of Trait Theory claimed the traits of effective leadership were inborn, that a person either had the traits or they did not. Later evolutions of Trait Theory eschewed this belief by focusing on personality traits derived from personality frameworks like the *Five-Factor Model* and *Myers-Briggs*. Trait Theories in the ICMT include:

- *Trait Theory (Carlyle/Galton)*, also known as Great Man Theory
- *Trait Theory (Kouzes/Posner)*

Behavioral Theories: These leadership theories suggest individuals become successful leaders by learning and adopting certain behaviors or practices. Behavioral Theories reject the notion that great leaders are born, arguing that leadership is a set of behaviors that a person may acquire. Behavioral Theories in the ICMT include:

- Blake and Mouton *Managerial Grid*

Contingency Theories: These leadership theories suggest what makes a leader effective is situationally dependent. In other words, a person may be an effective leader in one situation but not in another. Contingency Theories in the ICMT include:

- *Fiedler's Contingency Theory*
- *Lewin's Leadership Styles*
- *Tannenbaum-Schmidt Leadership Continuum Model*
- *Path-Goal Theory*
- *Vroom-Yetton Decision Model*
- *Situational Leadership Theory*

Transformational Theories: These leadership theories perceive effective leadership as one in which the leader works with a group or team of individuals to achieve objectives. These theories typically describe an inclusive style of leadership whereby leaders integrate the thoughts and feelings of those around them to achieve success.

Transactional Theories: These leadership theories describe leaders who use rewards and incentives to achieve cooperation.

Functional Theories: These leadership theories argue that effective leaders are ones who contribute to group effectiveness. They suggest leadership is not the sole responsibility of a single leader, but of the collective. Therefore, the effective leader is one who contributes to positive group behaviors. Functional Theories in the ICMT include:

- *Action-Centered Leadership*
- *Five Leadership Practices*

Relational Leadership Theories: These leadership theories suggest that effective leadership focuses on cultivating relationships between leaders and followers. Relational Theories in the ICMT include:

- *Leader-Member Exchange Theory*
- Rost's *Postindustrial Leadership Theory*
- *Charismatic Leadership Theory*
- *Participative Leadership Theory*

Sources[176]

LEAP MODEL

Certification Available: no
Certification Required: no
Assessments: no
Proprietary: no
Client: individuals
Cost: not applicable
Category: reflection, change (ind.)

The origin of the LEAP Model remains ambiguous. Further complicating the matter, research reveals "LEAP Model" refers to a variety of different frameworks. This entry pertains to the LEAP Model associated with *Cognitive Behavioral Coaching (CBC)*. This means the model explores the client's thoughts and feelings about change.

The LEAP Model is a simple process designed to help clients through a period of transition. The fundamental belief of this framework is that the beginning of one thing marks the end of something else, a perspective shared with other frameworks like *Bridges' Transition Model*.

Even when the client faces positive change (e.g., promotion, birth of a new child, etc.), it is important for the client to reflect on what they may lose when the change takes effect. This reflective process is meant to maximize learning from the change experience and to better position the client for the changes to come.

The LEAP Model provides a four-step framework to help the client reflect and consider the consequences of change prior to, during, and after the change occurs.

Step 1—Letting go: During the first step of the process, the client reflects on how the changes will affect their status quo. Any transition, especially a significant one, typically results in changes to the client's status quo. Therefore, it is important for the client to identify the nuances of how this transition will change their day-to-day life. The client's ability to let go of the old status quo is essential if they are to embrace the new status quo.

For example, a client receives a promotion to a senior leader position. This leads to increased responsibilities and job demands. The client should explore what this means for them.

Step 2—Ending: Just as change may introduce new elements to a client's life, it may also remove others. The client should therefore expect that any transition will inevitably mean the loss of something, which may result in the client grieving.

For example, a new promotion may result in better pay and benefits, but the added responsibility of leadership may affect personal relationships at the office. The client may perceive the changes in these personal relationships as a loss.

The second stage is not about thinking negatively, rather it is about bringing awareness to all the consequences of change. This awareness can help the client prepare for what is to come.

Step 3—Adjusting: The third step involves the client applying what they have learned to better help them adapt to the new status quo. By understanding the positive and negative consequences of transition, clients can adjust their perceived sense of self, their expectations, and their thoughts and feelings about the transition.

Step 4—Positive beginnings: The final step involves the client exploring what the new status quo looks like. When the transition is positive, clients tend to skip the first steps, jumping straight to step 4, which can lead them to regret the transition later. When this happens, a client may say they did not anticipate the outcome when they accepted the transition.

For clients facing undesirable change, reaching step 4 can prove daunting but not impossible. Helping the client see all perspectives may facilitate their experience, allowing them to process the change and find acceptance.

Professionals seeking additional information on this LEAP Model will find limited resources available. This entry derives from Helen Whitten's 2011 book, *Cognitive Behavioural Coaching Techniques for Dummies*.

Sources[177]

LEARNED HELPLESSNESS THEORY

Certification Available: no
Certification Required: no
Assessments: no
Proprietary: no
Client: individuals
Cost: not applicable
Category: confidence/resilience, self-actualization

Developed in the 1960s by psychologists Martin Seligman and Steven F. Maier, the Theory of Learned Helplessness provides a framework for exploring a client's sense of helplessness. They describe helplessness as a mindset in which people believe they have no ability to influence or change their current circumstances; therefore they do not even try to effect change.

The Learned Helplessness Theory framework consists of three specific aspects which facilitate an exploration of helplessness. They call these aspects Explanatory Styles because they examine the client's perception of the situation.

Solvability: This aspect refers to the client's perceptions of whether it is possible to solve the problem or issue, and their opinion on who could solve the issue or fix the problem. The client's perceptions may fall under one of two categories.

• **Universal helplessness**: This applies to clients who believe that nothing or no one can solve the problem. This is a sense of total helplessness.

• **Personal helplessness**: This applies to clients who believe that someone could help them, but they cannot help themselves. The client believes the problem has a solution, but the solution is beyond them.

Focus: This aspect refers to the client's perceptions regarding the cause, scale, and scope of the issue on their life. The client's perceptions may fall under one of two categories.

• **Global helplessness**: This applies to clients who believe the issue spans multiple aspects of their life. They feel they have no control over anything.

• **Specific helplessness**: This applies to clients who believe the issue focuses on a specific aspect of their life. They feel confident in other aspects of their life, just not this one.

Temporal: This aspect refers to the frequency and duration of the client's experienced sense of helplessness. The client's perceptions may fall under one of two categories.

• **Chronic helplessness**: This applies to clients whose sense of helplessness has persisted over a long period of time and is a continuous presence in their life. In extreme cases, the learned helplessness may go back to childhood.

• **Transient helplessness**: This applies to clients whose sense of helplessness is short-lived, recent, or nonrecurrent.

An examination of a client's perceptions using this framework helps the coach determine if the client's learned helplessness is appropriate for coaching or more appropriate for therapy. Clients with helplessness characterized as Universal, Global, or Chronic should consider therapy. Conversely, clients whose learned helplessness is Personal, Specific, or Transient may benefit from coaching.

Subsequent research into learned helplessness has shown a connection between this phenomenon and depression, making it even more important for coaches to be ready to refer the client to a clinical professional when appropriate.

A fundamental aspect of this theory is the belief that people learn helplessness, that they are not born with this mindset. Helplessness is a state of mind acquired through experiences. Just as one learns helplessness, they can unlearn it. For some clients, it may become necessary to explore their current environment and how it may contribute to their sense of helplessness.

Coaching clients with learned helplessness can prove daunting. Professionals seeking additional information will find much written on the topic, including Seligman and Maier's 1993 book, *Learned Helplessness: A Theory for the Age of Personal Control*, co-authored by Christopher Peterson.

Sources[178]

LEARNED OPTIMISM THEORY

Certification Available: no
Certification Required: no
Assessments: yes (LOT, ASQ)
Proprietary: no
Client: individuals
Cost: not applicable
Category: confidence/resilience, self-actualization

Developed by psychologist Martin Seligman, Learned Optimism Theory suggests that individuals have the capacity to adjust their cognitive processing to foster a positive perception of themselves and their life experiences. Thus, this theory falls under the umbrella of *Positive Psychology Coaching*.

An evolution of *Learned Helplessness Theory*, Learned Optimism offers a framework for understanding which cognitive processes influence a person's tendency toward pessimism and provides strategies for teaching individuals how to adjust these processes to facilitate optimism.

The Learned Optimism framework consists of three cognitive processes which contribute to a client's sense of pessimism or optimism.

Focus of selective attention: This pertains to an individual's tendency to favor one type of information over another. This may include preferential biases for negative information, positive information, or the inability to see positive information.

A popular analogy to explain this is (1) the glass is half full, (2) the glass is half empty, or (3) the glass has almost no water in it, the latter representing a person who focuses on the absence of a positive element.

Locus of control: This pertains to the cognitive process by which individuals assess their ability to control or influence an outcome. Pessimistic individuals tend to perceive negative events as beyond their ability to control. The less control a person feels, the greater the pessimism. This, in turn, impacts an individual's sense of self-efficacy and self-confidence, further affecting their perceptions of future events.

Attribution: This pertains to the cognitive process that enables an individual to assign responsibility for an outcome. For example, a pessimistic individual may explain their poor performance as the result of not being smart enough.

Pulling from Learned Helplessness Theory, Learned Optimism includes a variation of the Explanatory Styles, called the 3 Ps. This provides a framework for helping clients explore options for improving optimism.

Personalization: This involves an exploration of the client's tendency to internalize setbacks as their fault alone or externalize them as the result of outside factors.

Pervasiveness: This pertains to how the client makes meaning of the event. The belief that a negative event has global implications (e.g., I'll never be good at anything) is prevalent among pessimists. Therefore, this domain involves the client's exploration of newer and more positive ways to look at the situation.

Permanence: This involves an exploration of the client's perceptions regarding the duration and permanence of the situation. Clients experiencing pessimism may perceive that they will always be bad at something, or that the situation is fixed and unchangeable.

There are a variety of tools, exercises, and instruments available to facilitate a client's exploration within this domain. These include the Attributional Style Questionnaire (ASQ) and the Learned Optimism Test (LOT). In addition, Seligman adopted from Albert Ellis's *ABCDE Model* to create his own *ABCDE Model (Seligman)* as an approach to facilitating Learned Optimism.

Professionals will find significant literature available on Learned Optimism, such as Seligman's 2006 book, *Learned Optimism: How to Change Your Mind and Your Life.*

Sources[179]

LEARNING ORGANIZATION

Certification Available: no
Certification Required: no
Assessments: no
Proprietary: no
Client: organizations
Cost: not applicable
Category: change (org.), problem-solving

Learning Organization is a term that carries different meaning for different people. We present two perspectives on learning organization—the first from MIT professor Peter M. Senge, the second by Harvard professor David A. Garvin.

Senge defines a learning organization as "an organization where people continually expand their capacity to create the results they truly desire, where new and expansive patterns of thinking are nurtured, where collective aspirations are set free, and where people are continually learning how to learn together." The fundamental component of a learning organization is the individual and their capacity for learning. Consequently, learning organizations are ones that provide an environment conducive to the individual's learning experience.

Senge provides a framework consisting of five disciplines for becoming a learning organization.

Discipline 1—Personal mastery: The organization creates an environment where individuals may reflect, develop a vision, and strive to accomplish personal goals.

Discipline 2—Shared vision: The organization, through a collaborative and integrative process, gives voice to all employees, allowing them to create a unified vision for the organization. Empowering employees to develop a vision free from directives and mandates allows each person to possess a sense of ownership in the vision.

Discipline 3—Mental models: The organization empowers employees to question the status quo and challenge assumptions. This allows them to broaden their perception of events, giving them a more accurate frame of reference from which to grow.

Discipline 4—Team learning: Organizations create an open environment where individuals can discuss issues free from criticism and judgment.

Discipline 5—Systems thinking: The final discipline involves employees exploring the complex relationships between variables of the organization. These include the relationships between departments, units, and individuals.

Other sources describe learning organizations as organizations which learn from past and present experiences, understand cause and effect, detect patterns and trends in data, and anticipate or prepare for the future. Harvard professor David A. Garvin describes the five main activities of a learning organization.

Systematic problem-solving: The use of scientific methods to collect, analyze, and assess relevant data and avoid or challenge assumptions and bias.

Experimentation: The use of testing to increase knowledge. This includes an exploration of what works, what does not work, and why.

Learning from past experiences: The ability to examine past efforts and projects, attempting to understand why they worked or did not work, so the organization may avoid repeating mistakes.

Learning from others: The ability to explore beyond the confines of the organization and look to others for lessons.

Transferring knowledge: The ability of the organization to disseminate knowledge throughout the organization.

The concept of a learning organization is far more complex than presented here. Professionals seeking additional information may consider Senge's 1990 book, *The Fifth Discipline: The Art and Practice of the Learning Organization.*

Sources[180]

LEAVITT'S SYSTEM MODEL

Certification Available: no
Certification Required: no
Assessments: no
Proprietary: no
Client: organizations
Cost: not applicable
Category: change (org.)

Developed in 1965 by management psychologist Harold J. Leavitt, Leavitt's System Model (LSM) provides a framework for exploring organizational change and assessing the potential systemic consequences of change on the organization.

The LSM framework consists of four interrelated components or domains. Changes to one component affect the other three. Professionals use this framework for examining the relationship between components and to better understand how changes in one domain affect the other domains.

Structure: This component (or domain) pertains to all aspects of an organization's structure. This includes the reporting hierarchy (i.e., chain of command), the method of grouping employees (i.e., departments, units), the formal and informal nature of the relationship between these groups, and the unique communication style of each group.

Structure also includes the flow of responsibilities, authorities, and accountability within and between all groups at all levels. Exploration of an organization's structure should consider the centralization or decentral-ization of work, the level of control at various echelons of the organization, and the state of delegation within the organization.

Task: This component focuses on how the organization performs its mission or produces its products or its services. This domain consists of two perspectives. The first perspective focuses on the employee, specifically the type of tasks they perform and how they perform them. The second aspect focuses on the tasks the organization performs. This includes how the organization measures progress and success.

Exploring this domain involves examining how each employee's action contributes to the product or service offered. This also requires an understanding of how each employee group contributes to the mission, as well as an assessment of the alignment between individual and organizational objectives and goals (i.e., whether the day-to-day performance measures are conducive to achieving the bigger goal).

People: This component focuses on the employees responsible for accomplishing the tasks identified in the second domain. Exploring this component includes understanding how everyone's skills, abilities, and knowledge contribute to mission success and task completion.

This also includes understanding each employee's motivation, the state of their professional development, and their training needs.

Technology: This component pertains to the tools employees use to accomplish their assigned tasks. This includes all available software, hardware, and equipment.

The LSM framework suggests that change to any component (e.g., introducing new technology) will inherently have a ripple effect, creating the need for change or adaptation in other domains (e.g., training for employees on the new technology, new metrics for ensuring compliance, and changes to how departments use the new technology).

Effectively using LSM requires a thorough and accurate understanding of each component as it applies to the organization. This depth of organizational and institutional knowledge is vital to facilitating lasting change within an organization by creating insight into how each component needs to adapt to embrace and support the change.

Also known as Leavitt's Diamond Model and Leavitt's Alignment Model, Leavitt's framework is among the oldest change management models available. Professionals seeking additional information will find significant literature available online.

Sources[181]

LEWIN'S BEHAVIOR EQUATION

Certification Available: no
Certification Required: no
Assessments: no
Proprietary: no
Client: individuals
Cost: not applicable
Category: change (ind.), behavioral styles, self-awareness

Developed in the 1930s by psychologist Kurt Lewin, his equation proposes that behavior is a function of the individual and their environment, frequently depicted by the formula $B = f(P,E)$. Also known as Lewin's Equation or Lewin's Formula, his model consists of three variables which help explain human behavior.

Person (P): This variable refers to the whole person (or personality) and includes a person's expectations, desires, fears, motivations, and predispositions. Another element within this variable is an individual's growth vs. fixed mindset and their receptivity to development and openness to new experiences. These elements cover both past and current experiences.

Environment (E): This variable refers to the individual's environment and includes their physical and social settings, social rules, social norms, and their primary and secondary cultures. The elements of environment influence multiple aspects of an individual's experiences and the way they process these experiences. Some sources refer to this variable as the Life Space.

Behavior (B): This variable refers to the individual's behavior, the observable manifestation of their thoughts, feelings, beliefs, and habits.

Function (f): This suggests that the elements of an individual's personality and their environment have a direct effect on how a person behaves.

Lewin's Equation offers many possibilities in considering the relationship between a person, their environment, and their behavior. One such possibility suggests that a person's behavior changes with the environment. Another suggests that behavioral change occurs when facets of an individual's personality change.

A key exploratory aspect of Lewin's Equation seeks to understand how much the individual influences their environment versus how much the environment influences the individual. At the heart of this question is one of the oldest debates in psychology, nature vs. nurture. Lewin suggests the issue is not one of either/or, rather it is both and to what degree. To that end, he further suggests that the answer is situation-dependent.

Lewin's Equation is a useful framework for clients struggling to understand their relationship with the environment. For example, a client may use Lewin's Equation to develop awareness of how their professional environment may affect their behavior at home.

Lewin's work can help leadership-level clients understand how their behaviors at work influence another person's environment, consequently affecting that person's behavior at work. This form of social awareness facilitates the client's leadership development.

Lewin's Equation is also useful with clients struggling to make personal changes. Often, clients having trouble making changes stick will discover ways their environment may prevent or impede their quest for lasting change.

Though seemingly simple, Lewin's theory is quite complex and derives from Gestalt Psychology, which suggests "the whole is greater than the sum of its parts." Both variables (personality and environment) consist of multiple elements which act as influencers of behavior. Thoroughly using Lewin's Equation requires a deep understanding of these elements.

Professionals seeking additional information will find significant literature available on the model, including Kurt Lewin's 1936 book, *Principles of Topological Psychology*.

Sources[182]

LEWIN'S CHANGE MANAGEMENT MODEL

> **Certification Available:** no
> **Certification Required:** no
> **Assessments:** no
> **Proprietary:** no
> **Client:** individuals
> **Cost:** not applicable
> **Category:** change (org.), change (ind.)

Developed circa 1947 by psychologist Kurt Lewin, his Change Management Model provides a framework for understanding the progression of organizational change. The model suggests change occurs in three sequential stages. Lewin uses an analogy of changing an ice cube to an ice cone to represent the stages. First, a person unfreezes the ice cube, then they shape the water into a cone (i.e., change), and then they refreeze the water into an ice cone.

Stage 1—Unfreeze: The first stage begins with the assumption that most individuals are naturally predisposed to seek equilibrium in their life (see *Consistency Theories* for more on this). This suggests people inherently anchor themselves to the status quo because it is a known commodity and therefore a source of safety, security, and comfort. Lewin argues that for change to even have a chance, it becomes necessary to agitate that equilibrium.

Upsetting the status quo requires drawing attention to aspects of the norm some may resist accepting. This can include bringing awareness to undesirable elements of the status quo or highlighting potential risks on the horizon that the status quo cannot address. Such tactics are necessary to help the client see how the status quo is less desirable than the change presented.

During the first stage, change managers and change agents must seek out supporters (i.e., develop a coalition) to help facilitate the change effort. They must convey details addressing the how and why of change through effective messaging. A successful first stage results in a workforce that is aware of the need for change, supports the change, and commits to adopting the change.

Stage 2—Change: The second stage involves change agents defining what the change will look like and how the change will occur. This requires planners to understand the complex relationship between multiple variables within the organization (see *Leavitt's System Model* for more information on these variables). Change agents should explore how change will impact the organization's processes, relationships, structure, and mission.

This stage is extremely complex and requires persistent communication with the workforce and all stakeholders, updating them on progress and adjustments to the change effort. This stage involves implementation of the change; therefore, it is important that leaders delegate and empower those charged with carrying out the change.

Stage 3—Refreeze: The final stage involves turning the desired change into the new status quo. Typically, this requires the organization to adjust its policies, processes, and culture to reinforce the change. Failure to make the appropriate adjustments presents the risk that some aspect of the organization may, intentionally or unintentionally, undermine the change effort.

Lewin's Change Management Model, also known as Lewin's 3-Stage Model of Change, would go on to influence future organizational change frameworks. Aspects of Lewin's model—like building a coalition, messaging the change, and challenging the status quo—manifest in other popular frameworks like *Kotter's Change Management Theory* and the *ADKAR Model*.

Some sources credit Lewin as the father of change management, and while his Change Management Model is very influential, today's practitioners consider it more of a philosophy than an actual process. Lewin's model is useful for clients preparing to undertake a large-scale change effort.

Professionals seeking additional information will find much written on Lewin's Change Management Model. The array of available literature includes articles supportive and critical of Lewin's model.

Sources[183]

LEWIN'S LEADERSHIP STYLES

Certification Available: no
Certification Required: no
Assessments: no
Proprietary: no
Client: individuals
Cost: not applicable
Category: leadership

Developed in the 1930s by psychologist Kurt Lewin, his theory proposes that an individual's approach to leadership falls under one of three distinct styles. Though Lewin advocates for one of these styles over the others, subsequent research places Lewin's Leadership Styles under the umbrella of *Contingency Theories*, suggesting that the best style is situationally dependent.

Authoritarian leadership: Also known as the Autocratic Style, this style describes a leader who maintains strict control over the decision-making process, often excluding others from providing input. This style of leader provides a clear and meticulous explanation of what needs to be done, how it is to be done, and when it is to be done.

Lewin considered this an undesirable style of leadership which produces mixed outcomes. The negative consequences, Lewin observed, include diminished creativity among followers, lower morale, higher absenteeism, and increased turnover.

Proponents of contingency theories of leadership, however, argue that the authoritarian approach is an ideal leadership style in crisis situations during which there is little time for collaborative decision-making.

Participative leadership: Also known as the Democratic Style, this style describes a leader who includes followers in the decision-making process. This does not mean followers make the decision, simply that they have input in the process.

Lewin considered this the ideal leadership style. He made several observations of groups working under the participative leadership style. Though they produced fewer results than those under an authoritarian leader, the results were of higher quality.

The benefits of participative leadership include higher morale among followers, an increased sense of ownership in decision outcomes, and improved employee engagement. Proponents of contingency theories caution that participative leadership is ill-suited for certain situations like a crisis.

Delegative leadership: Also known as the Laissez-Faire Style, this style describes a leader who provides little guidance to followers, instead relying on the initiative of followers to carry out the tasks associated with the mission. Lewin considered this the least effective style, having observed a considerable lack of productivity among groups under this style of leadership and a significant decrease in the quality of their results.

Additionally, Lewin observed followers subjected to delegative leadership appeared directionless, lacked motivation, and were unable to function independently.

Contingency theorists believe this style of leadership has some merit and is better suited in situations where followers are mature, well experienced, and who require room to create and experiment. Critics of Lewin's model argue the term "Delegative" is misleading, as delegation is the deliberate empowerment of people, and what Lewin describes here is the careless abdication of power to followers.

As with many of Lewin's theories, the Leadership Styles framework would go on to influence future leadership theories. The three styles manifest in several popular frameworks used today.

It is important to note that Lewin's observations were based on children. Subsequent research applied Lewin's theory to adult professionals, which determined that no one style was best, hence its inclusion among contingency theories.

Though more comprehensive leadership models exist, Lewin's Leadership Styles remains a popular framework for examining leadership.

Sources[184]

LIKERT'S FOUR MANAGEMENT SYSTEMS

Certification Available: no
Certification Required: no
Assessments: no
Proprietary: no
Client: individuals, organizations
Cost: not applicable
Category: leadership

Created in the 1960s by social psychologist Rensis Likert, the Four Management Systems provides a framework for examining an individual's leadership style. The model consists of four levels he called the four systems, which can describe the organization's overall leadership culture.

Likert, who created the widely used Likert scale (i.e., "on a scale of 1–10…"), applies the four systems of management using a scale of 1–4. System 1 represents the least desirable approach to leadership and management. System 4 represents the most desirable approach.

System 1—Exploitative-authoritative: Characterizes a hierarchal approach to leadership with power and authority relegated to the highest levels of the organization. Leaders dictate the roles and responsibilities of employees, communication flows one way from the top down, and employees have zero input in decisions.

Employees under this system have little to no voice and experience motivation through fear of punishment. They have limited trust in leaders, peers, or others within the organization. System 1 leadership leads to lower employee engagement, lower morale, decreased creativity, and a lack of innovation.

System 2—Benevolent-authoritative: Characterizes a "master-servant" relationship that is just as autocratic as System 1 leaders. However, System 2 leaders use rewards to induce motivation as opposed to the fear-based motivation of System 1. The relationship between employees and frontline managers improves with System 2, though there remains little to no communication between employees and upper management. The sparse information that reaches upper management often serves only to satisfy what leaders want to hear.

The level of trust is slightly better in System 2, with some authority delegated to mid-management, though it remains denied to those at the lowest level.

System 3—Consultative-democratic: Leaders in this system have greater trust in their followers, often including them in decision-making discourse. Communication is open across most, if not all, levels of the organization. Though decision-making authority remains with senior leadership, employees have a voice with which to influence decision-making.

System 3 combines rewards and participation to motivate employees. In other words, a System 3 approach views inclusion as a source of motivation.

System 4—Participative-democratic: Considered the most satisfying leadership approach by employees, System 4 involves a complete integration of the workforce. Where System 3 allowed employees an opportunity to influence decision-making, System 4 empowers them to make decisions. This requires full trust as well as open and transparent communication across all levels of the organization.

Characterized by a collective sense of ownership, responsibility, and purpose, System 4 embraces a concept called **Linking Pins**. These are individuals who possess enhanced responsibilities, skills, and experiences who serve as members of more than one team. Their presence on multiple teams allows them to link the efforts of disparate teams into a more integrative and efficient effort.

Also called Likert's Management Theory, his model is more complex than presented here and includes an exploration of seven key variables within each system (leadership, motivation, communication, influence, decision-making, goal setting, and control). Professionals seeking additional information may consider Likert's 1961 book, *New Patterns of Management*.

Sources[185]

LOCKE'S GOAL-SETTING THEORY

Certification Available: no
Certification Required: no
Assessments: no
Proprietary: no
Client: individuals
Cost: not applicable
Category: employee engagement, goal setting, motivation

Developed in 1968 by psychologist Edwin A. Locke, Goal-Setting Theory provides a framework to explain individual motivation in the workplace with an emphasis on the creation of goals. Locke's model consists of five principles necessary for effective goal setting.

Clarity: Goals should possess a sufficient level of specificity and clarity so that stakeholders and employees understand the tasks expected of them. This includes defining the role of each person in goal attainment. Clarity also serves to ensure everyone participating in the effort shares a common understanding of the goal and what constitutes successful goal attainment.

Challenge: The goal should possess a proper balance of difficulty and achievability. Goals that are too easy will demotivate employees; conversely, goals that are too difficult will demoralize employees. Hence, goals should consist of a balance between difficulty level and achievability. This requires a deep understanding of the capabilities and limitations of employees in carrying out the tasks necessary to achieve the goal. When prop-

erly balanced, challenging goals will provide a sense of accomplishment for employees once completed.

Commitment: Everyone participating in goal attainment must have voice and ownership in the effort to establish a sense of commitment to the effort. Employees must buy in to the goal from the beginning. To achieve this, goal setters must ensure everyone understands the importance of the goal to both the organization and its employees.

A strong commitment requires accountability. This means participants should understand the relationship between their individual responsibilities and how their behavior impacts the larger effort and those around them.

Feedback: A critical element of goal setting involves developing a mechanism for employees to track their progress and see tangible outcomes from their efforts. Key to this is the use of effective and meaningful feedback, which can reinforce accountability and foster continued momentum.

Task complexity: Effective goal setting may require deconstructing the goal into smaller objectives, sometimes called chunking. This is particularly important when the goal or associated tasks become highly complex or complicated.

Occasionally, it may become necessary to adjust the timeframe of goal attainment to allow sufficient time to achieve the individual objectives.

Some sources characterize Locke's Goal-Setting Theory as the predecessor to the *SMART Model for Goal Setting*. This is understandable, given that many aspects of Locke's model manifest in that and other frameworks.

Locke's research on individual motivation continues to provide valuable insight. Locke determined that employees who have a say in establishing their company's goals, or in how they might achieve those goals, have higher motivation to contribute to the effort. In this, Locke discovered one of the earliest pieces of evidence highlighting the relationship between employee voice and employee engagement.

Professionals seeking additional information will find significant literature available on Locke's Goal-Setting Theory, including his 1968 research paper, "Toward a Theory of Task Motivation and Incentives."

Sources[186]

MANAGERIAL GRID MODEL

Certification Available: no
Certification Required: no
Assessments: no
Proprietary: no
Client: individuals, groups
Cost: not applicable
Category: leadership

Developed in the 1960s by professors Robert R. Blake and Jane S. Mouton, the Managerial Grid is a framework designed to help classify leadership behaviors. The Managerial Grid is based on two key dimensions: the leader's concern for **people** (which includes their needs, interests, and personal development), and their concern for **results** (which includes productivity, achievement, and efficiency). These dimensions form the basis for the five leadership styles.

Impoverished management (low results and low people): These leaders care little for achieving mission success or creating a satisfying work environment for their people. Characterized as indifferent, noncommittal, and apathetic, they typically only care about preserving what they have (i.e., status quo) and avoiding accountability for any mistakes they make. Most consider this style the least effective form of leadership.

Produce-or-perish management (high results but low people): These leaders view their employees as a means to an end, a necessary component to achieve success and nothing more. Characterized as autocratic or authoritarian, these managers typically adopt a strict adherence to rules, policies, and procedures. They prefer to motivate people through fear by punishing those who fail to perform. These leaders produce good results in the beginning, but over time their results slip as morale drops and employee engagement decreases.

Middle-of-the-road management (medium results and medium people): These leaders strive to maintain the status quo. Characterized as average leaders or middle-of-the-road managers, they are conflict avoidant and fearful of straying too far from the established norm. Consequently, innovation and creativity do not thrive under these leaders. This style of leadership results in average performances from individuals who feel indifferent about their work.

Country club management (low results but high people): These leaders prioritize people over results, erroneously believing that a happy workforce will produce significant results. Characterized as friendly, easygoing, and responsive to subordinates' needs, these leaders try to limit conflict between themselves and their employees. This style of leadership often results in marginal or below-average outcomes. The lack of accountability, direction, and focus leads to performance shortcomings.

Team management (high results and high people): These leaders are passionate about results and their people. Characterized as empowering, motivating, and driven, these leaders clearly and unambiguously articulate their expectations for employees, ensuring they have all the resources they need to achieve the desired results. These leaders create a sense of ownership among their people, recognizing that employees who have a voice in decision-making feel empowered and will produce greater results.

Years after its initial introduction, Blake added two more leadership styles to the framework.

Paternalistic management: These leaders vacillate between country club management and produce-or-perish management. They will offer support and encouragement to employees but do not like having their position or decisions challenged.

Opportunistic management: This describes leaders who place their needs before others. A leader of this form moves from one style of leadership to another based on what benefits them in the moment.

Professionals seeking additional information will find much written on the framework, including Blake and Mouton's 1964 book, *The Managerial Grid: The Key to Leadership Excellence.*

Sources[187]

MASLOW'S HIERARCHY OF NEEDS

Certification Available: no
Certification Required: no
Assessments: no
Proprietary: no
Client: individuals, groups
Cost: not applicable
Category: motivation

Introduced in 1943 by noted psychologist Abraham Maslow, his Hierarchy of Needs provides a framework for understanding, characterizing, and prioritizing the needs of human beings. Maslow's work advanced our understanding of the relationship between an individual's needs, motivations, and behaviors.

Maslow's framework consists of five levels visually depicted as a pyramid. Though presented as a hierarchy, Maslow emphasized that people could move up and down the pyramid in nonsequential ways.

Level 1—Physical needs: These are essential to human survival and include food, water, warmth, and sleep. Positioned at the bottom of the pyramid, the prolonged absence of any one of these needs will lead to catastrophic results.

Level 2—Safety needs: These needs influence an individual's sense of comfort and well-being. They include personal security, sufficient employment, good health, personal property, and adequate resources.

Level 3—Social needs: These address an individual's community needs, which include family, friends, love, and a sense of belonging.

Level 4—Esteem needs: These needs influence an individual's perception of self, also called "Ego." These include recognition, status, and respect.

Level 5—Self-actualization: Positioned at the top of the pyramid, these needs address an individual's sense of self and include the need to improve oneself and to be the best that one can be.

The five levels are consolidated into two groups based on the relationship between the need and the motivation.

• Deficiency needs: These pertain to those needs that, when left unsatisfied, increase motivation. For example, when a person's need for food is unmet, their motivation to get food goes up. The needs that fall under this classification are Physical, Safety, Social, and Esteem.

• Growth need: These pertain to needs, that when met, increase a person's motivation. For example, when a person's need to learn a new skill is satisfied, their motivation to apply the skill goes up. The need which falls under this classification is Self-actualization.

Maslow's Hierarchy of Needs is among the most widely known models of motivation, influencing subsequent motivation theories like Alderfer's *Existence, Relatedness, and Growth Theory (ERG)* and leadership theories like Douglas McGregor's *Theory X and Theory Y.*

Despite its popularity, there is growing opposition to Maslow's theory. Critics claim there is insufficient scientific testing to support the theory. Following Maslow's death, researchers set out to test his theory, with results failing to fully support the model. Critics also note that Maslow's theory fails to account for differences between individualist and collectivist culture, suggesting that the model as originally presented does not apply cross-culturally.

Regardless, most agree, Maslow's theory changed the way we view motivation. Though his original theory remains a subject of controversy, the subsequent research into the model has led to the development of new theories.

Variations of Maslow's theory exist, sometimes referred to as Maslow's Extended Theory of Hierarchy of Needs. These include additional levels like **Mate Acquisition**, **Mate Retention**, **Parenting**, **Cognitive**, **Aesthetic**, and **Transcendence**.

Professionals seeking additional information may consider Maslow's 1943 paper, "A Theory of Human Motivation," and his 1954 book, *Motivation and Personality.*

Sources[188]

MAYO'S MOTIVATION THEORY

Certification Available: no
Certification Required: no
Assessments: no
Proprietary: no
Client: groups, organizations
Cost: not applicable
Category: motivation, teaming

Developed during the 1920s by Harvard professor George Elton Mayo, his Motivation Theory provides a framework to explain the primary sources of employee motivation. Based on numerous experiments, including the famous Hawthorne study (see *Hawthorne Effect*), Mayo concluded that employee motivation derives from internal and relational sources.

Mayo's experiments suggest that the group or workforce collective plays a much larger role in motivating and influencing workplace behavior than previously thought. He identified two dimensions, the combination of which can characterize the productivity and effectiveness of performance.

Dimension 1—Group norm: This dimension pertains to the rules of behavior established by the group. These include behaviors deemed positive and those considered negative.

Dimension 2—Group cohesiveness: This pertains to how well the group gets along and includes camaraderie and sense of belonging.

These two dimensions result in four possible characterizations of group behavior.

• Norms (LOW), Cohesiveness (LOW): This is a nonfunctional and ineffective collective. Individuals in this type of group achieve nothing and lack motivation to perform. Groups that fall into this category will not last long.

• Norms (LOW), Cohesiveness (HIGH): This group, though highly cohesive, tends to perpetuate negative behaviors among its members. They often fail to achieve objectives despite getting along so well. This can include groups with an "us vs. them" attitude, often viewing their own organization as an adversary.

• Norms (HIGH), Cohesiveness (LOW): Members within this type of group tend to work toward goal attainment as individuals, not as a team. For this reason, they produce positive results, albeit limited. This can include a group that assigns each person a task to accomplish independent of the collective (i.e., stovepipe).

• Norms (HIGH), Cohesiveness (HIGH): These groups have the highest positive impact because people motivate each other to succeed. Individuals cooperate as a team to achieve shared goals.

Mayo's work is among the first to challenge the long-standing belief that an employee's primary source of motivation derives from pay. His observations shed light on the importance of relational leadership to employee motivation.

Also known as Mayo's Theory of Human Relations and Mayo's Theory of Management, his work provided valuable insight into employee job satisfaction, engagement, and motivation. Much of his work manifests in the popular theories of leadership and motivation we see today.

Mayo made several important observations through his experiments, including the observation that workplace rules and regulations affect employee attitudes. He also observed that when managers fail to pay regular attention to workers, the risk of underproduction and poor performance goes up.

Through his work, Mayo discovered that an employee's motivation, satisfaction, and productivity increase with recognition and involvement. This speaks to an employee's need for appreciation and a sense of control in what they do and how they do it.

Sources[189]

McCLELLAND'S THEORY OF NEEDS

Certification Available: no
Certification Required: no
Assessments: no
Proprietary: no
Client: individuals, groups, teams
Cost: not applicable
Category: motivation

Developed in the 1960s by psychologist David McClelland, his Theory of Needs provides a framework of three motivations he believed apply to all people. McClelland suggested that individuals learn these motivations through life; hence the theory is also known as Learned Needs Theory or Acquired Needs Theory. Because McClelland's Theory builds upon *Maslow's Hierarchy of Needs*, it is also known as Human Motivation Theory.

The Theory of Needs suggests that regardless of our age, gender, or culture, every person is a blend of these three distinct needs, with one need emerging as the dominant motivator. The relationship between these motivators shapes an individual's leadership, followership, teaming, and workplace engagement.

Achievement: Individuals with a strong need to achieve want to get things done right and efficiently. They seek out reasonably challenging goals, meaning they tend to avoid easy tasks because any resulting achievements would fail to satisfy their sense of accomplishment. They also avoid overly difficult tasks because they may fail.

Individuals motivated by a need to achieve need to consistently complete tasks and see progress, no matter how small. Calculated risk-takers with high energy, these individuals favor working alone and require honest and balanced feedback. At times, they may feel frustrated or become bored if they do not see progress.

Affiliation: Individuals with a strong need for affiliation desire a sense of belonging which, in turn, drives an individual to seek out admiration or approval from their peers. They prefer to work in a collaborative environment as opposed to a competitive one.

Characteristically, these individuals tend to go along with the group and avoid rocking the boat. Conflict avoidant, they avoid risky situations and will often blindly follow the group. Despite these questionable characteristics, individuals motivated by affiliation can serve as the glue that holds a team together and are an essential part of the team's culture.

Power: Individuals with a strong need for power possess a motivation to influence and control others and attain status. They desire competition because of the status that comes with winning.

Characteristically, these individuals possess high risk tolerance, are tenacious, persistent, and desire praise, recognition, and status. Their need to control others or the team can be both a blessing and a curse. They can keep a team focused and on track, but they can also stymie creativity and diminish morale.

McClelland's Theory of Needs has broad utility as a lens through which to explore leadership styles, feedback approaches, and team construct development. Application of McClelland's Theory of Needs follows a simple two-step process.

• Identify driver (motivational needs): This involves observing an individual to determine their preferential motivator. Though McClelland's Theory does not provide a formal assessment, professionals may incorporate external assessments to facilitate this step.

• Structure approach: Once a client understands the motivations of their employees, they can adjust their leadership style to better resonate with them.

McClelland's Theory of Needs is more complex than presented here and includes its influence on leadership styles, communication preferences, and feedback approaches.

Professionals seeking additional information will find much written on the topic, including McClelland's 1961 book, *The Achieving Society*.

Sources[190]

McGRATH'S TIME, INTERACTION, AND PERFORMANCE THEORY

Certification Available: no
Certification Required: no
Assessments: no
Proprietary: no
Client: teams
Cost: not applicable
Category: teaming

Developed in 1991 by social psychologist Joseph E. McGrath, the Time, Interaction, and Performance Theory (TIP) provides a typology for analyzing group development and performance. This typology consists of four modes of operation (or activities) the group undertakes to achieve project goals.

Mode I—Inception: This mode involves activities relevant to the initial undertaking of the task or project. This includes establishing project goals and defining the parameters of the project.

Mode II—Technical problem-solving: This mode involves activities the group undertakes to overcome practical obstacles preventing project success. These practical problems include challenges stemming from limitations in technology and equipment, among others.

Mode III—Conflict resolution: This mode involves activities the group undertakes to overcome policy, procedural, or personal obstacles impeding the project's success. This can include conflict surrounding how to approach a task or policy constraints which impede the group's ability to act.

Mode IV—Execution: This mode involves all activities core to accomplishing the mission and achieving the project goals.

McGrath emphasizes that the modes of operation are potential forms of activity. Specifically, he states that while the Inception and Execution modes are necessary and that all teams engage in these two modes, not all teams will need to engage in Problem-Solving or Conflict Resolution. Only when the team encounters a problem will they need to engage in Mode II or III.

The TIP typology also includes three functions that occur within each mode of operation. These functions speak to how well the team performs in furtherance of the project objectives and maintains the health of the group and its members.

Production: These are actions individual members take in direct support of accomplishing project objectives.

Well-being: These involve actions which maintain group relationships, build trust and rapport, and increase morale among members.

Member support: These functions directly contribute to the individual needs of group members. This includes ensuring clarity of role and purpose, as well as ensuring members have what they need to actively support the project.

Though success does not require all four modes of operation, groups must engage in all three functions. In other words, a team will not achieve success if individual members do not have their needs met, distrust runs high among members, or individuals do not contribute to advancing the project.

The four modes of operation and the three functions create a total of 12 nodes. Often depicted in a matrix format, the 12 nodes provide a construct for examining team development and performance.

TIP Theory suggests that different teams may choose different paths to arrive at the same outcome. The temporal aspect of this theory implies that unless circumstances dictate otherwise, teams will choose the easiest route, or the path of least resistance.

TIP Theory is more complex than presented here. Professionals seeking additional information will find most information available on the subject relegated to academic sources. McGrath published multiple books exploring team dynamics, including his 2000 book, *Small Groups as Complex Systems*, co-authored by H. Arrow and J. L. Berdahl.

Sources[191]

McKINSEY 7S MODEL

Certification Available: yes (multiple vendors)
Certification Required: no
Assessments: no
Proprietary: no
Client: organizations
Cost: pricing varies
Category: change, crisis management, culture

Developed in the 1970s by McKinsey & Company consultants Tom Peters and Robert Waterman, the 7S Model provides a framework for the examination of an organization's design, efficacy, and ability to adapt. The model identifies 7 interrelated elements essential to organizational effectiveness. The core of the 7S Model suggests that organizational success necessitates the alignment of all seven of these elements.

The 7 elements consolidate into two categories, the first being the hard elements. These consist of aspects of the organization that are tangible and easy to quantify. The second category is that of soft elements, which include intangible aspects of the organization that are difficult to measure.

Strategy (hard): This element pertains to the organization's plan to create and maintain a competitive advantage. While there is no single one-size-fits-all strategy, certain characteristics are common to effective strategies. These include being forward-looking (5 years or more), having a well-defined mission and vision, and proper alignment with the other elements.

Structure (hard): This element pertains to the hierarchy of an organization and includes reporting flow, chain of command, and delegation of roles, responsibilities, and accountabilities across departments, units, and sections of the company. This may also include the use of organizational charts.

Systems (hard): This element pertains to how the organization gets things done and includes policies and processes that dictate how individuals carry out the organization's mission. These processes span every aspect of the organization, from human resources to customer support.

Shared values (soft): This element pertains to the organization's core values, culture, and purpose. These include the norms and standards of the company and its employees. Visual depictions of the 7S Model show this element at the heart of the 7 elements.

Style (soft): Considered an aspect of culture, this element pertains to the styles of leadership used across all levels of management. This includes the code of conduct used by leaders and the nature of relationships between leaders and their followers.

Staff (soft): This element pertains to the individual members of the organization, and includes their recruitment, training, and development. This construct considers the diversity of members, the quality of talent management, and the reward systems used to incentivize members.

Skills (soft): This pertains to the core competencies and capabilities of the individual members of an organization.

The 7S Model is useful with clients whose organizations are considering change or struggling with competition. Though originally developed for McKinsey & Company, there are many resources freely available online to facilitate the application of this model. These include matrixes, worksheets, and question guides.

The McKinsey 7S Model is included in the crisis management category because several models for crisis management (see *Crisis Management Model [G. Herrero/Pratt]*) recommend monitoring the organization's baseline as a means of early warning and early detection. The McKinsey 7S Model is a useful model for analyzing a company to determine this baseline.

Professionals seeking additional information on the 7S Model may consider Peters' and Waterman's 1982 book, *In Search of Excellence: Lessons from America's Best-Run Companies*. Multiple vendors offer training in the 7S Model at diverse price points and in different formats. Interested professionals should thoroughly examine their options before selecting a program.

Sources[192]

MERRILL-REID SOCIAL STYLES

Certification Available: yes
Certification Required: no
Assessments: yes (Social Style Profile, others)
Proprietary: no
Client: individuals, groups
Cost: pricing varies
Category: personality type, communication

Developed in the 1960s by industrial organizational psychologists David W. Merrill and Roger Reid (and based on the work of Dr. James W. Taylor), the Merrill-Reid Social Styles (MRSS) provide a framework for characterizing and categorizing individual personality.

The model classifies four personality styles based on two dimensions: the individual's style of responsiveness and their style of assertiveness.

Dimension 1—Responsiveness: This dimension pertains to an individual's tendencies for emotional regulation and their preference for people or tasks.

- On one side of the spectrum, individuals are task oriented, exercise strict emotional control, and show diminished concern for the feelings of others.

- On the other side of the spectrum, individuals are people oriented, they display emotions, and they incorporate the feelings of others in goal attainment.

Dimension 2—Assertiveness: This dimension pertains to the way an individual influences those around them. This includes the amount of effort a person puts forth and their preferred style of influencing others.

- On one side of the spectrum, individuals are less aggressive, and their influence is subtle and indirect, typically by using questions or inquiry.

- On the other side of the spectrum, individuals are more aggressive, their influence is direct and explicit, typically from telling or directing others.

Analytical: Characterized as organized, methodical, and structured, these individuals value precision and accuracy. They seek out all available data prior to making decisions. The analytical person values neatness, order, and conformity to rules and standards. At times, these individuals may appear indecisive, picky, critical, and slow to act. These individuals tend to be exacting, industrious, persistent, and serious.

Driver: Characterized as goal driven, action oriented, and result seeking, these individuals possess discipline and act decisively, efficiently, and independently. At times, these individuals may appear dominating, harsh, unwilling to cooperate, and averse to listening.

Expressive: Characterized as sociable, enthusiastic, and possessing exceptional interpersonal skills, these individuals strive for the inclusivity of others. Others describe them as outgoing and friendly. At times, these individuals may appear impulsive, dramatic, egotistical, and undisciplined.

Amiable: Characterized as cooperative, they value security though they may avoid conflict. Described as dependable and agreeable, they prefer working with teams to working alone. At times, these individuals may appear awkward, dependent, pliable, and overly conforming.

The Merrill-Reid Social Styles framework, also known as the Four Social Styles and the Merrill-Reid Personality Styles, shares similarities with other models of personality like *DISC,* which also explores an individual's personal and public projection of personality and their preferences for communication.

MRSS includes multiple assessments, which vary in price and certification requirements based on the originator of the assessment. One example is the Social Style Profile assessment, which is proprietary to Tracom. Another, the Social Styles Inventory, is available for free online.

Professionals seeking additional information on the MRSS framework will find much written on the model, including Merrill and Reid's 1981 book, *Personal Styles and Effective Performance.*

Sources[193]

MIND STYLES MODEL

Certification Available: no
Certification Required: no
Assessments: yes (Gregorc Style Delineator)
Proprietary: no
Client: individuals
Cost: pricing not available
Category: learning/development

Developed in 1969 by educator Anthony F. Gregorc, the Mind Styles Model (MSM) provides a framework for identifying and characterizing an individual's learning preferences.

The model consists of a four-quadrant matrix which classifies learning preferences based on an individual's perceptual preferences for receiving and ordering or processing information.

Perceptual preference: This dimension pertains to how an individual grasps, receives, or perceives information.

  • **Concrete perceptions**: This is the ability to take in information, absent hidden meaning, using the five senses.

  • **Abstract perceptions**: This is the ability to find meaning in conceptual or theoretical information using intuition and imagination.

Ordering preference: This dimension pertains to the individual's preferences for arranging or processing information they receive.

  • **Sequential ordering**: This is a preference for information presented in a linear, chronological, or logical fashion.

  • **Random ordering**: This is a preference for indiscriminate information.

The combination of these two dimensions results in a matrix of four learning preferences.

Concrete sequential: This learner prefers that information follow a logical and ordered sequence, such as those found within structured lesson plans. They prefer a controlled learning environment and may struggle to learn in chaotic surroundings. Working with groups, especially ones with unpredictable individuals, may cause distress for these learners.

Concrete random: This learner enjoys using experimentation to find answers. They are comfortable taking risks and prefer working independently. These learners resist overly restrictive environments, excessive rules, and monotonous routines, as well as having to redo problems they've already solved.

Abstract sequential: This learner prefers analyzing information prior to acting. They need sufficient time to explore a concept and understand it before deciding on a course of action. These learners may struggle if forced to work with people of differing opinions or with teams requiring emotional connections. They tend to resist repetitive tasks and social interactions requiring diplomacy.

Abstract random: This learner prefers working in groups or with people and building relationships. They thrive in highly personalized environments. These learners may struggle if compelled to explain or advocate a position, compete with others, or work with authoritarian personalities.

Though originally called the Energic Model of Styles, in 1984 Gregorc revised the model based on years of research, leading to the framework we see today. The Mind Styles Model includes an instrument called the Gregorc Style Delineator, which assesses an individual's preferences within the framework's four quadrants. Professionals should exercise caution; unofficial versions of the assessment exist online for free. However, the Gregorc Style Delineator is the only official assessment.

Despite decades of use, critics of the Mind Styles Model question the efficacy of both the model and its assessment. Professionals seeking additional information on the Mind Styles Model may consider Gregorc's 1986 book: *An Adult's Guide to Style*.

Sources[194]

MITROFF'S CRISIS MANAGEMENT MODEL AND PORTFOLIO MODEL

Certification Available: no
Certification Required: no
Assessments: no
Proprietary: no
Client: organizations
Cost: not applicable
Category: crisis management

Developed by crisis management expert Ian Mitroff in 1994, the Crisis Management Model and Portfolio Model (CMPM) provides two interrelated frameworks to facilitate organizations working to enhance their ability to prevent, prepare for, or overcome crisis events.

The first framework, called the Crisis Management Model, identifies five stages of crisis management, consisting of two proactive stages (pre-crisis) and three reactive stages (crisis and post-crisis).

Stage 1—Crisis signal detection: This involves the organization proactively seeking signs or indicators of a potential crisis on the horizon, be it an internal crisis or external crisis. Mitroff's research shows that nearly 75% of crises smolder and "slowly unfold from ignored or undetected warning signals."

Stage 2—Probing and prevention: This involves the organization proactively planning for possible crises and practicing or exercising these plans to test for vulnerabilities. While it is impossible to account for all possibilities, an effective level of preparation considers a variety of different crises.

Stage 3—Damage containment: This reactive stage involves the organization taking action to contain the damage to prevent it from spreading to other aspects of the organization. This includes the use of effective internal and external communication and an accurate examination of cause and effects.

Stage 4—Recovery: This stage involves the organization's efforts to return to a pre-crisis state. This stage may occur during the crisis as the organization works to address the cause of the crisis.

Stage 5—Learning: The final phase involves the organization members reviewing their performance and identifying lessons and best practices to prepare themselves for future crises. This after-action allows the organization to develop new business practices.

The second framework, called the Portfolio Model, suggests that crises fall into one of five categories called "clusters." The model involves developing two portfolios, one drawing from a crisis within each cluster, the other focusing on preventive actions from within each cluster.

Cluster 1—Strategic: This involves the integration of crisis management into organizational philosophy and leadership excellence. Adopting crisis planning, training, and exercises as common practice and increasing diversity within leadership positions in an organization to meet a crisis should one arise.

Cluster 2—Technical/Structural: The organization should incorporate crisis management into business policies and processes. Including CM in employee handbooks and manuals and soliciting external experts for new and unbiased insight strengthens the organization's ability to respond during a crisis.

Cluster 3—Evaluation/Diagnosis: Establish programs to foster the proactive identification of crisis indicators. Conduct a system review to determine an organization's blind spots to identify and address a potential crisis in its early stages.

Cluster 4—Communication: Develop and practice crisis management communication plans, including internal and external communication.

Cluster 5—Psychological/Cultural: Establish mechanisms to provide employee support during and after the crisis. Create a culture that values whistleblowers and encourages employees to come forward with concerns.

One of the most comprehensive and widely used crisis management models, CMPM is significantly more complex than presented here. Professionals seeking additional information may consider Mitroff's 2004 book, *Crisis Leadership: Planning for the Unthinkable.*

Sources[195]

MORPHOLOGICAL ANALYSIS

Certification Available: no
Certification Required: no
Assessments: no
Proprietary: no
Client: individuals, teams
Cost: not applicable
Category: problem-solving, decision-making

Created in the 1960s by astrophysicist Fritz Zwicky, Morphological Analysis provides a methodical framework for solving complex problems. Sources vary on the precise number of steps in Zwicky's model; some offer as few as three steps while others identify as many as six. Despite these differences, the process remains fundamentally the same. We present one variation of this process.

Step 1—Deconstruct the problem: This step involves the principle of analysis by deconstruction. In this, the client dissects the problem to identify its core elements, characteristics, and parameters. If appropriate, the client may assign values to these parameters.

Step 2—Construct the matrix: Also called a Zwicky Box, Morphological Table, or Multidimensional Matrix. In this step, the client creates a table with each param-eter representing a column of the table. Under each parameter, the client lists the characteristics, elements, or alternatives to the parameter. Consequently, each cell of the table represents a variable in a potential solution.

Step 3—Create combinations: In the third step, the client synthesizes forced relationships by combining elements across columns, specifically one cell (or variable) from each column. Depending on the number of parameters and cells, this can result in many different possibilities or relationships.

Step 4—Explore the possibilities: In the final step, the client explores the various combinations, eliminating those deemed inappropriate, ineffective, or undesirable. The client can do this by ruling out combinations that are impossible or inconsistent. The combinations that remain represent the most viable solutions or options.

To facilitate the fourth step, the client may use the concept of Cross-Consistency Assessment (CCA), which involves the use of a separate matrix (e.g., spreadsheet) to allow the client to quickly identify and rule out inconsistent or impossible combinations.

Additionally, the model takes into consideration the possibility that the presence of certain variables may preclude or require the presence of other variables. The CCA matrix will also highlight these rules when appropriate.

The Morphological Analysis framework differs from other popular problem-solving models in that it does not isolate and discard elements or parameters for being trivial or unimportant. The model assumes that solution generation requires the consideration of all variables and avoids prematurely omitting elements before determining the nature of the relationship between variables.

Though widely used in technical and scientific fields, Morphological Analysis has broad utility in other fields, including innovation, product development, complicated decision-making, and more. The framework is useful for clients facing complex challenges or problems that require careful consideration. Zwicky's approach also works with teams engaged in problem-solving.

Professionals seeking additional information will find much written about Morphological Analysis, sometimes called General Morphological Analysis. This includes Zwicky's 1967 paper, "The Morphological Approach to Discovery, Invention, Research, and Construction."

Sources[196]

MOTIVATION THEORIES (GENERAL ENTRY)

Certification Available: no
Certification Required: no
Assessments: no
Proprietary: no
Client: individuals, teams
Cost: not applicable
Category: motivation

Motivation theories is an umbrella term for a collection of theories that seek to explain the driving forces behind human behavior. These drivers include biological, extrinsic, and intrinsic forces.

Most motivational specialists agree that, outside of basic survival needs, each person is a distinct combination of wants and desires. This means that what motivates one person may not motivate another. These differences, and the relationship between wants and needs, have led to multiple theories of human motivation. We can group the vast array of motivation theories into three categories.

Content Theories of Motivation: These theories attempt to define and explain motivation. Also called Need-Based Theories of Motivation, they include the following theories.

- *Maslow's Hierarchy of Needs*
- *Existence, Relatedness, and Growth Theory*
- *McClelland's Theory of Needs*
- *Two-Factor Theory*
- *Job Demands-Control Model*
- *Job Demands-Resource Model*
- *Theory X and Theory Y*
- *Theory Z*

Process Theories of Motivation: These theories attempt to explain how motivation occurs, describing it as a rational process. These include the following theories.

- *Expectancy Theory of Motivation*
- *Equity Theory of Motivation*
- *Locke's Goal-Setting Theory*
- *Reinforcement Theory*

Cognitive Theories: Though not specifically focusing on motivation, these theories provide insight into how our way of thinking and perceiving the world influences our motivations. Some consider these theories relational to motivation theories, but not the same. They include the following.

- *Cognitive Dissonance Theory*
- *Heider's Balance Theory*
- *Newcomb's Symmetry Theory*
- *Congruity Theory*

It is important for professionals to consider the environment when exploring the available literature. You will find books and articles on motivation within specific industries like business, sports, and art, as well as personal and professional motivation.

Motivation theories are essential to a variety of business topics, including organizational change, individual change, conflict resolution, negotiation, career advancement, leadership development, and more.

Sources[197]

MOTIVATIONAL INTERVIEWING

Certification Available: yes (multiple vendors)
Certification Required: no
Assessments: no
Proprietary: no
Client: individuals
Cost: pricing varies
Category: change (ind.), coaching model

Developed in 1983 by psychologists William R. Miller and Stephen Rollnick, Motivational Interviewing (MI) is "a collaborative, goal-oriented style of communication with a particular attention to the language of change." The MI framework consists of five core principles and a four-step process.

Principle 1—Express empathy through reflective listening.

Principle 2—Explore discrepancies between the client's desired goals, their values, and their current behavior.

Principle 3—Avoid judgment and confrontation.

Principle 4—The coach should adjust to meet the client's level of resistance instead of opposing it.

Principle 5—Be an active supporter of the client's self-efficacy and optimism.

The following process facilitates motivational-based discourse between the coach and client.

Step 1—Engaging: The bedrock of MI, in this stage the coach and client work to develop a healthy and productive relationship. Effectively engaging the client requires the coach to embrace the five principles and practice active listening, empathy, and have a genuine desire to understand the client. A successful first step results in a deep level of rapport between coach and client.

Step 2—Focusing: In this step, the coach and client agree to an agenda. This requires that the client discuss their goals and desires related to change. During this stage, the coach requests permission from the client to pursue possible paths or topics for exploration with the client.

Step 3—Evoking: This stage focuses heavily on the exploration of a client's reasons for seeking change, the experiences that motivate their desire for change, and their perceptions of change. Discourse in this stage seeks insight into the client's relationship to and with change and the catalysts for change, real or perceived.

Step 4—Planning: The final stage focuses on the client's effort to develop an actionable strategy or plan for change. This includes the client's self-assessment regarding their ability to follow through on change and their commitment to it.

Motivational Interviewing hinges on a belief that the client inherently possesses the resources, faculties, and skills to change. Thus, MI relies on a collaborative partnership between coach and client to identify and capitalize on the client's strengths to foster change. Through a nonjudgmental relationship, the coach provides expertise on the change process while the client serves as an expert of self.

MI includes a variety of skill sets key to the coach's success with the client. These skills include the use of open-ended questions to facilitate the client's insight, affirmations to encourage the client, reflection to foster the client's growth, and the careful and effective exchange of information between coach and client.

Though born of clinical therapy, MI consists of many of the same skills, characteristics, beliefs, and processes as coaching. For this reason, the ICMT includes MI as a model for coaching.

Heavily influenced by James Prochaska's *Transtheoretical Model (TTM)*, MI originally focused on addiction. However, like the Transtheoretical Model, Motivational Interviewing has broad utility and applies to a variety of individual change efforts.

Motivational Interviewing is more complex than presented here. Multiple vendors offer certification and training in MI. Professionals seeking additional information may consider Miller and Rollnick's 2012 book, *Motivational Interviewing: Helping People Change* (3rd edition).

Sources[198]

MYERS-BRIGGS PERSONALITY MODEL

Certification Available: yes (M & B Company)
Certification Required: yes
Assessments: yes (MBTI, others)
Proprietary: yes (Myers and Briggs Foundation)
Client: individuals
Cost: $2,895
Category: personality type

Developed in the 1940s by the mother-daughter team of Katharine Briggs and Isabel Briggs Myers, the Myers-Briggs Personality Model provides a framework for identifying and characterizing individual personalities. Derived from the works of noted psychologist Carl Jung, the Myers-Briggs model classifies personality types based on four dimensions.

Introversion (I) vs. **Extraversion (E)**: This dimension pertains to the source of a person's energy. Does a person derive their energy from their inner world or their outer world? Extroverts find energy from the external world, often through socializing or spending time with others. Introverts, on the other hand, derive their energy from within, often by spending time alone.

Sensing (S) vs. **Intuition (N)**: This dimension pertains to an individual's preferences for gathering and using information. Sensors collect information from their five senses and prefer to focus on facts and logic while those who favor intuition prefer to make meaning from the patterns and trends in the information.

Thinking (T) vs. **Feeling (F)**: This dimension pertains to an individual's preferences for decision-making. Those who favor thinking adopt a more analytical approach to decision-making, focusing on logic and reason. Those who adopt a feeling approach consider the thoughts and feelings of others when making decisions. They will also consider their personal values and the emotional impact on those around them.

Judging (J) vs. **Perceiving (P)**: This dimension pertains to an individual's observable behaviors or how they interact with the external world. Those with judging tendencies present as structured, ordered, disciplined, and organized. Those with perceiving tendencies present as spontaneous, flexible, and open to new experiences.

According to the theory of Myers-Briggs, though we may occasionally share in both aspects of each dimension, every person demonstrates a preference. The combination of preferences results in 16 possible personality types, each coded and given a label to reflect the characteristics of the personality. For example, a person whose preferences are Introversion, Intuition, Feeling, and Judging receives the coding of INFJ and the label the Advocate. Other frameworks, like *Keirsey's Four Temperaments*, use a similar coding system.

To identify a person's personality type under the Myers-Briggs framework, the model offers several assessments, the principal one being the Myers-Briggs Type Indicator (MBTI), a self-report questionnaire. Professionals will find free Myers-Briggs–based assessments online; however, these typically lack the depth and accuracy of the formal MBTI instrument.

Myers-Briggs is one of the oldest and most popular personality models; however, it is not without controversy. Some denounce the use of Myers-Briggs (and other similar personality assessments) in hiring practices. Critics also question the scientific validity of the model and its principal assessment. Despite these criticisms, the Myers-Briggs Model can provide a source of awareness, growth, and development for clients.

Myers-Briggs is proprietary to The Myers and Briggs Foundation. Formal use of the framework or its associated assessments requires certification. Multiple vendors offer training in MBTI under the umbrella of the Myers-Briggs Company. Course options include self-paced, virtual, and in-person options.

The Myers-Briggs Personality framework is significantly more complex than presented here. Professionals seeking additional information will find much written on the model, including Isabel Briggs Myers and Peter B. Myers' 1980 book, *Gifts Differing: Understanding Personality Types*. For an alternative perspective, consider Merve Emre's 2018 book, *Personality Brokers: The Strange History of Myers-Briggs and the Birth of Personality Testing*.

Sources[199]

NEUROSCIENCE-BASED COACHING

Certification Available: yes (multiple)
Certification Required: yes
Assessments: no
Proprietary: yes (program specific)
Client: groups, teams, organizations
Cost: $3,000–$4,000
Category: coaching model

Neuroscience-Based Coaching (NBC) is a style of coaching founded in the science of how the brain works. NBC is based on research that seeks to better understand the regions of the brain, the nature of the relationship between these regions, and how these regions function. In addition, neuroscience includes the examination of concepts like fight, flight, freeze, neuroplasticity, neurochemical composition, and neuropath development (also known as wiring or rewiring).

An important source of modern neuroscience information comes from the advancement of neuroimaging technology which allows scientists to see the different areas of the brain activate in response to a variety of stimuli. This technology, in conjunction with evolutionary biology, allows researchers to better understand how a person's brain function influences their response or reaction to certain situations.

Knowledge born of neuroscience can help clients better understand themselves and their connection to the world around them. Several key neuroscience principles worth knowing include the following.

• Our brain's wiring influences how we process the world and our experiences. This includes our unique capacity for pattern recognition and our use of heuristics (i.e., mental shortcuts).

• The differences in wiring between two people mean they can go through the same event but have two different experiences and interpretations of that same event.

• The brain's pathway for processing an external stimulus leads first to the emotional center before reaching the cognitive center. In other words, we tend to experience an emotional reaction to an external stimulus before we form a thought about that stimulus.

• Some areas of the brain are hardwired while others are elastic and can be molded and changed with experience (i.e., plasticity). This means some people can change on a fundamental level based on their experiences.

• The question is no longer one of nature *or* nurture, but of nature *and* nurture and to what degree. Put another way, both a person's genetics and their environment interact to influence and shape their brain, which in turn shapes their behavior.

• Memories are imperfect. A variety of factors can distort memory, including emotions, which can modify perceptions of the experience and alter how a brain stores the event as a memory.

Neuroscience-Based Coaching is incredibly complex and far more intricate than presented here. Professionals seeking to adopt neuroscience into their coaching practice should seek formal training.

Certification in neuroscience is available through several vendors, including the Brain-Based Coaching Certificate offered by the NeuroLeadership Institute. Another program is the Neuroscience Coaching Program offered by the International Coaching Community. These programs offer training at different price points. Professionals should research the options before selecting.

Neuroscience-Based Coaching, also called Brain-Based Coaching, includes a variety of coaching models and approaches like the *RESULTS Coaching Model* and the *SCARF Model,* both developed by David Rock, who also founded the NeuroLeadership Institute.

Professionals seeking additional information on Neuroscience-Based Coaching will find much written on the topic, including David Rock and Al H. Ringleb's 2013 book, *Handbook of Neuroleadership*.

Sources[200]

NEWCOMB'S SYMMETRY THEORY

Certification Available: no
Certification Required: no
Assessments: no
Proprietary: no
Client: individuals
Cost: not applicable
Category: conflict, communication, influence

Introduced in 1953 by social psychologist Theodore Newcomb, his Symmetry Theory (NST) falls under the umbrella of *Consistency Theories*, which suggest that people inherently seek equilibrium between their attitudes, thoughts, beliefs, values, behaviors, and feelings. NST examines the use of communication between individuals to achieve and maintain equilibrium in relationships.

NST derives from *Heider's Balance Theory*, but unlike Heider's theory (which focuses on the consequences of an imbalance on the relationship between individuals), NST looks at how individuals use communication to reestablish symmetry in the relationship.

Like Heider, Newcomb provides a formulaic representation of his theory using three variables. Newcomb's formula uses different labels than Heider does to reflect the variables involved.

Prime person (A): This is the individual experiencing balance or imbalance. This person is the message sender.

Other person (B): This is the person with whom the Prime person has a relationship, be it positive or negative. This person is the message receiver.

Issue, idea, object (X): This is the subject or topic of the message.

The focus of Newcomb's theory centers on the strength of the relationship between the person sending the message and the person receiving the message. NST also considers how strongly the person sending the message feels about the issue contained within the message.

Newcomb's Symmetry Theory suggests that the stronger the connection between the person sending the message and the person receiving the message, the more likely the sender will use communication to influence the recipient's opinion of the issue to align with their own. Thus, maintaining a balance between both parties.

In the event the person sending the message is unable to influence the recipient's opinion of the issue, the threat of an imbalance may compel the sender to adjust their own thoughts and feelings about either the other recipient or the issue to protect the balance.

Contributing to NST is another of Newcomb's theories, the **Similarity Principle**. His research indicated that individuals tend to associate with or join groups that possess similar ideologies, beliefs, or politics. When NST and the Similarity Principle combine, it becomes difficult to adjust the attitudes, thoughts, and feelings of insular groups because members do not value the opinions of outsiders. Thus, limiting the outsider's ability to influence a person's thoughts and feelings about the issue.

NST is a useful lens with clients looking to explore strained relationships that may result from diverging beliefs. In the realm of organizational change, NST is useful when developing a communication strategy in support of a change initiative, especially when social and group identities may oppose or resist change efforts.

Professionals seeking additional information will find much written on NST, including Newcomb's 1961 book, *The Acquaintance Process*.

Alternative names for NST include the ABX Model of Communication, Newcomb's Model of Communication, and the ABX Symmetry Model.

Sources[201]

NUDGE THEORY

Certification Available: no
Certification Required: no
Assessments: no
Proprietary: no
Client: individuals, groups
Cost: not applicable
Category: bias, decision-making, influence

The principles of Nudge Theory are based on the work of Nobel Prize winner, psychologist, and economist Daniel Kahneman and psychologist Amos Nathan Tversky. Nudge Theory is a complex construct that seeks to explain how heuristics and bias affect decision-making and problem-solving. The theory explores multiple facets of the human mind susceptible to manipulation which, in turn, may influence behavioral change.

Nudge Theory presents three facets, biases, habits, and cognitive boundaries, which influence decision-making. The three facets represent opportunities for someone to influence or nudge a person to make a better or more desirable decision. The authors call this process of influencing the facets **Choice Architecture**.

Choice Architecture is a method of subtly persuading a consumer to select a particular product while maintaining the consumer's sovereign right to choose. In other words, Nudge Theory seeks to help people make better decisions for themselves without restricting their freedom of choice.

For example, the government of Spain changed their organ donation policy from an opt-in to an opt-out policy. Spanish citizens retain the right to opt out if they desire. The decision to shift the program to an opt-out strategy stems from the assumption that most people are not making an explicit decision to donate or not, but simply lack the motivation to spend the time and energy to opt in or out. By shifting the consumer's decision from an opting-in choice to an opting-out choice, Spain became the world leader in organ donation.

It is important to emphasize that Choice Architecture is about influencing or encouraging changes in behavior, not forcing it. Though Nudge Theory should facilitate the best interests of the decision-maker, there are many examples where individuals use these concepts to exploit the decision-maker. The authors call these more nefarious applications of Nudge Theory "**Sludge**."

Nudge Theory includes an examination of 15 heuristics or biases which affect decision-making. These represent potential vulnerabilities which others may target to deliberately influence us. These include the following.

Anchoring: the tendency to adopt the first information we receive as fundamental, from which we compare all subsequent information received.

Framing: when someone presents information to us in a way intended to persuade how we feel about it.

Loss aversion: when the fear of losing something outweighs the pleasure of gaining.

Priming: when a series of thematically similar stimuli influences our anticipation, expectation, or perception of subsequent information.

Nudge Theory incorporates Kahneman's *Dual Process Theory* to explain how System 1 (automatic quick thinking) and System 2 (deliberate meticulous thinking) impact decision-making. In other words, Nudge Theory explains how reactive thought and methodical thought affect our ability to make decisions.

Though based in behavioral economics, Nudge Theory has broad utility in marketing, strategy, and public policy. Nudge Theory offers clients a framework for exploring the topic of manipulation and influence, especially with clients who believe they are the victims of deliberate manipulation.

Nudge Theory is significantly more complex than presented here. Professionals seeking additional information may consider Nobel Prize winner Richard H. Thaler and legal scholar Cass Sunstein's 2008 book, *Nudge: Improving Decisions About Health, Wealth, and Happiness.*

Sources[202]

OASIS CONVERSATION

Certification Available: yes (Potentials)
Certification Required: yes
Assessments: no
Proprietary: yes (Potentials)
Client: individuals
Cost: $2,000
Category: communication, coaching model, feedback

Developed in 2006 by organizational psychologist Ann Van Eron, OASIS Conversation provides a framework for engaging in positive and productive discourse. The model consists of the open mindset principle and a five-step process which facilitate meaningful conversations.

According to OASIS, achieving an open mindset requires four elements.

Open mind: This is a genuine curiosity about the other person, their experiences, their thoughts, and their feelings. Genuine curiosity is essential because a curious mind is less susceptible to preemptive judgment. The presence of judgment undermines productive and meaningful conversations and can lead one party to shut down.

Open heart: This is a deep level of compassion for the other person which serves as the essential ingredient for empathy. The ability to feel for and with another person provides the foundation for enhanced understanding between two conversing parties.

Open gut: This is courage. Such courage is necessary to maintain an open mindset in the face of anxiety, anger, and fear. A thread that runs through all elements of an open mindset, courage serves as a source of personal empowerment and resolve to face the issues or topics central to the conversation.

Open hands: This is a warm and welcoming state of acceptance for others. The absence of judgment and the presence of acceptance promotes rapport, an essential component of meaningful discourse.

Once established, the open mindset positions a person to undertake specific steps and behaviors that facilitate productive conversations. The acronym OASIS reflects these steps.

Step 1—Observations: This is the ability to take notice and bring attention to patterns, trends, and themes, mindful to separate facts from assumptions. The capacity to make distinctions in our observations helps us identify and focus on what is essential.

Step 2—Awareness: This is the ability to recognize what we think and feel, to notice a moment while the moment is happening. Put another way, this speaks to our awareness of the things that influence us emotionally or may alter our perspectives.

Step 3—Shift: This is the ability to act on the awareness we possess. Once you recognize the presence of an emotion, assumption, or other variable influencing your perceptions or feelings of someone else, shifting involves taking a step back and adjusting your mindset to regain proper perspective, often adopting a mindset of curiosity.

Step 4—Importance: This is the ability to manage the conversation and adjust the focus to topics which are important to all parties.

Step 5—Solution: This is the ability to use conversation to seek a shared resolution or a common understanding with others. Identifying and developing resolution requires an exploration of possibilities, options, and expectations.

Though not a formal coaching model, the OASIS framework offers a process comparable to many coaching models. For this reason, we include OASIS in the category of coaching models. The fundamental principles of OASIS have utility in multiple styles of conversation, including feedback sessions.

Professionals seeking formal training may consider OASIS Moves, the official training workshop from Ann Van Eron's company, Potentials. Professionals seeking additional information may consider Van Eron's 2016 book, *OASIS Conversations: Leading with an Open Mindset to Maximize Potential.*

Sources[203]

OODA LOOP

Certification Available: no
Certification Required: no
Assessments: no
Proprietary: no
Client: individuals
Cost: not applicable
Category: decision-making, problem-solving

Developed in the 1950s by US Air Force Colonel John Boyd, the OODA Loop provides a framework commonly associated with high-stakes decision-making and problem-solving. The model consists of four multifaceted steps, using the acronym OODA to reflect these steps. It is important to note that each step in the OODA Loop involves a series of complex variables which influence the process.

Step 1—Observe: This is the act of collecting information and data to inform the decision-making process. Depending on the nature of the decision, this data may include intelligence about the environment, the industry, competitors, and resource availability. When applied to problem-solving, the first step involves identifying the components of the problem, then using those components to define the problem.

When analyzing the collected data, it is important to contextualize the information to better understand the relationship between various data points and how they influence the bigger picture. In essence, this is the interconnected system of variables that make up our environment.

Step 2—Orient: This is the act of orienting one's focus to see the world as it is. To accomplish this, it is important to be aware of and mitigate any bias or preconceptions which negatively influence one's view of the world. The more accurate a person's view of the world, the more accurate their decision.

This step, considered the most complex in the OODA Loop, involves a multitude of variables that can distort a person's view of the world. These include the following:

- Culture: This defines a person's social norms, informs their sense of right and wrong, and what constitutes appropriate behavior.

- Genetics: This applies to a person's temperament, their predisposition for feeling a certain way in response to stimuli. Research indicates temperament is partially inherited.

- Heuristics and pattern recognition: These are the mental models a person adopts on a subconscious level that influence what information they accept or reject and may distort how they process data.

- New information: This is a person's level of receptivity to new data, even after they draw a conclusion. Are they open to receiving new information, even if that information contradicts their assumptions?

Step 3—Decide: This is the act of envisioning and formulating multiple possibilities or options for consideration and the eventual selection of one course of action for testing.

Step 4—Act: This is the act of deliberately executing the decision.

A continuous and ever-present element of the OODA Loop process is the **Feedback Loop**. This requires an individual to seek out all relevant information resulting from the OODA Loop process and the decision. This information allows the individual to adjust course based on the data.

Also known as the Boyd Cycle, some sources frequently misrepresent it as a linear process. However, the OODA Loop is a complex, multifaceted, iterative cycle. Those using the framework correctly will find themselves frequently moving back and forth through the process based on the data.

The OODA Loop is significantly more complex than presented here. Surprisingly, Boyd wrote very little about his decision-making model. Much of our understanding comes from his notes and a few surviving presentations. Many strategists, leaders, and business process experts have studied Boyd's work and written extensively on the topic.

OODA Loop remains widely used in military and commercial organizations around the world.

Sources[204]

ORGANIZATIONAL SUPPORT THEORY

Certification Available: no
Certification Required: no
Assessments: yes (SPOS)
Proprietary: no
Client: individuals
Cost: not applicable
Category: employee engagement, motivation

Developed in 1986 by psychologist Robert Eisenberger and other scholars, Organizational Support Theory (OST) provides a framework for exploring the employee-organization relationship with an emphasis on the perceptions of employees, specifically their opinion of the organization's behavior toward them.

OST explores three aspects from the employee's perspective.

Employee attribution: This is the explanation an employee uses to rationalize why the organization treats them the way it does.

Social exchange: This is the reciprocity between the employee and the organization. The employee gives effort, work, and loyalty to the organization in return for tangible benefits and social resources.

Self-enhancement: These are the socio-emotional needs of the employee. This aspect examines how many of those needs the organization satisfies. Put another way, is the employee getting sufficient approval, affiliation, and esteem from the organization?

These aspects form the foundation of OST, called **Perceived Organizational Support (POS)**. This is the overarching perception or sentiment an employee forms about the organization's behavior toward them. This sentiment includes their opinion of how well the organization appreciates the employee's contribution to the mission and how well it cares for the employee. Often, the behavior of an individual perceived to represent the organization (e.g., a supervisor) translates to how the organization feels.

Studies show these perceptions have a critical impact on employee engagement, motivation, performance, and absenteeism. In addition, research suggests employees with a high POS tend to suffer lower stress at work and spend less time away from work.

Research based on Organizational Support Theory identified a variety of ways an organization may enhance POS. These include the following.

- Fairness: Employees who perceive greater fairness tend to have higher POS. What constitutes "fair" changes from person to person and is based on rank, position, experience, and performance.

- Supervisor support: Supervisors who provide explicit personal and professional support to their employees foster higher POS among employees. Studies show that employees tend to see the values and behaviors of their supervisors as an indication of the organization's values. How the supervisor treats them reflects how the organization feels about them.

- Organizational rewards: Adequate and thoughtful rewards typically result in higher POS. This means providing practical benefits employees will use. This includes consideration of when to apply intrinsic vs. extrinsic rewards.

- Job conditions: Employees who perceive their working conditions as suitable to support the task are more likely to have a higher POS.

OST is a lens through which to explore the organizational environment and culture. The framework also facilitates an examination of the impact of leadership styles, employee engagement, and especially employee perceptions on the organization.

Professionals adopting OST may find utility in the framework's formal assessment, the Survey of Perceived Organizational Support.

Professionals seeking additional information will find much written on the topic, including Eisenberger's 2011 book, *Perceived Organizational Support: Fostering Enthusiastic and Productive Employees*.

Sources[205]

OSKAR COACHING MODEL

Certification Available: no
Certification Required: no
Assessments: no
Proprietary: no
Client: individuals, groups, teams
Cost: not applicable
Category: coaching model

Developed in 2002 by coaches Mark McKergow and Paul Z. Jackson, the OSKAR Coaching Model provides a framework for solutions-focused coaching sessions. This means the coaching effort centers more on developing solutions to the problem than on the problem itself.

Like other coaching models, the OSKAR coaching process strives to help the client bridge the gap between where they are and where they want to be through a combination of goal setting, action taking, and reflection. The acronym, OSKAR, represents the five-step process used to achieve success.

Step 1—Outcome: During this step, the client defines their objective, purpose, or expectation for the coaching session. Critical to this is the client's ability to thoughtfully articulate their desired goals and intentions to the coach. This includes conveying their vision for the future. The client should consider the changes they hope to see stemming from the coaching relationship.

Step 2—Scale: This step requires the client to assess their current progress toward achieving their goal. This is not a formal measurement, rather it is the client's perception of where they are and what remains. Some clients may possess accurate perceptions of their progress while others may overestimate their position.

Coaches following the OSKAR Model will often use a Likert scale (1–10) to help measure the client's perception of their progress. This, in turn, will serve as a gauge for both the client and coach in future steps of the process.

Step 3—Know-how: During this step, the client considers the resources and skills they believe essential to achieving their goal. The intention of this step is to help clients identify the skills and resources they currently possess and those they believe they will need. Identifying their current capabilities and those capabilities they will need is essential to the client's plan of action (step 4).

For coaches who used the Likert scale during the second step, they may ask the client what skills are necessary to advance them one step further. In other words, if the client feels they are at a 5, what resources do they need to reach a 6?

A variation of OSKAR changes "know-how" to "change and consequences," making it the OSCAR Model. This change encourages the client to evaluate different courses of action while increasing their awareness of outcomes.

Step 4—Affirm + Action: This step consists of two aspects. The first, affirm, involves the client identifying which existing behaviors positively facilitate their progress. The client then reaffirms their commitment to continue these behaviors. In essence, this aspect is about the client examining what is working.

The second aspect, action, involves the client identifying new behaviors they believe will advance them closer to their goal. This step seeks to help the client capitalize on their momentum and progress.

Step 5—Review: In the final step, the client assesses the efficacy of their effort to move toward their goal. Step 5 discourse focuses on the client evaluating the impact of their actions and prepares them for any new actions and behaviors based on their own personal observations and assessments.

In addition to its use in executive coaching, the OSKAR Model is useful for leaders adopting a "leader as coach" approach to leadership. Professionals using the OSKAR Model advocate its value in addressing performance and behavioral problems within teams and groups.

Professionals seeking additional information on the OSKAR Model will find much written on the topic, including McKergow and Jackson's 2007 book, *The Solutions Focus: Making Coaching and Change Simple.*

Sources[206]

OUTCOMES COACHING MODEL

Certification Available: no
Certification Required: no
Assessments: no
Proprietary: yes (Partners Team Development)
Client: individuals, groups, teams
Cost: not applicable
Category: coaching model

Developed in the early 2000s by performance management coach Allan Mackintosh, the OUTCOMES Coaching Model provides a framework for coaching. The model consists of an eight-step process for enhancing performance and facilitating individual, group, and team development.

Step 1—Objectives: During the first step, the client works to identify, define, and articulate their expectations and goals for coaching. This includes goals for both the overall coaching relationship and each individual coaching session.

Step 2—Understand the reason: In this step, the coach and client explore the client's rationale behind the goal or objective they selected. Understanding why the client feels driven or compelled to achieve this goal may reveal misconceptions, misperceptions, and misguided intentions. These insights can help the client improve their goal setting and decision-making, helping them to focus on a more meaningful outcome.

Step 3—Take stock of the present situation: During this step, clients determine where they are in relation to their goal. Are they starting from scratch, or have they achieved a measure of progress they can build from? The intent of this step is to determine where the client is at the current moment.

Step 4—Clarify the gap: Knowing where the client is, and where they want to go, the client may now take measure of the gap between. Exploring this gap enables the client to develop an idea of the journey which is before them and allows them to prepare accordingly.

Step 5—Options generation/analysis: This is the creative process whereby the client considers multiple possible courses of action which may advance them toward their goal. It is important that clients create a robust list of possible actions. This will allow them to make a more meaningful comparison between options.

Step 6—Motivate to action: During this step, the client makes a commitment to see their plan through to its logical conclusion. It is important that the client recognize if their motivation to succeed results from a genuine desire to achieve the goal or is in response to what others expect of them. A client acting solely based on the expectations of others will likely lose commitment and fall short of their goal.

Step 7—Enthusiasm and encouragement: In this stage, the coach (or manager using the model) should display enthusiasm for the client's effort. Encouragement is essential to helping the client maintain the momentum necessary to achieve their goals.

Step 8—Support: During the final step, the client identifies the kind of support they will require to help them in their journey. This may include support from the coach, a manager or supervisor, as well as those within the client's social and professional network.

Like many coaching frameworks, the foundation of the OUTCOMES Coaching Model emerged from Sir John Whitmore's *GROW Coaching Model*. And like these models which follow the GROW framework, this process seeks to help a client recognize where they are, where they want to be, and then bridge the gap between them.

The OUTCOMES Coaching Model offers one of the more comprehensive frameworks to facilitate the coaching process. In addition to supporting the coaching process, the OUTCOMES Coaching Model is useful for leaders who wish to adopt a "leader as coach" approach to leading.

Professionals seeking additional information about the OUTCOMES Coaching Model may consider Mackintosh's 2003 book, *The Successful Coaching Manager: A Manager's Guide to Coaching Individuals and Teams Effectively*.

Sources[207]

PARTICIPATIVE LEADERSHIP THEORY

> **Certification Available:** no
> **Certification Required:** no
> **Assessments:** no
> **Proprietary:** no
> **Client:** individuals
> **Cost:** not applicable
> **Category:** leadership

Participative Leadership Theory, though called a theory, is a nebulous term that holds different meanings for different people. Some sources define Participative Leadership Theory as an umbrella theory that includes a variety of leadership styles; others suggest it is a leadership style in and of itself.

Because of this ambiguity, sources cannot agree on attribution. Many different theorists, working independent of one another, contributed to our general understanding, including Henry Landsberger, Kurt Lewin, and Abraham Maslow.

Despite its obscure origins, most sources agree on the characteristics which describe the participative style of leadership. These include some of the following.

- The leader facilitates open discourse with all members of the team and solicits their collective input.

- The leader empowers all team members by providing them a voice to express their point of view, concerns, and opinions.

- The leader shares information openly and equitably among all members of the team.

- The leader considers the recommendations of each member, though the leader remains responsible for making the decision.

Using the above characteristics, one may identify examples of participative leadership styles contained in broader theories of leadership. Examples of participative leadership styles that manifest in other theories include the following.

- From *Fiedler's Contingency Theory*: the Relationship-Oriented leadership style and the Leader-Member Relations aspect of situational orientation.

- From *Goleman's Six Styles of Leadership*: the Democratic leadership style and the Coaching leadership style.

- From the *Hoy-Tarter Decision-Making Model*: the Integrator role, Parliamentarian role, and Solicitor role.

- From *Lewin's Leadership Styles*: the Participative Leadership style, also known as the Democratic Leadership style.

- From *Tannenbaum-Schmidt Leadership Continuum Model*: the Consults style, Joins style, and Delegates style.

In addition, singular theories of leadership also share a connection to participative leadership, including the following.

- *Relational Leadership Theory*

- *Servant Leadership Theory*

Because participative leadership focuses on the inclusion of employees into the organization's mission, aspects of the theory may provide an important lens when exploring topics like employee engagement and morale.

One of the earliest documented uses of the term participative leadership comes from the Hawthorne Western Electric experiments of the 1930s (see *Hawthorne Effect*). The experiment intended to shed light on elements affecting employee engagement. During these experiments, researchers attributed changes in employee behavior to the presence of observers.

Critics of the theory question its utility, with many arguing that a participative leadership style is not appropriate for all circumstances. Situations with limited time and high stakes may not be suitable for this style of leadership.

Sources[208]

PATH-GOAL THEORY

Certification Available: no
Certification Required: no
Assessments: no
Proprietary: no
Client: individuals
Cost: not applicable
Category: leadership

Developed in 1971 by Robert House and John Antonakis (later revised in 1996), Path-Goal Theory provides a framework for exploring leadership with an emphasis on the relationship between leadership style and the employee. Put simply, Path-Goal Theory is about how leaders motivate their employees to accomplish goals.

Path-Goal Theory consists of four major leadership styles. According to the theory, the best style depends on the unique needs of each employee and the situation.

Directive path-goal clarifying leader: This style describes leaders who inform employees of their expectation for them, explain which procedures and processes they should follow, and establish a timeframe for task completion. This leadership style is ideal for situations in which the employee's role is ambiguous yet intrinsically rewarding, or the employee is new to the job. Applied in the wrong situation, this behavior risks micromanagement, real or perceived.

Achievement-oriented leader: This style describes leaders who set challenging goals for their people, estab-lish high expectations of them, and show confidence in their ability to achieve objectives. These leaders actively support the continuous improvement of their people. This leadership style is ideal for situations where employ-ees feel insufficiently challenged or experience boredom. Achievement-oriented leaders are common in high-skill professions like sales, engineering, technology, the sci-ences, and entrepreneurship.

Participative-leader: This style describes leaders who consult with employees prior to making decisions. This "employee inclusive" approach to leadership is most effec-tive with employees who are personally involved in their work and possess a willingness to share their thoughts and experiences with others. Employees who consistently make poor decisions or fail to follow procedure may benefit from this style of leadership as it provides an opportunity for the leader to "coach" or "mentor" the employee by including them in the decision-making process.

Supportive-leader: This style describes leaders who focus on satisfying the employee's needs and preferences. This approach to leadership is effective in situations where employees face tasks that are psychologically or physically demanding by offering encouragement and support. New and inexperienced teams may also benefit from a support-ive leadership approach.

An aspect central to Path-Goal Theory is the need for leaders to deeply understand their employees, their wants, and their needs. This level of awareness is necessary for the model to work. Therefore, this theory is useful when working with clients who possess depth of knowledge about those who follow them.

Path-Goal Theory falls under the umbrella of *Contingency Theories* of leadership, suggesting that effective leaders adapt their leadership style and leadership behavior based on the needs of employees and the work environment. This means that effective leaders are constantly adopting different types of leadership behaviors based on the situation and the follower.

Professionals exploring contingency theories of leadership may also consider *Fiedler's Contingency Theory*, which focuses on the leadership-situation relationship, or the *Vroom-Yetton Decision Model*, which focuses on the leadership/decision-making relationship.

Variations of Path-Goal Theory exist which provide additional leadership styles; however, the original four styles are those listed here. Professionals seeking additional information may consider House's 1975 paper, "Path-Goal Theory of Leadership," co-authored by T.R. Mitchell; or Antonakis' 2004 book, *The Nature of Leadership*, co-authored by A.T. Cianciolo and R.J. Sternberg.

Sources[209]

PENDLETON FEEDBACK MODEL

Certification Available: no
Certification Required: no
Assessments: no
Proprietary: no
Client: individuals
Cost: not applicable
Category: feedback

Introduced in 1984 by psychologist and business school professor David Pendleton, the Pendleton Model provides a simple framework for conducting effective and meaningful feedback sessions. Like many feedback models, the Pendleton framework, also known as Pendleton's Rules, first emerged in the field of health and medical education. The model consists of four steps that combine the recipient's self-evaluation and the provider's observations.

Step 1—What worked (from the recipient's POV): During this step, the feedback provider asks the recipient to share their opinion of what they thought went well. This includes the recipient identifying what skills, experiences, and knowledge they believe contributed to their positive performance.

It is important to remember that some people find it difficult to speak of themselves in a positive way. The source of this type of sensitivity varies greatly from person to person; regardless of the source, the result often creates discomfort and anxiety for the person. In these cases, it is important to help the recipient explore the positive aspects of their performance in a thoughtful manner, avoiding a forceful approach.

Step 2—What worked (from the provider's POV): During the second stage, the provider offers their perspective of what the recipient did well. It is important that some of the provider's observations reinforce the recipient's perceptions of self. This requires striking a balance; too much or too little reinforcement can compromise the process, risk damaging rapport, and potentially shut down the client's receptivity to further feedback.

Step 3—What could you improve upon (from the recipient's POV): In this step, the provider asks the recipient to identify areas for improvement. It is important to note that sources differ on the appropriate way to phrase this stage of the process. Carelessly wording the question may lead the recipient to feel judged.

Some of the recommended language for this step in the process includes "what didn't work," "what would you do differently next time," "what could you improve upon," and "what could be done better."

Idiosyncratic differences mean it is important for the provider to know the recipient and tailor the wording based on what will resonate for them.

Step 4—What could you improve upon (from the provider's POV): In the final step, the provider shares their perspective on areas for improvement. Again, it is important that the provider capitalize on the recipient's observations to bolster the recipient's self-perception.

The model's emphasis on fostering the recipient's learning through a collaborative feedback process makes it a useful framework for recipients seeking to develop self-awareness. By allowing the recipient to self-identify first, the provider may use the recipient's own language and observation to reinforce learning points. Additionally, a skilled provider can help the recipient to see things they may have overlooked, improving the recipient's self-evaluative abilities.

Variations of the Pendleton Model exist which include an additional fifth step in the framework. In these cases, there is no consistency regarding the fifth step or its order in the process. Some variations add a new step to the beginning of the process, while others add a new step to the end. The lack of consistency and the use of different labels suggest these are not formal variations of the model.

Professionals seeking depth of knowledge may consider Pendleton's 1984 book, *The Consultation: An Approach to Learning and Teaching.*

Sources[210]

PERFORMANCE-VALUES MATRIX

Certification Available: no
Certification Required: no
Assessments: no
Proprietary: no
Client: individuals, organizations
Cost: not applicable
Category: leadership, values

Developed in the 1980s by former GE CEO Jack Welch, the Performance-Values Matrix provides a framework for exploring individual manager or leader effectiveness within an organization. Also known as the Jack Welch Matrix, the framework examines management/leadership efficacy across two dimensions: results and behaviors.

Results (also called **performance**): This dimension pertains to the manager's ability to produce the outcomes necessary for success.

Behaviors (also called **values**): This dimension pertains to the manager's alignment with the company's values. In other words, does the manager's behavior support or undermine the firm's core values?

The two dimensions result in a four-quadrant matrix with each quadrant representing a specific type of manager.

Type 1: This is the ideal manager, capable of achieving goals and producing the desired results while behaving in a manner consistent with the organization's values. With this type of manager, Welch said, "Sky's the limit."

Type 2: This manager behaves in a manner consistent with the organization's values; however, they are unable to consistently reach goals or produce the desired results. Of this manager Welch said, "Gone."

Type 3: An ineffective manager, this leader is unable to produce the desired results and frequently engages in behavior that undermines the organization's values. Senior leaders often remove type 3 managers from leadership roles. Welch said he might give this type of manager "another chance, or two."

Type 4: This manager produces the desired results and consistently achieves positive outcomes; however, their behavior is inconsistent with the organization's values. Jack Welch considered this the most difficult manager to have in the company because they produce the numbers, but they represent a threat to the culture and stability of the company. Too frequently, senior leaders will overlook the deficiencies of type 4 managers because they produce results. In time, this will lead to a decrease in employee engagement and morale. Welch advocated removing these managers from the organization immediately.

The placement of management types within the matrix provides further insight into the style and nature of management. The upper level of the matrix denotes individuals who produce the desired results, with those on the lower level signifying individuals who fail to achieve their assigned objectives. Management types on the right side of the matrix denote individuals whose behaviors align with the organization's core values, while those on the left side are inconsistent with or contradict the organization's core values.

Jack Welch used his matrix to emphasize the courage organizations must possess to not only remove type 4 managers, but to make the reason explicit. According to Welch, it is important to ensure that removing these managers, although producing results, is for failure to share in the organization's values. This reinforces the organization's commitment to its values.

Though the Performance-Values Matrix does not provide a formal or quantitative assessment to evaluate manager performance, the framework is useful for clients seeking to explore the efficacy of individual management performance. Put another way, Welch's framework functions as a lens through which to characterize and explore management styles. It is important to note that assessments based on the Performance-Values Matrix exist but are not official or formal assessments.

Professionals seeking additional information will find much written on the Performance-Values Matrix, including Jack Welch's note to investors in *GE's Annual Report from 2000*.

Sources[211]

PERMA MODEL

Certification Available: yes
Certification Required: no
Assessments: no
Proprietary: yes (Seligman)
Client: individuals
Cost: pricing not available
Category: coaching model, confidence/resilience

Developed by noted psychologist Martin E. P. Seligman, the PERMA Model provides a framework for exploring the components necessary for positive individual growth, happiness, and well-being, something Seligman called "flourishing."

The PERMA Model consists of five elements necessary for achieving lasting well-being.

Positive emotion: This component includes an array of factors like hope, joy, compassion, and love. These elements are essential to undoing the damaging effects caused by negative emotions.

Helping the client achieve positive emotions can involve varying degrees of complexity, depending on the client. A common approach involves the client openly acknowledging gratitude for the good things in their life, self-forgiveness, and a forgiveness of others for past mistakes.

Engagement: This element involves being present in the moment and fully committing to the activities and tasks at hand.

Clients who experience high levels of engagement use their skills and strengths to overcome challenges. For them, the activity is its own reward, and they benefit from the act on a deeply intrinsic level. For those struggling in this domain, they may abandon their effort at the first sign of negativity.

Relationships: This component pertains to the health and authenticity of the client's relationships. These include personal, familial, and professional relationships.

Exploring this domain may include the client's consideration of how loved, supported, and valued they feel from their relationships. Conversely, the client may also consider how they love, support, and value others.

Meaning: This element pertains to the individual's need to serve something greater than themselves. This includes their sense of purpose, ideas, beliefs, and values. Acknowledging their purpose can facilitate a client's journey to happiness and improved well-being.

Accomplishments: This element pertains to the client's triumphs in endeavors that are intrinsically rewarding. These triumphs require perseverance and goal attainment. This component incorporates the client's mastery of their experience, self-motivation, self-confidence, and self-efficacy.

The PERMA Model falls under the umbrella of *Positive Psychology Coaching (PPC)*. Though listed here as a coaching model, the framework is less a structure for coaching and more a structure for understanding the elements needed for flourishing. Put another way, following the PERMA Model can help clients achieve a greater sense of happiness and well-being.

Variations of the PERMA Model exist, which include the PERMA-H and PERMA+ Models. The former (H) refers to **Health,** while the latter (+) includes **Optimism**, **Physical activity**, **Nutrition**, and **Sleep**.

It is important to note that certain factors can counteract a client's ability to follow the PERMA Model, inhibiting their ability to experience positive outcomes and potentially indicating a larger issue. These factors include temperament, trauma, and psychopathologies. When present in the client, these issues are the domain of therapy, not coaching.

PERMA, also called the PERMA Theory of Well-Being, is more complex than presented here. Certification in PERMA and Positive Psychology Coaching is available from multiple vendors. Professionals seeking additional information may consider Seligman's 2011 book, *Flourish: A Visionary New Understanding of Happiness and Well-Being.*

Sources[212]

PERSONALITY MODELS (GENERAL ENTRY)

Category: personality type

Personality models provide us with frameworks to better understand ourselves and others. They serve to educate, inform, increase a client's self-awareness, and allow them to improve their relationship with themselves and the world around them.

Personality assessments can help professionals categorize and characterize a client's personality through a form of "testing." These assessments serve as a conduit to help clients determine where they fall within the different personality frameworks.

Sources claim over 2,500 personality models and assessments exist in the US, though sources vary greatly on how to best categorize or characterize these models. Some make distinctions based on the type of assessment, self-report vs. checklist vs. interview-based. Others make distinctions based on the possible number of outcomes (e.g., DISC has 4 outcomes, MBTI has 16, and Enneagram has 27).

The philosophers of ancient Mesopotamia and Greece were among the first documented theorists of human behavior. They strove to better understand the human mind: to know why people think, feel, and behave the ways they do. They lacked the technology to image the brain or map genetics, and they relied primarily on observation. This led to interesting theories, like the belief that personality correlates to the balance of blood, phlegm, and bile in the body.

The ancients were astute observers of human behavior. These observations led philosophers to recognize a pattern of four types of behavior. Though scholars of the time used different labels to describe this pattern, the two most popular were Hippocrates (blood, black bile, yellow bile, and phlegm) and Plato (artistic, sensible, intuitive, and reasoning).

Though the names changed over the years, many modern personality frameworks still follow a four-style type model. These include *Business Chemistry, DISC, TetraMap,* and *Keirsey's Four Temperaments.*

Other personality models recognize more than four styles. These include the *Five-Factor Model,* the *Enneagram of Personality, Myers-Briggs Personality Model,* and others.

Though each framework varies in popularity and application, there is no universally accepted personality model or assessment. Every framework has critics who question the scientific rigor or efficacy of the model or the assessment.

Personality frameworks can develop a client's awareness of self and others; however, they also present a risk when used inappropriately. Without proper training and careful debriefing, personality assessments may leave clients feeling anxious or distressed about the results of their assessment.

For years, organizations used personality assessments in their hiring practices. Recently, clinical, legal, and human resource professionals began rejecting the use of personality assessments as a factor in hiring due to growing evidence that personality tests discriminate against persons with certain conditions like autism.

Professionals should exercise caution when using personality models or their associated assessments. Coaches should use these frameworks to create awareness, facilitate insight, and help clients better understand aspects of their behavior. Coaches should not use personality assessments as diagnostic instruments.

Professionals seeking additional information on the risks associated with personality assessments may consider Annie Murphy Paul's 2004 book, *The Cult of Personality: How Personality Tests Are Leading Us to Miseducate Our Children, Mismanage Our Companies, and Misunderstand Ourselves.*

For a scientific emphasis on personality testing, professionals may consider R.J. Cohen, W.J. Schneider, R. Tobin, M. Swerdlik, and E. Sturman's 2022 text, *Psychological Testing and Assessment: An Introduction to Tests and Measurement.* (10th edition).

Sources[213]

POLARITY MANAGEMENT MODEL

Certification Available: yes
Certification Required: yes (for official use)
Assessments: yes (Polarity Assessment)
Proprietary: yes (Polarity Partnerships)
Client: individuals, groups
Cost: $3,000–$4,000
Category: polarities

Developed in 1975 by psychologist Barry Johnson, the Polarity Management Model provides a framework for exploring and addressing the conflict that arises between competing polarities.

According to Johnson, polarities are two diametrically opposed yet interdependent internal issues which can compete for dominance. When one issue becomes overly dominant, it creates an imbalance which leads to internal and external conflict.

Leadership often involves competing polarities. Examples of polarities leaders may struggle with include the following:

- Leading—Delegating
- Confidence—Humility
- Accountability—Latitude
- Strength—Vulnerability
- Tough-minded—Empathetic

Johnson argues that traditional problem-solving approaches do not work with polarities and often make the situation worse. This is because, unlike traditional problems that have solutions and foster an "either/or" style of thinking, polarity issues are unsolvable or have multiple right answers. Therefore, when dealing with polarities, the ideal approach is one that seeks to manage the issues and reestablish balance.

When exploring polarities, it is important to avoid labeling one belief or feeling right and the other wrong. Each polarity represents both a potential strength and a potential risk depending on circumstances. The Polarity Management Model, therefore, helps the client find a balance between competing polarities.

Achieving the proper balance requires a shift in the client's mindset from one of "either/or" to one of "both/and." This moves the client from viewing the issue as a choice between two options to one of envisioning a life in which both exist. Though simple in concept, in practice Polarity Management can prove challenging, especially when the client experiences intense emotions resulting from the conflict.

Using Polarity Management effectively requires developing a client's awareness of the competing polarities, recognizing the strengths and vulnerabilities of each polarity, exploring the relationship between each polarity and the client's desires and fears, and creating a vision for balance.

To facilitate the client's journey toward balance, Johnson created the Polarity Map, a four-quadrant matrix which serves as a conduit for discourse and exploration. When properly used, the Polarity Map is a source of insight for the client and fosters greater awareness of the issues at hand, and it allows the client to see the relationship between the variables involved.

The Polarity Management Model and the Polarity Map are among the most popular and frequently used frameworks in the coaching industry. Multiple variations of the Polarity Map exist; some incorporate other tools and theories into the process. For example, one version of the Polarity Map includes the use of SWOT Analysis to facilitate a deeper exploration of the strengths and weaknesses of each polarity.

The Polarity Management Model includes tools (Polarity Map), assessments (Polarity Assessment), and an expanded application of the model called Polarity Approach to Continuity and Transformation (PACT). PACT applies the Polarity Management Model on an enterprise-wide scale.

Professionals seeking additional information will find much written on the topic of polarities, including Johnson's 1992 book, *Polarity Management: Identifying and Managing Unsolvable Problems.* Another resource is the 2019 book by Emerson and Lewis, *Navigating Polarities: Using Both/And Thinking to Lead Transformation.*

Sources[214]

POOLE'S MULTIPLE SEQUENCE MODEL

Certification Available: no
Certification Required: no
Assessments: no
Proprietary: no
Client: groups, teams
Cost: not applicable
Category: teaming, communication

Developed in 1983 by communications professor Marshall Scott Poole, Poole's Multiple Sequence Model (MSM) provides a complex framework for exploring and understanding group-based decision-making.

Through his research, Poole discovered that contrary to most theories on teaming (e.g., *Tuckman's Stages of Group Development*), small group decision-making is not a linear process. Instead, he found small group decision-making consists of activities that do not follow a specific sequence.

Poole's Multiple Sequence Model consists of three "tracks" of communication which Poole says may repeat or happen at any time in the communication process. These tracks may occur in clusters, moving from track to track multiple times in a single day based on the needs of the group. The combination of these interweaving tracks characterizes the group's communication style.

Task track (also known as the **period of understanding**): While on this track, the group spends time learning about the task at hand, formulating goals and objectives, and exploring possible problem-solving processes. According to MSM, a group may revisit this track many times as the project evolves. As they learn new information, members of the group may adjust their approach to task completion, or revise their goals and objectives.

Relational track: This track focuses on the interpersonal relationships between group members and typically involves members getting to know each other, forming friendships, and learning about one another's strengths. During a project, a group may stop working on the task and start working on relationships. According to MSM, this may happen multiple times over the course of the project. For example, a group may randomly take a break from the job at hand to laugh, joke, or chitchat about their weekend plans.

Topic track: This track focuses on the major themes or issues that emerge during the project and often stems from the group's work. Typically, these issues affect the way the group communicates and may lead the group to other tracks.

In addition to the three tracks, MSM includes the concept of **breakpoints**—transition points where the group moves from one track to another. Through his research, Poole identified three types of breakpoints.

Normal breakpoint: This is a natural transition from one track to another or a seamless shift in focus.

Delay breakpoint: This seemingly redundant transition involves shifting from one track to the topic track to reexamine the group's position. Often, this includes a recycling of information already covered in prior discussions. A delay breakpoint can feel like retreading old ground.

Disruption breakpoint: This is a transition based on conflict.

Arguably the most important aspect of MSM is the idea that group dynamics do not follow a prescriptive or formulaic sequence. Factors like group composition, task structure, and conflict management influence how and when groups move across tracks.

Poole's Multiple Sequence Model is a useful framework or lens through which to examine how a group communicates and engages in problem-solving.

Professionals seeking additional information will find most literature on MSM derives from academic sources. For more information on Poole's research into group communication, consider his 2021 book, *The Emerald Handbook of Group and Team Communication Research*.

Sources[215]

POSITIVE COACHING MODEL

Certification Available: no
Certification Required: no
Assessments: no
Proprietary: no
Client: individuals, groups
Cost: not applicable
Category: coaching model

Developed in 2004 by psychologist Vincenzo Libri, the POSITIVE Coaching Model (PCM) provides a comprehensive 8-stage process for coaching.

Stage 1—Purpose: During the first step, the client establishes their expectations for coaching, both for the individual session and the coaching relationship. This includes what they want to get from the coaching experience, which often requires the coach to use narrative-inducing questions to encourage the client's exploration of their desires and goals.

Stage 2—Observation: The second stage involves the client exploring their status quo or present state of being. The observation stage seeks to reveal insight into the client's current reality, identify the people involved in the client's current reality, and the issues or challenges facing the client. PCM encourages clients to focus on both the positive and negative aspects of their situation.

Stage 3—Strategy/SMART: During the third stage, the client formulates a vision and goal for their desired state of being and develops a strategy to achieve this goal. Like many coaching models, PCM adopts the *SMART Model for Goal Setting*. The client should develop goals that are specific, measurable, attainable, relevant, and time-bound.

Stage 4—Insight: The fourth stage is about exploring the client's emotional connection to their goals. Through this stage, the client begins to understand their level of motivation and commitment to achieving their goals. If motivation is low, it might indicate the goal does not intrinsically satisfy them. In such cases, the client may need to reconsider their goals. If this happens, the client returns to stage 3.

Stage 5—Team: In this stage, the client considers what interpersonal support could help them achieve their desired goals. This requires the client to explore their social network for allies and supporters to facilitate their motivation and accountability.

Stage 6—Initiate: The sixth stage marks the first time the client takes concrete steps toward achieving their goals. It is important that the client explore actions that are meaningful to goal attainment. Discourse in this stage typically involves the client considering how and when they intend to start.

Stage 7—Value: This stage involves the client acknowledging and appreciating their efforts toward goal attainment. If a client's goals take time, it may become difficult for the client to recognize their own progress. In this case, the coach can help the client see the impact of their small wins. Like *Kotter's Change Management Theory*, PCM advocates "win early, win often."

Stage 8—Encourage: During the final stage, the coach continues to provide encouragement for the client. As the client pursues their goals, they will experience good days and bad days; through it all, the coach can be a source of encouragement.

Like many of the coaching models presented in this compendium, PCM derives from Sir John Whitmore's *GROW Coaching Model*. The eight stages of PCM provides a robust and methodical framework for coaches who need or want more structure in their coaching sessions.

It is important to note that the POSITIVE Coaching Model is different from and unrelated to *Positive Psychology Coaching*. Professionals seeking additional information may consider Libri's book, *Your POSITIVE Life*.

Sources[216]

POSITIVE INTELLIGENCE

> **Certification Available:** yes
> **Certification Required:** yes
> **Assessments:** yes (Saboteur Assessment)
> **Proprietary:** yes (Positive Intelligence)
> **Client:** individuals, groups
> **Cost:** pricing not available
> **Category:** coaching model, resilience, self-actualization

Developed by executive coach Shirzad Chamine, Positive Intelligence provides a framework for exploring the relationship between a person's mindset and their well-being. Positive Intelligence helps clients identify and explore two mental modes that may influence their happiness, well-being, and ability to thrive.

Saboteur mode: This is the negative mode, which may include the following mindsets.

- Avoider: This mindset focuses on the positive while evading the negative. This style of saboteur avoids conflict and suppresses negative emotions.

- Controller: Driven by anxiety, this mindset leads a person to take charge of people and situations. These saboteurs relish conflict and easily intimidate others.

- Hyper-achiever: This mindset depends on achievement for validation and self-respect. This style of saboteur is hypercompetitive and goal oriented.

- Hyper-rational: This mindset perpetuates the methodical analysis of every aspect of life. Intensely focused, this style of saboteur tends to regulate emotional displays, leading others to perceive them as cold.

- Hyper-vigilant: This mindset is constantly fearful of the dangers in life. These types of saboteurs are skeptical, cynical, suspicious, and full of doubt.

- Judge: This saboteur fixates on every mistake, no matter how small, and is hypercritical and judgmental of self.

- Pleaser: This type of saboteur seeks acceptance through excessive pleasing and rescuing, losing sight of their own needs.

- Restless: This is a mindset driven to seek excitement. Easily distracted, this type of saboteur avoids unpleasant feelings in favor of new stimulation.

- Stickler: A mindset driven to achieve perfection, this style of saboteur is sarcastic and self-righteous. Hypercritical of self and others, they possess very high standards.

- Victim: These saboteurs seek attention through emotional or bad behaviors. Characterized as temperamental, they are prone to pouting and sulking.

Sage mode: The positive mode, which may include one or more of the following mindsets and behaviors.

- Empathize: a mindset of compassion for self and others.

- Explore: a mindset of curiosity and open-mindedness.

- Innovate: a mindset driven to create new perspectives.

- Navigate: a mindset to choose new paths that align with values.

- Activate: a mindset to act without saboteur interference.

Positive Intelligence includes multiple assessments to measure a person's Positive Intelligence, or PQ. The concept of Positive Intelligence falls under the umbrella of *Positive Psychology Coaching (PPC)* and is significantly more complex than presented here. Certification is available through Chamine's company Positive Intelligence and through third-party vendors.

Professionals seeking additional information may consider Chamine's 2012 book, *Positive Intelligence: Why Only 20% of Teams and Individuals Achieve Their True Potential and How You Can Achieve Yours*.

Sources[217]

POSITIVE PSYCHOLOGY COACHING

Certification Available: yes (multiple vendors)
Certification Required: no
Assessments: no
Proprietary: no
Client: individuals, groups
Cost: pricing varies
Category: coaching model

Developed by noted psychologist Martin E. P. Seligman in 1998, Positive Psychology Coaching (PPC) is a style (or philosophy) of coaching, rooted in science, that facilitates the client's personal growth and development. PPC includes many different coaching models and methodologies, like the *RAW Model, PERMA Model, 6M Foundations, Positive Intelligence,* and others.

Coaches who follow a style of Positive Psychology Coaching tend to focus on tools, assessments, and models backed by scientific inquiry and supported by academic research. As psychologist Suzy Green explains it, "Positive psychology is the science of us at our best."

A common misconception of PPC is that practitioners focus solely on the positive aspects of the client's situation to the exclusion of the negative. This may be true for some practitioners; however, fundamentally, PPC acknowledges the powerful role a negative can play in helping a client flourish. Some clinical practitioners even encourage their clients to openly acknowledge and appreciate the negative side of their human existence/nature.

Practitioners of PPC seek to achieve a balance between negative and positive based on the needs of the client. For example, some clients may require more attention to the negative, like exploring weaknesses and vulnerabilities to further develop resilience and self-awareness. Meanwhile, other clients may benefit from focusing on the positive, like clients experiencing self-doubt or a diminished sense of self-efficacy.

A research paper published in May 2020 examined a sampling of coaching models used by PPC practitioners and discovered a pattern within these processes. The authors called this pattern the Positive Psychology Coaching Model. This model is not a formal framework and therefore not included as an independent entry.

The paper determined that the Positive Psychology Coaching Model consists of five phases further supported by three continuous processes.

Phase 1: Creating the relationship
Phase 2: Strength profiling and feedback
Phase 3: Develop an ideal vision of self
Phase 4: Goal setting and execution
Phase 5: Concluding or recontracting

The five phases of the Positive Psychology Coaching Model are like other coaching processes presented in this compendium, so we will not delve into the details of each phase. Instead, we will focus on the three continuous processes which apply across the entire lifecycle of the Positive Psychology Coaching Model.

Learning transfer: Throughout the course of using any coaching model under the PPC style, the client should transfer what they learn from the coaching process to the workplace, while taking ownership of the learning process (i.e., real-world application of what they learn).

Action tracking (continuous evaluation): This process focuses on how the client will measure or determine the success of the coaching process. This includes monitoring both goal achievement and well-being.

Empowerment (reframing, reinforcement): This process is complex and involves helping the client maintain an emotional connection to their goals, reframing setbacks as opportunities, and maintaining a sense of control in the process.

Many of the coaching frameworks that fall under the umbrella of Positive Psychology Coaching offer formal training and certification. Professionals seeking additional information on Positive Psychology Coaching may consider the 2018 book, *Positive Psychology Coaching in Practice,* edited by Suzy Green and Stephen Palmer.

Sources[218]

POSTINDUSTRIAL LEADERSHIP THEORY

Certification Available: no
Certification Required: no
Assessments: no
Proprietary: no
Client: individuals
Cost: not applicable
Category: leadership

Developed in the early 1990s by professor of leadership studies Joseph C. Rost, Postindustrial Leadership Theory provides a framework consisting of four principles that foster effective leadership. According to Rost, "Leadership is an influence relationship among leaders and followers who intend real changes that reflect their mutual purposes." This belief underlies all four principles.

Relationship of influence: According to Rost, the relationship between a leader and a follower is one of mutual influence. Rost diverged from older leadership theories of the time, which often defined leadership as one individual directing others. On this topic, he suggests that a direct or dictatorial approach to leadership is less effective than styles which depend on subtle guidance or interpersonal influence.

Leadership is not based on authority: This principle suggests that everyone shares in the function of leadership, not just the individual designated as the leader. Again, Rost deviated from preindustrial leadership theories that defined leadership as the people with designated authority to lead.

Change sought by both parties: According to this principle, both leaders and their followers seek some form of change. Though leaders and followers may not initially seek the same changes, both see value in changing the status quo on some level.

Mutual purpose: The fourth principle of Postindustrial Leadership Theory suggests that both leaders and their followers must strive to agree and share in the changes. Initially, the changes sought may differ between leader and follower; however, through discourse and collaboration, they may reach common ground and agree to a shared goal.

Postindustrial Leadership Theory proposes that effective leaders should consider the shared goals and values of everyone involved. They should foster collaboration between themselves and their employees, giving voice and empowering everyone to mutual benefit.

Rost developed Postindustrial Leadership Theory as an alternative to the prevailing preindustrial theories of the time. To differentiate his theory from preindustrial theories, he focused on the relationship between individuals instead of the authorities of leadership like we see in *Lewin's Leadership Styles*. Rost also emphasized the importance of mindsets over competencies, and consciousness over models. Postindustrial Leadership Theory classifies as both a *Relational Leadership Theory* and a *Functional Leadership Theory*.

In challenging preindustrial leadership theories, Rost argued against a prevailing belief that leadership is unteachable. He believed there is a strong connection between how leaders think and how they behave, a belief backed by subsequent research. Therefore, he argued, one person may train another to develop their relationship-building skills and in so doing, effectively teach leadership.

Much of the literature available on Postindustrial Leadership Theory derives from academic repositories and may require paid access to retrieve. Professionals seeking additional information on Postindustrial Leadership Theory may consider Rost's 1991 book, *Leadership for the 21st Century*.

In the development of his book, Rost reviewed over a thousand texts and other literary sources on the topic of leadership. This allowed Rost to examine multiple theories of leadership and the research approaches used to develop them. From this, Rost highlights several problems with the leadership studies behind these theories.

In addition to Rost's Postindustrial Leadership Theory, professionals may also explore *Relational Leadership Theory*, which shares similar characteristics.

Sources[219]

PRACTICE COACHING MODEL

Certification Available: no
Certification Required: no
Assessments: no
Proprietary: no
Client: individuals, groups
Cost: not applicable
Category: coaching model

Developed in 2007 by psychologist Stephen Palmer, the PRACTICE Coaching Model provides a framework for coaching based on *Cognitive Behavioral Coaching*. Considered a solutions-based approach to coaching, the PRACTICE Model uses techniques designed to foster the client's ability to examine the problem, develop solutions, and implement them.

The framework consists of seven steps represented by the acronym PRACTICE.

Step 1—Problem identification: During the first step, the client explores the problem or issue. Their goal is to seek clarity and understanding by examining the construct of the problem. This involves identifying the components which make up the problem and determining the underlying causes which precipitate the problem.

Step 2—Realistic goals: In the second step, the client articulates their desired goals and expectations. This includes what they wish to achieve during the overall coaching relationship and in each individual coaching session. Like other coaching models, this model advocates using the *SMART Model for Goal Setting*.

Step 3—Alternative solutions: During the third step, the client explores all possible options which may address the problem or issue at hand. It is important that the client avoid evaluating or passing judgments on these options.

The focus should remain on identifying as many viable solutions as possible. Critical to this step is the client's ability to embrace the idea that most problems have multiple solutions and their ability to resist going with the first option that comes to mind without considering other options first.

Step 4—Consideration of consequences: In the fourth step, the client explores all potential outcomes that may result from each option. The client should consider both positive and negative consequences to ensure a realistic and holistic perspective. This exploration is vital to the decision-making process because it allows the client to make better-informed decisions.

Step 5—Target most feasible solution: During the fifth step, the client prioritizes the list of options and then eliminates the less desirable options. The client does this by using their knowledge and assessment of outcomes to determine which options may yield the most undesirable results. By considering the consequences (both positive and negative), the client can narrow down the possibilities until they can decide on the best course of action.

Step 6—Implementation of Chosen solution: In the sixth step, the client chooses the solution they believe most appropriate. Then, the client develops a strategy for implementing the selected solution. This involves creating an action plan consisting of small or incremental actions they can engage in to move them closer to their goals. Clients should create a thoughtful plan, one that incorporates measurable indicators of progress and intrinsic rewards to foster motivation.

Step 7—Evaluation: In the final step, the client examines their progress to determine what, if any, changes they should make to their plan. This requires an honest examination of the ways their progress aligns and deviates from their expectations.

The PRACTICE Coaching Model is among the more comprehensive coaching frameworks included in the ICMT. Because this model falls under the umbrella of Cognitive Behavioral Coaching, following this process requires a frequent understanding of the client's feelings.

Professionals seeking additional information on the PRACTICE Coaching Model will find minimal literature available online. Though not specific to the model, Stephen Palmer authored several books on the topic of coaching, including *The Coaching Relationship: Putting People First* (2010).

Sources[220]

PROLONGED ADAPTATION STRESS SYNDROME

> **Certification Available:** no
> **Certification Required:** no
> **Assessments:** no
> **Proprietary:** no
> **Client:** individuals
> **Cost:** not applicable
> **Category:** stress mgt., confidence/resilience

Developed in 1997 by psychologist Katherine Benziger and brain function specialist Arlene R. Taylor, Prolonged Adaptation Stress Syndrome (PASS) provides a framework to identify the consequences of protracted exposure to an energy-exhaustive lifestyle. Put another way, PASS can help clients determine the physiological and psychological costs associated with prolonged exposure to a high-stress environment.

PASS identifies eight potential consequences or indicators. Multiple variables influence how many of these outcomes a client may experience, including length of exposure to the stressful environment, access to support networks and coping mechanisms, the client's level of resilience, and more.

Fatigue: When tasked to perform functions counter to an individual's cognitive preferences or when facing stressful experiences, the brain works overtime to perform. This can lead to exhaustion. Typically, when the brain experiences exhaustion, sleep can facilitate recovery; however, when exposure is prolonged, sleep interruption may occur. This decreases quality sleep and REM, which consequently prevents the necessary recovery from taking place, leading to fatigue.

Hypervigilance: Continuous exposure to a high-stress environment can lead a person's reticular activating system to put them in a persistent state of heightened alertness, further taxing the body and the mind.

Immune system suppression: A common physiological consequence of hypervigilance and prolonged stress exposure is a decrease in the efficacy of the body's immune system. This often slows the client's ability to heal and increases the risk of illness.

Reduced function of the frontal lobes: Overtaxing the brain can lead clients to experience diminished cognitive functions. For some, this manifests as a decrease in creative and artistic ability, while in others it involves an inability to effectively think logically and analytically.

Altered neurochemistry: Studies suggest that prolonged stress exposure can alter hormone levels in the body, leading to real medical consequences.

Memory problems: Linked with changes in neurochemistry, a client may find it difficult to recall short-term and long-term memories. This process may also manifest with a client experiencing frequent "foggy brain" moments.

Discouragement and depression: Prolonged stress exposure can, over time, alter a client's perception of their life. This can lead them to develop a sense of hopelessness and even depression.

Self-esteem problems: Clients may experience an altered negative view of self. This may manifest as clients seeing themselves as the victim or as the offender.

The sources of PASS are many. In coaching, it is not uncommon to see this among clients who present very differently from their true self while at work. This behavior, sometimes called false typing, creates a significant source of stress that can lead to PASS.

Prolonged Adaptation Stress Syndrome is distinctly different from *General Adaptation Syndrome*, and the two should not be confused. Additionally, Taylor emphasizes that while the symptoms of PASS are like those of post-traumatic stress (PTS), PTS is a clinical diagnosis. Taylor developed the concept of PASS to apply to those who do not meet the clinical criteria for a PTS diagnosis.

Professionals seeking additional information may consider Taylor and Benziger's 1999 paper, "The Physiological Foundations of Falsification of Type and PASS."

Sources[221]

PUNCTUATED EQUILIBRIUM MODEL

Certification Available: no
Certification Required: no
Assessments: no
Proprietary: no
Client: groups, teams
Cost: not applicable
Category: teaming

Developed in 1988 by professor of organizational behavior Connie J.G. Gersick, the Punctuated Equilibrium Model provides a framework for understanding team development with an emphasis on the impact of time-based requirements on developmental progression. Put another way, the model suggests that time pressures associated with a project deadline can influence the speed and progression of team development. The framework consists of two phases and a transition period between phases.

Phase 1: The first phase begins with the group's first meeting. During phase 1, the group dedicates time to learning about one another, setting the tone for group behavior, and establishing expectations for group performance. The group may not spend much time or energy working on the task itself; instead members may focus on identifying the tasks required for success and deciding how to best accomplish each task. During phase 1, group members engage in a significant amount of socialization as they work to acclimate to one another. This may require up to half of the project's allotted time.

• Transition: This is a period of adjustment that takes place exactly halfway through the time allotted. Sometimes called the group's "midlife crisis," this transition occurs because the team realizes they have used half of the allotted time, with little to no progress. This realization also leads the group to evaluate the contributions of its members, leading to another reality: some of the team members are not performing as expected. The transition period may also lead a team to question earlier assumptions from phase 1 about the tasks needed to succeed.

As the reality of their current situation sets in, the group develops a sense of urgency (or even panic) about the remaining tasks, which fosters a surge in momentum toward goal attainment.

During the transition period, the group may revisit these tasks and reexamine the best way to achieve the group's goals within the limited timeframe left. This results in a new plan of action, which serves as the foundation for phase 2.

Phase 2: The second phase begins when the group acts on its new plan of action. During this phase, the group develops a renewed sense of commitment and an enhanced level of focus on completing the tasks in a manner consistent with the new plan. This means groups in phase 2 demonstrate greater efficiency and progress more rapidly than they did in phase 1.

Phase 2 marks the final stage in the Punctuated Equilibrium Model. Completion of the project marks the completion of phase 2.

Studies on the Punctuated Equilibrium Model showed teams given a specific amount of time to work on a project will behave one way for the first half of their allotted time; then, halfway through, they will experience a transition before entering the second phase. Researchers also observed significant differences in team behavior from phase 1 to phase 2.

The Punctuated Equilibrium Model derives from Punctuated Equilibrium, a similarly named theory of biological evolution developed by Niles Eldredge and Stephen J. Gould. Like biological evolution, the Punctuated Equilibrium Model suggests group development is static for potentially long periods of time, but when change occurs, it does so in short, rapid, and radical spurts. It is through this belief that this model rejects the notion that groups follow easily defined stages of progression like those presented in *Tuckman's Stages of Group Development*.

Professionals seeking additional information will find much written on the Punctuated Equilibrium Model, including Gersick's 1988 paper, "Time and Transition in Work Teams: Toward a New Model of Group Development."

Sources[222]

RADICAL CANDOR FRAMEWORK

Certification Available: yes
Certification Required: no
Assessments: no
Proprietary: yes (Radical Candor LLC)
Client: individuals
Cost: $59
Category: feedback, communication

Developed in 2017 by executive coach Kim Scott, Radical Candor provides a framework to help leaders deliver more meaningful and caring feedback. The Radical Candor framework consists of two behavioral dimensions which form a matrix, resulting in four styles of communication behavior.

Behavioral Dimensions

- **Care personally**: This dimension focuses on your level of care and concern for the welfare of your team, the people they are responsible for, and the work they do. To care deeply means doing more than just making yourself available to the team and requires a leader get to know each member of their team individually.

- **Challenge directly**: This dimension focuses on how you engage and challenge your team. This includes how you motivate them to their best work, and how you communicate with them. Challenging effectively means being direct and honest, and tough but not mean.

These two dimensions form a matrix that characterizes four styles of communication. It is important to note that the four styles characterize behaviors, not people. People may adopt one behavior in one setting and another style in a different circumstance.

Radical candor: The ideal style of communication behavior, it involves adopting an open and direct style of feedback that combines honesty and compassion. This is the ability to challenge someone directly while simultaneously showing you care about them. Radical candor often requires time and practice to acclimate to the discomfort and anxiety that sometimes accompanies this approach.

Ruinous empathy: This behavior occurs when your positive feelings for a person influence you to withhold or obfuscate your feedback to spare their feelings. This behavior is high on Care Personally, but low on Challenge Directly.

Obnoxious aggression: This behavior results when you care less about the person and more about the message. Characterized as brutal honesty, this is the act of challenging the person directly without showing any care or concern for them. This behavior is low on Care Personally, and high on Challenge Directly.

Manipulative insincerity: The most caustic and damaging of the four behaviors, this communication behavior is insincere and callous. Characterized as passive-aggressive or backstabbing, this may include deceptive feedback intended to mislead or cause harm. This typically occurs when the person cares little for the other person and has little interest in providing direct and honest feedback. This behavior is low on both Care Personally and Challenge Directly.

For those who intend to adopt Radical Candor, Scott recommends first letting people know of your intentions to use the framework and solicit their feedback. She recommends explaining the framework using the organization's own vocabulary, so everyone understands. Second, apply the concepts of Radical Candor in the feedback you deliver. In essence, set the example. Scott offers tools to help you gauge your progress using Radical Candor. Third, create processes that encourage a commitment of feedback between members of the team.

Professionals seeking additional information may consider Scott's 2017 book, *Radical Candor: How to Get What You Want by Saying What You Mean*. In addition to her book, Scott offers a variety of information and resources through her personal website and her company's website. Professionals interested in training may consider the Radical Candor self-paced e-course program.

Sources[223]

RAW MODEL OF FLOURISHING

Certification Available: yes
Certification Required: no
Assessments: no
Proprietary: no
Client: individuals, groups
Cost: $330 AUD (The Positivity Institute)
Category: coaching model, confidence/resilience

Developed by psychologists Suzy Green and Stephen Palmer, the RAW Model of Flourishing provides a framework for exploring the symbiotic relationship between multiple variables essential to an individual's ability to flourish and thrive in life.

The RAW Model focuses on the concept of "flourishing," a term born of *Positive Psychology Coaching*. This is a complex construct that explains what it means to feel well and happy. The model examines the relationship between the essential aspects or variables of a client's state of being that, in turn, influence their happiness and sense of wellness.

The RAW Model of Flourishing explores three dimensions of a client's state of being, happiness, and wellness. Experiencing a positive state of being requires a balance between these three dimensions. The symbiotic relationship between these variables means each one affects the others. When an imbalance exists, it affects the client's happiness and wellness.

Dimension 1—Resilience: This dimension pertains to the client's ability to recover quickly from challenges and setbacks.

Dimension 2—Achievement: This dimension pertains to the client's drive to strive, achieve, or accomplish a goal; typically, through effort, courage, or skill.

Dimension 3—Well-being: This dimension pertains to the client's present state of being. This includes their level of comfort, happiness, and health.

One way to use the RAW Model involves exploring the client's current situation through the optic of these three dimensions. For example, clients exploring why they are experiencing a lack of joy or fulfillment despite being on the verge of achieving long sought-after goals may discover they sacrificed well-being and resilience in favor of achievement, thereby creating an imbalance.

When confronted with an imbalance, the coach may use the **WAR Model of Withering** to help the client reestablish balance. This framework consists of three lenses that a client may use to examine their situation.

Well-being sabotage: This lens involves exploring the client's experience to identify behaviors that sabotage their well-being. This may include lack of exercise, poor sleep, drinking caffeine before bed, excessive consumption of depressants like alcohol, and more.

Achievement blocking: This lens seeks to identify the behaviors that serve as roadblocks to the client's ability to achieve goals. This may include procrastination, excuse making, avoidance, lack of commitment, and more.

Resilience undermining: The final lens allows the client to identify the behaviors that undermine their resilience. These may include unrealistic expectations, an overly idealistic mindset, rigid perfectionist beliefs, and more.

The RAW Model of Flourishing is more complex than presented here. Professionals seeking formal training in this, or similar models, like the *PERMA Coaching Model*, may consider certification in the field of Positive Psychology Coaching. Dr. Suzy Green offers certification through her company, the Positivity Institute.

Professionals seeking additional information on the RAW Model will find much written on the framework and the topic of flourishing, including Green and Palmer's 2018 book, *Positive Psychology Coaching in Practice*.

Sources[224]

RECOGNITION-PRIMED DECISION MODEL

Certification Available: no
Certification Required: no
Assessments: no
Proprietary: no
Client: individuals
Cost: not applicable
Category: decision-making

Developed in the 1980s by psychologists Gary Klein, Roberta Calderwood, and Ann Clinton-Cirocco, the Recognition-Primed Decision Model (RPD) provides a framework for exploring how people make decisions in high-stress, high-stakes situations using intuition and heuristics. The RPD Model derives from research on high-stakes decision-making in the US Army and other demanding professions.

The RPD process consists of three steps that incorporate the use of situational assessments and mental simulation.

Step 1—Experience the situation: The client examines the current situation, exploring multiple aspects of their experience and making useful observations. This requires that the client gather relevant data to determine what is happening and why, often by listening to those around them.

Step 2—Analyze the situation: The client reflects on their observations, comparing the current situation to previous experiences. This requires that the client engage in "compare and contrast" analysis. During this analysis, the client may ask questions like "What aspects of this situation surprised me?" "What aspects of this situation did I see coming?" and "Have I experienced anything like this before?"

The intent of step 2 is for the client to identify a common frame of reference to previous experiences. When no experience compares to the current situation, the individual often chooses the closest alternative. In this, the second step incorporates the use of heuristics.

Step 3—Implement the decision: During the final step, the client explores possible courses of action, one at a time, using a form of cognitive modeling that involves intuition and imagination. The client may run through multiple mental simulations for a single option. This will help the client determine if the action makes sense or if they need to consider a different solution.

RPD encourages clients to thoroughly consider one course of action at a time until they reach the one that makes sense. This approach deviates from traditional decision-making models that encourage clients to develop a robust list of options, then explore the efficacy of each issue. Often, decision-makers do not have the time to generate and consider multiple options and must go with the first logical course of action.

Fundamental to the RPD Model is the idea that a person's past experiences influence their ability to make high-stakes decisions. RPD suggests that individuals facing difficult decisions often rely on a combination of pattern recognition and past experiences (heuristics) to facilitate the decision-making process.

Training professionals who incorporate the RPD Model into leadership development programs often focus on the individual's capacity for experiential learning. Improving the individual's ability to learn from and leverage past experiences will foster their decision-making skills. Examples of experiential learning approaches include mentoring programs or shadow programs where new leaders follow senior leaders and observe their decision-making process in a variety of situations.

Another method of experiential-based learning involves the use of reality-based scenarios designed to simulate actual experiences. For example, new agent trainees at the FBI often conduct training exercises at the famed Hogan's Alley, a mock town consisting of real buildings including a bank, pharmacy, motel, apartment, homes, and businesses. The scenarios presented derive from actual events. Adding to the realistic environment, trainees use real firearms loaded with paint rounds, creating a more realistic experience.

Professionals seeking additional information may consider Klein's 1999 book, *Sources of Power: How People Make Decisions*.

Sources[225]

REINFORCEMENT THEORY

Certification Available: no
Certification Required: no
Assessments: no
Proprietary: no
Client: individuals
Cost: not applicable
Category: motivation, employee engagement, influence

Developed in 1957 by psychologist Burrhus Frederic Skinner, Reinforcement Theory (RT) provides a framework for exploring and understanding human behavior. The fundamental principle of RT suggests that people tend to engage in behavior that produces desirable outcomes while avoiding behavior that results in undesirable outcomes.

The Reinforcement Theory framework classifies conditioning variables which influence behavior in two dimensions. The first dimension categorizes variables based on whether they increase desirable behavior or decrease undesirable behavior.

Reinforcements: These are conditioning variables that seek to increase, reinforce, or establish desirable behavior.

Punishments: These conditioning variables seek to decrease, deter, or eliminate undesirable behavior.

The second dimension classifies variables based on whether they introduce a stimulus or remove one as a means of influence.

Positive (+): These consist of variables or actions that introduce a stimulus. It has nothing to do with the stimulus being positive or negative.

Negative (-): These consist of variables or actions that remove a stimulus. It has nothing to do with the stimulus being positive or negative.

The outcome of these two dimensions results in a matrix which helps identify and understand the methods of motivating or conditioning behavior.

Positive reinforcement: the act of introducing a desirable stimulus to encourage the continuation of desirable behavior.

For example, a manager may provide bonuses to employees who achieve their quotas. Other examples include time-off awards, employee of the month, and promotions.

Negative reinforcement: the act of removing an undesirable stimulus as a reward for desirable behavior.

For example, a manager may decrease their oversight of employees who demonstrate desirable behavior. Other examples include removing an employee from probation, removal of restrictions, and the elimination of micromanagement.

Positive punishment: the act of introducing an undesirable stimulus in response to undesirable behavior. This is typically what we know as punishment.

For example, a manager may place an employee on probation which requires frequent oversight and progress checks. Other examples include suspension or an increase in undesirable assignments.

Negative punishment: the act of removing a desirable stimulus in response to undesirable behavior.

For example, a manager may prohibit an employee from using the company car until they correct their behavior. Other examples include pay reduction and time off without pay

Also called Behaviorism or the Theory of Operant Conditioning, Reinforcement Theory is based on Edward Thorndike's Law of Effect. Like other theories on this subject, RT is not without controversy and criticism.

Professionals seeking additional information will find a wealth of literature available on the topic, including Skinner's earliest work on the subject featured in his 1938 book, *The Behavior of Organisms*. For a different perspective of Skinner's work, consider Lauren Slater's 2004 book, *Opening Skinner's Box: Great Psychological Experiments of the 20th Century*.

Sources[226]

RELATIONAL LEADERSHIP THEORY

Certification Available: no
Certification Required: no
Assessments: no
Proprietary: no
Client: individuals, organizations
Cost: not applicable
Category: leadership

Relational Leadership Theory (RLT) is an umbrella term that refers to the collection of theories which contribute to the view of leadership as a social construct. RLT is distinct from other theories of leadership in that it views leadership as a social process of interconnected relationships and not as an individual-centric product. In other words, leadership lies in the relationship between individuals and the organization, not the characteristics, personality, or authority of a single person.

Research in Relational Leadership Theory is nascent, so there are differing perspectives and views regarding what constitutes relational leadership. Each of these distinct perspectives provides a unique lens through which coach and client may explore leadership as a social construct.

A popular framework for Relational Leadership Theory defines it as the study of leadership as a social influence process. This version presents two lenses to facilitate the examination of leadership as a social construct. The first focuses on the relationships between people while the second explores the relatedness or connection to the larger social system or organization.

Entity: This lens explores the relationships between people by examining the relevant social processes from the perspective of individual perceptions, cognitions, attributes, and behaviors as people engage in relationship activities. Put another way, the entity perspective focuses on the attributes of individuals as they build and maintain relationships.

Theories that adopt a similar perspective typically focus on the "one-on-one" and "one-on-many" relationships. These include the relationship between the leader and follower as well as that of the leader and group or collective.

Theories adopting a similar perspective include *Leader-Member Exchange Theory*, Rost's *Postindustrial Leadership Theory*, and *Charismatic Leadership Theory*.

In addition to leadership theories, there are numerous social and psychosocial theories which support the entity approach to leadership study. These include theories on the relational and collective self and those on social networking.

Relational: This lens explores leadership as a social process of organizational design, the construct of a constantly evolving and dynamic ever-changing ecosystem of relationships that is the greater organization. Where the entity approach focuses on the individual's perspective of the relationship, the relational approach looks at the connection with and to the larger collective.

Several schools of thought adopt a similar perspective, including relational constructionism, lateral relationships (Sayles), and Drath and Murrell's relational leadership. Collectively, these theories support a larger, more holistic approach to studying the social construct of leadership. These theories examine the nature and style of the communication that forms the relationships, cultures, and values.

Relational Leadership Theory is among the newer theories of leadership, and emergent literature continues to offer insight into this unique perspective on leadership study. Professionals seeking additional information may consider the academic publications of business school professor Mary Uhl-Bien or leadership professor Megan Reitz, who wrote about Relational Leadership Theory in her 2015 book, *Dialogue in Organizations: Developing Relational Leadership.*

Sources[227]

RENEWAL CYCLE

Certification Available: yes (Hudson Inst.)
Certification Required: yes
Assessments: no
Proprietary: yes
Client: individuals, groups
Cost: $14,500–$15,500
Category: change (ind.), coaching model

Developed in the early 1990s by educator Frederic M. Hudson, the Renewal Cycle provides a framework consisting of four phases that characterize the individual's journey to adopt change. Fundamental to the Renewal Cycle is the belief that the change adoption journey is cyclical, not linear. The change experience is a never-ending process; as clients grow and develop, they will move back and forth across phases.

Phase 1—Go for it or **Heroic period**: Considered an ideal state, phase 1 clients present as focused, driven, and excited. They experience a sense of fulfillment because their life has purpose and meaning. While in phase 1, clients typically do not seek change because they feel like everything is turning out perfect for them. As with all things in life, change is inevitable. No one can remain in phase 1 forever, and eventually the bliss of phase 1 gives way to phase 2.

Phase 2—Doldrums period: In phase 2, clients experience restlessness, detachment, disenchantment, and anxiety as they grapple with their transition out of phase 1 (i.e., loss of their ideal state). Phase 2 may come about due to a change in the environment or a change in the client's priorities. When the status quo changes, this can create a misalignment between the client's needs and wants and what they get from the status quo.

Clients in phase 2 often feel stuck or suffocated and may act compulsively. Phase 2 clients can articulate what they don't want, but they often struggle to identify what they do want.

Out of frustration, a client may adopt small changes to try to get back to phase 1. Hudson called these **mini-transitions** and cautioned these actions were short-lived. Once the client accepts that achieving phase 1 requires more significant change, they are ready to move into phase 3.

Phase 3—Cocooning period: In phase 3 the client tends to be more introspective and internally focused. This period of self-examination can be scary for the client and often requires patience, commitment, courage, and creativity.

During phase 3, the client revisits their values and reevaluates what is important to them. A client may discover that long-held beliefs or values no longer serve them, or that old goals should give way to new desires.

This is a deeply personal period for the client as they reflect on who they are and what they want. As the client begins to see the changes needed, they start to let go of the past and embrace the future. At this point they are ready to move to phase 4.

Phase 4—Getting ready period: During the final phase, the client experiments with the changes they identified in phase 3. Characterized as a period of "trying on the change," the client seeks to determine if the change fits. This requires the client to possess the courage to take risks, be willing to fall, and have the strength to get back up. As the client explores and adjusts, these new changes will lead them back to phase 1.

Hudson's framework is also known as Hudson's Cycle of Renewal and Change, the Hudson Change Model, and Hudson's Transition Model. Variations of the model exist which use different labels, and some even reorder the phases. There is also a version of the model designed for use with teams and organizations.

Professionals seeking to incorporate the Renewal Cycle may obtain certification through the Hudson Institute. Those seeking additional information may consider Hudson's 1994 book, *Life Launch: A Passionate Guide to the Rest of Your Life*, co-authored by Pamela D. McLean. For information on the Renewal Cycle-based Hudson Coaching method, see McLean's 2012 book, *The Completely Revised Handbook of Coaching*.

Sources[228]

RESULTS/RESULTS COACHING MODEL

```
Certification Available: no
Certification Required: no
Assessments: no
Proprietary: no
Client: individuals, groups
Cost: not applicable
Category: coaching model
```

The Results Coaching Model refers to two distinctly different frameworks (Results vs. RESULTS). The ICMT presents both under this entry. The first, Results Coaching Model, developed in 1996 by neuroscientist David Rock, provides a framework of principles for coaching under the umbrella of *Neuroscience-Based Coaching*, also known as Brain-Based Coaching.

David Rock's Results-Based Coaching incorporates a combination of positive psychology, change theories, adult learning theories, and systems theories. This provides coaches with a roadmap for conducting meaningful neuroscience-based coaching relationships.

The Results Coaching Model consists of five core principles. Throughout the process, the coach seeks permission from the client to challenge them.

Principle 1—Self-directed learning: For coaching to be meaningful, the client must decide the focus of the process and drive the discourse. Though the coach supports the client, it is the client who ultimately decides what to focus on and what decisions to make.

Principle 2—Solutions focused: The emphasis of this style of coaching lies in focusing on the positive (solution), not the negative (problem). This is due to a concern that focusing too much on the problem is counterproductive to the client.

Principle 3—Positive feedback: Acknowledging the client's progress throughout the coaching relationship is essential and involves the use of positive reinforcement to help the client gain and maintain momentum.

Principle 4—Stretch: Help the client identify and pursue challenging goals. This is particularly important for clients who tend to focus on simple short-term goals.

Principle 5—Structure: Have clearly identifiable steps within a systematic process or approach to goal attainment so that both coach and client understand what is expected.

The second model, developed by business coach Wayne Farrell, uses the acronym RESULTS. This framework consists of a seven-step process.

Step 1—Reason: Exploring the client's reasons for seeking out coaching is critical to anticipating the client's potential level of commitment. A client who self-selects for coaching may commit to the process more than one forced to receive coaching.

Step 2—Establish: Review the coaching agreement, set both the client's and coach's expectations for coaching, and identify the client's goals.

Step 3—Self-awareness: Use open-ended, narrative-inducing questions to facilitate the client's exploration of self.

Step 4—Understanding: Help the client explore their relationship to the environment by developing an enhanced understanding of self. Investigate the reciprocal effects between the client and their environment.

Step 5—Learning: Capitalize on the client's inherent resources and capacity to succeed.

Step 6—Time to reflect: Provide the client sufficient time to contemplate and explore what they have learned from coaching to facilitate their personal and professional growth.

Step 7—Success: No matter how big or small, the coach and client must celebrate the client's success. This builds momentum and positivity.

Professionals interested in learning more about the neuroscience version of the model may explore *The Five Levels of Focus* and *SCARF Model*.

Sources[229]

ROLFE'S REFLECTIVE LEARNING

Certification Available: no
Certification Required: no
Assessments: no
Proprietary: no
Client: individuals
Cost: not applicable
Category: reflection

Developed in 2001 by nursing professor Gary Rolfe, Rolfe's Reflective Learning provides a framework to facilitate reflection on past experiences with the intention of learning from them.

Rolfe's Reflective Learning segments the experiential learning process into three parts.

Part 1—What: The first part of Rolfe's reflective process involves the use of questions designed to facilitate the client's exploration of the event or experience. These questions should provide the client a conduit to examine important details like a description of the experience (i.e., what happened), the people involved, and an objective explanation of how each person (including the client) behaved.

Questions that explore the experience include the following:

- What happened?
- What was my role during the event/incident?
- What actions/behaviors did I take?
- What was I trying to achieve?
- What were the consequences of my actions?

Part 2—So what: The second part of Rolfe's framework uses questions designed to help the client learn from their experience. In this step, the client seeks to make meaning from the experience by gaining insight into their relationship with others, the organization, and the many cultures influencing everyone involved. Questions that facilitate this exploration include the following:

- What was I feeling during the experience?
- When did I become aware of my feelings?
- What knowledge might have helped me in this situation?
- What can I learn about myself from how I handled the situation?

Part 3—Now what: The final step in Rolfe's process involves the client's exploration of how they can apply the lessons learned from the experience to benefit them going forward. Questions that facilitate this exploration include the following:

- If confronted with a similar situation in the future, how would I like to respond?
- Knowing what I know now, how can I prepare myself for the next time this may happen?
- What do I need to remember so that I may respond to the situation the way I would like?

A popular application of Rolfe's Reflective Learning involves its use in reflective writing. The framework provided by Rolfe's model is useful for those who prefer journaling or storytelling as a means of reflection.

Rolfe's model, like *Driscoll's Reflection Cycle*, is based on *Borton's Model of Reflection*, which also uses the "what, so what, now what" approach. The similarity of these three models makes it difficult to distinguish between them. Much of the available literature appears to present these models in near identical fashion.

Professionals considering incorporating one of these frameworks into practice should explore all three of the above models. Each one presents a number of useful questions coaches may adopt to facilitate the client's reflection.

Professionals seeking additional information will find much written on this and similar frameworks, including Rolfe's 2001 book, *Critical Reflection for Nurses and the Helping Professions: A User's Guide*, co-authored by Melanie Jasper and Dawn Freshwater.

Sources[230]

RUMMLER-BRACHE METHODOLOGY

Certification Available: yes
Certification Required: recommended
Assessments: no
Proprietary: yes (Rummler-Brache Group)
Client: organizations
Cost: $4,495
Category: change (org.)

Developed in the 1980s by management systems theorist and organizational psychologists Geary Rummler and Alan Brache, the Rummler-Brache Methodology (RPM or BPM) is a constellation of concepts, tools, and frameworks designed to facilitate organization-wide process improvement.

The RPM framework allows professionals to analyze organizations, assess their business processes, and redesign and implement new improvements.

This multifaceted and complex methodology consists of two dimensions: the Three Levels of Performance and Performance Needs, which form the Performance Matrix.

Three Levels of Performance

Level 1—Organizational: a macro view of the organization, including the organization's relationship with the market, the major functions of the organization, strategies, goals, metrics, and deployment of resources.

Level 2—Process: how the organization accomplishes its mission, including an examination of all operational processes in use.

Level 3—Individual: the employees tasked with executing the many processes.

Performance Needs

• **Goals**: the alignment of standards and expectations for performance and achievement.

• **Design**: the thoughtful consideration of how goals interconnect and reinforce each other in furtherance of the organization's mission.

• **Management**: the practices that ensure goals are relevant and satisfied.

Performance Matrix

Combining the Three Levels of Performance and the Performance Needs results in the Performance Matrix, sometimes called the Nine Variables Model. This matrix identifies nine distinct but interconnected variables that can improve an organization's efficiency and effectiveness.

1. Organization-Goals
2. Organization-Design
3. Organization-Management
4. Process-Goals
5. Process-Design
6. Process-Management
7. Individual-Goals
8. Individual-Design
9. Individual-Management

RPM also uses a six-phase **Process Improvement Methodology** which provides a structured approach to analyzing and assessing an organization.

Phase 0: Performance improvement planning
Phase 1: Project definition
Phase 2: Is analysis and should design
Phase 3: Managing implementation and change
Phase 4: Process management
Phase 5: Managing the organization as an adaptive system

The Rummler-Brache Methodology is significantly more intricate and complex than presented here and includes a variety of tools, resources, and software designed to facilitate application of the model. Effectively using the methodology and its supporting resources requires training from the Rummler-Brache Group, a subsidiary of Pritchett LP.

Professionals seeking additional information on the Rummler-Brache Methodology may consider Rummler and Brache's 1990 book, *Improving Performance: How to Manage the White Space on the Organization Chart.*

Sources[231]

SCARF MODEL

Certification Available: yes
Certification Required: yes
Assessments: yes (SCARF Assessment)
Proprietary: yes (NeuroLeadership Institute)
Client: individuals
Cost: $4,100–$5,995
Category: self-awareness, confidence/resilience

Introduced in 2008 by neuroscientist Dr. David Rock, the SCARF Model provides a framework for understanding the complex relationship between the biology of the brain and its impact on human social behaviors.

Two assumptions underpin the SCARF Model. First, our natural tendency to minimize exposure to threats and maximize opportunities for reward governs our social behavior. Second, many of the neural networks used for basic survival needs (i.e., food and water) activate in our pursuit of rewards and avoidance of threats. Together, these principles suggest that many of our social behaviors result from primal reactions.

The SCARF Model identifies five domains that represent the human social experience. Through these domains, clients may explore their social relationships and develop an increased level of self-awareness.

Status: This is about a person's perceived relative importance to others and includes their place in the seniority or pecking order within a group. Though an individual's explicit achievements may enhance their status (i.e., rank and title), their perceptions and inferences may undermine their sense of status.

For example, a person receiving advice may perceive the feedback as critical of their performance, thus an indication of diminishing status. In response, they may treat this feedback as a threat and react accordingly.

Certainty: This pertains to the individual's need to predict the near-term future. A person's vulnerability in this domain varies in intensity from person to person. However, most people facing uncertainty experience some measure of anxiety and discomfort.

For example, employees who do not know what management expects of them may perceive the anxiety as an unbearable threat and act accordingly.

Autonomy: This is about a person's sense of control over their self and their environment. For many, this includes the availability of choices. When a person feels they have little or no choice, they may perceive their autonomy as threatened and act accordingly.

For example, individuals who highly value autonomy tend to experience the most visceral reaction when micromanaged.

Relatedness: This is a determination of who is "in" and who is "out" of a group. The natural tendency for human beings is to seek out "tribes" or groups we can associate with and belong to. When left unsatisfied, this can lead a person to feel alone.

For example, a person left out by a group can feel rejected, thus experiencing intense emotions which subsequently affect that person's behavior.

Fairness: This is a perception that seeks to classify exchanges between people and organizations as equitable and fair. When a person perceives an organization's behavior toward them as unfair, they may react to the organization as a threat.

For example, a person who believes a boss favors one or two employees over everyone else may develop the mindset that "the boss only listens to them." This may result in the individual classifying their boss and the favored employees as threats, which in turn will affect how they react to them.

The NeuroLeadership Institute (owned by Dr. David Rock) offers different certifications within the neuroscience coaching field. Professionals seeking additional information on the model may consider Dr. Rock's 2008 article, "SCARF: A Brain-Based Model for Collaborating with and Influencing Others."

Sources[232]

SCHEIDEL-CROWELL SPIRAL MODEL

Certification Available: no
Certification Required: no
Assessments: no
Proprietary: no
Client: groups
Cost: not applicable
Category: teaming, decision-making

Developed in the 1960s by communications researchers Thomas Scheidel and Laura Crowell, the Spiral Model provides a conceptual understanding of the generation and evolution of ideas within a group setting. Scheidel and Crowell's research focused heavily on the interpersonal communication between group members as they generated ideas and made decisions.

Scheidel and Crowell's research yielded several observations. In one, they noted that once a member of the group presented an idea, the collective would communicate about the idea as a means of exploring the option, adding to it, subtracting from it, or adjusting as the conversation progressed.

Researchers used this pattern to formulate coding for their study. The behaviors receiving specific coding included the introduction of an idea, the restatement of the idea, a clarification of the idea, adding to or subtracting from the idea, extensions of the idea, an agreement or disagreement with the idea, and others.

Using the above coding system, Scheidel and Crowell noted that approximately 25% of group discourse focused on the creative aspect of idea generation. These behaviors include creating the idea, modifying it, adding to it, subtracting from it, and synthesizing it to form an advanced idea.

The group spent another 25% of their discourse focused on clarifying and substantiating the idea. Evaluating the idea occupied another 25% of group conversation. Scheidel and Crowell did not characterize the remaining 25%. Some believe this is a result of behavior inconsequential to the study, while others suggest this may involve the discourse needed for group consolidation, a behavior they did not code.

In another observation, they noted that as groups generated ideas, the group would reject some of the less favorable ideas while selecting others for further development, but not necessarily in a linear fashion. In other words, the group might sideline good ideas as they explore other possible options, only to return to these good ideas later. They called this phenomenon Spiraling.

In this observation, the Spiral Model deviated from other models of the 1960s that presented group decision-making as a linear process. Scheidel and Crowell argued that group decision-making occurs in a circular and reciprocal process. Put another way, groups (teams) do not function in a purely efficient way, nor is their path from goal setting to goal achievement a direct one. They may go forward or backward at any time. They may also repeat past discourse or activities.

Readers will notice the Spiral Model does not include a formal structure or framework. The nonlinear and seemingly random processes groups follow during idea generation make it difficult to identify a set pattern.

Frequently compared to *Tuckman's Stages of Group Development*, the Spiral Model and Tuckman's work focus on two different aspects of group dynamics, making a direct comparison dubious. Scheidel and Crowell's model focuses on how groups develop their ideas, while Tuckman's examines how groups develop their social structure and task order.

Professionals seeking additional information on the Spiral Model will find limited information available. Much of the Spiral Model's utility has fallen within academic research; accordingly, most of the literature available derives from academic sources.

Sources[233]

SCHEIN'S CAREER ANCHORS

Certification Available: yes
Certification Required: no
Assessments: yes (Career Anchors Assessment)
Proprietary: no
Client: individuals
Cost: pricing not available
Category: values, employee engagement

Developed between the 1970s and 1980s by former MIT Sloan School of Management professor Edgar Schein, Career Anchors provides a framework for understanding an individual's perceptions and preferences for career selection. Because these preferences speak to an individual's core motivations, we include this in the category of values and employee engagement.

Schein's Career Anchors consists of eight constructs or themes that characterize an individual's career preferences. These preferences stem from a person's values, abilities, and motivations.

Technical/Functional preference: These are individuals who find value and satisfaction from developing and enhancing their expertise and skills in a specific area. Those with this preference enjoy the challenge of successfully completing stimulating tasks requiring skill.

Managerial preference: These individuals prefer to engage in high-level problem-solving, often from a position of elevated responsibility where they can leverage relationships to achieve success. They enjoy collaborating with individuals and prefer focusing on the strategic perspective more than the tactical.

Autonomy preference: These are individuals who prefer doing things their own way with minimal interference from others. They tend to push the boundaries of their organization's rules, which can make them ideal out-of-the-box thinkers.

Security/Stability preference: These individuals value stability and consistency in their work. They want to become comfortable with a role and be able to plan their life around this constant variable. If forced to transition jobs, they will seek professional opportunities that are most like their previous role.

Entrepreneurial preference: Unlike the Autonomy preference, individuals with an Entrepreneurial preference prefer to work alone. They enjoy brainstorming, creating something new, and innovating. Like those favoring a Managerial preference, they prefer to be in charge.

Service to a Cause preference: These are individuals driven to find ways to help people or have an impact on what they perceive as a greater good. They inherently seek out opportunities to make a difference in their community, often through public service or not-for-profits.

Pure Challenge preference: These are individuals motivated strictly by the experience of confronting and overcoming challenges. They relish tasks and problems that push their abilities and test them. Though like those with a Technical preference, individuals with a Pure Challenge preference derive their satisfaction from the task, not in the quality of their skill.

Lifestyle preference: These are individuals who favor jobs that can integrate into their whole life. This is not the same thing as work-life balance, rather it is about how the career fits into their way of living.

Schein's Career Anchors is a popular model for helping clients facing significant career changes or pivots. Schein's official assessment is available online from John Wiley & Sons. Clients may register online, take the assessment, and receive a multi-page report which explains the significance of the results. The assessment is also available in a booklet from Schein's website as well as third-party vendors. Professionals seeking to become a certified assessment administrator will find details on the Career Anchors website.

Though administering the formal assessment requires authorization, other assessments and exercises based on Schein's framework are freely available online. For additional information on this model, consider Schein's 2013 book, *Career Anchors* (4th Edition).

Sources[234]

SCHÖN'S MODEL OF REFLECTION

Certification Available: no
Certification Required: no
Assessments: no
Proprietary: no
Client: individuals
Cost: not applicable
Category: reflection

Developed in the 1980s by MIT professor Donald Schön, Schön's Model of Reflection provides a framework for reflection focusing on how an individual's implicit knowledge impacts their experience. Schön believed a person's intuition, which he viewed as tacit knowledge, plays a pivotal role in how a person behaves during the experience.

Schön's Model of Reflection consists of three components: Knowing in Action, Reflection in Action, and Reflection on Action. The distinction between Reflection in Action and Reflection on Action makes Schön's framework unique among models of reflection.

Knowing in Action: Commonly referred to as implicit or tacit knowledge, this pertains to the individual's intuitive ability to perform a task or handle a situation. Schön believed that reflecting on actions dependent on tacit knowledge can help an individual make this knowledge explicit, thus opening doors for growth and development.

For example, a person able to hold dynamic and engaging meetings without any forethought or prior planning likely possesses some implicit or intuitive knowledge that fosters this ability. Reflecting on the underlying knowledge may indicate (and make explicit) the behaviors contributing to their ability to hold successful meetings. Making the implicit explicit allows both the individual and others to benefit from the knowledge.

Reflection on Action: This involves an exploration of how tacit or intuitive abilities (knowing in action) may have contributed to the outcome of an experience. During this stage of reflection, the client considers possible changes for the future, which includes the use of counterfactual thinking. Put another way, the client thinks about how they might have handled the situation differently and how they might handle a similar situation in the future.

For example, a client is running a meeting and realizes that participants are not engaged. The client pushes through with the meeting and afterwards contemplates why participants seemed uninterested. The client considers various factors and realizes that his meetings typically involve him speaking to participants but not soliciting their feedback. Based on this, the client plans to adjust future meetings by asking participants for their opinion.

Reflection in Action: This is the component which makes Schön's framework unique among models of reflection. Schön believed it was important for individuals to reflect on an experience as it was unfolding. The oft-used expression, "recognizing the moment while you're in the moment," captures this concept.

One benefit of this is its ability to help a client make deliberate adjustments in response to the unexpected as it is happening instead of defaulting to inaction or reaction. Some refer to this component as "thinking on your feet."

For example, a client is running a meeting and notices that participants are not engaged. The client reflects in the moment by considering the possible factors at play and then adjusts his style to reengage participants by asking their opinion about the topic on the table.

Critics of Schön's model argue that reflecting in the moment may create overwhelming anxiety for some individuals and that the model itself lacks sufficient process to enable clients to understand how to conduct reflection. Despite these criticisms, Schön's model remains a prominent framework for reflection and an essential component of *Learning Organizations* based on his work with Harvard professor Chris Argyris.

Professionals seeking depth of knowledge on Schön's Model of Reflection may consider Schön's 1983 book, *The Reflective Practitioner: How Professionals Think in Action.*

Sources[235]

SCIENTIFIC MANAGEMENT THEORY

Certification Available: no
Certification Required: no
Assessments: no
Proprietary: no
Client: individuals
Cost: not applicable
Category: employee engagement, motivation

Developed in the early 1900s by management consultant Frederick Winslow Taylor, Scientific Management Theory is one of the first theories of management ever conceived. Taylor conducted numerous experiments to identify a better way to maximize employee efficiency and productivity. Also known as Taylorism and Taylor's Motivation Theory, his model would revolutionize management and influence future frameworks on employee engagement and management.

Scientific Management Theory consists of four guiding principles that facilitate more effective management and consequently a more efficient workforce.

Principle 1: Develop a science for each element of the work. During the 1900s, workers typically learned to perform tasks based on inconsistent on-the-job training, by observing others, and from guesswork. Taylor recommended deconstructing each task into its base elements or components. Using the scientific method, managers should determine the most effective and efficient way to execute each element of the task. This will allow managers to establish a process that is both effective and efficient which they may share with employees. Ultimately, this will ensure a consistent approach to task completion across the workforce.

Principle 2: Scientifically select, train, and develop each worker. Mindful of the knowledge, skills, and abilities needed to perform each task, managers should identify the best fit for the job by considering the capability and motivation of each candidate. Second, use science to train employees to perform the task. Explain concepts to ensure all employees possess a shared and consistent understanding. Finally, commit to employee development to ensure that those capable of performing multiple different tasks can do so when needed.

Principle 3: Cooperate with and observe workers so management may respond to inefficiencies and inconsistencies in worker performance as they arise.

Principle 4: Divide work responsibilities among employees. Delegating responsibilities among workers in a logical fashion so that no single worker bears responsibility for too much of the manufacturing process prevents burnout and fosters ownership.

Since its introduction, critics of Scientific Management Theory have questioned the validity of the theory. They cite several erroneous assumptions; among these, Taylor's belief that money is the sole and universal motivator for all workers. In fact, Scientific Management Theory ignores all other needs of the worker. Many argue his omission of intrinsic motivators is a serious flaw in his theory. Another assumption is Taylor's belief that every task has only one right way of completion. In this, Taylor rejected the idea that there might be many ways of accomplishing a task.

A primary oversight of Taylor's theory is that workers perform functions individually, not as a team. In fact, Taylorism rejects the idea of teamwork along with other holistic approaches to task accomplishment.

Despite these significant shortcomings, Taylor's theory is not without merit. After all, it was Taylor who first advocated use of the scientific method in the workplace specifically in hiring, training, and task performance. Taylor's work involved calculating the time it took to perform elements of each task, a function widely used today in project planning and project management.

Scientific Management Theory is more complex than presented here. Professionals interested in learning more may consider Taylor's 1911 book, *The Principles of Scientific Management*.

Sources[236]

SEEDS MODEL

Certification Available: no
Certification Required: no
Assessments: no
Proprietary: yes (NeuroLeadership Institute)
Client: individuals
Cost: not applicable
Category: bias, decision-making

Developed by Christine Cox, Heidi Grant Halvorson, Matthew D. Lieberman, and David Rock of the NeuroLeadership Institute, the SEEDS Model provides a framework for understanding and mitigating unconscious bias in decision-making.

The model amalgamates roughly 150 different types of cognitive bias into five general categories, with each category requiring a distinct approach to resolution.

Similarity bias: This a preferential bias for those we determine to be like us, or a prejudicial bias against those we determine to be different from us. Biases within this category typically stem from "in-group" and "out-group" perceptions (see *Social Identity Theory*). Similarity Bias commonly manifests in decisions involving selection, hiring, recruiting, and promotion.

Expedience bias: This form of cognitive bias can stem from a desire to alleviate the discomfort associated with an unknown (or uncertainty) or a need to find resolution in a timely manner. Often, this results in a dependence on heuristics, a set of mental shortcuts that facilitate rapid decision-making (see *Dual Process Theory*). Expedience bias commonly manifests in decisions involving judgments about people. In other words, we tend to fill gaps in our knowledge about people with assumptions, often mistaking these assumptions for facts.

Experience bias: This form of cognitive bias stems from the belief that our perceptions of the world are synonymous with reality. Put another way, it is the belief that our understanding of the world around us is accurate, and we may fail to consider that others possess different perceptions. This bias often manifests in decisions we make about how the social world works.

Distance bias: This form of bias involves the physical and temporal proximity of a person, things, or issue to us. The expression "out of sight, out of mind" captures this bias. When a person or object is closer to us, we tend to hold a preferential bias for that person or object. This bias often manifests in decisions that require us to seek input from others, leaving us to sometimes omit input from those not conveniently situated close to us.

Safety bias: This form of cognitive bias suggests that motivation stemming from a fear of loss outweighs motivation derived from the benefit of gaining something. Put another way, losing a good thing feels worse than finding a good thing feels good. This bias manifests often in high-risk decisions.

The SEEDS Model provides a three-step process to facilitate mitigation of these biases.

Step 1—Accept: Bias is a natural part of the human condition. Because we want to see ourselves in a positive light, we may reject the idea that we have bias. The first step in this process is acknowledging that bias is a natural biological function applicable to all humans. In some cases, we may possess some awareness of our biases and in others we may remain completely unaware.

Step 2—Label: Using the five forms of bias presented by the SEEDS Model, identify which bias is presently manifesting. Labeling the bias based on its characteristics allows a person to better determine how to overcome the bias.

Step 3—Mitigate: Once the bias is labeled, select the measures appropriate for the specific bias at play. Depending on the bias, this may include seeking insight from third parties, buying time to fully process thoughts and feelings, or adopting another position on the issue or topic.

Professionals seeking additional information may consider Cox, Halvorson, Lieberman, and Rock's 2015 article, "Breaking Bias Updated: The SEEDS Model," featured in the *NeuroLeadership Journal*.

Sources[237]

SELF-DETERMINATION THEORY

Certification Available: no
Certification Required: no
Assessments: yes (GCOS, IMI, IAF, others)
Proprietary: no
Client: individuals, groups
Cost: not applicable
Category: motivation, engagement, resilience

Developed in the early 1980s by psychologists Edward Deci and Richard Ryan, Self-Determination Theory (SDT) provides an expansive framework to facilitate an exploration of human motivation and individual self-determination.

SDT suggests three innate universal psychological needs motivate all human beings.

• Need for competence: When an individual believes they possess a sufficient mastery of skills, they are more likely to strive for goals.

• Need for relatedness (connection): Individuals inherently need to experience a sense of belonging or connection to others.

• Need for autonomy: Individuals need to feel in control of their own behaviors, goals, and destiny. This need provides a sense of ownership, which is critical to individual self-determination.

SDT classifies motivation into three distinct forms. The theory suggests that each form of motivation is a continuum, with individuals regularly moving along the continuum.

• Intrinsic form: This refers to motivations that provide internal enjoyment or benefit to the individual.

• Extrinsic form: This refers to motivations that provide an external benefit or reward. This form of motivation typically involves a measure of societal influence.

• Amotivation form: This refers to a general lack of either intrinsic or extrinsic motivation. Amotivated individuals have little to no drive and often struggle to satisfy any of their needs.

Studies in Self-Determination Theory indicate that providing an extrinsic reward for acts that are inherently intrinsic may lower an individual's self-determination and undermine their motivation overall, a phenomenon known as the **Overjustification Effect**. For this reason, SDT advocates the use of intrinsic rewards over extrinsic as much as possible.

According to the Center for Self-Determination Theory, six mini-theories form the foundation for SDT. See *Self-Determination Theory: Mini-theories* for more information.

1—Cognitive Evaluation Theory (CET)
2—Organismic Integration Theory (OIT)
3—Causality Orientations Theory (COT)
4—Basic Psychological Needs Theory (BPNT)
5—Goal Contents Theory (GCT)
6—Relationships Motivation Theory (RMT)

SDT research suggests that helping clients improve their self-determination requires a client to establish a greater sense of control or ownership in their life choices and decisions. Because of this, SDT is highly useful in leadership, life, happiness, and performance coaching. SDT also provides utility when discussing employee engagement.

As with many models, SDT works well when integrated with other frameworks. For example, there is research to suggest that self-determination improves with increased self-awareness and self-regulation, two major components of emotional intelligence. Therefore, it makes sense that when working with a client on improving self-determination, one might consider incorporating techniques and tools from *Emotional Intelligence* in their coaching effort.

Self-Determination Theory includes several informal assessments and tools. Professionals seeking additional information will find much written on the theory, including Deci and Ryan's 1985 book *Intrinsic Motivation and Self-Determination in Human Behavior*.

Sources[238]

SELF-DETERMINATION THEORY: MINI-THEORIES

> **Category:** motivation, engagement, resilience

Self-Determination Theory (SDT), created in the 1980s by psychologists Edward Deci and Richard Ryan, provides a framework for exploring human motivation and the individual's capacity for self-determination. The underlying foundation of Self-Determination Theory consists of six subtheories, also called mini-theories. The combination of these mini-theories adds depth to the SDT framework and facilitates its use as a resource for coaching.

Theory 1—Cognitive Evaluation Theory (CET): This subtheory focuses on the effect of social contexts on intrinsic motivations (e.g., how external consequences affect internal motivation). CET highlights the risk of using extrinsic rewards with intrinsic acts; the result is an overall decreased sense of motivation, a phenomenon known as the Overjustification Effect or Motivational Crowding Theory. CET is more complex than presented here and requires further exploration prior to adoption into practice.

Theory 2—Organismic Integration Theory (OIT): This subtheory focuses on extrinsic motivations and how individuals internalize these motivations by making intrinsic associations. Put another way, the more internalized a person's extrinsic motivations, the more autonomous a person's behavior. The "value" an individual ascribes to the performance of an activity affects how they execute that activity. OIT is more complex than presented here and includes descriptions of four types of extrinsic motivations at differing levels of autonomy.

Theory 3—Causality Orientations Theory (COT): This subtheory seeks to explain individual differences in how people orient to their environment and regulate their behaviors in response to their environment. COT identifies three types of causality orientations.

- Autonomy: person acts out of an interest in what is happening.

- Control: person acts for rewards, gains, or approval.

- Impersonal or Amotivated: person acts because of anxiety over competence.

Causality Orientations Theory suggests people have a certain amount of each orientation.

Theory 4—Basic Psychological Needs Theory (BPNT): This subtheory introduces the three universal psychological needs to SDT (Competence, Relatedness, Autonomy). BPNT argues that all three needs are essential, and failure to meet any one need will result in functional consequences.

Theory 5—Goal Contents Theory (GCT): This subtheory introduces the distinction between intrinsic motivations (e.g., community, family, personal growth) and extrinsic motivations (e.g., money, appearance, fame). GCT research suggests extrinsic motivations are associated with decreased wellness and diminished well-being.

Theory 6—Relationships Motivation Theory (RMT): This subtheory focuses on the Relatedness need from BPNT Theory and explores how a person's relationships and the groups they belong to influence or affect their motivation. Studies in RMT indicate that not only do relationships satisfy the relatedness need but they also impact the autonomy and competence needs. RMT further suggests that the highest quality relationships are the ones in which each partner supports the relatedness, competence, and autonomy needs of the other.

Practical use of Self-Determination Theory requires a deep understanding of the six subtheories. These provide useful constructs for clients struggling to find the motivation for change or experiencing challenges making change last. SDT and its foundational subtheories offer utility for clients exploring the issue of employee engagement and employee motivation.

Professionals seeking additional information may consider Deci and Ryan's 2016 book, *Self-Determination Theory: Basic Psychological Needs in Motivation, Development, and Wellness.*

Sources[239]

SELF-EFFICACY THEORY

Certification Available: no
Certification Required: no
Assessments: yes (SES, SSES, TSES)
Proprietary: no
Client: individuals
Cost: not applicable
Category: resilience, self-awareness, stress mgt.

Developed in 1977 by psychologist Albert Bandura, Self-Efficacy Theory (SET) provides a framework for exploring the relationship between a person's perceived ability to face and overcome obstacles and their actual ability to do the same.

Self-Efficacy Theory suggests that a person's sense of efficacy influences how they manage the stress and anxiety that comes from challenges. The higher the individual's self-efficacy, the greater their ability to work through challenges and obstacles on their own terms.

Self-Efficacy Theory consists of two key determinants of behavior. These form the construct of an individual's perceived abilities.

Self-efficacy: This component applies to the individual's belief in their capability to execute the behaviors necessary to achieve their desired goals. Put another way, does the individual believe they possess the skills and abilities needed to succeed in life?

Outcome expectancy: This component pertains to the individual's perceptions surrounding the positive and negative consequences of performing the behavior. This perception hinges on the individual's belief that a specific action will result in a specific outcome.

An individual derives their sense of self-efficacy from four sources. The role of specific sources varies from person to person. In effect, the four sources act as spectra, the combination of which influences a person's sense of self-efficacy.

Mastery experiences: This refers to the experiences gained from practicing and performing. Through the successes and failures of these experiences, people learn what they are capable of accomplishing.

Vicarious experiences: This is learning by observing others, like role models. Watching other people who possess a healthy sense of self-efficacy can impart some of those positive beliefs to an individual.

Verbal persuasion: This refers to the impact words can have on a person's sense of self. Individuals receiving positive verbal affirmations feel motivated to strive and often believe they can achieve (self-efficacy). Further research indicates verbal persuasion applies to self-talk (e.g., how we talk to ourselves).

Emotional and psychological states: This refers to the general health and well-being of the whole person. The presence of anxiety or depression can have a profound effect on a person's sense of self-efficacy. Individuals struggling with an emotional or psychological challenge may need to consider therapy as these issues typically exceed the boundaries of coaching.

Other variations of SET provide a fifth potential source of self-efficacy, **Imaginal experience**. This pertains to the individual's ability to imagine or envision future successes.

Self-Efficacy Theory is a subtheory of Bandura's larger construct, *Social Cognitive Theory*, which explains how people regulate their behavior to achieve and maintain desired goals.

SET is very useful when working with clients who struggle with issues of self-confidence, resilience, fear of change, and stress management.

Widely used in both clinical and coaching settings, Self-Efficacy Theory has broad utility across industries including education, health care, entrepreneurship, and performance coaching, as well as working with individuals with special needs.

Professionals seeking additional information may consider Bandura's 1997 book, *Self-Efficacy: The Exercise of Control.*

Sources[240]

SELF-PERCEPTION THEORY

Certification Available: no
Certification Required: no
Assessments: no
Proprietary: no
Client: individuals
Cost: not applicable
Category: polarities, self-awareness

Developed in the late 1960s by social psychologist Daryl Bem, Self-Perception Theory (SPT) seeks to explain how people form attitudes about the world around them by examining the relationship between thoughts/beliefs and behavior.

Two key assumptions form the core of Self-Perception Theory. The first is that people develop an awareness of their thoughts, beliefs, and attitudes by observing their own behavior and the circumstances surrounding their behavior. Second, when internal cues to a person's thoughts, beliefs, and attitudes are weak, that person is in the same position as when they are observing and judging others by their behavior.

Self-Perception Theory suggests that a person's attitudes are based on inferences they make of their own behavior. Put another way, we determine what our attitudes are about something based on how we behave toward that thing.

For example, a close friend may share some exceptionally good news, but for some reason we might find ourselves becoming tense, agitated, and flush. We might avoid them at a social event that night. By observing our reactions, we might consider that our behavior is the result of feeling jealous about our friend's good fortune.

Self-Perception Theory–based research suggests that a person's behavior can influence their attitude about something. In one study, participants smiled at themselves in a mirror for a time before reading a comic strip. Those who smiled prior to reading the cartoon (behavior) reported finding the comic more humorous (attitude) than those who did not smile in the mirror.

In another example, multiple studies have shown that when one person smiles frequently at another person, this can lead the smiler to feel more positively about the person they smile at. In professions like sales, marketing, law enforcement, and others, smiling is a technique used to both build rapport with someone and increase the presence of genuinely positive sentiment between parties.

Some sources present Self-Perception Theory as an alternative to the popular *Cognitive Dissonance Theory (CDT)*, which states that people inherently seek consistency between their thoughts, feelings, and behaviors. But others argue that SPT complements cognitive dissonance. Where CDT explains how people may change their attitudes when a conflict between beliefs arises, SPT explains how a person forms their initial attitude in the first place.

We include Self-Perception Theory in the category of self-awareness because it speaks to a person's ability to make observations of their own behavior, attribute the behavior to some thought, feeling, or belief, and form an understanding of the overall attitude that influenced the behavior.

We also include SPT in the category of polarities because clients exploring competing priorities must consider their thoughts, feelings, and beliefs about the issues creating conflict for them. SPT can provide clients with a perspective to consider when exploring their attitudes about competing issues of importance.

Professionals will find Self-Perception Theory shares a connection with other theories and techniques commonly encountered in coaching. For example, when engaging in behavioral change efforts, a coach may encourage a client to initially seek out small incremental changes. Some call this the Foot in the Door Technique. By performing a single small behavior, a client may reflect on that behavior and discover an existing, albeit subconscious, positive attitude that will increase their chances for engaging in larger, more meaningful behaviors in the future.

Professionals seeking additional information may consider Bem's 1972 article, "Self-Perception Theory," featured in *Advances in Experimental Social Psychology*.

Sources[241]

SERVANT LEADERSHIP THEORY

> **Certification Available:** no
> **Certification Required:** no
> **Assessments:** no
> **Proprietary:** no
> **Client:** individuals, organizations
> **Cost:** not applicable
> **Category:** leadership

Introduced in the 1970s by leadership theorist Robert K. Greenleaf, Servant Leadership Theory (SLT) describes a style of leadership in which the leader is fundamentally a servant first—a servant to those who follow and a servant to a greater purpose or mission. SLT suggests that before a person experiences the desire to lead, there first exists a desire to serve.

Since its introduction, many theorists have built upon Greenleaf's work. This led to the identification of ten characteristics or attributes of effective servant leaders.

Listening: Servant leaders use listening as a tool for demonstrating respect for others and as the first step in including others in problem-solving.

Empathy: Servant leaders accept people for who they are; they maintain an open mind and use empathy to understand people and their differences instead of rejecting them.

Healing: Servant leaders strive to understand and make whole each person they serve. This includes understanding the equality and equity needs of each person.

Awareness: Servant leaders possess an awareness of their own values and an understanding of how their values impact those who follow them.

Persuasion: Servant leaders use subtle influence, not position power or authority, to guide and build consensus among those they serve.

Conceptualization: Servant leaders create an inspirational vision for the future that others can embrace and achieve.

Foresight: Servant leaders can anticipate problems lurking over the horizon.

Stewardship: Servant leaders establish a positive relationship between those they serve (their followers), their organization, and society.

Commitment to growth of people: Servant leaders strive to uplift those they serve so they may be "taller than they would be otherwise."

Building community: Servant leaders provide opportunities for those they serve to connect in meaningful ways across the organization. They build a sense of community and belonging for all.

Servant Leadership Theory describes the behavioral pattern of a leader who prioritizes the well-being of employees above all else. This philosophy manifests in the expression "leaders take care of their people; in turn, their people take care of the mission."

Since its introduction in the 1970s, SLT has continued to grow in popularity. Many Fortune 500 companies and leadership coaches tout Servant Leadership Theory as one of the best approaches to leadership alongside *Transformational Leadership Theory*, *Relational Leadership Theory*, and the *Full Range Leadership Model*.

As with many theories, critics question the efficacy of SLT, citing a lack of empirical evidence. This is because much of the available literature on Servant Leadership Theory presents evidence limited to anecdotal observations. Some urge caution when touting SLT, as it requires a level of authenticity that can be difficult for some to achieve, and in many cases, developing a servant leadership style requires a significant amount of time and commitment.

Professionals seeking additional information on Servant Leadership Theory will find much written on the topic, including Greenleaf's 1971 book, *The Servant as Leader*.

Sources[242]

SEVEN TRANSFORMATIONS OF LEADERSHIP

Certification Available: yes
Certification Required: yes
Assessments: yes (GLP)
Proprietary: yes (Global Leadership Associates)
Client: individuals
Cost: $3,100
Category: leadership

Introduced in 2005 by leadership consultant David Rooke and management professor William R. Torbert, the Seven Transformations of Leadership provides a framework for exploring the stages of an individual's leadership development. A person may transition across levels based on the situation.

Also known as Torbert's Action Logics, the theory consists of seven levels, or action logics, in ascending order from the lowest (least effective) to highest (most effective). Each stage has its unique strengths, and professionals should avoid using labels like "good" or "bad" when describing the stages. Research into the seven levels provides an estimate of the percentage of the population represented by each level, reflected in parentheses.

Level 1—Opportunist (5%): These leaders are self-serving and highly manipulative. Often described as hostile and deceptive, they are frequently vindictive.

Level 2—Diplomat (12%): These leaders are conflict avoidant and seek to integrate with the status quo. Described as not wanting to rock the boat, they are loyal but status conscious.

Level 3—Expert (38%): These leaders desire accuracy of knowledge and value a perfect performance. Described as critical and dogmatic, they relish problem-solving.

Level 4—Achiever (30%): These leaders are results driven. Described as dedicated to the mission or objective, they hold themselves and others to high standards.

Level 5—Redefining (10%): Formerly known as Individualists, these leaders see a bigger picture, allowing them to identify and resolve gaps in the organization's structure. Described as collaborative, they embrace change.

Level 6—Transforming (4%): Formerly known as the Strategist, these leaders possess the courage to be vulnerable. Described as highly aware of self and others, they often recognize opportunities others miss.

Level 7—Alchemical (1%): Formerly known as the Alchemist, these leaders possess the ability to put themselves aside and see multiple perspectives. They build and manage complex relationships and are capable of linear and associative thought. They can lead society-wide transformation efforts.

Unlike other theories of leadership that focus on factors like traits, personalities, or behavior, the Seven Transformations concentrates on action logics. In other words, the theory explores leadership based on how leaders make meaning of themselves, the world around them, and their relationships.

Since its introduction in 2005, the theory has undergone several modifications, which included changes to some of the labels. This is important, as professionals may encounter both the original and current versions of the framework.

To facilitate the use of the Seven Transformations, Torbert developed an assessment called the Global Leadership Profile (GLP), formerly known as the Leadership Development Profile (LDP).

Critics of the Seven Transformations question the efficacy of the model, as they do many of the leadership theories contained in the ICMT. They argue against the linear nature of the framework, suggesting leaders do not need to transition through each level to become Alchemical.

Professionals seeking additional information may consider Rooke and Torbert's 2005 *Harvard Business Review* article, "Seven Transformations of Leadership." Formal certification in the model and its associated assessment is available from Torbert's company, Global Leadership Associates.

Sources[243]

SIMPLEXITY

Certification Available: yes
Certification Required: no
Assessments: yes (CPSP)
Proprietary: no
Client: individuals, groups, teams
Cost: $495–$3,995
Category: problem-solving, change (org.)

ntroduced in 1981 by organizational psychologist Marino "Min" Sidney Basadur, Simplexity provides a framework for problem-solving and innovation. The Simplexity framework consists of eight steps which occur over three phases. Though presented here as a linear process, the framework is iterative. This means the process repeats until the user fully solves the problem.

Phase 1: Problem Formulation

Step 1—Problem finding: Identify existing problems and opportunities or those looming on the horizon. This proactive step includes a combination of analytical processes like a needs assessment or customer feedback analysis to help define the issues.

Step 2—Fact finding: This involves a methodical examination of the identified problem, which requires collecting all relevant data and information about the problem. It is critical that problem-solvers consider multiple diverse perspectives to ensure a holistic picture. Useful sources of information include survey results, formal feedback, and interviews.

Step 3—Problem definition: This involves an analysis of the data collected during step 2 and seeks to pinpoint the root source of the problem and distinguish cause from effect. This

distinction ensures the process focuses on the root cause of the problem and not the symptoms that result from the problem.

Phase 2: Solution Formulation

Step 4—Idea finding: This involves the formulation of multiple ideas and potential solutions using techniques like brainstorming. It is critical that problem-solvers avoid preemptive judgment or criticism when generating ideas.

Step 5—Evaluation and selection: This involves the use of techniques designed to evaluate and prioritize options. Exploring the merits and risks of each option allows problem-solvers to select the option they believe will yield the desired results.

Phase 3: Solution Implementation

Step 6—Action planning: This involves an exploration of the selected option so problem-solvers may identify the specific tasks or actions required to implement the option successfully. Problem-solvers should be as methodical as possible during this step.

Step 7—Gaining acceptance: Implementing any solution to a problem inherently requires change. Therefore, problem-solvers should consider the best way to build and maintain support for the changes to come. This exploration should include social factors like organizational culture, stakeholder motivation, and employee sentiment to ensure buy-in.

Step 8—Action taking: The final step involves executing the actions identified in steps 6 and 7. According to the framework, upon completing step 8, problem-solvers return to step 1 to continue refining the problem and its solution.

Simplexity, also known as the Simplex Process Model, Simplex Creative Problem-Solving, and the Simplexity Thinking System is more complex than shown here. The framework includes an assessment, the Basadur Creative Problem-Solving Profile Inventory (CPSP), which explores how members of a team prefer to think during the process of innovation.

Professionals seeking additional information may consider Dr. Basadur's 1995 book, *The Power of Innovation*. Formal training and certification in Simplexity are available from multiple vendors, including Dr. Basadur's firm, Basadur Applied Innovation. Professionals interested in certification should further explore all options, as vendors offer different levels of certification at different price points.

Sources[244]

SIROTA'S THREE-FACTOR THEORY

Certification Available: no
Certification Required: no
Assessments: no
Proprietary: no
Client: individuals, groups, teams
Cost: not applicable
Category: employee engagement, motivation

Developed in 2005 by social psychologist David Sirota, the Three-Factor Theory provides a framework for understanding how companies can foster employee motivation. Also known as the ACE Model, Sirota's framework consists of three factors and multiple elements to explain the nuances of employee motivation.

Sirota's Three-Factor Theory derives from millions of surveys, from which he identified three factors shared among all motivated and enthusiastic employees.

Factor One—Equity/Fairness: Sirota discovered that most employees possess the expectation that their organization will treat them equally and fairly, both compared to one another and to the bigger picture of basic human values. Sirota identified three elements critical to an employee's perception of equity and fairness.

• **Physiological**: Employees should have a sense of safety at work. This requires the use of safety protocols, the presence of a comfortable work environment, and a workload that does not damage the health or well-being of the employee.

• **Economic**: Organizations should compensate employees and provide benefits that are market competitive and anticipatory of inflation. Additional forms of remuneration include the use of meaningful bonuses and the presence of job security.

• **Psychological**: Employees want to feel respected by the organization. They want a management structure that

is both credible and consistent (i.e., not a rotating door of leaders every few months). They also desire flexibility and understanding in the form of reasonable accommodation for special needs (i.e., family emergencies).

Factor Two—Achievement: Employees want to feel a sense of accomplishment from both their individual work and the collective work stemming from the organization's mission. Six elements comprise achievement.

• **Challenge level**: The difficulty of the work should sufficiently challenge employees without being impossible.

• **New skills**: Employees should have every opportunity to acquire new skills and seek professional development.

• **Ability to perform**: Employees require empowerment and support to perform their tasks.

• **Perceived importance**: Employees need to see the value of their contributions to the organization's mission.

• **Recognition**: Employees must receive acknowledgment for their performance.

• **Company pride**: Employees must possess a sense of pride in the organization's mission.

Factor Three—Camaraderie: Drawing from the basic human need for belonging, most employees want to feel like their organization is a community that accepts them. A single element influences this factor.

• **Culture of acceptance**: An organization's culture should strive for the inclusion of all members and an openness to empower individual voices. Doing this creates a sense of teaming which is essential to a strong and accepting culture.

In 2013, Sirota's Dynamic Alignment Model emerged from his Three-Factor Theory. Professionals seeking additional information will find much written about the Three-Factor Theory, including Sirota's 2005 book, *The Enthusiastic Employee: How Companies Profit by Giving Workers What They Want.*

Sources[245]

SITUATION, BEHAVIOR, IMPACT MODEL

Certification Available: no
Certification Required: no
Assessments: no
Proprietary: yes (CCL)
Client: individuals
Cost: not applicable
Category: feedback

Created by the Center for Creative Leadership (CCL), the Situation, Behavior, Impact Model (SBI) provides a simple framework to help leaders provide relevant and meaningful feedback. The model consists of three steps which guide users to provide both negative and positive feedback.

Step 1—Situation: Describe, in specific terms, where the observed behavior occurred. Include the specific date and time, if possible, and any other details that describe the situation. During this step, it is important to avoid passing judgment or making attributions.

Step 2—Behavior: Describe the behavior, focusing on what you observed and not your perceptions or opinions of why the behavior occurred. As in step 1, avoid passing judgments.

Step 3—Impact: Describe how the observed behavior made you feel or influenced your thinking. It is important to avoid judgment or risk shutting down the recipient. For example:

Feedback with judgment: "When you cut me off at the meeting, that was rude and arrogant."

Feedback using SBI: "At this morning's meeting, I was trying to make a point when you interrupted me, changing the subject before I could share my point of view. That made me feel frustrated and unappreciated."

After its initial development, the Center for Creative Leadership refined the SBI model by adding a fourth step, Intent. This led to the expanded SBII version.

Step 4—Intent: Ask the recipient about the intention behind the observed behavior. This transforms a one-way feedback session into a two-way conversation, allowing the recipient an opportunity to share their perspective, which may provide new information or insight for the provider and may lead to a more desirable outcome. For example:

Feedback using SBII: "At this morning's meeting, I was trying to make a point when you interrupted me, changing the subject before I could share my point of view. That made me feel frustrated and unappreciated. Can you help me understand what happened?"

An example of how the SBII approach may provide insight that changes the way the provider sees this experience: "I'm sorry about that. I got the sense the boss was becoming agitated about the state of this project and was looking to jump on anyone who didn't see it the way he did, and I didn't want you to step on that land mine."

The two-way conversational nature of the SBII Model requires the provider to be emotionally prepared for the recipient's possible responses. Just because SBII invites the recipient to respond does not mean they will provide a logical or rational explanation for their behavior. SBII discourse may reveal deeper issues, and if the provider is unprepared to handle them, they could lead to less desirable outcomes.

The SBI and SBII Models are among many similar feedback models included in *The Infourge Compendium of Models and Theories*, like *BEEF, BIFF, BOOST, COIN,* and many others. Due to the similarities between these feedback models, professionals should explore each framework thoroughly prior to adoption. One difference between SBII and other feedback models is its emphasis on the recipient's intentions over the impact of their behavior.

There is no certification in the SBI or SBII Model; however, the Center for Creative Leadership integrates these frameworks into larger training programs like their Better Conversations and Coaching Level 1 Program.

Professionals seeking additional information will find literature on the SBI and SBII Models freely available online. See the sources section for this entry for recommended articles.

Sources[246]

SITUATIONAL LEADERSHIP THEORY

Certification Available: yes
Certification Required: yes
Assessments: no
Proprietary: yes
Client: individuals
Cost: pricing not available
Category: leadership

Developed in 1969 by behavioral scientist Dr. Paul Hersey and business consultant Ken Blanchard, Situational Leadership Theory (SLT) argues against the idea that there is a single universally effective leadership style. Breaking from traditional leadership theories of its time, Situational Leadership Theory suggests that the most effective leadership approach depends on the situation. Also known as the Hersey-Blanchard Model, SLT falls under the umbrella of *Contingency Theories* of leadership.

According to SLT, several variables can affect which style of leadership is most appropriate for a given situation. Among the most influential variables are the characteristics and traits of those who might follow a prospective leader, specifically their readiness and willingness to perform the task, face the challenge, or achieve the mission. Consequently, leaders need to adapt their leadership style based on the needs of followers.

In 1979, Blanchard and Hersey went separate ways, resulting in the creation of two versions of Situational Leadership Theory. Hersey retained the original version, now called Situational Leadership, which is proprietary to the Center for Leadership Studies. Blanchard's version, simply called SLII, is proprietary to The Ken Blanchard Company.

Both models provide a framework consisting of four distinct styles of leadership which characterize the behaviors of leaders. Though the models are fundamentally similar, users will notice differences in the labels used to describe the four styles. These four behaviors also share similarities with other models like the *Tannenbaum-Schmidt Leadership Continuum Model*.

- The four leadership styles according to Hersey's Situational Leadership: **Delegating**, **Participating**, **Selling**, **Telling**.

- The four leadership styles according to Blanchard's SLII: **Delegating**, **Supporting**, **Coaching**, **Directing**.

Both models include an additional framework useful for exploring the characteristics of followers. This enables leaders to develop an enhanced understanding of those who follow them.

- The followership framework for Hersey's Situational Leadership: **Performance Readiness** (4 levels)

- The followership framework for Blanchard's SLII: **Development** (4 levels)

SLT is useful because of its emphasis on followers. It offers both coach and client a lens through which to examine and consider the perspective of those who follow the client. Developing awareness of the follower's unique combination of needs may allow the client to enhance their ability to consider other points of view and adapt their leadership style accordingly.

Though similar, there are philosophical differences between the two versions, and readers will need to examine both to determine which is appropriate for their practice. Formal use of Situational Leadership and SLII requires training and certification.

Both sets of frameworks are significantly more complex than presented here. Professionals seeking additional information on Situational Leadership or SLII will find much written on these models, including Hersey and Blanchard's 1969 book on the original SLT: *Management of Organizational Behavior: Leading Human Resources*.

For those seeking more information on Situational Leadership, consider Hersey's 1984 book: *The Situational Leader*.

For those seeking more information on SLII, consider Blanchard's 1985 book: *Leadership and the One-Minute Manager*.

Sources[247]

SIX PRINCIPLES OF INFLUENCE

Certification Available: yes
Certification Required: yes
Assessments: no
Proprietary: yes
Client: individuals, groups
Cost: pricing not available
Category: influence

Introduced in the early 1980s by psychologist Robert Cialdini, the Six Principles of Influence provides a framework for understanding how to more effectively influence or persuade others.

The six principles of Cialdini's framework can help clients improve their relationships at work, enhance their effectiveness at obtaining cooperation, and allow them to establish rapport more efficiently with others.

Principle 1—Reciprocity: Sometimes articulated as "give a little to get a little," this principle suggests that when people receive something (e.g., a gift, a service, a gesture), they experience a sense of obligation to return the favor.

To make the principle of reciprocity even more effective, it helps if what is given is both personal and unexpected. Professional interviewers may use this principle with interviewees having trouble sharing details about their personal life. For example, the interviewer may volunteer that they have two kids who love to play soccer. This may entice the interviewee to share some detail about their personal life outside of work.

Principle 2—Scarcity: This principle, a fundamental component of microeconomics, simply states that the less available something is, the more people want it. Leveraging scarcity to influence others often involves bringing attention to the rarity of an opportunity.

Principle 3—Authority: This principle suggests people perceived as credible or knowledgeable experts can more easily influence others. Leveraging authority might include establishing bona fides through a display of diplomas on a wall or the use of many abbreviations after one's name.

Principle 4—Consistency: This principle is based on the natural tendency for people to maintain consistency of thought and behavior (see *Consistency Theories*). Leveraging consistency can involve linking a person's values to the behavior you want to see from them so that their new behavior reinforces their values (i.e., consistency of behavior).

Principle 5—Liking: This principle suggests a person will respond more positively to a person they like than one they do not. Leveraging the liking principle may involve finding something you have in common to facilitate rapport.

Principle 6—Social proof: Also called Consensus, this principle suggests we have a natural tendency to look to others when determining how to behave. Leveraging social proof often involves group norms and behaviors.

Recently, Cialdini revised his framework to include another principle. Professionals may encounter the newer model, Seven Principles of Influence, when collaborating with other coaches and clients.

Principle 7—Unity: This principle is an expansion of the liking principle and involves the shared identity between two people. Leveraging unity involves understanding a person's need for belonging (see *Maslow's Hierarchy of Needs*).

Cialdini's framework, along with models like *Nudge Theory*, are popular among marketing and advertising professionals. The model has utility with clients trying to find their voice, increase their influence in team meetings, or build rapport with colleagues. For leadership-level clients, Cialdini's framework can serve as a lens to explore leadership behaviors intended to influence and inspire employees.

Professionals seeking additional information on the Six Principles may consider Cialdini's 1984 book, *Influence: The Psychology of Persuasion,* and his 2016 book, *Pre-Suasion: A Revolutionary Way to Influence and Persuade.* For those seeking formal certification, Cialdini offers training through his company, Influence at Work, and their Principles of Persuasion workshops.

Sources[248]

SMART MODEL FOR GOAL SETTING

Certification Available: no
Certification Required: no
Assessments: no
Proprietary: no
Client: individuals, groups, teams
Cost: not applicable
Category: goal setting

Developed in the early 1980s by George T. Doran, Arthur Miller, and James Cunningham, the SMART Model for Goal Setting provides a framework for developing meaningful goals to help individuals achieve a desired outcome. The model, further popularized by Robert S. Rubin and Peter Drucker, enjoys widespread use today.

The SMART Model consists of five steps designed to help individuals explore, identify, and define goals.

Step 1—Specific: Effective goals and objectives should contain sufficient specificity to eliminate the risk of misunderstandings or misinterpretations. An ambiguous goal may lead stakeholders to unintentionally move toward different outcomes or inadvertently undermine each other.

Effective goals must possess clarity and define what the desired end state looks like, who will play a role in achieving the goal and how, why the goal is important, and where the pursuit of the goal will take place.

Step 2—Measurable: Effective goals and objectives must include measurable elements so the individual may track their progress and recognize key milestones. Considerations during this step include explicit tangible metrics like how much, how many, or other observable and measurable metrics. A common coaching question to facilitate this step is "How will you know if you are successful?"

Step 3—Achievable: An effective goal or objective must be realistic. Considerations during this step include how the individual will achieve the goal and what steps they will take to succeed. If the individual struggles to answer this question, then it may indicate the goal is not achievable.

Step 4—Relevant: Effective goals and objectives must be meaningful to the client. During this step, the individual should consider why the goal is important to them, how the goal benefits them, if this is the right goal for them, and how success might affect them.

Step 5—Time-Bound (or timely): An effective goal should include a specific deadline or timeframe. In addition to helping individuals track their progress, the presence of a timeline helps individuals hold themselves accountable. Discourse during this step may include breaking the effort into chunks of time like monthly, quarterly, or annually.

Organizational psychologist Robert Rubin revised the SMART Model to expand the framework. This version of the model, called SMARTER, adds two additional steps.

Step 6—Evaluated: As individuals pursue their goal, they must frequently and consistently evaluate their progress against the measures they identified in step 2.

Step 7—Reviewed: Other variations of the model call this step Readjust. During this step, individuals adjust their effort based on the progress as measured in step 6.

The SMART Model for Goal Setting is a useful framework for clients struggling to set goals for coaching or professional development.

SMART is among the most well-known and widely used frameworks for goal setting. The model's broad utility has allowed it to easily integrate with other frameworks and theories like the *Transtheoretical Model (TTM)*, *Intentional Change Theory (ICT)*, and *Locke's Goal-Setting Theory*.

Professionals seeking additional information on the SMART Model for Goal Setting will find an almost endless number of books and articles written on the process, along with subtle variations to facilitate the process in different circumstances.

Sources[249]

SMYTH'S MODEL OF REFLECTION

Certification Available: no
Certification Required: no
Assessments: no
Proprietary: no
Client: individuals
Cost: not applicable
Category: reflection

Developed in the late 1980s by professor of education John Smyth, his Model of Reflection provides a framework designed to help teachers reflect on their teaching style with an emphasis on how and why they teach the way they do. Smyth's model has broad utility and applies across multiple professions, particularly in coaching. We present Smyth's framework from the perspective of professional coaching. In some cases, we pull directly from Smyth's own words but substitute the label of coach for teacher.

Smyth's Model of Reflection consists of four stages. Professionals may use the framework to reflect on a specific coaching session or as a means of reflecting on their broader coaching style. Additionally, a coach may elect to use Smyth's model individually or in a collaborative fashion with a group of peers.

Stage 1—Describing (What did I do?): The first step involves the coach exploring their coaching actions, both deliberate and unintentional, to identify patterns. Smyth encourages journaling to capture concrete coaching events which will assist in pattern recognition. Codifying these events will also allow the coach to identify elements or factors that may negatively influence or limit their coaching.

Stage 2—Informing (What does this mean?): During the second step, the coach examines the narrative of their coaching style to identify "theories in use," also called mental models. These are behaviors that result from decisions occurring just below conscious awareness.

Through a process of meaning-making, the coach identifies the knowledge, principles, and beliefs driving their coaching behaviors (i.e., why they coach the way they do).

Stage 3—Confronting (How did I come to be like this?): In the third stage, the coach (or group) examines the origin of these mental models to identify underlying cultural, political, social, and psychological variables influencing the coach's adherence to these models. This examination may include the coach's personal beliefs pertaining to the value of coaching.

During this process, the coach may compare their style to existing coaching frameworks to provide context for certain coaching behaviors. For example, a coach's decision to directly challenge a client in session may result from their use of the *FACTS Coaching Model*, which encourages the coach to directly challenge the client and create tension in the coaching relationship. Alternatively, a coach may determine that this coaching behavior results from a general sensitivity to people who "make excuses."

Stage 4—Reconstructing (How might I do things differently?): During the final stage, the coach brings everything together to compare how their coaching actions align with their values and beliefs for coaching. Does the coach feel they are the type of coach they want to be or not? If not, how do they become the coach they strive to be? Reconstructing concludes with the coach considering how they will use their new insight to influence their coaching style going forward.

Smyth's model is distinct from other models of reflection because it does not focus on a single event or behavior, but on a pattern of behavior which, in turn, pertains to a larger style of teaching (coaching). The ability to explore existing theories to help characterize and explain coaching behaviors further contributes to the model's effectiveness and relevance.

Smyth's Model of Reflection is slightly more involved than presented here. The framework includes multiple questions designed for each stage in the process to facilitate the coach's personal reflection. Smyth's model also includes questions for peer groups to foster a collaborative approach to reflection in support of the coach.

Professionals seeking additional information may consider Smyth's 1989 article, "Developing and Sustaining Critical Reflection in Teacher Education."

Sources[250]

SOCIAL COGNITIVE THEORY

Certification Available: no
Certification Required: no
Assessments: no
Proprietary: no
Client: individuals
Cost: not applicable
Category: learning, change (ind.)

The origins of Social Cognitive Theory (SCT) date back to the 1960s when psychologist Albert Bandura developed its proto version, Social Learning Theory (SLT). The original SLT consisted of five constructs. In 1986, Bandura added a sixth construct when he revised the theory into Social Cognitive Theory.

SCT helps to explain how people regulate and maintain their behavior over time. SCT proposes that behavioral learning occurs in a social context influenced by social reinforcement. Put another way, the theory suggests that individuals learn and regulate their behavior by watching others and seeing the consequences of their behaviors.

Construct 1—Reciprocal determinism: This refers to the dynamic and reciprocal interactions between three key variables (the person, their environment, and their behavior). These three factors continually interact and influence each other. Most people (person) strive for a sense of agency by exerting control (behavior) over key events in their life (environment).

Construct 2—Behavioral capability: Refers to a person's ability to perform behavior based on their knowledge, skills, and experiences. To perform a behavior, a person must know what to do and how to do it.

Construct 3—Observational learning: Refers to the individual's ability to observe and replicate behavior seen in others (called modeling behavior).

Construct 4—Reinforcements: Refers to the internal or external responses to an individual's behavior. These responses influence whether a person continues or discontinues the behavior. This construct captures the reciprocal relationship between the individual and their environment.

Construct 5—Expectations: Refers to the anticipated outcome from a behavior. This is subjective to the individual and typically derives from previous experiences.

Construct 6—Self-efficacy: Refers to the person's confidence in their ability to perform the behavior. See *Self-Efficacy Theory* for more detailed information.

Social Cognitive Theory involves the principle of **modeling**, a mediational process for replicating observed behavior that includes four components.

- Attention: the extent to which a person observes or notices another person's behavior.

- Retention: the extent to which a person remembers the behavior and how accurately they remember it.

- Reproduction: the extent to which a person can replicate the behavior (physically, emotionally, cognitively).

- Motivation: the extent to which the individual has the will to perform the behavior.

It is important to note that variations of SCT exist which use different labels. One version presents seven constructs: self-efficacy, behavioral capability, expectations, expectancies, self-control, observational learning, and reinforcements.

Social Cognitive Theory is useful with clients considering behavioral changes in how they lead. These may include the style in which they deliver feedback, how they delegate responsibility, or how they manage conflict. For clients new to leadership, SCT provides a framework to help them engage in meaningful modeling (deep change) vs. mimicry (shallow impersonation).

Professionals seeking additional information may consider Bandura's 2023 book (published posthumously), *Social Cognitive Theory: An Agentic Perspective on Human Nature*. Alternatively, those interested in Bandura's earlier work on SLT may consider his 1977 book, *Social Learning Theory*.

Sources[251]

SOCIAL EXCHANGE THEORY

> **Certification Available:** no
> **Certification Required:** no
> **Assessments:** no
> **Proprietary:** no
> **Client:** individuals
> **Cost:** not applicable
> **Category:** communication, conflict

Developed in 1958 by sociologist George Homans, Social Exchange Theory (SET) suggests that people calculate the value of their relationships using a form of cost-benefit analysis. Since its introduction in 1958, many researchers have contributed to the theory, including John W. Thibaut, Harold H. Kelley, Claude Lévi-Strauss, and many others.

Born from a combination of behaviorism and economics, Social Exchange Theory depends on four critical assumptions.

Assumption 1—Humans inherently seek out rewards in the form of benefits or profits, while avoiding punishments like costs.

Assumption 2—People initiate relationships with the intention of maximizing profit and minimizing costs.

Assumption 3—People often try to anticipate the potential profits and costs of a relationship before initiating a connection.

Assumption 4—Generally, people believe the cost-to benefit ratio of a relationship will change over time.

Given these assumptions, Social Exchange Theory suggests individuals will continue to pursue a relationship so long as they believe the value of the relationship exceeds the cost. When the cost of a relationship exceeds the reward, a person will either change the nature of the relationship to minimize the cost, or they will end the relationship.

When exploring cost vs. benefit, it is important to note that individuals will differ on what constitutes a cost or a benefit. This is largely based on the individual's needs, wants, and motivations. Costs relate to anything the individual perceives as a negative in the relationship. Benefits are those elements of the relationship perceived as positive.

A person assessing the cost/benefit of a potential relationship may make two types of comparisons.

Comparison Level (CL): Refers to a person's perception of what benefits they believe they should or might get from a specific potential relationship. The CL is subjective, meaning that a person's prior relationship experiences may influence their perceptions of what they can expect from a potential relationship. A person with poor past relationships may have lower expectations than a person with a history of close and meaningful relationships.

Comparison Levels of Alternatives (CLalt): This involves a person comparing an existing relationship to a potential new relationship. During this comparison, a person considers if a different relationship offers better benefits or costs less than an existing one. The relationship with the best profit margin (i.e., greatest benefit with the least cost) may win out.

A person's CLalt is a factor that may influence the stability of their relationships. A person who sees no better option for reward or who fears solitude will remain in their current relationships.

Social Exchange Theory is a popular framework in social work; however, it has broad utility and applies to all relationships, including professional relationships and teaming. For this reason, we include SET in the ICMT.

Social Exchange Theory is more complex than presented here and includes a number of additional concepts and considerations like reciprocity, power dynamics, risk and uncertainty, equality, cultural implications, and leadership.

Professionals seeking additional information on Social Exchange Theory will find much written on the theory, including the 1980 book, *Social Exchange: Advances in Theory and Research*, authored by K.J. Gergen, M.S. Greenberg, and R.H. Willis.

Sources[252]

SOCIAL FACILITATION

Certification Available: no
Certification Required: no
Assessments: no
Proprietary: no
Client: individuals
Cost: not applicable
Category: influence, teaming

First observed in 1898 by psychologist Norman Triplett, Social Facilitation is the phenomenon whereby an individual's performance improves when in the presence of others. Triplett first observed this phenomenon while watching cyclists train for competition. He noticed that individual performance improved when cyclists trained as a group as compared to training solo. In 1920, psychologist Floyd Allport coined the term Social Facilitation to describe Triplett's observations.

Two forms of Social Facilitation exist, each one describing a different source of enhanced performance.

Social Facilitation (Co-Action Effects): This form of Social Facilitation describes the performance enhancement that results when an individual executes a task in the presence of one or more individuals executing the same task. Examples of Co-Action Effects include team sports, groups working together to accomplish a shared task, and musicians within an orchestra.

Social Facilitation (Audience Effects): This form of Social Facilitation describes the performance enhancement that results when an individual executes a task while other people watch. Examples of this include athletes and musicians performing in front of a crowd.

Early experiments in Social Facilitation led to contradictory and conflicting results. In some cases, subject performance improved in the presence of others, while in other experiments subject performance deteriorated. In 1965, psychologist Robert Zajonc discovered the reason for this.

Zajonc determined that an individual's level of mastery over the task was the key determinant in whether performance improved or worsened when in the presence of others. When individuals possessed mastery of the task, they showed notable improvements in performance when in the presence of others.

Conversely, those for whom the task was new or difficult demonstrated decreased performance in the presence of others. Researchers called this phenomenon **Social Inhibition**. Therefore, a person's skill level in the task determines if Social Facilitation or Social Inhibition takes place.

Academics studying the phenomenon of Social Facilitation and Social Inhibition identified three variables that can affect a person's performance when in the presence of others.

Affective factors (self): It is not the presence of others that influences performance, but the fear of their judgment that induces enhanced/diminished performance.

Physiological factors (feeling): The presence of other people can create an intense emotional state within the performer, often in the form of anxiety and stress.

Cognitive factors (thought): The presence of others may distract or take focus away from the task at hand, making it difficult to concentrate.

Not everyone responds the same way when performing in the presence of others. In team settings, some individuals may underperform because they feel less responsibility to perform. In some cases, individuals may decrease their level of effort in expectation that other members of the team will pick up the slack. Researchers called this phenomenon **Social Loafing**.

Professionals interested in theories that explore how individual behavior changes in the presence of others may consider the *Hawthorne Effect*.

Social Facilitation is more complex than presented here and integrates other theories like Yerkes-Dodson Law, Activation Theory, Alertness Hypothesis, Drive Theory, and Self-Presentation Theory. Professionals seeking depth of knowledge will find much written on the topic, including Allport's 1920 paper, "The Influence of the Group upon Association and Thought."

Sources[253]

SOCIAL IDENTITY THEORY

Certification Available: no
Certification Required: no
Assessments: no
Proprietary: no
Client: individuals
Cost: not applicable
Category: communication, conflict

Developed in the 1970s by social psychologists Henri Tajfel and John Turner, Social Identity Theory (SIT) provides a framework for exploring the complex interplay between our sense of self (personal identity) and our sense of belonging to the social world (social identity). Social Identity Theory consists of three constructs, called **Cognitive Processes**, that shed light on the complexity of this relationship.

Social categorization: This is the cognitive process that allows us to organize and group ourselves and others. Then, we may define ourselves and others based on these groupings. A person may belong to several groups. In these cases, the social situation determines which identity asserts itself in the moment.

When conducting social categorization, a person may classify self and others into two categories. The first is the **in-group**. This classification applies to the group a person identifies with or belongs to, often called "us." The second is the **out-group**. This classification applies to any group the individual does not belong to, often called "them."

By definition, a group is any collective which a person may belong to or identify with. The number of potential groups is almost endless and includes those defined by religion, race, ethnicity, political affiliation, social class, sports teams, hobbies, and more.

Social categorization is a natural act based on the human need to define and understand our environment. A key part of understanding our world lies in how we identify and label the things around us, including people and groups. These labels, in turn, can lead us to form generalizations and stereotypes.

Social identification: This describes the cognitive process whereby a person begins to assimilate aspects of their behavior to conform with the group they identify with. This happens when a person adjusts their behavior based on their assumptions of how other members within the group behave.

Social comparison: This is the cognitive process by which an individual compares their group to other groups. To protect their self-image, the individual must perceive their in-group as having a higher status than the out-group. The need for one's group to stand superior to another often leads to prejudice and can blind members to important truths.

The default for most people is to maintain a positive image of the group to which they belong. When evidence emerges calling into question the integrity of the group, members may reject the evidence without proper consideration because the alternative damages the individual's social and personal identity. This phenomenon leads to confirmation bias.

Though a natural act, the three cognitive processes are prone to inaccuracy. People often overstate the similarities between in-group members while exaggerating the differences between their group and out-groups. This contributes to prejudice and bias. Further complicating matters, a person may affiliate another person with a group they do not identify with.

Social Identity Theory is useful for clients dealing with issues of racism and prejudice. Though not a solution, SIT provides valuable insight to help us understand some of the variables which contribute to these problems. The SIT framework can open new pathways for exploration.

Social Identity Theory is more complex than presented here and includes additional concepts like individual-mobility belief system, social change belief system, social competition, social creativity, and more. Professionals seeking additional knowledge will find much written on the topic, including Tajfel's 1981 book, *Human Groups & Social Categories: Studies in Social Psychology*.

Sources[254]

SOCIAL INTELLIGENCE

Certification Available: yes
Certification Required: no
Assessments: yes (ESCI, SEIP)
Proprietary: no
Client: individuals
Cost: pricing varies
Category: emotional intelligence

The concept of Social Intelligence (SI) first emerged in the work of psychologist Edward Thorndike during the 1920s. Originally defined as the ability to understand and manage human relationships, psychologist Daniel Goleman later refined the definition to include "being intelligent of relationships and in relationships."

Though many sources claim social intelligence is distinct from emotional intelligence, most agree that social intelligence is part of the emotional intelligence ecosystem. In other words, the two concepts are interrelated and, in some frameworks, overlap.

This resulted in several versions of SI, each offering subtly different labels and perspectives. One of the most popular versions of social intelligence is that of Daniel Goleman, which consists of two dimensions and eight facets.

Social awareness: This dimension pertains to how you respond to others. Social awareness consists of four facets that influence one's social awareness.

- **Primal empathy:** the ability to sense other people's feelings.

- **Attunement:** the ability to listen with full receptivity.

- **Empathetic accuracy:** the ability to understand another's thoughts and intentions.

- **Social cognition:** the ability to understand how the social world works.

Social facility: This dimension pertains to one's ability to have smooth social interactions and consists of the following four facets.

- **Synchrony:** the ability to interact with another person meaningfully and smoothly.

- **Self-presentation:** the ability to know how you (and your behavior) come across to others.

- **Influence:** the ability to shape the outcome of social interactions.

- **Concern:** the ability to care about the needs of other people.

Some forms of social intelligence theory incorporate additional concepts which elucidate on the complexity of SI. These theories may include constructs like Socially Desirable Responding (SDR), which explain how an individual's positive bias may influence their social behavior. Following are two types of SDR:

Impression management (conscious act): the intentional act of presenting a favorable picture of oneself. In this, the person knows they are deceiving others.

Self-deceptive enhancement (subconscious act): the unintentional, yet honest, act of presenting a favorable picture of oneself. In this, people genuinely believe what they present about themselves because they cannot see the truth about themselves.

Social intelligence frameworks are useful for clients looking to integrate with existing social cultures, networks, teams, or environments more effectively. SI constructs can help clients explore the way they connect to the social world around them and help them process their social experiences, especially when they encounter challenges "fitting in."

The array of social intelligence frameworks available make the theory too complex to present here. Professionals seeking formal training in SI will find many courses available by multiple vendors. Those seeking additional information may consider Goleman's 2006 book, *Social Intelligence: The New Science of Human Relationships*, or K. Albrecht's 2005 book, *Social Intelligence: The New Science of Success*.

Sources[255]

SOCIAL NORMS THEORY

Certification Available: no
Certification Required: no
Assessments: no
Proprietary: no
Client: individuals, groups, organizations
Cost: not applicable
Category: influence, change (org.)

Though the term "social norms" dates to the early 1930s, the modern theory emerged in 1986 from the work of sociologist H. Wesley Perkins and psychologist Alan Berkowitz. Social Norms Theory (SNT) suggests that a person's perceptions or beliefs about how other people think, feel, and behave will influence their own thoughts, feelings, and behavior.

Fundamental to SNT is the concept of social norms, defined as "rules and standards that are understood by members of a group, and that guide or constrain social behaviors without the force of law." The presence of social norms establishes what is appropriate and inappropriate behavior for group members but can also become obstacles to organizational and cultural change efforts.

Social Norms Theory includes three core concepts and three common inaccuracies that explain how individuals may experience explicit and implicit influence from the group.

Perceived norms: These are the perceptions a person forms about how and why the other members of the group think, feel, and behave the way they do.

Actual norms: This is how the other members of the group really think, feel, and behave.

Misperceptions: This represents the gap between the individual's perceived norms and the actual norms of the group.

The presence of these misperceptions may lead a person (or a group) to form several inaccurate beliefs about their group or other groups. Social Norms Theory posits that an individual's misperceptions are the greatest influence on their behavioral decisions. The three most common inaccuracies include the following.

- **Pluralistic ignorance**: This occurs when multiple members of a group incorrectly believe that their peers think, feel, or behave differently than they really do.

- **False consensus**: This occurs when members of a group incorrectly believe that other members think, feel, and behave the same way they do when in fact they do not.

- **False uniqueness**: Occurs when members of a group overestimate or exaggerate the differences between their own behavior and that of the group.

Other concepts often associated with Social Norms Theory include the proximity principle, elaboration principle, and the reciprocity principle. These explain how individuals may come to identify with preexisting groups or form new groups.

Though research in Social Norms Theory heavily focused on the impact of peer influence on college students' use of alcohol, the results proved applicable across a wide range of ages and situations, demonstrating the utility of the framework in understanding the complex relationship between a person's perceptions of their group and their behavior.

Social Norms Theory is popular in many fields, including marketing and advertising. In coaching, SNT is useful to help clients explore how their perceptions (and misperceptions) of their group (or other groups) influence their own thoughts, feelings, and behavior.

Social Norms Theory is more complex than presented here. Those searching for similar theories may also consider *Social Identity Theory* and the *Six Principles of Influence*. Professionals seeking additional information will find an array of literature available that examines SNT in different contexts.

For example, in his 2018 book, *Social Norms and the Theory of the Firm: A Foundational Approach*, Douglas E. Stevens explores the effect of SNT on the organization (Agency Theory).

Sources[256]

SOFT SYSTEMS METHODOLOGY

Certification Available: no
Certification Required: no
Assessments: no
Proprietary: no
Client: groups, organizations
Cost: not applicable
Category: problem-solving

Developed in the 1960s by management professor Peter Checkland, Soft Systems Methodology (SSM) provides a useful framework for solving ill-defined or ambiguous problems.

The philosophical basis for SSM suggests human beings are complex and illogical, further suggesting people can form vastly different perceptions of the same shared event. These differences of interpretation can introduce ambiguity to a problem. In these cases, recognizing and solving the problem requires a different approach from more traditional problem-solving methodologies.

SSM consists of a seven-step process to facilitate the examination of an ambiguous problem.

Step 1—Understanding the situation: The first step involves developing a shared understanding of the peripheral circumstances surrounding the problem, not the examination of the problem itself. This is a broad exploration of environmental factors contributing to the problem, which is crucial, since not all stakeholders may perceive the existence of a problem, let alone be able to define it. Some may even perceive the problem as a good thing.

Successfully executing the first step requires gathering relevant information and exploring all stakeholder perspectives to identify patterns among the different perceptions. In group settings, this may necessitate a skilled facilitator to guide discourse. The conclusion of this step results in the acceptance or rejection of a problem's existence, and a decision to respond to the problem.

Step 2—Expressing the problem: People come from different experiences, which may influence their interpretation of a shared event. The second step seeks to bridge the gap between these different perspectives by defining the problem clearly and concisely to facilitate a shared understanding.

A common technique to enable this step, called Rich Picture, involves individuals drawing a picture displaying the various components, aspects, and relationships of the relevant problem.

Step 3—Naming the relevant systems: For each component identified in the Rich Picture, develop a **Root Definition**. This is a statement which expresses the desired state of the component as a transformative process.

To facilitate this step, SSM provides a process called CATWOE which requires users to identify six specific elements within each definition. The acronym stands for customer, actor, transformation process, worldview, owner, and environment. The presence of all six elements in each root definition will allow users to accomplish the next step.

Step 4—Build conceptual models of relevant systems: Using the root definitions, develop a conceptual model that defines how to best achieve the desired state for each component.

Step 5—Compare models with real world: Determine the efficacy and practicality of each model by comparing them to the problem as expressed in step 2.

Step 6—Define possible changes: Using the outcomes from step 5, adjust the models to enhance their efficacy in addressing the problem.

Step 7—Take action: The final step involves executing the conceptual models to address the problem.

SSM is substantially more complex than presented here. Adding a measure of ambiguity to the framework (ironic, no?), several sources define the seven steps using different labels. Some sources even distill the process to five steps. Professionals seeking additional information may consider Checkland's 1990 book, *Soft Systems Methodology in Action*, co-authored with J. Scholes.

Sources[257]

SPACE COACHING MODEL

```
Certification Available: yes
Certification Required: no
Assessments: no
Proprietary: no
Client: individuals
Cost: not applicable
Category: coaching model, self-awareness, stress mgt.
```

Developed in 2002 by occupational psychologist Nick Edgerton, the SPACE Coaching Model is a five-step framework designed to help clients develop their self-awareness and better understand the relationship between their thoughts, feelings, and actions.

Step 1—Social context: The first step involves the client's exploration of their situation, issue, or triggering event. This requires the client to consider all relevant factors influencing the situation, like the role of personal and organizational culture on the situation, as well as the personalities and perceptions of those involved.

Step 2—Physiology: During this step, the client considers their somatic reaction to the event or situation. A physiological reaction may also occur before an event takes place (e.g., the client may experience intense feelings about an upcoming speaking engagement).

The client's exploration in this domain should include all forms of physiological responses, such as heart rate, breathing rate, perspiration, temperature, etc.

Step 3—Action: The third step involves the client exploring their behaviors, specifically those actions that created or exacerbated the situation as well as behaviors they did not engage in which contribute to the situation. Put another way, the client considers what they did and did not do that influenced the situation.

During this stage of exploration, the client may discover avoidant or self-defeating behaviors previously unknown to them. Bringing awareness to these behaviors can allow the client to address them through coaching.

Step 4—Cognition: During the fourth step, the client examines the thought processes, perceptions, and expectations that influenced their experience of the issue, situation, or event.

The client's exploration during this stage of the process may reveal counterproductive thoughts as well as biases which negatively contribute to the issue. The client may also uncover conflict between their values and the issue at hand.

Step 5—Emotion: The final stage in the process involves the client's exploration of their emotions during and following the event. During this stage, the client considers how emotions may have influenced the event.

Because of its emphasis on the relationship between a person's thoughts, feelings, and behaviors, the SPACE Coaching Model falls under the umbrella of *Cognitive Behavioral Coaching (CBC)*. Consequently, the model's fundamental philosophy suggests that what a client thinks about something influences how they feel about that thing, and how they feel about that thing influences how they respond to that thing. By the coach helping the client develop a greater awareness in the domains of thoughts, feelings, and behavior, the client can better adapt to achieve their desired outcomes.

Variations of the SPACE Model exist which adopt different labels to describe the process. Moreover, there is an obscure and unrelated coaching model also called the SPACE Coaching Model which stands for Success, Possibilities, Awareness, Choice, and Empowerment. This version is not a CBC-based model.

In addition to developing self-awareness, the SPACE Model provides a framework to help clients understand and manage variables affecting their stress levels.

Professionals seeking additional information may consider Edgerton's and psychologist Stephen Palmer's 2005 article, "SPACE: A Psychological Model for Use within Cognitive Behavioral Coaching, Therapy, and Stress Management." It is worth noting that Stephen Palmer also developed the CBC-based *PRACTICE Coaching Model*.

Sources[258]

STAGE GATE PROCESS

Certification Available: yes
Certification Required: yes
Assessments: no
Proprietary: yes (Stage Gate International)
Client: organizations
Cost: pricing not available
Category: problem-solving

Developed in 1988 by innovation researcher and business school professor Robert G. Cooper, the Stage Gate Process provides a framework for facilitating meaningful and efficient innovation.

The Stage Gate Process consists of six stages, and four gates situated between the stages. Each gate represents a decision point in the process (i.e., project go/no-go). By design, each gate gets progressively more challenging as the level of scrutiny and examination increases.

Stage 0—Discovery: Characterized as a period of exploration, during this stage the team considers potential opportunities for innovating new products, services, or processes. Stage 0 involves brainstorming techniques, idea generation, and exercises to spur creativity. The goal of stage 0 is to generate a list of potential innovations for further exploration. The period between stage 0 and stage 1 is the only transition without a gate.

Stage 1—Scope: Using the list from stage 0, the team begins a preliminary investigation into the feasibility of each idea. The intent of stage 1 is to better define each of the potential innovation opportunities and assess their respective viability. The goal of stage 1 is to narrow the list of ideas to the ones with the greatest potential and present these findings to leadership.

Gate 1: During this first gate, leadership conducts a gentle review of the ideas submitted by the team. The ensuring decision-making process must consider the team's analysis, their conclusion, and the justifications for their recommendations.

The purpose of the first gate is for leadership to determine if the project should proceed to the next stage or if they need to terminate the project.

Stage 2—Business case: During this stage, also called the **Design** phase, the team conducts an in-depth examination of all logistical, financial, administrative, and resources requirements needed to successfully execute the project. This should also include a cross-organization feasibility assessment to determine how the innovation will impact other aspects of the organization. The goal of this stage is to design a robust and comprehensive project management plan.

Gate 2: A more intensive and rigorous review than gate 1, leaders evaluate the team's project plan against a detailed scorecard to ensure quality control and project viability. Leaders then decide to approve the project to the next stage or terminate the project based on these results.

Stage 3—Develop: During this stage, the team executes the project plan, which requires developing the new product, service, or process. This includes alpha prototyping the innovation, developing new policies to support the product, service, or process. The goal of this stage is to create a sample of the new product, service, or process for testing.

Gate 3: Leaders evaluate the alpha test results and determine go/no-go for continuation.

Stage 4—Test and validate: Sometimes called the **Scale-Up** stage, this involves testing the new product or service with the target market. The goal of this stage is to learn from the alpha test and adapt the product, service, or process into a beta prototype for testing.

Gate 4: Leaders evaluate the beta test results and determine go/no-go for continuation.

Stage 5—Launch: The final stage marks the full-scale launch of the product, service, or process.

Also known as the Phase Gate Model, Waterfall Model, or Tollgate Model, the Stage Gate Process is significantly more complex than presented here. Professionals seeking additional information may consider Cooper's 2009 book, *Generating Breakthrough New Product Ideas: Feeding the Innovation Funnel*, co-authored with S.J. Edgett.

Stage Gate International provides services based on this model. Pricing is available upon request.

Sources[259]

STAR/AR METHOD

Certification Available: no
Certification Required: no
Assessments: no
Proprietary: no
Client: individuals
Cost: not applicable
Category: feedback

Developed by leadership consulting firm Development Dimensions International (DDI), the STAR/AR Method provides a framework for delivering effective and meaningful feedback. Additionally, the model also serves as a framework for conducting recruiting interviews; however, this entry focuses solely on the feedback aspect of the model.

The STAR Method consists of five steps.

Step 1—Situation/Task: During the first step, the provider articulates the subject of the feedback, often a task or situation.

For a task, the provider asks the recipient to recall who assigned the task, their understanding of the task, and any explicit and implicit guidance provided to them. This allows the provider to identify any misconceptions or misunderstandings on the part of the recipient.

For a situation, the provider asks the recipient to describe the event, including when and where the situation took place and who was present. The recipient should attempt to recall the experience absent attributions or judgments.

Step 2—Action: During this step, the provider explores the recipient's behavior. In the case of a task, the provider asks the recipient to describe the actions they took to accomplish the task, including the rationale for their approach (i.e., what they did and why they did it).

For a situation, the provider asks the recipient to describe what they said and did leading up to and during the event. This includes how they held themselves (i.e., body language) and tone of voice. The recipient should include what other people said and did during the situation.

Step 3—Results: This step centers on the consequences of the actions taken. For a task, the provider and recipient examine the consequences of the recipient's behavior in explicit terms. Did the action result in the intended outcomes? Did the action move the recipient closer to their goal?

For a situation, the recipient explores the observable results of their behavior during the situation. They consider the possible impacts from alternative perspectives (i.e., how the other person may have perceived or felt in response to the recipient's actions).

Step 4—Alternative Action: In this step, the recipient explores alternative courses of action they might have taken. For a task, this involves the recipient exploring alternative steps they could have taken which might have resulted in better outcomes.

For a situation, the recipient considers alternative ways they might have handled the situation, or how they could have responded differently.

Step 5—Alternative Result: Given these alternative courses of action, the recipient then considers how each action might have produced different results. For both tasks and situations, the recipient considers the potential consequences of these alternative actions. The idea is that a recipient who believes there might have been a better course of action is more likely to behave differently should a similar event occur in the future.

The STAR Method is one among many feedback models included in this compendium and among a small group of virtually identical processes. (See *BIFF, BEEF, BOOST, SBI.*)

Because many of the models are similar in their design and intent, professionals should familiarize themselves with these frameworks as both clients and collaborating coaches will likely possess awareness of one or more of these frameworks.

Sources[260]

START, STOP, CONTINUE MODEL

Certification Available: no
Certification Required: no
Assessments: no
Proprietary: no
Client: groups, teams
Cost: not applicable
Category: feedback, change (ind.)

The Start, Stop, Continue Model—also called Stop, Start, Continue Analysis—is a multipurpose framework that can facilitate effective feedback, meaningful change, and process improvement. Though the origins of the model are ambiguous, available literature suggests the framework has been around for some time.

As a framework for change and process improvement, the Start, Stop, Continue Model can help teams distinguish which existing tasks, processes, or projects work from those that do not work. This examination also allows the team to identify uncompleted or pending tasks.

As a feedback tool, the model allows the provider to identify aspects of the recipient's performance that should continue, behaviors the recipient should cease, and more desirable behaviors the recipient should implement.

The Start, Stop, Continue Model consists of three stages.

Stage 1—Start: The first stage of the process begins with the team discussing what actions or behaviors are missing from the task or project that would provide value added. The team designates these missing components as new actions which require implementation.

As a feedback tool, this stage focuses on the specific behaviors the provider does not see but wishes to see from the recipient. For example, a supervisor may want the employee to include them on emails they send to supervisors in other departments.

Stage 2—Stop: The second stage of the process involves the team examining existing actions or behaviors to determine which ones are not working. This includes identifying pain points or aspects of the project or process unnecessary or detrimental to the organization or team's effort. The team then recommends terminating these harmful behaviors immediately.

As a feedback tool, this stage involves the provider calling specific attention to the recipient's problematic behaviors which require the recipient's attention.

Stage 3—Continue: The final stage involves the team identifying those aspects of the process or behaviors that are working and should continue.

As a feedback tool, this involves the provider highlighting the recipient's actions or behaviors that are positive and beneficial, ones the provider wishes to see continued.

Variations of the model exist which present the same process but in a different sequence. Regardless of which version professionals use, the model recommends beginning the process with the stage that seems appropriate to the situation.

The Start, Stop, Continue Model has broad utility, and as a result, there are a variety of exercises based on the model. Some of these include games designed to foster team development while simultaneously allowing the collective to better understand aspects of the organization's mission. Several practitioners who use the Start, Stop, Continue Model recommend using the model in combination with other frameworks like SWOT Analysis.

Professionals seeking additional information will find much written about the Start, Stop, Continue Model. Sources provide insight into a variety of different applications for the framework and include an array of exercises for different situations.

Sources[261]

STEPLADDER MODEL

Certification Available: no
Certification Required: no
Assessments: no
Proprietary: no
Client: groups, teams
Cost: not applicable
Category: decision-making, problem-solving, teaming

Developed in 1992 by organizational psychologists Steven Rogelberg, Janet Barnes-Farrell, and Charles Lowe, the Stepladder Model provides a framework to facilitate group-based decision-making by minimizing the risk of *Groupthink* on the decision-making process. This fosters more thoughtful and meaningful discourse among group members.

The Stepladder Model consists of five steps designed to mitigate the risk of groupthink in two ways. First, it dedicates time for individuals to consider the problem and formulate ideas on their own before sharing their thoughts with the group. Second, the process allows individuals to share their ideas with the group without prior knowledge of how other members think.

Step 1—Explain the problem: During the first step, a facilitator or neutral party defines the problem for each person individually and separate from the group. This allows each member to form their own initial thoughts without the influence of other people's reactions. It is important that whoever explains the problem uses precisely the same language and explanation with each person. Despite this, individual members will likely form slightly different interpretations of the problem. The process leverages these different perspectives to add value during group discourse.

Next, allow each person time to contemplate and reflect on the issue or problem and formulate ideas and opinions. This includes the individual's thoughts regarding possible solutions. The outcome of this step represents a person's genuine thoughts and feelings about the issue before the group has a chance to influence the individual.

Step 2—Build the ladder: For the second step, select two individuals from the group to serve as core members. These two individuals come together in a private setting to discuss the issue or problem. During this discourse they explore their respective understandings of the issue at hand and share their ideas on possible solutions.

Step 3—Continue the process: Once the first two members of the group complete their discourse, introduce a third member to the group. It is critical the new member share their thoughts about the issue and their ideas before the original core members. In this way, the new member can contribute a point of view free from group influence.

Once the third member has fully shared their point of view, then the group mutually discusses all options and perspectives freely.

Step 4—Complete the ladder: Like the previous step, add another member to the group and ensure they present their perspective first and fully before the group discussion begins.

Repeat this step for each member, allowing time for each new member to share their ideas before group discussions.

Step 5—Make a decision: Once all group members have an opportunity to share their individual ideas, the group may transition to the final step, making the decision.

This requires the group to consider all the independent ideas, look for patterns among the possible solutions, discuss the viability of these solutions, prioritize, and finally select the course of action or solution.

The Stepladder framework is useful when dealing with strong personalities that tend to negatively influence the participation of other group members.

The Stepladder Model is a simple but effective framework to use in group-based decision-making. Professionals exploring this model will find various worksheets and tools designed to facilitate the process.

Sources[262]

STEPPPA COACHING MODEL

Certification Available: no
Certification Required: no
Assessments: no
Proprietary: no
Client: individuals
Cost: not applicable
Category: coaching model

Developed in 2003 by executive coach and business school professor Angus McLeod, the STEPPPA Coaching Model provides a framework to help coaches conduct meaningful coaching sessions.

STEPPPA consists of a seven-step coaching model that actively incorporates the client's emotional experience into the coaching process.

Step 1—Subject: During the first step, the client explores various topics they feel appropriate for coaching. It is important for the client to bring up topics voluntarily, as some subjects may elicit intense emotions. Through this step, the client defines their boundaries for the coaching contract (agreement), which then influences the coaching agenda and helps the client remain focused on what is important to them.

Step 2—Target identification: During this step, the client establishes their target goal for coaching. Sometimes a client may already know what they want to achieve but struggle to reach the desired outcome. In these cases, the coach works with the client to explore the obstacles that undermine the client's efforts, which might include unrealistic goals, poorly defined goals, insufficient motivation, or missing tasks. For clients without a predetermined goal, the coach works with them to identify meaningful goals. In this, STEPPPA advocates using the *SMART Model for Goal Setting*.

Step 3—Emotions: This step is what distinguishes STEPPPA from other coaching models. Simply put, emotions drive human behavior; they serve as significant moti-

vators and demotivators. Emotions influence most of the important choices and decisions a client faces. The STEPPPA Model advises coaches to factor this into their coaching process and cautions that ignoring the role of emotion in the client's experience risks compromising their ability to achieve the goal.

Step 4—Perception and choice: To facilitate this step in the process, the model defines a client's Conscious Perception as how they view their issues and goals. Understanding the client's perception of the subject and possible solutions is central to helping them expand their perceptions. Doing so allows the client to increase the choices and options available to them. A broader perspective may give the client new insight to adjust their goals in favor of a more desirable outcome. Along the way, the client should make decisions and take ownership for each choice they make.

Step 5—Plan: During the fifth step, the client begins to strategize a plan for how they intend to achieve their goal. It is important the client follow the principles of effective planning, which include setting measurable objectives that move them toward their goal, establishing a timeline for action, and creating a mechanism for personal accountability.

Step 6—Pace: An excited client may attempt to move too quickly through the plan. Doing so risks poor execution or a failure to achieve specific tasks. A client lacking motivation may move too slowly, risking a loss of momentum, which may lead them to abandon the entire effort. Therefore, the client should establish a logical and reasonable pace for implementing their plan. The coach and client should revisit this pace often to ensure the client is not moving too fast or too slow. This is not an isolated step, but a thread that runs through the entire effort.

Step 7—Adapt (or Act): During the final step, the client reviews their plan and reflects on how they feel about what they developed and their progress thus far. The intention of this step is to ascertain the client's level of commitment to their plan. Based on this, the client may want to adjust their plan.

Professionals seeking additional information will find sufficient literature on the STEPPPA Model available online.

Sources[263]

SYNECTICS

Certification Available: no
Certification Required: no
Assessments: no
Proprietary: yes (SynecticsWorld)
Client: individuals, teams
Cost: not applicable
Category: problem-solving

Developed in the 1950s by business consultant George M. Prince and psychologist William J.J. Gordon, Synectics is both a theory and a process for problem-solving. In this entry, we present the theory of Synectics for creative problem-solving. The process of using Synectics in problem-solving we reserve for *The Infourge Compendium of Tools and Techniques*.

The study of Synectics began when Prince and Gordon set out to understand the psychology behind why some meetings were more productive than others. The duo recorded thousands of hours of meetings in which teams discussed topics focused on product development and problem-solving. The pair examined the recordings and identified several patterns among the meetings considered most successful. This led to three observations.

- When people become aware of the psychological processes affecting their behavior, creative output increases.

- The emotional component of creative behavior overshadows the intellectual component.

- Harnessing both the emotional and irrational components of creative behavior can boost creative output.

Prince and Gordon chose to name their theory Synectics from the Greek word for "the joining together of different and apparently irrelevant elements." They did this because Synectics pushes a team to set aside what they already know and search for what is odd and overlooked.

This leads to the first phase of Synectics, making the familiar strange. To accomplish this, a team must dissect the problem to discover seemingly unrelated connections between elements of the problem. This requires a set of techniques they call "analogies." These analogies range from the basic to the highly creative and fantastical.

Direct analogy: This involves the team making a comparison between two objects that are similar but possess different circumstances. Example: comparing an organization's ecosystem to a rainforest ecosystem.

Personal analogy: This approach requires the team to adopt the perspective of the persons most affected by the problem to help them develop empathy. Example: I am the frustrated customer complaining to the company.

Symbolic analogy: This technique involves using poetic comparisons that appear contradictory but provide new ways of looking at the issue. Example: This problem is an open secret in our organization.

Fantasy analogy: This approach involves looking for an unrealistic situation with impossible solutions. Example: How can I be in two places at once?

Games with words: This involves establishing associations with words linked to the problem.

Games to render laws ineffective: This technique involves changing the laws of nature and physics to determine the effect on the problem. Example: If mass did not increase with speed, how could we travel at the speed of light?

After using analogies to explore the problem, the second phase of Synectics involves making the strange familiar. This involves analyzing the actual problem, identifying the significant elements, and applying models to make sense of the relationship between these elements.

The theory of Synectics is more complex than presented here. Different sources offer diverse perspectives on the theory, its process, and its application. Professionals seeking additional information may consider Gordon's 1961 book, *Synectics: The Development of Creative Capacity*.

Sources[264]

SYSTEMATIC INVENTIVE THINKING

> **Certification Available:** yes
> **Certification Required:** no
> **Assessments:** no
> **Proprietary:** no
> **Client:** individuals, groups
> **Cost:** pricing not available
> **Category:** problem-solving

Developed in the 1990s by professors Jacob Goldenberg and Roni Horowitz, Systematic Inventive Thinking (SIT) provides a methodical approach to problem-solving based on the *Theory of Inventive Problem-Solving*. While many popular problem-solving theories advocate out-of-the-box thinking, SIT encourages "thinking within the box" and proposes a framework for doing so in a meaningful and creative way.

Systematic Inventive Thinking consists of five distinct approaches designed to facilitate problem-solving and innovation. The SIT process begins by applying each approach to an existing product or service.

Subtraction: This approach involves examining the product or service on a cellular level and removing a component from the product or service, something typically seen as essential. Users then consider the potential applications of the remaining components. For example, streamlining TV remote controls by removing scores of buttons in favor of a single unidirectional cursor button.

Multiplication: This approach involves copying and then altering an existing component of the product or service. This approach requires two conditions: First, copy a component which already exists as part of the product or service (i.e., do not add a new component). Second, change or modify the duplicated component. For example, razor companies added additional blades to the once single-blade razor (copying an existing component), then they angled the extra blades differently (modification) to raise the hair as it cuts, leaving a closer shave.

Division: This approach involves dividing the components of a product or service either by functionality or other categorization and rearranging them to achieve new uses. For example, in the 1990s audio manufacturers divided and rearranged the components of a car's CD/radio in such a way as to allow users to remove the face of the system when not in use to prevent theft.

Task unification: This approach involves exploring the potential for using a product's or service's components in ways other than originally intended. Sometimes referred to as "two birds, one stone." For example, defrosting filaments in windshields are, by design, intended to defrost the windshield. However, innovative thinking has resulted in the product serving a dual purpose as an antenna for radios, thereby negating the need for tall rods protruding from a vehicle's hood or trunk.

Attribute dependency: This approach involves an exploration of the relationship between attributes of a product or service and the attributes of the environment. In cases where this relationship exists, consider scenarios in which the relationship does not exist. In cases where this relationship does not exist, consider scenarios in which they might. For example, there is no relationship between standard prescription eyeglasses and sunlight; however, innovators explored establishing such a relationship by developing lenses that alter their color when exposed to light, thus creating transition lenses.

Fundamental to Systematic Inventive Thinking are six axioms. These include the belief that creativity is a logical process that one can learn and practice, and that contradictions are a path (not an obstacle) to creativity.

Systematic Inventive Thinking is significantly more complex than presented here and includes additional principles, approaches, and tools to facilitate the process, such as online software and mobile apps. Professionals seeking additional information may consider Goldenberg's 2013 book, *Inside the Box: A Proven System of Creativity for Breakthrough Results*, co-authored with Drew Boyd. Additionally, Drew Boyd offers training in Systematic Inventive Thinking through online videos and courses.

Sources[265]

SYSTEMS THEORY

> **Certification Available:** no
> **Certification Required:** no
> **Assessments:** no
> **Proprietary:** no
> **Client:** individuals, groups
> **Cost:** not applicable
> **Category:** problem-solving, change (org. & ind.)

Systems Theory is a broad term, often attributed to biologist Karl Ludwig von Bertalanffy (circa 1930), that describes the interdisciplinary and transdisciplinary study of multiple systems within a larger system. Put another way, Systems Theory examines how smaller systems interact and form larger systems.

Like Gestalt Theory (1912), Systems Theory suggests that the whole is greater than the sum of its parts. For this reason, Bertalanffy cautions against focusing solely on a single component of a larger system when exploring these relationships.

In a coaching context, Systems Theory explores the relationship between the many variables of a client's life. For example, a client experiencing significant stress at work may want to explore the relationship between the variables creating stress, the variables helping them manage stress, and the variables giving them purpose. This may reveal new insight, allowing the client to make more meaningful changes.

Systems Theory may require consideration of multiple theories to facilitate an exploration of these relationships. For example, a coach working with a client struggling to fit in at work may want to explore the relationship between their client's need for belonging (*Maslow's Hierarchy of Needs*), how the client characterizes and groups people at work (*Social Identity Theory*), and how they handle conflict between the group's beliefs and culture, and their own (*Affective-Cognitive Consistency Model*).

Systems Theory, also known as General Systems Theory, has utility in many different fields, including biology, psychology, ecology, physics, mathematics, medicine, and more.

In addition to working with individual clients, Systems Theory is an important concept for professionals working with organizations. A company is a complex combination of multiple systems, working independently, interrelatedly, and in some cases interdependently. Whether conducting a needs assessment or designing an enterprise change effort, it is imperative that professionals develop a deep understanding of how these systems interact with each other as part of the larger system.

Though not a formal framework, some sources offer a structure consisting of several elements.

Inputs: These represent what goes into the system to sustain it, feed it, or drive it. In organizations, this might include hiring, budget allocations, and resource acquisitions.

Outputs: These are what come out of the system, either as a by-product or waste. In organizations, this might include the products or services produced by the company.

Process: This is the operation or active relationship that takes inputs and transforms them into outputs. In organizations, these include cradle-to-grave processes for how organizations hire and incentivize employees, what raw materials employees receive, what actions they perform to produce the organization's products or services, and the relationship between the organization and the customer.

Feedback loop: This element includes the process by which the organization maintains quality and ensures consistency of outputs. This requires measurements to allow the organization to quickly identify risks and flaws in the process or inputs that could jeopardize the outputs.

Systems Theory is useful in problem-solving, analyzing complex systems, and understanding complicated relationships.

Professionals seeking additional information will find much written on the topic. Keep in mind the literature segments by field, with psychology and sociology closest to coaching.

Sources[266]

T7 MODEL OF TEAM EFFECTIVENESS

<table>
<tr><td>Certification Available: no</td></tr>
<tr><td>Certification Required: no</td></tr>
<tr><td>Assessments: yes (Team Architect)</td></tr>
<tr><td>Proprietary: yes (Korn Ferry)</td></tr>
<tr><td>Client: teams</td></tr>
<tr><td>Cost: pricing not available</td></tr>
<tr><td>Category: teaming</td></tr>
</table>

Developed in 1995 by leadership researchers Michael Lombardo and Robert Eichinger, the T7 Model of Team Effectiveness provides a framework for determining team effectiveness based on research of over 300 teams and more than 3,200 participants across 50 organizations.

The T7 Model consists of seven factors and multiple dimensions that affect the performance and efficacy of teams. These factors bifurcate into internal factors and external factors.

Internal factors: These variables concern the team itself.

• **Thrust**: This refers to the team's goal and if the team shares in that goal. According to the model, effective teams must possess a shared sense of purpose. This factor consists of several dimensions, including thrust management, thrust clarity, and thrust commitment. These speak to how well the members manage their goals and objectives and how well they understand them.

• **Trust**: This refers to the level of confidence team members have in one another and their ability to support each other. Dimensions of trust include trust in communication, trust in action, and trust inside the team.

• **Talent**: This refers to the collective ability of the team to achieve the mission by examining the combined skills of team members. Dimensions of talent include talent acquisition and enhancement, as well as talent allocation and deployment.

• **Teaming skills**: This refers to the group's ability to operate effectively as a team by considering their interpersonal relationships and level of cohesion. Dimensions of teaming skills include resource management, team learning, decision-making, conflict resolution, team atmosphere, and managing processes.

• **Task skills**: This refers to the ability of the team to execute the work necessary to achieve the team's goals. Dimensions of task skills include focusing, assignment flexibility, measurement, and delivering the goods.

External factors: These are variables outside of the team that influence its ability to function.

• **Team-leader fit**: This considers the degree to which the team's leader supports members, addresses their needs, and guides them.

• **Team support from the organization**: This refers to the level of support and empowerment organizational leaders give the team.

According to the T7 Model of Team Effectiveness, all seven factors are essential to a successful team. A deficiency in any one variable may diminish the overall effectiveness of the team.

Korn Ferry touts the T7 Model, and its associated assessment (Team Architect), as "one of the most comprehensive assessments of team effectiveness in literature." Though proprietary to Korn Ferry, a cursory search of available training and certification courses did not reveal any programs specific to the T7 Model. It is likely the model is a component within a larger course like Korn Ferry's Building Effective Teams.

The T7 Model of Team Effectiveness is more complex than presented here. Professionals seeking additional information will find much written on the topic online, including Korn Ferry Institute's comparative analysis of the T7 Model with other teaming frameworks.

Professionals may also consider Lombardo's 1996 book, *FYI For Your Improvement: A Guide for Development and Coaching for Learners, Managers, Mentors, and Feedback Givers*, co-authored by Robert W. Eichinger.

Sources[267]

TANNENBAUM-SCHMIDT LEADERSHIP CONTINUUM MODEL

Certification Available: no
Certification Required: no
Assessments: no
Proprietary: no
Client: individuals
Cost: not applicable
Category: leadership

Developed in 1958 by psychologists Robert Tannenbaum and Warren Schmidt, the Tannenbaum-Schmidt Leadership Continuum Model (LCM) provides a framework characterizing seven styles of leadership. The fundamental belief underlying LCM suggests that the best way to lead depends on the situation. For this reason, LCM falls under the umbrella of Contingency Theories. See *Contingency Theories* for more information.

The Leadership Continuum Model explores leadership by examining the relationship between the level of authority a leader uses and the level of freedom granted followers. LCM research suggests that leadership styles using a high level of authority tend to afford followers the least amount of freedom. As leaders move along the continuum and use less authority, they afford greater freedom to followers.

LCM consists of seven leadership behaviors, placed on a continuum from left to right: most authoritative (least freedom) to least authoritative (most freedom). Each style includes a combination of strengths and limitations, and the model argues that effective leaders are ones capable of reading the situation to select the most appropriate style.

Tells: This style of leadership uses the most amount of authority and typically entails the leader identifying the problem, developing a solution, and telling followers what to do and how to do it. Characterized as intense micromanagement, this style does not afford the followers any opportunity to participate in decision-making. As with each style, this form of leadership has utility in certain situations, though it can be detrimental if it is the only style a leader possesses.

Sells: In this style, the leader makes the decision but provides followers with an explanation for how he came to his conclusion. This style gets its name because the leader will try to sell the decision to followers, so they understand how the decision is in their best interest, hopefully mitigating any resistance.

Suggests: In this style, the leader identifies the problem and makes the decision, but asks followers if they have any questions or concerns about the tentative decision put forth. This gives followers a little more say into the process. Like the Sell style, this style also explains the decision, but the leader does so to ensure followers understand the reasons behind the decision, not to sell the decision.

Consults: In this style, the leader seeks input from followers in the decision process. This marks the first point in the continuum where followers can impact and change the decision before the leader makes a conclusion.

Joins: In this style, the leader presents the problem and invites followers to find a solution. This is the first truly collaborative approach to problem-solving in the LCM. Here, the leader does not offer or imply a solution or decision but allows followers to form recommendations.

Delegates: In this style, the leader outlines the problem and empowers the team to develop a solution. The leader remains responsible for the outcome, but the team makes the decision.

Abdicates: In this style, the leader allows followers to explore and define the problem and develop the solution. The leader remains responsible for the outcome.

LCM is a useful framework when working with clients who have a tendency for extreme micromanagement or macro-management. Professionals seeking additional information may consider Tannenbaum and Schmidt's 1973 *Harvard Business Review* article, "How to Choose a Leadership Pattern."

Sources[268]

TASKS OF MOURNING

Certification Available: no
Certification Required: no
Assessments: no
Proprietary: no
Client: individuals
Cost: not applicable
Category: change (ind.)

Developed by psychologist J. William Worden, his Tasks of Mourning provides a framework for exploring the grieving process. Unlike other grief frameworks, like the Kübler-Ross Model, Worden's Tasks of Mourning does not view grief as a set of stages but as a series of tasks necessary to effectively process grief.

The Tasks of Mourning consists of four distinct nonlinear tasks. A person may move from task to task in no order, sometimes revisiting a previous task as needed. Though presented from the optic of death, Worden and others remind us that grief is not solely the domain of death. We present the Tasks of Mourning from a more common coaching perspective.

Task 1—Accept the reality of loss: Loss comes in many forms, like the loss of a job, a lost opportunity for promotion, a valued team member leaving, or the failure of a project. Clients may experience some denial, refusing to accept the loss. They may also minimize the significance of the loss to avoid the pain.

The circumstances surrounding the loss may contribute to the difficulty of processing and accepting the loss. For example, a client losing a promotion to a colleague they trained may feel betrayed or bitter, further complicating the grieving process.

Task 1 involves the client acknowledging their loss and the reactions that follow (e.g., denial, minimizations, projections, blame, etc.). This includes accepting that change

is happening, and they can choose to take an active role in shaping how that change affects them.

Task 2—Process the pain of grief: Significant change or loss can involve intense feelings, often characterized as pain. Worden identified dozens of reactions to grief, grouping them into four categories.

- Feelings: These include the emotions (e.g., sadness, anger, etc.) and sentiments (e.g., shock, numbness, loneliness, etc.) that result from the impact of grief.

- Physical sensations: These are the physiological reactions to grief and include tightness in the chest, difficulty breathing, and muscle weakness.

- Cognitions: These are the consequences of grief on our thoughts (e.g., confusion, difficulty focusing, etc.) and beliefs (e.g., spirituality, fairness, equity, etc.).

- Behaviors: These include the outward manifestations of grief (e.g., loss of sleep, crying, avoiding people/places, loss of temper, etc.).

Task 3—Adjust to a world without the deceased: This task involves the client exploring how to adapt to a status quo that acknowledges their loss. Often, this requires that the client learn new skills, change priorities, create a new vision for their life and the future, and develop mechanisms to facilitate moving forward in a healthy and productive way.

Task 4—Find an enduring connection with the deceased in the midst of embarking on a new life: The final task involves the client finding equilibrium or balance. This does not mean the pain of the loss disappears, rather it simply means the client has discovered how to move forward in a healthy and productive way, succeeding in life, without their loss dominating them.

Though more commonly associated with grief therapy, the Tasks of Mourning have utility in a variety of coaching styles and circumstances. These including helping clients passed over for promotion, fired from their position, losing a desirable project, or regretting a past decision.

Professionals seeking additional information may consider Worden's 1982 book, *Grief Counseling and Grief Therapy*.

Sources[269]

TDODAR MODEL

Certification Available: no
Certification Required: no
Assessments: no
Proprietary: no
Client: individuals
Cost: not applicable
Category: decision-making, problem-solving

The TDODAR Model provides a framework for decision-making and problem-solving. Though the origins of the model remain unclear, TDODAR is commonly associated with the aviation industry as a process to help aircraft crew make effective decisions when facing high-stakes emerging or unexpected problems.

The TDODAR Model consists of a six-step process designed to facilitate decision-making during a crisis.

Step 1—Time: The first step involves the client considering the presence of time constraints (e.g., how much time is available for decision-making). Acknowledging how much time they have can help prevent panic from overtaking the client's decision-making process.

Step 2—Diagnosis: The second step involves developing a deep understanding of the problem by exploring the issue and examining what is happening and why (i.e., work the problem). Frameworks to differentiate cause and effect are useful in this step, and some may benefit from including techniques designed to mitigate confirmation bias.

Step 3—Options: During this step, the client considers multiple courses of action that may address or solve the problem. The Options stage requires creativity, so the client may benefit from techniques designed to facilitate brainstorming and out-of-the-box thinking.

Step 4—Decide: In this stage, the client assesses the potential efficacy of each option and prioritizes them. The client may find it useful to incorporate external frameworks that can facilitate the prioritization and selection of the ideal option, the one which makes most sense.

Step 5—Act or assign: Once the client selects an option, they are ready to execute or take action on the option. This step often includes delegating tasks to the appropriate individuals to ensure a successful outcome. This requires awareness of the capabilities and limitations of others.

Step 6—Review: As the client executes the selected option, they will need to examine the results to determine if the effort is producing the desired results. If not, the client will need to repeat the process to find another solution.

Readers may perceive missing steps in the framework, like developing an action plan for executing the solution. Remember, the TDODAR Model facilitates crisis-based problem-solving in aviation. Problems in these circumstances often require rapid decision-making and do not afford much time for planning. To that end, the TDODAR Model may not be an appropriate framework for large-scale organizational problem-solving.

Professionals seeking additional information on the TDODAR Model will find much written on this process.

Sources[270]

TEAM EVOLUTION AND MATURATION MODEL

Certification Available: no
Certification Required: no
Assessments: no
Proprietary: no
Client: groups, teams
Cost: not applicable
Category: teaming

Developed in 1994 by researchers Ben B. Morgan, Eduardo Salas, and Albert S. Glickman, the Team Evolution and Maturation Model (TEAM) provides a framework to explain the process of team development. The model suggests that team development is neither linear nor inherently predictable. In other words, teams may move back and forth across stages at different times influenced by a variety of factors.

The TEAM Model consists of nine stages, seven central and two supplemental.

Stage 1—Preforming (supplemental): This stage focuses on external environmental forces compelling the group to form. These forces may include constraints, issues, problems, demands, or other factors which drive the need for team creation. This occurs before a team forms and serves as the foundation for the experience to come.

Stage 2—Forming (central): During this stage, individuals come together to form the team. The characteristics of individual behaviors in this stage suggest uncertainty and an overabundance of politeness as individuals seek to find their place within the group.

Stage 3—Storming (central): As individuals grow more comfortable with the team, they become more forthcoming with their opinions and feelings, which may lead to conflict. Potentially adding to this conflict, some will compete for formal and informal positions within the group.

Stage 4—Norming (central): As resolution emerges and the conflict abates, team members begin to settle into their respective roles and accept each other.

Stage 5—Performing I (central): In this stage the team makes initial progress toward their goals, though their efforts are inefficient.

Stage 6—Reforming (central): Recognizing their inefficiencies in the previous stage, the team may adjust individual roles, change process implementation, or change team membership to improve efficiency.

Stage 7—Performing II (central): Having effected changes in the previous stage, the team begins performing more efficiently, moving them quickly to their goals.

Stage 8—Conforming (central): During this stage, individual team members complete their assignments; collectively, the team achieves its goals.

Stage 9—Deforming (supplemental): In the final stage, having achieved its goals, the team disbands (i.e., the team loses its identity and ceases to exist). Individuals may depart the team separately or collectively.

The TEAM Model incorporates other frameworks to help characterize the types of activities, called tracks, the team undertakes. See *Poole's Multiple Sequence Model* for more information.

• Task track: encompasses all discourse and activities focused on achieving the team's goals and objectives. These may include establishing and exploring policies, processes, procedures, tools, and courses of action.

• Interpersonal track: encompasses all discourse and activities focused on developing relationships between team members. This may include rapport building, learning about one another, and forming social bonds.

The TEAM Model is one of the more holistic models on teaming as it combines the fundamentals of several preexisting theories to form a more robust framework for how teams come together, function, and succeed.

Professionals seeking additional information may consider the 1993 *Journal of General Psychology* article, "An Analysis of Team Evolution and Maturation."

Sources[271]

TETRAMAP

<table>
<tr><td>Certification Available: yes</td></tr>
<tr><td>Certification Required: yes</td></tr>
<tr><td>Assessments: yes</td></tr>
<tr><td>Proprietary: yes (TetraMap)</td></tr>
<tr><td>Client: individuals, groups</td></tr>
<tr><td>Cost: $2,500</td></tr>
<tr><td>Category: communication, personality type</td></tr>
</table>

Developed in 2000 by corporate training professionals Yoshimi Brett and Jon Brett, TetraMap provides a framework for understanding individual personality types and their communication preferences. A unique aspect of TetraMap lies in its use of nature as a metaphor to characterize personalities and preferences.

The framework consists of four personality types, linked to the elements Earth, Air, Water, and Fire. The use of these labels avoids any negatively biased or positively biased associations. The neutrality of these descriptors means individuals can process their results without the risk of unintentionally assigning inaccurate meaning to the outcomes.

Earth (firm like the mountain): Characteristically, individuals of the Earth element are confident, time-driven, factual, and bold. These individuals value setting goals, striving for goal attainment, and sometimes seek to control their environment.

When Earth types communicate, they may use bullet points to convey facts and save time. They sometimes use significant gesticulations when speaking. To others, an Earth type can seem blunt, excessively direct, and overly goal-focused.

Air (clear like the wind): Characteristically, individuals of the Air element are highly focused, orderly, and logical.

These individuals value accuracy and strive for quality in everything they say and do.

When Air types communicate, they focus heavily on empirical data, statistics, and evidence. In action, they want sufficient time to perform a task correctly. To others, an Air type may appear picky or hypercritical.

Water (calm like a lake): Characteristically, individuals of the Water element are empathic, consistent, steadfast, patient, and loyal. They prefer to focus on people and maintaining harmony in their relationships.

Water types tend to work well with teams and take a genuine interest in how others are feeling. This often makes them the glue that can hold a team together. To others, a Water type can appear hesitant in word and deed.

Fire (bright like the sun): Characteristically, individuals of the Fire element are colorful and full of personality. They love variety and value exploring the possibilities in life. They possess an innate sense of fun and seek to inspire others.

Fire types have lots of ideas, are highly energetic, and ambitious. To others, a Fire type may appear disruptive and unfocused.

The philosophy of TetraMap suggests that while we possess aspects of all four elements, we develop a preference for one or two elements.

According to the Bretts, unlike other personality frameworks, TetraMap is not rooted in psychological theories of personality. This is because the framework is not a clinical or diagnostic tool. TetraMap, by design, provides an easy-to-understand set of characteristics of personality that individuals may use to better understand themselves and others, and foster their ability to adapt to their environment.

Like many of the personality frameworks contained in the ICMT, TetraMap has broad utility. The framework can help clients enhance their self-awareness, develop their leadership skill sets, facilitate individual and organizational change, manage conflict, and improve communication with others.

Use of TetraMap and its associated assessment requires certification. Professionals seeking additional information will find much written on the model, including the Bretts' book, *TetraMap: Develop People and Business the Way Nature Intended.*

Sources[272]

TGROW COACHING MODEL

Certification Available: no
Certification Required: no
Assessments: no
Proprietary: no
Client: individuals, groups
Cost: not applicable
Category: coaching model

Developed in the 2000s by executive coach Myles Downey, the TGROW Coaching Model provides a five-step framework for coaching that expands upon Sir John Whitmore's *GROW Model.*

Downey improved upon Whitmore's model by adding a new first step. In Whitmore's GROW Model, the process begins with the client identifying their goals, whereas Downey's process begins with the client exploring all the potential topics that interest them.

The addition of this new step helps the client consider all relevant topics before initiating goal setting. This may also limit the chances a client changes their focus halfway through the coaching relationship.

Step 1—Topic: During the first step of Downey's coaching process, the client describes all the relevant issues they may wish to discuss. The model encourages clients to explore the scale and scope of each issue to understand the relationship between the topic and their life. In other words, the relative impact of each issue on the client.

During this stage, it is important that the coach help the client reflect on which issues may be less relevant than others. To do this, clients might consider factors such as which issues have the most profound effect on them personally or professionally, which issues they can most easily change, and which ones they are struggling with the most. Then the client selects the issue they want to focus on during coaching.

Step 2—Goal: During the second step, the client works to identify goals or envision a desired end state pertaining to the issue. The client should include both short-term and long-term goals that will help them make progress on the issue facing them.

The TGROW Model recommends the client establish concrete and measurable goals. Because goal development is an ongoing process, the coach should periodically check in with the client to gauge their feelings about the goals they set.

Step 3—Reality: During this step, the client explores where they are now. In other words, the current reality of their situation. This type of exploration may include feedback from leaders, peers, and direct reports. Additionally, the client may reflect on multiple interactions or events which describe the status quo.

The third step is crucial to helping clients identify potential misconceptions they may have about the situation, themselves, or others.

Step 4—Options: During this step, the client applies creativity to identify multiple potential solutions to the problem or issue at hand. These solutions may include changes in behavior, reframing perceptions, or changing their environment.

The TGROW Model encourages coaches to challenge clients to think outside and inside the box. Clients who struggle with creativity may benefit from techniques designed to foster imaginative thinking. Other versions of the TGROW Model call this step **Obstacles**.

Step 5—Will: During the final step in the process, clients consider how they intend to execute the options they identified in the fourth step.

To increase the chances of a successful outcome, the client should make their commitment to action explicit to the coach and to those within their social and professional network who can serve to encourage them and hold them accountable. Other versions of the model call this step **Wrap-Up** or **Way Forward**

Professionals seeking additional information on the TGROW Model may consider Downey's 2003 book, *Effective Coaching: Lessons from the Coach's Coach.*

Sources[273]

THE PLATINUM RULE

Certification Available: no
Certification Required: no
Assessments: no
Proprietary: no
Client: individuals, groups, teams
Cost: not applicable
Category: personality type, communication

Developed in the late 1990s by business professionals Tony Alessandra and Michael J. O'Connor, the Platinum Rule provides a framework for classifying personalities through an examination of communication styles.

The principle underlying the Platinum Rule suggests that one should "treat others as they want to be treated." This contrasts with the popular and long-held Golden Rule, "treat others as you wish to be treated."

The Golden Rule suggests that everyone shares the same preference for how they wish others to treat them. The Platinum Rule, however, implies that each person possesses a unique set of preferences, expectations, and needs for how they wish others to treat them. Therefore, using the Platinum Rule requires us to develop a deeper understanding of others, and their wants and needs as it pertains to how we treat them.

The Platinum Rule framework consists of four types of personalities based on a person's style of communication.

Director: Characterized as no-nonsense, this type of personality prefers to be in control of people and situations. They often adopt a style of communication described as clear and direct.

Driven to achieve, individuals of this type are comfortable taking risks, often undertaking daunting challenges and pushing boundaries. It is not uncommon to hear them say, "It is better to ask for forgiveness than permission."

These individuals tend to be more aggressive, impatient, and task oriented. Others may perceive these individuals as stubborn and insensitive despite their ability to accomplish great things.

Socializer: These individuals are gregarious, outgoing, and social. They crave the limelight and thrive on admiration and acknowledgment.

Often characterized as warm, charming, and persuasive, their charisma enables them to influence and rally people to support their cause. This type of person can motivate people to participate in the task at hand.

Others may perceive Socializers as impatient, with short attention spans. At times, they may appear aloof, though they despise being alone.

Relator: These individuals are warm and personable. Considered the most people friendly of the four categories, they make excellent friends and great listeners.

As members of the team, they will share in the responsibility and work. Others may perceive them as risk averse and inflexible to changing environments. Their need to maintain the safety and comfort of the status quo can make them ill-equipped to adapt in a changing environment.

Thinker: These individuals are systematic and analytical in their approach to problem-solving. They focus more on content, accuracy, and details than style. Typically, Thinkers do not engage in showmanship.

These individuals tend to control their emotions, though they can become uncomfortable around those with flashy or gregarious personalities.

The four behavioral styles in the Platinum Rule framework share similarities with other models contained in this compendium, like *DISC*, *Merrill-Reid Social Styles*, and *TetraMap*, among others.

Professionals seeking additional information on the Platinum Rule may consider Alessandra and O'Connor's 1998 book, *The Platinum Rule: Discover the Four Basic Business Personalities and How They Can Lead You to Success.*

Sources[274]

THEORIES AND SCHOOLS OF PSYCHOLOGY

Certification Available: no
Certification Required: no
Assessments: no
Proprietary: no
Client: individuals
Cost: not applicable
Category: coaching model

There is an indelible link between psychology and coaching. With few exceptions, many of the approaches, techniques, theories, and assessments used in coaching derive from research born of psychology. Many of the theories presented in *The Infourge Compendium of Models and Theories* derive from one or more of the seven major schools of psychology, also called the Grand Theories of Psychology.

Structuralism: Considered the first school of psychology, Structuralism breaks down the mental process into its most basic components. Developed by Wilhelm Wundt, this style emphasizes the technique of introspection as a means of examining one's thoughts in an objective manner.

Functionalism: Developed by William James, the Functional school focuses on the role mental processes play for a person. For comparison, Structuralism tries to understand what mental process is in play, while Functionalism tries to understand what function the mental process serves. Put another way, this school explores the purpose of thoughts and behaviors.

Gestalt Psychology: Developed by Max Wertheimer, Wolfgang Köhler, and Kurt Koffka, this school famously advocated that the whole is greater than the sum of its parts. The Gestalt approach examines the whole of an individual's experience, believing that it is important to identify the patterns that exist within a person's experience.

Behaviorism: Developed by John Watson, B.F. Skinner, and Ivan Pavlov, Behaviorism suggests that environmental or external forces, not internal forces, explain human behavior.

Psychoanalysis: Developed by Sigmund Freud, this school of psychology focuses on the ability of the unconscious mind to influence a person's behavior.

Humanistic Psychology: Developed by Abraham Maslow, Carl Rogers, and Clark Moustakas, this school of psychology focuses on helping people achieve their full potential. Humanistic Psychology would later play a significant role in the development of Positive Psychology.

Cognitive Psychology: This school explores the mental processes involved with how people think, perceive, remember, and learn.

The popularity and utility of these psychological approaches vary. Regardless, each school of psychology has played an important role in the evolution of psychology. Consequently, professionals may notice these schools of psychology as they manifest in coaching.

For example, Cognitive Psychology significantly influenced development of *Cognitive Behavioral Coaching*, while Humanistic Psychology influenced the growth of *Positive Psychology Coaching*.

It is important to note that several sources make a distinction between traditional coaching and coaching psychology. They define coaching psychology as coaching based on one of the grand theories of psychology. Other sources, however, suggest that most traditional coaching styles can be attributed to one or more of the schools of psychology. These latter sources argue that coaching psychology is simply the application of coaching within a clinical or therapy setting.

Professionals seeking to learn more about the relationship between these schools of psychology and coaching will find a variety of thought pieces, blogs, and editorials on the topic freely available online.

Sources[275]

THEORIES OF CONFLICT (GENERAL ENTRY)

Certification Available: no
Certification Required: no
Assessments: no
Proprietary: no
Client: individuals, groups
Cost: not applicable
Category: conflict

Conflict is a common theme in coaching and may derive from internal or external sources and occur between individuals and groups. The origin of conflict, the personalities of those involved, the motivations driving behavior, and the various types of conflict prevent a one-size-fits-all approach to resolution. In fact, this has led to several different types of approaches: those that strive for conflict resolution, conflict management, and conflict transformation.

A number of theories exploring conflict exist, allowing coaches to evaluate the conflict and select the most appropriate framework for the situation. Each theory offers a slightly different approach to conflict, whether it is resolution, management, or transformation.

Social psychologist Morton Deutsch developed the **Theory of Cooperation and Competition**, also called the **Cooperative Model**. A common framework in negotiations, the Cooperative Model strives to help competing parties strike a balance between cooperation and competition to seek out a win-win solution. Instead of splitting the pie 50/50, leaving no one truly happy, this approach encourages parties to work together to increase the size of the pie.

The **Principled Negotiation Model**, developed by professors Roger Fisher and William Ury, strives for conflict resolution by separating the person from the conflict. This framework facilitates a pragmatic approach to conflict, requiring an intense exploration of the driving forces behind each party's position. By understanding the party's rationale for their position, it can be easier to find resolution.

The **Human Needs Model**, developed by professor John W. Burton, sees conflict emerging when one or both parties perceive their needs threatened. This approach involves identifying which need is threatened and restructuring the relational dynamic between parties so productive discourse may occur. Unlike the more pragmatic Principled Negotiation Model, the Human Needs Model includes the emotional side of conflict.

The **Strategy of Conflict**, from professor Thomas C. Schelling, adopts a game theory perspective on conflict. Though his work focuses on high-stakes conflict between nations, his work has utility in coaching. Schelling's treatise on the subject goes beyond the traditional belief that conflict is about winning and includes consideration for rational and irrational behaviors.

Social psychologist Donald Campbell coined the term **Realistic Conflict Theory** to explain how hostility between individuals and groups arises from conflicting goals and the competition for limited resources. When combined with in-group/out-group identities, this leads to prejudice and discrimination, further exacerbating the conflict, making resolution difficult at best.

When exploring conflict, it helps to consider how different sources characterize the types of conflict. One characterization identifies two types of conflict. **Cognitive Conflict**, considered healthy conflict, focuses on the issue and involves objective debate. This form of conflict is essential to positive growth and the development of people, groups, and organizations. **Affective Conflict**, considered unhealthy conflict, involves personal attacks against the other party. This form of conflict creates mistrust and can lead to anger and hatred.

Many approaches to conflict offer a litany of techniques to address specific challenges that may arise. For example, when confronting spiraling negativity or position inflexibility, coaches may try perspective-taking exercises designed to help parties consider the other party's point of view.

Professionals will find no shortage of books, articles, and literature on conflict, including The Arbinger Institute's *The Anatomy of Peace,* and the 2020 book, *The Handbook of Conflict Resolution: Theory and Practice* by P.T. Coleman, M. Deutsch, and E.C. Marcus.

Sources[276]

THEORY OF INVENTIVE PROBLEM-SOLVING

Certification Available: yes (Altshuller Institute for TRIZ Studies)
Certification Required: no
Assessments: no
Proprietary: no
Client: individuals, groups, teams
Cost: $4,250
Category: problem-solving

Developed in 1946 by engineer Genrich S. Altshuller, the Theory of Inventive Problem-Solving (TRIZ) provides a complex and multifaceted framework for problem-solving and innovation. To form his theory, Altshuller conducted an examination of patents to identify patterns in how developers overcame problems and created new ideas. His research revealed three patterns that would influence his Theory of Inventive Problem-Solving.

• Problems and their solutions repeat across industries and sciences.

• Patterns of technical evolution repeat across industries and sciences.

• Innovations use scientific effects outside of the field from which they were developed.

TRIZ is complex, consisting of multiple facets like the 40 Principles of Problem-Solving (also known as the 40 Inventive Principles), the Separation Principles, and the 76 Standard Solutions. The complexity of TRIZ precludes us from including all facets in this compendium. Instead, we present TRIZ's simple four-step process for problem-solving which captures the fundamental approach used in all facets of Altshuller's theory.

Step 1—Define and generalize the problem: This involves the client defining their problem, then generalizing it to facilitate a comparison with other problems. The act of generalizing the problem allows the client to identify and compare the problem across industries and sciences.

Step 2—Find a comparable problem: During this step, the client seeks out problems with similar characteristics.

Step 3—Explore the similar problem's solution: In this step, the client explores the successful solutions used for similar problems. This step introduces TRIZ's 40 Principles of Problem-Solving.

Step 4—Adapt the solution: In the final step, the client considers how to adapt the similar problem's solution to their problem.

TRIZ also includes the concept of Contradictions. This occurs when innovation pertaining to one principle (of the 40 Principles of Problem-Solving) creates a problem with another principle. For example, a company wants to increase storage in a product's hard drive (this is one principle), but doing so means the weight (principle) and size (another principle) of the product go up.

TRIZ classifies Contradictions into two categories:

Technical contradictions: These are traditional trade-offs, like the example above. To get something desired means getting something else you do not want.

Inherent (or physical) contradictions: These typically involve polarities. In other words, the issue is not a matter of either-or but one of both and to what degree. For example, the client wants a hot cup of coffee, but not so hot it burns their tongue.

Though developed for engineers and scientists, many aspects of TRIZ have utility beyond these fields. For example, several of the 40 Principles can help clients examine solutions to a problem by removing or adding elements to the situation, combining potential solutions, and considering measures to protect the client in the event they encounter the problem again.

TRIZ is significantly more complex than presented here and includes matrixes which can help clients engage their problems using a structured approach. Professionals seeking additional information may consider Altshuller's 1994 book, *And Suddenly the Inventor Appeared: TRIZ, the Theory of Inventive Problem-Solving*. Additionally, the Altshuller Institute for TRIZ Studies offers certification courses.

Sources[277]

THEORY OF PLANNED BEHAVIOR

Certification Available: no
Certification Required: no
Assessments: no
Proprietary: no
Client: individuals
Cost: not applicable
Category: change (ind.)

Developed in 1985 by psychologist Icek Ajzen, the Theory of Planned Behavior (TPB) provides a framework for understanding and predicting human behavior by examining a client's beliefs, attitudes, and social influences. TPB evolved from the Theory of Reasoned Action, developed in 1980 by Ajzen and psychologist Martin Fishbein.

The Theory of Planned Behavior consists of three variables (alternative versions identify up to six variables) which can predict the likelihood a person will engage in a specific behavior (i.e., adopt change).

Attitude: This is the client's subjective evaluation (i.e., thoughts and feelings) about the new behavior. The client forms a favorable or unfavorable assessment based on all available knowledge and any existing prejudices/biases. The client considers the pros and cons of the new behavior, while being influenced by their preconceptions, and then formulates a sentiment regarding the new behavior. The client's attitude plays a key role in determining the likelihood they will commit to change.

Subjective Norm: This is the client's perception of how others will judge the new behavior. The attitudes of friends and family can influence how a client thinks and feels about the new behavior. Those closest or the people most important to the client often carry the greatest influence.

An expanded version of the TPB framework builds off Subjective Norm by including **Social Norms** as a variable. This applies to behaviors deemed appropriate by culture and society which further influence a person's perception of the new behavior.

Exploring the relationship between the client's thoughts and feelings and how others may influence them can help the client make conscious decisions about the new behavior.

Perceived Behavioral Control: This is the extent to which the client believes they can perform the new behavior. This factor is multifaceted and includes the person's perception of their abilities, the availability of resources to support the new behavior, and their sense of control.

Other versions of the framework expand upon Perceived Behavioral Control with the addition of **Perceived Power** (or **Control Beliefs**). This is the client's perception of factors (real or imagined) that may impede their ability to perform the new behavior.

Exploring the client's confidence in their ability to perform the new behavior can lead the client to seek out new skills to improve their abilities.

The Theory of Planned Behavior suggests that these variables influence the client's **Behavioral Intention**, their level of motivation to perform the new behavior. When all the variables are positive, a person's intention to perform the new behavior goes up. Through an exploration of these three variables, we can better predict the client's orientation for behavioral achievement.

Though heavily focused on clinical applications, the theory offers broad utility for coaching. Coaches working with clients engaged in change may use TPB as a conduit to explore the likelihood the client will adopt the changes.

Professionals interested in TPB may also consider *Consistency Theory*, the *Health Belief Model*, *Self-Efficacy Theory*, and the *Transtheoretical Model*.

Professionals seeking additional information will find significant literature available on the Theory of Planned Behavior. This includes Ajzen's 1985 article, "From Intentions to Actions: A Theory of Planned Behavior." Additionally, Ajzen and Fishbein published several books which incorporate TPB, including their 2009 book, *Predicting and Changing Behavior: The Reasoned Action Approach*.

Sources[278]

THEORY U

Certification Available: yes (Presencing Institute/
U-School)
Certification Required: no
Assessments: no
Proprietary: no
Client: individuals, organizations
Cost: pricing not available
Category: change (ind.), leadership

Developed in the early 2000s by MIT lecturer Otto Scharmer, Theory U provides a framework for change described as letting go of the past to realize the future as it is happening. Practitioners of Theory U tout its relevance as a change management model, a framework for leadership, a form of systems thinking, and a method for living a more fulfilling life.

Visually depicted as an arrow in the shape of the letter "U," the client's journey takes them from the left side of the U to the right. To comprehend Theory U, it helps to understand the underlying concept of the **Blind Spot**. This is the belief that we are blind to the deeper dimensions of leadership, change, and social interactions, which Scharmer calls **Source Dimensions**. It is the Blind Spot that Theory U seeks to explore.

Theory U consists of the five movements and the seven leadership capacities. As clients journey through the five movements, they simultaneously improve within the seven leadership capacities.

Movement 1—Co-Initiating: This involves building common intent by opening the mind and being receptive to others and to life. Clients do this by listening to themselves and others.

Movement 2—Co-sensing: This involves clients opening their heart and observing what the world is telling them.

Movement 3—Presencing: The client connects to their source of inspiration (i.e., the world within). This is the process of letting go of ego, self, and the past.

Movement 4—Co-creating: This involves the client envisioning what is possible by exploring the future.

Movement 5—Co-evolving: The client embodies the vision through action.

Leadership Capacity 1—Listening: creating the space to listen to self and others.

Leadership Capacity 2—Observing: suspending judgments to allow for honest observations.

Leadership Capacity 3—Sensing: fine-tuning an open mind, heart, and will.

Leadership Capacity 4—Presencing: connecting to the deepest part of self, which requires letting go of ego and the past.

Leadership Capacity 5—Crystalizing: committing to purpose and change through visioning.

Leadership Capacity 6—Prototyping: integrating thought and feeling in the context of experimenting and learning by doing.

Leadership Capacity 7—Performing: moving from discussing and visualizing change to creating change.

Theory U is significantly more complex than presented here and includes a multifaceted exploration of the client's somatic experience. Scharmer's framework can help clients develop the skills necessary for letting go of the past, allowing them to embrace the future. Additionally, the Presencing Institute offers several tools to facilitate the application of Theory U on its website.

Professionals seeking additional information may consider one of Scharmer's many publications, like his 2007 book, *Theory U: Leading from the Future as it Emerges*.

The Presencing Institute, via the U-School for Transformation, offers an extensive certification program for interested professionals.

Sources[279]

THEORY X AND THEORY Y

Certification Available: no
Certification Required: no
Assessments: no
Proprietary: no
Client: individuals, organizations
Cost: not applicable
Category: motivation, leadership

Developed in 1960 by social psychologist Douglas McGregor, Theory X and Theory Y provides a framework to explain how a manager's beliefs about employee motivation affect their management style. The model consists of two diametrically opposed styles, each based on a set of assumptions a manager may have about employee motivations.

Theory X: This style describes managers who possess a pessimistic view of their people. Consequently, they adopt a more authoritarian approach to leadership.

Key assumptions underlying Theory X include the belief that workers inherently dislike their work, they lack motivation, and they have no natural incentive to perform. Managers who embrace these assumptions adapt their managerial behaviors accordingly. These include the direct and meticulous control of worker task performance (i.e., micromanagement) and the overdependent use of extrinsic rewards (i.e., money) to encourage performance.

Another assumption held by Theory X managers is the belief that people prefer their style of management because it frees them from the burden of responsibility. This assumption hinges on the belief that workers lack the creativity and intelligence to solve the organization's problems, viewing such tasks with great anxiety.

Theory X managers tend to rely heavily on the threat of punishment to discourage undesirable behavior. For this reason, Theory X managers present as autocratic, authoritarian, coercive, and/or dictatorial.

Theory Y: This style describes managers who possess an optimistic view of their people. Consequently, they adopt a participative approach to leadership.

Key assumptions underlying Theory Y include the belief that workers possess sufficient self-motivation to accomplish the organization's goals, especially when working on tasks of their own initiative. Additionally, Theory Y suggests that employees inherently assume responsibility for their work and find it intrinsically rewarding.

Theory Y managers tend to adopt a hands-off approach to leading, encourage employees to collaborate, and include them in decision-making. This style of leadership recognizes and capitalizes on the employees' intrinsic motivations.

Unlike Theory X managers, who use feedback as a means of criticizing undesirable behavior, Theory Y managers use feedback to reinforce and encourage desirable behavior.

Often associated with *Maslow's Hierarchy of Needs*, Theory X and Theory Y suggest that managers following the Theory X style tend to focus on satisfying the individual's basic needs (e.g., job security, pay), while those adopting the Theory Y style focus more on the individual's higher-level needs (e.g., a sense of belonging or the opportunity to increase self-esteem through achievement).

Theory X and Theory Y apply to organizational culture as much as individual leadership style. In this, McGregor's work is useful in exploring and characterizing the managerial culture of an organization.

McGregor points out that while it may seem Theory Y is the preferred approach, neither is universally correct. He argues that the environment and situation play a role in determining which approach to management is most appropriate. For this reason, Theory X and Theory Y fall under the umbrella of *Contingency Theories*.

Professionals seeking additional information on Theory X and Theory Y will find a significant amount of literature available, including McGregor's 1960 book, *The Human Side of Enterprise*.

Sources[280]

THEORY Z

Certification Available: no
Certification Required: no
Assessments: no
Proprietary: no
Client: individuals, groups, teams
Cost: not applicable
Category: motivation, engagement

Developed in 1981 by business management professor William Ouchi, Theory Z provides insight into the impact of culture on employee motivation and engagement. Specifically, Theory Z explores how Japanese culture affects employee motivation compared to that of American culture.

Through his research, Ouchi determined that Japan's collectivist culture played a significant role in fostering the efficacy of Japanese management. By contrast, American culture is one of individualism, and until Ouchi's work, many believed the two were incompatible. Professor Ouchi, however, believed it was possible for American companies to obtain similar levels of management efficiencies while still respecting an individual's independence.

To prove his point, he created Theory Z, a hybrid management approach combining Japanese philosophy with American cultural values. Theory Z consists of several principles or considerations for creating and sustaining employee engagement. The following represents a selection of these principles.

Job for life: Ouchi noticed that organizations which adopt the mindset "everyone is replaceable" tend to treat their employees as cogs, discarding them at will. For employees, it creates a perception the organization does not care for them or about them, and their job is a temporary short-term event. This perpetuates an employee mindset that undermines loyalty.

Theory Z proposes organizations shift their mindset to promote the idea their jobs are for life. Create the environment and expectation that employee positions should last. Treating employees as members of a collective (or family) changes their perception so they no longer see themselves as replaceable cogs but as vital members who require care and nurturing.

Employee voice: Organizations should encourage their employees to contribute to decision-making, as this will give them a sense of ownership in the work and the mission. Empowering employees to voice their concerns creates an environment where they feel appreciated and heard. For those within individualist cultures, the ability to voice one's thoughts and for others to listen is an essential source of motivation.

Accountability: Organizations should hold individuals accountable (both for good and bad), but do so in the context of the greater organization. Highlight the individual's performance, positive or negative, and its impact on others within the organization, the customer, and the mission. Accountability, when done correctly, is not about calling people out; rather it demonstrates that managers care about each person and their performance.

Growth and development: Theory Z encourages organizations to provide developmental opportunities for employees so they may acquire new skills and abilities. They should ensure employees also have opportunities to move around within the company. This principle satisfies an employee's intrinsic motivation for new experiences.

Extensive literature explores multiple aspects of Theory Z, including the Theory Z Worker, the Theory Z Leader, and the Theory Z Organization. Sources offer insight into considerations for clients seeking to create a Theory Z Organization.

Heavily influenced by Douglas McGregor's *Theory X and Theory Y,* Theory Z's exploration of culture's impact on employee motivation and engagement makes it a useful resource for organizational and leadership development.

Professionals seeking additional information may consider Ouchi's 1981 book, *Theory Z: How American Business Can Meet the Japanese Challenge.*

Sources[281]

THOMAS KILMANN MODEL

Certification Available: yes
Certification Required: yes
Assessments: yes (TKI)
Proprietary: yes (The Myers-Briggs Company)
Client: individuals, groups, teams
Cost: $875–$1,100
Category: conflict

The Thomas Kilmann Model (TKM), developed in the 1970s by management professors Kenneth Thomas and Ralph H. Kilmann, provides a framework for understanding and characterizing individual approaches to conflict management.

The Thomas Kilmann Model explores conflict management across two dimensions, resulting in a framework consisting of five distinct conflict management styles.

Dimension 1—Assertiveness: This is the degree to which a client tries to satisfy their own needs when conflict arises. Individuals high on assertiveness tend to adopt uncompromising positions, while those low on assertiveness welcome compromise.

Dimension 2—Cooperativeness: This is the degree to which a client tries to satisfy the other person's needs. Highly cooperative individuals strive to understand the other person's point of view, while those low on cooperation care little for what the other person desires.

Style 1—Avoiding: Characterized as unassertive and uncooperative, individuals adopting this style of conflict management avoid conflict altogether either because they have no stake in the conflict or because conflict creates unbearable anxiety. Signs of a conflict-avoidant style include sidestepping the issue, postponing plans to discuss the issue, or abruptly withdrawing from the discussion.

Style 2—Accommodating: Characterized as unassertive but highly cooperative, individuals adopting this style of conflict management try to satisfy the needs of other people at the cost of their own, often leading others to perceive them as submissive or selfless. Signs of an accommodating style include giving away too much of the pie to the other person, appearing to forsake one's own needs, wants, or desires, and overly acquiescing to the other party.

Style 3—Competing: Characterized as assertive but uncooperative, individuals adopting this style of conflict management try to satisfy their own needs at the expense of the other party. This style is power- and position-oriented. Signs of a competing style include vying for as much of the pie as possible, leaving less for the other person, wanting to have the last word, and viewing the conflict as a zero-sum game.

Style 4—Compromising: Characterized as moderately assertive and cooperative, individuals adopting this style of conflict management strive to find a solution which satisfies an equal portion of both side's needs. Both parties gain and lose equally. Signs of a compromising style include splitting the difference, portioning the pie evenly, and that neither party feels wholly satisfied or unhappy.

Style 5—Collaborating: Characterized as assertive and cooperative, individuals adopting this style of conflict management work to meet the desires of both parties. Signs of a collaborative style include a win-win mindset, expanding the size of the pie so everyone gets what they want, and a genuine desire for both parties to work together in creative fashion to find an ideal solution.

Widely used in negotiations, group coaching, and crisis management, the Thomas Kilmann Model allows individuals to understand their natural predisposition to conflict management, identify the preferred conflict management style of others, and adapt accordingly.

The Thomas Kilmann Model includes several tools and assessments, including the Thomas Kilmann Conflict Mode Instrument (TKI) for individuals and groups. TKM is proprietary to the Myers-Briggs Company, and incorporating the model formally into practice requires training and certification.

Professionals seeking additional information on the Thomas Kilmann Model may consider their 1976 article found on ResearchGate, "Thomas-Kilmann Conflict MODE Instrument."

Sources[282]

THREE-DIMENSIONAL MODEL OF ATTRIBUTION

Certification Available: no
Certification Required: no
Assessments: no
Proprietary: no
Client: individuals
Cost: not applicable
Category: bias, change (ind.), employee engagement, motivation

Developed by social psychologist Bernard Weiner, the Three-Dimensional Model of Attribution builds upon Fritz Heider's *Attribution Theory* by exploring the relationship between attribution and achievement. Put another way, Weiner's model examines how a person's attributions (a product of their perceptions) can affect their ability to perform and succeed.

To understand the Three-Dimensional Model of Attribution, it helps to know the three principles underlying the model. These explain how a person makes attributions of another person's behavior and how they make attributions to the outcome of a task or situation.

Principle 1: A person making attribution of another's behavior follows a three-step process.

Step 1—The person observes actual behavior; it is real, not imagined.

Step 2—The person determines the behavior is deliberate, not forced or accidental.

Step 3—The person attributes the behavior to either internal or external causes.

Principle 2: When reflecting on the outcome of a task or situation, a person may consider four variables when attributing success or failure.

- Effort: the amount of energy put forth to accomplish a task.

- Ability: the skill required to accomplish a task.

- Difficulty: the degree to which a task is challenging.

- Luck: the role of chance in an outcome.

Principle 3: When reflecting on the outcome of a task or situation, a person may consider three variables affecting their behavior in relation to their performance.

- Locus of control: This pertains to a person's perception that the cause of an outcome is either internal or external. If the person believes they are responsible, then their attribution is internal. If they believe someone or something else is responsible, then their attribution is external.

- Stability: This pertains to a person's perception of whether the cause of an outcome is consistent over time or a singular event. If the cause persists, it is stable. If the cause is isolated, then it is unstable.

- Controllability: This pertains to a person's perception that the cause is within their ability to influence. If they believe the cause is beyond their control, it is not controllable. If they can influence the cause, it is controllable.

A person's determination or belief on each of the three variables will influence their attitudes, motivation, and sense of self-efficacy. This, in turn, affects the person's ability to perform.

The Three-Dimensional Model of Attribution suggests that when a person attributes behaviors or causes to factors beyond their control, assigns responsibility to others, or believes the causes of failure persist, then a person may experience decreased motivation to perform a task.

Weiner's model has broad utility in coaching and is useful for exploring employee motivation, personal change, and individual goal attainment. The model also provides a framework for challenging a client's assumptions, their cognitive processes, and bias when making attribution or assigning blame for an outcome.

Professionals seeking additional information on the Three-Dimensional Model of Attribution will find much written on the topic, including Weiner's 1986 book, *An Attributional Theory of Motivation and Emotion*.

Sources[283]

TICHY'S TPC MODEL

Certification Available: no
Certification Required: no
Assessments: no
Proprietary: no
Client: groups, organizations
Cost: not applicable
Category: change (org.)

Developed in the early 1980s by management consultant Noel Tichy, the TPC Model provides a comprehensive framework to facilitate change management within organizations. The TPC Model consists of three key dynamics and nine "change levers" used to foster change.

The three key dynamics provide a framework for understanding the forces influencing the organization. These include factors internal and external to the organization. Identifying and understanding the forces influencing the organization provides valuable information to support decision-making and strategy development.

Dynamic 1—Technical: This involves the exploration of an organization's structure, policies, doctrine, technological advancements, product portfolio, and more. The technical dynamic seeks to understand how changes to the economic ecosystem (e.g., economic conditions and industry forces) affect how the organization functions. For example, an organization may wish to analyze the impact of new technology advancements on how the organization conducts business.

Dynamic 2—Political: This involves an examination of the sources prompting the organization to consider change. These can include issues associated with the distribution and use of power, forces influencing decision-makers, and the allocation of limited resources. Exploring the political

dynamic requires an understanding of both macro and micro perspectives.

Other considerations within the political dynamic include the relationship between the organization and the environment, and the relationship between elements within the organization. These relationships are significant sources of influence, guiding the organization.

Dynamic 3—Cultural: This involves an exploration of the values and beliefs influencing the organization and people involved. These can include external cultural dynamics provoking change, like the country where the firm is based, and internal cultural dynamics like organizational culture.

Once change agents understand the three dynamics, they may begin to effect change using the nine levers. Each lever represents an element essential to successful change.

Lever 1—External interface of the organization's external environment (input)

Lever 2—Mission

Lever 3—Strategy (Vision)

Lever 4—Managing organizational mission and strategy processes

Lever 5—Task

Lever 6—Prescribed networks (formal organizational structure)

Lever 7—Organizational processes

Lever 8—People

Lever 9—Emergent networks (informal organizations)

To manipulate these levers, change agents have three fundamental tools available to them. These include the use of strategy tools like goal setting, mission statements, and vision statements; the use of structural tools like management processes, metrics, and chain of command; and the use of human resource tools like recruiting, selection, performance reviews, and rewards.

Tichy's TPC Model is more complex than presented here. Professionals seeking additional information may consider Tichy's 1983 book, *Managing Strategic Change.*

Sources[284]

TOXIC POSITIVITY

Certification Available: no
Certification Required: no
Assessments: no
Proprietary: no
Client: groups, organizations
Cost: not applicable
Category: self-awareness, stress management

The term Toxic Positivity describes the excessive or inappropriate use of well-intentioned positivity which avoids, rejects, suppresses, invalidates, or minimizes a person's negative emotions or experiences. As grief expert David Kessler says, "Toxic positivity is positivity given in the wrong way, in the wrong dose, at the wrong time."

The sources of toxic positivity vary, but some of the most common reasons a person engages in toxic positivity may include anxiety or discomfort stemming from another person's pain, a lack of social skills to deal with a person's negative feelings, low empathy for the person, or a general lack of awareness of how to handle or support a person experiencing intense negative feelings.

Indications you are engaging in toxic positivity toward another person include the following.

• Minimizing another person's negative feelings through the use of positive quotes and sayings like "stay positive," "everything happens for a reason," and "pull yourself up by your bootstraps." This also includes the popular statement, "If I can do it, so can you."

• Telling a person what they should be grateful for instead of validating their feelings.

• Shaming another for not feeling gratitude or positivity.

• Dismissing a person's feelings with statements like "it is what it is."

Indications you are engaging in toxic positivity toward yourself include masking your true feelings, dismissing negative emotions to be "tough," and feeling guilty for feeling bad.

The consequences of toxic positivity are real and can lead to serious physical, health, and psychological effects. These include an overwhelming sense of shame for feeling bad or negative that can result in depression, loss of sleep, and a sense of diminished self-worth.

Additionally, people exposed to prolonged toxic positivity may begin to suppress their feelings or isolate themselves from others.

Most theories of adult development and psychology emphasize the important role of experiential learning to a person's personal and professional growth. Some of the most significant life-changing experiences come from negative events. The presence of toxic positivity risks compromising a person's ability to meaningfully process these experiences and learn from them.

It is important to note that there is no definitive line between being positive and being toxically positive. As with many things, toxic positivity is not typically a single act, but a pattern of behavior. This behavior can be deliberate or accidental, directed at others or at one's self.

Techniques to avoid toxic positivity include considering your own feelings about someone else's negative emotions, giving thought to the most appropriate way to respond before responding, listening without judgment, validating the other person's emotion, and most importantly, adopting the mindset that "it is okay to not be okay."

For coaches who use Positive Psychology Coaching, it is important to remember that positive coaching does not avoid negative emotions or experiences but leverages them to foster the client's growth.

Professionals seeking additional information on Toxic Positivity will find much written about the concept, including the 2022 book, *Toxic Positivity: Keeping It Real in a World Obsessed with Being Happy*, written by psychotherapist Whitney Goodman.

Sources[285]

TRAIT THEORY (CARLYLE/GALTON)

Certification Available: no
Certification Required: no
Assessments: no
Proprietary: no
Client: individuals
Cost: not applicable
Category: leadership

Developed in the mid-1800s by historian Thomas Carlyle, his theory suggests leadership traits are innate; leaders are born, not made. Attempting to demonstrate his point, Carlyle presented detailed studies of history's greatest leaders as examples of the "natural-born leader." These included Julius Caesar and Alexander the Great, among others.

A fundamental aspect of early Trait Theory is the belief that the attributes of exceptional leaders derive from their genetic makeup. Individuals without inborn leadership qualities could not learn or develop the necessary leadership skills. In the late 1860s, noted polymath Sir Francis Galton further contributed to this notion when he described leadership as "an immutable property endowed to extraordinary individuals."

Trait Theory endured unchallenged for nearly a century until the mid-1900s, when leadership theorists and academics began to question the efficacy of Carlyle's theory. Trait Theory opponents questioned Carlyle's research, observing that among the leaders he studied, the only shared inborn trait among them was being born with status.

Other countervailing arguments highlight the critical fact that all the leaders Carlyle studied lived during a period and place where leadership was determined by title which, in turn, was determined based on bloodline, gender, race, or religious affiliation, not skill or quality.

Over the ensuing years, leadership theorists have excoriated Trait Theory, citing a lack of scientific evidence. Using Galton's own concept of "nature vs. nurture" against him, theorists determined that leadership is not a matter of one or the other but involves a combination of both factors. While some may possess inborn skills that may foster leadership, they alone do not make the leader.

In 1948, psychologist Ralph Melvin Stogdill released the findings of his 40-year research project into Trait Theory and discovered that leadership occurred in all people, and not just special people.

In the late 1970s, Stogdill made additional discoveries which further contravened the fundamental beliefs of Trait Theory. These include a determination that physical characteristics were not singularly critical for leadership efficacy, and that leadership ability can manifest in the young (classic Trait Theory argued that leadership was the domain of the mature).

It is important to point out that one of the key architects of classic Trait Theory, Francis Galton, was a noted proponent of scientific racism (the belief that scientific evidence exists to support or justify racism) and was an avowed pioneer of eugenics (he believed in improving the quality of a population by excluding what he perceived to be inferior groups of people). The presence of these belief systems undoubtedly influenced Galton's work in this field.

Discredited in its original form, classic Trait Theory evolved from the initial belief that genetics determines leadership. Almost two hundred years after its development, an alternative version of Trait Theory emerged. See *Trait Theory (Kouzes/Posner)*.

We include Trait Theory in the ICMT because it is one of the first theories of leadership and it demonstrates evolution in the field of leadership science.

Professionals may encounter variations of this theory, as it is also known as the Great Man Theory, the Great Person Theory, and the more colorful Big Beast Theory.

Professionals interested in a critical review of Trait Theory may consider Harrison Sachs' 2020 essay, "Why the Trait Theory Approach to Leadership Is Illogical … Issues That Arise from Determining Leadership Potential."

Sources[286]

TRAIT THEORY (KOUZES/POSNER)

> **Certification Available:** yes (The Leadership Challenge)
> **Certification Required:** no
> **Assessments:** no
> **Proprietary:** no
> **Client:** individuals
> **Cost:** $1,400–$2,400 (depending on course)
> **Category:** leadership

Developed in the 1980s by leadership researchers James Kouzes and Barry Posner, their version of Trait Theory provides a framework consisting of multiple traits observed in effective leaders.

Kouzes and Posner's theory is distinct and separate from the classic *Trait Theory (Carlyle/Galton)* of leadership. In their original work on Trait Theory, Carlyle and Galton examined historical figures recognized for their leadership styles. They studied available texts to identify the traits of these leaders. This approach left them vulnerable to the inaccuracies of historical accounts which often lacked precision due to embellishment or bias.

Rather than examine past leaders, Kouzes and Posner's approach focused on the characteristics people wanted from their leaders. In other words, they asked people to profile their ideal leader. Using a combination of surveys and interviews of hundreds of individuals at various levels of leadership, Kouzes and Posner identified dozens of traits respondents associated with effective leadership. Following are some of the most frequently listed traits:

- Honest
- Forward-Looking
- Inspirational
- Competent

- Fair-Minded
- Supportive
- Broad-Minded
- Intelligent
- Straightforward
- Dependable
- Adaptable/Flexible
- Assertive
- Courageous
- Creative
- Decisive
- Responsible
- Emotionally Stable
- Achievement Oriented
- Personable
- Trustworthy
- Understanding of Follower Needs

Kouzes and Posner's work in Trait Theory eventually led them to develop a new framework called the *Five Leadership Practices*. Readers will notice that the traits identified in the authors' research form the foundations for each of the five practices identified in their framework.

- Model the way
- Inspire shared vision
- Challenge the process
- Enable others to act
- Encourage the heart

Opponents of Trait Theory argue that although many effective leaders possess the traits identified by Kouzes and Posner, not all who possess these traits are good leaders. In other words, the presence of these traits is no guarantee of effective leadership.

Professionals seeking additional information on Kouzes and Posner's Trait Theory will find much written on the subject, though sources vary on their use of labels and characterizations of the theory. It is important that readers make their own distinctions between classic Trait Theory and general theories of trait-based leadership which examine the characteristics associated with effective leadership.

It is important to note that while classic Trait Theory (Carlyle and Galton) holds little validity by today's standards, Kouzes and Posner's Trait Theory provides an optic through which to examine leadership.

Use of Trait Theory does not require certification; however, use of Kouzes and Posner's Five Leadership Practices and its associated assessment instrument does require certification. Professionals seeking additional information may consider Kouzes and Posner's 2012 book, *The Leadership Challenge: How to Make Extraordinary Things Happen in Organizations.*

Sources[287]

TRANSACTIONAL LEADERSHIP THEORY

Certification Available: no
Certification Required: no
Assessments: no
Proprietary: no
Client: individuals
Cost: not applicable
Category: leadership

Introduced in 1947 by sociologist Max Weber, Transactional Leadership Theory (TLT) describes a style of leadership in which leaders motivate followers using a system of extrinsic rewards and punishments. Weber's theory portrays this style of leadership as a series of transactional exchanges between the leader and followers. These exchanges involve the leader offering followers a reward to motivate them or dissuade undesirable behaviors.

Also known as Management Theory, several assumptions form the foundation of Transactional Leadership Theory.

• People perform better under a strong and well-defined chain of command.

• Extrinsic rewards are the most effective motivators.

• Punishments provide the most effective deterrence for undesirable performance.

• Employees require close monitoring to ensure compliance and quality of work.

• Employees lack self-motivation.

Leaders favoring a transactional style of leadership may present one or more of the following observable characteristics.

• Manages by micromanagement.

• Strict and inflexible adherence to policy.

• Prioritizes metrics over employee needs.

• Overly reliant on rewards to motivate employees.

• Resistant to change.

Several noted leadership theorists contributed to the development of Transactional Leadership Theory, including James MacGregor Burns (1970s), Bernard Bass (1980s), and Bruce Avolio and Jane Howell (1990s). These contributions led to the identification of three major dimensions of TLT.

Contingent reward: occurs when leaders incentivize employees to perform as expected by linking rewards to goal achievement.

Active management by exception: occurs when leaders continuously monitor employee performance to anticipate problems and issue corrective guidance as needed.

Passive management by exception: occurs when leaders limit direct involvement with employees until they observe employees failing to meet standards or goals.

Critics of TLT call into question some of the assumptions which underlie the theory. They cite studies which strongly suggest that intrinsic rewards are far more effective at motivating employees than extrinsic rewards. Additionally, critics reject the assumption that all employees lack self-motivation.

While some sources present Transactional Leadership Theory in a negative light, transactional leadership is neither good nor bad. Proponents of TLT cite multiple examples of both effective and ineffective transactional leaders. For example, transactional leadership has proven effective during crisis situations but ineffective in circumstances where creativity is necessary. For this reason, some categorize Transactional Leadership Theory under the umbrella of *Contingency* or *Situational Leadership Theories*. In other words, transactional leadership is effective in some circumstances, but not all.

Perhaps the most significant contribution of TLT is its inclusion in the *Full Range Leadership Model (FRLM)*, one of the most popular leadership frameworks. Professionals seeking to add depth of knowledge will find a wide range of literature freely available.

Sources[288]

TRANSFORMATIONAL LEADERSHIP THEORY

Certification Available: no
Certification Required: no
Assessments: no
Proprietary: no
Client: individuals
Cost: not applicable
Category: leadership

Developed in 1973 by sociologist James Downton, Transformational Leadership Theory (TLT) suggests that effective leaders are ones who inspire and motivate their people to create and sustain meaningful change. The theory further implies that when combined with a collaborative approach, this style is transformative for both leader and follower.

Since its introduction, several noted academics have contributed to the development of Transformational Leadership Theory, including historian James MacGregor Burns and industrial psychologist Bernard Bass. In the 1980s, Bass developed a framework to capture the four elements he believed constituted a transformational leader. He called these elements the **4 I's**.

Element 1—Idealized Influence (II): This element explores the different ways a leader may attempt to influence others within the group. Ideally, these leaders set the example (i.e., they walk the walk), and in so doing become a role model for others in the group. The phrase "do as I do" best exemplifies this behavior.

The leader who encapsulates idealized influence sets clear goals and establishes a sense of belonging for others. Consequently, this leader is well respected by members of the group.

Element 2—Intellectual Stimulation (IS): This element explores the different ways a leader challenges the status quo. On one level, this pertains to how they as individuals challenge the status quo, but also how they as leaders inspire others to do so. Leaders effective in IS encourage others to be creative and seek out new ways of doing things by creating an open and diverse environment.

Element 3—Inspirational Motivation (IM): This element explores the different ways a leader motivates others. Leaders effective in IM enhance the performance of others by inspiring and raising morale. This includes motivating and obtaining each person's commitment.

Element 4—Individualized Consideration (IC): This element explores the different ways leaders create a diverse environment while addressing the unique needs of each person. Leaders effective in IC listen to each person, act as mentors or coaches (as appropriate), and foster trust. Individual consideration also includes leaders nurturing future leaders.

TLT suggests transformational leadership occurs when leaders and followers raise one another to increased levels of performance and achievement. Transformational leadership does not happen overnight. To develop this skill set requires work and dedication. Transformational Leadership Theory recognizes that not all personality types can become this type of leader; however, improvement is possible for most leaders.

Transformational Leadership Theory is a useful framework for leadership-level clients, specifically as a lens for examining one's own leadership behaviors and those of other leaders. Such an application allows the client to observe, draw comparisons, and adapt.

The Transformational Leadership Theory is one-third of Bernard Bass' *Full Range Leadership Model*, along with Max Weber's *Transactional Leadership Theory* and Kurt Lewin's *Laissez-faire Leadership Theory*.

Professionals seeking additional information on Transformational Leadership Theory may consider James MacGregor Burns' 1978 book, *Leadership*, and his 2003 book, *Transforming Leadership*. Additionally, readers may also consider Bernard Bass' 1998 book, *Transformational Leadership: Industrial, Military, and Educational Impact*.

Sources[289]

TRANSFORMATIVE LEARNING THEORY

Certification Available: no
Certification Required: no
Assessments: no
Proprietary: no
Client: individuals
Cost: not applicable
Category: bias, learning/development

Developed in the 1970s by sociologist Jack Mezirow, Transformative Learning Theory (TLT) provides a framework to explain the impact of a person's worldview on their ability to learn new things. Mezirow's theory suggests a person's worldview consists of two dimensions.

Dimension 1—Habits of mind: This dimension encompasses a person's broad, abstract, and habitual ways of thinking, feeling, and acting as influenced by a set of codes. These codes derive from cultural, social, educational, economic, and political sources.

Dimension 2—Points of view: This dimension encompasses the constellation of beliefs, judgments, values, and attitudes that manifest from habits of mind.

Mezirow argues that habits of mind are resilient and more resistant to change than points of view. TLT proposes two primary ways of changing worldview, either through the repeated critical examination of multiple points of view, or through a powerful catalyst (i.e., significant event).

Transformative Learning Theory implies the drive to make sense of the world is a natural part of the human condition; however, once established, that worldview is difficult to change. Through his research, Mezirow identified several phases a person may experience during transformative learning. These phases are not formal, linear, or sequential, meaning it is not necessary to experience each phase for transformative learning to take place. Different sources may use different labels and terminology to describe these phases.

Phase 1—Disorienting dilemma: This involves a learner discovering the possibility that their initial thoughts or beliefs may not be correct. As the name suggests, this creates discomfort for the learner and drives them to make sense of the experience (what and why), sometimes leading to an "aha" moment.

Phase 2—Self-examination: As the learner seeks to make sense of their experience, they may engage in critical self-reflective analysis. This may include the learner questioning how their existing worldview contributed to the dilemma.

Phase 3—Critical assessment of assumptions: In this phase, the learner examines how their assumptions might be incorrect.

Phase 4—Recognition others have similar experiences: This phase involves the learner realizing their journey is not entirely unique by acknowledging others with similar experiences.

Phase 5—Exploration of new roles and options: As the learner acquires knowledge and skills, they begin to seek new roles and positions compatible with their newly acquired skills.

Transformative Learning Theory includes five additional phases (definitions omitted due to length): **Develop Plan of Action**, **Acquire Knowledge to Action Plan**, **Execute the Plan**, **Building Confidence and Competence in New Role**, and **Reintegration**.

Transformative Learning Theory is a useful framework because it relies heavily on critical thinking and reflection. TLT is useful with clients experiencing deep-rooted bias, prejudice, cultural assimilation/integration challenges, or struggling with sense-making.

Transformative Learning Theory is more complex than presented here and includes a bevy of considerations for developing curricula that foster transformative learning. Additional aspects of TLT include types of learning (e.g., communicative, instrumental, etc.) and developing self-efficacy.

Professionals seeking to develop their knowledge of Transformative Learning Theory may consider Mezirow's 1991 book, *Transformative Dimensions of Adult Learning*.

Sources[290]

TRANSTHEORETICAL MODEL

Certification Available: no
Certification Required: no
Assessments: no
Proprietary: no
Client: individuals
Cost: not applicable
Category: change (ind.)

Developed in the 1970s by James Prochaska and Carlo Di Clemente, the Transtheoretical Model (TTM) provides a framework to explain the internal process for individual change.

The original Transtheoretical Model consisted of five stages, with an additional stage emerging years later.

Stage 1—Pre-contemplation: During this stage, clients are not considering change, often because they are unaware a problem exists.

Stage 2—Contemplation: During stage 2, clients consider the idea of change through an intense, methodical, and honest exploration of self and situation. The result of stage 2 may see the client deciding for or against the need for change.

Stage 3—Preparation: Should clients determine change is appropriate, they begin preparing for change. This includes consideration of where they are, where they want to be, and what actions will help them bridge the gap.

Stage 4—Action: During the fourth stage, clients execute the steps they identified in stage 3. This stage requires the client to build and maintain momentum.

Stage 5—Maintenance: During the fifth stage, clients reinforce the adopted changes with support from the coach and their social support network, as well as by acknowledgment of their successes.

Stage 6—Termination: Stage 6 occurs when the adopted changes become the new norm. Once in stage 6, regression is highly unlikely.

Variations of the Transtheoretical Model exist which include the optional stage, **Relapse**. This occurs when the client reverts to old habits or behavior.

The principles underlying the Transtheoretical Model suggest that a client's development occurs along two dimensions. Horizontal development involves the client's growth within their current stage. Vertical development involves the client progressing to the next stage in the process. Effectively using the TTM in coaching requires focusing on the client's horizontal development over their vertical. Put another way, the most important stage is the stage the client is in. Help the client get the most from their current stage, and their transition to the next stage will take care of itself.

Prochaska and Di Clemente developed the Transtheoretical Model to identify the stages of addiction recovery; however, the model is fundamental and has broad application, including weight loss, smoking cessation, and reaction control.

The Transtheoretical Model can help coaches determine where a client is in their readiness and willingness to embrace the changes that may come with coaching, allowing the coach to adapt accordingly. The principles of TTM may also help clients seeking to improve their leadership style through behavioral change.

The Transtheoretical Model works best when combined with other theories, tools, and approaches. For example, a client in stage 2 is considering the idea of change. During stage 2, clients often encounter their biases for or against change. To maximize the learning potential from stage 2, the coach might consider using tools and approaches designed to shed light on bias, adopt alternative perspectives, and encourage creative thinking.

The Transtheoretical Model is more complex than presented here (see *Transtheoretical Model: Processes of Change*). Professionals seeking additional information may consider Prochaska and Di Clemente's 1994 book, *Changing for Good: A Revolutionary Six-Stage Program for Overcoming Bad Habits and Moving Your Life Positively Forward*, co-authored by J.C. Norcross.

Sources[291]

TRANSTHEORETICAL MODEL: PROCESSES OF CHANGE

Category: change (ind.)

The complexity of the Transtheoretical Model (TTM) consists of multiple subprocesses that facilitate an individual's behavioral change effort. The following represent aspects of the TTM most relevant to coaching.

When faced with change, a client will process the experience across three distinct but interrelated dimensions.

Cognitive Dimension: how the client thinks about change.

Affective Dimension: how the client feels about change.

Evaluative Dimension: how the client determines the value or meaning of change.

Where the client falls within each dimension affects their experience at each stage of the TTM. To better explain the Transtheoretical Model process, the framework consists of ten subprocesses or actions that encapsulate the client's experience during the change effort.

Consciousness Raising: This involves increasing the client's awareness of the benefits of change while acknowledging the consequences of maintaining any unhealthy behaviors.

Dramatic Relief: This is the exploration of the client's emotional arousal concerning change, be it positive or negative. This includes their emotional response to the idea of change in general and their feelings about the specific changes facing them.

Self-Reevaluation: This involves a self-examination to determine if the change is part of who the client wants to be. This may require that the client revisit their values and beliefs.

Environmental-Reevaluation: During this process, the client explores the social implications of maintaining the status quo. In other words, if the client does not change, how will this affect those around them?

Social-Liberation: This approach involves the client's exploration of examples which indicate society's support for the change.

Self-Liberation: This is the client's self-evaluation of their capacity and capability to perform the change (see *Self-Efficacy Theory*).

Helping Relationships: This process involves the client identifying existing relationships that can foster and encourage them throughout the change effort.

Counter-Conditioning: This involves the client exploring behaviors to substitute for the problematic behavior (i.e., what the client can do in lieu of current behaviors).

Reinforcement-Management: This process helps the client develop a reward system to encourage their change.

Stimulus-Control: This involves the client's examination of environmental variables which can foster change and those that can undermine their efforts.

Though we present these as processes, it is more accurate to say these are characterizations of processes. Each conceptually describes a process, but it is up to the coach to select the appropriate tools and techniques to effect the process. For example, to help a client raise their consciousness, a coach may use several techniques designed to foster a client's internal and external self-awareness. Alternatively, clients considering reinforcement management may benefit from resources designed to help identify a client's intrinsic motivations and needs.

The subprocesses and techniques that support the Transtheoretical Model are extensive and complex. Professionals seeking additional information may consider Prochaska and Di Clemente's 1994 book, *Changing for Good: A Revolutionary Six-Stage Program for Overcoming Bad Habits and Moving Your Life Positively Forward*, co-authored by J.C. Norcross.

Sources[292]

TRIUNE BRAIN MODEL

Certification Available: no
Certification Required: no
Assessments: no
Proprietary: no
Client: individuals
Cost: not applicable
Category: learning/development, self-awareness

Developed in the 1960s by neuroscientist Paul MacLean, the Triune Brain Model framework organizes the human brain into a hierarchy of three distinct regions, each responsible for a specific set of functions. MacLean ordered the three regions of the brain and their associated functions based on their order of evolutionary development.

Basal ganglia: This is the oldest portion of the brain, responsible for basic survival and body functions such as heart rate, respiratory function, and body temperature. The basal ganglia are also known as the Primal Brain or Reptilian Brain.

Limbic system: This is the reactive portion of the brain responsible for "fight, flight, or freeze." The limbic system is also known as the Emotional Brain or Paleomammalian Brain.

Neocortex: This is the part of the brain responsible for higher thought and functions like language, creativity, imagination, logic, and abstract thought. The neocortex is also known as the Rational Brain or Neomammalian Brain.

The theory of Triune Brain suggests that each region of the brain evolved sequentially, one region on top of the previously existing region. It is important to note that many in the scientific community reject this notion. Neuroscience-based research contravenes the idea that newer brain structures developed on top of older brain structures, instead suggesting that these regions evolved simultaneously. This stems from research based on advancements in neuroimaging which conflict with the associations made by the Triune Brain Model.

In another aspect of controversy, the Triune Brain implies that the three regions of the brain follow a hierarchy, with a higher region able to assert control over the others. Opponents argue that just because the neocortex sits atop the hierarchy does not mean it exerts control over the other regions. For example, a person may attempt to hold their breath (an action driven by the neocortex), but eventually the basal ganglia will assert control and force the lungs to take in air.

Despite growing evidence calling into question the model, the Triune Brain Model persists because many find it provides insight into the triad relationship between body, heart, and mind.

Conceptually, the Triune Brain Model may prove a useful framework for helping clients understand why they may react versus respond in certain situations. However, this model is but one lens through which coach and client may explore the effect of their experiences on their perceptions and resulting behaviors.

Professionals seeking additional information on the Triune Brain Model may consider MacLean's 1990 book, *The Triune Brain in Evolution.*

Sources[293]

TUBBS SYSTEMS MODEL

Certification Available: no
Certification Required: no
Assessments: no
Proprietary: no
Client: teams
Cost: not applicable
Category: teaming, decision-making

Developed by management professor Stewart L. Tubbs, the Tubbs Systems Model (TSM) provides a framework to explain how groups come together and make decisions.

The Tubbs Systems Model includes four stages of team development and a process consisting of three variables.

Stage 1—Orientation: The group forms, members learn about one another, and explore the parameters of the project. During this stage, members engage in discourse designed to examine the goal or problem. Additionally, the team explores the strengths, skills, and capabilities of the team.

Stage 2—Conflict: As team members continue to learn about one another, they will inevitably encounter misunderstandings, miscommunications, and misalignments between individual member priorities and perspectives. Conflict is a normal and often healthy occurrence in group development. However, left unmanaged, conflict can devastate group dynamics.

Stage 3—Consensus: In the third stage, the team resolves the conflict in favor of compromise. This involves members establishing a common ground, often based on a shared sense of purpose. Consensus marks the most productive stage, where the team moves toward its goals.

Stage 4—Closure: In the last stage, the team reaches a final decision regarding task completion or problem solution. During this stage, the individual members reaffirm their commitment to the process and the outcome.

The Tubbs Systems Model identifies three variables which influence the group's decision-making process across the four stages.

Variable 1—Inputs: The first variable affecting the group's decision-making process pertains to external factors such as any project parameters (e.g., budget, timeline, etc.), the organization's culture, and the policies affecting employee behavior. Other external variables include personal issues and behavioral characteristics individual members bring with them, like personality traits, values, beliefs, and attitudes.

Variable 2—Throughputs: The second variable focuses the group's internal processing of inputs. Put another way, this involves how the group incorporates these variables in their thought process. Throughputs also include individual behaviors which impact interactions between group members (and possibly lead to conflict).

Variable 3—Outputs: The final variable pertains to the outcome of the group's effort. This relates to both the actual result of the group's work and the personal growth of individual team members.

Considered a linear framework, Tubbs Systems Model suggests that groups must transition sequentially from one stage to the next, without jumping stages. TSM, like any framework on teaming, has strengths and limitations. Critics of Tubbs Systems Model argue that most groups will not achieve consensus, especially in the presence of intense emotion, high-stakes decisions, or crisis.

Professionals seeking additional information on Tubbs Systems Model may consider Tubbs' book, *A Systems Approach to Small Group Interaction*, now in its 11th edition. Additionally, professionals may consider Tubbs' book, *Human Communication: Principles and Contexts*, 13th edition.

Sources[294]

TUCKMAN'S STAGES OF GROUP DEVELOPMENT

Certification Available: no
Certification Required: no
Assessments: no
Proprietary: no
Client: teams, groups
Cost: not applicable
Category: teaming

Developed in 1965 by psychologist Bruce Wayne Tuckman, the Stages of Group Development provides a framework to explain how individuals form teams capable of achieving a common goal. The original model consisted of four stages. Then in 1977, Tuckman revised the framework, adding a fifth stage to create the model we see today, also known as the FSNPA Model.

Stage 1—Forming: The first stage in the process involves the introduction of individuals to the team. During this stage, each person will seek to answer a host of questions about themselves and others. These include what does the team expect of me, how will I fit in, why was I selected for this team, what is in it for me, and what do the other members of the team bring to the table. In the first stage, uncertainty runs high; therefore most people tend to be overly polite until they get a better sense of their teammates.

Discourse in stage 1 focuses principally on relationships as members seek to better understand the background and experiences of one another. Secondarily, the team may discuss aspects of the project like timelines, parameters, and goals. During this stage, the members of the team attempt to determine their individual roles and responsibilities.

Stage 2—Storming: In this stage, as individuals become more comfortable with one another, the tendency for overly polite behavior subsides in favor of expressing true feelings. This often leads to conflict between team members, sometimes over trivial issues.

Though some forms of conflict are healthy, left unchecked, conflict may spill over into the team's work, leading the team to resist the assigned project. Furthermore, members may compete for specific roles within the group. Even when the group has a designated leader, members may vie for the functional leadership role.

Stage 3—Norming: As the conflict abates and individuals begin to settle into their roles, team members finally become comfortable with each other. With the initial conflict behind them, they can accept their differences and see the value of what each person brings to the project.

Stage 4—Performing: In this stage, the team coalesces, moving efficiently toward goal achievement. Should conflict arise in this stage, high-performance teams seek quick and meaningful resolution, allowing them to continue working on the project.

Stage 5—Adjourning: In the final stage, the team achieves its purpose or goal and disbands.

Professionals using Tuckman's model should keep in mind several key points about the framework.

- The amount of time in a stage varies from team to team.

- Though originally presented as a linear model, research now suggests that the process is dynamic, so teams may regress to a previous stage.

- A team may get stuck and never move beyond a stage.

Tuckman's model is among the most widely known frameworks of teaming. It provides a valuable lens through which to explore group dynamics. For example, when examining a team in the forming stage, it is helpful to consider the way individuals joined the team. Those directed to participate may react differently (or behave differently at each stage) than those who self-select or volunteer.

Tuckman's Stages of Group Development, as presented here, is simple and easy to use. Though Tuckman never published a book on his model, others have. One to consider is D.B. Egolf and S.L. Chester's 2013 book, *Forming Storming Norming Performing: Successful Communication in Groups and Teams*, 3rd edition.

Sources[295]

TWO-FACTOR THEORY

Certification Available: no
Certification Required: no
Assessments: no
Proprietary: no
Client: individuals
Cost: not applicable
Category: motivation, engagement

Developed in the 1950s by psychologist Frederick Herzberg, the Two-Factor Theory provides a multi-faceted framework for understanding job satisfaction and motivation. The Two-Factor Theory, also called Herzberg's Motivation-Hygiene Theory, consists of two factors that influence an employee's sense of job satisfaction and job dissatisfaction.

Factor 1—Motivation: These are factors that positively contribute to an employee's sense of job satisfaction. They include an employee's needs like the need for achievement, recognition, responsibility, advancement, and development.

Factor 2—Hygiene: These are factors that contribute to an employee's sense of job dissatisfaction. They include the policies that guide the work, the quality of supervision, the employee's relationship to peers and supervisors, the work conditions, and the employee's salary.

The philosophical underpinnings of Two-Factor Theory suggest a lack of job satisfaction is not the same thing as job dissatisfaction. Herzberg's research revealed that the factors that contribute to job satisfaction were not the same as, or related to, the factors that contribute to job dissatisfaction.

Therefore, the absence of job satisfaction factors does not lead to job dissatisfaction; it merely results in a lack of job satisfaction.

And the absence of job dissatisfaction factors does not lead to job satisfaction; it simply means the individual is not dissatisfied.

The distinction between job dissatisfaction and a lack of satisfaction leads to another significant principle of Herzberg's research: remedying the cause of dissatisfaction will not create satisfaction.

Therefore, Herzberg offers two considerations for leaders seeking to improve employee motivation and engagement.

• First, eliminate or mitigate the factors that contribute to employee job dissatisfaction. This includes reviewing policies to ensure they are conducive to supporting the employee's work. Ensure salaries are fair and competitive to industry standards. Evaluate employee work conditions and make changes favorable to employees.

• Second, create the necessary conditions for job satisfaction. Recognize employee successes and describe the impact of employee contributions on the mission. Ensure employees have sufficient opportunities for advancement and professional development.

The Two-Factor Theory is useful with clients facing challenges with employee engagement and motivation. The model provides a relevant lens through which to consider and explore the impact of the client's organizational environment on employee engagement.

While the Two-Factor Theory has enjoyed decades of acceptance, some question the validity of the theory, citing limitations in Herzberg's model and his research. Recent research indicates a shift in what constitutes job satisfaction and dissatisfaction, further calling into question the efficacy of Two-Factor Theory.

Professionals seeking additional information may consider the book *The Motivation to Work*, authored by Frederick Herzberg, Bernard Mausner, and Barbara Bloch Snyderman in 1959.

Sources[296]

UNCERTAINTY REDUCTION THEORY

Certification Available: no
Certification Required: no
Assessments: no
Proprietary: no
Client: individuals
Cost: not applicable
Category: communication

Developed in 1975 by professors Charles Berger and Richard Calabrese, their Uncertainty Reduction Theory (URT) provides a framework to explain how uncertainty between two people may lead to anxiety and what actions a person may take to reduce uncertainty. The theory suggests that when two people possess significant uncertainties about each other, this may lead to discomfort and anxiety. Consequently, they will seek to learn as much as possible to minimize their uncertainties about each other.

The Uncertainty Reduction Theory framework identifies several types of uncertainty that explain the sources of anxiety and insecurity in social interaction.

Partner uncertainty: This is a person's inability to predict the thoughts, feelings, or behaviors of a specific individual, sometimes labeled "the other person."

Self-uncertainty: This is a person's inability to explain or predict their own feelings, thoughts, and behaviors, sometimes labeled "self-awareness."

Relational uncertainty: This is a person's lack of confidence in their ability to predict or explain issues associated with a given relationship.

Cognitive uncertainty: This is a category that applies to uncertainties of not knowing what another person is thinking, or what we ourselves are thinking.

Behavioral uncertainty: This is a category that applies to the uncertainties of being unable to predict or understand another person's behaviors or our own.

Research in Uncertainty Reduction Theory led to the formation of seven axioms that provide greater insight into the implications of uncertainty.

- The more people talk, the more uncertainty decreases.

- The more people display positive nonverbal behavior (e.g., smiling), the more uncertainty decreases.

- When uncertainty levels decrease, so too does information-seeking behavior.

- Lower levels of uncertainty produce higher levels of intimacy in communication.

- Higher levels of uncertainty produce higher levels of reciprocity.

- Similarities between parties reduce uncertainty.

- Increases in uncertainty levels decrease liking.

Over time, URT has evolved to encompass most forms of communication between people. In fact, the theory suggests that the concepts apply far beyond strangers. For example, even in established relationships, there are moments when one might experience uncertainty about how the other person feels about them.

URT is useful with clients new to an organization or who are struggling to process their social anxiety about the uncertainties of new and existing relationships.

Uncertainty Reduction Theory is more complex than presented here and includes additional considerations like sources of motivation for reducing uncertainty, strategies for reducing uncertainty, and the stages of relational development.

Professionals seeking additional information will find much written on Uncertainty Reduction Theory, including Berger's 1982 book, *Language and Social Knowledge: Uncertainty in Interpersonal Relations (Social Psychology of Language)*.

Sources[297]

VAK/VARK LEARNING PREFERENCE MODEL

> **Certification Available:** no
> **Certification Required:** no
> **Assessments:** yes (many)
> **Proprietary:** no
> **Client:** individuals
> **Cost:** not applicable
> **Category:** learning/development

Developed in the 1920s, the VAK Learning Preference Model, also known as the Visual-Auditory-Kinesthetic Learning Styles Model, provides a framework for understanding and characterizing personal learning preferences. The original model suggested that learning occurs through three modalities: visual, auditory, and kinesthetic. In 1987, teacher Neil Fleming added a fourth modality, reading/writing. This led to the current version of the model, VARK.

Visual modality: For the learner who prefers a visual modality, information resonates more deeply when they can see it. These learners favor demonstrations, pictures, videos, diagrams, and handouts. Indicators that a person may prefer visual learning include frequent highlighting in books, color coding ideas and concepts, and the substantial use of sticky notes.

Visual learners often demonstrate creative or artistic tendencies. Potential challenges for visually dominant learners include visual distractions like sitting near a window that looks out to a bustling courtyard.

Auditory modality: For the learner who prefers an auditory modality, information resonates more deeply when they can hear it. These learners favor listening to lectures, audio books, and group discussions. Indicators a person may prefer auditory learning include frequently discussing their ideas with others, seeking group study vs. self-study, and memorizing information so they may recite it verbally.

Auditory learners are sensitive to a speaker's tone and pitch. Potential challenges for auditory learners include sound-based distractions like sudden announcements, TV noise, and music.

Reading/Writing modality: For learners of this modality, information resonates more deeply when they can read or write it for themselves. Like visual learners, they take notes; however, the impact is not from seeing their notes but from the act of writing them. Thus, a key indicator of this style is effusive note-taking. Even when presented with hard copies of detailed slides, they will take significant notes.

Reading/writing learners may struggle when confronted with poorly written text. They may also become frustrated when rushed to make notes.

Kinesthetic modality: For the learner who prefers a kinesthetic modality, information resonates more deeply when combined with a physical experience. In other words, they learn by doing, using their hands or their bodies. Key indicators a person may favor kinesthetic learning include frequent doodling, or a penchant for activities that involve physical performance or action. A common challenge for kinesthetic learners is their susceptibility to boredom, leading to them becoming restless and fidgety.

According to the VARK Model, a person's preferences may vary depending on the situation, the subject matter, and the medium through which the material is presented. The model recognizes that while a person may have a strong preference for a single style, most people rely on a combination of styles.

Understanding the four preferences and where the client falls within these modalities will allow professionals to tailor their coaching approach in a way that resonates with the client.

The VARK Learning Preference Model includes a variety of assessments to help identify an individual's learning preferences. Many of these assessments are freely available online.

Professionals seeking additional information on the VARK Model may consider the 2010 book, *Understanding Learning Styles: Making a Difference for Diverse Learners*, by K. Allen, J. Scheve, and V. Nieter.

Source[298]

VERTICAL THINKING MODEL

Certification Available: yes
Certification Required: yes
Assessments: no
Proprietary: yes (The de Bono Group)
Client: individuals
Cost: $5,200
Category: problem-solving

Developed in the 1960s by noted psychologist Edward de Bono, the Vertical Thinking Model describes an analytical and methodical approach to problem-solving. The Vertical Thinking Model consists of several characteristics describing a logic-driven approach to solving problems.

Sequential: Vertical thinkers adopt a linear approach to understanding the problem, often working chronologically or procedurally. This includes exploring the events leading up to the problem in the order they occurred. In situations where a failure occurred despite an established process, vertical thinkers will explore the actions of those involved in executing the process in the same sequence laid out by the process.

When using a specific problem-solving process, vertical thinkers will commit themselves to accomplishing a single step properly before moving to the next step in the process.

Facts-driven: Vertical thinkers are meticulous about which details they consider while examining a problem and forming a solution. They only accept information they know is true or factual and dismiss everything else. This means they avoid assumptions as much as possible.

Exclusion: Vertical thinkers take into consideration the relevance of information. If the information or data does not appear relevant, they will discount it.

Reason: Vertical thinkers strive to establish and understand the relationship between concepts and variables. Using logic and reason, they formulate connections between multiple factors and how those factors contributed to the problem. This allows vertical thinkers to draw conclusions about the cause of the problem, helping them identify possible solutions.

Analytical: Vertical thinkers draw heavily from their ability to process and analyze data. This is a complex endeavor that involves identifying patterns and trends within the data. Their analysis seeks to make meaning of these patterns and trends.

De Bono developed Vertical Thinking as an antithesis to the creative-based *Lateral Thinking Model*. Though presented in the ICMT as two separate entries, the Lateral Thinking Model and Vertical Thinking Model are two halves of de Bono's problem-solving framework. It is important to note that there is no right or wrong approach. Both approaches present distinct advantages. For this reason, it is worth considering both models when addressing a problem.

Organizations considering a team-based approach to problem-solving may find utility in de Bono's models. Having a mix of individuals representing both styles of thought can enhance solution development.

To facilitate the integration of both Lateral and Vertical Thinking Models in group settings, de Bono created the Six Thinking Hats technique, a framework that allows groups to be simultaneously creative and methodical in their approach to problem-solving.

The Vertical Thinking Model is more complex than presented here. Professionals seeking formal training may consider one of de Bono's many authorized providers.

Professionals seeking additional information on Vertical Thinking may consider one of Edward de Bono's many published works, including his 1967 book, *The Use of Lateral Thinking*, and his 1970 book, *Lateral Thinking: Creativity Step by Step*.

Sources[299]

VERTICAL-HORIZONTAL LEADERSHIP DEVELOPMENT

Certification Available: yes
Certification Required: no
Assessments: yes (many)
Proprietary: no
Client: individuals
Cost: pricing varies
Category: learning/development

Vertical-Horizontal Leadership Development (VHLD) provides a multidimensional approach to leadership development and training. More philosophy than framework, VHLD suggests that leadership growth occurs on two levels, each requiring different approaches to training.

Horizontal dimension: This dimension involves the skills, abilities, tools, and competencies associated with leadership. Specific skill sets within the horizontal dimension include communication techniques, problem-solving methods, decision-making processes, conflict management approaches, and more. A common analogy used to describe this dimension: "Horizontal development involves adding water to the leader's cup."

Vertical dimension: This dimension involves developing the leader's mindset and worldview. This includes challenging what a leader knows, how they know it, and transforming the way leaders think and behave. A common analogy used to describe this dimension: "Vertical development involves increasing the size of the leader's cup."

Fostering vertical development requires a different training approach than horizontal development. For example, training focusing on horizontal development may adopt more traditional instructional methodologies, such as teaching new skills in a typical classroom environment. Vertical development, on the other hand, requires a more complex approach that may involve facilitated peer-to-peer or group discourse or experiential learning.

Various sources offer differing perspectives and definitions of VHLD. One version, from the Center for Creative Leadership, identifies three conditions necessary for effective vertical development.

Heat experiences: These are experiences that disrupt a leader's habitual way of thinking, causing them to consider the possibility that their current worldview is inadequate. Because individuals inherently seek out equilibrium between their thoughts, feelings, and behaviors (see *Consistency Theories*), the leader may begin to explore newer and better ways to make sense of the experience.

Colliding perspectives: This involves exposing the leader to individuals who possess worldviews, cultures, and backgrounds different from their own. Experiencing different perspectives challenges the leader's own assumptions and points of view, leading them to question their existing perspectives.

Elevated sense-making: This involves the use of a mentor, coach, facilitator, or confidant to challenge the leader and help them explore their worldview and make sense of their experience.

Though the origins of VHLD are ambiguous, over the years many scholars and professionals have contributed to the development and propagation of the concept, like Jennifer Garvey Berger, Bill Joiner, and Stephen Josephs. Readers will notice many similarities between VHLD and theories of learning like the *Transformative Learning Theory* and *Kegan's Theory of Adult Development*.

The concept of Vertical-Horizontal Leadership Development is broad, with many organizations offering their unique VHLD programs, processes, and models. These include the *Seven Transformations of Leadership Model*, *Ego Development Theory*, *Leadership Maturity Framework*, and Harvard University's *Immunity to Change* Program among many others.

Professionals seeking additional information on VHLD will find a vast array of literature available, including Ryan Gottfredson's book, *The Elevated Leader: Level Up Your Leadership Through Vertical Development*, and M.F. Tucker and Lori Tucker-Eccher's book, *Horizontal and Vertical: Meeting the Global Talent Challenge*.

Sources[300]

VROOM-YETTON DECISION MODEL

Certification Available: no
Certification Required: no
Assessments: no
Proprietary: no
Client: individuals
Cost: not applicable
Category: leadership, decision-making

Developed in 1973 by professors Victor H. Vroom and Philip W. Yetton, the Vroom-Yetton Decision Model (VYDM) provides a framework to facilitate an examination of the three-way relationship between leadership style, the situation, and the decision-making process. The VYDM consists of five leadership decision-making styles and a framework of questions designed to help leaders determine the most appropriate decision-making style.

Decision Styles

- **Autocratic type 1 (AI):** The leader makes the decision alone.

- **Autocratic type 2 (AII):** The leader collects information from some followers (but does not share the problem), then makes the decision alone.

- **Consultative type 1 (CI):** The leader shares the problem with certain followers individually, then makes the decision alone after hearing individual input.

- **Consultative type 2 (CII):** The leader shares the problem with relevant followers as a group, then makes the decision alone after hearing group input and discussion.

- **Group-based type 2 (GII):** The leader presents the problem to followers as a group and seeks ideas from them through brainstorming. The leader accepts the decision by the group without forcing his idea.

To help leaders determine which decision-making style is appropriate for the situation, the VYDM provides seven questions.

- How important is the technical quality of the decision?

- Do I have enough information to make the decision?

- Is the problem well structured (i.e., well defined, clear, organized, lends itself to problem-solving, time-limited)?

- How critical is subordinate acceptance to implementation or outcome?

- Would my subordinates accept the decision if I made it myself?

- Do my subordinates have a personal stake in the solution?

- Will there be conflict among subordinates when trying to reach a solution?

In 1988, professor Arthur Jago collaborated with Vroom and Yetton on revisions to the model. These revisions formed the Vroom-Yetton-Jago Decision Model.

The VYDM is useful with clients facing significant decisions. It can help them explore the relevant variables and determine which decision-making style is most appropriate for the situation.

As a framework for leadership, VYDM suggests that effective decision-making is based on the situation, not the traits of the leader. Therefore, a leadership style appropriate for one situation may be a liability in another. This belief means VYDM falls under the umbrella of *Contingency Theories*.

The Vroom-Yetton Decision Model is unique among contingency theories. Compared to other frameworks like the *Fiedler Contingency Model,* which looks at the relationship between leadership style and the favorableness of the situation, the Vroom-Yetton Model looks at the relationship between leadership style, the situation, and the decision.

Professionals seeking additional information may consider Victor Vroom and Philip Yetton's 1973 book, *Leadership and Decision-Making.*

Sources[301]

WEBER'S THEORY OF AUTHORITY

> **Certification Available:** no
> **Certification Required:** no
> **Assessments:** no
> **Proprietary:** no
> **Client:** individuals
> **Cost:** not applicable
> **Category:** leadership

Developed in the early 1900s by sociologist Max Weber, the Theory of Authority suggests that there are three possible types of authority which empower leaders. From these three types of power, Weber developed his theories of leadership: *Transactional Leadership Theory, Charismatic Leadership Theory,* and *Transformational Leadership Theory.*

Weber's Theory of Authority, also called Tripartite Classification of Authority, emphasized the sources of power from which leaders could rule, or dominate (in his words). These three foundations each present strengths and vulnerabilities for leaders, none of them inherently good or bad.

Charismatic Authority: Weber defined this as devotion to the exemplary character of an individual person. This type of authority is beneficial in that it is revolutionary and those who follow the charismatic leader do so vigorously and wholeheartedly. Those with Charismatic Authority have the capacity to lead great change efforts.

In early history, leaders imbued with Charismatic Authority were those professing anointment by a higher power or seen as godly themselves. However, recent history has given us many examples of leaders whose Charismatic Authority derived from their ability to inspire others, to give hope, and to communicate in effective ways.

Leadership authority derived from charisma is often short-lived and leaves little in the way of formal tradi-tions and stability. Another vulnerability of Charismatic Authority is with succession. Because it derives from the personality of a single leader, when that leader dies, it can leave a void in leadership, which paves the way for one of the other two types of authority to emerge.

Traditional Authority: This form of authority derives from tradition and culture. According to Weber, Traditional Authority depends on the sanctity of the status quo. Examples of Traditional Authority include any form of government in which title and leadership is hereditary. A potential strength of Traditional Authority is the presence of stability and preservation of tradition. Additionally, this form of authority typically provides for social order.

However, leaders imbued with Traditional Authority can use their power to exploit those who follow them, which can lead to greater inequality and inequity. The lack of accountability found in most forms of Traditional Authority governments can lead to moral corruption.

Legal Authority: Defined as authority derived from the rule of law, legal or natural. Weber sometimes referred to this as Bureaucratic Authority since he believed the methodical practices, policies, and regulations of a bureaucracy best represented this form of authority. A strength of Legal Authority is that obedience and loyalty are not to a single person, but to a system of governance. Another benefit is that leaders imbued with Legal Authority are accountable to the very laws and rules which grant their authority. To break them risks undermining their own authority. The most common examples of this style of authority are democratic governments.

A vulnerability of Legal Authority rests in its dependence on consensus to enact new laws and rules. This can diminish a leader's ability to address a crisis quickly and efficiently.

Professionals seeking additional information may consider Weber's article, "The Three Types of Legitimate Rule," published posthumously in 1922 (in English in 1958).

Sources[302]

WESTLEY AND MACLEAN'S MODEL OF COMMUNICATION

Certification Available: no
Certification Required: no
Assessments: no
Proprietary: no
Client: individuals
Cost: not applicable
Category: communication, influence

Presented in 1957 by professors Bruce Westley and Malcolm S. MacLean Jr., their Model of Communication was among the first communication-centric theories to suggest that the environment, not the speaker, begins the communication process.

Westley and MacLean's Model of Communication applies to communication on two levels: interpersonal communication and mass communication. The model consists of four actors and four variables which help explain the process.

Four actors: These represent the core entities involved in communication.

• **Environment**: the catalyst for communication. This is an event or environmental condition which creates the need for communication. Example: An employee trying to leave work cannot because the car next to hers parked too close and she cannot get into her car. This is an event which precipitates the need to communicate.

• **Message sender**: the person formulating and sending the message (written or verbal). Example: The employee who could not get into her car initiates a conversation with her supervisor about the issue.

• **Gatekeeper**: the person who edits or controls dissemination of the message. The gatekeeper actor is more often present in mass communication settings than interpersonal. Example: In this case, the supervisor is the gatekeeper. She decides to send an office-wide email asking people to be more considerate when parking. She (the supervisor) can alter the sender's initial (verbal) message to create a more diplomatic and impactful message (written).

• **Message receiver**: the people who receive the message. Example: The message receivers are the employees of the office.

Four variables: These represent the factors that influence the communication process.

• **Sensory experience**: the ways we receive messaging from the environment. Is the catalyst something we saw, heard, or inferred? The sensory conduit can influence our perception and interpretation of the stimulus. Example: The employee with the blocked car (a small hybrid) may perceive this as a personal offense because the offending vehicle is a large pickup truck.

• **Sender object orientation**: the beliefs, culture, and background of the sender may influence development of the message. Example: The employee with the blocked car has felt unappreciated at work for some time, which further influences her perception of this event.

• **Receiver object orientation**: the beliefs, culture, and background of the receiver may influence how the person receives the message. Example: Employees at the office have long struggled with the poor condition of the parking lot. This influences their receptivity to any management messaging about the parking situation.

• **Feedback**: the responses from receivers to the gatekeeper and/or sender. Example: Employees advise the supervisor that the parking slots are not regulation size; they are too narrow.

Westley and MacLean's Model of Communication is a useful framework to explore organization-wide communication strategies with clients. The model is more complex than presented here. Professionals will find numerous academic articles freely available online.

Sources[303]

WORKING GENIUS

Certification Available: no
Certification Required: no
Assessments: yes (Working Genius Assessment)
Proprietary: yes (Table Group)
Client: individuals, groups, teams
Cost: not applicable
Category: personality styles, teaming

Developed in the 2020s by management expert Pat Lencioni, the Working Genius provides a dual-purpose framework useful for developing insight into aspects of an individual's personality and as a productivity tool to help teams and organizations ensure the right people are in the right positions.

The Working Genius framework consists of six types (personality aspects) or stages (productivity).

Type 1—Wonder: This form of genius pertains to individuals who contemplate the world around them. They consider why things are the way they are, they explore opportunities for improvement, and ask themselves if there is a better way. Though not problem-solvers, they often think about problem-solving.

As a conduit for productivity, most work begins with curiosity, asking questions about the status quo, and a desire to understand the "why" behind everything. They see the potential in things by thinking about them.

Type 2—Invention: This form of genius pertains to imaginative individuals inspired to create new ideas and find new ways of doing things. If wonder geniuses identify problems, invention geniuses dive into solving them.

If wonder geniuses imagine, then invention geniuses create. They create ideas by working things out.

Type 3—Discernment: This form of genius pertains to individuals capable of seeing patterns, form, and structure. They possess instinct and an ability to evaluate and test the ideas invention geniuses create. They can determine the efficacy and validity of an idea with little data.

Type 4—Galvanizing: This form of genius pertains to individuals able to bring people together and inspire them to implement the idea. They promote the idea by motivating others, provoking them to action.

Type 5—Enablement: This form of genius pertains to individuals with an uncanny ability to anticipate the needs of others and provide needed support in seeing the idea realized. Natural responders, they proactively work to actualize the idea by helping others accomplish their goals.

Type 6—Tenacity: This form of genius pertains to individuals who enjoy bringing projects to their natural conclusion. If momentum begins to fade, this type of genius will see realization of the idea completed without pause and ensure that others follow through.

According to Lencioni, we each possess two primary working geniuses, two working competencies (not as strong as genius but still effective), and two working frustrations (areas of weakness). To help clients determine which of the six types apply as geniuses, competencies, and frustrations, Lencioni developed the 6 Types of Working Genius Assessment. He also created a worksheet called the WIDGET Tally Team Map for use with groups and teams.

The Working Genius framework is a useful resource for clients struggling with building effective team constructs or leveraging teams to carry out complex projects. The six types of geniuses provides a lens through which to explore and consider candidates for future teaming opportunities.

The Working Genius framework is new; consequently, literature on the topic remains limited. Professionals seeking additional information may consider Lencioni's 2022 book, *The 6 Types of Working Genius: A Better Way to Understand Your Gifts, Your Frustrations, and Your Team.*

Sources[304]

SOURCES

1   4A Model for Stress Management

Conway, A. (2021, March 8). *The 4 A's of stress relief.* Retrieved from the Mayo Clinic: https://www.mayoclinichealthsystem.org/hometown-health/speaking-of-health/the-4-as-of-stress-relief

Avram, R. (2017, October 27). *The 4 A's of stress management.* Retrieved from the Minute School: https://www.minuteschool.com/2017/10/the-4-as-of-stress-management/

Whitten, H. (2009). *Cognitive behavioural coaching techniques for dummies.* Wiley.

Sparks, D. (2019, April 24). *Mayo mindfulness: Try the 4 A's for stress relief.* Retrieved from the Mayo Clinic: https://newsnetwork.mayoclinic.org/discussion/mayo-mindfulness-try-the-4-as-for-stress-relief/

The 4 A's of stress management. (n.d.). Retrieved from Pain Scale: https://www.painscale.com/article/the-4-a-s-of-stress-management

The 4 A's of stress management. (n.d.). Retrieved from Jai Medical Systems: https://www.jaimedicalsystems.com/4-as-of-stress-management/

Singh, A. (2021, March 15). *4 A's of stress management to cope with stress.* Retrieved from Calm Sage: https://www.calmsage.com/practice-4-as-of-stress-management/

2   4C Model for Mental Toughness

Lyons, P. *The 4 C's of mental toughness.* (n.d.). Retrieved from Wellness Daily: https://www.wellnessdaily.com.au/expert/the-4-c-s-of-mental-toughness

4 C's of mental toughness. (n.d.). Retrieved from Rokman: https://rokman.co.uk/blogs/articles/4-cs-of-mental-toughnes

Sport and the 4 C's of mental toughness. (n.d.). Retrieved from Ebrary.net: https://ebrary.net/1925/philosophy/sport_four_mental_toughness

Strycharczyk, D. (2017, November 14). *Commitment: The second of the 4 C's of mental toughness.* Retrieved from AQR International: https://aqrinternational.co.uk/video-aqr-ceo-doug-strycharczyk-gives-overview-commitment-second-c-4cs-mental-toughness

What is mental toughness? (n.d.). Retrieved from Human Kinetics: https://canada.humankinetics.com/blogs/excerpt/what-is-mental-toughness

3   4MAT Learning Styles

McCarthy, B. (1990, October). *Using the 4MAT system to bring learning styles to schools.* Retrieved from the Association for Supervision and Curriculum Development: http://www.ascd.org/ASCD/pdf/journals/ed_lead/el_199010_mccarthy.pdf

4MAT. (n.d.). Retrieved from the Peak Performance Center: https://thepeakperformancecenter.com/educational-learning/learning/preferences/learning-styles/4mat/

4MAT. (n.d.). Retrieved from the 4MAT Group: http://www.4mat.eu/method-learning-styles.aspx

4MAT overview. (n.d.). Retrieved from About Learning: https://aboutlearning.com/about-us/4mat-overview/

4MAT learning styles info. (n.d.). Retrieved from About Learning: https://aboutlearning.com/free-resources/4mat-learning-styles-info/

4   4S Coaching Model

The 4 S's: A comprehensive program for coaching people with ADD. (n.d.). Retrieved from ADDvisor.com: http://www.addvisor.com/the-four-ss.html

ADHD coaching certification. (n.d.). Retrieved from Mentor Coach LLC: https://www.mentorcoach.com/certification/adhd-coaching-certification/

Coleman, S., & Sussman, S. (n.d.). *The 4 S's: A comprehensive program for coaching people with ADHD.* Retrieved from ADDers.org: http://www.adders.org.uk/info9.htm

5   4 Territories Coaching Model

The 4 territories model. (n.d.). Retrieved from Dr. Mike Munro Turner: https://www.mikethementor.co.uk/blog/change-model

The 3W4T model of supervision. (n.d.). Retrieved from Dr. Mike Munro Turner: https://www.mikethementor.co.uk/blog/the-3w4t-model-of-supervision

Newell, D., & Turner, M. M. (2008, January). A model of coaching for renewal. *International Journal of Mentoring and Coaching*, 6(1), 94–100. Retrieved from Squarespace: https://static1.squarespace.com/static/56c58f7ee32140c4f701a476/t/5c27542 903ce64cdbb239044/1546081324001/Renewal_EMCC_Journal_volume_VI_issue_1_February_2008.pdf

6   5 Elements of Cooperative Learning

Gaille, B. (2015, July 18). *8 pros and cons of cooperative learning*. Retrieved from Brandon Gaille: https://brandongaille.com/8-pros-and-cons-of-cooperative-learning/

What is cooperative learning? (n.d.). Retrieved from the Science and Education Center at Carleton College: https://serc.carleton.edu/introgeo/cooperative/whatis.html

Johnson and Johnson's thoughts on cooperative learning. (n.d.). Retrieved from Teachnology Inc.: https://www.teach-nology.com/currenttrends/cooperative_learning/johnson_and_johnson/

McDuffee, S. (2014, July 14). *5 elements of cooperative learning activities help your team learn substantially more*. Retrieved from LinkedIn Pulse: https://www.linkedin.com/pulse/20140714163307-9761051-5-elements-of-cooperative-learning-activities-help-your-team-learn-substantially-more/

7   5 Voices

Everyone speaks. Not everyone is heard. (n.d.). Retrieved from 5 Voices System: https://5voices.com

5 voices certified coach. (n.d.). Retrieved from GiANT University: https://www.giantuniversity.com/5-voices

Why different types of leadership are critical to successful decision making. (n.d.). Retrieved from 5 Voices System: https://5voices.com/leadership-voices/different-types-of-leadership/

You have a leadership voice, discover it today. (n.d.). Retrieved from Kate Davis: https://www.katedavis.net/5-voices-workshops

Kubicek, J., & Cockram, S. (n.d.). *5 voices: How to communicate effectively with everyone you lead*. Retrieved from Twelve Mavens: https://assets.website-files.com/5eb411c68cf2c678c014d489/5f5807852ab120fbf5c0c1f3_5Voices.pdf

You have a leadership voice—Discover it today. (n.d.). Retrieved from Long Table Consulting: https://www.longtableconsulting.com/5-voices

The Glasses Guy. (n.d.). *Find your voice! What are the 5 voices?!?* [Video]. Retrieved from YouTube: https://www.youtube.com/watch?v=M5fexbKYAkM

8   6M Foundations of Flourishing

The Positivity Institute workplace services kit. (n.d.). Retrieved from The Positivity Institute: https://www.thepositivityinstitute.com.au/wp-content/uploads/2017/04/PI_Workplace-Services-Kit.pdf

Green, S. (Host). (2020). *The positivity prescription with Dr. Suzy Green* (episodes 1–6) [Audio podcast]. Retrieved from Apple Podcasts: https://podcasts.apple.com/au/podcast/the-positivity-prescription-with-dr-suzy-green/id1530323097

The positivity prescription with Dr. Suzy Green. (2020, May 19). Retrieved from the Me-Suite: https://www.the-me-suite.com/podcast/positivity-rx

Dunn, C. (Host). (2021, February 21). *The positivity prescription* (episode 56) [Audio podcast]. In Crappy to Happy. LiSTNER. https://cassdunn.com/podcast/

9   7 Cs of Effective Communication

Wroblewski, M.T. (2019, April 24). 7 C's of effective business communication. *Houston Chronicle*: https://smallbusiness.chron.com/7-cs-effective-business-communication-114.html

Seven C's of effective communication. (n.d.). Retrieved from Management Study Guide: https://www.managementstudyguide.com/seven-cs-of-effective-communication.htm

The seven C's of communication. (2017, June 28). Retrieved from Education Executive: https://edexec.co.uk/the-seven-cs-of-communication/

Does your business writing contain the 7 C's of effective communication? (n.d.). Retrieved from Hurley Write Inc.: https://www.hurleywrite.com/Blog/77947/Does-Your-Business-Writing-Contain-the-7-Cs-of-Effective-Communication

The 7 C's of communication. (n.d.). Retrieved from the World of Work Project: https://worldofwork.io/2019/07/the-7-cs-of-communication/

Rongala, A. (2021, July 17). *7 Cs of effective communication with example*. Retrieved from Invensis: https://www.invensislearning.com/blog/7-rules-of-effective-communication-with-examples/

10 7-Eyed Supervision Model

Abramska, M. (2020, August 26). *The 7 eyed model of supervision: A map to navigate your coaching supervision*. Retrieved from the International Centre for Coaching Supervision: https://iccs.co/blog/the-seven-eyed-model-a-map-to-navigate-your-coaching-supervision-practice/

Turner, M. (n.d.). *The 7-eyed supervision model*. Retrieved from Mike the Mentor: https://www.mikethementor.co.uk/blog/the-7-eyed-supervision-model

Eustace, M. (n.d.). *The seven-eyed supervision model*. Retrieved from Living Therapy: https://www.livingtherapy.co.uk/seven-eyed-model

The seven-eyed model of supervision: A guide for coaches. (n.d.). Retrieved from Personal Coaching Information: https://www.personal-coaching-information.com/seven-eyed-model.html

Adamson, F. (2017). *The seven-eyed model of supervision: A systemic perspective to knowledge building and increased effectiveness*. Retrieved from Mindful Leaders: http://mindful-leaders.com/wp-content/uploads/2017/08/The-Seven-Eyed-Model-of-Supervision.pdf

11 8 Cs of Self-Leadership

Sullivan, J. (2010). *The 8 C's*. Retrieved from Reid Stell Counseling: https://www.reidstellcounseling.com/uploads/1/3/9/3/13938466/r_schwartz_the_8_cs_worksheet.pdf

8 C's: Self-energy qualities. (n.d.). Retrieved from Don Elium Psychotherapy: http://www.don-elium-psychotherapy.com/connectedness

Baran, K. (2020, April 8). *The 8 C's*. Retrieved from Kerim Baran: https://kerimbaran.com/2020/04/08/the-8-cs/

The center for self-leadership. (n.d.). Retrieved from Good Therapy: https://www.goodtherapy.org/training-courses/internal-family-systems.html

Rizzo, A. (2021, November 22). *Self in IFS therapy: What it is, what are the 8 C's and the 5 P's of self*. Retrieved from Therapy with Allesio: https://www.therapywithallesio.com/articles/self-in-ifs-therapy-what-it-is-what-are-the-8-cs-and-the-5-ps-of-self

12 8 Disciplines of Problem-Solving (8D)

What are the 8 disciplines (8D)? (n.d.). Retrieved from the American Society for Quality: https://asq.org/quality-resources/eight-disciplines-8d

Introduction to eight disciplines of problem solving (8D). (n.d.). Retrieved from Quality-One International: https://quality-one.com/8d/

Faircloth, S. (2015, December 9). *How to use the 8D method to find the root cause of nonconformances*. Retrieved from Ease Inc.: https://www.ease.io/how-to-use-the-8d-method-to-find-the-root-cause-of-nonconformances/

The 8D problem solving process. (n.d.). Retrieved from Operational Excellence Consulting: https://www.operational-excellence-consulting.com/174_asics-point-spike_ryEV.html

8D problem solving process. (n.d.). Retrieved from Smooth Operations in the Far East: https://www.sofeast.com/glossary/8d-problem-solving-process/

Gomex, B. (2019, September 6). *Leverage the 8 disciplines*. Retrieved from Rever: https://reverscore.com/8d-problem-solving/

Peterson, O. (2019, November 29). *8D chess: How to use the 8 disciplines for problem solving*. Retrieved from Process Street: https://www.process.st/8d/

13 8 Factors of Engagement

Engagement. (n.d.). Retrieved from Sicora Consulting: https://sicoraconsulting.com/engagement/

Employee engagement. (n.d.). Retrieved from Sicora Consulting: https://sicoraconsulting.com/employee-engagement/

8 factors of employee engagement individual profile. (n.d.). Retrieved from Sicora Consulting: https://sicoraconsulting.com/8-factors-promotion/

Dr. Robert T. Sicora. (n.d.). Retrieved from Sicora Consulting: https://sicoraconsulting.com/dr-robert-t-sicora/

Sicora, R.T., Stepanek, C., Gravholt, D., & Baker, A. (2019, November 11). *8 factors of engagement: Historical white paper and analysis*. Retrieved from TTI Success Insights: https://images.ttisi.com/wp-content/uploads/research/2020/03/23144622/SCI-8FE.pdf

Sicora, R.T. (2016, October 20). *8 factors of engagement*. Retrieved from LinkedIn Pulse: https://www.linkedin.com/pulse/8-factors-engagment-robert-t-sicora-ed-d-/

14 ABC Model of Behavior (Bijou)

BetterHelp Editorial Team. (2023, October 30). *Understanding the antecedent behavior consequence model*. Retrieved from Betterhelp: https://www.betterhelp.com/advice/behavior/understanding-the-antecedent-behavior-consequence-model/

ABC model. (n.d.). Retrieved from Psychology Tools: https://www.psychologytools.com/resource/abc-model/

What are the ABCs of behavior? (n.d.). Retrieved from the Applied Behavior Analysis Programs Guide: https://www.appliedbehavioranalysisprograms.com/faq/what-are-the-abcs-of-behavior/

Webster, J. (2020, January 29). *ABC: Antecedent, behavior, consequence.* Retrieved from Thoughtco: https://www.thoughtco.com/abc-antecedent-behavior-and-consequence-3111263

Gilmore, H. (2017, July 4). *ABC's of behavior (antecedent-behavior-consequence).* Retrieved from PsychCentral: https://pro.psychcentral.com/child-therapist/2017/07/abcs-of-behavior-antecedent-behavior-consequence/

Smith, S.D. (2021, September 24). *The benefits of training parents to use antecedent-behavior-consequence charts.* Retrieved from Autism Spectrum News: https://autismspectrumnews.org/the-benefits-of-training-parents-to-use-antecedent-behavior-consequence-charts/

15 ABCDE Model (Ellis)

Wright, S. (2022, April 15). *All about rational emotive behavior therapy (REBT).* Retrieved from Psych Central: https://psychcentral.com/lib/rational-emotive-behavior-therapy/

Roberts, A. (2016, January 31). *ABCDE model: Improving emotional intelligence.* Retrieved from Master Facilitator: http://masterfacilitator.com/abcde-model-improving-emotional-intelligence/

Schenck, L.K. (n.d.). *Gaining control is as easy as A-B-C-D-E.* Retrieved from Mindfulness Muse: https://www.mindfulnessmuse.com/cognitive-behavioral-therapy/gaining-control-is-as-easy-as-a-b-c-d-e

The ABCDE approach to faulty cognitions. (n.d.). Retrieved from the University of Connecticut: https://nrcgt.uconn.edu/underachievement_study/school-perceptions/sp_section14/

Matei, M. (2014, October 3). *Research paper: Rational emotive behavioral approach and the ABCDE model.* Retrieved from The International Coach Academy: https://coachcampus.com/coach-portfolios/research-papers/monica-matei-rational-emotive-behavioral-approach-and-the-abcde-model/

Ramzan, T. (2020, July 2). *Describe the ABCDE model of REBT. Also describe the ABCDE model of treatment.* Retrieved from Medium: https://medium.com/@noormohammadwarriach/describe-the-abc-model-of-rebt-also-briefly-describe-the-abcde-model-of-treatment-913b4c043e2c

Mahoney, T. (2019, November 16). *How I use Albert Ellis's "ABCDE" method to stay motivated.* Retrieved from Medium: https://medium.com/med-daily/how-i-use-albert-elliss-abcde-method-to-stay-motivated-f22107c0633f

Selva, J. (2018, March 8). *What is Albert Ellis' ABC model in CBT theory?* Retrieved from Positive Psychology: https://positivepsychology.com/albert-ellis-abc-model-rebt-cbt/

McLeod, S. (2023, October 20). *Cognitive behavioral therapy (CBT): Types, techniques, uses.* Retrieved from Simply Psychology: https://www.simplypsychology.org/cognitive-therapy.html

Nunez, K. (2020, April 17). *What is the ABC model in cognitive behavioral therapy?* Retrieved from Healthline: https://www.healthline.com/health/abc-model#benefits-and-examples

The ABCDE coaching model: A simple summary. (2019, June). Retrieved from the World of Work Project: https://worldofwork.io/2019/06/abcde-coaching-model/

16 ABCDE Model (Seligman)

Selva, J. (2018, March 8). *What is Albert Ellis' ABC model in CBT theory?* Retrieved from Positive Psychology: https://positivepsychology.com/albert-ellis-abc-model-rebt-cbt/

Robson, P. (n.d.). *The "ABCDE" method for changing your mind—for the better.* Retrieved from Wishful Thinking Works: https://wishfulthinkingworks.com/what-2/the-quotabcdequot-method-for-changing-your-mind-for-the-better/

Taylor, J. (n.d.). *Learned helplessness and the ABCDE model.* Retrieved from Habits for Wellbeing: https://www.habitsforwellbeing.com/learned-helplessness-and-the-abcde-model/

Cherry, K. (2021, June 28). *Using learned optimism in your life.* Retrieved from Verywell Mind: https://www.verywellmind.com/learned-optimism-4174101

Nickol, C. (2021, February 27). *ABCDE model of optimism—How to become more optimistic.* Retrieved from Work Grow Thrive: https://workgrowthrive.com/abcde-model-of-optimism-how-to-become-more-optimistic-psycap-3/

Wood, S. (2017, May 11). *Optimism: A proven 5-step model to upgrade your thinking system.* Retrieved from Great Managers: https://www.greatmanagers.com.au/learned-optimism/

Haralambous, P. (2016, February 14). *Learning to be optimistic (ABCDE model).* Retrieved from LinkedIn Pulse: https://www.linkedin.com/pulse/learning-optimistic-abcde-model-paula-haralambous/

Shepherd, W. (2011). *Reframing adversity.* Retrieved from the University of Washington: https://www.washington.edu/admin/hr/publications/email/pod/convio/leadingedge/sp11/leadingedge-adversity.html

Romano, J. (2017, September 18). *Conquer negativity: It's as easy as ABCDE.* Retrieved from Medium: https://medium.com/@LiveTREW/conquer-negativity-its-as-easy-as-abcde-e7511cd8d061

17 Acceptance and Commitment Therapy

Ackerman, C. (2017, March 1). *How does acceptance and commitment therapy (ACT) work?* Retrieved from Positive Psychology: https://positivepsychology.com/act-acceptance-and-commitment-therapy/

Harris, R. (n.d.). *Embracing your demons: An overview of acceptance and commitment therapy.* Retrieved from Psychotherapy.net: https://www.psychotherapy.net/article/Acceptance-and-Commitment-Therapy-ACT#section-six-core-principles-of-act

Hayes, S. (n.d.). *Acceptance and commitment therapy.* Retrieved from the Association for Contextual Behavioral Science: https://contextualscience.org/act

Archer, R. (2022, January 7). *Acceptance and commitment training.* Retrieved from Working with ACT: https://workingwithact.com/category/acceptance-and-commitment-training-act/

Acceptance and commitment therapy. (2018, February 12). Retrieved from GoodTherapy: https://www.goodtherapy.org/learn-about-therapy/types/acceptance-commitment-therapy

Dewane, C. (2008). *The ABCs of ACT—Acceptance and commitment therapy.* Retrieved from Social Work Today: https://www.socialworktoday.com/archive/090208p36.shtml

Acceptance and commitment therapy. (2022, March 21). Retrieved from Psychology Today: https://www.psychologytoday.com/us/therapy-types/acceptance-and-commitment-therapy

Glasofer, D. (2023, August 23). *What is acceptance and commitment therapy?* Retrieved from Verywell Mind: https://www.verywellmind.com/acceptance-commitment-therapy-gad-1393175

18 ACHIEVE Coaching Model

The ACHIEVE coaching model: A simple summary. (n.d.). Retrieved from the World of Work Project: https://worldofwork.io/2019/08/the-achieve-coaching-model/

Lea, S. (2022, February 16). *What is the ACHIEVE model?* Retrieved from Businessballs: https://www.businessballs.com/coaching-and-mentoring/achieve-model/

Dembkowski, S., & Eldridge, F. (2004). *The ACHIEVE coaching model.* Retrieved from the Coaching and Mentoring Network: http://www.coachingnetwork.org.uk/information-portal/Articles/pdfs/CtC3.pdf

ACHIEVE coaching model (pros, cons, examples). (2022, March 26). Retrieved from Coach 4 Growth: https://www.coach4growth.com/coaching-skills/coaching-models/achieve-coaching-model/

19 Action-Centered Leadership Model (ACL)

Functional leadership model. (n.d.). Retrieved from Toolshero: https://www.toolshero.com/leadership/functional-leadership-model/

Functional leadership. (n.d.). Retrieved from Accipio: https://www.accipio.com/eleadership/mod/wiki/view.php?id=1658

Shead, M. (n.d.). *The functional leadership model.* Retrieved from Leadership 501: http://www.leadership501.com/functional-leadership-model/20/

Michelini, A. (2016, November). *Functional leadership model.* Retrieved from DocShare: http://docshare01.docshare.tips/files/30741/307419369.pdf

Chapman, A. (2022, January 11). *What is action centered leadership?* Retrieved from Businessballs: https://www.businessballs.com/leadership-models/action-centred-leadership-john-adair/

Action centered leadership: John Adair. (n.d.). Retrieved from Expert Program Management: https://expertprogrammanagement.com/2011/08/action-centred-leadership-john-adair/

20 Action Learning

Action learning and group coaching. (n.d.). Retrieved from Personal Coaching Information.com: https://www.personal-coaching-information.com/action-learning-and-group-coaching.html

Action learning model. (n.d.). Retrieved from Personal Coaching Information: https://www.personal-coaching-information.com/action-learning-model.html

Carson, B. (2014, September 4). *Action learning coaching: How to be a catalyst for transformation.* Retrieved from the Association for Talent Development: https://www.td.org/insights/action-learning-coaching-how-to-be-a-catalyst-for-transformation

Norman, C. (2017, December 12). *How action learning sets can support a culture of coaching in organizations.* Retrieved from the International Coaching Federation: https://coachfederation.org/blog/action-learning-sets-can-support-culture-coaching-organizations

McNamara, C. (2022, August 1). *What is action learning?* Retrieved from the Management Library: https://managementhelp.org/blogs/personal-and-professional-coaching/2013/03/10/what-is-action-learning/

Marquardt, M.J. (n.d.). *The coach as catalyst for action learning.* Retrieved from the World Institute for Action Learning: https://wial.org/wp-content/uploads/The_Coach_as_Catalyst_for_Action_Learning.pdf

Certifications for action learning coaches. (n.d.). Retrieved from the World Institute for Action Learning: https://wial.org/certification/calc-courses/

Sahni, S. (2015, March 30). *Action learning with impact.* Retrieved from Harvard Business Publishing: https://www.harvardbusiness.org/action-learning-with-impact/

Chadwick, P. (2017, January 10). *An executive education process fit for the 21st century.* Retrieved from IEDP.com: https://www.iedp.com/articles/action-learning-explained/

21 Adaptive Leadership

Ramalingam, B., Nabarro, D., Oqubay, A., Carnall, D.R., & Wild, L. (2020, September 11). 5 principles to guide adaptive leadership. *Harvard Business Review.* https://hbr.org/2020/09/5-principles-to-guide-adaptive-leadership

What is adaptive leadership? (2021, January 5). Retrieved from Western Governors University: https://www.wgu.edu/blog/what-adaptive-leadership2101.html#close

Srivastava, Y. (2022, June 23). *Principles and examples of adaptive leadership.* Retrieved from BetterUp: https://www.betterup.com/blog/adaptive-leadership

What is adaptive leadership: Definition and Heifetz principles. (2021, January 27). Retrieved from WDHB: https://wdhb.com/blog/what-is-adaptive-leadership/

Wale, H. (2023, May 11). *Adaptive leadership.* Retrieved from the Corporate Finance Institute: https://corporatefinanceinstitute.com/resources/management/adaptive-leadership/

Michaels, G. (2023, June 28). *Adaptive leadership: Principles and a framework for the future.* Retrieved from Atlassian: https://www.atlassian.com/blog/leadership/adaptive-leadership

Herrity, J. (2023, February 3). *What is adaptive leadership?* Retrieved from Indeed: https://www.indeed.com/career-advice/career-development/adaptive-leadership

Heifetz, R., Grashow, A., & Linsky, M. (2009). *The practice of adaptive leadership: Tools and tactics for changing your organization and the world.* Harvard Business Press.

22 ADKAR Model

The Prosci ADKAR model. (n.d.). Retrieved from Prosci: https://www.prosci.com/adkar/adkar-model

ADKAR model of change (Prosci). (n.d.). Retrieved from Toolshero: https://www.toolshero.com/change-management/adkar-model/

What is the ADKAR model and how to use it. (2018). Retrieved from Tallyfy: https://tallyfy.com/adkar-model/

Using the ADKAR change management model. (n.d.). Retrieved from Lucidchart: https://www.lucidchart.com/blog/using-the-adkar-model-for-change-management

Bridges, M. (2018, December 7). *How to use the ADKAR model to manage change the right way.* Retrieved from Medium: https://medium.com/@mark.bridges/how-to-utilize-the-adkar-model-to-manage-change-the-right-way-d3b58679f92f

Malhotra, G. (2023, August 21). *ADKAR model, what is it and how to use it.* Retrieved from WhatFix: https://academy.whatfix.com/adkar-model-what-is-it-and-how-to-use-it/

23 Affective-Cognitive Consistency Model (ACCM)

Cognitive consistency theories. (n.d.). Retrieved from Encyclopedia.com: https://www.encyclopedia.com/social-sciences/encyclopedias-almanacs-transcripts-and-maps/cognitive-consistency-theories

Theories of attitude change. (2001, August 3). Retrieved from the Association for Educational Communications and Technology: http://members.aect.org/edtech/ed1/34/34-03.html

Wilbert, M. L. (1972). *An investigation of attitude consistency.* Retrieved from the Institute of Educational Sciences: https://files.eric.ed.gov/fulltext/ED070984.pdf

Kruglanski, A., Jasko, K., Milyavsky, M., Chernikova, M., Webber, D., Pierro, A., & di Santo, D. (n.d.). *Cognitive Consistency Theory in social psychology: A paradigm reconsidered.* Retrieved from Google: https://www.google.com/l?sa=t&rct=j&q=&esrc=s&source=web&cd=&ved=2ahUKEwiJ6cKSxY73AhW8oXIEHaj8BMY4ChAWegQIJxAB&url=https%3A%2F%2Fpsyarxiv.com%2Fyjz3r%2Fdownload%2F%3Fformat%3Dpdf&usg=AOvVaw0oQQSMC1DWkqpY7ZZNlVCs

Simon, D., Snow, C., & Read, S. (2004). The redux of cognitive consistency theories: Evidence judgements by constraint satisfaction. *Journal of Personality and Social Psychology, 86*(6), 814–837. http://www.communicationcache.com/uploads/1/0/8/8/10887248/the_redux_of_cognitive_consistency_theories-_evidence_judgments_by_constraint_satisfaction.pdf

Petty, R.E., Fabrigar, L.R., & Wegener, D.T. (2003). Emotional factors in attitudes and persuasion. In R.J. Davidson, K.R. Scherer, & H.H. Goldsmith (Eds.), *Handbook of Affective Sciences,* 752–772. Oxford University Press. Retrieved from Richard Petty: https://richardepetty.com/wp-content/uploads/2019/01/2003-emotion-pettyfabrigarwegener.pdf

24 After-Action Review

After Action Review process. (n.d.). Retrieved from Mindtools: https://www.mindtools.com/pages/article/newPPM_73.htm

Darling, M., Parry, C., & Moore, J. (2005, July–August). Learning in the thick of it. *Harvard Business Review*. https://hbr.org/2005/07/learning-in-the-thick-of-it

Hearn, S. (2019, March 26). *After Action Review*. Retrieved from Better Evaluation: https://www.betterevaluation.org/en/evaluation-options/after_action_review

After Action Review (AAR). (n.d.). Retrieved from Army Study Guide: https://www.armystudyguide.com/content/powerpoint/Training_the_force_presentations/after-action-review-aar-2.shtml

Henshaw, T. (2012, April). *After Action Reviews*. Retrieved from the Wharton School of Business: https://executiveeducation.wharton.upenn.edu/thought-leadership/wharton-at-work/2012/04/after-action-reviews/

The leader's guide to after-action reviews (AAR). (2013, December). Retrieved from US Army Combined Arms Center-Training: https://pinnacle-leaders.com/wp-content/uploads/2018/02/Leaders_Guide_to_AAR.pdf

25 Agile Methodology

Rigby, D., Sutherland, J., & Takeuchi, H. (2016, May). Embracing Agile: How to master the process that's transforming management. *Harvard Business Review*. https://hbr.org/2016/05/embracing-agile

Laoyan, S. (2022, October 15). *What is Agile methodology?* Retrieved from Asana: https://asana.com/resources/agile-methodology#

Peek, S. (2023, October 23). *What is Agile scrum methodology?* Retrieved from Business News Daily: https://www.businessnewsdaily.com/4987-what-is-agile-scrum-methodology.html

Coursera. (2023, July 27). *What is Agile and when to use it*. Retrieved from Coursera: https://www.coursera.org/articles/what-is-agile-a-beginners-guide

What is Agile methodology in project management? (n.d.). Retrieved from Wrike: https://www.wrike.com/project-management-guide/faq/what-is-agile-methodology-in-project-management/

Arun, R. (2023, October 19). *What is Agile methodology in software development*. Retrieved from SimpliLearn: https://www.simplilearn.com/tutorials/agile-scrum-tutorial/what-is-agile

The Agile coach. (n.d.). Retrieved from Atlassian: https://www.atlassian.com/agile

Sacolick, I. (2022, April 6). *What is Agile methodology? Modern software development explained*. Retrieved from InfoWorld: https://www.infoworld.com/article/3237508/what-is-agile-methodology-modern-software-development-explained.html

Agile 101. (n.d.). Retrieved from Agile Alliance: https://www.agilealliance.org/agile101/

Agile methodology: What is it, how it works, and why it matters. (n.d.). Retrieved from LucidSpark: https://lucidspark.com/blog/what-is-agile-methodology

What is Agile methodology? (2022, July 19). Retrieved from Red Hat: https://www.redhat.com/en/devops/what-is-agile-methodology

Abeythilake, U. (2022, June 11). *Agile methodology*. Retrieved from Medium: https://medium.com/@abeythilakeudara3/agile-methodology-106270809c99

26 AGS Change Management Framework

The journey of a change manager & change team. (2021). Retrieved from OCM Solutions: https://www.ocmsolution.com/AGS-Guides-and-Plans/The-Journey-of-a-Change-Manager-AGS-Framework.pdf

Top change management model & template. (n.d.). Retrieved from OCM Solutions: https://www.ocmsolution.com/change-management-approach/

Indeed Editorial Team. (2022, December 2). *Change management methodology: Definition and 13 types*. Retrieved from Indeed: https://www.indeed.com/career-advice/career-development/change-management-methodology

A best change management process. (n.d.). Retrieved from Airiodion Consulting: https://www.airiodionconsulting.com/a-best-change-management-process/

27 AID Feedback Model

The AID feedback model. (n.d.). Retrieved from Revolution Learning and Development: https://www.revolutionlearning.co.uk/article/the-aid-feedback-model/

The AID model. (n.d.). Retrieved from The Leadership Coaches: https://www.theleadershipcoaches.co.uk/post/the-aid-model

Feedback: Giving and receiving powerful feedback. (n.d.). Retrieved from The Real Human: https://therealhuman.co.uk/wp-content/uploads/2019/04/AID-feedback-model.pdf

Landsberg, M. (2015). *The tao of coaching: Boost your effectiveness at work by inspiring and developing those around you.* IPS-Profile Books.

Big Ideas Growing Minds. (2019, November 25). *The AID model by Max Landsberg* [Video]. Retrieved from YouTube: https://www.youtube.com/watch?v=Ve7EaSwW2Bw

Roberts, A. (2020, March 21). *AID feedback model.* Retrieved from Andi Roberts: https://andiroberts.com/aid-feedback-model/

Henderson, I. (2019, November 8). *AID feedback model.* Retrieved from Eagle Training: https://eagletraining.co.uk/2019/11/08/aid-feedback-model-feedback-training/

28 AIM Change Management Methodology

The AIM methodology. (n.d.). Retrieved from Implementation Management Associates: https://www.imaworldwide.com/aim-change-management-methodology

Alsher, P. (2017, November 9). *AIM vs. the ADKAR model: Comparing change management methodologies.* Retrieved from Implementation Management Associates: https://www.imaworldwide.com/blog/aim-vs.-the-adkar-model-comparing-change-management-methodologies

Harrison, D. (2019, September 18). *Leading people through business changes: The AIM methodology explained.* Retrieved from Implementation Management Associates: https://www.imaworldwide.com/blog/leading-people-through-business-changes-the-aim-methodology-explained

Change management methodologies. (2016). Retrieved from Change Actions: https://www.changeactions.com/single-post/2016/07/11/the-change-management-methodologies

Best change management methodologies & models. (n.d.). Retrieved from Airiodion Global Services: https://www.airiodion.com/organizational-change-management-methodologies/#AIM-Change-Framework

Change management methodology: Definition and 13 types. (2022, December 2). Retrieved from Indeed.com: https://www.indeed.com/career-advice/career-development/change-management-methodology

29 Appreciative Coaching Model

Moore, C. (2019, May 21). *18 appreciative inquiry workshops, training, and courses.* Retrieved from Positive Psychology: https://positivepsychology.com/appreciative-inquiry-workshops/

Menard, J. (2023, June 2). *The 4 D's of appreciative inquiry: A positive model and process for change.* Retrieved from The Coaching Tools Company: https://www.thecoachingtoolscompany.com/4-ds-appreciative-inquiry-model-process-for-change-by-julia-menard/

Appreciative coaching explained. (n.d.). Retrieved from Toolshero: https://www.toolshero.com/management/appreciative-coaching/

30 Appreciative Inquiry Model

The 5-Step appreciative inquiry process. (n.d.). Retrieved from the University of Waterloo: https://uwaterloo.ca/partnerships-in-dementia-care/getting-started-culture-change/5-step-appreciative-inquiry-process

What is appreciative inquiry? A short guide to the appreciative inquiry model and process. (2017, May 9). Retrieved from Benedictine University: https://cvdl.bcn.cdu/blog/what-is-appreciative-inquiry/

Appreciative inquiry. (n.d.). Retrieved from Organizing Engagement: https://organizingengagement.org/models/appreciative-inquiry/

What is appreciative inquiry? (n.d.). Retrieved from David Cooperrider: https://www.davidcooperrider.com/ai-process/

Moore, C. (2019, April 27). *What is appreciative inquiry?* Retrieved from Positive Psychology: https://positivepsychology.com/appreciative-inquiry/

Tocino-Smith, J. (2019, May 21). *How to apply appreciative inquiry: A visual guide.* Retrieved from Positive Psychology: https://positivepsychology.com/appreciative-inquiry-process/

31 ARROW Coaching Model

The ARROW coaching model: A quick reference guide. (n.d.). Retrieved from Teachable Inc.: https://cdn.fs.teachablecdn.com/s9p5QCrSaXDTlp1vuW9A

Thomson, S. (2018, January 11). *The coaching model library: An introduction.* Retrieved from the Training Journal: https://www.trainingjournal.com/articles/features/coaching-model-library-introduction

Libri, V. (2004, July). Beyond GROW: In search of acronyms and coaching models. *The International Journal of Mentoring and Coaching,* 2(1), via HumanExcellence: https://humanexcellence.com.au/images/POSITIVE-MODEL.pdf

McChristie, S. (2016, April 15). *Session 7: Coaching at work, part 2.* Retrieved from Blog-McChristie: https://blog.mcchristie.com/tag/arrow/

Krcivoj, I. (2019, October 7). *Coaching model: ARROW.* Retrieved from Coach Campus: https://coachcampus.com/coach-portfolios/coaching-models/ivana-krcivoj-arrow/

32 Atkins Murphy Model of Reflection (AMMR)

Models of reflection. (2023, October 17). Retrieved from LA Trobe University: https://latrobe.libguides.com/reflectivepractice/models

Atkins Murphy model. (n.d.). Retrieved from The Open University: https://www.open.edu/openlearn/education-development/learning-teach-becoming-reflective-practitioner/content-section-6.3

Using a model of reflection. (n.d.). Retrieved from the Online Network of Irish Nurses and Midwives: http://www.nurse2nurse.ie/Upload/NA4874Models%20of%20Reflection.pdf

Atkins and Murphy. (n.d.). Retrieved from Physiopedia: https://www.physio-pedia.com/File:Atkins_and_Murphy.JPG

Nichola, B. (2016, May 2). *Guide to models of reflection: When and why you should use different ones.* Retrieved from Life Long Learning with Occupational Therapy: https://lifelonglearningwithot.wordpress.com/2016/05/02/different-models-of-reflection-using-them-to-help-me-reflect/

All Answers Ltd. (2018, November). *Atkins Murphy model of reflection.* Retrieved from Nursing Answers: https://nursinganswers.net/reflective-guides/atkins-and-murphy.php

33 Attribution Theory

McLeod, S. (2023, June 11). *Attribution theory in psychology: Definition and examples.* Retrieved from Simply Psychology: https://www.simplypsychology.org/attribution-theory.html

Attribution theory. (n.d.). Retrieved from Shippensburg University: http://webspace.ship.edu/ambart/psy_220/attributionol.htm

Attribution theory. (n.d.). Retrieved from Instructional Design: https://www.instructionaldesign.org/theories/attribution-theory/

Hopper, E. (2018, September 30). *Attribution theory: The psychology of interpreting behavior.* Retrieved from ThoughtCo.: https://www.thoughtco.com/attribution-theory-4174631

Cherry, K. (2023, May 19). *Understanding attribution in social psychology.* Retrieved from Verywell Mind: https://www.verywellmind.com/attribution-social-psychology-2795898

American Psychological Association. (n.d.). Attribution theory. In *APA dictionary of psychology*: https://dictionary.apa.org/attribution-theory

Attribution theory. (n.d.). Retrieved from Ifioque.com: https://ifioque.com/interpersonal-skills/attribution-theory

34 Barrett Model

The Barrett model. (n.d.). Retrieved from the Barrett Values Center: https://www.valuescentre.com/barrett-model/

Wiedemann, C. (n.d.). *Theoretical support for the Barrett model.* Retrieved from the Barrett Values Center: https://www.valuescentre.com/resource-library/theoretical-support-barrett-model/

Barrett certification. (n.d.). Retrieved from the Barrett Values Center: https://compass.valuescentre.com/bvc-certification/

Barrett model, a great motivation theory. (n.d.). Retrieved from Toolshero: https://www.toolshero.com/psychology/barrett-model/

Lea, S. (2022, February 21). *Seven levels of leadership consciousness.* Retrieved from Businessballs: https://www.businessballs.com/self-awareness/seven-levels-of-leadership-consciousness/

35 Basadur Profile

Mind Tools Content Team. (n.d.). *How good is your problem solving?* Retrieved from MindTools: https://www.mindtools.com/aoubxrt/how-good-is-your-problem-solving

Basadur profile: Products and pricing. (n.d.). Retrieved from Basadur Profile: https://basadurprofile.com/products/pricing/#!/profile/

Basadur profile. (n.d.). Retrieved from Basadur Profile: https://basadurprofile.com

FAQs and support. (n.d.). Retrieved from Basadur Profile: https://basadurprofile.com/support/faq/#!/profile/0/

The profile. (n.d.). Retrieved from Basadur Profile: https://www.basadur.com/the-profile/

The Basadur profile team report. (n.d.). Retrieved from Basadur Profile: https://www.basadur.com/wp-content/uploads/2023/04/Basadur-Profile-For-Teams.pdf

Online assessment tool: Discover your innovation style by Dr. Min Basadur. (n.d.). Retrieved from the Disruptive Innovation Hub: https://www.disruptiveinnovation.io/courses/bprofile

Shedroff, N. (n.d.). Basadur profiles. Retrieved from Nathan.com: https://nathan.com/tool-basadur-profiles/

Koach.net. (2019, November 11). Which of these is your problem solving style? Retrieved from Medium: https://medium.com/@contact_56580/which-of-these-is-your-problem-solving-style-857401256154

36 BASIC ID Model

Lazarus, C. (2014, February 16). Seven ways to become a better you. Retrieved from Psychology Today: https://www.psychologytoday.com/us/blog/think-well/201402/seven-ways-become-better-you

Lazarus, C. (2019, November 30). Multimodal therapy: A unifying approach to psychotherapy. Retrieved from Psychology Today: https://www.psychologytoday.com/us/blog/think-well/201911/multimodal-therapy-unifying-approach-psychotherapy

BASIC ID. (n.d.). Retrieved from All About Counseling: https://edu505counseling.weebly.com/sample-basic-id.html

American Psychological Association. (2007, August). Multimodal therapy [Video]. Retrieved from the American Psychological Association: https://www.apa.org/pubs/videos/4310817

Whitten, H. (2009). Cognitive behavioural coaching techniques for dummies. Wiley.

Cuncic, A. (2022, January 25). What is multimodal therapy? Retrieved from Verywell Mind: https://www.verywellmind.com/what-is-multimodal-therapy-5216156

37 BEEF Feedback Model

Powerful performance feedback models and how they can help your company. (n.d.). Retrieved from Lucidchart: https://www.lucidchart.com/blog/performance-feedback-models

BEEF feedback model. (n.d.). Retrieved from the Isle of Man Office of Human Resources: https://hr.gov.im/media/1497/beefmodel.pdf

Giving constructive feedback—The BEEF model. (n.d.). Retrieved from If Development: http://www.if-dev.co.uk/wp-content/uploads/2013/07/BEEF-Feedback.pdf

Laurel, D. (2016, November 14). Tip #647: Feedback models ABC through BET. Retrieved from Laurel and Associates: https://www.laurelandassociates.com/tip-647-feedback-models-abc-through-bet/

Morrison, M. (2015, October 3). COBS or CORBS feedback model for performance management. Retrieved from RapidBi: https://rapidbi.com/cobs-or-corbs-feedback-model-for-performance-management/

Stratton, R. (2019, April 24). Use the BEEF model to correct employee behavior. Retrieved from Blue Gem Learning: https://www.bluegemlearning.com/post/use-the-b-e-e-f-model-to-correct-employee-behaviour

38 Behavioral EQ Model

The Behavioral EQ training model. (n.d.). Retrieved from TRACOM: https://tracom.com/emotional-intelligence-training/behavioral-eq-model

Mulqueen, C. (n.d.). Behavioral EQ: Putting emotional intelligence to work. Retrieved from Business2Community: https://www.business2community.com/wp-content/uploads/2014/06/BEQ_Whitepaper-TRACOM.pdf

Emotional intelligence: Behavioral EQ. (n.d.). Retrieved from John K. Whitehead and Associates: https://johnkwhitehead.ca/what-we-do/social-styles/behavioral-eq/

What's BEQ model? (n.d.). Retrieved from Mentor Top Solutions: https://www.mentortopsolutions.ro/behavioural-eq/whats-beq-model/

Mulqueen, C. (n.d.). Behavioral EQ explorations: Building relationships. Retrieved from Mentor Top Solutions: https://www.mentortopsolutions.ro/media/Emotional-Intelligence-Explorations-Building-Relationships-Whitepaper-Behavioral-EQ-W.pdf

Freifeld, L. (2012, September 10). Behavioral EQ: The next generation of emotional intelligence. Training magazine: https://trainingmag.com/behavioral-eq-the-next-generation-of-emotional-intelligence/

Richmond, A. (2022, March 6). Boosting emotional intelligence. Retrieved from Career Intelligence: https://career-intelligence.com/boosting-emotional-intelligence/

What is behavioral intelligence? (2020, October 1). Retrieved from The Coeus Creative Group: https://www.coeuscreativegroup.com/2020/10/01/what-is-behavioral-intelligence/

Gaffney, C.R. (2014, January 15). A brief history of behavioral intelligence. Retrieved from Behavioral Intelligence at Work: https://www.behavioral-intelligence.com/2014/01/15/a-brief-history-of-behavioral-intelligence/

Boyatzis, R.E. (2018, August 13). The behavioral level of emotional intelligence and its measurement. Frontiers in Psychology, 9, Issue 1438. https://www.frontiersin.org/articles/10.3389/fpsyg.2018.01438/full

39 Behavioral Learning Theory (BLT)

What is the behavioral learning theory? (2020, May 29). Retrieved from Western Governor's University: https://www.wgu.edu/blog/what-behavioral-learning-theory2005.html

McLeod, S. (2023, October 11). *Behaviorist approach to psychology.* Retrieved from Simply Psychology: https://www.simplypsychology.org/behaviorism.html

Cherry, K. (2022, November 7). *What is behaviorism?* Retrieved from Verywell Mind: https://www.verywellmind.com/behavioral-psychology-4157183

Horne, C. (2023, September 20). *Behavioral theory or behavioral psychology? How behavior and personality intersect.* Retrieved from BetterHelp: https://www.betterhelp.com/advice/behavior/behavioral-theory-behavioral-psychology-or-behaviorism-how-behavior-and-personality-intersect/

Behavioral and cognitive theories. (n.d.). Retrieved from CourseHero: https://www.coursehero.com/study-guides/wmopen-lifespandevelopment/behavioral-and-cognitive-theories/

Behavioral theories. (n.d.). Retrieved from Richards On The Brain: https://www.richardsonthebrain.com/behavioral-theories

40 Belbin's Team Role Theory

The nine Belbin team roles. (n.d.). Retrieved from Belbin Associates: https://www.belbin.com/about/belbin-team-roles

Belbin's team roles. (n.d.). Retrieved from MindTools: https://www.mindtools.com/pages/article/newLDR_83.htm

Moultrie, J. (n.d.). *Belbin's team roles.* Retrieved from Cambridge University: https://www.ifm.eng.cam.ac.uk/research/dmg/tools-and-techniques/belbins-team-roles/

Mackechnie, P. (n.d.). *Belbin team role theories.* Retrieved from Notion Business Coaching: https://www.businesscoaching.co.uk/files/belbin_team_role_theories.pdf

Belbin's team role theory. (2021, August 13). Retrieved from Harappa Learning: https://harappa.education/harappa-diaries/belbins-team-roles-theory/

The 9 Belbin team roles. (2023, March 16). Retrieved from Indeed: https://www.indeed.com/career-advice/career-development/belbin-team-roles

Channell, M. (2021, October 21). *Belbin's team roles: How can team roles improve performance in the workplace?* Retrieved from Training Services Wales Ltd.: https://www.tsw.co.uk/blog/leadership-and-management/belbins-team-roles/

41 Benziger's Thinking Styles

Chapman, A. (2022, February 21). *What is Benziger's personality assessment model?* Retrieved from Businessballs.com: https://www.businessballs.com/self-awareness/benziger-personality-assessment/

Personality types: Testing and theory. (2023, October 4). Retrieved from Live Positive: https://livepositive.space/personality-types-testing-and-theory/

What is your brain type? (2012, February 4). Retrieved from Identity and Type: https://identityandtype.wordpress.com/tag/katherine-benziger/

Personality theories, types, and tests. (n.d.). Retrieved from Martabolette Stecher Inst.: http://www.stecherinsti.com/wp-content/uploads/2018/02/e-stimate_Personality-theories-types-and-tests.pdf

Thinking styles assessment. (n.d.). Retrieved from Zen-Tools: https://www.zen-tools.net/thinking-styles.html

Personality quiz. (n.d.). Retrieved from Zen-Tools: https://www.zen-tools.net/personality-quiz.html

Taylor, A. (n.d.). *Brain models.* Retrieved from Arlene Taylor: https://www.arlenetaylor.org/images/pdfs/Brain%20Models-130724.pdf

Katherine Benziger. (n.d.). Retrieved from the Australian Centre for Leadership for Women: https://aclw.org/wp-content/uploads/2020/01/02-Katherine-Benziger.pdf

Newcomb, J. (n.d.). *The Benziger thinking styles assessment.* Retrieved from Focused Solutions: https://focusedcoach.com/the-benziger-thinking-styles-assessment-btsa/

42 BIF/BIFFOF/BIFF Feedback Models

Eddy, B. (2011). *BIFF: A quick response to high conflict people.* HCI Press. Retrieved from Google Books: https://books.google.com/books?hl=en&lr=&id=O_miBkpsbUwC&oi=fnd&pg=PA9&dq=BIFF+Feedback+Model&ots=07PD8_Sqei&sig=Kzwlj-NYwPE9rcuVMIbSy-W3zD4#v=onepage&q=BIFF%20Feedback%20Model&f=false

Rethinking feedback: The RBI-BIF feedback model. (n.d.). Retrieved from Head, Heart, and Hands Engagement: http://www.headheartandhandsengagement.com/rethinking-feedback---the-r-b-i-b-i-f-feedback-model.html

Czernik, A. (n.d.). *Feedback with impact and integrity.* Retrieved from Inspired Executives: https://www.inspired-executives.com/wp-content/uploads/2017/06/Download_Feedback_neu.pdf

Challenging negative behaviour. (2011, March 29). Retrieved from Toolbox HR: https://www.toolbox.com/hr/hr-careers-skills/blogs/challenging-negative-behaviour-032911/

Tomlinson, J. (2014, April 22). *BIF: A simple feedback model.* Retrieved from John Tomlinson: https://johnrtomlinson.com/2014/04/22/bif-a-simple-feedback-model/

Planning and giving feedback. (n.d.). Retrieved from Persona People Management Ltd.: http://www.personapm.co.uk/wp-content/uploads/2015/09/Planning-Giving-Feedback.pdf

Roberts, A. (n.d.). *Feedback models hub.* Retrieved from Andi Roberts: https://andiroberts.com/feedback-models-hub/

43 Birkman Method

The Birkman method. (n.d.). Retrieved from Birkman International Inc.: https://birkman.com/the-birkman-method/

Signature certification. (n.d.). Retrieved from Birkman International Inc.: https://store.birkman.com/collections/get-certified

Birkman personality tests. (n.d.). Retrieved from Practice Aptitude Tests: https://www.practiceaptitudetests.com/birkman-personality-tests/

What is the Birkman method personality test? (2023, June 22). Retrieved from Psychometric Success: https://psychometric-success.com/aptitude-tests/test-types/birkman-test

The Birkman method personality test. (2023, June 8). Retrieved from WikiJob: https://www.wikijob.co.uk/aptitude-tests/test-types/birkman-method-personality-test

The Birkman method. (n.d.). Retrieved from Terry Hildebrandt and Associates LLC.: https://terryhildebrandt.com/birkman-method/

Birkman personality test: Method, report, and question types. (n.d.). Retrieved from Job Test Prep: https://www.jobtestprep.com/birkman-test-prep#breakdown-of-the-birkman-method

The Birkman method personality test: A simple introduction. (n.d.). Retrieved from the World of Work Project: https://worldofwork.io/2019/05/the-birkman-method/

Birkman method. (n.d.). Retrieved from ToolsHero: https://www.toolshero.com/psychology/birkman-method/

44 Bloom's Taxonomy (Revised)

Armstrong, P. (2010). *Bloom's taxonomy.* Retrieved from Vanderbilt University Center for Teaching: https://cft.vanderbilt.edu/guides-sub-pages/blooms-taxonomy/

Forehand, M. (2011, December 11). *Bloom's taxonomy.* Retrieved from Vanderbilt University Center for Teaching: https://cft.vanderbilt.edu/wp-content/uploads/sites/59/BloomsTaxonomy-mary-forehand.pdf

Heick, T. (2021, August 14). *Bloom's taxonomy is a hierarchal framework for cognition and learning objectives.* Retrieved from TeachThought: https://www.teachthought.com/learning/what-is-blooms-taxonomy-a-definition-for-teachers/

Revised Bloom's taxonomy. (n.d.). Retrieved from Iowa State University Center for Excellence in Learning and Teaching: https://www.celt.iastate.edu/teaching/effective-teaching-practices/revised-blooms-taxonomy/

Bloom's taxonomy. (n.d.). Retrieved from the University of Waterloo Centre for Teaching Excellence: https://uwaterloo.ca/centre-for-teaching-excellence/teaching-resources/teaching-tips/planning-courses-and-assignments/course-design/blooms-taxonomy

Shabatura, J. (2022, July 26). *Using Bloom's taxonomy to write effective learning objectives.* Retrieved from the University of Arkansas: https://tips.uark.edu/using-blooms-taxonomy/

Bloom's revised taxonomy. (n.d.). Retrieved from Colorado College: https://www.coloradocollege.edu/other/assessment/how-to-assess-learning/learning-outcomes/blooms-revised-taxonomy.html

What is Bloom's taxonomy? (n.d.). Retrieved from Bloomstaxonomy.net: https://www.bloomstaxonomy.net

Bloom's taxonomy. (n.d.). Retrieved from the University of Central Florida: https://fctl.ucf.edu/teaching-resources/course-design/blooms-taxonomy/

45 BOOST Feedback Model

Roberts, A. (n.d.). *BOOST feedback model.* Retrieved from Andi Roberts: http://masterfacilitator.com/boostleadershipfeedback/

What you should know about BOOST informal feedback model. (n.d.). Retrieved from Upraise: https://upraise.io/blog/know-boost-informal-feedback-model/

BOOST feedback model. (n.d.). Retrieved from The University of California Irving Human Resources: https://www.hr.uci.edu/partnership/merit/interactive/story_content/external_files/BOOSTFINALresource.pdf

BOOST employee performance with constructive feedback. (2015, May 13). Retrieved from Primalogik: https://primalogik.com/blog/boost-employee-performance-with-constructive-feedback/

Ryder, N. (2014, September 24). *BOOST—The best feedback.* Retrieved from Nathan Ryder: http://www.nathanryder.co.uk/2014/09/boost-the-best-feedback/

The BOOST feedback model. (n.d.). Retrieved from Revolution Learning and Development: https://www.revolutionlearning.co.uk/article/the-boost-feedback-model/

46 Borton's Model of Reflection

Dabell, J. (2018, August 5). *Borton's model of reflection.* Retrieved from John Dabell: https://johndabell.com/2018/08/05/models-of-reflection/

Borton's development framework. (n.d.). Retrieved from Physiopedia.com: https://www.physio-pedia.com/Borton%27s_Development_Framework

McClean, T. (2019). *Models for reflection.* Retrieved from The Institute: http://theinstitute.gg/CHttpHandler.ashx?id=117767&p=0

Reflective practice toolkit. (n.d.). Retrieved from the University of Cambridge: https://libguides.cam.ac.uk/reflectivepracticetoolkit/models

Driscoll by Borton. (n.d.). Retrieved from the University of Nottingham: https://www.nottingham.ac.uk/nmp/sonet/rlos/placs/critical_reflection/models/driscoll.html

Models (or frameworks) of reflection. (n.d.). Retrieved from the University of Nottingham: https://www.nottingham.ac.uk/nmp/sonet/rlos/placs/critical_reflection/models/index.html

Reflective practice. (n.d.). Retrieved from TUS Library: https://lit.libguides.com/reflective-practice-tips/models

47 Bridges' Transition Model

Bridges' transition model. (n.d.). Retrieved from William Bridges Associates: https://wmbridges.com/about/what-is-transition/

How to use Bridges' transition model to facilitate change. (n.d.). Retrieved from Tallyfy: https://tallyfy.com/bridges-transition-model/

Change management brief. (n.d.). Retrieved from the Ontario Center of Excellence for Child and Youth Mental Health: https://www.cymh.ca/resource-hub-files/t_change_william_bridges_transitional_model.pdf

Bridges' transition model. (n.d.). Retrieved from MindTools: https://www.mindtools.com/pages/article/bridges-transition-model.htm

Bridges' transition model for change: A summary. (n.d.). Retrieved from the World of Work Project: https://worldofwork.io/2019/07/bridges-transition-model-for-change/

Airiodion, O., & Crolley, F. (n.d.). *Bridges' transition model for change: All you need to know.* Retrieved from Airiodion Global Services: https://www.airiodion.com/bridges-transition-model/

48 Brookfield Model of Reflection

Miller, B. (2010, March). *Brookfield's four lenses: Becoming a critically reflective teacher.* Retrieved from The University of Sydney: https://valenciacollege.edu/faculty/development/courses-resources/documents/brookfield_summary.pdf

Reflective model according to Brookfield. (n.d.). Retrieved from Dr. Nicole Brown: https://www.nicole-brown.co.uk/reflective-model-according-to-brookfield/

Brookfield lens two: Learners' eyes. (2013, December). Retrieved from the Oxford Centre for Staff and Learning Development: https://radar.brookes.ac.uk/radar/items/8dfa1c7d-d4ca-457b-b52c-9568cfd8d867/1/?attachment.uuid=f160b1bf-1138-439b-a808-415a87ccd550&attachment.stream=true

Dabell, J. (2018, August 19). *The lenses model of reflection.* Retrieved from John Dabell: https://johndabell.com/2018/08/19/models-of-reflection-4/

All Answers Ltd. (2018, November). *Brookfield's reflective model.* Retrieved from Nursing Answers: https://nursinganswers.net/reflective-guides/brookfield-reflective-model.php

49 Burke-Litwin Change Model

The Burke-Litwin organizational change framework: A simple summary. (n.d.). Retrieved from the World of Work Porject: https://worldofwork.io/2019/07/the-burke-litwin-organizational-change-framework/

Burke-Litwin: Understanding drivers for change. (n.d.). Retrieved from the University of Exeter: https://www.exeter.ac.uk/media/universityofexeter/humanresources/documents/learningdevelopment/understanding_drivers_for_change.pdf

Burke-Litwin: The performance and change model. (n.d.). Retrieved from Accipio Ltd: https://www.accipio.com/eleadership/mod/wiki/view.php?id=1848

Burke-Litwin model of organizational change. (n.d.). Retrieved from Toolshero: https://www.toolshero.com/change-management/burke-litwin-model/

Abbas, T. (2020, April 6). *Burke-Litwin model of change.* Retrieved from Change Management Insight: https://changemanagementinsight.com/burke-litwin-model-of-change/

Burke-Litwin model of organizational performance and change. (2021, October 29). Retrieved from CIO Wiki: https://cio-wiki.org/wiki/Burke-Litwin_Model_of_Organizational_Performance_and_Change

Robinson, J. (2019, December 16). *The Burke-Litwin change model: Today's most influential model on organizational change.* Retrieved from Flevyblog: https://flevy.com/blog/the-burke-litwin-change-model-todays-most-influential-model-on-organizational-change/

Cuofano, G. (2023, October 12). *The Burke-Litwin model in a nutshell.* Retrieved from Four Week MBA: https://fourweekmba.com/burke-litwin-model/

50 Burnett Model of Crisis Management

Marker, A. (2020, July 20). *Models and theories to improve crisis management.* Retrieved from SmartSheet: https://www.smartsheet.com/content/crisis-management-model-theories

Boudreaux, B. (2005). *Exploring a multi-stage model of crisis management: Utilities, hurricanes, and contingency.* Retrieved from the University of Florida: https://ufdcimages.uflib.ufl.edu/UF/E0/01/04/86/00001/boudreaux_b.pdf

Burnett's model of crisis management–1998. (n.d.). Retrieved from Guru Nanak Khalsa Institute of Technology and Management: https://gnkitm.ac.in/blog/Burnett-s-Model-of-Crisis-Management-1998

Vargo, J., & Seville, E. (2011, September). Crisis strategic planning for SMEs: Finding the silver lining. *International Journal of Production Research—Creating Resilient SMEs, Special Issue,* 49(18), 5619–5635. Retrieved from Resilient Organizations: https://resorgs.org.nz/wp-content/uploads/2017/07/crisis_strategic_planning_for_smes.pdf

Ritchie, B.W. (2003, April 1). Chaos, crises and disasters: A strategic approach to crisis management in the tourism industry. *Tourism Management,* 25, 669–683. Retrieved from Virtual University of Pakistan: https://vulms.vu.edu.pk/Courses/MGMT729/Downloads/Chaos_Crises_and_Disasters_a_Strategic_A.pdf

51 Business Chemistry

Business Chemistry infographic. (n.d.). Retrieved from Deloitte: https://www2.deloitte.com/content/dam/Deloitte/us/Documents/process-and-operations/us-business-chemistry-infographic.pdf

Deloitte's Business Chemistry. (n.d.). Retrieved from MindTools: https://www.mindtools.com/pages/article/Deloitte-Business-Chemistry.htm

McKinney, M. (2018, September 3). *Business Chemistry: What type are you?* Retrieved from Leadership Now: https://www.leadershipnow.com/leadingblog/2018/09/business_chemistry_what_type_a.html

Marks, A. (2020, June 23). Virtual teamwork: It's all about (business) chemistry. *The Wall Street Journal:* https://deloitte.wsj.com/articles/virtual-teamwork-its-all-about-business-chemistry-01592938928

Johnson Vickberg, S.M., & Christfort, K. (2019, January). Pioneers, drivers, integrators, and guardians. *Harvard Business Review Special Issue: The Brain Science Behind Business,* 28–37.

52 Carper's Fundamental Ways of Knowing

Nursing's fundamental patterns of knowing. (n.d.). Retrieved from Nurse Key: https://nursekey.com/nursings-fundamental-patterns-of-knowing/

Carper's ways of knowing essay examples. (n.d.). Retrieved from Online Nursing Papers: https://onlinenursingpapers.com/carpers-ways-of-knowing-essay-examples/

Chinn, P. (2018, September 15). *Fundamental patterns of knowing in nursing.* Retrieved from Nursology: https://nursology.net/nurse-theorists-and-their-work/fundamental-patterns-of-knowing-in-nursing/

Carper, B. (1978). *Fundamental patterns of knowing in nursing.* Retrieved from Jones and Bartlett LLC.: http://samples.jbpub.com/9780763765705/65705_CH03_V1xx.pdf

Thorne, S. (2020, June 21). *Rethinking Carper's personal knowing for 21st century nursing.* Retrieved from the Wiley Online Library: https://onlinelibrary.wiley.com/doi/10.1111/nup.12307

53 CEDAR Feedback Model

Wildman, A. (n.d.). *CEDAR feedback model.* Retrieved from Anna Wildman: https://www.annawildman.com/cedar-feedback-model.html

The CEDAR feedback model: Feedback in a coaching style. (n.d.). Retrieved from the World of Work Project: https://worldofwork.io/2019/07/the-cedar-feedback-model/

Nemeth, B. (2018, May 31). *3 ways to give effective feedback everytime.* Retrieved from Session Lab: https://www.sessionlab.com/blog/effective-feedback-models/

Roberts, A. (n.d.). *CEDAR feedback model.* Retrieved from Andi Roberts: https://andiroberts.com/feedback-models-hub/

Collaborative feedback: The CEDAR feedback model. (2018). Retrieved from MindTools: https://www.mindtools.com/media/ Images/Infographics/Collaborative_Feedback_Infographic-Final.pdf

54 Charismatic Leadership Theory

Lee, S. (2020, July 30). *What is charismatic leadership?* Retrieved from Torch Leadership Labs: https://torch.io/blog/what-is-charismatic-leadership/

What is charismatic leadership? Leading through personal conviction. (2014, November 25). Retrieved from St. Thomas University: https://online.stu.edu/articles/education/what-is-charismatic-leadership.aspx

Charismatic leadership theory. (n.d.). Retrieved from Psychology iResearchnet: http://psychology.iresearchnet.com/industrial-organizational-psychology/leadership-and-management/charismatic-leadership-theory/

What is charismatic leadership? (2021, March 23). Retrieved from Western Governor's University: https://www.wgu.edu/blog/charismatic-leadership2103.html#close

Luenendonk, M. (2020, July 25). *Charismatic leadership guide: Definition, qualities, pros and cons, examples.* Retrieved from Cleverism: https://www.cleverism.com/charismatic-leadership-guide/

Gayan, G. (2023, September 19). *7 best characteristics and benefits of charismatic leadership style.* Retrieved from Vantage Circle: https://blog.vantagecircle.com/charismatic-leadership/

Perry, E. (2021, November 30). *How to tap into heart and soul to lead with more charisma.* Retrieved from BetterUp: https://www.betterup.com/blog/charismatic-leadership

55 CIGAR Coaching Model

Warner, J. (2012, October 19). *Using "models" to assist the coaching process.* Retrieved from Ready to Manage: http://blog.readytomanage.com/using-models-to-assist-the-coaching-process/

Hawkes, T. (2018, January 15). *Coaching models explored: CIGAR.* Retrieved from the Training Zone: https://www.trainingzone.co.uk/deliver/coaching/coaching-models-explored-cigar

Giving feedback: Useful models. Retrieved from Potential Unearthed Ltd.: https://www.potentialunearthed.co.uk/wp-content/uploads/2017/09/Feedback-Models.pdf

Blackbyrn, S. (2022, April 15). *Coaching model: 3 models you must use for success.* Retrieved from the Coach Foundation: https://sai.coach/blog/coaching-model-2/

Biro, K. (2019, August 23). *Coaching models overview.* Retrieved from Coach Campus: https://coachcampus.com/coach-portfolios/research-papers/kincso-biro-an-overview-of-coaching-models/

56 CLEAR Coaching Model

Turner, M.M. (n.d.). *The CLEAR model.* Retrieved from Mike the Mentor: https://www.mikethementor.co.uk/blog/the-clear-model

The CLEAR coaching model: A simple summary. (n.d.). Retrieved from the World of Work Project: https://worldofwork.io/2019/06/the-clear-coaching-model/

Lea, S. (2022, February 16). *CLEAR model.* Retrieved from Businessballs: https://www.businessballs.com/coaching-and-mentoring/clear-model/

CLEAR coaching model by Peter Hawkins. (n.d.). Retrieved from Personal Coaching Information: https://www.personal-coaching-information.com/clear-coaching-model.html

Thomson, S. (2018, March 19). *The coaching model library: CLEAR.* Retrieved from the Training Journal: https://www.trainingjournal.com/articles/features/coaching-model-library-clear

57 Co-Active Coaching Model

What is Co-Active? (n.d.). Retrieved from the Co-Active Training Institute: https://coactive.com/about/what-is-coactive/

The Co-Active coaching model. (n.d.). Retrieved from Crowe Associates Ltd.: https://www.crowe-associates.co.uk/coaching-and-mentoring-skills/the-co-active-coaching-model/

Preuss, D. H., (2013, January). *What is Co-Active coaching?* Retrieved from A Bigger Game Today: https://abiggergame.today/files/resources/WhatIsCoActiveCoaching_DPreuss_A4.pdf

The Co-Active coaching model explained. (n.d.). Retrieved from Leadership Coaching: https://leadershipcoaching.gr/the-co-active-model-explained-4-cornerstones-5-contexts-3-principles/

Kimsey-House, H., Kimsey-House, K., Sandahl, P., & Whitworth, L. (2018). *Co-Active coaching: The proven framework for transformative conversations at work and in life, 4th Edition.* Nicholas Brealey Publishing.

58 COACH Model

Coaching mastery certification program. (n.d.). Retrieved from Creative Results Management: https://www.creativeresultsmanagement.com

Webb, K. (n.d.). *How to improve your results with the COACH model.* Retrieved from Keith Webb: https://keithwebb.com/how-to-improve-your-results-with-the-coach-model/

Webb, K. (n.d.). *The Coach model.* Retrieved from Keith Webb: https://keithwebb.com/coach-model/

Webb, K. (n.d.). *The Coach model.* Retrieved from ABWE International: https://farran.abwe.org/uploads/9/7/1/2/97128822/the_coach_model_summary.pdf

59 Coaching Models (general entry)

Warner, J. (2012, October 19). *Using models to assist the coaching process.* Retrieved from Ready to Manage: http://blog.readytomanage.com/using-models-to-assist-the-coaching-process/

Coaching and mentoring. (n.d.). Retrieved from the Sieger Group: https://www.siegergroups.com/corporate-training/pdf/coaching-and-mentoring.pdf

Coaching models. (2015, November 2). Retrieved from Being a Coach: https://cobbep.wordpress.com/tag/coaching/

60 Cognitive Behavioral Coaching (CBC)

Lea, S. (2022, February 16). *What is cognitive behavioral coaching?* Retrieved from Businessballs: https://www.businessballs.com/coaching-and-mentoring/cognitive-behavioural-coaching/

Smith, R. (n.d.). *What is cognitive behavioral coaching?* Retrieved from Multibriefs Exclusive Articles: https://www.multibriefs.com/briefs/exclusive/what_is_cognitive_behavioral_coaching.html#.X0p6rC2z2QI

Myers, C. (n.d.). *Cognitive behavioral coaching techniques for health coaches.* Retrieved from ACE Fitness: https://www.acefitness.org/education-and-resources/professional/certified/august-2019/7339/cognitive-behavioral-coaching-techniques-for-health-coaches/

CBT coaching approaches. (n.d.). Retrieved from Crowe Associates ltd.: http://www.crowe-associates.co.uk/coaching-tools/cbt-coaching-approaches/

McMahon, G. (n.d.). *Coaching that works for you.* Retrieved from Gladeana McMahon: http://www.cognitivebehaviouralcoachingworks.com

McMahon, G., & Williams, P. (2016, June). *Cognitive behavioral coaching* [Audio]. Retrieved from the Institute for Life Coach Training: https://www.lifecoachtraining.com/resources/listen/cognitive_behavioral_coaching

Whitten, H. (2009). *Cognitive behavioral coaching techniques for dummies.* Wiley & Sons.

61 Cognitive Dissonance Theory (CDT)

McLeod, S. (2023, October 24). *What is cognitive dissonance theory?* Retrieved from Simply Psychology: https://www.simplypsychology.org/cognitive-dissonance.html

Cherry, K. (2022, November 7). *What is cognitive dissonance?* Retrieved from Verywell Mind: https://www.verywellmind.com/what-is-cognitive-dissonance-2795012

Vaidis, D., & Bran, A. (2019, May 29). Respectable challenges to respectable theory: Cognitive dissonance theory requires conceptualization clarification and tools. *Frontiers in Psychology* 10: https://www.frontiersin.org/articles/10.3389/fpsyg.2019.01189/full

Harmon-Jones, E., Mills, J. (2019) *An introduction to cognitive dissonance theory and an overview of current perspectives on the theory.* Retrieved from the American Psychological Association: https://www.apa.org/pubs/books/Cognitive-Dissonance-Intro-Sample.pdf

Villines, Z. (2023, May 23). *Cognitive dissonance: What to know.* Retrieved from Medical News Today: https://www.medicalnewstoday.com/articles/326738#how-to-resolve

Cognitive dissonance. (n.d.). Retrieved from Psychology Today: https://www.psychologytoday.com/us/basics/cognitive-dissonance

Cognitive dissonance (Festinger). (n.d.). Retrieved from Instructional Design: https://www.instructionaldesign.org/theories/cognitive-dissonance/

Suls, J. (n.d.). Cognitive dissonance of Leon Festinger. Retrieved from *Britannica*: https://www.britannica.com/biography/Leon-Festinger/Cognitive-dissonance

62 COILED Feedback Model

The COIN feedback model. (n.d.). Retrieved from the World of Work Project: https://worldofwork.io/2019/07/the-coin-coiled-feedback-models/

63 COIN Feedback Model

The COIN conversation model. (n.d.). Retrieved from MindTools: https://www.mindtools.com/pages/article/COIN.htm

The COIN feedback model. (n.d.). Retrieved from the World of Work Project: https://worldofwork.io/2019/07/the-coin-coiled-feedback-models/

Make team feedback more effective with COIN conversations. (n.d.). Retrieved from Sean Glaze Great Results Teambuilding: https://greatresultsteambuilding.net/make-team-feedback-effective-coin-conversations/

COIN communications framework. (n.d.). Retrieved from Training Resources for the Environmental Community: https://www.trec.org/wp-content/uploads/2020/04/COIN-Communications-Framework-v819.pdf

64 Communication Theory of Identity

Hecht, M., & Choi, H. (n.d.). Chapter 8: The communication theory of identity as a framework for health message design, 137–152. Retrieved from Sage Publishing: https://in.sagepub.com/sites/default/files/upm-binaries/43569_8.pdf

Mahetsu, G., & Kustiawan, E. (2016, August 15). *What you need to know about: Communication theory of identity.* Retrieved from Binus University: https://communication.binus.ac.id/2016/08/15/what-you-need-to-know-about-communication-theory-of-identity/

Hecht, M., & Jung, E. (2004). Elaborating the communication theory of identity: Identity gaps and communication outcomes. *Communication Quarterly,* 52(3), 265–283. Retrieved from Taylor & Francis Online: https://www.tandfonline.com/doi/abs/10.1080/01463370409370197?journalCode=rcqu20

65 Competing Values Framework (CVF)

Lawrence, K. (n.d.). *Teaching the competing values framework.* Retrieved from the University of Michigan: http://kathla.people.si.umich.edu/Teaching_the_Competing_Values_Framework_(handout).pdf

Cameron, K. (n.d.). *An introduction to the competing values framework.* Retrieved from the RCF Group: https://www.thercfgroup.com/files/resources/an_introduction_to_the_competing_values_framework.pdf

About the organizational culture assessment instrument (OCAI). (n.d.). Retrieved from OCAI Online: https://www.ocai-online.com/about-the-Organizational-Culture-Assessment-Instrument-OCAI

DeGraff, J. (n.d.). *The competing values assessment overview.* Retrieved from the Denver Metro Chamber Leadership Foundation: https://denverleadership.org/wp-content/uploads/2016/01/Competing-Values-Framework.pdf

Cameron, K., & Quinn, R. (2011). *Competing values framework.* Retrieved from the Cultural Competence Learning Institute: https://community.astc.org/ccli/resources-for-action/supporting-documents/competing-values-framework

The competing values framework. (n.d.). Retrieved from Changing Minds: http://changingminds.org/explanations/culture/competing_values.htm

Competing values framework. (n.d.). Retrieved from Value Based Management: https://www.valuebasedmanagement.net/methods_quinn_competing_values_framework.html

Cameron, K., & Quinn, R. (2011). *Diagnosing and changing organizational culture: Based on the competing values framework.* John Wiley and Sons. Retrieved from Google: https://www.google.com/books/edition/Diagnosing_and_Changing_Organizational_C/D6gWTf02RloC?hl=en&gbpv=1

66 Congruity Theory

American Psychological Association. (n.d.). Congruity theory. In *APA dictionary of psychology:* https://dictionary.apa.org/congruity-theory

American Psychological Association. (n.d.). Consistency theory. In *APA dictionary of psychology:* https://dictionary.apa.org/consistency-theory

Heider's Balance, Newcomb's Symmetry, Osgood's Congruity, and Cognitive Dissonance Theories. (2012, September 17). Retrieved from Mass Communication Talk: https://www.masscommunicationtalk.com/heiders-balance-newcombs-symmetry-osgoods-congruity-cognitive-dissonance-theories.html

Congruity theory. (n.d.). Retrieved from Oxford Reference: https://www.oxfordreference.com/view/10.1093/oi/authority.20110803095632235

Buckley, P. J., Cross, A., & De Mattos, C. (2015, December). The principle of congruity in the analysis of international business cooperation. *International Business Review,* 24(6), 1048–1060. DOI: http://dx.doi.org/10.1016/j.ibusrev.2015.04.005

Gordon, J. (2023, October 8). *Congruity theory explained.* Retrieved from The Business Professor: https://thebusinessprofessor.com/en_US/management-leadership-organizational-behavior/congruity-theory-explained

67 Consistency Theories (general entry)

Trepte, S. (2013, January 26). *Consistency theories.* Retrieved from the Wiley Online Library: https://onlinelibrary.wiley.com/doi/abs/10.1002/9781405186407.wbiecc125.pub2

Nelson, T. (n.d.). *Cognitive consistency theories.* Retrieved from Encyclopedia.com: https://www.encyclopedia.com/social-sciences/encyclopedias-almanacs-transcripts-and-maps/cognitive-consistency-theories

American Psychological Association. (n.d.). Consistency theory. In *APA dictionary of psychology*: https://dictionary.apa.org/consistency-theory

Consistency theory. (n.d.). Retrieved from Changing Minds: http://changingminds.org/explanations/theories/consistency_theory.htm

Russo, J. E., & Chaxel, A.E. (2017, July 26). *Cognitive consistency theories.* Retrieved from Oxford Bibliographies: https://www.oxfordbibliographies.com/view/document/obo-9780199828340/obo-9780199828340-0195.xml

Consistency theories. (n.d.). Retrieved from iResearchnet: http://communication.iresearchnet.com/exposure-to-communication-content/consistency-theories/

Cognitive consistency. (n.d.). Retrieved from iResearchnet: http://psychology.iresearchnet.com/social-psychology/attitudes/cognitive-consistency/

68 Contingency Theories (general entry)

Brooks, C. (2023, November 1). *Contingency management theory explained.* Retrieved from Business.com: https://www.business.com/articles/contingency-management-theory/

The contingency theory of leadership explained. (2015, January 9). Retrieved from Villanova University: https://www.villanovau.com/resources/leadership/leadership-and-contingency-theory/

Contingency theory of leadership: Definition and models. (2023, March 10). Retrieved from Indeed.com: https://www.indeed.com/career-advice/career-development/contingency-theory-of-leadership

Virkus, S. (2009). *Contingency theory.* Retrieved from Tallinn University: https://www.tlu.ee/~sirvir/Leadership/Leadership%20Models/contingency_theory.html

69 Core Model for Critical Reflection

McClean, T. (2019). *Models for reflection.* Retrieved from The Institute: http://theinstitute.gg/CHttpHandler.ashx?id=117767&p=0

Chapter 8: The art of reflection. (n.d.). Retrieved from Extend Your Thinking: https://datsoftlyngby.github.io/soft2017fall/UFO/TheArtOfReflection.pdf

How to develop your reflective writing. (n.d.). Retrieved from The University of Sunderland: https://library.sunderland.ac.uk/images/internal-websites/uls/skills-for-learning/images/pdfs/How-to...develop-your-reflective-writing.pdf

70 Correspondent Inference Theory

Correspondent inference theory. (n.d.). Retrieved from Iresearchnet: http://psychology.iresearchnet.com/social-psychology/social-psychology-theories/correspondent-inference-theory/

Shrestha, P. (2017, November 17). *Correspondent inference theory.* Retrieved from Psychestudy: https://www.psychestudy.com/social/correspondent-inference-theory

Kelley's covariation model. (2023, September 21). Retrieved from Practical Psychology: https://practicalpie.com/kelleys-covariation-model/

Correspondent inference theory. (n.d.). Retrieved from Ifioque: https://www.ifioque.com/social-psychology/correspondent-inference-theory

Correspondent inference theory. (n.d.). Retrieved from Changing Minds: http://changingminds.org/explanations/theories/correspondent_inference.htm

Correspondent inference theory. (n.d.). Retrieved from Psychology Wiki: https://psychology.fandom.com/wiki/Correspondent_inference_theory

American Psychological Association. (n.d.). Correspondent inference theory. In *APA dictionary of psychology*: https://dictionary.apa.org/correspondent-inference-theory

Correspondent inference theory explained. (n.d.). Retrieved from Health Research Funding: https://healthresearchfunding.org/correspondent-inference-theory-explained/

McLeod, S. (2023, June 11). *Attribution theory in psychology: Definition and examples.* Retrieved from Simply Psychology: https://www.simplypsychology.org/attribution-theory.html

Parkinson, B. (n.d.). *Chapter 3: Social perception and attribution*. Retrieved from Blackwell Publishing: https://www. blackwellpublishing.co.uk/content/hewstonesocialpsychology/chapters/chapter3.pdf

71 Crisis Management Model (G-Herrero/Pratt)

Crisis management model. (n.d.). Retrieved from Management Study Guide: https://www.managementstudyguide.com/crisis-management-model.htm

Crisis management models. (n.d.). Retrieved from Course Hero: https://www.coursehero.com/file/p4rsmh7/34-Crisis-Management-Models-First-Gonzalez-Herrero-and-Pratt-Model-They/

Marker, A. (2020, July 20). *Models and theories to improve crisis management*. Retrieved from Smartsheet: https://www.smartsheet.com/content/crisis-management-model-theories

Public affairs crisis management in a multi-service atmosphere. (n.d.). Retrieved from The University of Oklahoma: https://www.ou.edu/deptcomm/dodjcc/groups/98C1/discuss.html

72 Crisis Management Models (general entry)

Marker, A. (2020, July 20). *Models and theories to improve crisis management*. Retrieved from Smartsheet: https://www.smartsheet.com/content/crisis-management-model-theories

73 Crisis Management Relational Model

Iyigun, O., & Yalcintas, M. (2018, July). A managerial evaluation of Syrian civil war on Turkish firms: Crisis management practices. *China-USA Business Review*, 17(7), 335–346. Retrieved from David Publishing Company: http://davidpublisher.org/Public/uploads/Contribute/5ba9e0527a40e.pdf

Marker, A. (2020, July 20). *Models and theories to improve crisis management*. Retrieved from Smartsheet.com: https://www.smartsheet.com/content/crisis-management-model-theories

Jaques, T. (2014, October 8). *The crisis after the crisis*. Retrieved from Melissa Agnes Crisis Management Strategist: https://melissaagnes.com/crisis-after-the-crisis/

74 Cultural Identity Theory

Cultural identity theory. (n.d.). Retrieved from Communicationtheory.org: https://www.communicationtheory.org/cultural-identity-theory/

Mahestu, G., & Kustiawan, E. (2016, June 29). *What you need to know about cultural identity theory*. Retrieved from Binus University: https://communication.binus.ac.id/2016/06/29/what-you-need-to-know-about-cultural-identity-theory/

Namita. (2018, March 27). *Stuart Hall's theory of cultural identity*. Retrieved from Medium: https://medium.com/@greyflak/stuart-halls-theory-of-cultural-identity-19c22f64721a

Bajracharya, S. (2018, January 7). *Cultural identity theory*. Retrieved from Businesstopia: https://www.businesstopia.net/communication/cultural-identity-theory

75 Cultural Intelligence (CQ)

Earley, P.C., & Ang, S. (2003). *Cultural intelligence: Individual interactions across cultures*. Stanford University Press.

About cultural intelligence. (n.d.). Retrieved from the Cultural Intelligence Center: https://culturalq.com/about-cultural-intelligence/

Get CQ certified online. (n.d.). Retrieved from the Cultural Intelligence Center: https://culturalq.com

Earley, P. C., & Mosakowski, E. (2004, October). Cultural intelligence. *Harvard Business Review*. https://hbr.org/2004/10/cultural-intelligence

Cultural intelligence: Working confidently in different cultures. (n.d.). Retrieved from MindTools: https://www.mindtools.com/pages/article/cultural-intelligence.htm

Cultural intelligence. (n.d.). Retrieved from The CQ Model: http://www.thecqmodel.com

Gozzoli, C., & Gazzaroli, D. (2018, July 10). The cultural intelligence scale: A contribution to the Italian validation. *Frontiers in Psychology*, 9: https://www.frontiersin.org/articles/10.3389/fpsyg.2018.01183/full

Farrell, J. (n.d.). *What is cultural intelligence?* Retrieved from Equality Works Group Ltd.: https://theewgroup.com/us/blog/what-is-cultural-intelligence/

What is cultural intelligence? (n.d.). Retrieved from Common Purpose: https://commonpurpose.org/knowledge-hub/what-is-cultural-intelligence/

76 Cultural Web

Mind Tools Content Team. (n.d.). *The cultural web*. Retrieved from MindTools: https://www.mindtools.com/a8im94b/the-cultural-web

Cultural web model: A strategy for corporate culture. (n.d.). Retrieved from Personio: https://www.personio.com/hr-lexicon/cultural-web-model/

Sridharan, M., Gajji, M., & Agrawal, S. (2022, January 11). *Cultural web – A model to align culture with strategy*. Retrieved from Think Insights: https://thinkinsights.net/strategy/cultural-web-model/

Nikoloska, V. (2023, July 11). *Cultural web model: What is it & how to use it?* Retrieved from Factorial: https://factorialhr.co.uk/blog/cultural-web/

Cultural web. (n.d.). Retrieved from The Leadership Centre: https://www.leadershipcentre.org.uk/artofchangemaking/theory/cultural-web/

Durevall, H. (2021, June 1). *What is the cultural web model?* Retrieved from Flair: https://flair.hr/en/blog/cultural-web-model/#how-do-you-use-the-cultural-web-model

The culture web. (n.d.). Retrieved from Squarespace: https://static1.squarespace.com/static/5ab0e7eee749404673aa499d/t/615440c29aad8c245b257d55/1632911682047/Forward+Institute+-+Culture+Web+.pdf

Cultural web analysis. (n.d.). Retrieved from the University of Leeds: https://deliveringresults.leeds.ac.uk/delivering-results-lifecycle/cultural-web-analysis/

Janse, B. (2018). *Cultural web analysis*. Retrieved from Toolshero: https://www.toolshero.com/management/cultural-web-analysis/

Cultural web model. (2023, July 12). Retrieved from Velents: https://www.velents.com/hr-glossary/culture-web-model

77 DECIDE Model

Kay, J. (n.d.). *The D.E.C.I.D.E. model*. Retrieved from Project School Wellness: https://www.projectschoolwellness.com/the-d-e-c-i-d-e-model-a-tool-for-teaching-students-how-to-making-healthy-decisions/

Guo, K. (2008, April). *DECIDE decision-making model*. Retrieved from the University of Montana: https://winapps.umt.edu/winapps/media2/wilderness/toolboxes/documents/safety/DECIDE%20Decision-Making%20Model.pdf

Kempster, H. (n.d.). *Different models of decision-making*. Retrieved from Future Learn: https://www.futurelearn.com/info/courses/career-success/0/steps/21290

Guo, K. (2008). DECIDE: A decision-making model for more effective decision making by health care managers. *The Health Care Manager, 27*(2), 118–127. Retrieved from the University of Hawai'i: https://dspace.lib.hawaii.edu/bitstream/10790/2991/1/guo.k-2008-0014.pdf

78 Deming Cycle

What is the plan-do-check-act (PDCA) cycle? (n.d.). Retrieved from the American Society for Quality: https://asq.org/quality-resources/pdca-cycle

PDCA (plan do check act). (n.d.). Retrieved from MindTools: https://www.mindtools.com/pages/article/newPPM_89.htm

Skhmot, N. (2017, August 5). *Using the PDCA cycle to support continuous improvement (Kaizen)*. Retrieved from The Lean Way: https://theleanway.net/the-continuous-improvement-cycle-pdca

How to apply the plan-do-check-act (PDCA) model to improve your business. (n.d.). Retrieved from Lucidchart: https://www.lucidchart.com/blog/plan-do-check-act-cycle

Hargrave, M. (2022, November 30). *What does PDCA stand for in business? Plan Do-Check-Act cycle*. Retrieved from Investopedia: https://www.investopedia.com/terms/p/pdca-cycle.asp

Arveson, P. (1998). *The Deming cycle*. Retrieved from The Balanced Scorecard Institute: https://balancedscorecard.org/bsc-basics/articles-videos/the-deming-cycle/

79 Denison Model

Daniel Denison. (n.d.). Retrieved from Denison Consulting: https://www.denisonconsulting.com/team/daniel-r-denison-ph-d/

Certification workshops. (n.d.). Retrieved from Denison Consulting: https://www.denisonconsulting.com/certification/

The Denison model: Diagnosing and building cultural alignment. (n.d.). Retrieved from Denison Consulting: https://www.denisonconsulting.com/the-denison-model-diagnosing-and-building-cultural-alignment/

Introduction to the Denison model. (n.d.). Retrieved from Denison Consulting: https://www.denisonconsulting.com/wp-content/uploads/2019/08/introduction-to-the-denison-model.pdf

Wahyuningsih, S. H., Sudiro, A., Troena, E. A., & Irawanto, D.W. (2019, March). Analysis of organizational culture with Denison's model approach for international business competitiveness. *Problems and Perspectives in Management, 17*(1),

142–151. Retrieved from Business Perspectives: https://businessperspectives.org/images/pdf/applications/publishing/templates/article/assets/11640/PPM_2019_01_Wahyuningsih.pdf

Kokina, I., & Ostrovska, I. (2013, December). The analysis of organizational culture with the Denison model. *European Scientific Journal, 1*, 362–368. Retrieved from the *European Scientific Journal:* https://core.ac.uk/download/pdf/236405832.pdf

The Denison model and DSCC. (n.d.). Retrieved from the Defense Logistics Agency: https://www.dla.mil/Portals/104/Documents/LandAndMaritime/Councils/The%20Denison%20Model%20and%20DSCC.pdf

Bremer, M. (2017, April 20). *Denison culture model.* Retrieved from the Organizational Cultural Assessment Instrument Online: https://www.ocai-online.com/blog/denison-culture-model

80 DESC Model

Marsh, E. (2018, December 18). *3 simple but powerful techniques for giving effective feedback.* Retrieved from T-Three Consulting Ltd: https://www.t-three.com/soak/insights/3-simple-but-powerful-techniques-for-giving-effective-feedback

Levey, S. (n.d.). *Giving feedback using the DESC model.* Retrieved from Target Training: https://www.targettraining.eu/feedback-desc-model/

Levey, S. (2014, June 23). *Giving feedback with the DESC model.* Retrieved from LinkedIn Pulse: https://www.linkedin.com/pulse/20140623213931-156563678-giving-feedback-with-the-desc-model/

Using DESC to make your difficult conversations more effective. (2016). Retrieved from Yale University: https://your.yale.edu/sites/default/files/adviformanagers_usingdesctomakeyourdifficultconversations.pdf

Sharon Anthony Bower, author, "The assertive advantage." (n.d.). Retrieved from The Howland Group: https://howlandgroup.com/bower.htm

81 Design Thinking

Design thinking. (n.d.). Retrieved from the Interaction Design Foundation: https://www.interaction-design.org/literature/topics/design-thinking

What is design thinking? (n.d.). Retrieved from IDEO U: https://www.ideou.com/blogs/inspiration/what-is-design-thinking

Design thinking defined. (n.d.). Retrieved from IDEO: https://designthinking.ideo.com

History (of design thinking). (n.d.). Retrieved from IDEO: https://designthinking.ideo.com/history#the-evolution-of-design-thinking

Liedtka, J. (2018, September–October). Why design thinking works. *Harvard Business Review:* https://hbr.org/2018/09/why-design-thinking-works

Linke, R. (2017, September 14). *Design thinking, explained.* Retrieved from the Massachusetts Institute of Technology Sloan School of Business: https://mitsloan.mit.edu/ideas-made-to-matter/design-thinking-explained

Stevens, E. (2023, January 4). *What is design thinking? A comprehensive beginner's guide.* Retrieved from the Career Foundry: https://careerfoundry.com/en/blog/ux-design/what-is-design-thinking-everything-you-need-to-know-to-get-started/

Stevens, E. (2020, January 30). *What is design thinking, and how do we apply it?* Retrieved from InVision: https://www.invisionapp.com/inside-design/what-is-design-thinking/

Han, E. (2022, January 18). *What is design thinking, and why is it important?* Retrieved from the Harvard Business School: https://online.hbs.edu/blog/post/what-is-design-thinking

82 DESTINY Model

Whitten, H. (2009). *Cognitive behavioural coaching techniques for dummies.* Wiley.

83 Diffusion of Innovation Theory (DOI)

Diffusion of innovation theory. (n.d.). Retrieved from the Ohio State University: Dept. of Communication: https://www.ou.edu/deptcomm/dodjcc/groups/99A2/theories.htm

Halton, C. (2023, June 16). *Diffusion of innovations theory: Definition and examples.* Retrieved from Investopedia: https://www.investopedia.com/terms/d/diffusion-of-innovations-theory.asp

Dearing, J. W., & Cox, J. G. (2018, February). *Diffusion of innovations theory, principles, and practice.* Retrieved from Health Affairs: https://www.healthaffairs.org/doi/10.1377/hlthaff.2017.1104

Diffusion of innovation. (2021, April 24). Retrieved from the Corporate Finance Institute: https://corporatefinanceinstitute.com/resources/knowledge/other/diffusion-of-innovation/

84 DISC

History of DiSC. (n.d.). Retrieved from DiSC Profile: https://www.discprofile.com/what-is-disc/history-of-disc/

William Marston. (n.d.). Retrieved from DISC Insights: https://discinsights.com/william-marston

What is DiSC? (n.d.). Retrieved from the Center for Internal Change: https://internalchange.com/what-is-disc/

DISC history. (n.d.). Retrieved from DISC Insights: https://discinsights.com/disc-history

What is DISC? (n.d.). Retrieved from Extended DISC: https://www.extendeddisc.org/what-is-disc/

85 Distributed Work's Five Levels of Autonomy

Mullenweg, M. (2020, April 10). *Distributed work's five levels of autonomy.* Retrieved from Matt Mullenweg: https://ma.tt/2020/04/five-levels-of-autonomy/

Glaveski, S. (2020, March 29). *The five levels of remote work—and why you're probably at level 2.* Retrieved from Medium: https://medium.com/swlh/the-five-levels-of-remote-work-and-why-youre-probably-at-level-2-ccaf05a25b9c

Dans, E. (2020, June 30). What if working from home could be different to how it's been until now? *Forbes:* https://www.forbes.com/sites/enriquedans/2020/06/30/what-if-working-from-home-could-be-different-to-how-its-been-until-now/?sh=4588d166980d

Verlinden, N. (n.d.). *Making distributed teams work: 5 levels of autonomous organizations.* Retrieved from the Academy to Innovate HR: https://www.digitalhrtech.com/distributed-teams/

The five levels of distributed work: Lesson from a 100% distributed company with 1000+ employees. (2022, July 15). Retrieved from Carrus.io: https://carrus.io/the-five-levels-of-distributed-work/

Distributed work's five levels of autonomy. (2020, June 3). Retrieved from HR Curator: https://hrcurator.com/2020/06/03/https-ma-tt-2020-04-five-levels-of-autonomy/

Mullenweg, M. (Host). (2020, April 15). *Matt Mullenweg with Sam Harris on distributed work's five levels of autonomy* [Audio podcast]. Retrieved from Matt Mullenweg's blog "Distributed": https://distributed.blog/2020/04/15/matt-mullenweg-sam-harris-five-levels-distributed-work/

86 Doblin's Ten Types of Innovation

Woods, T. (2021, May 21). *The ten types of innovation framework, and how to use it.* Retrieved from Hype Innovation: https://blog.hypeinnovation.com/using-the-ten-types-of-innovation-framework

Khandelwal, N. (2016, February 6). *Understanding Doblin's 10 types of innovation with examples.* Retrieved from Medium: https://medium.com/@hwabtnoname/understanding-doblin-s-10-types-of-innovations-with-examples-2da595cea601

Nieminen, J. (2020, August 13). *The ten types of innovation framework explained.* Retrieved from Viima Solutions: https://www.viima.com/blog/ten-types-of-innovation

Doblin—10 types of innovation. (n.d.). Retrieved from Innovating Society: https://innovatingsociety.com/doblin-10-types-of-innovation/

Desjardins, J. (2020, July 1). *10 types of innovation: The art of discovering a breakthrough product.* Retrieved from Visual Capitalist: https://www.visualcapitalist.com/10-types-of-innovation-the-art-of-discovering-a-breakthrough-product/

87 Drexler-Sibbet Team Performance Model

Rodgers, D. (2021, June 23). *Drexler-Sibbet team performance model: Does it work?* Retrieved from BState: https://bstate.com/2021/06/23/drexler-sibbet-team-performance-model/

Loehr, A. (2018). *Want to build excellent teams? Try this efficient model.* Retrieved from Anne Loehr: https://www.anneloehr.com/2018/04/05/build-excellent-teams-try-efficient-model/

Render, J. (2019, June 13). *Drexler and Sibbet's team performance model.* Retrieved from Agile-Mercurial: https://agile-mercurial.com/2019/06/13/drexler-and-sibbets-team-performance-model/

Stephan, F. (2017, May 19). *Drexler/Sibbet team performance model.* Retrieved from Kaizenko: https://www.kaizenko.com/drexler-sibbet-team-performance-model/

The Drexler/Sibbet team performance model. (n.d.). Retrieved from The Grove Consultants International: https://www.thegrove.com/methodology/team-performance-model

Process models. (n.d.). Retrieved from David Sibbet: https://davidsibbet.com/process-models/

88 Dreyfus Model

Patterson, R. (2020, July 17). *Use the Dreyfus model to learn new skills.* Retrieved from College Info Geek: https://collegeinfogeek.com/dreyfus-model/

Khan, A. (2018, April 2). *The five Dreyfus model stages.* Retrieved from 360PMO Project Management Consulting Inc.: https://www.360pmo.com/the-five-dreyfus-model-stages/

Stalburg, C. M. (n.d.). *Dreyfus model: Skill acquisition.* Retrieved from the University of Michigan: https://open.umich.edu/sites/default/files/downloads/0203-f13-ms-coursera-imhpe-cstalburg_dryefus_model-cleared.pdf

Peña, A. (2010, June 14). The Dreyfus model of clinical problem-solving skills acquisition: A critical perspective. *Medical Education Online*, 15, Retrieved from the US National Library of Medicine: https://www.ncbi.nlm.nih.gov/pmc/articles/PMC2887319/

Novice to expert: The Dreyfus model of skill acquisition. (2005). Retrieved from Stan Lester Developments: http://devmts.org.uk/dreyfus.pdf

Dreyfus, S. E. (2004). The five-stage model of adult skill acquisition. *Bulletin of Science, Technology, and Society,* 24(3), 177–181. Retrieved from Boston University Medical Campus: https://www.bumc.bu.edu/facdev-medicine/files/2012/03/Dreyfus-skill-level.pdf

89 Driscoll's Reflection Cycle

Driscoll (by Borton). (n.d.). Retrieved from the University of Nottingham: https://www.nottingham.ac.uk/nmp/sonet/rlos/placs/critical_reflection/models/driscoll.html

Know the Driscoll model of reflection. (2020, January 22). Retrieved from All Assignment Help: https://www.allassignmenthelp.co.uk/blog/driscoll-model-of-reflection/

Reflective practice toolkit. (n.d.). Retrieved from the University of Cambridge: https://libguides.cam.ac.uk/reflectivepracticetoolkit/models

Nichola B. (2016, May 2). *Guide to models of reflection: When and why you should use different ones.* Retrieved from Life-Long Learning with OT: https://lifelonglearningwithot.wordpress.com/2016/05/02/different-models-of-reflection-using-them-to-help-me-reflect/

Jason, S. (2020, January 25). *Driscoll's model of reflection.* Retrieved from Make My Assignments: http://www.makemyassignments.co.uk/blog/driscolls-model-of-reflection/

90 DRiV Model

DRiV certification. (n.d.). Retrieved from OKA: https://oka-online.com/products/driv/

DRiV model: The six factors. (2020, December 11). Retrieved from OKA: https://oka-online.com/blog-driving-into-2021/driv-model-the-six-factors/

The science. (n.d.). Retrieved from DRiV Insights (Leadership Worth Following): https://drivinsights.com/the-science/

DRiV insights. (n.d.). Retrieved from LinkedIn: https://www.linkedin.com/company/drivinsights/

OKA. (2021, April 1). *Understanding the DRiV assessment* [Video]. Retrieved from YouTube: https://www.youtube.com/watch?v=UtgKMq7SNTU

OKA. (2021, December 21). *Understanding DRiV scores* [Video]. Retrieved from YouTube: https://www.youtube.com/watch?v=VI351_cP5wI

OKA. (2021, September 30). *DRiV assessment overview* [Video]. Retrieved from YouTube: https://www.youtube.com/watch?v=DxVmG123w5c

91 Dual Process Theory (Kahneman)

Dual process theory. (n.d.). Retrieved from Behavioral Science Solutions Ltd.: https://www.behavioraleconomics.com/resources/mini-encyclopedia-of-be/dual-system-theory/

Pettinger, T. (n.d.). *Dual-system theory.* Retrieved from Economics Help: https://www.economicshelp.org/blog/glossary/dual-system-theory/

Grayot, J. D. (2020, February). Dual process theories in behavioral economics and neuroeconomics: A critical review. *Review of Philosophy and Psychology,* 11, 105–136. Retrieved from Springer Link: https://link.springer.com/article/10.1007/s13164-019-00446-9

Tolbert, L. (2023, May 1). *Dual process theory: Analyzing our thought process for decision-making.* Retrieved from CXL: https://cxl.com/blog/dual-process-theory/

Dual process theory. (n.d.). Retrieved from Conceptually: https://conceptually.org/concepts/dual-processing-theory

92 Dunbar's Number

Ro, C. (2019, October 9). *Dunbar's number: Why we can only maintain 150 relationships.* Retrieved from the BBC: https://www.bbc.com/future/article/20191001-dunbars-number-why-we-can-only-maintain-150-relationships

Konnikova, M. (2014, October 7). The limits of friendship. *The New Yorker.* https://www.newyorker.com/science/maria-konnikova/social-media-affect-math-dunbar-number-friendships

Maintaining relationships: The fallacy of Dunbar's number. (2021, April 19). Retrieved from Contacts+: https://www.contactsplus.com/blog/maintaining-relationships

Your brain limits you to just five BFFs. (2016, April 29). Retrieved from MIT Technology Review: https://www.technologyreview.com/2016/04/29/160438/your-brain-limits-you-to-just-five-bffs/

Burkus, D. (2018, August 8). *Dunbar's number doesn't represent the average number of social connections.* Retrieved from Quartz: https://qz.com/work/1351400/dunbars-number-doesnt-represent-the-average-number-of-social-connections/

Goff, S. (n.d.). *Theory: Dunbar's number.* Retrieved from Beautifultrouble.org: https://beautifultrouble.org/theory/dunbars-number/

Makovsky, K. (2014, August 7). Dunbar's number: A key to networking. *Forbes:* https://www.forbes.com/sites/kenmakovsky/2014/08/07/dunbars-number-and-the-need-for-relationship-management/?sh=20ea831b397b

93 Dunn and Dunn Learning Styles

Harrington-Atkinson, T. (2017, November 10). *Dunn and Dunn learning style—1975.* Retrieved from Paving the Way: https://tracyharringtonatkinson.com/dunn-and-dunn-learning-style/

The Dunn and Dunn learning styles inventory model. (n.d.). Retrieved from Learning Abled Kids: https://learningabledkids.com/learning-styles/dunn-dunn-learning-style-model

Dunn and Dunn learning styles. (n.d.). Retrieved from Shmoop: https://www.shmoop.com/teachers/teaching-learning-styles/learning-styles/dunn-and-dunn.html

Learning styles: Dunn and Dunn model. (n.d.). Retrieved from The American Teaching English to Speakers of Other Languages Institute: http://americantesol.com/DunnLearningStyles.pdf

Love2Learn Idaho. (2017, May 1). *Do you know the 5 elements of a learning style?* Retrieved from Medium: https://medium.com/love2learnidaho/do-you-know-the-5-elements-of-a-learning-style-7721c10e358c

Medlin, R. G. (n.d.). *Learning style and academic achievement in homeschooled children.* Retrieved from Stetson University: https://www.stetson.edu/artsci/psychology/media/medlin-learning-styles.pdf

94 Edmondson's Theory of Teaming

The importance of teaming. (2012, April 25). Retrieved from the Harvard Business School Working Knowledge Newsletter: https://hbswk.hbs.edu/item/the-importance-of-teaming

Edmondson, A. C. (2013, December 17). The three pillars of a teaming culture. *Harvard Business Review* (online): https://hbr.org/2013/12/the-three-pillars-of-a-teaming-culture

BenedictineCVDL. (2018, July 6). *What is teaming? Amy Edmondson-Harvard University* [Video]. Retrieved from YouTube: https://www.youtube.com/watch?v=sZZHkqIY0Fo

Edmondson, A. C. (2012). *Teaming: How organizations learn, innovate, and compete in the knowledge economy.* John Wiley & Sons.

95 Effort-Reward Imbalance Model

Notelaers, G., Törnroos, M., & Salin, D. (2019, February 25). Effort-reward imbalance: A risk factor for exposure to workplace bullying. *Frontiers in Psychology,* 10: https://www.frontiersin.org/articles/10.3389/fpsyg.2019.00386/full

Stanhope, J. (2017). Effort-reward imbalance questionnaire. *Occupational Medicine,* 67(4), 314–315. Retrieved from Oxford Academic: https://academic.oup.com/occmed/article/67/4/314/3858140

Effort-reward imbalance at work: Theory, measurement, and evidence. (2008). Retrieved from Dusseldorf University: http://www.mentalhealthpromotion.net/resources/theorie_measurement_evidence.pdf

Wigger, E. (2011, January 26). *Effort-reward model.* Retrieved from Unhealthywork.org: https://unhealthywork.org/effort-reward-imbalance/effort-reward-model/

Van Vegchel, N., de Jonge, J., Bosma, H., & Schaufeli, W. (2005). Reviewing the effort-reward imbalance model: Drawing up the balance of 45 empirical studies. *Social Science and Medicine,* 60, 1117–1131, https://www.wilmarschaufeli.nl/publications/Schaufeli/223.pdf

96 Ego Development Theory (Loevinger)

Armstrong, T. (2020, January 31). *The stages of ego development according to Jane Loevinger.* Retrieved from the American Institute for Learning and Human Development: https://www.institute4learning.com/2020/01/31/the-stages-of-ego-development-according-to-jane-loevinger/

Gautam, S. (n.d.). *Ego development: The nine stages theory of Loevinger.* Retrieved from The Mouse Trap: https://the-mouse-trap.com/2007/12/24/ego-devlopment-the-nine-stages-theory-of-loevinger/

Jane Loevinger. (n.d.). Retrieved from Jrank.org: https://reference.jrank.org/psychology/Jane_Loevinger.html

Loevinger's stages of ego development. (n.d.). Retrieved from Psychology-Wiki: https://psychology.fandom.com/wiki/Loevinger%27s_stages_of_ego_development

Suchman, N., McMahon, T., DeCoste, C., Castiglioni, N., & Luthar, S. (2008). Ego development, psychopathology, and parenting problems in substance-abusing mothers. *American Journal of Orthopsychiatry*, 78(1), 20–28. Retrieved from the National Library of Medicine: https://www.ncbi.nlm.nih.gov/pmc/articles/PMC2729054/

Licensure Exams. (2015, December 1). *Stages of ego development—Loevinger* [Video]. Retrieved from YouTube: https://www.youtube.com/watch?v=vQNXXpxT-pM

Kowalski, K. (n.d.). *An introduction to ego development theory by Susanne Cook-Greuter (EDT Summary)*. Retrieved from SLOWW: https://www.sloww.co/ego-development-theory-cook-greuter/

97 EI Ability Model (Mayer, Salovey, Caruso)

Salovey and Mayer's emotional intelligence theory. (2020, July 14). Retrieved from Exploring Your Mind: https://exploringyourmind.com/salovey-mayers-emotional-intelligence-theory/

The Mayer-Salovey-Caruso emotional intelligence test (MSCEIT). (n.d.). Retrieved from the Consortium for Research on Emotional Intelligence in Organizations: http://www.eiconsortium.org/measures/msceit.html

Lea, S., & Howell, D. (2020, September 3). *What is emotional and social intelligence?* Retrieved from Businessballs.com: https://www.businessballs.com/self-awareness/main-theories-of-emotional-and-social-intelligence-esi/

Craig, H. (2019, January 30). *The theories of emotional intelligence explained*. Retrieved from Positive Psychology: https://positivepsychology.com/emotional-intelligence-theories/

Fiori, M., Antonietti, J-P., Mikolajczak, M., Luminet, O., Hansenne, M., & Rossier, J. (2014, June 5). What is the ability emotional intelligence test (MSCEIT) good for? An evaluation using item response theory. *PloS One*, 9(6), e98827. Retrieved from the National Library of Medicine: https://www.ncbi.nlm.nih.gov/pmc/articles/PMC4046984/

98 EI Competencies Model (Bar-On)

Craig, H. (2023, April 7). *The theories of emotional intelligence explained*. Retrieved from Positive Psychology: https://positivepsychology.com/emotional-intelligence-theories/

Bar-On, R. (n.d.). *The Bar-On model of social and emotional intelligence*. Retrieved from the Consortium for Research on Emotional Intelligence in Organizations: http://www.eiconsortium.org/reprints/bar-on_model_of_emotional-social_intelligence.htm

Lea, S., & Howell, D. (2020, September 3). *What is emotional and social intelligence?* Retrieved from Businessballs.com: https://www.businessballs.com/self-awareness/main-theories-of-emotional-and-social-intelligence-esi/

99 EI Performance Model (Goleman)

Craig, H. (2023, April 7). *The theories of emotional intelligence explained*. Retrieved from Positive Psychology: https://positivepsychology.com/emotional-intelligence-theories/

Emotional & social competency inventory (ESCI). (n.d.). Retrieved from Korn Ferry: https://www.kornferry.com/insights/learning/trainings-and-certifications/esci-emotional-and-social-competency-inventory

Lea, S., & Howell, D. (2020, September 3). *What is emotional and social intelligence?* Retrieved from Businessballs.com: https://www.businessballs.com/self-awareness/main-theories-of-emotional-and-social-intelligence-esi/

Goleman, D., & Boyatzis, R. (2017, February 6). Emotional intelligence has 12 elements. Which do you need to work on? *Harvard Business Review*. https://hbr.org/2017/02/emotional-intelligence-has-12-elements-which-do-you-need-to-work-on

Overview of EI. (n.d.). Retrieved from the Goleman Consulting Group: https://golemanconsultinggroup.com

Goleman, D. (n.d.). *An EI-based theory of performance*. Retrieved from the Consortium for Research on Emotional Intelligence in Organizations: https://www.eiconsortium.org/pdf/an_ei_based_theory_of_performance.pdf

100 EI Trait Model (Petrides)

Agnoli, S., Mancini, G., Andrei, F., & Trombini, E. (2019, July 30). The relationship between trait emotional intelligence, cognition, and emotional awareness: An interpretive model. *Frontiers in Psychology*, 10: https://www.frontiersin.org/articles/10.3389/fpsyg.2019.01711/full

Alegre, A., Perez-Escoda, N., & Lopez-Cassa, E. (2019 April 24). The relationship between trait emotional intelligence and personality. Is Trait EI really anchored within the big five, big two, and big one frameworks? *Frontiers in Psychology*, 10: https://www.frontiersin.org/articles/10.3389/fpsyg.2019.00866/full

Siegling, A., Furnham, A., & Petrides, K.V. (2015, February). Trait emotional intelligence and personality: Gender-invariant linkages across different measures of the big five. *Journal of Psychoeducational Assessment*, 33(1), 57–67. Retrieved from the US National Library of Medicine: https://www.ncbi.nlm.nih.gov/pmc/articles/PMC4361496/

Petrides, K.V. (2011). Ability and trait emotional intelligence. In *The Wiley-Blackwell Handbook of Individual Differences* (1st ed.),

656–678. Retrieved from TEIQue inc.: http://www.psychometriclab.com/adminsdata/files/Trait%20EI%20-%20HID.pdf

Emotional intelligence: The three models. (n.d.). Retrieved from Emotional Intelligence: http://theimportanceofemotionalintelligence.weebly.com/the-3-models.html

Emotional intelligence: The ability model. (n.d.). Retrieved from the Universalclass.com: https://www.universalclass.com/articles/self-help/emotional-intelligence/emotional-intelligence-the-ability-model.htm

Trait emotional intelligence questionnaire (TEIQue). (n.d.). Retrieved from the Consortium for Research on Emotional Intelligence in Organizations: http://www.eiconsortium.org/measures/teique.html

The trait model of emotional intelligence. (n.d.). Retrieved from Free Management Books: http://www.free-management-ebooks.com/faqpp/measuring-04.htm

101   Elaboration Likelihood Model (ELM)

Bitner, M. J., & Obermiller, C. (1985). The elaboration likelihood model: Limitations and extensions in marketing. *Advances in Consumer Research*, 12, 420–425. https://www.acrwebsite.org/volumes/6427/volumes/v12/NA-12

Elaboration likelihood model. (n.d.). Retrieved from Communication Theory: https://www.communicationtheory.org/elaboration-likelihood-model/

Yocco, V. (2014, July 1). *Persuasion: Applying the elaboration likelihood model to design.* Retrieved from A List Apart: https://alistapart.com/article/persuasion-applying-the-elaboration-likelihood-model-to-design/

Hopper, E. (2019, July 3). *What is the elaboration likelihood model in psychology?* Retrieved from ThoughtCo.: https://www.thoughtco.com/elaboration-likelihood-model-4686036

Geddes, J. (2016). *Elaboration likelihood model theory: How to use ELM.* Retrieved from the Interaction Design Foundation: https://www.interaction-design.org/literature/article/elaboration-likelihood-model-theory-using-elm-to-get-inside-the-user-s-mind

Elaboration likelihood model. (n.d.). Retrieved from Jack Westin: https://jackwestin.com/resources/mcat-content/theories-of-attitude-and-behavior-change/elaboration-likelihood-model

Behavior Works Australia. (n.d.). *The elaboration likelihood model of persuasion.* Retrieved from the North Dakota Prevention and Resource Media Center: https://prevention.nd.gov/files/bingedrinking/ELM%20-%20Australia.pdf

102   Emotional Intelligence (general entry)

Craig, H. (2019, January 30). *The theories of emotional intelligence explained.* Retrieved from Positive Psychology: https://positivepsychology.com/emotional-intelligence-theories/

Cherry, K. (2023, May 2). *Emotional intelligence: How we perceive, evaluate, express, and control emotions.* Retrieved from Verywell Mind: https://www.verywellmind.com/what-is-emotional-intelligence-2795423

Truninger, M., Fernandez-i-Marin, X., Batista-Foguet, J. M., Boyatzis, R. E., & Serlavos, R. (2018, September 7). The power of EI competencies over intelligence and individual performance: A task-dependent model. *Frontiers in Psychology*, 9: https://www.frontiersin.org/articles/10.3389/fpsyg.2018.01532/full

Winter, T. (2011, October 28). *The history of emotional intelligence.* Retrieved from Human Performance Technology: https://blog.dtssydney.com/the-history-of-emotional-intelligence

Bradberry, T., & Greaves, J. (2009). *Emotional intelligence 2.0.* TalentSmart.

103   Enneagram of Personality

The nine Enneagram type descriptions. (n.d.). Retrieved from the Enneagram Institute: https://www.enneagraminstitute.com/type-descriptions

Alexander, M., & Schnipke, B. (2020, March 6). The Enneagram: A primer for psychiatry residents. *The American Journal of Psychiatry*, 15(3), 2–5, https://psychiatryonline.org/doi/full/10.1176/appi.ajp-rj.2020.150301

What are the nine Enneagram types? (n.d.). Retrieved from Personality Path: https://personalitypath.com/enneagram/9-personality-types/

Booth, J. (2023, October 17). The 9 Enneagram personality types: Strengths, weaknesses, and more. *Forbes.* https://www.forbes.com/health/mind/enneagram-types/

Cherry, K. (2022, July 21). *What is the Enneagram of personality?* Retrieved from Verywell Mind: https://www.verywellmind.com/the-enneagram-of-personality-4691757

104   Equity Theory of Motivation (Adams)

Employee motivation theories: Stacey Adams equity theory. (n.d.). Retrieved from Your Coach: https://www.yourcoach.be/en/employee-motivation-theories/stacey-adams-equity-theory.php

Equity theory: Keeping employees motivated. (n.d.). Retrieved from Expert Program Management: https://expertprogrammanagement.com/2017/06/equity-theory/

A guide to equity theory of motivation. (2023, February 22). Retrieved from Indeed: https://www.indeed.com/career-advice/career-development/equity-theory-of-motivation

Adams' equity theory of motivation: A simple summary. (n.d.). Retrieved from the World of Work Project: https://worldofwork.io/2019/02/adams-equity-theory-of-motivation/

Adams' equity theory. (n.d.). Retrieved from MindTools: https://www.mindtools.com/pages/article/newLDR_96.htm

105   Existence, Relatedness, and Growth Theory

ERG theory. (n.d.). Retrieved from Oxford Reference: https://www.oxfordreference.com/view/10.1093/oi/authority.20110803095756477

Alderfer's ERG theory of motivation: A simple summary. (n.d.). Retrieved from the World of Work Project: https://worldofwork.io/2019/02/alderfers-erg-theory-of-motivation/

Quigley, S. P. (2015, March 18). *Existence, relatedness, growth theory of motivation.* Retrieved from Value Transformation LLC.: https://www.valuetransform.com/existence-relatedness-growth-erg-theory-motivation/

Alderfer, C. (n.d.). *Existence, relatedness, growth theory.* Retrieved from What Is Human Resources: http://www.whatishumanresource.com/existence-relatedness-growth-erg-theory

American Psychological Association. (n.d.). Existence, relatedness, growth theory. In *APA dictionary of psychology*: https://dictionary.apa.org/existence-relatedness-and-growth-theory

Alderfer's ERG theory. (n.d.). Retrieved from Lumen Learning: https://courses.lumenlearning.com/wm-introductiontobusiness/chapter/alderfers-erg-theory/

106   Expectancy Theory of Motivation

Expectancy theory of motivation. (n.d.). Retrieved from Management Study Guide: https://www.managementstudyguide.com/expectancy-theory-motivation.htm

Expectancy theory. (n.d.). Retrieved from Expert Program Management: https://expertprogrammanagement.com/2018/10/expectancy-theory/

Expectancy theory of motivation: Guide for managers. (2023, February 3). Retrieved from Indeed.com: https://www.indeed.com/career-advice/career-development/expectancy-theory-of-motivation

Expectancy theory. (n.d.). Retrieved from Lumen Learning, Introduction to Business Module 10 (Motivating Employees): https://courses.lumenlearning.com/wm-introductiontobusiness/chapter/expectancy-theory/

Vroom's expectancy theory. (n.d.). Retrieved from the University of Cambridge Institute of Manufacturing Management Technology Policy: https://www.ifm.eng.cam.ac.uk/research/dstools/vrooms-expectancy-theory/

Vroom expectancy motivation theory. (n.d.). Retrieved from YourCoach BVBA: https://www.yourcoach.be/en/employee-motivation-theories/vroom-expectancy-motivation-theory.php

Shrestha, P. (2017, November 17). *Expectancy theory of motivation.* Retrieved from Psychestudy.com: https://www.psychestudy.com/general/motivation-emotion/expectancy-theory-motivation

Vroom's expectancy theory of motivation: Valence, instrumentality, and expectancy. (n.d.). Retrieved from the World of Work Project: https://worldofwork.io/2019/02/vrooms-expectancy-theory-of-motivation/

Motivational theories. (n.d.). Retrieved from the University of Tennessee: https://mightymustangsutk.weebly.com/expectancy-value-theory.html

Wigfield, A., & Gladstone, J. (2019, March 25). What does expectancy-value theory have to say about motivation and achievement in times of change and uncertainty? *Motivation in Education at a Time of Global Change, 20*, 15–32. Retrieved from Emerald.com: https://www.emerald.com/insight/content/doi/10.1108/S0749-742320190000020002/full/html

107   Eysenck's PEN Model

Knežević, G., Lazarević, L.B., Purić, D., Bosnjak, M., Teovanović, P., Petrović, B., & Opačić, G. (2019, June). Does Eysenck's personality model capture psychosis-proneness? A systematic review and meta-analysis. *Personality and Individual Differences, 143*, 155–164. Retrieved from Science Direct: https://www.sciencedirect.com/science/article/pii/S0191886919300832

PEN model. (1999). Retrieved from Personality Research: http://www.personalityresearch.org/pen.html

Shukla, U. (2022, December 12). *Eysenck's PEN model of personality.* Retrieved from Tutorials Point: https://www.tutorialspoint.com/eysenck-s-pen-model-of-personality

Van Kampen, D. (2009, December). Personality and psychopathology: A theory-based revision of Eysenck's PEN model. *Clinical Practice and Epidemiology in Mental Health, 5*, 9–21. Retrieved from the National Library of Medicine: https://www.ncbi.nlm.nih.gov/pmc/articles/PMC2858518/

Bhushan, N.J. (2019, June 13). *Eysenck's personality model*. Retrieved from Medium: https://medium.com/@jhansibhushann/eysenks-personality-model-f6ad709014ea

Ergünes, H. (2018, April). *The review of five empirical studies: To what extent contemporary findings provide biological evidence for Eysenck's PEN model*. Retrieved from Research Gate: https://www.researchgate.net/publication/325780034_The_review_of_five_empirical_studies_To_what_extent_contemporary_findings_provide_biological_evidence_for_Eysenck%27s_PEN_Model

Eysenck's personality inventory. (n.d.). Retrieved from Community Health Solutions: https://chsresults.com/blog/test/eysencks-personality-inventory-epi-extroversionintroversion/

Free Eysenck personality test (online). (n.d.). Retrieved from Psychology Test: https://psychology-test.net/eysenck-epi-scoring-online-test/

Russin, S., & Condon, D.M. (2016, December 8). *Eysenck personality questionnaire*. Retrieved from The SAPA Project: https://www.sapa-project.org/blogs/EysenckPersonalityQuestionnaire.html

Eysenck, H.J., & Eysenck S.B.G. (1964). *Manual of the Eysenck personality inventory*. Hodder and Stoughton. Retrieved from the Genetic Epidemiology, Translational Neurogenomics, Psychiatric Genetics and Statistical Genetics Laboratory: https://genepi.qimr.edu.au/contents/p/staff/1964_Eysenck_Manual.pdf

108   FACTS Coaching Model

Welcome to the world of challenging coaching. (n.d.). Retrieved from Challenging Coaching: https://challengingcoaching.co.uk

Blakey, J., & Day, I. (n.d.). *Challenging coaching: Going beyond traditional coaching to face the FACTS: Part 1: Feedback*. Retrieved from Challenging Coaching: https://challengingcoaching.co.uk/wp-new/wp-content/uploads/2012/02/FACTS-Model-Feedback.pdf

Blakey, J., & Day, I. (n.d.). *Challenging coaching: Going beyond traditional coaching to face the FACTS: Part 2: Accountability*. Retrieved from Challenging Coaching: https://challengingcoaching.co.uk/wp-new/wp-content/uploads/2012/02/FACTS-Model-Accountability.pdf

Day, I. (2012, July). *The 'Olympic' approach to setting and achieving courageous goals*. Retrieved from Challenging Coaching: https://challengingcoaching.co.uk/wp-new/wp-content/uploads/2012/07/Association-for-Coaching-Courageous-Goals-Article.pdf

Blakey, J., & Day, I. (n.d.). *Challenging coaching: Going beyond traditional coaching to face the FACTS: Part 4: Tension*. Retrieved from Challenging Coaching: https://challengingcoaching.co.uk/wp-new/wp-content/uploads/2012/02/FACTS-Model-Tension.pdf

Blakey, J., & Day, I. (n.d.). *Challenging coaching: Going beyond traditional coaching to face the FACTS: Part 5: Systems thinking*. Retrieved from Challenging Coaching: https://challengingcoaching.co.uk/wp-new/wp-content/uploads/2012/02/FACTS-Model-Systems-Thinking.pdf

Blakey, J., & Day, I. (n.d.). *Challenging coaching: Going beyond traditional coaching to face the FACTS: Part 6: ZOUD*. Retrieved from Challenging Coaching: https://challengingcoaching.co.uk/wp-new/wp-content/uploads/2012/02/FACTS-Model-Zone-of-Uncomfortable-Debate.pdf

Sharma, N. (2018, March 20). *FACTS-based coaching technique for agile leaders to enter the ZOUD*. Retrieved from Medium: https://medium.com/@just4nagesh/facts-based-coaching-technique-for-agile-leaders-to-enter-into-the-zoud-4dc31efb3f4d

Proffitt, N. (2016, June 9). *Face the coaching facts*. Retrieved from Proffitt Management Solutions: https://proffittmanagement.com/face-the-coaching-facts/

Day, I., & Blakey, J. (n.d.). *Challenging coaching: Going beyond traditional coaching to face the FACTS*. Retrieved from Dan Roberts Group: https://danrobertsgroup.com/wp-content/uploads/2018/02/ChallengeCoaching.pdf

The personal development collection: Self-study workbook: Coaching. (n.d.). Retrieved from the University of Nottingham: https://training.nottingham.ac.uk/Public/Coaching-Skills-Workbook.pdf

Blakey, J., & Day, I. (n.d.). *Challenging coaching summary and review*. Retrieved from Lifeclub: https://lifeclub.org/books/challenging-coaching-john-blakey-and-ian-day-review-summary

109   Felder-Silverman Learning Styles

Felder-Silverman. (n.d.). Retrieved from The Peak Performance Center: https://thepeakperformancecenter.com/educational-learning/learning/preferences/learning-styles/felder-silverman/

Index of learning styles. (n.d.). Retrieved from The Peak Performance Center: https://thepeakperformancecenter.com/educational-learning/learning/preferences/learning-styles/felder-silverman/index-of-learning-styles/

Learning styles and index of learning styles. (n.d.). Retrieved from North Carolina State University College of Engineering: https://www.engr.ncsu.edu/stem-resources/legacy-site/learning-styles/

Graf, S., Viola, S., Leo, T., & Kinshuk. (2007). In-depth analysis of the Felder-Silverman learning styles dimensions. *Journal of Research on Technology in Education,* 40(1), 79–93. Retrieved from the Institute of Education Science: https://files.eric.ed.gov/fulltext/EJ826065.pdf

Teaching and learning styles. (n.d.). Retrieved from Shmoop: https://www.shmoop.com/teachers/teaching-learning-styles/learning-styles/felder-silverman.html

The Felder-Silverman learning styles model. (n.d.). Retrieved from Study.com: https://study.com/academy/lesson/the-felder-silverman-learning-styles-model.html

Felder, R., & Brent, R. (n.d.). *Index of learning styles.* Retrieved from Resources for Teaching and Learning STEM: https://educationdesignsinc.com/index-of-learning-styles/

Felder, R., & Soloman, B. (n.d.). *Index of learning styles questionnaire.* Retrieved from North Carolina State University: https://www.webtools.ncsu.edu/learningstyles/

El-Bishouty, M., Aldraiweesh, A., Alturki, U., Tortorella, R., Yang, J., Chang, W., Graf, S., & Kinshuk. (2018, November 2.). Use of Felder and Silverman learning styles model for online course design. *Educational Technology Research and Development,* 67, 161–177. Retrieved from SpringerLink: https://link.springer.com/article/10.1007/s11423-018-9634-6

110   Fiedler's Contingency Theory

Brooks, C. (2023, November 1). *Contingency management theory explained.* Retrieved from Business.com: https://www.business.com/articles/contingency-management-theory/

The contingency theory of leadership explained. (2015, January 9). Retrieved from Villanova University: https://www.villanovau.com/resources/leadership/leadership-and-contingency-theory/

Contingency theory of leadership: Definition and models. (2023, March 10). Retrieved from Indeed.com: https://www.indeed.com/career-advice/career-development/contingency-theory-of-leadership

Virkus, S. (2009). *Leadership models: Contingency theory.* Retrieved from Tallinn University: https://www.tlu.ee/~sirvir/Leadership/Leadership%20Models/contingency_theory.html

111   Fink's Crisis Management Model

Marker, A. (2020, July 20). *Models and theories to improve crisis management.* Retrieved from Smartsheet Inc.: https://www.smartsheet.com/content/crisis-management-model-theories

Boudreaux, B. (2005). *Exploring a multi-stage model of crisis management: Utilities, hurricanes, and contingency.* Retrieved from the University of Florida: https://ufdcimages.uflib.ufl.edu/UF/E0/01/04/86/00001/boudreaux_b.pdf

Kamei, K. (2019). Crisis management. In Abe, S., Ozawa, M., & Kawata, Y. (Eds), *Science of Societal Safety. Trust,* vol. 2. Springer. https://doi.org/10.1007/978-981-13-2775-9_13

The four stages of a crisis. (n.d.). Retrieved from the Washington State Department of Commerce: http://mystartup365.com/links/crisis/crisis-planner-3/

112   Fisher's Theory of Decision Emergence

Fisher's theory of decision emergence. (n.d.). Retrieved from The Team Building Company: https://www.teambuilding.co.uk/theory/fishers-theory-of-decision-emergence.html

Fisher's model: Small group communication. (n.d.). Retrieved from Communicationtheory.org: https://www.communicationtheory.org/fishers-model-small-group-communication/

Organizational behavior. (n.d.). Retrieved from Ebrary.net: https://ebrary.net/3069/management/tubbs_systems_model

Interact system model of decision emergence. (n.d.). Retrieved from A First Look at Communication Theory: https://www.afirstlook.com/docs/intersys.pdf

Fisher, A. (2009, June 2). Decision emergence: Phases in group decision-making. *Speech Monographs,* 37(1), 53–66. Retrieved from Taylor & Francis Online: https://www.tandfonline.com/doi/abs/10.1080/03637757009375649

113   Five Dynamics of Teamwork and Collaboration

Udoagwu, K. (2020, May 28). *6 different team effectiveness models to understand your team better.* Retrieved from Wrike.com: https://www.wrike.com/blog/6-different-team-effectiveness-models/

LaFasto, F., & Larson, C. (2001). *When teams work best.* Retrieved from LeadershipHQ: https://leadershiphq.files.wordpress.com/2011/02/when-teams-work-best1.pdf

Team dynamics—Frank LaFasto. (n.d.). Retrieved from the Team Building Company: https://www.teambuilding.co.uk/theory/team-dynamics-frank-lafasto.html

Kukhnavets, P. (2021, March 9). *What team effectiveness model will make a team perform better?* Retrieved from Hygger: https://hygger.io/blog/team-effectiveness-model-will-make-team-perform-better/#5-lafasto-and-larson-model

8 models of team effectiveness. (2018, June 12). Retrieved from Riter: https://medium.com/@RiterApp/8-models-of-team-effectiveness-3a3b84efb3ae

Muslihat, D. (2023, October 27). *7 popular team effectiveness models and what they are best suited for.* Retrieved from Zenkit Blog: https://zenkit.com/en/blog/7-popular-team-effectiveness-models-and-what-theyre-best-suited-for/

How to choose a team effectiveness model. (2020, February 11). Retrieved from SpriggHR: https://sprigghr.com/blog/hr-professionals/how-to-choose-a-team-effectiveness-model/

Driving team effectiveness. (2016). Retrieved from Korn Ferry: https://www.kornferry.com/content/dam/kornferry/docs/pdfs/driving-team-effectiveness.pdf

O'Neill, M. (2018, October 2). *The 8 best team effectiveness models and how they work.* Retrieved from Samewave.com: https://www.samewave.com/posts/team-effectiveness-models

Tamiru, N. (2023, June). *Team dynamics: Five keys to building effective teams.* Retrieved from Think With Google: https://www.thinkwithgoogle.com/intl/en-gb/consumer-insights/consumer-trends/five-dynamics-effective-team/

114   The Five Dysfunctions of a Team

Lencioni, P.M. (2002). *The five dysfunctions of a team.* Wiley.

The five dysfunctions of a team. (2021, April 27). Retrieved from Executive Agenda: https://www.executiveagenda.com/resources/blog/five-dysfunctions-team#

Overcoming the 5 dysfunctions in a team. (2019, March 5). Retrieved from Then Somehow: https://www.thensomehow.com/dysfunctions-of-a-team/

The five dysfunctions of a team. (n.d.). Retrieved from What You Will Learn: https://www.whatyouwilllearn.com/book/the-five-dysfunctions-of-a-team/

Zartler, J. (2017, September 7). *Lencioni's 5 dysfunctions of a team.* Retrieved from Medium: https://medium.com/taskworld-blog/lencionis-5-dysfunctions-of-a-team-330d58b2cd81

115   Five Factor Model of Personality (OCEAN)

Five-factor model of personality. (n.d.). Retrieved from Psychologist World: https://www.psychologistworld.com/personality/five-factor-model-big-five-personality

Lim, A. (2023, November 5). *Big five personality traits: The 5-factor model of personality.* Retrieved from Simply Psychology: https://www.simplypsychology.org/big-five-personality.html

Grice, J. (2023, August 7). Five-factor model of personality. Retrieved from *Britannica*: https://www.britannica.com/science/five-factor-model-of-personality

Workplace big five profile. (n.d.). Retrieved from Paradigm Personality Labs: https://paradigmpersonality.com/products/workplace-big-five-profile/

Janse, B. (2018). *Big five personality test.* Retrieved from Toolshero.com: https://www.toolshero.com/psychology/big-five-personality-test/

The big five personality test. (n.d.). Retrieved from the World of Work Project: https://worldofwork.io/2019/03/the-big-five-personality-test/

Cherry, K. (2023, March 11). *What are the big five personality traits?* Retrieved from Verywell Mind: https://www.verywellmind.com/the-big-five-personality-dimensions-2795422

Big five personality test. (2019, August 2). Retrieved from the Open-Source Psychometrics Project: https://openpsychometrics.org/tests/IPIP-BFFM/

116   Five Leadership Practices

LPI coach training online. (n.d.). Retrieved from The Leadership Challenge: https://www.leadershipchallenge.com/landingpages/lpi-coach-training-february-2021.aspx

Scouller, J., & Chapman, A. (2020, September 3). *Practices of exemplary leadership—Kouzes and Posner.* Retrieved from Businessballs.com: https://www.businessballs.com/leadership-models/five-practices-of-exemplary-leadership-kouzes-and-posner/

Scouller, J., & Chapman, A. (2020, September 3). *Trait theory—Kouzes and Posner.* Retrieved from Businessballs.com: https://www.businessballs.com/leadership-models/trait-theory-kouzes-and-posner/

Posner, B. (2017, August 2). 5 practices of exemplary leadership. Retrieved from *Success*: https://www.success.com/5-practices-of-exemplary-leadership/

The five practices of exemplary leadership. (n.d.). Retrieved from FlashPoint Inc.: https://www.flashpointleadership.com/the-five-practices-of-exemplary-leadership

Kouzes, J.M., & Posner, B. (2013). The five practices of exemplary leadership: How ordinary people make extraordinary things happen. In Kessler, E.H. (Ed.), *Encyclopedia of Management Theory*. Sage. Retrieved from Santa Clara University: https://scholarcommons.scu.edu/cgi/viewcontent.cgi?article=1029&context=mgmt

117   Five Levels of Focus Model

Bence, B. (2014, February 3). *Where do you place your focus as a leader?* Retrieved from Brenda Bence: https://www.brendabence.com/blog/2014/02/03/where-do-you-place-your-focus-as-a-leader/

Kailanto, J. (2016, July 25). *Where is your focus: Vision, process, or details?* Retrieved from Coach Jarkko: https://coachjarkko.com/2016/07/25/where-is-your-focus-vision-process-or-details/

Choose your focus. (2016, October 13). Retrieved from Coaching for Growth: https://www.coaching4growth.co.nz/blog/2016/10/13/choose-your-focus

Sari, J. (2019). *Focus model.* Retrieved from Toolshero.com: https://www.toolshero.com/personal-development/focus-model/

Goldstein, A. (2016, March 22). *How to be focused: Using the 5 levels of focus* [Video]. Retrieved from YouTube: https://www.youtube.com/watch?v=WPm5ccysNV0

Beck, D. (2012). *Brilliant leadership based on brain science.* Retrieved from the Fundraising Institute of Australia: https://fia.org.au/wp-content/uploads/2018/05/Brilliant_Leadership_Based_on_Brain_Science_-_Dominique_Beck.pdf

118   Formula for Change

Nieuwenburg, J. (n.d.). *The formula for change.* Retrieved from W⁵ Coaching: https://w5coaching.com/formula-change/

The Beckhard-Harris formula for change. (2019, May 21). Retrieved from Humanperf Software: https://www.humanperf.com/en/blog/nowiunderstand-glossary/articles/beckhard-harris-formula-for-change

Blixt, A., Eggers, M., James, S., Loup, R., & Tolchinsky, P. (2018, April 19). Kathleen D. Dannemiller: Unleashing the magic in organizations. In Szabla D.B., Pasmore W.A., Barnes M.A., & Gipson A.N. (Eds.), *The Palgrave handbook of organizational change thinkers*. Palgrave Macmillan. Retrieved from Springer Link: https://link.springer.com/referenceworkentry/10.1007%2F978-3-319-52878-6_38#citeas

119   Four-Dimensional Model of Virtual Teams

Juneja, P. (n.d.). *Four-dimensional model of virtual teams.* Retrieved from Management Study Guide: https://www.managementstudyguide.com/four-dimensional-model-of-virtual-teams.htm

Lipnack, J., & Stamps, J. (2000). *Virtual teams: People working across boundaries with technology:* Chapter 6. John Wiley & Sons. Retrieved from NetAge: http://www.netage.com/pub/books/VirtualTeams%202/CHAPTERS%20PDF/chapter06.pdf

Lipnack, J., & Stamps, J. (2000). *Virtual teams: People working across boundaries with technology:* Chapter 7. John Wiley & Sons. Retrieved from NetAge: http://www.netage.com/pub/books/VirtualTeams%202/CHAPTERS%20PDF/chapter07.pdf

Lipnack, J., & Stamps, J. (2000). *Virtual teams: People working across boundaries with technology:* Chapter 8. John Wiley & Sons. Retrieved from NetAge: http://www.netage.com/pub/books/VirtualTeams%202/CHAPTERS%20PDF/chapter08.pdf

Lipnack, J., & Stamps, J. (2000). *Virtual teams: People working across boundaries with technology:* Chapter 9. John Wiley & Sons. Retrieved from NetAge: http://www.netage.com/pub/books/VirtualTeams%202/CHAPTERS%20PDF/chapter09.pdf

Lipnack, J., & Stamps, J. (2000). *Virtual teams: People working across boundaries with technology:* Chapter 12. John Wiley & Sons. Retrieved from NetAge: http://www.netage.com/pub/books/VirtualTeams%202/CHAPTERS%20PDF/chapter12.pdf

Geisler, B. (2002). *Virtual teams.* Retrieved from New Foundations: https://www.newfoundations.com/OrgTheory/Geisler721.html

Ludden, P., Ledwith, A., & Lee-Kelley, L. (2012, July 18). *A typology framework for virtual teams.* Retrieved from the Project Management Institute: https://www.pmi.org/learning/library/typology-framework-virtual-teams-6398

Kim, S. (2004). *Team development of virtual teams.* Retrieved from the Institute of Education Sciences: https://files.eric.ed.gov/fulltext/ED492488.pdf

120   Four-Factor Theory of Leadership

Hernandez, J.G. (2015). *The four-factor theory of leadership.* Retrieved from Jesus Gil Hernandez: http://jesusgilhernandez.com/2015/12/14/the-four-factor-theory-of-leadership/

Carson, N. (2021, January 1). Four factors of the theory of leadership. Retrieved from *USA Today*: https://yourbusiness.azcentral.com/four-factors-theory-leadership-11715.html

Taylor, J.C. (1971). An empirical examination of a four-factor theory of leadership using smallest space analysis. *Organizational Behavior and Human Performance, 6,* 249–266. Retrieved from the University of Michigan: https://deepblue.lib.umich.edu/bitstream/handle/2027.42/33661/0000171.pdf;jsessionid=E7DE37F1A0F7CF385B735E5FF174280C?sequence=1

Martin, G. (2017, October 15). *Becoming a better leader: The four-factors theory of leadership.* Retrieved from LinkedIn Pulse:

https://www.linkedin.com/pulse/becoming-better-leader-four-factors-theory-martin-faim-face/

Four-factor theory of leadership. (n.d.). Retrieved from Toolshero: https://www.toolshero.com/leadership/four-factor-theory-of-leadership/

Bowers, D.G., & Seashore, S.E. (1967). *Peer leadership within work groups.* Retrieved from the University of Michigan: https://isr.umich.edu/wp-content/uploads/historicPublications/Peerleadership_2282_.PDF

121   Four Stages of Competence Model

Conscious competence learning model. (n.d.). Retrieved from Businessballs.com: https://www.businessballs.com/self-awareness/conscious-competence-learning-model/

The four stages of competence. (n.d.). Retrieved from Mercer Community College: https://www.mccc.edu/~lyncha/documents/stagesofcompetence.pdf

The four stages of competence. (n.d.). Retrieved from Training Industry: https://trainingindustry.com/wiki/strategy-alignment-and-planning/the-four-stages-of-competence/

The conscious competence ladder. (n.d.). Retrieved from MindTools: https://www.mindtools.com/pages/article/newISS_96.htm

Zaki, Z. (2017, January 26). *The four stages of competence.* Retrieved from Medium: https://medium.com/@zainabz/the-four-stages-of-competence-ee5c6046b205

The conscious competence learning model. (n.d.). Retrieved from Expert Program Management: https://expertprogrammanagement.com/2012/08/the-conscious-competence-learning-model/

122   FUEL Coaching Model

FUEL coaching model: Why, when, how, examples. (2023, August 4). Retrieved from Coach 4 Growth: https://www.coach4growth.com/coaching-skills/coaching-models/fuel-coaching-model/

Zenger, J. (Host). (2022, July 12). *FUEL: A proven framework for coaching with Kathleen Stinnett* (Episode 82). [Audio Podcast]. https://zengerfolkman.com/episode-30-fuel-a-proven-framework-for-coaching-2/

Polemis, J. *FUEL Coaching framework.* (n.d.). Retrieved from New York University Coaching for Leadership: https://wp.nyu.edu/coaching/tools/fuel-model/

FUEL coaching model. (n.d.). Retrieved from the Peak Performance Center: https://thepeakperformancecenter.com/development-series/skill-builder/interpersonal/coaching-for-performance/coaching-model/fuel-coaching-model/

123   Full Range Leadership Model (FRLM)

Barbuto Jr., J. E., & Cummins-Brown, L. L. (2007). *Full range leadership.* Retrieved from the University of Nebraska-Lincoln: https://extensionpublications.unl.edu/assets/html/g1406/build/g1406.htm

The full range leadership model. (2012, June 9). Retrieved from My News Desk: https://www.mynewsdesk.com/se/ledarskapscentrum/blog_posts/the-full-range-leadership-model-13176

Theoretical spotlight: Full range leadership model. (n.d.). Retrieved from Complete Dissertation by Statistics Solutions: https://www.statisticssolutions.com/theoretical-spotlight-full-range-leadership-model/

Lindberg, C. (2022, August 18). *The full range leadership model.* Retrieved from Leadership Ahoy: https://www.leadershipahoy.com/full-range-leadership-model/

Sanchez, B. M. (2020, April 10). *Full range leadership model.* Retrieved from LinkedIn Pulse: https://www.linkedin.com/pulse/full-range-leadership-model-benjamin-martinez-sanchez/

124   Functional Leadership Models

Functional leadership model. (n.d.). Retrieved from Toolshero: https://www.toolshero.com/leadership/functional-leadership-model/

Shead, M. (n.d.). *The functional leadership model.* Retrieved from Leadership501: http://www.leadership501.com/functional-leadership-model/20/

10 functional leadership characteristics. (n.d.). Retrieved from Y Scouts: https://yscouts.com/10-functional-leadership-characteristics/

Functional leadership model. (2016, November). Retrieved from DocShare: http://docshare01.docshare.tips/files/30741/307419369.pdf

What is action-centered leadership? (n.d.). Retrieved from Businessballs.com: https://www.businessballs.com/leadership-models/action-centred-leadership-john-adair/

125   Fundamental Interpersonal Relations Orientation Theory

Fundamental interpersonal relations orientation (FIRO). (n.d.). Retrieved from the Myers-Briggs Company: https://www.themyersbriggs.com/en-US/Products-and-Services/FIRO

Thompson, H.L. (2000). *FIRO element B and psychological type*. Retrieved from High Performing Systems Inc.: https://www.hpsys.com/articles/why_firo_elementb.htm

Fundamental interpersonal relations orientation (FIRO). (n.d.). Retrieved from the Myers-Briggs Company: https://asia.themyersbriggs.com/instruments/firo/

Blackman, C. (n.d.). *A brief summary of FIRO theory*. Retrieved from The Human Element Sweden: https://www.thesweden.se/files/FIRO-a_brief_summary_of_firo_theory.pdf

Blackman, C. (2008). *A brief summary of FIRO theory*. Retrieved from The Human Element: https://thehumanelement.com/wp-content/uploads/2020/06/T966US_2019_02-1.pdf

FIRO. (n.d.). Retrieved from The Human Element: https://www.thehumanelement.com/firo-theory/

Practitioner training | The Human Element. (n.d.). Retrieved from The Human Element: https://www.thehumanelement.com/practitioner-training-the-human-element/

Wagner, R. (n.d.). *The fundamental interpersonal relations orientation (FIRO) of people*. Retrieved from Tiba Management: https://www.tiba.de/en/the-fundamental-interpersonal-relations-orientation/

Fundamental interpersonal relations orientation. (n.d.). Retrieved from Psychology Concepts: https://psychologyconcepts.com/fundamental-interpersonal-relations-orientation/

126   Gardner's Theory of Multiple Intelligences

Marenus, M. (2023, October 24). *Howard Gardner's theory of multiple intelligences*. Retrieved from Simply Psychology: https://www.simplypsychology.org/multiple-intelligences.html

Cherry, K. (2023, March 11). *Gardner's theory of multiple intelligences*. Retrieved from Verywell Mind: https://www.verywellmind.com/gardners-theory-of-multiple-intelligences-2795161

Multiple intelligences: What does the research say? (2016, July 20). Retrieved from Edutopia: https://www.edutopia.org/multiple-intelligences-research

Howard Gardner's theory of multiple intelligences. (2020). Retrieved from Northern Illinois University Center for Innovative Teaching and Learning: https://www.niu.edu/citl/resources/guides/instructional-guide/gardners-theory-of-multiple-intelligences.shtml

Multiple intelligences. (n.d.). Retrieved from the American Institute for Learning and Human Development: https://www.institute4learning.com/resources/articles/multiple-intelligences/

Herndon, E. (2018, February 6). *What are multiple intelligences and how do they affect learning?* Retrieved from Cornerstone University: https://www.cornerstone.edu/blog-post/what-are-multiple-intelligences-and-how-do-they-affect-learning/

Smith, M. (2008). *Howard Gardner, multiple intelligences and education*. Retrieved from Infed Org: https://infed.org/mobi/howard-gardner-multiple-intelligences-and-education/

Howard Gardner's theory of multiple intelligences. (n.d.). Retrieved from Northern Illinois University Faculty Development and Instructional Design Center via the Autism Empowerment Organization: http://www.autismempowerment.org/wp-content/uploads/2013/12/Howard-Gardner-Theory-of-Multiple-Intelligences.pdf

127   General Adaptation Syndrome

Edwards, R. (2023, October 18). *What is general adaptation syndrome?* Retrieved from Verywell Health: https://www.verywellhealth.com/general-adaptation-syndrome-overview-5198270

What is general adaptation syndrome? (2017). Retrieved from Healthline: https://www.healthline.com/health/general-adaptation-syndrome#takeaway

Burgess, L. (2023, July 17). *What to know about general adaptation syndrome*. Retrieved from Medical News Today: https://www.medicalnewstoday.com/articles/320172

Ohwovoriole, T. (2022, January 11). *General adaptation syndrome: How your body responds to stress*. Retrieved from Verywell Mind: https://www.verywellmind.com/general-adaptation-syndrome-gad-definition-signs-causes-management-5213817

Lucille, H. (2023). *General adaptation syndrome stages*. Retrieved from Integrative Therapeutics: https://www.integrativepro.com/articles/general-adaptation-syndrome-stages

128   Gibbs' Reflective Cycle

Gibbs' reflective cycle. (2020, November 11). Retrieved from the University of Edinburgh: https://www.ed.ac.uk/reflection/reflectors-toolkit/reflecting-on-experience/gibbs-reflective-cycle

Gibbs' reflective cycle. (n.d.). Retrieved from MindTools: https://www.mindtools.com/pages/article/reflective-cycle.htm

Gibbs' reflective cycle. (2020, June). Retrieved from the University of Cumbria: https://my.cumbria.ac.uk/media/MyCumbria/Documents/ReflectiveCycleGibbs.pdf

Ruby. (2018, May 1). *Gibbs—Reflective cycle model (1988)*. Retrieved from The e-Learning Network: https://www.eln.io/blog/gibbs-reflective-cycle-model-1988

Coombs, J. (n.d.). *Nurses and midwives reflection process.* Retrieved from Working Well Solutions: https://workingwellsolutions. com/reflection-gibbs-model-applied-example/

Reflective practice toolkit. (n.d.). Retrieved from the University of Cambridge: https://libguides.cam.ac.uk/ reflectivepracticetoolkit/models

129   Goleman's Six Styles of Leadership

Lindberg, C. (2023, January 23). *The six leadership styles by Daniel Goleman.* Retrieved from Leadership Ahoy: https://www. leadershipahoy.com/the-six-leadership-styles-by-daniel-goleman/

Sands, L. (2020, July 24). *The six styles of leadership: Where do you fit?* Retrieved from Breathe: https://www.breathehr.com/en-gb/blog/topic/business-leadership/the-six-styles-of-leadership-where-do-you-fit

Leadership styles. (n.d.). Retrieved from Skillsyouneed.com: https://www.skillsyouneed.com/lead/leadership-styles.html

Casali, E. (2015, May 13). *The six styles of leadership.* Retrieved from Intenseminimalism.com: https://intenseminimalism. com/2015/the-six-styles-of-leadership/

Goleman, D. (2000, March–April). Leadership that gets results. *Harvard Business Review,* 82–83. Retrieved from Montana State University: https://www.montana.edu/engagement/organizations/solc/The%20Six%20Leadership%20Styles.pdf

Leadership Styles—Daniel Goleman et al. (2016). Retrieved from Blackpool Teaching Hospitals: https://www.bfwh.nhs.uk/ onehr/wp-content/uploads/2016/02/Leadership-Styles-V1.pdf

Benincasa, R. (2012, May 29). 6 leadership styles and when you should use them. *Fast Company:* https://www.fastcompany. com/1838481/6-leadership-styles-and-when-you-should-use-them

130   Groupthink

Groupthink. (n.d.). Retrieved from Psychology Today: https://www.psychologytoday.com/us/basics/groupthink

Cherry, K. (2022, November 12). *How groupthink impacts our behavior.* Retrieved from Verywellmind.com: https://www. verywellmind.com/what-is-groupthink-2795213

Avoiding groupthink. (n.d.). Retrieved from Mindtools.com: https://www.mindtools.com/pages/article/newLDR_82.htm

What is groupthink? (n.d.). Retrieved from Corporate Finance Institute: https://corporatefinanceinstitute.com/resources/ careers/soft-skills/groupthink-decisions/

Schmidt, A. (2023, November 3). Groupthink. Retrieved from *Britannica:* https://www.britannica.com/science/groupthink

Kenton, W. (2022, December 5). *What is groupthink? Definition, characteristics, and causes.* Retrieved from Investopedia.com: https://www.investopedia.com/terms/g/groupthink.asp

Ethics unwrapped: Groupthink. (n.d.). Retrieved from the University of Texas-Austin: https://ethicsunwrapped.utexas.edu/ glossary/groupthink

131   GROW Coaching Model

The GROW model. (n.d.). Retrieved from Performance Consultants International Ltd.: https://www.performanceconsultants. com/grow-model

GROW coaching model. (n.d.). Retrieved from Your Coach BV.: https://www.yourcoach.be/en/coaching-tools/grow-coaching-model.php

Elsey, E-L. (2023, May 2). *The GROW model explained for coaches.* Retrieved from The Coaching Tools Company: https://www. thecoachingtoolscompany.com/the-grow-model-explained-for-coaches-questions-tips-more/

Wilson, C. (n.d.). *The GROW model.* Retrieved from Culture at Work: https://www.coachingcultureatwork.com/the-grow-model/

Miller, K. (2020, April 3). *What is the GROW coaching model?* Retrieved from Positive Psychology: https://positivepsychology. com/grow-coaching-model/

132   GROWTH Coaching Model

John Campbell. (n.d.). Retrieved from GROWTH Coaching International: https://www.growthcoaching.com.au/team-member/john-campbell/

Munro, C. (2017). *From relationships to results: Coaching using the GROWTH model.* Retrieved from GROWTH Coaching International: https://www.growthcoaching.com.au/media/documents/Coaching_using_the_GROWTH_model.pdf

Campbell, J., & van Nieuwerburgh, C. (2018). Chapter 3: The GROWTH coaching system, In *The leader's guide to coaching in schools.* Corwin. https://uk.sagepub.com/sites/default/files/upm-assets/87600_book_item_87600.pdf

Campbell, J. (n.d.). *3 ways to help sustain commitment towards goals.* Retrieved from GROWTH Coaching International: https:// www.growthcoaching.com.au/resource/3-ways-to-help-sustain-commitment-towards-goals/

About GCI. (n.d.). Retrieved from GROWTH Coaching International: https://www.growthcoaching.com.au/about/

Acha, K. (2018, August 2). *The GROWTH model of coaching*. Retrieved from Kenneth Acha Ministries: https://www.kennethmd.com/the-growth-model-of-coaching/

133   GRPI Model

Tartell, R. (2016, February 4). Understand teams by using the GRPI model. Retrieved from *Training* Magazine: https://trainingmag.com/trgmag-article/understand-teams-using-grpi-model/

Kholghi, B. (n.d.). *The GRPI model for effective teams—Easy explained with examples.* Retrieved from Coaching Online: https://www.coaching-online.org/grpi/

Goal roles process and interpersonal relations (GRPI). (n.d.). Retrieved from What is Sigma Six: https://www.whatissixsigma.net/grpi/

The GRPI model for effective teams. (n.d.). Retrieved from Hinteregger: https://www.hinteregger.de/grpi-model-for-effective-teams/

What is the GRPI model? (n.d.). Retrieved from Businessballs.com: https://www.businessballs.com/leading-teams/the-grpi-model/

Raue, S., Tang, S-H., Weiland, C., & Wenzlik, C. (2013, February 2). *The GRPI model—An approach for team development.* Retrieved from the SE Group: https://www.google.com/rl?sa=t&rct=j&q=&esrc=s&source=web&cd=&cad=r-ja&uact=8&ved=2ahUKEwjhvKiJkajtAhXytlkKHe3tCzoQFjAMegQIHhAC&url=https%3A%2F%2Fhsrc.himmelfarb.gwu.edu%2Fcgi%2Fviewcontent.cgi%3Ffilename%3D0%26article%3D1017%26context%3Delearning%26type%3Dadditional&usg=AOvVaw0uGOj5bBYqDXTAyZ7A8O4a

134   Hackman's Model of Team Effectiveness

Haas, M., & Mortensen, M. (2016, June). The secrets of great teamwork. *Harvard Business Review:* https://hbr.org/2016/06/the-secrets-of-great-teamwork

Models of team effectiveness. (2018, June). Retrieved from Riter: https://riter.co/blog/models-of-team-effectiveness

Udoagwu, K. (2022, May 28). *6 different team effectiveness models to understand your team better.* Retrieved from Wrike.com: https://www.wrike.com/blog/6-different-team-effectiveness-models/

Richard Hackman's 'five factor model.' (n.d.). Retrieved from Free Management Books: http://www.free-management-ebooks.com/faqld/development-03.htm

O'Neill, M. (2018, October 2). *The 8 best team effectiveness models and how they work.* Retrieved from Samewave.com: https://www.samewave.com/posts/team-effectiveness-models

Hackman's group effectiveness model. (n.d.). Retrieved from Psychology Wiki: https://psychology.wikia.org/wiki/Hackman%27s_group_effectiveness_model

How to choose a team effectiveness model. (2020, February 11). Retrieved from SpriggHR: https://sprigghr.com/blog/hr-professionals/how-to-choose-a-team-effectiveness-model/

135   Handy's Four Types of Culture

Handy's four types of organizational culture. (n.d.). Retrieved from the Chartered Management Institute: https://switcheducation.com/wp-content/uploads/2017/06/SEB_LYO_Handy.pdf

Juneja, P. (n.d.). *Charles Handy model of organizational culture.* Retrieved from Management Study Guide: https://www.managementstudyguide.com/charles-handy-model.htm

Charles Handy's model of organizational culture. (n.d.). Retrieved from MBA Knowledge Base: https://www.mbaknol.com/management-principles/charles-handys-model-of-organizational-culture/

Teaching guide: Handy's culture. (n.d.). Retrieved from AQA: https://www.aqa.org.uk/resources/business/as-and-a-level/business-7131-7132/teach/teaching-guide-handys-culture

Mind Tools Content Team. (n.d.). *Handy's four types of culture.* Retrieved from MindTools: https://www.mindtools.com/ass-7geb/handys-four-types-of-culture

Handy's model of organizational culture. (2018, February 27). Retrieved by Tutor 2 U: https://www.tutor2u.net/business/reference/models-of-organisational-culture-handy

Handy model of organizational culture. (n.d.). Retrieved from Toolshero: https://www.toolshero.com/management/handy-model/

136   Hawthorne Effect

Cherry, K. (2023, July 6). *How the Hawthorne effect worked.* Retrieved from Verywell Mind: https://www.verywellmind.com/what-is-the-hawthorne-effect-2795234

Kenton, W. (2022, June 15). *Hawthorne effect definition: How it works and is it real.* Retrieved from Investopedia: https://www.investopedia.com/terms/h/hawthorne-effect.asp

McCambridge, J., Witton, J., & Elbourne, D. R. (2014, March). Systematic review of the Hawthorne effect: New concepts are needed to study research participation effects. *Journal of Clinical Epidemiology, 67*(3), 267–277. https://doi.org/10.1016/j.jclinepi.2013.08.015

Belyh, A. (2020, July 25). *Participative leadership guide: Definition, qualities, pros and cons, examples.* Retrieved from Cleverism: https://www.cleverism.com/participative-leadership-guide/

137 Health Belief Model

LaMorte, W. W. (2022). *The health belief model.* Retrieved from the Boston University Medical Center: https://sphweb.bumc.bu.edu/otlt/mph-modules/sb/behavioralchangetheories/behavioralchangetheories2.html

The health belief model. (n.d.). Retrieved from the Rural Health Information Hub: https://www.ruralhealthinfo.org/toolkits/health-promotion/2/theories-and-models/health-belief

Boskey, E. (2023, April 7). *How the health belief model influences your behaviors.* Retrieved from Verywell Mind: https://www.verywellmind.com/health-belief-model-3132721

Limbu, Y. B., Gautam, R. K., & Pham, L. (2022, June). The health belief model applied to COVID-19 vaccine hesitancy: A systematic review. *Vaccines, 10*(6), 973. Retrieved from the National Library of Medicine: https://www.ncbi.nlm.nih.gov/pmc/articles/PMC9227551/

138 Heider's Balance Theory

Roundy, L. (n.d.). *Balance theory in psychology: Definition and examples.* Retrieved from Study.com: https://study.com/academy/lesson/balance-theory-in-psychology-definition-examples.html

Heider's balance theory. (n.d.). Retrieved from Toolshero.com: https://www.toolshero.com/psychology/heiders-balance-theory/

Balance theory. (n.d.). Retrieved from Changingminds.org: http://changingminds.org/explanations/theories/balance_theory.htm

Balance theory. (n.d.). Retrieved from Psychology.iresearchnet.com: http://psychology.iresearchnet.com/social-psychology/social-psychology-theories/balance-theory/

Balance theory. (n.d.). Retrieved from Wikia.org: https://psychology.wikia.org/wiki/Balance_theory

Fritz Heider. (n.d.). Retrieved from Wikia.org: https://psychology.wikia.org/wiki/Fritz_Heider

139 Helical Model of Communication

Bajracharya, S. (2018, January 11). *Helical model of communication.* Retrieved from Businesstopia: https://www.businesstopia.net/communication/helical-model-communication

Helical model of communication. (n.d.). Retrieved from Communication Theory: https://www.communicationtheory.org/helical-model-of-communication/

Cuofano, G. (2023, October 13). *What is the helical model of communication? The helical model of communication in a nutshell.* Retrieved from Four Week MBA: https://fourweekmba.com/helical-model-of-communication/

Drew, C. (2023, March 18). *5 features of Dance's helical model of communication.* Retrieved from Helpful Professor: https://helpfulprofessor.com/helical-model-of-communication/

Juneja, P. (n.d.). *Helical model of communication.* Retrieved from Management Study Guide: https://www.managementstudyguide.com/helical-model-of-communication.htm

Nadkarni, P. S. (2021, August 13). *Helix model of communication.* Retrieved from Hub Pages: https://discover.hubpages.com/technology/Helix-Model-of-Communication

What is Frank Dance's communication model? (2020, March 24). Retrieved from Reference.com: https://www.reference.com/business-finance/frank-dance-s-communication-model-adabb2fb53f626fe

140 Heron's Six Categories of Intervention

Lea, S. (2020, September 3). *Origins of Heron's six categories of intervention.* Retrieved from Businessballs.com: https://www.businessballs.com/coaching-and-mentoring/herons-six-categories-of-intervention/

Ross, P. (2017, October 8). *John Heron's six category intervention-analysis.* Retrieved from the Nursing Education Network: https://nursingeducationnetwork.net/2017/08/10/john-herons-six%E2%80%90category-intervention-analysis/

Blakey, J. (2012, July 20). *Heron's six categories of intervention.* Retrieved from Challenging Coaching: https://challengingcoaching.co.uk/herons-six-categories-of-intervention/

Intervention styles questionnaire. (n.d.). Retrieved from Challenging Coaching: https://challengingcoaching.co.uk/wp-new/wp-content/uploads/2012/08/Heron-questionniare.pdf

Heron, J. (2001). *Helping the client: A creative practical guide.* Sage Publications. Retrieved from the South Pacific Centre for Human Inquiry: https://johnheron-archive.co.uk/wp-content/uploads/2020/03/Helping-the-Client-ff.pdf

141   Herrmann's Whole Brain Model

The whole brain thinking methodology. (n.d.). Retrieved from Herrmann Global LLC: https://www.thinkherrmann.com/how-it-works

Herrmann certification workshops. (n.d.). Retrieved from Herrmann Global LLC: https://www.thinkherrmann.com/upcoming-hbdi-certification-workshops

What we do (HBDI). (n.d.). Retrieved from Herrmann Global LLC (Australia): https://www.herrmann.com.au/what-is-whole-brain-thinking/

The whole brain model. (n.d.). Retrieved from the Peak Performance Center: https://thepeakperformancecenter.com/educational-learning/learning/preferences/thebrain/hbdi/whole-brain-model/

Faust, K. (2019, May 23). *Herrmann brain dominance instrument: HBDI overview.* Retrieved from LEADx: https://leadx.org/articles/hbdi-herrmann-brain-dominance-instrument/

Isiramen, O. (2020, September 22). *What is the whole brain thinking approach?* Retrieved from Coaching with Omozua: https://www.omozua.com/4679/whole-brain-thinking/

142   Heuristic-Systematic Model of Information Processing

Heuristic-systematic model of information processing. (n.d.). Retrieved from Psychologywiki: https://psychology.wikia.org/wiki/Heuristic-systematic_model_of_information_processing

Trumbo, C. (1999, June). Heuristic-systematic information processing and risk judgement. *Risk Analysis,* 19, 391–400. Retrieved from Springer Link: https://link.springer.com/article/10.1023%2FA%3A1007092410720

Heuristic-systematic model of persuasion. (n.d.). Retrieved from Psychology Research Net: http://psychology.iresearchnet.com/social-psychology/social-influence/heuristic-systematic-model-of-persuasion/

Baumeister, R. F., & Vohs, K. D. (2007). Heuristic-systematic model of persuasion. In *Encyclopedia of Social Psychology,* 429–430. SAGE Publications. https://sk.sagepub.com/reference/socialpsychology/n256.xml

Chaiken, S. (1980). Heuristic versus systematic information processing and the use of source versus message cues in persuasion. *Journal of Personality and Social Psychology,* 39(5), 752–766. Retrieved from the University of North Carolina at Chapel Hill: https://fbaum.unc.edu/teaching/articles/jpsp-1980-Chaiken.pdf

143   Honey and Mumford Learning Styles

Ruby. (2017, August 1). *Honey and Mumford learning styles.* Retrieved from the E-Learning Network: https://www.eln.io/blog/honey-and-mumford-learning-styles

Rosewell, J. (2005). *Learning styles.* Retrieved from The Open University: https://www.open.edu/openlearn/ocw/pluginfile.php/629607/mod_resource/content/1/t175_4_3.pdf

Honey and Mumford learning styles. (n.d.). Retrieved from Businessballs.com: https://www.businessballs.com/self-awareness/honey-and-mumfords-learning-styles/

Clark, D. (2011, July 12). *Honey and Mumford's learning styles questionnaire.* Retrieved from Big Dog & Little Dog's Performance Juxtaposition: http://www.nwlink.com/~donclark/hrd/styles/honey_mumford.html

Watson, E. (2019, May 10). *Honey and Mumford learning style theory.* Retrieved from The Classroom: https://www.theclassroom.com/honey-mumford-learning-style-theory-10038576.html

Honey Mumford. (n.d.). Retrieved from The Peak Performance Center: https://thepeakperformancecenter.com/educational-learning/learning/preferences/learning-styles/honey-mumford/

144   Hoy-Tarter Decision-Making Model

Noppe, R., Yager, S., Webb, C., & Sheng, B. (2013, March). Decision-making and problem-solving practices of superintendents confronted by district dilemmas. *NCPEA International Journal of Educational Leadership Preparation,* 8(1), 103–120. Retrieved from the Institute of Education Sciences: https://files.eric.ed.gov/fulltext/EJ1012999.pdf

Zane, E. (2016, January 18). *Are you a good team leader? And why you may be better off alone.* Retrieved from EBZ Coaching: https://www.edoardo-binda-zane.com/team-leader/

Kartik. (2023, March 24). *What is the Hoy-Tarter model of decision-making?* Retrieved from Digital Gyan: https://digitalgyan.org/what-is-hoy-tarter-model-of-decision-making/

145   Human Synergistics International Circumplex (HSI)

The human synergistics circumplex. (n.d.). Retrieved from Human Synergistics International: https://www.humansynergistics. com/about-us/the-circumplex

The circumplex. (n.d.). Retrieved from Human Synergistics International: https://www.humansynergistics.com/Files/HTML5/ Circumplex/index.html

Accreditation. (n.d.). Retrieved from Human Synergistics International: https://www.humansynergistics.com/training/ workshop-calendar

Ray, R., & Cooke, R. A. (2011, October). *A tale of two departments: The impact of leadership on change.* Retrieved from the Organizational Development Network (Baltimore, Maryland): https://cdn.ymaws.com/www.odnetwork.org/resource/ resmgr/2011_conf_ppts/c12_-_tale_of_two_department.pdf

146   IBM Design Thinking Model (DTM)

Enterprise design thinking. (n.d.). Retrieved from IBM: https://www.ibm.com/design/approach/design-thinking/

Apply design thinking to complex teams, problems, and organizations. (n.d.). Retrieved from IBM: https://www.ibm.com/design/thinking/

Elmansy, R. (2016, February 18). *IBM design thinking model: A shift toward big enterprises.* Retrieved from Designorate: https:// www.designorate.com/ibm-design-thinking/

Cutler, A. (2016, January 21). *IBM design thinking: A framework to help teams continuously understand and deliver.* Retrieved from LinkedIn Pulse: https://www.linkedin.com/pulse/ibm-design-thinking-framework-help-teams-continuously-adam-cutler/

Stinson, L. (2016, January 21). IBM's got a plan to bring design thinking to big business. *Wired:* https://www.wired. com/2016/01/ibms-got-a-plan-to-bring-design-thinking-to-big-business/

147   IDEA Feedback Model

Nemeth, B. (2018, May 31). *3 ways to give effective feedback everytime.* Retrieved from SessionLab: https://www.sessionlab.com/ blog/effective-feedback-models/

What is a feedback model? (2022, June 24). Retrieved from Indeed: https://www.indeed.com/career-advice/career-development/feedback-model

Bhasin, H. (2020, November 28). *7 powerful types of feedback models.* Retrieved from Marketing91: https://www.marketing91. com/feedback-models/

Stover, J. (2017, May 18). *The IDEA feedback model.* Retrieved from SlideShare: https://www.slideshare.net/JeremyStoverPCC/ giving-feedback-with-idea

148   Identity Management Theory

Identity management theory. (n.d.). Retrieved from Communicationtheory.org: https://www.communicationtheory.org/identity-management-theory/

Merrgian, G. (2017, December 13). *Identity management theory.* Retrieved from Wiley Online Library: https://onlinelibrary.wiley. com/doi/abs/10.1002/9781118783665.ieicc0038

Table, A. (2016). Transitions in polyamorous identity and intercultural communication: An application of identity management theory. *Electronic Theses and Dissertations,* 4883. Retrieved from the University of Central Florida: https:// stars.library.ucf.edu/cgi/viewcontent.cgi?article=5883&context=etd

149   Immunity to Change

Changing for the better. (n.d.). Retrieved from the Harvard Graduate School of Continuing Education: https://www.gse.harvard. edu/hgse100/story/changing-better

Mind Tools Content Team. (n.d.). *Immunity to change.* Retrieved from MindTools: https://www.mindtools.com/a4l75hx/ immunity-to-change

Kegan, R., & Lahey, L. (2001, November). The real reason people won't change. *Harvard Business Review:* https://hbr. org/2001/11/the-real-reason-people-wont-change

Brown, B. (Host). (2022, November 21). *Lisa Lahey on immunity to change, part 1* [Audio podcast]. Retrieved from Brené Brown: https://brenebrown.com/podcast/immunity-to-change-part-1-of-2/

Immunity to change. (n.d.). Retrieved from Zen Tools: https://www.zen-tools.net/immunity-to-change.html

150   Innovation Funnel

Innovation funnel. (n.d.). Retrieved from the University of Cambridge: https://www.ifm.eng.cam.ac.uk/research/dstools/ innovation-funnel/

Luenendonk, M. (2016, August 10). *Innovation funnel*. Retrieved from Cleverism: https://www.cleverism.com/lexicon/innovation-funnel-definition/

Hoehn, R. (2020, February 3). *Which innovation funnel should I use?* Retrieved from Innovation Management: https://innovationmanagement.se/2020/02/03/what-innovation-funnel-should-i-use/

The innovation funnel. (n.d.). Retrieved from The Desai Group: http://www.desai.com/our-approach/innovation-funnel.php

Etiemble, F. (2019, August 26). *Q&A with an executive: How to feed an innovation funnel*. Retrieved from Strategyzer: https://www.strategyzer.com/blog/qa-with-an-executive-how-to-feed-an-innovation-funnel

Why innovation funnels don't work and why rockets do. (2007). Retrieved from The Marketing Society: https://www.marketingsociety.com/the-library/why-innovation-funnels-dont-work-and-why-rockets-do

Barber, T. (2011, June 4). *The innovation funnel: Bringing ideas to life*. Retrieved from GreenBook: https://www.greenbook.org/mr/market-research-news/the-innovation-funnel-bringing-ideas-to-life/

151 Innovation Management

Nieminen, J. (2023, May 4). *Innovation management—The ultimate guide*. Retrieved from Viima Solutions Oy: https://www.viima.com/blog/innovation-management

Birkinshaw, J., & Mol, M. (2006, July 1). *How management innovation happens*. Retrieved from MIT Sloan Management Review: https://sloanreview.mit.edu/article/how-management-innovation-happens/

152 Integral Theory

Manson, M. (n.d.). *The rise and fall of Ken Wilber*. Retrieved from Mark Manson: https://markmanson.net/ken-wilber

Welcome to the integral approach. (n.d.). Retrieved from Integral+Life: https://integrallife.com/what-is-integral-approach/

Zampella, T. V. (2018, June 26). *Integral theory: From behaving to belonging, part 1*. Retrieved from the Bhāvanā Learning Group: https://www.bhavanalearning.com/integral-theory-behaving-belonging-part1/

Zampella, T. V. (2021, May 26). *Integral theory: Learning and Leadership, Part 2*. Retrieved from Medium: https://tonyvzampella.medium.com/integral-theory-learning-and-leadership-part-2-f5b882338960

What is integral theory? (n.d.). Retrieved from the Integral European Conference: https://integraleuropeanconference.com/integral-theory/

Edwards, R. (2021, July 1). *Ken Wilber fundamentals: The attitudes/stages of development*. Retrieved from the Great Updraft: https://thegreatupdraft.com/ken-wilber-fundamentals-altitudes-of-development-explained/

Armstrong, T. (2020, February 5). *The stages of life according to Ken Wilber*. Retrieved from the American Institute for Learning and Human Development: https://www.institute4learning.com/2020/02/05/the-stages-of-life-according-to-ken-wilber/

Integral theory. (n.d.). Retrieved from Spiral Dynamics Integral Nederland: https://spiraldynamicsintegral.nl/en/about-sdi/integral-theory/

Segatori, S. (2017, July 3). *What is integral philosophy, integral theory?* Retrieved from Medium: https://medium.com/@ssegatori/what-is-integral-philosophy-integral-theory-5c6b0ccc7724

What is integral theory? (n.d.). Retrieved from Integral Agile Journal: https://integralagile.com/what-is-integral-theory

153 Integrated Model of Group Development

Wheelan's integrated model of group development. (n.d.). Retrieved from O'Reilly: https://www.oreilly.com/library/view/the-little-book/9780273785262/html/chapter-045.html

Creating effective teams—The detailed curation. (n.d.). Retrieved from Hyper Island: https://www.hyperisland.com/blog/creating-effective-teams-the-detailed-curation

Wheelan's integrated model of group development. (n.d.). Retrieved from Ebrary: https://ebrary.net/3071/management/wheelans_integrated_model_group_development

Puscasu, A. (2023, May 1). *8 best team building methods series – Wheelan and Locke methods*. Retrieved from Ape: http://apepm.co.uk/the-8-best-team-building-methods-wheelan-and-locke/

Chapter 2: Group Development, 15–32. (n.d.). Retrieved from Jones & Bartlett Learning: http://samples.jbpub.com/9781284112009/9781284112009_CH02_PASS03.pdf?TSPD_101_R0=089de8e4f9ab2000863ae0df6b345eabb-d4828ee844743bf61d77a2bfc98b4f666f6b81f3ea6fae60867ee2164143000244739624fed00775b653e000216c02b036be-4f30aeb919d13f6bea5340d3b374f326a49e51a77aff4a8e6ccf39b4e23

154 Intentional Change Theory

Intentional change theory: The five steps of personal change. (n.d.). Retrieved from the World of Work Project: https://worldofwork.io/2019/04/intentional-change-theory/

Intentional change theory: Achieving manageable, meaningful change. (n.d.). Retrieved from MindTools: https://www.mindtools.com/pages/article/intentional-change-theory.htm

Boyatzis, R. (2017, February 21). *The five stages of intentional change theory.* Retrieved from Key Step Media: https://www.keystepmedia.com/intentional-change-theory/

Boyatzis, R. (2006). An overview of intentional change from a complexity perspective. *Journal of Management Development, 25*(7), 607–623. Retrieved from Penn State University: https://citeseerx.ist.psu.edu/viewdoc/download?doi=10.1.1.465.3613&rep=rep1&type=pdf

Boyatzis, R., Smith, M., & Van Oosten, E. (2019, September–October). Coaching for change. *Harvard Business Review.* https://hbr.org/2019/09/coaching-for-change

155   Internal Family Systems Model

Internal family systems tool. (n.d.). Retrieved from Crowe & Associates: https://www.crowe-associates.co.uk/coaching-tools/ifs-coaching-tool/

Internal family systems background. (n.d.). Retrieved from Crowe & Associates: http://www.crowe-associates.co.uk/wp-content/uploads/2017/03/Internal-Family-Systems.pdf

Schwartz, R. (2020, July 2). *Internal family systems and coaching* (episode 62). [Audio podcast]. Retrieved from Coaches Rising: https://www.coachesrising.com/podcast/internal-family-systems-and-coaching/

About IFS. (n.d.). Retrieved from Kirin Alolkoy: https://kirinalolkoy.com/about-ifs/

IFS and coaching. (n.d.). Retrieved from Kirin Alolkoy: https://kirinalolkoy.com/articles/

Schwartz, R. (n.d.). *A brief introduction to the internal family systems model.* Retrieved from Kira Freed: http://www.kirafreedcoaching.com/wp-content/uploads/2010/08/IFS_Intro_Schwartz.pdf

What is internal family systems? (n.d.). Retrieved from the IFS Institute: https://ifs-institute.com

Richard C. Schwartz, PhD—The founder of internal family systems. (n.d.). Retrieved from the IFS Institute: https://ifs-institute.com/about-us/richard-c-schwartz-phd

IFS training programs. (n.d.). Retrieved from the IFS Institute: https://ifs-institute.com/trainings

156   Job Demands-Control Model

Towler, A. (2020, December 9). *The job demand-control-support model: What it is and why it matters to cope with workplace stress.* Retrieved from CQ Net: https://www.ckju.net/en/dossier/job-demand-control-support-model-what-it-and-why-it-matters-cope-workplace-stress

Job demand control model by Robert Karasek. (n.d.). Retrieved from Toolshero: https://www.toolshero.com/human-resources/job-demand-control-model/

Mind Tools Content Team. (n.d.). *The demand-control model of job stress.* Retrieved from MindTools: https://www.mindtools.com/ar3h9eb/the-demand-control-model-of-job-stress

Gameiro, M., Chambel, M.J., & Carvalho, V.S. (2020, November 29). A person-centered approach to the job demands-control model: A multifunctioning test of addictive and buffer hypotheses to explain burnout. *International journal of environmental research and public health, 17*(23), 8871. Retrieved from the National Library of Medicine: https://www.ncbi.nlm.nih.gov/pmc/articles/PMC7730790/

Dowling, J. (2020, June 16). *Job demand control theory and the experience of working remotely during COVID.* Retrieved from LinkedIn Pulse: https://www.linkedin.com/pulse/job-demand-control-theory-experience-working-remotely-jennifer/

157   Job Demands-Resources Model

The JD-R model. (n.d.). Retrieved from MindTools: https://www.mindtools.com/pages/article/job-demands-resources-model.htm

Schaufeli, W. B., & Taris, T. W. (2014). *Chapter 4: A Critical Review of the Job Demands-Resources Model: Implications for Improving Work and Health.* Retrieved from Wilmar Schaufeli: https://www.wilmarschaufeli.nl/publications/Schaufeli/411.pdf

De Carlo, A., Girardi, D., Falco, A., Dal Corso, L., & Di Sipio, A. (2019, May 21). When does work interfere with teachers' private life? An application of the job demands-resources model. *Frontiers in Psychology,* 10: https://www.frontiersin.org/articles/10.3389/fpsyg.2019.01121/full

The JD-R model. (n.d.). Retrieved from Accipio: https://www.accipio.com/eleadership/mod/wiki/view.php?id=1929

Tummers, L. G., & Bakker, A. B. (2021, September 30). Leadership and job demands-resources theory: A systematic review. *Frontiers in Psychology,* 12: https://www.frontiersin.org/articles/10.3389/fpsyg.2021.722080/full

158   John Dewey's Reflective Thinking

Farra, H. (1988, March). The reflective thought process: John Dewey revisited. *The Journal of Creative Behavior*, 22(1), 1–8. Retrieved from Wiley Online Library: https://onlinelibrary.wiley.com/doi/abs/10.1002/j.2162-6057.1988.tb01338.x

Reflective thinking: RT. (n.d.). Retrieved from the University of Hawai'i: https://www.hawaii.edu/intlrel/pols382/Reflective%20Thinking%20-%20UH/reflection.html

Reflective thinking. (n.d.). Retrieved from Lumen Learning: https://lumen.instructure.com/courses/218897/pages/linkedtext54355?module_item_id=5007253

Porntaweekul, S., Raksasataya, S., & Nethanomsak, T. (2016, March 23). Developing reflective thinking instructional model for enhancing students' desirable learning outcomes, *Educational Research and Reviews*, 11(6), 238–251. Retrieved from ERIC Educational Resource Center: https://files.eric.ed.gov/fulltext/EJ1094371.pdf

Popova, M. (2014). *How we think: John Dewey on the art of reflection and fruitful curiosity in an age of instant opinions and information overload*. Retrieved from Brainpickings.org: https://www.brainpickings.org/2014/08/18/how-we-think-john-dewey/

Genç, B. (n.d.). *The nature of reflective thinking and its implications for in-service teacher education*. Retrieved from DergiPark: https://dergipark.org.tr/tr/download/article-file/50165

159   John Dewey's Theory of Education

John Dewey's pedagogy: A summary. (2023, February 16). Retrieved from TeachThought: https://www.teachthought.com/learning/pedagogy-john-dewey-summary/

John Dewey. (n.d.). Retrieved from PBS: https://www.pbs.org/onlyateacher/john.html

Piedra, A. M. (2018, February 1). *The tragedy of American education: The role of John Dewey*. Retrieved from The Institute of World Politics: https://www.iwp.edu/articles/2018/02/01/the-tragedy-of-american-education-the-role-of-john-dewey/

Cherry, K. (2023, July 25). *Biography of John Dewey*. Retrieved from Verywell Mind: https://www.verywellmind.com/john-dewey-biography-1859-1952-2795515

Sikandar, A. (2016, February). John Dewey and his philosophy of education. *Journal of Education and Educational Development*, 2(2), 191. Retrieved from ResearchGate: https://www.researchgate.net/publication/314967156_John_Dewey_and_His_Philosophy_of_Education/link/58c7f725aca2723ab165bf82/download

Gouinlock, J. S. (2023, October 16). John Dewey: American philosopher and educator. Retrieved from *Britannica*: https://www.britannica.com/biography/John-Dewey

160   Johns' Model for Structured Reflection

Johns model of reflection (MSR). (n.d.). Retrieved from Toolshero.com: https://www.toolshero.com/personal-development/johns-model-of-reflection/

Johns model of reflection. (n.d.). Retrieved from the Reflective Practice Community: https://reflectiononthetin.files.wordpress.com/2013/02/johnsmodelofreflection.pdf

Guide to models of reflection—When and why should you use different ones? (2016, May 2). Retrieved from Lifelong Learning with Occupational Therapy: https://lifelonglearningwithot.wordpress.com/2016/05/02/different-models-of-reflection-using-them-to-help-me-reflect/

Chiplin, J., & Stavric, V. (2017). *Models of reflection*. Retrieved from Physiotherapy New Zealand: https://pnz.org.nz/Attachment?Action=Download&Attachment_id=770

Models of reflection. (n.d.). Retrieved from La Trobe University: https://latrobe.libguides.com/reflectivepractice/models

All Answers Ltd. (2021, February 8). *Reflection theories for nursing practice*. Retrieved from Nursinganswers.net: https://nursinganswers.net/reflections/reflection-theories-for-nursing-practice.php

161   Kaizen

Do, D. (2017, August 5). *What is continuous improvement (Kaizen)?* Retrieved from The Lean Way: https://theleanway.net/what-is-continuous-improvement

Bhasin, H. (2019, January 10). *What is Kaizen—The philosophy of Kaizen explained*. Retrieved from Marketing91: https://www.marketing91.com/kaizen/

Kotelnikov, V. (n.d.). *Problem solving process at Toyota*. Retrieved from Breakthrough e-Coach: http://www.1000ventures.com/business_guide/crosscuttings/problem_solving_toyota_7steps.html

Drever, B. (2015, July 14). *Why Kaizen is superior for rapid problem solving*. Retrieved from the Acuity Institute: https://acuityinstitute.com/why-kaizen/

Kohlman, K. (2013, September 16). *Eight steps to practical problem solving*. Retrieved from Kaizen-News: https://www.kaizen-news.com/eight-steps-practical-problem-solving/

Priyadarshini, I. (2019, July 19). *Kaizen and Kanban: The most desirable problem-solving methods of agile.* Retrieved from Temenos+Agility: https://www.visiontemenos.com/blog/kaizen-and-kanban-the-most-desirable-problem-solving-methods-of-agile

162   Katzenbach and Smith Team Effectiveness Model

Katzenbach and Smith. (n.d.). Retrieved from Praxis Framework Ltd.: https://www.praxisframework.org/en/library/katzenbach-and-smith

Udoagwu, K. (2022, May 28). *6 different team effectiveness models to understand your team better.* Retrieved from Wrike: https://www.wrike.com/blog/6-different-team-effectiveness-models/

Katzenbach, J.R., & Smith, D.K. (1993, April). The discipline of teams. *Harvard Business Review.* https://hbr.org/1993/03/the-discipline-of-teams-2

O'Neill, M. (2018, October 2). *The 8 best team effectiveness models and how they work (with examples).* Retrieved from Samewave Ltd.: https://www.samewave.com/posts/team-effectiveness-models

Kukhnavets, P. (2021, March 9). *What team effectiveness model will make a team perform better?* Retrieved from Hygger LLC.: https://hygger.io/blog/team-effectiveness-model-will-make-team-perform-better/#katzenbach-and-smith-model

Qualities of high-performance teams—Katzenbach and Smith. (2018, August 4). Retrieved from the Team Building Portal: https://www.teambuildingportal.com/articles/effective-teams/qualities-high-performance-teams

163   Kegan's Theory of Adult Development

Morad, N. (2017, September 28). *Part 1: How to be an adult—Kegan's theory of adult development.* Retrieved from Medium: https://medium.com/@NataliMorad/how-to-be-an-adult-kegans-theory-of-adult-development-d63f4311b553

Morad, N. (2017, November 20). *Part 2: How to be an adult—Kegan's theory of adult development.* Retrieved from Medium: https://medium.com/@NataliMorad/part-2-how-to-be-an-adult-kegans-theory-of-adult-development-ddf057b4517b

How consciousness develops adequate complexity to deal with a complex world: The subject-object theory of Robert Kegan. (n.d.). Retrieved from Terry Patten: https://terrypatten.typepad.com/iran/files/KeganEnglish.pdf

Girgis, F., Lee, D. J., Goodarzi, A., & Ditterich, J. (2018, January 23). Toward a neuroscience of adult cognitive development theory. *Frontiers in Neuroscience,* 12: https://www.frontiersin.org/articles/10.3389/fnins.2018.00004/full

Possert, J. (2017, October 29). *The three most relevant stages of human development in the modern world.* Retrieved from the Library of Concepts: https://libraryofconcepts.wordpress.com/2017/10/29/three-most-relevant-stages-of-human-development-nowadays-kegan-13/

164   Keirsey's Four Temperaments

Learn about the four temperaments. (n.d.). Retrieved from the Keirsey Group: https://keirsey.com/temperament-overview/

About Keirsey assessments. (n.d.). Retrieved from the Keirsey Group: https://keirsey.com/assessments/about/

Personality theories and types. (n.d.). Retrieved from Businessballs.com: https://www.businessballs.com/self-awareness/personality-theories-and-types/

Harper, H. (2021, January 22). *What is the Keirsey temperament sorter?* Retrieved from The Career Project: https://www.thecareerproject.org/blog/what-is-the-keirsey-temperament-sorter/

Keirsey temperaments. (n.d.). Retrieved from The Peak Performance Center: https://thepeakperformancecenter.com/educational-learning/learning/preferences/keirsey-temperaments/

Keirsey, D.M. (n.d.). *Keirsey temperament vs. Myers-Briggs types.* Retrieved from the Edge of Order: http://edgeoforder.org/difference.html

Thomas, J. (2020, February 25). *What can the Keirsey temperament sorter reveal about you?* Retrieved from Better Help: https://www.betterhelp.com/advice/temperament/what-can-the-keirsey-temperament-sorter-reveal-about-me/

165   Kelley's Covariation Model

Covariation model. (n.d.). Retrieved from Ifioque.com: https://www.ifioque.com/social-psychology/covariation-theory

Kelley's covariation model. (2023, September 21). Retrieved from Practical Psychology: https://practicalpie.com/kelleys-covariation-model/

McLeod, S. (2023, June 11). *Attribution theory in psychology: Definition & examples.* Retrieved from Simply Psychology: https://www.simplypsychology.org/attribution-theory.html

Shrestha, P. (2017, November 17). *Covariation model.* Retrieved from Psychestudy: https://www.psychestudy.com/social/covariation-model

Kelley's covariation model. (n.d.). Retrieved from Iresearchnet: https://psychology.iresearchnet.com/social-psychology/social-cognition/kelleys-covariation-model/

Babsy, W. (2018, April 4). *Kelley's covariation model*. Retrieved from Wanda Babsy Social Psychology: http://wakandabapsy. blogspot.com/2018/04/kelleys-covariation-model.html

What constitutes a 'jerk'? (2021, February 19). Retrieved from Psych 424 Blog, Pennsylvania State University: https://sites.psu. edu/aspsy/tag/kelleys-covariation-model/

166   Kolb's Experiential Learning Cycle

Chapman, A. (2020, September 30). *Kolb's learning styles*. Retrieved from Businessballs.com: https://www.businessballs.com/ self-awareness/kolbs-learning-styles/

Brown, N. (n.d.). *Reflective model according to Kolb*. Retrieved from Dr. Nicole Brown: https://www.nicole-brown.co.uk/ reflective-model-according-to-kolb/

McLeod, S. (2023, October 24). *Kolb's learning styles and experiential learning cycle*. Retrieved from SimplyPsychology: https:// www.simplypsychology.org/learning-kolb.html

McPheat, S. (2023, August 8). *What are Kolb's learning styles? The 1984 model explained and applied*. Retrieved from Skillshub: https://www.skillshub.com/what-are-kolbs-learning-styles/

The four stage learning cycle by David Kolb. (n.d.). Retrieved from The Training Thinking: https://thetrainingthinking.com/en/the-four-stage-learning-cycle-by-david-kolb/

Kurt, S. (2020, December 28). *Kolb's experiential learning theory and learning styles*. Retrieved from Educational Technology: https://educationaltechnology.net/kolbs-experiential-learning-theory-learning-styles/

David Kolb's learning cycle. (n.d.). Retrieved from the Center for Teaching at the University of Iowa: https://teach.its.uiowa.edu/ sites/teach.its.uiowa.edu/files/docs/docs/David_Kolbs_Learning_Cycle_ed.pdf

What is experiential learning? (n.d.). Retrieved from the Institute for Experiential Learning: https://experientiallearninginstitute. org/resources/what-is-experiential-learning/

Cherry, K. (2022, October 7). *Kolb's theory of learning styles*. Retrieved from Verywellmind.com: https://www.verywellmind. com/kolbs-learning-styles-2795155

167   Kotter's Change Management Theory

The 8 steps for leading change. (n.d.). Retrieved from Kotter Inc.: https://www.kotterinc.com/8-steps-process-for-leading-change/

Juneja, P. (n.d.). *Kotter's 8 step model of change*. Retrieved from Management Study Guide: https://www.managementstudyguide. com/kotters-8-step-model-of-change.htm

How to implement change with Kotter's 8-step change model. (n.d.). Retrieved from Lucidchart: https://www.lucidchart.com/blog/ kotters-8-step-change-model

Kotter, J. P. (1996). *Leading Change*. Harvard Business School Press.

Kotter, J. P. (2011). What leaders really do. *Harvard Business Review: 10 Must Reads on Leadership*. Harvard Business Review Press.

Kotter, J. P. (2011). Leading change. *Harvard Business Review: 10 Must Reads on Change Management*. Harvard Business Review Press.

168   Kübler-Ross Change Curve

Kübler-Ross change curve. (n.d.). Retrieved from the Elisabeth Kübler-Ross Foundation: https://www.ekrfoundation.org/5-stages-of-grief/change-curve/

Kübler-Ross change curve. (n.d.). Retrieved from Change Quest: https://www.changequest.co.uk/resources/kubler-ross-change-curve/

Belyh, A. (2022, January 20). *Understanding the Kübler-Ross change curve*. Retrieved from Cleverism: https://www.cleverism.com/ understanding-kubler-ross-change-curve/

The change curve. (n.d.). Retrieved from the University of Exeter: https://www.exeter.ac.uk/media/universityofexeter/ humanresources/documents/learningdevelopment/the_change_curve.pdf

Malik, P. (2022, February 24). *The Kübler-Ross change curve in the workplace (2023)*. Retrieved from Whatfix: https://whatfix.com/ blog/kubler-ross-change-curve/

169   Kübler-Ross Model

The five stages of grief. (2022, June 7). Retrieved from Psycom: https://www.psycom.net/depression.central.grief.html

Connelly, M. (2020, September 12). *Kubler-Ross five stage model*. Retrieved from the Change Management Coach: https://www. change-management-coach.com/kubler-ross.html

The Kubler-Ross model. (n.d.). Retrieved from Huntington's Disease Society of America: https://hdsa.org/wp-content/ uploads/2015/02/13080.pdf

Clarke, J. (2023, March 15). *How the five stages of grief can help process a loss*. Retrieved from Verywell Mind: https://www.verywellmind.com/five-stages-of-grief-4175361

Kübler-Ross change curve. (n.d.). Retrieved from the Elisabeth Kübler-Ross Foundation: https://www.ekrfoundation.org/5-stages-of-grief/change-curve/

5 stages of grief. (n.d.). Retrieved from the Elisabeth Kübler-Ross Foundation: https://www.ekrfoundation.org/5-stages-of-grief/5-stages-grief/

170   Ladder of Inference

The ladder of inference. (n.d.). Retrieved from Mindtools.com: https://www.mindtools.com/pages/article/newTMC_91.htm

The ladder of inference. (n.d.). Retrieved from The Systems Thinker: https://thesystemsthinker.com/the-ladder-of-inference/

King, L. (2013, September 26). *The ladder of inference: Why we jump to conclusions and how to avoid it*. Retrieved from Synergy Commons: https://synergycommons.net/resources/the-ladder-of-inference/

The ladder of inference. (2023, November 3). Retrieved from Management Consulted: https://managementconsulted.com/the-ladder-of-inference/

The ladder of inference. (n.d.). Retrieved from Skills You Need: https://www.skillsyouneed.com/ips/ladder-of-inference.html

171   Laissez-faire Leadership (LFL)

What is laissez-faire leadership? How autonomy can drive success. (2014, November 25). Retrieved from St. Thomas University: https://online.stu.edu/articles/education/what-is-laissezfaire-leadership.aspx

Cherry, K. (2022, November 14). *What is laissez-faire leadership?* Retrieved from Verwell Mind: https://www.verywellmind.com/what-is-laissez-faire-leadership-2795316

Ainomugisha, G. (n.d.). *Management style: Guide to laissez-faire leadership*. Retrieved from 6Q: https://inside.6q.io/laissez-faire-leadership/

Herrity, J. (2023, February 3). *What is laissez-faire leadership? (Plus advantages and tips)*. Retrieved from Indeed: https://www.indeed.com/career-advice/career-development/laissez-faire-leadership

Five main principles of laissez-faire leadership. (n.d.). Retrieved from Status: https://status.net/articles/laissez-faire-leadership/

What is laissez-faire leadership? (2020, June 29). Retrieved from the Western Governors University: https://www.wgu.edu/blog/what-laissez-faire-leadership2006.html#close

172   Laser Coaching Model

Laser coaching module. (n.d.). Retrieved from the World Coach Institute: http://worldcoachinstitute.homestead.com/1._Laser_Coaching_Module.pdf

Walsh, D. (n.d.). *Laser coaching*. Retrieved from Des Walsh: https://www.deswalsh.com/laser-coaching/

Canfield, J. (n.d.). *8 step laser coaching model*. Retrieved from Jack Canfield: https://www.jackcanfield.com/images/stories/8_Step_Laser_Coaching_Model.pdf

Rentschler, M. (Host). (2020, January 15). *How to laser coach and effectively close a coaching conversation: Jim Smith, PCC. (No. 167)*. [Audio podcast]. Retrieved from the Star Coach Show: https://starcoachshow.com/167-how-to-laser-coach-and-effectively-close-a-coaching-conversation-jim-smith-pcc/

Sherman, T. (2017, March 1). *Laser coaching*. Retrieved from The Sherman Partnership: https://www.tsp-uk.co.uk/leadership-coaching/carrying-out-the-coaching/laser-coaching/

Franklin, M. (n.d.). *Laser-focused coaching*. Retrieved from the Life Coaching Group: https://www.lifecoachinggroup.com/training/lasercoach.php

Coaching model: Laser. (2012, July 2). Retrieved from Coach Campus: https://coachcampus.com/coach-portfolios/coaching-models/hagit-hoffman-laser/

Edgerton, N., & Palmer, S. (2005, December). SPACE: A psychological model for use within cognitive behavioral coaching, therapy, and stress management. *The Coaching Psychologist*, 2(2), 25–31. Retrieved from ResearchGate: https://www.researchgate.net/publication/322509343_SPACE_A_psychological_model_for_use_within_cognitive_behavioural_coaching_therapy_and_stress_management

Laser focused coaching. (n.d.). Retrieved from the Cape Cod Young Professionals Organization: https://capecodyoungprofessionals.org/resources/laser-focused-coaching

173   Lateral Thinking Model

Lateral thinking techniques. (n.d.). Retrieved from the Peak Performance Center: https://thepeakperformancecenter.com/educational-learning/thinking/types-of-thinking-2/lateral-thinking/lateral-thinking-techniques/

Davis, M. (2022, October 10). *The most undervalued problem-solving tool? Lateral thinking*. Retrieved from Big Think: https://bigthink.com/mind-brain/lateral-thinking?rebelltitem=3#rebelltitem3

Lateral thinking (de Bono). (n.d.). Retrieved from the Instructional Design: https://www.instructionaldesign.org/theories/lateral-thinking/

Lateral thinking. (n.d.). Retrieved from Idea Connection: https://www.ideaconnection.com/thinking-methods/lateral-thinking-00012.html

What is lateral thinking? (n.d.). Retrieved from Success at School: https://successatschool.org/advicedetails/609/examples-of-lateral-thinking-skills

Lateral thinking. (n.d.). Retrieved from Edward de Bono Ltd.: https://www.lateralthinking.com

174   Leader-Member Exchange Theory

Leader-member exchange theory (LMX). (n.d.). Retrieved from Toolshero.com: https://www.toolshero.com/management/leader-member-exchange-theory-lmx/

Leader-member exchange theory. (n.d.). Retrieved from Mindtools.com: https://www.mindtools.com/pages/article/leader-member-exchange.htm

Leadership-member exchange theory (LMX). (n.d.). Retrieved from Management Study Guide: https://managementstudyguide.com/lmx-theory.htm

Power, R.L. (2013, September). *Leader-member exchange theory in higher and distance education*. Retrieved from Athabasca University: http://www.irrodl.org/index.php/irrodl/article/view/1582/2631

Burkus, D. (2010, March 11). *Leader-member exchange theory*. Retrieved from Davidburkus.com: https://davidburkus.com/2010/03/leader-member-exchange-theory/

Leader-member exchange (LMX) theory. (n.d.). Retrieved from Changingminds.org: http://changingminds.org/explanations/theories/leader_member_exchange.htm

Caison Bagg, K.A. (2017, October 7). *My understanding of the LMX theory*. Retrieved from Penn State University: https://sites.psu.edu/leadership/2017/10/07/my-understanding-of-the-lmx-theory/

175   Leadership Maturity Framework

Integral Life. (2018, March 20). *The stages of leadership maturity* [Video]. Retrieved from YouTube: https://www.youtube.com/watch?v=jO46PjA__N0

Handelsman, A. (2017, December 3). *Episode 70: Later stages of leadership maturity with Susanne Cook-Greuter* [Audio podcast]. Retrieved from Amiel Handelsman: https://amielhandelsman.com/amiel-show-070-susanne-cook-greuter/

Bronzert, J. (2020, June 5). *Vertical development: The intersection of change and leadership*. Retrieved from Change Management Review: https://www.changemanagementreview.com/vertical-development-the-intersection-of-change-and-leadership-5/

Cook-Greuter, S. (2004). Industrial and commercial training: Making the case for a developmental perspective. *Industrial and Commercial Training*, 36(7), 1–10. Retrieved from Vertical Development: http://www.verticaldevelopment.com/wp-content/uploads/2018/05/1.-Cook-Greuter-Making-the-case-for-a-developmental-perspective.pdf

Cook-Greuter, S., & Sharma, B. (2018, March 18). *The stages of leadership maturity*. Retrieved from Integral Life: https://integrallife.com/stages-leadership-maturity/#

Metcalf, M. (2015, September 21). *Leadership maturity and vertical development*. Retrieved from Innovative Leadership Institute: https://www.innovativeleadershipinstitute.com/leadership-maturity-and-vertical-development/

Metcalf, M. (2016, August 30). What is the path for leadership maturity? *Forbes*. https://www.forbes.com/sites/forbescoachescouncil/2016/08/30/what-is-the-path-for-leadership-maturity/?sh=1b21b7151b6c

Ganti, B. (2017, February 23). *Are you a leader? Find out more about ways to develop maturity*. Retrieved from Integral European Conference: https://integraleuropeanconference.com/2017/02/23/are-you-a-leader-find-out-more-about-ways-to-develop-maturity/

The leadership maturity framework. (n.d.). Retrieved from the Vertical Development Academy: http://www.verticaldevelopment.com

Kowalski, K. (n.d.). *An Introduction to Ego Development Theory by Susanne Cook-Greuter (EDT Summary)*. Retrieved from SLOWW: https://www.sloww.co/ego-development-theory-cook-greuter/

176   Leadership Theories (general entry)

Functional leadership model. (n.d.). Retrieved from Toolshero: https://www.toolshero.com/leadership/functional-leadership-model/

Leadership styles. (n.d.). Retrieved from Businessballs.com: https://www.businessballs.com/leadership-models/

Cherry, K. (2022, May 23). *The major leadership theories*. Retrieved from Verywell Mind: https://www.verywellmind.com/leadership-theories-2795323

177   LEAP Model

Whitten, H. (2011). *Cognitive behavioural coaching techniques for dummies*. Wiley.

178   Learned Helplessness Theory

Cherry, K. (2023, April 11). *What causes learned helplessness?* Retrieved from Verywell Mind: https://www.verywellmind.com/what-is-learned-helplessness-2795326

Nolen, J.L. (2022, September 27). Learned helplessness. Retrieved from *Britannica*: https://www.britannica.com/science/learned-helplessness

Ackerman, C. E. (2018, March 24). *Learned helplessness: Seligman's theory of depression*. Retrieved from PositivePsychology: https://positivepsychology.com/learned-helplessness-seligman-theory-depression-cure/

Maier, S. F., & Seligman, M. E. P. (2016, July). Learned helplessness at fifty: Insights from neuroscience. *Psychological Review*, 123(4), 349–367. Retrieved from the US National Library of Medicine: https://www.ncbi.nlm.nih.gov/pmc/articles/PMC4920136/

Leonard, J. (2023, May 23). *What is learned helplessness?* Retrieved from Medical News Today: https://www.medicalnewstoday.com/articles/325355#theory

Seligman, M. E. P. (1972). *Learned helplessness*. Retrieved from the University of Pennsylvania: https://ppc.sas.upenn.edu/sites/default/files/learnedhelplessness.pdf

Learned helplessness. (n.d.). Retrieved from Psychology Today: https://www.psychologytoday.com/us/basics/learned-helplessness

179   Learned Optimism Theory

Moore, C. (2023, October 13). *Learned optimism: Is Martin Seligman's glass half full?* Retrieved from Positive Psychology: https://positivepsychology.com/learned-optimism/

Cherry, K. (2021, June 28). *Using learned optimism in your life*. Retrieved from Verywellmind.com: https://www.verywellmind.com/learned-optimism-4174101

Baum, E. (2022, December 16). *What is learned optimism?* Retrieved from 7 Summit Pathways: https://7summitpathways.com/blog/learned-optimism/

Popova, M. (n.d.). *Learned optimism: Martin Seligman on happiness, depression, and the meaningful life*. Retrieved from Brainpickings.org: https://www.brainpickings.org/2012/06/28/learned-optimism-martin-seligman/

Zimmerman, J. (n.d.). *Learned optimism*. Retrieved from Cruzio.com: http://www2.cruzio.com/~zdino/psychology/seligman.optimism.htm

180   Learning Organization

Building a learning organization. (2022, September 14). Retrieved from ELM Learning: https://elmlearning.com/blog/what-is-a-learning-organization/

Lannon, C. (n.d.). *Learning organizations: From invention to innovation*. Retrieved from The Systems Thinker: https://thesystemsthinker.com/learning-organizations-from-invention-to-innovation/

Garvin, D. A. (1993, July–August). Building a learning organization. *Harvard Business Review*. https://hbr.org/1993/07/building-a-learning-organization

Chandele, T. (2020). *The journey to become a learning organization*. Retrieved from the Society for Human Resource Management Executive Network: https://www.shrm.org/executive/resources/people-strategy-journal/fall2020/pages/feature-chandele.aspx

Wengroff, J. (2021, July 23). *What is a learning organization?* Retrieved from Cognota: https://cognota.com/blog/what-is-a-learning-organization/

Leadership and the learning organization. (n.d.). Retrieved from Knowledge Management Tools: http://www.knowledge-management-tools.net/leadership-and-the-learning-organization.html

Hill. J. (2021, July 27). *The benefits of a learning organization culture*. Retrieved from Bloomfire: https://bloomfire.com/blog/benefits-learning-organization-culture/

Smith, M.K. (2019, October 19). *The learning organization: Principles, theory, and practice*. Retrieved from Infed: https://infed.org/the-learning-organization/

181   Leavitt's System Model

Leavitt's diamond: Understanding the factors involved in change. (n.d.). Retrieved from Accipio Ltd.: https://www.accipio.com/eleadership/mod/wiki/view.php?id=1837

Tahir, U. (2020, January 10). *What is Leavitt's diamond model?* Retrieved from Change Management Insight: http://changemanagementinsight.com/what-is-leavitts-diamond-model/

Leavitt's alignment model. (n.d.). Retrieved from CIO Wiki: https://cio-wiki.org/wiki/Leavitt%27s_Alignment_Model

Robinson, J. (2019, November 28). *How to use Leavitt's diamond to achieve change.* Retrieved from Flevy Blog: https://flevy.com/blog/how-to-use-leavitts-diamond-to-achieve-change/

Thakur, S. (2011, July 31). *Leavitt's diamond: An interactive approach to change.* Retrieved from Bright Hub Project Management: https://www.brighthubpm.com/change-management/122495-a-look-at-the-components-of-leavitts-diamond/

Leavitt's diamond: An integrated approach to change. (n.d.). From MindTools Club, retrieved from the University of Sao Paulo: https://edisciplinas.usp.br/pluginfile.php/1769799/mod_resource/content/3/texto%2001%20-%20Leavitts%20Diamond%20-%20An%20Integrated%20Approach%20to%20Change.pdf

Leavitt's diamond: An integrated approach to change. (n.d.). Retrieved from Lapaas Digital Marketing Lab: https://lapaas.com/leavitts-diamond-an-integrated-approach-to-change/

Leavitt's diamond. (2016). Retrieved from Management Mania: https://managementmania.com/en/leavitts-diamond

182   Lewin's Behavior Equation

Lewin's behavior equation: A simple model of human behavior. (n.d.). Retrieved from the World of Work Project: https://worldofwork.io/2019/07/lewins-behavior-equation/

Lewin's equation. (n.d.). Retrieved from Psychology Wiki: https://psychology.wikia.org/wiki/Lewin%27s_Equation

Kurt Lewin's psychological field theory. (2020, February 13). Retrieved from Psychology Notes HQ: https://www.psychologynoteshq.com/psychological-field-theory/

Clear, J. (n.d.). *This simple equation reveals how habits shape your health, happiness, and wealth.* Retrieved from James Clear: https://jamesclear.com/lewins-equation

Praveen, SA. (2021, May 27). *The forgotten behavior equation.* Retrieved from Medium: https://medium.com/atypical-psychology/the-forgotten-behavior-equation-part-1-d0d3829dfe3

183   Lewin's Change Management Model

Lewin's change management model. (n.d.). Retrieved from Mindtools.com: https://www.mindtools.com/pages/article/newPPM_94.htm

Raza, M. (2019, November 5). *Lewin's 3 stage model of change explained.* Retrieved from BMC: https://www.bmc.com/blogs/lewin-three-stage-model-change/

Bridges, M. (2019, February 22). *Lewin 3-step change management model: A simple and effective method to institute change that sticks.* Retrieved from Mark Bridges: https://mark-bridges.medium.com/lewin-3-step-change-management-model-a-simple-and-effective-method-to-institute-change-that-sticks-c0274316748d

Hussain, S. T., Lei, S., Akram, T., Haider, M., Hussain, S.H., & Ali, M. (2018, September–December). Kurt Lewin's change model: A critical review of the role of leadership and employee involvement in organizational change. *Journal of Innovation and Knowledge,* 3(3), 123–127, https://www.sciencedirect.com/science/article/pii/S2444569X16300087

Lewin's 3-stage model of change: unfreezing, changing, refreezing. (n.d.). Retrieved from Study.com: https://study.com/academy/lesson/lewins-3-stage-model-of-change-unfreezing-changing-refreezing.html

What makes Lewin's change theory ideal for businesses. (n.d.). Retrieved from Lucidchart.com: https://www.lucidchart.com/blog/lewins-change-theory

Kurt Lewin's change management model: The planned approach to organizational change. (n.d.). Retrieved from Management Study Guide: https://www.managementstudyguide.com/kurt-lewins-change-management-model.htm

Understanding Lewin's change management model. (n.d.). Retrieved from Visual Paradigm Online: https://online.visual-paradigm.com/knowledge/business-design/understand-lewins-change-management-model/

Cummings, S., Bridgman, T., & Brown, K. (2016). Unfreezing change as three steps: Rethinking Kurt Lewin's legacy for change management. *Human Relations,* 69(1), 33–60, https://journals.sagepub.com/doi/10.1177/0018726715577707

184   Lewin's Leadership Styles

Cherry, K. (2023, June 27). *How to lead: 6 leadership styles and frameworks.* Retrieved from Verywellmind.com: https://www.verywellmind.com/leadership-styles-2795312

Lewin's leadership theory explained. (2022, June 2). Retrieved from Leadership & Performance Partners: https://leadershipandperformance.com.au/leadership-development/lewins-leadership-theory-explained/

Leadership styles. (n.d.). Retrieved from Mindtools.com: https://www.mindtools.com/pages/article/newLDR_84.htm

Lewin's leadership styles. (n.d.). Retrieved from Changingminds.org: http://changingminds.org/disciplines/leadership/styles/lewin_style.htm

Scouller, J., & Chapman, A. (2020, September 3). *What is Lewin's 3-style model of leadership?* Retrieved from Businessballs.com: https://www.businessballs.com/leadership-models/leadership-styles-3-style-model-kurt-lewin/

Leadership styles. (n.d.). Retrieved from Lumen Learning: https://courses.lumenlearning.com/wm-organizationalbehavior/chapter/leadership-styles/

185   Likert's Four Management Systems

Likert's management systems. (n.d.). Retrieved from Businessballs.com: https://www.businessballs.com/organisational-culture/likerts-management-systems/

Likert's four systems of management. (n.d.). Retrieved from Business Jargons: https://businessjargons.com/likerts-four-systems-management.html

Four management systems. (2015, October 29). Retrieved from Global NP Solutions: https://globalnpsolutions.com/2015/10/four-management-systems/

Likert's management system. (n.d.). Retrieved from Management Study Guide: https://www.managementstudyguide.com/likerts-management-system.htm

Clayton, M. (2016, November 8). *Rensis Likert: Participative management.* Retrieved from Management Pocketbooks: https://www.pocketbook.co.uk/blog/tag/likerts-four-management-systems/

Management systems. (2018, March 25). Retrieved from Learnmanagement2: https://www.learnmanagement2.com/Likert.htm

Rensis Likert's 4 management systems. (n.d.). Retrieved from Green On The Inside: https://www.greenontheinside.net/rensis-likert-s-4-management-systems-essay-example/

Venkatesh. (n.d.). *Likert's management systems and leadership.* Retrieved from Your Article Library: https://www.yourarticlelibrary.com/leadership/likerts-management-systems-and-leadership/53328

186   Locke's Goal-Setting Theory

Moore, C. (2023, September 20). *What is Locke's goal setting theory of motivation?* Retrieved from Positive Psychology: https://positivepsychology.com/goal-setting-theory/

What is goal-setting theory? (n.d.). Retrieved from Go Strengths: https://gostrengths.com/what-is-goal-setting-theory/

Locke's goal-setting theory. (n.d.). Retrieved from MindTools: https://www.mindtools.com/pages/article/newHTE_87.htm

Cui, Y. (n.d.). *Goal-setting theory.* Retrieved from Pressbooks: https://opentext.wsu.edu/theoreticalmodelsforteachingandresearch/chapter/goal-setting-theory/

187   Managerial Grid Model

The Blake Mouton grid. (n.d.). Retrieved from MindTools: https://www.mindtools.com/pages/article/newLDR_73.htm

De Bruin, L. (2020, March 22). *Blake and Mouton managerial grid: A behavioral approach towards management and leadership.* Retrieved from B2U: https://www.business-to-you.com/blake-mouton-managerial-grid/

Juneja, P. (n.d.). *Blake and Mouton's managerial grid.* Retrieved from Management Study Guide: https://managementstudyguide.com/blake-mouton-managerial-grid.htm

Blake and Mouton leadership grid. (n.d.). Retrieved from Make A Dent Leadership: https://makeadentleadership.com/blake-and-mouton/

Blake and Mouton's managerial grid. (n.d.). Retrieved from Business Jargons: https://businessjargons.com/blake-moutons-managerial-grid.html

Blake and Mouton's managerial grid: A simple summary. (n.d.). Retrieved from the World of Work Project: https://worldofwork.io/2019/03/blake-and-moutons-managerial-grid/

Blake and Mouton managerial grid. (n.d.). Retrieved from Businessballs.com: https://www.businessballs.com/leadership-models/behavioural-leadership-managerial-grid-blake-and-mouton/

188   Maslow's Hierarchy of Needs

McLeod, S. (2023, October 24). *Maslow's hierarchy of needs.* Retrieved from SimplyPsychology: https://www.simplypsychology.org/maslow.html

Kenrick, D. T., Griskevicius, V., Neuberg, S. L., & Schaller, M. (2010, May). Renovating the pyramid of needs: Contemporary extensions built upon ancient foundations. *Perspectives on psychological science: A journal of the Association for Psychological Science*, 5(3), 292–314. Retrieved from the US National Library of Medicine: https://www.ncbi.nlm.nih.gov/pmc/articles/PMC3161123/

Cherry, K. (2023, November 7). *Is Maslow's hierarchy of needs still relevant?* Retrieved from Verywell Mind: https://www.verywellmind.com/updating-maslows-hierarchy-of-needs-2795269

Cherry, K. (2022, August 14). *Maslow's hierarchy of needs*. Retrieved from Verywell Mind: https://www.verywellmind.com/what-is-maslows-hierarchy-of-needs-4136760

Render, J. (2019, June 20). *Abraham Maslow's expanded hierarchy of needs*. Retrieved from Agile-Mercurial: https://agile-mercurial.com/2019/06/20/abraham-maslows-expanded-hierarchy-of-needs/

Hopper, E. (2020, February 24). *Maslow's hierarchy of needs explained*. Retrieved from ThoughtCo.: https://www.thoughtco.com/maslows-hierarchy-of-needs-4582571

MasterClass. (2021, June 7). *A guide to the 5 levels of Maslow's hierarchy of needs*. Retrieved from MasterClass: https://www.masterclass.com/articles/a-guide-to-the-5-levels-of-maslows-hierarchy-of-needs#deficiency-needs-vs-growth-needs-on-maslows-hierarchy

Kremer, W., & Hammond, C. (2013, September 1). *Abraham Maslow and the pyramid that beguiled business*. Retrieved from the BBC: https://www.bbc.com/news/magazine-23902918

CFI Team. (2022, April 21). *Maslow's hierarchy of needs*. Retrieved from the Corporate Finance Institute: https://corporatefinanceinstitute.com/resources/knowledge/other/maslows-hierarchy-of-needs/

Burton, N. (2012, May 23). *Our hierarchy of needs*. Retrieved from Psychology Today: https://www.psychologytoday.com/us/blog/hide-and-seek/201205/our-hierarchy-needs

189 Mayo's Motivation Theory

Peek, S. (2023, March 23). *Management theory of Elton Mayo*. Retrieved from Business.com: https://www.business.com/articles/management-theory-of-elton-mayo/

Minute Tools Content Team. (2018, May). *Mayo's motivation theory | Hawthorne effect*. Retrieved from Expert Program Management: https://expertprogrammanagement.com/2018/05/mayos-motivation-theory-hawthorn-effect/

Ward, P. (2021, August 29). *Elton Mayo management theories*. Retrieved from NanoGlobals: https://nanoglobals.com/glossary/elton-mayo-management-theories/

Motivation – Mayo (Human relations school). (2021, March 22). Retrieved from Tutor2U: https://www.tutor2u.net/business/reference/motivation-mayo-human-relations-school

Mahesh. (2023, June 3). *What is human relations theory?* Retrieved from BokasTutor: https://bokastutor.com/human_relations_theory/

Elton Mayo's theory of management explained. (n.d.). Retrieved from Health Research Funding: https://healthresearchfunding.org/elton-mayos-theory-of-management-explained/

Gordon, J. (2023, October 20). *Human relations theory of management—Explained*. Retrieved from The Business Professor: https://thebusinessprofessor.com/en_US/management-leadership-organizational-behavior/human-relations-theory-of-management

190 McClelland's Theory of Needs

McClelland's human motivation theory. (n.d.). Retrieved from MindTools: https://www.mindtools.com/pages/article/human-motivation-theory.htm

McClelland's achievement-based motivational theory and models. (2020, September 3). Retrieved from Businessballs.com: https://www.businessballs.com/improving-workplace-performance/david-mcclelland-achievement-motivation/

Kukreja, S. (n.d.). *McClelland's theory of needs*. Retrieved from Management Study HQ: https://www.managementstudyhq.com/mcclellands-theory-of-needs-power-achievement-and-affiliation.html

McClelland's acquired needs motivation theory. (n.d.). Retrieved from the World of Work Project: https://worldofwork.io/2019/02/mcclellands-motivation-theory/

Beecher A. (2020, April 2). *McClelland's achievement motivation theory*. Retrieved from Medium: https://medium.com/@aleiabeecher/mcclellands-achievement-motivation-theory-5ad1f867953

McClelland's achievement and acquired needs theory. (n.d.). Retrieved from YourCoach BVBA: https://www.yourcoach.be/en/employee-motivation-theories/mcclelland-achievement-and-acquired-needs-motivation-theory.php

McClelland's theory of needs. (n.d.). Retrieved from NetMBA: http://www.netmba.com/mgmt/ob/motivation/mcclelland/

McClelland's needs theory. (n.d.). Retrieved from Business Jargons: https://businessjargons.com/mcclellands-needs-theory.html

191 McGrath's Time, Interaction, and Performance Theory (TIP)

Forte, A., Kittur, N., Larco, V., Zhu, H., Bruckman, A., & Kraut, R. (2012, February). *Coordination and beyond: Social functions of groups in open content production*. Retrieved from Andrea Forte: http://andreaforte.net/ForteKitturCSCW12.pdf

McGrath's time, interaction, and performance theory (TIP). (n.d.). Retrieved from Ebrary: https://ebrary.net/3070/management/mcgraths_time_interaction_performance_theory

Beranek, P. (2012). *Time, interaction, and performance in online student teams: A training approach*. Retrieved from IATED Digital

Library: https://library.iated.org/view/BERANEK2012TIM

Grudin, J. (n.d.). *McGrath and the behaviors of groups (BOGs)*. Retrieved from Penn State University: http://citeseerx.ist.psu.edu/viewdoc/download?doi=10.1.1.188.2253&rep=rep1&type=pdf

192   McKinsey 7S Model

McKinsey 7-S framework: Making every part of your organization work in harmony. (n.d.). Retrieved from MindTools: https://www.mindtools.com/pages/article/newSTR_91.htm

Enduring ideas: The 7S framework. (2008, March 1). Retrieved from McKinsey & Company: https://www.mckinsey.com/business-functions/strategy-and-corporate-finance/our-insights/enduring-ideas-the-7-s-framework#

Cost transformation model: McKinsey framework. (2018, August 2). Retrieved from the Chartered Global Management Accountant: https://www.cgma.org/resources/tools/cost-transformation-model/mckinsey-framework.html

Jurevicius, O. (2023, April 13). *McKinsey 7S model*. Retrieved from Strategic Management Insight: https://strategicmanagementinsight.com/tools/mckinsey-7s-model-framework.html

What is the McKinsey 7S model? (n.d.). Retrieved from the Corporate Finance Institute: https://corporatefinanceinstitute.com/resources/knowledge/strategy/mckinsey-7s-model/

What is the McKinsey 7S model? (n.d.). Retrieved from LucidChart: https://www.lucidchart.com/blog/mckinsey-7s-model

McKinsey 7S Model framework. (n.d.). Retrieved from OCM Solution: https://www.airiodion.com/mckinsey-7s-model-framework/

Athuraliya, A. (2023, January 10). *The easy guide to the McKinsey 7S model*. Retrieved from Creately: https://creately.com/blog/diagrams/mckinsey-7s-model-guide/

193   Merrill-Reid Social Styles

The social style model. (n.d.). Retrieved from the TRACOM Group: https://tracom.com/social-style-training/model

Farrington, J. (2013, May 13). *The 4 social styles*. Retrieved from ALM Global LLC.: https://www.thinkadvisor.com/2013/05/13/the-4-social-styles/

Merrill-Reid social personality styles in the world of work. (n.d.). Retrieved from the World of Work Project: https://worldofwork.io/2019/06/merrill-reid-social-personality-styles/

Clayton, M. (2017, April 18). *David Merrill & Roger Reid: Social styles*. Retrieved from Management Pocketbooks: https://www.pocketbook.co.uk/blog/2017/04/18/david-merrill-roger-reid-social-styles/

Social styles. (n.d.). Retrieved from Changing Minds: http://changingminds.org/explanations/preferences/social_styles.htm

Trigon Systems Consultants. (n.d.). *Social styles*. Retrieved from SoftEd-Skills Consulting Group: https://www.softed.com/assets/Uploads/Resources/Business-Analysis/Social-styles.pdf

Social style. (n.d.). Retrieved from Psychology Wiki: https://psychology.wikia.org/wiki/Social_style

194   Mind Styles Model

Gregorc mind styles model. (n.d.). Retrieved from The Peak Performance Center: https://thepeakperformancecenter.com/educational-learning/learning/preferences/learning-styles/gregorc-mind-styles-model/

Mind Styles—Anthony Gregorc. (n.d.). Retrieved from SUNY Cortland: https://web.cortland.edu/andersmd/learning/gregorc.htm

Harrington-Atkinson, T. (2017, November 8). *Gregorc mind styles*. Retrieved from Tracy Harrington-Atkinson: http://tracyharringtonatkinson.com/gregorc-mind-styles-model/

Gregorc learning styles. (n.d.). Retrieved from Study.com: https://study.com/academy/lesson/gregorc-learning-styles.html

Gregorc, A. (n.d.). *Anthony F. Gregorc, PhD (Books)*. Retrieved from Anthony Gregorc: https://www.anthonyfgregorc.com/publications

Gregorc, Anthony—The mind styles model. (2008). Retrieved from The Structure of Concern Project: http://paei.wikidot.com/gregorc-anthony-the-mind-styles-model

195   Mitroff's Crisis Management Model and Portfolio Model

Marker, A. (2020, July 20). *Models and theories to improve crisis management*. Retrieved from Smartsheet: https://www.smartsheet.com/content/crisis-management-model-theories

A need for more crisis management knowledge. (n.d.). Retrieved from Ongoing Crisis Communication: https://in.sagepub.com/sites/default/files/upm-assets/59529_book_item_59529.pdf

Jabeen, R. (2018). *Organizational crisis management*. Retrieved from the University of Vaasa: https://osuva.uwasa.fi/bitstream/handle/10024/1003/osuva_8004.pdf?sequence=1&isAllowed=y

Pauchant, T., Mitroff, I., & Lagadec, P. (2008). Toward a systematic crisis management strategy: Learning from the best examples in the US, Canada, and France. In Arjen Boin (Ed.), *Crisis management* (Vol. 2). Sage. Retrieved from The Institute of Risk Management: https://theisrm.org/public-library/Boin%20-%20Crisis%20Management%20(Book).pdf

Boudreaux, B. (2005). *Exploring a multi-stage model of crisis management: Utilities, hurricanes, and contingency.* Retrieved from the University of Florida: https://ufdcimages.uflib.ufl.edu/UF/E0/01/04/86/00001/boudreaux_b.pdf

Mitroff, I., Shrivastava, P., & Udwadia, F. (1987). Effective crisis management. *The Academy of Management Executive,* 1(4), 283–292. Retrieved from Researchgate: https://www.researchgate.net/publication/285064922_Effective_Crisis_Management

Dinkin, D. (2007). *Organizational crises in local North Carolina public health agencies: A crisis typology and assessment of organizational preparedness* [Dissertation]. University of North Carolina at Chapel Hill. Retrieved from Core: https://core.ac.uk/download/pdf/210604919.pdf

Shrivastava, P., & Mitroff, I. (1987, Spring). Strategic management of corporate crises. *Columbia Journal of World Business,* 5–11. Retrieved from Athens University of Economics and Business: http://www2.aueb.gr/users/siomkos/docs/articles/shrivastava_mitroff.pdf

Wang, J. (2007). *Organizational learning and crisis management.* Retrieved from https://files.eric.ed.gov/fulltext/ED504551.pdf

Commonwealth Club. (2010, February 24). *Dirty rotten strategies: How we trick ourselves and others into solving the wrong problems precisely* [Video]. Retrieved from WordPress: https://daviding.wordpress.com/2016/04/03/ian-mitroff-type-3-errors-type-4-errors/

196   Morphological Analysis

Morphological analysis—A problem solving method by an astrophysicist who discovered dark matter. (2018, August 1). Retrieved from North Star: https://northstar.greyb.com/morphological-analysis/

Lang, L. (2020, December 27). *Morphological Zwicky boxes vs feature models.* Retrieved from Medium: https://recontextualization.medium.com/morphological-zwicky-boxes-vs-feature-model-2348e5d978ad

Morphological analysis. (n.d.). Retrieved from IdeaConnection: https://www.ideaconnection.com/thinking-methods/morphological-analysis-00026.html

Morphological analysis (problem-solving). (n.d.). Retrieved from Psychology Wiki: https://psychology.fandom.com/wiki/Morphological_analysis_(problem-solving)#Illustration_of_the_need_for_Morphological_Analysis

Markov, S. (2018, January 28). *Morphological analysis.* Retrieved from Genvive: https://geniusrevive.com/en/morphological-analysis/

Barbu, B., & Purton, S. (2017). *Morphological analysis – Big words, simple idea.* Retrieved from the North Atlantic Treaty Organization via Google: https://www.google.com/url?sa=t&rct=j&q=&esrc=s&source=web&cd=&cad=rja&uact=8&ved=2a-hUKEwj6vKWfvbj9AhUXFVkFHWTWA384ChAWegQIBxAB&url=https%3A%2F%2Fwww.sto.nato.int%2F-publications%2FSTO%2520Meeting%2520Proceedings%2FSTO-MP-SAS-OCS-ORA-2017%2FMP-SAS-OCS-ORA-2017-03-3.pdf&usg=AOvVaw1fRdCW7T_aRqMVK1LXhUlC

197   Motivation Theories (general entry)

Souders, B. (2023, September 19). *20 most popular theories of motivation in psychology.* Retrieved from Positive Psychology: https://positivepsychology.com/motivation-theories-psychology/

Motivation theories. (n.d.). Retrieved from Knowledge Hut: https://www.knowledgehut.com/tutorials/project-management/motivation-theories

Sands, L. (2023, August 31). *What are motivation theories?* Retrieved from Breathe: https://www.breathehr.com/en-gb/blog/topic/employee-engagement/what-are-motivation-theories

Chapter 5: Theories of motivation. (2012). Retrieved from Saylor Academy: https://saylordotorg.github.io/text_organizational-behavior-v1.1/s09-theories-of-motivation.html

Theories about motivation. (n.d.). Retrieved from Lumen Learning: https://courses.lumenlearning.com/waymaker-psychology/chapter/theories-about-motivation/

198   Motivational Interviewing

Understanding motivational interviewing. (2019). Retrieved from the Motivational Interviewing Network of Trainers: https://motivationalinterviewing.org/understanding-motivational-interviewing

Center for Substance Abuse Treatment. *Enhancing motivation for change in substance abuse treatment.* (1999). (Treatment Improvement Protocol (TIP) Series, No. 35.) Chapter 3—Motivational interviewing as a counseling style. Retrieved from the National Center for Biotechnology Information: https://www.ncbi.nlm.nih.gov/books/NBK64964/

Hall, K., Gibbie, T., & Lubman, D. (2012, September). Motivational interviewing techniques: Facilitating behaviour change in the general practice setting. *Australian Family Physician,* 41(9), 660–667. Retrieved from The Royal Australian College of General Practitioners: https://www.racgp.org.au/afp/2012/september/motivational-interviewing-techniques/

A Definition of motivational interviewing. (n.d.). Retrieved from Ozaukee County: https://www.co.ozaukee.wi.us/DocumentCenter/View/8185/Definition-of-Motivation-Interviewing?bidId=

Souders, B. (2023, September 19). *17 motivational interviewing questions and skills.* Retrieved from Positive Psychology: https://positivepsychology.com/motivational-interviewing/

CrossFit. (2022, March 4). *Motivational interviewing for behavior change with Dr. Stephen Rollnick* [Video]. Retrieved from YouTube: https://www.youtube.com/watch?v=YKwmjYDIa98

199   Myers-Briggs Personality Model

MBTI certification. (n.d.). Retrieved from the Myers-Briggs Company: https://www.themyersbriggs.com/en-US/Get-Certified/MBTI-Certification

Myers-Briggs overview. (n.d.). Retrieved from the Myers & Briggs Foundation: https://www.myersbriggs.org/my-mbti-personality-type/mbti-basics/

Cunningham, L. (2012, December 14). Myers-Briggs: Does it pay to know your type? *The Washington Post:* https://www.washingtonpost.com/national/on-leadership/myers-briggs-does-it-pay-to-know-your-type/2012/12/14/eaed51ae-3fcc-11e2-bca3-aadc9b7e29c5_story.html

Cherry, K. (2023, October 31). *How the Myers-Briggs type indicator works.* Retrieved from Verywell Mind: https://www.verywellmind.com/the-myers-briggs-type-indicator-2795583

Personality puzzler: Is there any science behind Myers-Briggs? (2018, November 8). Retrieved from the University of Pennsylvania Wharton School of Business: https://knowledge.wharton.upenn.edu/article/does-the-myers-briggs-test-really-work/

200   Neuroscience-Based Coaching

North America brain-based coaching program. (n.d.). Retrieved from the NeuroLeadership Institute: https://individuals.neuroleadership.com/brain-based-coaching

Beverly, D. (2015, January 1). *The what, why, and how of brain-based coaching.* Retrieved from Dan Beverly: https://danbeverly.com/brain-based-coaching/

Introduction to brain-based coaching. (n.d.). Retrieved from Life Coach Training: https://www.lifecoachtraining.com/programs/all_courses/introduction-to-brain-based-coaching

Heyns-Nell, C. (2023). *Brain-based coaching and mentoring.* Retrieved from Udemy: https://www.udemy.com/course/brain-based-coaching-and-mentoring/

UCDavis CPE-Human Services. (2019, April 29). *Brain-based coaching* [Video]. Retrieved from YouTube: https://www.youtube.com/watch?v=Hgnb8aaATnE

ICF accredited coach certification and applied neuroscience training. (n.d.). Retrieved from the Brain First Training Institute: https://www.brainfirsttraininginstitute.com

Course 3: Neuroscience tools for coaches. (n.d.). Retrieved from the School of Coaching Mastery: https://www.schoolofcoachingmastery.com/coaching-with-neuroscience

Rock, D. (2006). A brain-based approach to coaching. *The International Journal of Coaching in Organizations,* 4(2), 32–44. Retrieved from David Rock: https://www.google.com/url?sa=t&rct=j&q=&esrc=s&source=web&cd=&cad=r-ja&uact=8&ved=2ahUKEwivv739zIfuAhWGVN8KHa9qCmA4ChAWMAV6BAgREAI&url=https%3A%2F%2Fresearchportal.coachfederation.org%2FDocument%2FPdf%2F2886.pdf&usg=AOvVaw3zy_-MKKC_Lx-oovQaAFk6

McKay, S. (2018, July 29). *7 principles of neuroscience every coach and therapist should know.* Retrieved from Dr. Sarah McKay: https://drsarahmckay.com/7-principles-neuroscience-every-coach-know/

201   Newcomb's Symmetry Theory (NST)

Heider's balance, Newcomb's symmetry, Osgood's congruity, and cognitive dissonance theories. (2012, September 17). Retrieved from Mass Communication Talk: https://www.masscommunicationtalk.com/heiders-balance-newcombs-symmetry-osgoods-congruity-cognitive-dissonance-theories.html

The Newcomb's model. (n.d.). Retrieved from Communication Theory: https://www.communicationtheory.org/the-newcomb's-model/

EduMania. (2018, November 22). *Newcomb's ABX symmetry model explained* [Video]. Retrieved from YouTube: https://www.youtube.com/watch?v=tQXYCmuqd88

202   Nudge Theory

What is nudge theory. (n.d.). Retrieved from Businessballs.com: https://www.businessballs.com/improving-workplace-performance/nudge-theory/

Prichard, S. (2018, April 20). *10 examples of nudge theory*. Retrieved from Skip Prichard: https://www.skipprichard.com/10-examples-of-nudge-theory/

Nudge. (n.d.). Retrieved from Behavioraleconomics.com: https://www.behavioraleconomics.com/resources/mini-encyclopedia-of-be/nudge/

Chu, B. (2018, January 13). What is nudge theory and why should we care? Explaining Richard Thaler's Nobel economics prize-winning concept. *The Independent*: https://www.independent.co.uk/news/business/analysis-and-features/nudge-theory-richard-thaler-meaning-explanation-what-it-nobel-economics-prize-winner-2017-a7990461.html

Hansen, P.G. (n.d.). *What is nudging?* Retrieved from the Behavioral Science & Policy Association: https://behavioralpolicy.org/what-is-nudging/

Choice architecture. (n.d.). Retrieved from Economics Help: https://www.economicshelp.org/blog/glossary/choice-architecture/

Sodha, S. (2020, April 26). Nudge theory is a poor substitute for hard science in matters of life or death. *The Guardian*: https://www.theguardian.com/commentisfree/2020/apr/26/nudge-theory-is-a-poor-substitute-for-science-in-matters-of-life-or-death-coronavirus

Groenewegen, A. (n.d.). *Nudging explained*. Retrieved from Behavioural Design: https://suebehaviouraldesign.com/nudging/

Sludge: When nudging is nefarious. (n.d.). Retrieved from the World of Work Project: https://worldofwork.io/2020/06/sludge/

203 OASIS Conversation

OASIS conversations. (n.d.). Retrieved from Potentials: https://oasisconversations.com/the-course/

Van Eron, A. (2016, November 21). *Cultivate an open mindset*. Retrieved from the Lead Change Group: https://leadchangegroup.com/cultivate-an-open-mindset/

Van Eron, A. (2016, October 18). *Are you open-minded?* Retrieved from the Lead Change Group: https://leadchangegroup.com/are-you-open-minded/

OASIS moves. (n.d.). Retrieved from Potentials: https://potentials.com/services/open-minded-conversations-oasis/

Kiger, P. (2016, November 2). *Featured instigator: Ann Van Eron*. Retrieved from the Lead Change Group: https://leadchangegroup.com/featured-instigator-ann-van-eron/

204 OODA Loop

Luft, A. (2020, March 17). *The OODA loop and the half-beat*. Retrieved from the Strategy Bridge: https://thestrategybridge.org/the-bridge/2020/3/17/the-ooda-loop-and-the-half-beat

The OODA loop: How fighter pilots make fast and accurate decisions. (n.d.). Retrieved from Farnam Street: https://fs.blog/ooda-loop/

Lewis, S. (2022, July). *OODA loop*. Retrieved from Tech Target: https://www.techtarget.com/searchcio/definition/OODA-loop

McKay, B., & McKay, K. (2023, July 1). *The tao of Boyd: How to master the OODA loop*. Retrieved from Art of Manliness: https://www.artofmanliness.com/character/behavior/ooda-loop/

The OODA loop. (n.d.). Retrieved from The Decision Lab: https://thedecisionlab.com/reference-guide/computer-science/the-ooda-loop/

Hightower, T. (n.d.). *Boyd's OODA loop and how we use it*. Retrieved from Tactical Response: https://www.tacticalresponse.com/blogs/library/18649427-boyd-s-o-o-d-a-loop-and-how-we-use-it

205 Organizational Support Theory

POS: Organizational support theory. (n.d.). Retrieved from Job Attitudes: http://whatsyourjobattitude.weebly.com/organizational-support-theory.html

Caesens, G., Stinglhamber, F., Demoulin, S., De Wilde, M., & Mierop, A. (2019, January). Perceived organizational support and workplace conflict: The mediating role of failure-related trust. *Frontiers in Psychology, 9*: https://www.frontiersin.org/articles/10.3389/fpsyg.2018.02704/full

Giorgi, G., Dubin, D., & Perez, J. F. (2016). Perceived organizational support for enhancing welfare at work: A regression tree model. *Frontiers in Psychology, 7*, 1770. Retrieved from the US National Library of Medicine: https://www.ncbi.nlm.nih.gov/pmc/articles/PMC5186753/

206 OSKAR Coaching Model

The OSKAR coaching framework. (n.d.). Retrieved from Mindtools: https://www.mindtools.com/pages/article/oskar-coaching-framework.htm

The OSKAR coaching model: A simple summary. (n.d.). Retrieved from World of Work Project: https://worldofwork.io/2019/08/the-oskar-coaching-model/

OSKAR coaching model: A solutions focused approach. (n.d.). Retrieved from Personal Coaching Information: https://www.personal-coaching-information.com/oskar-coaching-model.html

Blackbyrn, S. (2023, October 8). *OSKAR coaching model: The definitive guide.* Retrieved from the Coach Foundation: https://coachfoundation.com/blog/definitive-guide-to-oskar-coaching-model/

McKergow, M., & Clarke, J. (n.d.). *Coaching with OSKAR.* Retrieved from The Centre for Solutions Focus at Work: https://sfwork.com/pdf/Coaching%20with%20OSKAR.pdf

The OSKAR model. (n.d.). Retrieved from Free Management Books: http://www.free-management-ebooks.com/faqch/models-11.htm

OSKAR—Solutions focused coaching model. (n.d.). Retrieved from Inspire: https://www.inspireculture.org.uk/documents/914/Empowering_Learners_-_Coaching_Models_and_Questioning_Approaches.pdf

Palmer, S. (2008). The PRACTICE model of coaching: Towards a solution-focused approach. *Coaching Psychology International: Society for Coaching Psychology*, 1(1), 4–8. Retrieved from Crowe Associates Ltd.: http://www.crowe-associates.co.uk/wp-content/uploads/2013/10/The_PRACTICE_model_of_coaching_towards_a_solution-focused_approach-2.pdf

207   OUTCOMES Coaching Model

Our vision. (n.d.). Retrieved from Partners Team Development: https://www.partnersteamdevelopment.com/vision

Warner, J. (2012, November 2). *Coaching process models.* Retrieved from Ready to Manage: https://blog.readytomanage.com/coaching-process-models/

Mackintosh, A. (2003). *The successful coaching manager: A manager's guide to coaching individuals and teams effectively.* Troubador Publishing Ltd. Retrieved from Google: https://www.google.com/books/edition/The_Successful_Coaching_Manager/3ATDCfgmc3QC?hl=en&gbpv=1&printsec=frontcover

Allison, S., & Harbour, M. (2009). *The coaching toolkit: A practical guide for your school.* Sage Publishing: https://uk.sagepub.com/sites/default/files/upm-binaries/26777_01_Allison_&_Harbour_CH_01.pdf

Biro, K. (2019, August 23). *Coaching models overview.* Retrieved from Coach Campus: https://coachcampus.com/coach-portfolios/research-papers/kincso-biro-an-overview-of-coaching-models/

Mackintosh, A., & compiled by Watson, K. (n.d.). *Coaching models: A compilation of coaching models, tools, and techniques.* Retrieved from My Own Coach via Google: https://www.google.com/url?sa=t&rct=j&q=&esrc=s&source=web&cd=&cad=rja&uact=8&ved=2ahUKEwiA9LL5wYT2AhWPd98KHfxlBMcQFnoECCwQAQ&url=https%3A%2F%2Fcpb-ap-se2.wpmucdn.com%2Fglobal2.vic.edu.au%2Fdist%2F9%2F34331%2Ffiles%2F2013%2F11%2FCoaching-Models-2cb4q32.doc&usg=AOvVaw3QaEkqTLBDcQlMNZtsI6d1

208   Participative Leadership Theory

Cherry, K. (2022, May 23). *The major leadership theories.* Retrieved from Verywell Mind: https://www.verywellmind.com/leadership-theories-2795323

What is participative leadership? (2021, February 19). Retrieved from Western Governors University: https://www.wgu.edu/blog/participative-leadership2102.html#close

Belyh, A. (2020, July 25). *Participative leadership guide: Definition, qualities, pros & cons, examples.* Retrieved from Cleverism: https://www.cleverism.com/participative-leadership-guide/

Participative leadership theory and decision-making style. (n.d.). Retrieved from Psychologia: https://psychologia.co/participative-leadership/

What is participative leadership theory. (2022, July 21). Retrieved from Indeed: https://www.indeed.com/career-advice/career-development/participative-leadership-theory

Participative leadership theories. (n.d.). Retrieved from TechnoFunc: https://www.technofunc.com/index.php/leadership-skills-2/leadership-theories/item/participative-leadership-theories

Root III, G. (2019, March 25). *The advantages of participative leadership.* Retrieved from Chron: https://smallbusiness.chron.com/advantages-participative-leadership-17629.html

209   Path-Goal Theory

Path-goal leadership theory. (n.d.). Retrieved from Performance Juxtaposition Site: http://www.nwlink.com/~donclark/leader/lead_path_goal.html

Anderson, P. (2016, June 29). *What is path goal theory?* Retrieved from Pennsylvania State University: https://sites.psu.edu/leadership/2016/06/29/what-is-path-goal-theory/

Contingency theory of leadership: Definition and models. (2023, March 10). Retrieved from Indeed: https://www.indeed.com/career-advice/career-development/contingency-theory-of-leadership

The contingency theory of leadership explained. (2015, January 9). Retrieved from Villanova University: https://www.villanovau. com/resources/leadership/leadership-and-contingency-theory/

210   Pendleton Feedback Model

Burgess, A., van Diggele, C., Roberts, C., & Mellis, C. (2020, December). Feedback in the clinical setting. *BMC Medical Education*, 20 (Suppl 2), 460. https://doi.org/10.1186/s12909-020-02280-5. Retrieved from US National Library of Medicine: https://www.ncbi.nlm.nih.gov/pmc/articles/PMC7712594/

Thorn, M. (2017, January 3). *The Pendleton method of giving feedback.* Retrieved from Exult: https://www.exult.co.nz/articles/ giving-feedback/

Chowdhury, R., & Kalu, G. (2004). *Learning to give feedback in medical education.* Retrieved from the Royal College of Obstetricians and Gynecologists: https://static1.squarespace.com/static/5cca2e3af8135a72cc6b2016/t/5e7e2476075b34 6ec3a382bd/1585325174782/SET+GO+Method+of+Giving+Feedback.pdf

Pendleton's rules. (n.d.). Retrieved from GP Training: https://www.gp-training.net/feedback/pendletons-rules-feedback/

Brown, C. (2021, November 24). *Improve employee feedback conversations with the Pendleton feedback model.* Retrieved from IntelliHR: https://intellihr.com/en-us/insights/pendleton-feedback-model

A method of delivering a great feedback session—Pendleton's rules. (n.d.). Retrieved from Coach Zone: https://www.thecoach.zone/a-method-of-delivering-a-great-feedback-session-pendletons-rules/

Feedback: Pendleton's rules. (n.d.). Retrieved from Medical Educators: https://www.medicaleducators.org/write/MediaManager/ Speakers/Steve_Capey_-_Feedback_Workshop_11th_July_2017.pdf

Pendleton's rules (of feedback). (n.d.). Retrieved from Scaling the Heights: https://www.scalingtheheights.com/wp-content/ resources/feedback/Pendleton-1.pdf

211   Performance-Values Matrix

Janse, B. (2019). *Jack Welch matrix.* Retrieved from Toolshero: https://www.toolshero.com/human-resources/jack-welch-matrix/

Jack Welch matrix. (n.d.). Retrieved from Management Mania: https://managementmania.com/en/jack-welch-matrix

Schoenbaum, B. (2015, May 12). *Jack Welch—progressive leadership—really!* Retrieved from Keystone Executive Search: http:// blog.keystonesearch.com/jack-welch-progressive-leadership-really

Belludi, N. (2008, February 6). *General Electric's Jack Welch identifies four types of managers.* Retrieved from Right Attitudes: https://www.rightattitudes.com/2008/02/06/jack-welch-four-types-of-managers/

Buchko, A.A., & Buchko, K.J. (2012, January). Values-based management or the performance-values matrix: Was Jack Welch right? *Journal of Business and Leadership: Research, Practice, and Teaching,* 8(1), 69–83. https://scholars.fhsu.edu/cgi/ viewcontent.cgi?article=1183&context=jbl

Welch, J. (2000). *GE annual report.* Retrieved from GE's Annual Reports: https://www.annualreports.com/HostedData/ AnnualReportArchive/g/NYSE_GE_2000.pdf

212   PERMA Model

Meade, E. (2023, October 13). *8 PERMA model activities and worksheets to apply with clients.* Retrieved from Positive Psychology: https://positivepsychology.com/happiness-wellbeing-coaching-perma/

Madeson, M. (2023, October 9). *Seligman's PERMA+ model explained: A theory of well-being.* Retrieved from Positive Psychology: https://positivepsychology.com/perma-model/

Ackerman, C. (2023, October 13). *What is flourishing in positive psychology?* Retrieved from Positive Psychology: https:// positivepsychology.com/flourishing/

Walker, P. (n.d.). *Applying PERMA to your everyday life.* Retrieved from the Institute of Positive Psychology Coaching: https:// theippc.com/applying-perma-your-everyday-life/

5 ways to happiness. (n.d.). Retrieved from Flow Coaching: https://flowcoaching.gr/5-ways-to-happiness/

PERMA model. (n.d.). Retrieved from the Corporate Finance Institute: https://corporatefinanceinstitute.com/resources/ careers/soft-skills/perma-model/

PERMA theory of well-being and PERMA workshops. (n.d.). Retrieved from the University of Pennsylvania: https://ppc.sas. upenn.edu/learn-more/perma-theory-well-being-and-perma-workshops

The PERMA model. (n.d.). Retrieved from MindTools: https://www.mindtools.com/pages/article/perma.htm

Bennett, T. (2018, November 20). *We flourish when we prioritize each element in the PERMA model.* Retrieved from Thriveworks Counseling: https://thriveworks.com/blog/prioritize-master-process-perma-model/

213   Personality Models (general entry)

Fosslien, L., & West, M. (n.d.). *An illustrated guide to categorizing yourself*. Retrieved from Susan Cain: https://quietrev.com/an-illustrated-guide-to-categorizing-yourself/

Herrity, J. (2023, July 31). *8 personality tests used in psychology (and by employers)*. Retrieved from Indeed: https://www.indeed.com/career-advice/career-development/types-of-personality-test

Stiefvater, S. (2022, April 21). *From Myers-Briggs to the big 5, here are the four models used to determine personality type*. Retrieved from Pure Wow: https://www.purewow.com/wellness/types-of-personalities

Harper, H. (2023, October 11). *The 23 best personality tests in ranking order (2023 update)*. Retrieved from Work Style: https://www.workstyle.io/best-personality-test

214   Polarity Management Model

Clark, L. (2018, December 17). *Navigating complexity: Managing polarities*. Retrieved from Harvard Business Publishing: https://www.harvardbusiness.org/navigating-complexity-managing-polarities/

Certification and licensing. (n.d.). Retrieved from Polarity Partnerships: https://www.polaritypartnerships.com/certifications-programs-index#Certifications

Polarity management 101: The solution to unsolvable problems. (2016, December 29). Retrieved from Triple Pundit: https://www.triplepundit.com/story/2016/polarity-management-101-solution-unsolvable-problems/20846

Johnson, B. (2005, May). *Polarity management: A summary introduction*. Retrieved from Rise Leaders: https://rise-leaders.com/wp-content/uploads/2019/07/Polarity-Management-Summary-Introduction.pdf

215   Poole's Multiple Sequence Model

Poole's model—Small group communication. (n.d.). Retrieved from Communication Theory: https://www.communicationtheory.org/pooles-model-small-group-communication/

Models of small group development. (n.d.). Retrieved from Old Dominion University: http://ww2.odu.edu/~tsocha/comm326/326-sp11-ch05.pdf

Group development. (n.d.). Retrieved from Wikizero: https://www.wikizero.com/en/Group_development

Poole's multiple sequence model. (2023, November 8). Retrieved from *Wikipedia*: https://en.wikipedia.org/wiki/Poole%27s_Multiple_Sequence_Model

216   POSITIVE Coaching Model

Zeeman, A. (2019). *POSITIVE model of coaching*. Retrieved from Toolshero: https://www.toolshero.com/management/positive-model-of-coaching/

217   Positive Intelligence

Chamine, S. (2012). *Positive intelligence: Why only 20% of teams and individuals achieve their true potential and how you can achieve yours*. Greenleaf Book Group Press.

About: Shirzad Chamine. (n.d.). Retrieved from Positive Intelligence: https://www.positiveintelligence.com/about/

Chamine, S. (2020, March 4). *How to 100X your coaching impact*. Retrieved from Positive Intelligence: https://www.positiveintelligence.com/how-to-100x-your-coaching-impact/

Sage power games. (n.d.). Retrieved from Positive Intelligence: https://support.positiveintelligence.com/article/143-power-games

Stangel, L. (2017, August 17). *Shirzad Chamine: Five strategies to challenge negative thoughts*. Retrieved from Stanford University Graduate School of Business: https://www.gsb.stanford.edu/insights/shirzad-chamine-five-strategies-challenge-negative-thoughts

Latif, S. (2023, October 9). *Positive intelligence: How to overcome saboteurs in coaching*. Retrieved from Positive Psychology: https://positivepsychology.com/positive-intelligence/

Meier, J.D. (n.d.). *The power of positive intelligence: Why PQ matters more than IQ and EQ*. Retrieved from Sources of Insight: https://sourcesofinsight.com/positive-intelligence-and-pq/

Positive intelligence coaching. (n.d.). Retrieved from Jacy Imilkowski: https://jacyimilkowski.com/pq/

Positive intelligence. (n.d.). Retrieved from The Challenge Coach: https://thechallengecoach.com/positive-intelligence-training

Meier, J.D. (n.d.). *How to build your positive intelligence with PQ reps*. Retrieved from Sources of Insight: https://sourcesofinsight.com/get-a-few-pq-reps-in/

218   Positive Psychology Coaching

Van Zyl, L.E., Roll, L.C., Stander, M. W., & Richter, S. (2020, May). Positive psychological coaching definitions and models: A systematic literature review. *Frontiers in Psychology*, 11: https://www.frontiersin.org/articles/10.3389/fpsyg.2020.00793/full

Mead, E. (2023 October 13). *12 positive psychology coaching certifications and trainings.* Retrieved from PositivePsychology: https://positivepsychology.com/positive-psychology-coaching-certification-training/

Mead, E. (2023, October 19). *Positive psychology coaching vs. life coaching: A comparison.* Retrieved from PositivePsychology: https://positivepsychology.com/positive-psychology-life-coaching/

Pennock, S.F. (2023, October 13). *8 advanced positive psychology coaching skills to explore.* Retrieved from PositivePsychology: https://positivepsychology.com/positive-psychology-coaching-skills/

Moore, C. (2023, October 13). *40+ positive psychology websites you should know about.* Retrieved from PositivePsychology: https://positivepsychology.com/positive-psychology-websites-overview-topics-themes-tests/

Positive psychology and coaching. (n.d.). Retrieved from MentorCoach: https://www.mentorcoach.com/positive-psychology-coaching/

219   Postindustrial Leadership Theory

Chodkowski, M., & Schindler, T. (2018, July 15). *Leadership in the 21st century: The post-industrial paradigm.* Retrieved from Inside Indiana Business: https://www.insideindianabusiness.com/story/38649905/leadership-in-the-21st-century-the-postindustrial-paradigm-dr-matthew-chodkowski-terry-schindler

Postindustrial leadership ahead. (n.d.). Retrieved from Prezi: https://prezi.com/tdlql9suu4vk/postindustrial-leadership/

220   PRACTICE Coaching Model

Palmer, S. (2008). *The PRACTICE model of coaching: Towards a solution-focused approach.* Retrieved from Crowe Associates: http://www.crowe-associates.co.uk/wp-content/uploads/2013/10/The_PRACTICE_model_of_coaching_towards_a_solution-focused_approach-2.pdf

Thomson, S. (2018, August 17). *The coaching model library: PRACTICE.* Retrieved from the Training Journal: https://www.trainingjournal.com/articles/features/coaching-model-library-practice

The PRACTICE coaching model. (2019, October 7). Retrieved from Abintus Ltd.: https://www.abintus.co.uk/the-practice-coaching-model/

IAFPD certificate in coaching. (n.d.). Retrieved from the Centre for Coaching: https://www.centreforcoaching.com/cert-in-coaching

Janse, B. (2021). *PRACTICE coaching model.* Retrieved from ToolsHero: https://www.toolshero.com/management/practice-coaching-model/

221   Prolonged Adaptation Stress Syndrome

Taylor, A. (n.d.). *Prolonged adaptive stress syndrome.* Retrieved from Realizations Inc.: https://www.arlenetaylor.org/articles-monographs/taylor-articles/adapting/7-prolonged-adaptive-stress-syndrome-pass

Cox, K. (2016, March 15). *PASS: Prolonged adaptive stress syndrome. Do you have it?* Retrieved from Road Mumma: https://roadmumma.com/pass-prolonged-adaptive-stress-syndrome/

What is Benziger's personality assessment model? (n.d.). Retrieved from Businessballs.com: https://www.businessballs.com/self-awareness/benziger-personality-assessment/

222   Punctuated Equilibrium Model

Puscasu, A. (2023, August 30). *The punctuated equilibrium model of group development.* Retrieved from ApePM: http://apepm.co.uk/punctuated-equilibrium/

Puscasu, A. (2023, August 29). *The five-stage team development model.* Retrieved from ApePM: http://apepm.co.uk/team-development-model/

Kaur, S. (n.d.). *Punctuated equilibrium model.* Retrieved from Sandeep Kaur: https://sandeepartly.wordpress.com/punctuated-equilibrium-model/

9.1 group dynamics. (n.d.). Retrieved from British Columbia Campus: https://pressbooks.bccampus.ca/obcourseweir/chapter/9-1-group-dynamics/

Punctuated equilibrium in groups. (n.d.). Retrieved from Changing Minds: http://changingminds.org/explanations/groups/punctuated_equilibrium.htm

Models of small group development. (n.d.). Retrieved from Old Dominion University: http://ww2.odu.edu/~tsocha/comm326/326-sp11-ch05.pdf

Rodriguez, J. (2013, December 13). *Punctuated equilibrium model*. Retrieved from Prezi: https://prezi.com/5mlbvdbqazwm/the-punctuated-equilibruim-model/

Fripp, G. (n.d.). *The punctuated equilibrium model*. Retrieved from My Organizational Behavior Study Guide: https://www.myorganisationalbehaviour.com/the-punctuated-equilibrium-model/

Gersick, C. J. G. (1988). Time and transition in work teams: Toward a new model of group development. *Academy of Management Journal*, 31(1), 9–41. Retrieved from the Massachusetts Institute of Technology: https://web.mit.edu/curhan/www/docs/Articles/15341_Readings/Group_Dynamics/Gersick_1988_Time_and_transition.pdf

223   Radical Candor Framework

A new management philosophy. (n.d.). Retrieved from Radical Candor LLC: https://www.radicalcandor.com/our-approach/

Scott, K. (n.d.). *3 ways to introduce radical candor's feedback framework to your organization*. Retrieved from Radical Candor LLC: https://www.radicalcandor.com/introduce-radical-candor-feedback/

Scott, K. (2016, April 13). *Radical candor: Improve your impromptu feedback*. Retrieved from Medium: https://kimmalonescott.medium.com/radical-candor-improve-your-impromptu-feedback-48c860070f87

Tong, B. (2018, June 13). *Radical candor: What is it, and how does it work?* Retrieved from Impact Hub: https://vienna.impacthub.net/2018/06/13/radical-candor-work/

Longenecker, R. (2019, February 7). *How to implement radical candor with employees*. Retrieved from Chief Sales Leader: https://www.chiefsalesleader.com/implementing-radical-candor/

McKinney, M. (2017, April 5). *Radical candor*. Retrieved from Leading Blog: https://www.leadershipnow.com/leadingblog/2017/04/radical_candor.html

Self-paced e-course. (n.d.). Retrieved from Radical Candor LLC: https://www.radicalcandor.com/services/

Kim Scott's radical candor one-on-one template. (n.d.). Retrieved from Hypercontext: https://hypercontext.com/agenda-templates/kim-scott-radical-candor-one-on-one

Dixita. (2020, April 28). *What is radical candor?* Retrieved from Matter: https://matterapp.com/blog/what-is-radical-candor

224   RAW Model of Flourishing

About the positivity institute. (n.d.). Retrieved from The Positivity Institute: https://thepositivityinstitute.com.au/about-pi/

The positivity institute: Workplace services kit. (n.d.). Retrieved from The Positivity Institute: https://www.thepositivityinstitute.com.au/wp-content/uploads/2017/04/PI_Workplace-Services-Kit.pdf

Conceição, J.M.C. (2020, May 11). *Positive psychology coaching: Applying science to coaching*. Retrieved from Medium: https://medium.com/@contact.josecc/positive-psychology-coaching-applying-science-to-coaching-f073aed9e987

Wang, W. (2019). *Integrating positive psychology coaching approach with embodiment: An integrative coaching model*. Retrieved from Otago Polytechnic: https://www.op.ac.nz/assets/OPRES/CAP-Wang-thesis.pdf

Ackerman, C.E. (2023, October 13). *What is flourishing in positive psychology?* Retrieved from PositivePsychology: https://positivepsychology.com/flourishing/

225   Recognition-Primed Decision Model

The recognition-primed decision (RPD) process. (2018, May 2). Retrieved from MindTools: https://nanopdf.com/download/the-recognition-primed-decision-rpd-process_pdf

Danial, S.N., Smith, J., Veitch, B., & Khan, F. (2019, October 11). On the realization of the recognition-primed decision model for artificial agents. *Human-Centric Computing and Information Sciences*, 9(36). Retrieved from Springer Link: https://link.springer.com/article/10.1186/s13673-019-0197-2

Recognition-primed decision-making model. (n.d.). Retrieved from Decision Making Confidence: https://www.decision-making-confidence.com/recognition-primed-decision-making-model.html

Gary Klein (n.d.). Retrieved from Gary Klein: https://www.gary-klein.com/rpd

Klein, G.A., Orasanu, J., Calderwood, R., & Zsambok, C.E. (1993). *Decision making in action: Models and methods*. Retrieved from MacroCognition: http://www.macrocognition.com/documents/Decision-Making-in-Action-Models-and-Methods-0316.pdf

226   Reinforcement Theory

Gordon, J. (2023, October 19). *Reinforcement theory*. Retrieved from The Business Professor: https://thebusinessprofessor.com/en_US/management-leadership-organizational-behavior/reinforcement-theory-of-motivation

McLeod, S. (2023, November 24). *Operant conditioning: What it is, how it works, and examples*. Retrieved from SimplyPsychology: https://www.simplypsychology.org/operant-conditioning.html

Juneja, P. (n.d.). *Reinforcement theory of motivation*. Retrieved from Management Study Guide: https://www.managementstudyguide.com/reinforcement-theory-motivation.htm

Employee motivation—Reinforcement theory. (n.d.). Retrieved from Tutorialspoint: https://www.tutorialspoint.com/employee_motivation/employee_motivation_reinforcement_theory.htm

Williams, L. (n.d.). *Reinforcement theory*. Retrieved from Lumen Learning: https://courses.lumenlearning.com/wm-introductiontobusiness/chapter/reinforcement-theory/

Barnett, T. (n.d.). *Reinforcement theory*. Retrieved from Reference for Business: https://www.referenceforbusiness.com/management/Pr-Sa/Reinforcement-Theory.html

Sarokin, D. (2019, May 8). *How can managers use reinforcement theory to motivate employees?* Retrieved from Chron: https://smallbusiness.chron.com/can-managers-use-reinforcement-theory-motivate-employees-18559.html

227   Relational Leadership Theory

Uhl-Bien, M. (2006, December). *Relational leadership theory: Exploring the social processes of leadership and organizing*. Retrieved from the University of Nebraska-Lincoln: https://core.ac.uk/download/pdf/188041337.pdf

Reitz, M. (2015). Leading questions: Dialogue in organizations: Developing relational leadership. *Leadership*, 13(4), 516–522. Retrieved from Sage Journals: https://journals.sagepub.com/doi/abs/10.1177/1742715015617864

Uhl-Bien, M., Ospina, S.M. (2012). *Advancing relational leadership research*. Retrieved from New York University: https://wagner.nyu.edu/files/leadership/12_Ospina_Uhl-Bien_Intro_Mapping_the_Terrain.pdf

Vriend, T., Said, R., Janssen, O., & Jordan, J. (2020, July 10). The dark side of relational leadership: Positive and negative reciprocity as fundamental drivers of follower's intended pro-leader and pro-self unethical behavior. *Frontiers in Psychology*, 11: https://www.frontiersin.org/articles/10.3389/fpsyg.2020.01473/full

228   Renewal Cycle

Faeth, F. (n.d.). *The cycle of renewal*. Retrieved from Faeth Coaching: https://faethcoaching.com/the-cycle-of-renewal/

Johnson, R.R. (n.d.). *How to engage patients in necessary change: A dead simple roadmap*. Retrieved from the Tucson Osteopathic Medical Foundation: https://www.tomf.org/gd-resources/downloads/Johnson3.pdf

Taylor, J. (2019, June 14). *When it's time to start over…* Retrieved from Medium: https://medium.com/@bluesky1001/when-its-time-to-start-over-8157e22a042f

Werner, M. (2011, September 27). *Hudson's cycle of change—Phase 4 "getting ready."* Retrieved from Werner Coaching and Consulting: https://wernercoaching.typepad.com/theleadershipnotebook/2011/09/hudsons-cycle-of-changephase-4-getting-ready.html

McLean, P. (2020, May 20). *The cycle of change in this astonishing moment*. Retrieved from the Hudson Institute: https://insights.hudsoninstitute.com/the-cycle-of-change-in-this-astonishing-moment

Hudson, F.M., McLean, P.D. (n.d.). *The cycle of renewal*. Retrieved from Janie-Transforms-Minds: https://janenotdoe.com/home/the-cycle-of-renewal/

Heckerman, J. (2006). *Relapse prevention: Understanding the predictable cycle of renewal*. Retrieved from Sober Transitions: https://sobertransitions.typepad.com/sobertransitions/files/Relapse_Prevention.pdf

229   Results/RESULTS Coaching Model

Coaching model: RESULTS. (2015, August 5). Retrieved from The International Coach Academy: https://coachcampus.com/coach-portfolios/coaching-models/wayne-farrell-r-e-s-u-l-t-s/

Dearing, V. (n.d.). *Focus on what you want*. Retrieved from Results Coaching Global: http://resultscoachingglobal.com/focus-on-what-you-want/

Farrell, W. (2014, September 8). *Results coaching: Part 2*. Retrieved from Coaching with NLP: https://www.coachingwithnlp.co/results-coaching-part-2/

230   Rolfe's Reflective Learning

What, so what, now what? (n.d.). Retrieved from FutureLearn: https://www.futurelearn.com/info/courses/career-smart-sell-yourself/0/steps/25057

Reflective model according to Rolfe et al. (n.d.). Retrieved from Dr. Nicole Brown: https://www.nicole-brown.co.uk/reflective-model-according-to-rolfe/

Rolfe's et al.'s (2001) reflective model. Retrieved from the University of Cumbria: https://my.cumbria.ac.uk/media/MyCumbria/Documents/ReflectiveModelRolfe.pdf

Dabell, J. (2018, August 26). *The 'so what' model of reflection*. Retrieved from John Dabell: https://johndabell.com/2018/08/26/models-of-reflection-5/

Reflective writing. (n.d.). Retrieved from Otago Polytechnic: https://www.op.ac.nz/assets/LearningAdvice/d0a1fac268/Reflective-writing.pdf

Reflective writing: Rolfe. (2023, October 12). Retrieved from the University of Hull: https://libguides.hull.ac.uk/reflectivewriting/rolfe

231   Rummler-Brache Methodology

The Rummler-Brache process improvement certification workshop. (n.d.). Retrieved from the Rummler-Brache Group: https://www.rummlerbrache.com/sites/default/files/process-improvement-training-workshop.pdf

Online process improvement certification. (n.d.). Retrieved from the Rummler-Brache Group: https://www.rummlerbrache.com

The Rummler-Brache process improvement and management methodology. (n.d.). Retrieved from the Rummler-Brache Group: https://www.rummlerbrache.com/rummler-brache-process-improvement-and-management-methodology

Dalto, J. (2020, September 17). *Human performance improvement (HPI) basics: The Rummler and Brache "nine variables" model.* Retrieved from Vector Solutions: https://www.vectorsolutions.com/resources/blogs/human-performance-improvement-hpi-basics-the-rummler-brache-nine-variables-model/

Business process change. (n.d.). Retrieved from TechTarget: https://cdn.ttgtmedia.com/searchDataManagement/downloads/Business_process_change.pdf

232   SCARF Model

David Rock's SCARF model: Using neuroscience to work effectively with others. (n.d.). Retrieved from Mindtools: https://www.mindtools.com/pages/article/SCARF.htm

Batista, E. (2010, March 25). *Neuroscience, leadership, and David Rock's SCARF model.* Retrieved from Ed Batista: https://www.edbatista.com/2010/03/scarf.html

The SCARF assessment. (n.d.). Retrieved from the NeuroLeadership Institute: https://neuroleadership.com/research/tools/nli-scarf-assessment/

5 ways to spark (or destroy) your employees' motivation. (2023, October 17). Retrieved from the NeuroLeadership Institute: https://neuroleadership.com/your-brain-at-work/scarf-model-motivate-your-employees

The SCARF model of engagement. (2021, March 8). Retrieved from Growth Engineering: https://www.growthengineering.co.uk/scarf-model/

Luenendonk, M. (2019, September 23). *How to collaborate with and influence people using the SCARF model.* Retrieved from Cleverism: https://www.cleverism.com/scarf-model-influence-people/

233   Scheidel-Crowell Spiral Model

Neer, M. R. (1981, May). Small group communication in the 1980s. *COMMUNICATION: Journal of the Communication Association of the Pacific, 10*(2), 42–78. Retrieved from the Institute of Educational Science: https://files.eric.ed.gov/fulltext/ED207092.pdf

Minahan, M. (2014). Chapter nineteen: Working with groups in organizations. In B.B. Jones & M. Brazzel (Eds.), *The NTL handbook of organization development and change: Principles, practices, and perspectives* (2nd ed.). Retrieved from Ebook Reading: https://ebookreading.net/view/book/EB9781118836163_32.html

Managing group meetings. (n.d.). Retrieved from the North American Council on Adoptable Children: https://www.nacac.org/help/parent-group/start-parent-group/managing-group-meetings/

234   Schein's Career Anchors

Lea, S. (2020, September 3). *What are Schein's career anchors?* Retrieved from Businessballs.com: https://www.businessballs.com/self-management/career-anchors-edgar-schein/

Morrison, M. (2016, August 5). *Career anchors—Edgar Schein.* Retrieved from RapidBI: https://rapidbi.com/careeranchors/

Schein's career anchors. (n.d.). Retrieved from ChangingMinds.org: http://changingminds.org/explanations/values/career_anchors.htm

Career anchors example profile. (2006). Retrieved from Career Anchors Online: https://www.careeranchorsonline.com/SCA/media/images/common/report_sample.pdf

Edgar Schein's career anchors online. (n.d.). Retrieved from Career Anchors Online: https://www.careeranchorsonline.com/SCA/startPage.do

Patricio, V. (2020, April 2). *Edgar Schein's career anchors.* Retrieved from Vasco Patricio Executive Coaching: https://vascopatricio.com/the-career-anchors/

Von Knobloch, K. (2019, June 6). *What are you aiming for in your career?* Retrieved from Share the Love: https://www.sharethelove.blog/selfcoaching/careeranchor/

235   Schön's Model of Reflection

Schön reflective model. (2018, November). Retrieved from NursingAnswers.net: https://nursinganswers.net/reflective-guides/schon-reflective-model.php

The Schön reflective model. (n.d.). Retrieved from the University of Hull: https://libguides.hull.ac.uk/reflectivewriting/schon

Getting started with reflective practice. (n.d.). Retrieved from Cambridge Assessment International Education: https://www.cambridge-community.org.uk/professional-development/gswrp/index.html

Smith, M.K. (2021, April 7). *Donald Schön: Learning, reflection, and change.* Retrieved from infed.org: https://infed.org/mobi/donald-schon-learning-reflection-change/

Buwert, P. (2012, December 18). *The reflective practitioner by Donald Schön.* Retrieved from Gray's Research Reading Group: https://graysreadinggroup.wordpress.com/2012/12/18/the-reflective-practitioner-by-donald-schon/

236   Scientific Management Theory

Frederick Taylor and scientific management. (n.d.). Retrieved from Mindtools.com: https://www.mindtools.com/pages/article/newTMM_Taylor.htm

Ward, P. (2021, October 3). *Frederick Taylor's principles of scientific management theory.* Retrieved from NanoGlobals: https://nanoglobals.com/glossary/scientific-management-theory-of-frederick-taylor/

Teeboom, L. (2018, October 15). Herzberg and Taylor's theories of motivation. *Houston Chronicle*: https://smallbusiness.chron.com/herzberg-taylors-theories-motivation-704.html

Tutor2u. (2018, February 18). *Motivation theory: Taylor* [Video]. Retrieved from Tutor2u: https://www.tutor2u.net/business/reference/motivation-taylor-scientific-management

Nasrudin, A. (2022, April 17). *Taylor's theory of motivation: How it works, principles, and criticisms.* Retrieved from Penpoin: https://penpoin.com/taylors-theory-of-motivation/

Early theories of motivation. (n.d.). Retrieved from Lumen Learning: https://courses.lumenlearning.com/suny-osintrobus/chapter/early-theories-of-motivation/

Peek, S. (2023, March 13). *The management theory of Frederick Taylor.* Retrieved from Business.com: https://www.business.com/articles/management-theory-of-frederick-taylor/

Harry4econ. (2011, May 18). *Motivation theories: Taylor.* Retrieved from IB Business: https://hrnistbusinessproject.wordpress.com/2011/05/18/motivation-theories-taylor/

Taylor theory of motivation commerce essay. (2018, November). Retrieved from UK Essays: https://www.ukessays.com/essays/commerce/taylor-theory-of-motivation-commerce-essay.php#citethis

237   SEEDS Model

The five biggest biases that affect decision-making. (2023, August 1). Retrieved from the NeuroLeadership Institute: https://neuroleadership.com/your-brain-at-work/seeds-model-biases-affect-decision-making/

What is the SEEDS model, and how can it be used to mitigate bias? (n.d.). Retrieved from Kinnu: https://kinnu.xyz/kinnuverse/science/cognitive-biases/how-to-mitigate-bias/

Discover and apply the SEEDS model to defeat bias in everyday decisions. (n.d.). Retrieved from You Can Now: https://www.ycn.org/resources/seeds

What is the SEEDS model? (n.d.). Retrieved from Consuunt: https://www.consuunt.com/seeds-bias-model/

Bugbounter. (2022, August 9). *The cybersecurity prejudice: The SEEDS model.* Retrieved from LinkedIn Pulse: https://www.linkedin.com/pulse/cybersecurity-prejudice-seeds-model-bugbounter/?trk=pulse-article_more-articles_related-content-card

Davidson, J. (2020, December 30). *Using the SEED model for performance feedback.* Retrieved from Medium: https://medium.com/swlh/using-the-seed-model-for-performance-feedback-7cb7a810e637

238   Self-Determination Theory

Theory. (n.d.). Retrieved from the Center for Self-Determination Theory: https://selfdeterminationtheory.org/theory/

Cherry, K. (2022, November 8). *What is self-determination theory?* Retrieved from Verywell Mind: https://www.verywellmind.com/what-is-self-determination-theory-2795387

Ackerman, C.E. (2023, September 20). *Self-determination theory and how it explains motivation.* Retrieved from Positive Psychology: https://positivepsychology.com/self-determination-theory/

239 Self-Determination Theory: Mini-theories

Theory. (n.d.). Retrieved from the Center for Self-Determination Theory: https://selfdeterminationtheory.org/theory/

The theory. (n.d.). Retrieved from the Center for Self-Determination Theory: https://selfdeterminationtheory.org/the-theory/

Cherry, K. (2022, November 8). *What is self-determination theory?* Retrieved from Verywell Mind: https://www.verywellmind.com/what-is-self-determination-theory-2795387

Ackerman, C.E. (2023, September 20). *Self-determination theory and how it explains motivation*. Retrieved from Positive Psychology: https://positivepsychology.com/self-determination-theory/

Jekel, J. (2021, May 1). *Self-determination (organismic integration theory)*. Retrieved from LinkedIn Pulse: https://www.linkedin.com/pulse/self-determination-organismic-integration-theory-joe-jekel/

240 Self-Efficacy Theory

Carey, M.P., Forsyth, A.D. (2009). *Teaching tip sheet: Self-efficacy*. Retrieved from the American Psychological Association: https://www.apa.org/pi/aids/resources/education/self-efficacy

Moore, C. (2023, April 26). *Albert Bandura: Self-efficacy and agentic positive psychology*. Retrieved from Positive Psychology: https://positivepsychology.com/bandura-self-efficacy/

Ackerman, C.E. (2023, April 26). *What is self-efficacy theory? (Incl. 8 examples & scales)*. Retrieved from Positive Psychology: https://positivepsychology.com/self-efficacy/

Lopez-Garrido, G. (2023, July 10). *Bandura's self-efficacy theory of motivation in psychology*. Retrieved from Simply Psychology: https://www.simplypsychology.org/self-efficacy.html

Cherry, K. (2023, February 27). *Self-efficacy and why believing in yourself matters*. Retrieved from Verywell Mind: https://www.verywellmind.com/what-is-self-efficacy-2795954

241 Self-Perception Theory

Self-perception theory. (n.d.). International Encyclopedia of the Social Sciences. Retrieved from Encyclopedia.com: https://www.encyclopedia.com/social-sciences/applied-and-social-sciences-magazines/self-perception-theory

Chakraborty, A. (n.d.). *Self-perception theory: What you do affects what attitudes you build*. Retrieved from Coffee and Junk: https://coffeeandjunk.com/self-perception-theory/

Self-perception theory. (n.d.). Retrieved from the Decision Lab: https://thedecisionlab.com/reference-guide/psychology/self-perception-theory

Psychology 104: Social psychology. (2023, November 21). *What is Bem's self-perception theory?* [Video]. Retrieved from Study.com: https://study.com/academy/lesson/self-perception-theory-definition-and-examples.html

Self-perception theory (Bem). (n.d.). Retrieved from Learning Theories: https://learning-theories.com/self-perception-theory-bem.html

Self-perception theory. (2022, March 13). Retrieved from Practical Psychology: https://practicalpie.com/self-perception-theory/

American Psychological Association. (n.d.). Self-perception theory. In *APA dictionary of psychology*: https://dictionary.apa.org/self-perception-theory

Self-perception theory. (n.d.). Retrieved from Alley Dog: https://www.alleydog.com/glossary/definition.php?term=Self-Perception+Theory

Huntington, C. (n.d.). *Self-perception: Definition, theory, and questions*. Retrieved from Berkeley Well-Being Institute: https://www.berkeleywellbeing.com/self-perception.html

Self-perception theory. (n.d.). Retrieved from Changing Minds: http://changingminds.org/explanations/theories/self-perception.htm

242 Servant Leadership Theory

Servant leadership theory. (2010, April 1). Retrieved from David Burkus: https://davidburkus.com/2010/04/servant-leadership-theory/

What is servant leadership? (n.d.). Retrieved from Robert K. Greenleaf Center for Servant Leadership: https://www.greenleaf.org/what-is-servant-leadership/

Smith, C. (2005, December 4). *Servant leadership: The leadership theory of Robert K. Greenleaf*. Retrieved from Boyden 75: https://www.boyden.com/media/just-what-the-doctor-ordered-15763495/Leadership%20%20Theory_Greenleaf%20Servant%20Leadership.pdf

Servant leadership: Putting your team first, and yourself second. (n.d.). Retrieved from Mindtools.com: https://www.mindtools.com/pages/article/servant-leadership.htm

Tarallo, M. (2018, May 17). *The art of servant leadership*. Retrieved from The Society of Human Resource Managers: https://

www.shrm.org/resourcesandtools/hr-topics/organizational-and-employee-development/pages/the-art-of-servant-leadership.aspx

What is servant leadership? (2014, November 25). Retrieved from St. Thomas University: https://online.stu.edu/articles/education/what-is-servant-leadership.aspx

Kenton, W. (2023, August 23). *Servant leadership: Characteristics, pros & cons, example.* Retrieved from Investopedia: https://www.investopedia.com/terms/s/servant-leadership.asp

Phipps, K. (2010). Servant leadership and constructive development theory: How servant leaders make meaning of service. *Journal of Leadership Education, 9*(2). https://journalofleadershiped.org/jole_articles/servant-leadership-and-constructive-development-theory-how-servant-leaders-make-meaning-of-service/

Lopez-Gomez, A. (2022, July 18). *What is servant leadership and how can it empower your team?* Retrieved from BetterUp: https://www.betterup.com/blog/servant-leadership-what-makes-it-different

243　Seven Transformations of Leadership

Rooke, D., & Torbert, W.R. (2005, April). Seven transformations of leadership. *Harvard Business Review.* https://hbr.org/2005/04/seven-transformations-of-leadership.

The seven transformations of leadership: A simple summary. (n.d.). Retrieved from World of Work: https://worldofwork.io/2019/07/the-7-transformations-of-leadership/

Mulder, P. (2019). *Seven transformations of leadership.* Retrieved from Toolshero: https://www.toolshero.com/leadership/seven-transformations-of-leadership/

Casali, E. (2021, June 3). *The seven transformations of leadership.* Retrieved from Intense Minimalism: https://intenseminimalism.com/2021/the-seven-transformations-of-leadership/

Torbert, W. (2020). *Warren Buffett's and your own seven transformations of leadership.* Retrieved from Global Leadership Associates: https://www.gla.global/wp-content/uploads/2020/09/Warren-Buffetts-and-Your-Own-Seven-Transformations-of-Leadership.pdf

Martin, G. (2017, December 12). *The seven transformations of leadership.* Retrieved from LinkedIn Pulse: https://www.linkedin.com/pulse/seven-transformations-leadership-professor-gary-martin-faim-face/

Levels of leadership development. (n.d.). Retrieved from Global Leadership Associates: https://www.gla.global/the-glp/levels-of-leadership-development/

244　Simplexity

Basadur, M. (2011, October 17). *The simplex process: A robust creative problem-solving process.* Retrieved from translatedby.com: https://translatedby.com/you/the-simplex-process-a-robust-creative-problem-solving-process/original/

A framework for creative problem solving, a pathway to innovation. (n.d.). Retrieved from Basadur Applied Innovation: https://www.basadur.com/simplexity/

Basadur, M. (n.d.). *Understanding the Basadur simplexity innovation system.* Retrieved from Disruptive Innovation Hub: https://www.disruptiveinnovation.io/courses/sip

Min Basadur. (2023, April 25). Retrieved from *Wikipedia:* https://en.wikipedia.org/wiki/Min_Basadur

What is the simplex process? (n.d.). Retrieved from Consuunt: https://www.consuunt.com/simplex-process/

The simplex process. (n.d.). Retrieved from Visual Paradigm Online: https://online.visual-paradigm.com/tabular/templates/the-simplex-process/

245　Sirota's Three-Factor Theory

Sirota's three-factor theory. (n.d.). Retrieved from Mindtools: https://www.mindtools.com/pages/article/newTMM_57.htm

Sirota's three-factor theory of employee motivation. (n.d.). Retrieved from ChangingMinds.org: http://changingminds.org/explanations/needs/sirota_three_factor.htm

Sirota, D., & Klein, D. (2013). *The enthusiastic employee: How companies profit from giving workers what they want* (2nd ed.), Chapter 1. Pearson Education Inc. Retrieved from InformIT: https://www.informit.com/articles/article.aspx?p=2120854&seqNum=3

Belyh, A. (2019, September 25). *Sirota's three-factor theory: Keeping employees enthusiastic.* Retrieved from Cleverism.com: https://www.cleverism.com/sirotas-three-factor-theory-keeping-employees-enthusiastic/

A brief introduction to Sirota's dynamic alignment model. (n.d.). Retrieved from Hogan Assessments: https://info.hoganassessments.com/hubfs/EL_Dyn_Alignment_Model.pdf

Meier, J.D. (n.d.). *Three-factor theory: Create enthusiasm in your work environment.* Retrieved from Sources of Insight: https://sourcesofinsight.com/three-factor-theory/

246   Situation, Behavior, Impact Model (SBI)

The situation-behavior-impact feedback tool. (n.d.). Retrieved from MindTools: https://www.mindtools.com/ay86376/the-situation-behavior-impact-feedback-tool

Fernandes, T. (2020, September 19). *The situation-behavior-impact feedback framework.* Retrieved from Medium: https://medium.com/pm101/the-situation-behavior-impact-feedback-framework-e20ce52c9357

Situation-behavior-impact. (n.d.). Retrieved from Untools: https://untools.co/situation-behavior-impact

The SBI feedback model: A simple summary. (n.d.). Retrieved from The World of Work Project: https://worldofwork.io/2019/07/sbi-feedback-model/

Improve talent development with our SBI feedback model. (2022, November 24). Retrieved from the Center for Creative Leadership: https://www.ccl.org/articles/leading-effectively-articles/hr-pipeline-a-quick-win-to-improve-your-talent-development-process/

Use situation-behavior-impact (SBI) to understand intent. (2022, November 18). Retrieved from the Center for Creative Leadership: https://www.ccl.org/articles/leading-effectively-articles/closing-the-gap-between-intent-and-impact/

247   Situational Leadership Theory

Kenton, W. (2023, June 10). *Hersey-Blanchard situational leadership model: How it works.* Retrieved from Investopedia.com: https://www.investopedia.com/terms/h/hersey-and-blanchard-model.asp

De Bruin, L. (2020, March 28). *Hersey and Blanchard situational leadership model: Adapting the leadership style to the follower.* Retrieved from Business to You: https://www.business-to-you.com/hersey-blanchard-situational-leadership-model/

Scouller, J., & Chapman, A. (2020, September 3). *What is situational leadership?* Retrieved from Businessballs.com: https://www.businessballs.com/leadership-models/situational-leadership-model-hersey-and-blanchard/

What is the Hersey-Blanchard model? (n.d.). Retrieved from the Corporate Finance Institute: https://corporatefinanceinstitute.com/resources/careers/soft-skills/hersey-blanchard-model/

Cherry, K. (2023, March 10). *Situational leadership theory.* Retrieved from Verywellmind.com: https://www.verywellmind.com/what-is-the-situational-theory-of-leadership-2795321

Juneja, P. (n.d.). *Hersey Blanchard model.* Retrieved from Managementstudyguide.com: https://www.managementstudyguide.com/hersey-blanchard-model.htm

Kruse, K. (2019, September 23). *Situational leadership theory in plain language: The landmark model from Paul Hersey and Ken Blanchard.* Retrieved from LEADx.org: https://leadx.org/articles/situational-leadership-theory-model-blanchard-hersey/

Hersey and Blanchard. (n.d.). Retrieved from Praxis Framework Ltd: https://www.praxisframework.org/en/library/hersey-and-blanchard

Situational leadership. (n.d.). Retrieved from The Center for Leadership Studies: https://situational.com/situational-leadership/

Situational leadership and SLII: Points of distinction. (n.d.). Retrieved from The Center for Leadership Studies: https://situational.com/blog/situational-leadership-and-slii-points-of-distinction/

SLII. (n.d.). Retrieved from The Ken Blanchard Companies: https://www.kenblanchard.com

248   Six Principles of Influence

Schenker, M. (2022, April 29). *How to use Cialdini's 7 principles of persuasion to boost conversions.* Retrieved from CXL: https://cxl.com/blog/cialdinis-principles-persuasion/

Cialdini's 6 principles of persuasion: A simple summary. (n.d.). Retrieved from the World of Work Project: https://worldofwork.io/2019/07/cialdinis-6-principles-of-persuasion/

Juma, A. (2015, December 7). *The 6 principles of influence: How to master persuasion.* Retrieved from Medium: https://alyjuma.medium.com/the-6-principles-of-influence-how-to-master-persuasion-2f8c581da38b

Cialdini's 6 principles of influence. (n.d.). Retrieved from Conceptually.org: https://conceptually.org/concepts/6-principles-of-influence

Sloan, M. (2020, November 5). *The six principles of influence and how to use them to become a 10X sales rep or marketer.* Retrieved from Drift: https://www.drift.com/blog/six-principles-of-influence/

Cialdini, R. (n.d.). *The science of persuasion: Seven principles of persuasion.* Retrieved from Influence at Work: https://www.influenceatwork.com/7-principles-of-persuasion/#unity

Cialdini, R. (2016, May 23). *The principles of persuasion aren't just for business.* Retrieved from Influence at Work: https://www.influenceatwork.com/principles-of-persuasion-are-not-just-for-business/

Cialdini, R. (1984). *Influence: The psychology of persuasion.* Harper Collins.

Birkett, A. (2016, September 7). *Cialdini's 7th persuasion principle: Using unity in online marketing.* Retrieved from CXL: https://cxl.com/blog/cialdini-unity/

249   SMART Model for Goal Setting

Setting S.M.A.R.T.E.R. goals: 7 steps to achieving any goal. (n.d.). Retrieved from WunderLust Worker: https://www.wanderlustworker.com/setting-s-m-a-r-t-e-r-goals-7-steps-to-achieving-any-goal/

Setting goals. (n.d.). Retrieved from Bard College: https://cce.bard.edu/files/Setting-Goals.pdf

Everything you need to know about SMART goals. (n.d.). Retrieved from Achieve It: https://www.achieveit.com/resources/blog/everything-you-need-to-know-about-smart-goals/

Caucci, S. (2021, June 26). *Why SMART goals are outdated (and why you should leave them in the past).* Retrieved from 1Huddle: https://1huddle.co/blog/outdated-smart-goals/

Haughey, D. (2014, December 13). *A brief history of SMART goals.* Retrieved from Project Smart: https://www.projectsmart.co.uk/smart-goals/brief-history-of-smart-goals.php

SMART goals. (n.d.). Retrieved from MindTools: https://www.mindtools.com/pages/article/smart-goals.htm

SMART goals. (2022, November 24). Retrieved from the Corporate Finance Institute: https://corporatefinanceinstitute.com/resources/knowledge/other/smart-goal/

Herrity, J. (2023, July 10). *How to write SMART goals in 5 steps (with examples).* Retrieved from Indeed: https://www.indeed.com/career-advice/career-development/smart-goals

250   Smyth's Model of Reflection

Dabell, J. (2018, August 12). *Smyth's model of reflection.* Retrieved from John Dabell: https://johndabell.com/2018/08/12/models-of-reflection-2/

Hill, D. (n.d.). *Critical reflection in early childhood education: A framework for personal and professional empowerment* [PowerPoint]. Retrieved from the University of Auckland via Google: https://www.google.com/url?sa=t&rct=j&q=&esrc=s&source=web&cd=&cad=rja&uact=8&ved=2ahUKEwi0moLQr5P2AhVnSjABHRYKDSIQFnoECDcQAQ&url=https%3A%2F%2Fcdn.auckland.ac.nz%2Fassets%2Feducation%2Fabout%2Fschools%2Fteprac%2Fdocs%2FPPT%2520Critical%2520reflection%2520AT%2520Symposium%252014_6_08.ppt&usg=AOvVaw0amVltha4ItNXpJAvmtWm5

McClean, T. (2019). *Models for reflection.* Retrieved from The Institute: http://theinstitute.gg/CHttpHandler.ashx?id=117767&p=0

Carlson, S. (2022, September 11). *Reflective practice in early childhood education.* Retrieved from Storypark: https://blog.storypark.com/2018/09/reflective-practice-in-early-childhood-education/

Smyth, J. (1989). Developing and sustaining critical reflection in teacher education. *Education and Culture, 9*(1), Article 2. Retrieved from Purdue University: https://docs.lib.purdue.edu/cgi/viewcontent.cgi?article=1388&context=eandc

Backyardbooks. (2015, June 10). *Reflective models.* Retrieved from Literacy NZ: https://literacynz.wordpress.com/2015/06/10/reflective-models/

251   Social Cognitive Theory

The social cognitive theory. (n.d.). Retrieved from the Boston University School of Public Health: https://sphweb.bumc.bu.edu/otlt/MPH-Modules/SB/BehavioralChangeTheories/BehavioralChangeTheories5.html

Social cognitive theory. (n.d.). Retrieved from Rural Health Information Hub: https://www.ruralhealthinfo.org/toolkits/health-promotion/2/theories-and-models/social-cognitive

McLeod, S. (2023, October 24). *Albert Bandura's social learning theory.* Retrieved from Simply Psychology: https://www.simplypsychology.org/bandura.html

Nickerson, C. (2023, October 10). *Albert Bandura's social cognitive theory: Definition & examples.* Retrieved from Simply Psychology: https://www.simplypsychology.org/social-cognitive-theory.html

252   Social Exchange Theory

What is social exchange theory? (2018, April 20). Retrieved from Tulane University: https://socialwork.tulane.edu/blog/social-exchange-theory

Nickerson, C. (2023, October 25). *Social exchange theory of relationships: Examples & more.* Retrieved from Simply Psychology: https://www.simplypsychology.org/what-is-social-exchange-theory.html

Cherry, K. (2023, May 8). *Understanding social exchange theory in psychology.* Retrieved from Verywell Mind: https://www.verywellmind.com/what-is-social-exchange-theory-2795882

Introduction to social exchange theory in social work. (2020, July). Retrieved from Online Master's in Social Work Program: https://www.onlinemswprograms.com/social-work/theories/social-exchange-theory/

Crossman, A. (2020, January 14). *Understanding social exchange theory.* Retrieved from ThoughtCo.: https://www.thoughtco.com/social-exchange-theory-3026634

253　Social Facilitation

McLeod, S. (2023, October 5). *Social facilitation theory in psychology*. Retrieved from Simply Psychology: https://www.simplypsychology.org/Social-Facilitation.html

Cuncic, A. (2023, April 12). *How social facilitation can improve your performance*. Retrieved from Verywell Mind: https://www.verywellmind.com/an-overview-of-social-facilitation-4800890

American Psychological Association. (n.d.). Social facilitation. In *APA dictionary of psychology*: https://dictionary.apa.org/social-facilitation

Hopper, E. (2019, September 26). *What is social facilitation?* Retrieved from ThoughtCo.: https://www.thoughtco.com/social-facilitation-4769111

Social facilitation. (n.d.). Retrieved from The Decision Lab: https://thedecisionlab.com/reference-guide/psychology/social-facilitation/

Shrestha, P. (2017, December 7). *Social facilitation theory*. Retrieved from Psychestudy: https://www.psychestudy.com/social/social-facilitation-theory

Ukezono, M., Nakashima, S., Sudo, R., Yamazaki, A., & Takano, Y. (2015, May). The combination of perception of other individuals and exogenous manipulation of arousal enhances social facilitation as an aftereffect: Re-Examination of Zajonc's drive theory. *Frontiers in Psychology, 6*:601: https://www.frontiersin.org/articles/10.3389/fpsyg.2015.00601/full

254　Social Identity Theory

McLeod, S. (2023, October 5). *Social identity theory in psychology (Tajfel & Turner, 1979)*. Retrieved from Simply Psychology: https://www.simplypsychology.org/social-identity-theory.html

Ellemers, N. (2023, October 10). Social identity theory. Retrieved from *Britannica*: https://www.britannica.com/topic/social-identity-theory

Vinney, C. (2019, July 21). *Understanding social identity theory and its impact on behavior*. Retrieved from ThoughtCo.: https://www.thoughtco.com/social-identity-theory-4174315

Harwood, J. (2020, June 13). *Social identity theory*. Retrieved from Wiley Online Library: https://onlinelibrary.wiley.com/doi/10.1002/9781119011071.iemp0153

Chi, R. B. (2015). *Understanding social identity theory*. The SISU Intercultural Institute "Intercultural Communication." Retrieved from Future Learn: https://www.futurelearn.com/info/courses/intercultural-communication/0/steps/11053

255　Social Intelligence

Riggio, R.E. (2014, July 1). *What is social intelligence? Why does it matter?* Retrieved from Psychology Today: https://www.psychologytoday.com/us/blog/cutting-edge-leadership/201407/what-is-social-intelligence-why-does-it-matter

Van Edwards, V. (n.d.). *9 social intelligence principles everyone can master*. Retrieved from the Science of People: https://www.scienceofpeople.com/social-intelligence/

Goleman, D., & Boyatzis, R. (2008, September). Social intelligence and the biology of leadership. *Harvard Business Review*. https://hbr.org/2008/09/social-intelligence-and-the-biology-of-leadership

Morin, A. (2020, April 7). *How to increase your social intelligence*. Retrieved from Verywell Mind: https://www.verywellmind.com/what-is-social-intelligence-4163839

Howell, D. (n.d.). *What is emotional and social intelligence?* Retrieved from Businessballs.com: https://www.businessballs.com/self-awareness/main-theories-of-emotional-and-social-intelligence-esi/

Goleman, D. (2006). *Social intelligence: The new science of human relationships*. Bantam Books.

256　Social Norms Theory

Social norms theory. (n.d.). Retrieved from the Boston University School of Public Health: https://sphweb.bumc.bu.edu/otlt/MPH-Modules/SB/BehavioralChangeTheories/BehavioralChangeTheories7.html

Dempsey, R.C., McAlaney, J., & Bewick, B.M. (2018, November 6). A critical appraisal of the social norms approach as an interventional strategy for health-related behavior and attitude change. *Frontiers in Psychology, 9*: https://www.frontiersin.org/articles/10.3389/fpsyg.2018.02180/full

Berkowitz, A.D. (n.d.). *An overview of the social norms approach*. Retrieved from Alan Berkowitz: http://www.alanberkowitz.com/articles/social%20norms%20approach-short.pdf

Hahn-Smith, S., & Springer, F. (2005). *Prevention tactics: Social norms theory*. Retrieved from the Center for Applied Research Solutions: https://www.cars-rp.org/publications/Prevention%20Tactics/PT8.9.05.pdf

Research theory. (n.d.). Retrieved from the Social Norms National Research and Resources: http://www.socialnormsresources.org/research/Theory.php

257　Soft Systems Methodology

Augustsson, H., Churruca, K., & Braithwaite, J. (2019, September 14). Re-energizing the way we manage change in healthcare: The case for soft systems methodology and its application to evidence-based practice. *BMC Health Services Research*, 19, 666. Retrieved from BMC Health Services Research: https://bmchealthservres.biomedcentral.com/articles/10.1186/s12913-019-4508-0

Burge, S. (2015). *An overview of the soft systems methodology*. Retrieved from Burge Hughes Walsh: https://www.burgehugheswalsh.co.uk/Uploaded/1/Documents/Soft-Systems-Methodology.pdf

Unit 6: Soft systems methodology. (n.d.). Retrieved from University College London: http://www0.cs.ucl.ac.uk/staff/A.Finkelstein/advmsc/6.pdf

Williams, B. (2005, December). *Soft systems methodology*. Retrieved from Bob Williams: http://www.bobwilliams.co.nz/ewExternalFiles/ssm.pdf

A look at soft systems methodology. (n.d.). Retrieved from the University of Missouri St. Louis: https://www.umsl.edu/~sauterv/analysis/F2015/Soft%20Systems%20Methodology.html.htm

Soft systems methodology. (n.d.). Retrieved from the University of Cambridge: https://www.ifm.eng.cam.ac.uk/research/dstools/soft-systems-methodology/

Islam, T. (2018, October 28). *Soft systems methodology for transforming the business analysis to software development architecture*. Retrieved from Medium: https://medium.com/@tariqul.islam.rony/using-soft-system-methodology-for-transforming-the-business-analysis-to-software-development-52482608bda4

Soft systems methodology. (n.d.). Retrieved from The Open University: https://www.open.edu/openlearn/ocw/mod/oucontent/view.php?id=65641&section=6

258　SPACE Coaching Model

Weiss, R., Edgerton, N., & Palmer, S. (2017, October). *The SPACE coaching model: An integrative tool for coach therapists*. Retrieved from Coaching Today via the Rowan Consultancy: http://www.rowan-consultancy.co.uk/Documents/RowanResources/TheSPACECoachingModel%20_CoachingTodayOct%202017.pdf

Wiliams, H., Palmer, S., & Edgerton, N. (2008). May the force be with you: Harnessing the power of the mind to combat stress by using the cognitive behavioral SPACE model of coaching, counselling, and training. *Stress News*, 20(3), 29–32. Retrieved from Stress News via Academia: https://www.academia.edu/3814718/Williams_H_Palmer_S_and_Edgerton_N_2008_May_the_force_be_within_you_Harnesing_the_power_of_the_mind_to_combat_stress_by_using_the_cognitive_behavioural_SPACE_model_of_coaching_counselling_and_training_Stress_News_20_3_29_32

Cognitive behavioral therapy: Using the SPACE model for assessment and intervention. (n.d.). Retrieved from the Center for Stress Management: https://www.managingstress.com/cbt-space

Palmer, S., & Edgerton, N. (2005, December). *SPACE: A psychological model for use within cognitive behavioral coaching, therapy, and stress management*. Retrieved from ResearchGate: https://www.researchgate.net/publication/322509343_SPACE_A_psychological_model_for_use_within_cognitive_behavioural_coaching_therapy_and_stress_management

Palmer, S. (2008). *The PRACTICE model of coaching: towards a solution-focused approach*. Retrieved from the Society for Coaching Psychology via Crowe Associates: http://www.crowe-associates.co.uk/wp-content/uploads/2013/10/The_PRACTICE_model_of_coaching_towards_a_solution-focused_approach-2.pdf

Coaching model: SPACE. (2016, March 20). Retrieved from Coach Campus: https://coachcampus.com/coach-portfolios/coaching-models/iani-bacula-space/

259　Stage Gate Process

What is the stage gate discovery-to-launch process? (n.d.). Retrieved from Stage Gate International: https://www.stage-gate.com/discovery-to-launch-process/

Edgett, S. J. (n.d.). *The stage-gate model: An overview*. Retrieved from Stage Gate International: https://www.stage-gate.com/blog/the-stage-gate-model-an-overview/

What is phase gate? (2019). Retrieved from Smartsheet: https://www.smartsheet.com/phase-gate-process

The #NowIUnderstand glossary: The stage gate model for greater effectiveness in your product development processes. (2018, November 5). Retrieved from Humanperf Software: https://www.humanperf.com/en/blog/nowiunderstand-glossary/articles/stage-gate-model

260　STAR/AR Method

STAR method. (n.d.). Retrieved from Development Dimensions International: https://www.ddiworld.com/solutions/behavioral-interviewing/star-method

How to use the STAR model to provide feedback. (n.d.). Retrieved from Grapevine Evaluations: https://www.grapevineevaluations.com/use-star-model-provide-feedback

Increase employee motivation with STAR feedback model. (n.d.). Retrieved from Insperity: https://www.insperity.com/blog/start-with-star-how-to-avoid-saying-things-that-kill-employee-motivation/

The STAR feedback model. (2010). Retrieved from the University of New Mexico: https://hr.unm.edu/docs/eod/the-star-feedback-model.pdf

Jesse. (2016, October 4). *How to use STAR feedback for evaluation in your performance review system.* Retrieved from Trakstar: https://www.trakstar.com/blog-post/use-star-feedback-performance-review-system/

Give feedback like a super coach. (n.d.). Retrieved from Reliabilityweb: https://reliabilityweb.com/articles/entry/give_feedback_like_a_super_coach1/

Give great feedback using the STAR model. (n.d.). Retrieved from BrightHub PM: https://www.brighthubpm.com/resource-management/118832-improve-your-company-effectiveness-using-the-star-model-for-feedback/

Powerful performance feedback models and how they can help your company. (n.d.). Retrieved from Lucidchart: https://www.lucidchart.com/blog/performance-feedback-models

Drew-Forster, A. (2018, March 13). *How to be a STAR when giving feedback.* Retrieved from Workology Co.: https://workologyco.com.au/star-giving-feedback/

261   Start, Stop, Continue Model

Start stop continue retrospective. (n.d.). Retrieved from the GroupMap: https://www.groupmap.com/map-templates/start-stop-continue-retrospective/

The stop, start, continue approach to feedback. (n.d.). Retrieved from the World of Work Project: https://worldofwork.io/2019/07/feedback-start-stop-continue/

Ciccarelli, D. (2016, February 2). Start, stop, continue tutorial. *Forbes*: https://www.forbes.com/sites/groupthink/2016/02/02/start-stop-continue-tutorial/?sh=37a502fe2798

Start stop continue template. (n.d.). Retrieved from Alignment: https://www.swotanalysis.com/stop-start-continue-how-to-guide

Van Edwards, V. (n.d.). *Stop, start, continue: The single best team building exercise.* Retrieved from the Science of People: https://www.scienceofpeople.com/start-stop-continue/

Start stop continue retrospective. (n.d.). Retrieved from Retrium: https://www.retrium.com/retrospective-techniques/start-stop-continue

Morrison, M. (2016, May 25). *Stop, start, continue change management model.* Retrieved from RapidBI: https://rapidbi.com/stopstartcontinuechangemodel/

Jordan, K. (2012, March 16). *Bag of tricks: Start/Stop/Continue.* Retrieved from PeopleResults: https://www.people-results.com/start-stop-continue/

Ivins, J. (2018, February 28). *How to do a start, stop, continue exercise with your UX team.* Retrieved from Medium: https://medium.com/@jessicaivins/how-to-do-a-start-stop-continue-exercise-with-your-ux-team-dba72271bec4

262   Stepladder Model

The stepladder technique. (n.d.). Retrieved from Toolshero: https://www.toolshero.com/decision-making/stepladder-technique/

The stepladder technique. (n.d.). Retrieved from Mindtools: https://www.mindtools.com/pages/article/newTED_89.htm

What is stepladder technique? (n.d.). Retrieved from Visual Paradigm Online: https://online.visual-paradigm.com/knowledge/brainstorming/what-is-stepladder-technique/

Making effective group decisions with the stepladder technique. (2021, May 12). Retrieved from SlideModel: https://slidemodel.com/stepladder-technique/

The stepladder technique. (n.d.). Retrieved from Expert Program Management: https://expertprogrammanagement.com/2011/04/the-stepladder-technique/

Stepladder technique: 5 useful decision-making guides. (2020, December 28). Retrieved from Lapaas Digital: https://lapaas.com/stepladder-technique-5-useful-decision-making-guides/

Cuofano, G. (2023, November 10). *What is the stepladder technique? The stepladder technique in a nutshell.* Retrieved from FourWeekMBA: https://fourweekmba.com/stepladder-technique/

263   STEPPPA Coaching Model

McLeod, A. (2004). *STEPPPA coaching model.* Retrieved from Angus McLeod: http://angusmcleod.com/wp-content/uploads/2016/01/STEPPPA_Coaching_Model.pdf

Thomson, S. (2018, February 14). *The coaching model library: STEPPPA.* Retrieved from the Training Journal: https://www.trainingjournal.com/articles/features/coaching-model-library-stepppa

Chapter 7: Coaching models. (n.d.). Retrieved from the Life Coach Certification Institute: https://www.lifecoachcertification.com/free-learning-center/coaching-models

STEPPPA model. (n.d.). Retrieved from Businessballs.com: https://www.businessballs.com/coaching-and-mentoring/stepppa-coaching/

Ospina Avendano, D. (2021). *STEPPPA coaching model.* Retrieved from Toolshero: https://www.toolshero.com/management/steppa-coaching-model/

264   Synectics

Pincot, L. (2018, October 28). *Synectics: Creative problem-solving.* Retrieved from ProjectManagement.com: https://www.projectmanagement.com/contentPages/wiki.cfm?ID=501956&thisPageURL=/wikis/501956/Synectics--creative-problem-solving#_=_

Company name. (n.d.). Retrieved from Syreon: https://syreon.eu/company-name/

Nolan, V. (n.d.). *Synectics as a creative problem-solving technique.* Retrieved from Synecticsworld Inc.: https://synecticsworld.com/synectics-as-a-creative-problem-solving-technique/

Castillo, E. (2019, March 18). *Innovation and creativity: Synectics and other methods.* Retrieved from Scribalo: https://scribalo.com/en/scribablog/innovation-and-creativity-synectics-and-other-creative-methods/

Synectics. (n.d.). Retrieved from TechTarget: https://whatis.techtarget.com/definition/synectics

Clayton, M. (2013, October 22). *The synectics problem-solving process.* Retrieved from Management Pocketbooks: https://www.pocketbook.co.uk/blog/2013/10/22/the-synectics-problem-solving-process/

Navarro, A. (2022, December 21). *Synectics and creativity equal problem-solving.* Retrieved from Exploring Your Mind: https://exploringyourmind.com/synectics-and-creativity-equal-problem-solving/

265   Systematic Inventive Thinking

Boyd, D. (n.d.). *Faculty guide to the systematic inventive thinking (SIT) method.* Retrieved from Drew Boyd: https://drewboyd.com/wp-content/uploads/2016/07/Faculty%20Instructional%20Manual.final.pdf

Systematic inventive thinking. (n.d.). Retrieved from Toolshero: https://www.toolshero.com/problem-solving/systematic-inventive-thinking-sit/

Boyd, D. (2013, April 29). *Systematic inventive thinking: Creativity happens inside the box using five simple techniques.* Retrieved from Psychology Today: https://www.psychologytoday.com/us/blog/inside-the-box/201304/systematic-inventive-thinking

Goldenberg, J., Horowitz, R., Levav, A., & Mazursky, D. (2003, March). Finding your innovation sweet spot. *Harvard Business Review.* https://hbr.org/2003/03/finding-your-innovation-sweet-spot

Explore and apply the SIT method. (n.d.). Retrieved from Drew Boyd: https://drewboyd.com/the-sit-method/

Method. (n.d.). Retrieved from SIT: https://www.sitsite.com/method/

266   Systems Theory

Universal systems model. (n.d.). Retrieved from the University of Houston: https://uh.edu/~jhansen/Chapter%201/UniversalSystemsModel.htm

Introduction to systems theory in social work. (2020, July). Retrieved from Online Masters in Social Work Programs: https://www.onlinemswprograms.com/social-work/theories/systems-theory-social-work/

Gibson, B. (2023, December 21). Systems theory. Retrieved from *Britannica:* https://www.britannica.com/topic/systems-theory

Gordon, J. (2023, November 20). *Systems theory of management explained.* Retrieved from The Business Professor: https://thebusinessprofessor.com/en_US/management-leadership-organizational-behavior/systems-theory-of-management

Heylighen, F., & Joslyn, C. (1992, November 1). *What is systems theory?* Retrieved from Principia Cybernetica: http://pespmc1.vub.ac.be/SYSTHEOR.html

Heil, A. (n.d.). *Systems theory.* Retrieved from Southern Illinois University Edwardsville: https://www.siue.edu/~adheil/Systems%20Theory%20Paper.pdf

Anderson, B.R. (2016). Improving healthcare by embracing systems theory. *The Journal of Thoracic and Cardiovascular Surgery,* 152, 593–594: https://www.jtcvs.org/article/S0022-5223(16)30001-0/pdf

What is systems theory? (n.d.). Retrieved from Environment and Ecology: http://environment-ecology.com/general-systems-theory/137-what-is-systems-theory.html

What is systems theory? (n.d.). Retrieved from IGI Global: https://www.igi-global.com/dictionary/culture-from-a-value-systems-perspective/29133

267   T7 Model of Team Effectiveness

7 popular team effectiveness models and what they're best suited for. (2023, October 27). Retrieved from Zenkit: https://zenkit.com/en/blog/7-popular-team-effectiveness-models-and-what-theyre-best-suited-for/

How to choose a team effectiveness model. (2020, February 11). Retrieved from SpriggHR: https://sprigghr.com/blog/hr-professionals/how-to-choose-a-team-effectiveness-model/

deBara, D. (2021, September 23). *4 team effectiveness models to understand your team better.* Retrieved from Trello: https://blog.trello.com/team-effectiveness-models

Udoagwu, K. (2022, May 28). *6 different team effectiveness models to understand your team better.* Retrieved from Wrike: https://www.wrike.com/blog/6-different-team-effectiveness-models/

The benefits and downsides of team performance models. (n.d.). Retrieved from Lucidspark: https://lucidspark.com/blog/team-performance-models

Frameworks for team effectiveness. (n.d.). Retrieved from Alchemy Research and Consultancy: https://alchemyresearch-consultancy.com/frameworks-for-team-effectiveness/

Kukhnavets, P. (2021, March 9). *What team effectiveness model will make a team perform better?* Retrieved from Hygger: https://hygger.io/blog/team-effectiveness-model-will-make-team-perform-better/#3-the-t7-model-of-team-effectiveness

8 models of team effectiveness. (2018, June 12). Retrieved from Medium: https://medium.com/@RiterApp/8-models-of-team-effectiveness-3a3b84efb3ae

O'Neill, M. (2018, October 2). *The 8 best team effectiveness models and how they work.* Retrieved from Samewave Ltd.: https://www.samewave.com/posts/team-effectiveness-models

Herrity, J. (2023, February 3). *11 team effectiveness models (plus tips for choosing one).* Retrieved from Indeed: https://www.indeed.com/career-advice/career-development/team-effectiveness-model

Driving team effectiveness. (2016). Retrieved from Korn Ferry: https://www.kornferry.com/content/dam/kornferry/docs/pdfs/driving-team-effectiveness.pdf

268   Tannenbaum-Schmidt Leadership Continuum Model

The Tannenbaum-Schmidt leadership continuum video. (n.d.). Retrieved from MindTools: https://www.mindtools.com/pages/videos/tannenbaum-schmidt-transcript.htm

Minute Tools Content Team. (2018). *Tannenbaum-Schmidt leadership continuum.* Retrieved from Expert Program Management: https://expertprogrammanagement.com/2018/11/tannenbaum-schmidt-leadership-continuum/

Tannenbaum, R., & Schmidt, W. H. (1973, May). How to choose a leadership pattern. *Harvard Business Review.* https://hbr.org/1973/05/how-to-choose-a-leadership-pattern

What is the Tannenbaum and Schmidt continuum? (n.d.). Retrieved from Businessballs.com: https://www.businessballs.com/leadership-models/leadership-behaviour-continuum-tannenbaum-and-schmidt/

269   Tasks of Mourning

Grief reactions, duration, and tasks of mourning. (2020, December 4). Retrieved from the US Department of Veterans Affairs: https://www.va.gov/WHOLEHEALTHLIBRARY/tools/grief-reactions-duration-and-tasks-of-mourning.asp

Worden's four tasks of mourning. (n.d.). Retrieved from Our House Grief Support Center: https://www.ourhouse-grief.org/grief-pages/grieving-adults/four-tasks-of-mourning/

Bates, D. (2019, November 8). *The 4 tasks of grieving.* Retrieved from Psychology Today: https://www.psychologytoday.com/us/blog/mental-health-nerd/201911/the-4-tasks-grieving

Williams, L. (2013, June 24). *Worden's four tasks of mourning.* Retrieved from What's Your Grief: https://whatsyourgrief.com/wordens-four-tasks-of-mourning/

The four tasks of mourning. (2021, June 2). Retrieved from the Momentous Institute: https://momentousinstitute.org/blog/the-four-tasks-of-mourning

Vasquez, A. (2022, April 29). *What are Warden's four tasks of mourning?* Retrieved from Cake: https://www.joincake.com/blog/wordens-tasks-of-mourning/

Four tasks of mourning. (n.d.). Retrieved from Grief Compass: https://griefcompass.com/four-tasks-of-mourning

The four tasks of mourning. (n.d.). Retrieved from Grieve Well: https://www.grievewell.com/for-supporters/the-four-tasks-of-mourning/

Terranova, J. (n.d.). *Four tasks of mourning: Worden.* Retrieved from Farewells: https://farewells.co.uk/four-tasks-of-mourning-worden/

270   TDODAR Model

TDODAR decision model for making difficult decisions under pressure. (2022, April 27). Retrieved from SlideModel: https://slidemodel.com/tdodar-decision-model/

Cuofano, G. (2023, October 10). *TDODAR decision model in a nutshell.* Retrieved from Four Week MBA: https://fourweekmba.com/tdodar-decision-model-in-a-nutshell/

TDODAR decision making model. (n.d.). Retrieved from Toolshero: https://www.toolshero.com/decision-making/tdodar-decision-making-model/

Mind Tools Content Team. (n.d.). *The TDODAR decision model.* Retrieved from MindTools: https://www.mindtools.com/pages/article/tdodar-decision-model.htm

Decision-making under pressure. (2018, April). Retrieved from Healing Circles Global: https://healingcirclesglobal.org/wp-content/uploads/2018/04/Decision-Making-Under-Pressure-Healing-Circles-Global.pdf

271   Team Evolution and Maturation Model

Shuffler, M. L., Salas, E., & Rosen, M. A. (2020, September 4). The evolution and maturation of teams in organizations: Convergent trends in the new dynamic science of teams. *Frontiers in Psychology,* 11: https://www.frontiersin.org/articles/10.3389/fpsyg.2020.02128/full

Morgan Jr., B. B., Salas, E., & Glickman, A. S. (1993). An analysis of team evolution and maturation. *The Journal of General Psychology,* 120(3), 277–291. Retrieved from Taylor & Francis Online: https://www.tandfonline.com/doi/abs/10.1080/00221309.1993.9711148

Morgan, Salas, and Glickman's team model. (n.d.). Retrieved from Ebrary: https://ebrary.net/3072/management/morgan_salas_glickmans_team_model

Salonen, L. (2012). *The developmental phases of groups: Does it get any better than Tuckman?* Retrieved from Consulting in Organizations: http://www.consultinginorganisations.org/signup/Developmental_phases_of_groups_Paper.pdf

Lundberg, P. (2009, August 28). *Forming, storming, norming, performing: A better model.* Retrieved from Organizational Excellence: http://orgexcel.blogspot.com/2009/08/forming-storming-norming-performing.html

272   TetraMap

TetraMap Admin. (n.d.). *What is TetraMap?* Retrieved from TetraMap: https://www.tetramap.com/what-is-tetramap/

Polzer-Debruyne, A. (n.d.). *Academic perspective.* Retrieved from TetraMap: https://www.tetramap.com/psychometric-assessment-tetramap/

TetraMap Admin. (n.d.). *Influences and differences.* Retrieved from TetraMap: https://www.tetramap.com/influences-and-differences/

TetraMap: Putting nature into communication. (2018, June 19). Retrieved from Upskills: https://upskills.co.nz/tetramap-putting-nature-into-communication/

273   TGROW Coaching Model

The TGROW coaching model by Myles Downey. (n.d.). Retrieved from A Guide to Coaching and Being Coached: https://www.personal-coaching-information.com/tgrow-coaching-model.html

Hawkes, T. (2018, March 1). *The coaching model library: TGROW.* Retrieved from the Training Journal: https://www.trainingjournal.com/articles/features/coaching-model-library-tgrow

The TGROW coaching model. (n.d.). Retrieved from Free Management Books: http://www.free-management-ebooks.com/faqch/models-10.htm

TGROW questioning examples. (n.d.). Retrieved from Accipio: https://www.accipio.com/eleadership/mod/wiki/view.php?id=1807

274   The Platinum Rule

Souerwine, H. (2019, April 26). *Making the platinum rule work for you.* Retrieved from the American Society of Administrative Professionals: https://www.asaporg.com/articles/communication/making-the-platinum-rule-work-for-you

Economy, P. (2016, March 17). *How the platinum rule trumps the golden rule every time.* Retrieved from Inc.: https://www.inc.com/peter-economy/how-the-platinum-rule-trumps-the-golden-rule-every-time.html

Holden, C. K. (2023, October 11). *What is the platinum rule and why it matters more than ever.* Retrieved from Career Contessa: https://www.careercontessa.com/advice/the-platinum-rule-at-work/

HRDQ Staff. (2022, September 22). *What is the platinum rule and how can leaders apply it?* Retrieved from HRDQ: https://hrdqstore.com/blogs/hrdq-blog/platinum-rule-how-apply

275   Theories and Schools of Psychology

Richards, J. (n.d.). *Behavioral theories.* Retrieved from Richards on The Brain: https://www.richardsonthebrain.com/behavioral-theories

Cherry, K. (2022, November 8). *What are psychological theories?* Retrieved from Verywell Mind: https://www.verywellmind.com/what-is-a-theory-2795970

Cherry, K. (2023, November 13). *Why do we need psychology theories?* Retrieved from Verywell Mind: https://www.verywellmind.com/the-purpose-of-psychology-theories-2795084

Cherry, K. (2022, August 3). *Erikson's stages of development.* Retrieved from Verywell Mind: https://www.verywellmind.com/erik-eriksons-stages-of-psychosocial-development-2795740

Cherry, K. (2023, February 27). *Schools of psychology: Main schools of thought.* Retrieved from Verywell Mind: https://www.verywellmind.com/psychology-schools-of-thought-2795247

276   Theories of Conflict (general entry)

Wilson, C.R. (2023, September 20). *14 conflict resolution strategies for the workplace.* Retrieved from Positive Psychology: https://positivepsychology.com/conflict-resolution-in-the-workplace/

Kostiukevych, Y. (2022, June 8). *Conflict resolution: A practical framework.* Retrieved from LinkedIn Pulse: https://www.linkedin.com/pulse/conflict-resolution-practical-framework-yura-kostiukevych/?trk=pulse-article

Schelling, T.C. (1960). *The strategy of conflict.* Harvard University Press. Retrieved from Elcenia: http://elcenia.com/iamapirate/schelling.pdf

Kleeberger, T. (2020, November 7). *A brief guide to conflict resolution.* Retrieved from Medium: https://medium.com/becominghuman-tylerkleeberger/a-brief-guide-to-conflict-resolution-3912ff245a1b

Deutsch, M. (2020). *Cooperation and competition.* Retrieved from Beyond Intractability: https://www.beyondintractability.org/artsum/deutsch-cooperation

Burton, J.W. (n.d.). *Conflict resolution: The human dimension.* Retrieved from The International Journal of Peace Studies: https://www3.gmu.edu/programs/icar/ijps/vol3_1/burton.htm

Lederach, J.P. (1995). *Preparing for peace: Conflict transformation across cultures.* Retrieved from Beyond Intractability: https://www.beyondintractability.org/artsum/lederach-preparing

Clark, I. (2016, March 25). *Fisher and Ury's four principles of negotiation.* Retrieved from the Atlas of Public Management: https://www.atlas101.ca/pm/concepts/fisher-and-urys-four-principles-of-negotiation/

277   Theory of Inventive Problem-Solving

Chaudhuri, A. (2014, January 21). *40 inventive principles, the most popular component of TRIZ innovation system.* Retrieved from SureSolv: https://suresolv.com/inventive-principles/40-inventive-principles-most-popular-component-triz-innovation-system

Hipple, J. (n.d.). *The use of TRIZ separation principles to resolve the contradictions of innovation practices in organizations.* Retrieved from Innovation-TRIZ: https://www.innovation-triz.com/papers/separation.html

What is TRIZ and how to use it in problem-solving. (2021, April 16). Retrieved from SlideModel: https://slidemodel.com/triz-problem-solving/

Mind Tools Content Team. (n.d.). *TRIZ: A powerful methodology for creative problem-solving.* Retrieved from MindTools: https://www.mindtools.com/pages/article/newCT_92.htm

What is TRIZ? (n.d.). Retrieved from Oxford Creativity: https://www.triz.co.uk/what-is-triz

Six sigma terms: What is TRIZ – The theory of inventive problem-solving? (2020, May 14). Retrieved from Six Sigma Daily: https://www.sixsigmadaily.com/triz-theory-of-inventive-problem-solving/

Zornes, T. (n.d.). *TRIZ – The theory of inventive problem-solving.* Retrieved from Six Sigma Study Guide: https://sixsigmastudyguide.com/theory-of-inventive-problem-solving-triz/

What is TRIZ? (2013, May 1). Retrieved from the University of Michigan Department of Chemical Engineering: http://umich.edu/~scps/html/07chap/html/powerpointpicstriz/Chapter%207%20TRIZ.pdf

278   Theory of Planned Behavior

The theory of planned behavior. (2022). Retrieved from Boston University School of Public Health: https://sphweb.bumc.bu.edu/otlt/mph-modules/sb/behavioralchangetheories/BehavioralChangeTheories3.html

Brookes, E. (2023, October 11). *The theory of planned behavior: Behavioral intention.* Retrieved from Simply Psychology: https://www.simplypsychology.org/theory-of-planned-behavior.html

Asare, M. (2015). Using the theory of planned behavior to determine the condom use behavior among college students. *American Journal of Health Studies, 30*(1), 43–50. Retrieved from the US National Library of Medicine: https://www.ncbi.nlm.nih.gov/pmc/articles/PMC4621079/

Mathew, M., Li, K., Kloosterman, J., Albright, A., & Taddesse, N. (n.d.). *Development of theory of planned behavior.* Retrieved from Lumen Learning: https://courses.lumenlearning.com/suny-buffalo-environmentalhealth/chapter/development-of-theory-of-planned-behavior/

Theory of planned behavior. (n.d.). Retrieved from Weebly: https://theoryofplannedbehavior.weebly.com/theory.html

QUT IFB101. (2015, March 8). *Theory of planned behaviour* [Video]. Retrieved from YouTube: https://www.youtube.com/watch?v=nZsxuD3gExE

279   Theory U

Theory U. (n.d.). Retrieved from the Presencing Institute: https://www.presencing.org/aboutus/theory-u

About Otto. (2023). Retrieved from Otto Scharmer: https://ottoscharmer.com/bio

McKinney, M. (2018, April 5). *The essentials of theory U.* Retrieved from Leadership Now: https://www.leadershipnow.com/leadingblog/2018/04/the_essentials_of_theory_u.html

Sensing the future with the theory U model. (2019, October 17). Retrieved from Trigger: https://trigger-project.eu/2019/10/17/sensing-the-future-with-the-theory-u-model/

Warrilow, S. (n.d.). *Theory U: Leading from the future as it emerges.* Retrieved from Strategies for Managing Change: https://www.strategies-for-managing-change.com/theory-u.html

Garvey, B. (2018, March 7). *Theory U: Explanation through example* [Video]. Retrieved from YouTube: https://www.youtube.com/watch?v=VuwBXaKA3tw

Systems Innovation. (n.d.). *Theory U* [Video]. Retrieved from YouTube: https://www.youtube.com/watch?v=WvNlfu4263Q

280   Theory X and Theory Y

Theory X and Theory Y. (n.d.). Retrieved from Mindtools: https://www.mindtools.com/pages/article/newLDR_74.htm

Morse, J., & Lorsch, J. (1970, May). Beyond Theory Y. *Harvard Business Review.* https://hbr.org/1970/05/beyond-theory-y

Juneja, P. (n.d.). *Theory X and Theory Y.* Retrieved from Management Study Guide: https://www.managementstudyguide.com/theory-x-y-motivation.htm

Douglas McGregor: Theory X and Theory Y. (2015, October). Retrieved from Chartered Management Institute via Switch Education for Business Ltd: https://switcheducation.com/wp-content/uploads/2017/06/SEB_LYO_McGregor_Thinker.pdf

Williams, L. (n.d.). *Reading: McGregor's Theory X and Theory Y.* Retrieved from Lumen Learning: https://courses.lumenlearning.com/wmintrobusiness/chapter/reading-douglas-mcgregors-theory-x-and-theory-y-2/

Kurt, S. (2021, October 11). *Theory X and Theory Y, Douglas McGregor.* Retrieved from Education Library: https://educationlibrary.org/theory-x-and-theory-y-douglas-mcgregor/

Cruz, A. (2021, December 15). *McGregor's Theory X and Theory Y explained.* Retrieved from Management 3.0: https://management30.com/blog/theory-x-y/

Theory X and Theory Y. (n.d.). Retrieved from Tutorialspoint: https://www.tutorialspoint.com/organizational_behavior/theory_x_and_y.htm

Barnett, T. (n.d.). *Theory X and Theory Y.* Retrieved from Reference for Business: https://www.referenceforbusiness.com/management/Str-Ti/Theory-X-and-Theory-Y.html

Surbhi, S. (2017, July 8). *Difference between Theory X and Theory Y.* Retrieved from Key Differences: https://keydifferences.com/difference-between-theory-x-and-theory-y.html

281   Theory Z

Theory Z by William Ouchi explained. (n.d.). Retrieved from ToolsHero: https://www.toolshero.com/leadership/theory-z/

Mind Tools Content Team. (n.d.). *Theory Z.* Retrieved from MindTools: https://www.mindtools.com/az62i70/theory-z

Sabater, V. (2022, October 3). *William Ouchi: Theory Z of leadership.* Retrieved from Exploring Your Mind: https://exploringyourmind.com/william-ouchi-theory-z-of-leadership/

Barnett, T. (n.d.). *Theory Z.* Retrieved from Reference for Business.com: https://www.referenceforbusiness.com/management/Str-Ti/Theory-Z.html

Theory X, Theory Y, and Theory Z. (n.d.). Retrieved from Course Sidekick: https://courses.lumenlearning.com/wmopen-introbusiness/chapter/reading-douglas-mcgregors-theory-x-and-theory-y-2/

Theory Z. (n.d.). Retrieved from Communication Theory: https://www.communicationtheory.org/theory-z/

Theory Z. (n.d.). Retrieved from KB Manage: https://www.kbmanage.com/concept/theory-z

282 Thomas Kilmann Model

Day, I. (2012, July 13). *Conflict and challenge (The Thomas Kilmann model)*. Retrieved from Challenging Coaching: https://challengingcoaching.co.uk/conflict-and-challenge/

Thomas, K.W., & Kilmann, R.H. (2010, March 2). *Thomas-Kilmann conflict mode instrument: Profile and interpretive report*. Retrieved from Skills One: https://www.skillsone.com/Pdfs/smp248248.pdf

Hampton, M. (n.d.). *Understanding conflict behavior strategies: The Thomas Kilmann model*. Retrieved from 6Q Blog: https://inside.6q.io/conflict-behavior-strategies/

Thomas-Kilmann conflict mode instrument. (n.d.). Retrieved from The Myers-Briggs Company: https://www.themyersbriggs.com/en-US/Products-and-Services/TKI

Thomas-Kilmann conflict mode instrument. (n.d.). Retrieved from Psychometrics: https://www.psychometrics.com/assessments/thomas-kilmann-conflict-mode/

283 Three-Dimensional Model of Attribution

Attribution theory. (n.d.). Retrieved from Instructional Design: https://www.instructionaldesign.org/theories/attribution-theory/

Three-dimensional model of attribution. (n.d.). Retrieved from Psychology Wiki: https://psychology.fandom.com/wiki/Three_dimensional_model_of_attribution

Shrestha, P. (2017, November 17). *Weiner attribution theory*. Retrieved from Psychestudy: https://www.psychestudy.com/social/weiner-attribution-theory

Hopper, E. (2018, September 30). *Attribution theory: The psychology of interpreting behavior*. Retrieved from Thought Co.: https://www.thoughtco.com/attribution-theory-4174631

Indeed editorial team. (2023, February 3). *What is attribution theory?* Retrieved from Indeed: https://www.indeed.com/career-advice/career-development/attribution-theory

284 Tichy's TPC Model

Managing strategic change (Tichy). (n.d.). Retrieved from Toolshero: https://www.toolshero.com/change-management/managing-strategic-change-tichy/

Strategy directive: Steps of Tichy for change in organizations. (n.d.). Retrieved from the Atlantic International University: http://courses.aiu.edu/Certificate/Strategy%20and%20Management%20Quality/Strategy%20Directive/Leccion%206/STRATEGY%20DIRECTIVE%20-%20Session%206.pdf

Ravy, S. (2015, October 12). *Model integration*. Retrieved from Penn State University: https://sites.psu.edu/sterlingravy/2015/10/12/blog-5-model-integration/

Lesson 5: This model is a perfect 10! (2016, February 16). Retrieved from Penn State University: https://sites.psu.edu/plealy582/2016/02/16/lesson-5-this-model-is-a-perfect-10/

285 Toxic Positivity

Quintero, S. (n.d.). *Toxic positivity: The dark side of positive vibes*. Retrieved from The Psychology Group: https://thepsychologygroup.com/toxic-positivity/

Cherry, K. (2023, May 15). *Toxic positivity—Why it's harmful and what to say instead*. Retrieved from Verywell Mind: https://www.verywellmind.com/what-is-toxic-positivity-5093958

Princing, M. (2021, September 8). *What you need to know about toxic positivity*. Retrieved from the University of Washington: https://rightasrain.uwmedicine.org/mind/well-being/toxic-positivity

Toxic positivity. (n.d.). Retrieved from Psychology Today: https://www.psychologytoday.com/us/basics/toxic-positivity

Villines, Z. (2021, March 31). *What to know about toxic positivity*. Retrieved from Medical News Today: https://www.medicalnewstoday.com/articles/toxic-positivity#avoiding-toxic-positivity

Cooks-Campbell, A. (2022, October 12). *Toxic positivity at work: Examples and ways to manage it*. Retrieved from BetterUp: https://www.betterup.com/blog/toxic-positivity

Bernstein, E. (2021, November 2). Toxic positivity is very real, and very annoying. *The Wall Street Journal*: https://www.wsj.com/articles/tired-of-being-told-cheer-up-the-problem-of-toxic-positivity-11635858001 (Paywall)

286 Trait Theory (Carlyle/Galton)

Scouller, J., & Chapman, A. (2020, September 3). *What is Carlyle and Galton's trait theory of leadership?* Retrieved from BusinessBalls.com: https://www.businessballs.com/leadership-models/trait-theory-carlyle-and-galton/

Belyh, A. (2020, July 25). *Trait theory of leadership guide*. Retrieved from Cleverism: https://www.cleverism.com/trait-theory-of-leadership-guide/

Gwen. (n.d.). *Leadership theories*. Retrieved from Leader Who Leads: http://www.leaderwholeads.com/leadership-theories.html

Freedom Learning Group. (n.d.). *Early trait approach*. Retrieved from Lumen Learning: https://courses.lumenlearning.com/wm-organizationalbehavior/chapter/early-trait-approach/

Leadership theory: The trait theory of leadership. (n.d.). Retrieved from IPL: https://www.ipl.org/essay/The-Leadership-Theory-The-Trait-Theory-Of-P3H4PQ74AJF6

The great man theory of leadership explained. (2015, January 8). Retrieved from Villanova University: https://www.villanovau.com/resources/leadership/great-man-theory/

Cherry, K. (2023, September 6). *What is the great man theory of leadership?* Retrieved from Verywell Mind: https://www.verywellmind.com/the-great-man-theory-of-leadership-2795311

Juneja, P. (n.d.). *Great man theory of leadership*. Retrieved from Managementstudyguide.com: https://www.managementstudyguide.com/great-man-theory.htm

The great man theory. (n.d.). Retrieved from Technofunc.com: https://www.technofunc.com/index.php/leadership-skills-2/leadership-theories/item/the-great-man-theory-of-leadership-2

287 Trait Theory (Kouzes and Posner)

Scouller, J., & Chapman, A. (2020, September 3). *What is Kouzes and Posner's trait theory of leadership*. Retrieved from Businessballs.com: https://www.businessballs.com/leadership-models/trait-theory-kouzes-and-posner/

Scouller, J., & Chapman, A. (2022, January 11). *What are the five practices of the exemplary leadership model?* Retrieved from Businessballs.com: https://www.businessballs.com/leadership-models/five-practices-of-exemplary-leadership-kouzes-and-posner/

Cherry, K. (2022, October 20). *Understanding the trait theory of leadership*. Retrieved from Verywell Mind: https://www.verywellmind.com/what-is-the-trait-theory-of-leadership-2795322

This is what it means to lead. (n.d.). Retrieved from The Leadership Challenge: https://www.leadershipchallenge.com/research/five-practices.aspx

Kouzes and Posner's leadership model. (2023, November 21). Retrieved from Study.com: https://study.com/academy/lesson/kouzes-posners-leadership-model.html

Kouzes and Posner leadership participation inventory model in transformational leadership. (n.d.). Retrieved from StudiousGuy: https://studiousguy.com/kouzes-and-posner-leadership-participation-inventory-model-in-transformational-leadership/

Abu-Tineh, A.M., Khasawneh, S.A., & Omary, A.A. (2009, Winter). Kouzes and Posner's transformational leadership model in practice: The case of Jordanian schools. *Journal of Leadership Education*, 7(3), 265–283, https://journalofleadershiped.org/wp-content/uploads/2019/02/7_3_Abu-Tineh_Khasawneh_Omary-1.pdf

288 Transactional Leadership Theory

Juneja, P. (n.d.). *Transactional leadership theory*. Retrieved from Management Study Guide: https://www.managementstudyguide.com/transactional-leadership.htm

Cherry, K. (2022, October 20). *How a transactional leadership style works*. Retrieved from Verywell Mind: https://www.verywellmind.com/what-is-transactional-leadership-2795317

Defining transactional leadership. (2021, March 10). Retrieved from Western Governors University: https://www.wgu.edu/blog/transactional-leadership2103.html#close

Lee, S. (2020, April 8). *What is transactional leadership?* Retrieved from Torch Leadership Labs: https://torch.io/blog/what-is-transactional-leadership/

Betz, M. (2021, August 6). *The transactional leadership style still has a place*. Retrieved from BetterUp: https://www.betterup.com/blog/transactional-leadership

Transactional vs. transformational leadership: What's the difference? (2021, November 22). Retrieved from Michigan State University: https://www.michiganstateuniversityonline.com/resources/leadership/transactional-vs-transformational-leadership/

What is transactional leadership? Definition and advantages. (2022, July 21). Retrieved from Indeed.com: https://www.indeed.com/career-advice/career-development/what-is-transactional-leadership

Leadership theories and styles. (2020, April 7). Retrieved from Western Governors University: https://www.wgu.edu/blog/leadership-theories-styles2004.html

10 leadership theories to master for managerial success in 2024. (2023, October 11). Retrieved from Simplilearn Solutions: https://www.simplilearn.com/top-leadership-theories-every-manager-should-know-article

Birt, J. (2023, March 10). *Guide to 6 top leadership theories and how to apply them*. Retrieved from Indeed.com: https://www.indeed.com/career-advice/career-development/leadership-styles-and-theories

5 leadership theories and how to apply them. (2017, August 15). Retrieved from Benedictine University: https://cvdl.ben.edu/blog/leadership_theories_part1/

289   Transformational Leadership Theory

Cherry, K. (2023, February 24). *How transformational leadership can inspire others.* Retrieved from Verywell Mind: https://www.verywellmind.com/what-is-transformational-leadership-2795313

Burkus, D. (2010, March 18). *Transformational leadership theory.* Retrieved from David Burkus: https://davidburkus.com/2010/03/transformational-leadership-theory/

Transformational leadership. (n.d.). Retrieved from Langston University: https://www.langston.edu/sites/default/files/basic-content-files/TransformationalLeadership.pdf

White, S.K. (2022, October 10). *What is transformational leadership? A model for motivating innovation.* Retrieved from CIO: https://www.cio.com/article/3257184/what-is-transformational-leadership-a-model-for-motivating-innovation.html

Ugochukwu, C. (2023, July 10). *Transformational leadership.* Retrieved from Simply Psychology: https://www.simplypsychology.org/what-is-transformational-leadership.html

290   Transformative Learning Theory

What is the transformative learning theory? (n.d.). Retrieved from Western Governors University: https://www.wgu.edu/blog/what-transformative-learning-theory2007.html

Christie, M., Carey, M., Robertson, A., & Grainger, P. (2015, April). Putting transformative learning theory into practice. *Australian Journal of Adult Learning, 55*(1), 9–28. Retrieved from https://files.eric.ed.gov/fulltext/EJ1059138.pdf.

Transformative learning (Jack Mezirow). (n.d.). Retrieved from InstructionalDesign.org: https://www.instructionaldesign.org/theories/transformative-learning/

Transformative learning. (2023, July 5). Retrieved from the Valamis Group: https://www.valamis.com/hub/transformative-learning

Transformative learning theory (Mezirow). (n.d.). Retrieved from LearningTheories.com: https://www.learning-theories.com/transformative-learning-theory-mezirow.html

Mezirow, J. (1997). Transformative learning: Theory to practice. *New Directions for Adult and Continuing Education, 74,* 5–12. Retrieved from the European Consortium of Liberal Arts and Science: https://www.ecolas.eu/eng/wp-content/uploads/2015/10/Mezirow-Transformative-Learning.pdf

291   Transtheoretical Model

The transtheoretical mode (stages of change). (n.d.). Retrieved from the Boston University School of Public Health: https://sphweb.bumc.bu.edu/otlt/mph-modules/sb/behavioralchangetheories/behavioralchangetheories6.html

The transtheoretical model. (n.d.). Retrieved from ProChange Behavior Solutions: https://prochange.com/transtheoretical-model-of-behavior-change/

Stages of change model (transtheoretical model). (n.d.). Retrieved from Rural Health Information Hub: https://www.ruralhealthinfo.org/toolkits/health-promotion/2/theories-and-models/stages-of-change

Brookes, E. (2023, November 9). *Transtheoretical model: Stages of health behavior change.* Retrieved from Simply Psychology: https://www.simplypsychology.org/transtheoretical-model.html

Theeboom, T., Van Vianen, A.E.M., & Beersma, B. (2017, August 8). A temporal map of coaching. *Frontiers in Psychology, 8:* https://www.frontiersin.org/articles/10.3389/fpsyg.2017.01352/full

292   Transtheoretical Model: Processes of Change

The transtheoretical mode (stages of change). (n.d.). Retrieved from the Boston University School of Public Health: https://sphweb.bumc.bu.edu/otlt/mph-modules/sb/behavioralchangetheories/behavioralchangetheories6.html

The transtheoretical model. (n.d.). Retrieved from ProChange Behavior Solutions: https://prochange.com/transtheoretical-model-of-behavior-change/

Stages of change model (transtheoretical model). (n.d.). Retrieved from Rural Health Information Hub: https://www.ruralhealthinfo.org/toolkits/health-promotion/2/theories-and-models/stages-of-change

Brookes, E. (2023, November 9). *Transtheoretical model: Stages of health behavior change.* Retrieved from Simply Psychology: https://www.simplypsychology.org/transtheoretical-model.html

Theeboom, T., Van Vianen, A.E.M., & Beersma, B. (2017, August 8). A temporal map of coaching. *Frontiers in Psychology, 8:* https://www.frontiersin.org/articles/10.3389/fpsyg.2017.01352/full

293 Triune Brain Model

The concept of the "triune brain." (2021). Retrieved from The Interaction Design Foundation: https://www.interaction-design.org/literature/article/the-concept-of-the-triune-brain

A theory abandoned but still compelling. (2008). Retrieved from Yale University School of Medicine: https://medicine.yale.edu/news/yale-medicine-magazine/a-theory-abandoned-but-still-compelling/

History module: The triune brain/limbic system model—what to keep, what to discard. (n.d.). Retrieved from The Brain from Top to Bottom: https://thebrain.mcgill.ca/flash/capsules/histoire_bleu09.html

Steffen, P.R., Hedges, D., & Matheson, R. (2022, April 1). The brain is adaptive, not triune: How the brain responds to threat, challenge, and change. Retrieved from *Frontiers in Psychiatry*, 13: https://www.frontiersin.org/articles/10.3389/fpsyt.2022.802606/full

294 Tubbs Systems Model

Tubbs systems model. (n.d.). Retrieved from Tools Hero: https://www.toolshero.com/management/tubbs-systems-model/

Trang, T. (2011, September 10). *Tubbs and Moss' model of human communication.* Retrieved from Thanh Trang: https://trangchuthanh.wordpress.com/2011/09/10/tubbs-moss-model-of-human-communication/

Larcher, B. (2007). *Group development models: A comparison.* Retrieved from Bob Larcher: https://boblarcher.com/GroupDevelopmentModels.pdf

Tubbs' theory—Small group communication. (n.d.). Retrieved from Communication Theory: https://www.communicationtheory.org/tubbs-theory-small-group-communication/

Tubbs' systems model. (n.d.). Retrieved from Ebrary: https://ebrary.net/3069/management/tubbs_systems_model

Hurt, A.C., & Trombley, S.M. (2007). *The punctuated – Tuckman: Towards a new group development model.* Retrieved from the Institute of Education Sciences: https://files.eric.ed.gov/fulltext/ED504567.pdf

295 Tuckman's Stages of Group Development

Tuckman's stages of group development. (n.d.). Retrieved from West Chester University: https://www.wcupa.edu/coral/tuckmanStagesGroupDelvelopment.aspx

Mind Tools Team. (n.d.). *Forming, storming, norming, and performing.* Retrieved from MindTools: https://www.mindtools.com/abyj5fi/forming-storming-norming-and-performing

Stein, J. (n.d.). *Using the stages of team development.* Retrieved from the Massachusetts Institute of Technology: https://hr.mit.edu/learning-topics/teams/articles/stages-development

The five stages of team development. (n.d.). Retrieved from Lumen Learning: https://courses.lumenlearning.com/suny-principlesmanagement/chapter/reading-the-five-stages-of-team-development/

296 Two-Factor Theory

Herzberg's motivation theory. (n.d.). Retrieved from Businessballs.com: https://www.businessballs.com/improving-workplace-performance/frederick-herzberg-motivation-theory/

Mind Tools Content Team. (n.d.). *Herzberg's motivators and hygiene factors.* Retrieved from MindTools: https://www.mindtools.com/pages/article/herzberg-motivators-hygiene-factors.htm

Herzberg's motivation-hygiene theory (two-factor theory). (n.d.). Retrieved from NetMBA: http://www.netmba.com/mgmt/ob/motivation/herzberg/

Nickerson, C. (2023, September 28). *Herzberg's two-factor theory of motivation-hygiene.* Retrieved from Simply Psychology: https://www.simplypsychology.org/herzbergs-two-factor-theory.html

Iyer, Y. (2022, June 10). *Herzberg's two-factor theory in project management.* Retrieved from Wrike: https://www.wrike.com/blog/what-is-herzbergs-two-factor-theory/#What-is-the-two-factor-theory

297 Uncertainty Reduction Theory

Uncertainty reduction theory. (n.d.). Retrieved from Master's in Communication: https://www.mastersincommunications.com/research/interpersonal-communication/uncertainty-reduction-theory

Uncertainty reduction theory. (n.d.). Retrieved from Communication Studies: https://www.communicationstudies.com/communication-theories/uncertainty-reduction-theory

Stiffler, L. (2023, November 21). *Uncertainty reduction: Theory, history & examples.* Retrieved from Study.com: https://study.com/academy/lesson/uncertainty-reduction-definition-theory-examples.html

Cuofano, G. (2023, October 17). *What is the uncertainty reduction theory? Uncertainty reduction theory in a nutshell.* Retrieved from Four Week MBA: https://fourweekmba.com/uncertainty-reduction-theory/

Bajracharya, S. (2018, February 17). *Uncertainty reduction theory*. Retrieved from Businesstopia: https://www.businesstopia.net/communication/uncertainty-reduction-theory-definition

Uncertainty reduction theory: Examples and definition. (n.d.). Retrieved from Tools Hero: https://www.toolshero.com/communication-methods/uncertainty-reduction-theory/

298   VAK/VARK Learning Preference Model

VAK learning styles. (n.d.). Retrieved from The Peak Performance Center: https://thepeakperformancecenter.com/educational-learning/learning/preferences/learning-styles/vak/

Mind Tools Content Team. (n.d.). *VAK learning styles*. Retrieved from MindTools: https://www.mindtools.com/pages/article/vak-learning-styles.htm

VAK learning styles: What are they and what do they mean? (2023, March 24). Retrieved from Engage Education: https://engage-education.com/aus/blog/vak-learning-styles-what-are-they-and-what-do-they-mean/#!

An introduction to VAK learning styles. (n.d.). Retrieved from Businessballs.com: https://www.businessballs.com/self-awareness/vak-learning-styles/

Different learning styles—What teachers need to know. (2021, June 28). Retrieved from The University of Kansas: https://educationonline.ku.edu/community/4-different-learning-styles-to-know

Visual, auditory, and kinesthetic learning styles (VAK). (n.d.). Retrieved from The Performance Juxtaposition Site: http://www.nwlink.com/~donclark/hrd/styles/vakt.html

Cherry, K. (2023, February 28). *Overview of VARK learning styles*. Retrieved from Verywell Mind: https://www.verywellmind.com/vark-learning-styles-2795156

299   Vertical Thinking Model

Authorized distributors. (n.d.). Retrieved from Edward de Bono Ltd.: https://www.debono.com/authorised-distributors

Jarad, M. (2017, January 17). *Thinking strategies: Vertical vs. horizontal*. Retrieved from LinkedIn Pulse: https://www.linkedin.com/pulse/thinking-strategies-vertical-vs-horizontal-malik-tubaishat/

Shoop, M. (2023, November 24). *What is vertical thinking?* Retrieved from The Health Board: https://www.thehealthboard.com/what-is-vertical-thinking.htm

Vertical thinking vs. horizontal thinking. (2019, May 17). Retrieved from Medium: https://medium.com/@tuba.virk2/vertical-thinking-vs-horizontal-thinking-546cad9ce369

What is vertical thinking? (n.d.). Retrieved from LifePersona: https://www.lifepersona.com/what-is-vertical-thinking

Peters, J. (2017, December 6). *Vertical thinking*. Retrieved from the European Interest Group on Creativity and Innovation. https://www.creativity-innovation.eu/vertical-thinking/

Rasidi, N.A.A.B., & Bendiala, W.A. (2014, February 26). *Lateral vs. vertical thinking*. Retrieved from SlideShare: https://www.slideshare.net/mieyanana/lateral-vs-vertical-thinking

Tuarez, J. (2021, February 22). *Linear thinking vs. lateral thinking (a complete guide)*. Retrieved from NeuroTray: https://neurotray.com/linear-thinking-vs-lateral-thinking/

Frey, C. (2003, February 10). *Think horizontally and vertically to solve your next creative challenge*. Retrieved from Innovation Management: https://innovationmanagement.se/2003/02/10/think-horizontally-and-vertically-to-solve-your-next-creative-challenge/

Burks, D.B. (2020, March 15). *Vertical thinking: Definition and 11 characteristics*. Retrieved from Virtual Psych Centre: https://virtualpsychcentre.com/vertical-thinking-definition-and-11-characteristics/

300   Vertical-Horizontal Leadership Development

Petrie, N. (2014). *Vertical leadership development, part I: Developing leaders for a complex world (Center for Creative Leadership)*. Retrieved from Kairos Consulting: https://kairosconsulting.com/wp-content/uploads/2016/06/CCL-VerticalLeadersPart1.pdf

Developing talent? You're probably missing vertical development. (2022, September 25). Retrieved from the Center for Creative Leadership: https://www.ccl.org/wp-content/uploads/2015/04/verticalLeadersPart2.pdf

Henley, D. (2020, January 31). Research says vertical development can make you a better leader. *Forbes*: https://www.forbes.com/sites/dedehenley/2020/01/31/vertical-development-can-make-you-a-better-leader-in-todays-world/?sh=5e9b104976ca

Vertical leadership development explained. (n.d.). Retrieved from Ideasforleaders.com: https://www.ideasforleaders.com/ideas/vertical-leadership-development-explained

Vertical leadership development. (n.d.). Retrieved from Nicholas Petrie LLC: https://www.nicholaspetrie.com/vertical-leadership-development

Harper, S. (2020, June 15). *The 7 transformations in vertical leadership development*. Retrieved from the Innovative Leadership Institute: https://www.innovativeleadershipinstitute.com/the-7-transformations-in-vertical-leadership-development/

Jones, H., Chesley, J., & Egan, T. (2020, January). Helping leaders grow up: Vertical leadership development in practice. *The Journal of Values-Based Leadership*, 13(1), 1–19. Retrieved from Valparaiso University: https://scholar.valpo.edu/cgi/viewcontent.cgi?article=1275&context=jvbl

    Also retrieved from the *Journal of Leadership Education*: https://journalofleadershiped.org/jole_articles/elevating-leadership-development-practices-to-meet-emerging-needs/

Bronzert, J. (n.d.). *Vertical development: The intersection of change and leadership*. Retrieved from Change Management Review: https://www.changemanagementreview.com/vertical-development-the-intersection-of-change-and-leadership-2/

Root, D. (2017, August 23). *Making vertical leadership work in your organization*. Retrieved from Eagle's Flight: https://www.eaglesflight.com/blog/making-vertical-leadership-work-in-your-organization

Vertical and horizontal leadership development. (n.d.). Retrieved from Global Leadership Associates: https://www.gla.global/project/vertical-and-horizontal-development/

Goldminz, I. (2016, July 4). *Vertical (leadership) development*. Retrieved from Medium: https://medium.com/org-hacking/vertical-leadership-development-petrie-217df6514250

Vertical development for effective leaders. (2017, August 29). Retrieved from Medium: https://medium.com/@actionableco/vertical-development-for-effective-leaders-f126f1575b98

Horizontal development vs. vertical development: What you need to know. (2023, January 3). Retrieved from CrossKnowledge Blog: https://blog.crossknowledge.com/horizontal-vertical-development/

Karthikeyan, C. (2017, April). A predictive analysis on the future of vertical leadership development: A leadership perspective. *International Journal of Research in Social Sciences*, 7(4), 468–503. Retrieved from ResearchGate: https://www.researchgate.net/publication/332933789_A_Predictive_Analysis_on_Future_of_Vertical_Leadership_Development_A_Leadership_Perspective

301   Vroom-Yetton Decision Model

Prochilo, P. (2015, March 16). *Leadership and decision making: The Vroom-Yetton model*. Retrieved from Fire Engineering: https://www.fireengineering.com/2015/03/16/199227/leadership-and-decision-making-the-vroom-yetton-model/#gref

Indeed editorial team. (2023, March 10). *Contingency theory of leadership: Definition and models*. Retrieved from Indeed: https://www.indeed.com/career-advice/career-development/contingency-theory-of-leadership

The contingency theory of leadership explained. (2015, January 9). Retrieved from Villanova University: https://www.villanovau.com/resources/leadership/leadership-and-contingency-theory/

Zane, E.B. (2016, January 18). *Are you a good team leader?* Retrieved from EBZ Coaching: https://www.edoardo-binda-zane.com/team-leader/

Mind Tools Content Team. (n.d.). *The Vroom-Yetton decision model*. Retrieved from MindTools: https://www.mindtools.com/adamhmy/the-vroom-yetton-decision-model

Cuofano, G. (2023, October 18). *Vroom-Yetton decision model explained*. Retrieved from Four Week MBA: https://fourweekmba.com/vroom-yetton-decision-model/

302   Weber's Theory of Authority

Leadership theories. (2023, September 26). Retrieved from Moneyzine: https://moneyzine.com/career-development/leadership-skill/leadership-theories/

Alan, Dr. (2020, October 5). *Applying Max Weber's charismatic leadership theory*. Retrieved from Expert Assignment Help: https://expertassignmenthelp.com/applying-max-webers-charismatic-leadership-theory/

Understanding Max Weber's charismatic leadership (n.d.). Retrieved from Social Student: https://www.socialstudent.co.uk/understanding-max-webers-charismatic-leadership/

Williams, D. (n.d.). *Max Weber: Traditional, legal, and charismatic authority*. Retrieved from Dana Williams: https://danawilliams2.tripod.com/authority.html

Peek, S. (2023, May 17). *The management theory of Max Weber*. Retrieved from Business.com: https://www.business.com/articles/management-theory-of-max-weber/

Power, domination, legitimation, and authority. (1999, October 12). Retrieved from University of Regina: https://uregina.ca/~gingrich/o12f99.htm

Max Weber on authority. (n.d.). Retrieved from Sociology Guide: https://www.sociologyguide.com/socio-short-notes/view-short-notes.php?id=44

Weber's theory of bureaucracy and authority. (n.d.). Retrieved from Babson College: https://faculty.babson.edu/krollag/org_site/encyclop/weber.html

303 Westley and MacLean's Model of Communication

Juneja, P. (n.d.). *Westley and MacLean's model of communication*. Retrieved from Management Study Guide: https://www.managementstudyguide.com/westley-maclean-model-of-communication.htm

Westley and MacLean's model of communication. (n.d.). Retrieved from Communication Theory: https://www.communicationtheory.org/westley-and-macleans-model-of-communication/

Bajracharya, S. (2018, January 11). *Westley and MacLean's model of communication*. Retrieved from Bussinesstopia: https://www.businesstopia.net/communication/westley-and-maclean-model-communication

Drew, C. (2023, August 12). *Westley and MacLean model of communication: 9 key elements*. Retrieved from HelpfulProfessor: https://helpfulprofessor.com/westley-maclean-model/

Westley and MacLean's model of communication. (2012, January 19). Retrieved from WeCommunication: https://wecommunication.blogspot.com/2012/01/westley-and-macleans-model-of.html

Westley and MacLean's model. (2012, September 14). Retrieved from RelivingMBAdays: https://relivingmbadays.wordpress.com/2012/09/14/westley-and-macleans-model/

Ullah, R. (2015, March 1). *Westley and MacLean's model of communication*. Retrieved from Mass Communication Theory: https://rahmanjmc.wordpress.com/category/communication-models/

Lacy, S. (1989, August). *The Westley-MacLean model revisited: An extension of a conceptual model for communication research*. Retrieved from Institute for Educational Sciences: https://files.eric.ed.gov/fulltext/ED312681.pdf

304 Working Genius

Lencioni, P. (2022, April). *How to introduce working genius to your team*. Retrieved from the Table Group: https://www.tablegroup.com/how-to-introduce-working-genius-to-your-team/

Kininmonth, C. (2023, May 24). *6 types of working genius: New leadership tool from Patrick Lencioni*. Retrieved from The Growth Faculty: https://www.thegrowthfaculty.com/blog/6typesofworkinggenius

McKinney, M. (2022, September 16). *The 6 types of working genius*. Retrieved from Leadership Now: https://www.leadershipnow.com/leadingblog/2022/09/the_6_types_of_working_genius.html

Parker, R. (2021, April 19). *The 6 types of working genius*. Retrieved from LinkedIn Pulse: https://www.linkedin.com/pulse/6-types-working-genius-ryan-parker/

Rahil, L. (2020, November 9). *6 types of working genius*. Retrieved from Medium: https://medium.com/illumination/6-types-of-working-genius-f9cc71f799d8